The American Revolutionary Series

AMERICAN AND FRENCH ACCOUNTS

OF THE

AMERICAN REVOLUTION

*The American Revolutionary Series
is published in cooperation with
The Boston Public Library*

The American Jew as Patriot, Soldier and Citizen

By
SIMON WOLF

With a New Introduction and Preface by
GEORGE ATHAN BILLIAS

GREGG PRESS
Boston 1972

Library of Congress Cataloging in Publication Data

Wolf, Simon, 1826-1923.
    The American Jew as patriot, soldier and citizen.

    (American Revolutionary series)
    Reprint of the 1895 ed.
    1. Jews in the United States—History. 2. United
States—History—Revolution—Jewish participation.
3. United States—History—Civil War—Jewish troops.
I. Title. II. Series.
E184.J5W8   1972   917.3'06'924   72-8739
ISBN 0-8398-2179-4

AMERICAN AND FRENCH ACCOUNTS OF THE AMERICAN REVOLUTION

W ho shall write the history of the American Revolution?" John Adams once asked. "Who can write it?" "Who will ever be able to write it?" Adams, however, had overlooked one important area. Materials were available for writing the military side of the struggle for independence. There existed many accounts, both primary and secondary, by the two prime protagonists in the war—the Americans and their French allies. This series is devoted to reprinting a selection of such works.

Books within the first category—personal accounts by officers and men who fought in the Continental army—were quite numerous in the historical literature. Although the age of universal public education in this country lay in the future, a surprising number of soldiers could read and write—a fact to which signatures on muster rolls can attest. Conscious that they were involved in an epoch-making event, many men kept a diary or journal in their knapsacks or wrote long letters home. These firsthand records made it possible to visualize the agonies of marching and fighting battles through the eyes of those who endured them. Equally important, these individual accounts often were more revealing than the official records. Such was the case in two of the works in this series—Caleb Stark's, *Memoir and Official Correspondence of General John Stark, with Notices of Several Other Officers of the Revolution,* and

v

Egbert Benson's, *Vindication of the Captors of Major Andre.*

A second primary source of utmost importance were army orderly books. The official purpose of these journals was to record the orders given by military commanders, the movement of units, and the disposition of forces during battle. Numerous other details of daily army life were also incorporated, such as the rations issued, sanitary measures taken, and the courts-martial conducted. By analyzing their contents carefully, however, one could read between the lines certain attitudes about which nothing had been written—the relations between officers and men, morale of troops, and reactions to recent military developments. From the book of general orders issued by Israel Putnam in the Hudson Highlands during the summer and fall of 1777, for example, one catches the shiver of apprehension that ran through his men as the invasion by General John Burgoyne from Canada got under way.

Among the secondary sources in this series, biographies rank high. The Revolutionary War produced not only a new nation but a host of heroes. From the study of the personal lives of participants, one can gain new insights regarding the struggle for independence. Elbridge H. Goss' two-volume work, *The Life of Colonel Paul Revere*, reveals that the Boston silversmith was a major figure in Massachusetts along with John Hancock and Sam Adams well before he took his famous midnight ride. Hancock himself is portrayed as a master organizer as well as a colorful political leader in Lorenzo Sears' biography, *John Hancock, the Picturesque Patriot.* George Rogers Clark, a controversial figure in American history has alternately been described as the heroic conqueror of the West and as a guerilla fighter with dubious motives. Clark's contributions as well as his motives are examined in the careful book by Consul W. Butterfield. One of the European military experts who served the American cause in a unique way was Thaddeus Kosciuszko, the Polish patriot, artilleryman, and engineer. His career, studied by Miecislaus Haiman—a scholar with a command of the Polish language—provides information that is not generally known.

The last category in the American secondary sources reprinted in this series represents certain books that have been out-of-print. Although it is an older work, Sydney G. Fisher's *The True History of the American Revolution* is still regarded as indispensable by many scholars because of its treatment of the Loyalists as well as its emphasis on the internal social divisions within the country during the conflict. Paul Allen's *A History of the American Revolution* is of interest because it reflects the attitude toward the Revolution by the generation that fought the so-called "second war for independence"—the War of 1812. The volume by Simon Wolfe, *The Jew as Patriot, Soldier, and Citizen,* is distinctly different; it stresses, among other things, the contribution of Jews to the revolutionary movement in America. Finally, Clarence Bennett's *Advance and Retreat to Saratoga* goes well beyond the limits indicated in its title; it describes the military actions in the Northern theater of operations from Arnold's ill-fated expedition to Quebec in 1775 to the equally disastrous British invasion by Burgoyne in 1777.

Although French military aid is generally conceded to have made America's independence possible, literary accounts of France's involvement in the war have been relatively few in number. For this reason, three works in this series deal with the subject directly or indirectly. Thomas Balch's book, *The French in America During the War of Independence of the United States,* makes a strong case for the traditional position that France's contribution to the American cause made the difference between victory and defeat. William M. Sloane in *The French War and the Revolution,* on the other hand, concludes that the foreign alliance was a mistake and that America might have been better advised to gain her independence by herself. Abbe Raynal, the French writer and historian, examines the question from another point of view in *The Revolution of America*. He contends that the Revolution had a great impact upon European intellectuals, and that America provided a model for the Old World to follow in molding a new and better society.

One common theme runs through most of the volumes reprinted in this series; the participants—American and French—and the commentators—past and present—were agreed that the Revolution was a profound event whose effects were destined to shape the future of world history.

PREFACE

SIMON WOLF of Washington, D.C., took four years to collect the materials contained in this volume. The aim of the book was to stress the contribution made by Jews not only during the Revolutionary era but in subsequent wars as well—the War of 1812, Mexican War, and Civil War. much of the volume is devoted to an alphabetical listing of the names of those who served in these conflicts. Many of the articles included were written for the American Jewish Historical Society and subsequently edited and collated by Louis E. Levy.

The information relating to Jewish patriots in the Revolution is of special interest. Jews not only risked their lives but their money as well in the cause for American independence, the author notes. The sketch of Haym Salomon by the well-known colonial scholar, Herbert Baxter Adams, shows that the Jewish patriot made heavy loans and suffered for his sacrifices after the war. The article by Max J. Kohler on Colonel David S. Franks describes the important services rendered by that officer who served as aide-de-camp to General Benedict Arnold and carried diplomatic dispatches to Europe for Congress.

Jewish patriots could be found throughout all the thirteen colonies, according to Wolfe. In Newport, Rhode Island, Aaron Lopez and Isaac Hart worked hard for American independence. Within New York City, six Jewish merchants signed their names to the non-importation agreement in 1770. Baltimore and Philadelphia had their own small groups of Jewish patriot supporters. In Savannah, Georgia, Mordecai Sheftall held responsible positions on both the state and national level, and served as Deputy Commissary General of the Issues to the Continental Troops in Georgia.

One of the most important sections of the work is the compilation of names of Jewish soldiers who served in the Continental army. This list contains the rank as well as name of each man who appeared on the regular army rolls.

Lewis Abraham, one of the contributors to the volume, collated all of the correspondence that could be found between George Washington and members of the Jewish faith. This correspondence gives some indication of the attitudes taken toward the Jews at the time.

The date of publication of this volume in itself is significant. The influx of Jewish immigrants from eastern Europe in the 1890's had given rise to anti-Semitism among American nativists as well as creating a split between the older and more established elements of Jewry and the newcomers. This work was an effort to refute the harsh charges of anti-Semites and to foster the idea of an integrated Jewish community in America by stressing the contributions of Jews to the Revolution and to the subsequent growth of the American nation.

As an early work in Jewish immigrant history, this book is both interesting and valuable. Although often uncritical and unreliable, it contains information that cannot be found elsewhere.

George Athan Billias
Clark University

The American Jew

AS

Patriot, Soldier and Citizen.

STATUE OF RELIGIOUS LIBERTY,
Fairmount Park, Philadelphia.

THE

AMERICAN JEW

AS

PATRIOT, SOLDIER AND CITIZEN

BY

SIMON WOLF

———————

EDITED BY

LOUIS EDWARD LEVY

———————

PHILADELPHIA

THE LEVYTYPE COMPANY

PUBLISHERS

NEW YORK—CHICAGO—WASHINGTON

BRENTANO'S

1895

"And Ye shall know the Truth and the Truth shall make you free."—John, Viii, 32.

To All

Who Love and Seek the Truth

This Work is Dedicated

BY

The Author.

Editor's Preface.

It were an error to suppose that prejudice is always the off-spring of ignorance, inasmuch as the reverse is very frequently true. Not seldom is ignorance the result of prejudice, through a willful refusal to recognize such facts as run counter to the latter. A more accurate simile would, therefore, be the likening of prejudice and ignorance to twins, of whom either may be the precursor of the other, and either one the stronger of the two. The prejudices which follow ordinary ignorance give way readily before increasing knowledge of the truth, but where prejudice is the elder of the twin vices, it is usually the most obstinate as well. "None so blind as those who will not see" is an old aphorism whose truth is universally recognized. This obstinate kind of prejudice is usually but a form of self-conceit, as the latter, in turn, is but another form of ignorance.

To combat one of the most obstinate of all obstinate prejudices, and to promote enlightenment on a subject whereof ignorance has become unpardonable, has been undertaken by Hon. Simon Wolf in the work before us. His impelling motive has been to enforce a recognition of the Jewish people as a militant factor in the upbuilding of the State, and of Judaism as a primal force in the furtherance of civilization, and he has chosen as his weapons the simple truth of history and the testimony of leaders among men.

A notable French writer remarks that " La vérité historique

(vii)

devrait être non moins sacrée que la religion.''* His words
are just; the truth of history should, indeed, be no less sacred
than that of religion. If this is true, and few or none will be
found to dispute the proposition, then the records of historic
truth may be regarded as part of the gospel of humanity. Such
they are, in fact; as the truths of history become disentangled
from the maze of sophistry and falsehood in which the passions
and follies of mankind envelop them, they teach us first of all
the lesson of charity and good-will to men.

The light of historic truth has been concentrated by Mr.
Wolf on the part taken by his co-religionists in the development
of our great republic. He shows us that the Jewish people of
the New World, like their ancestors and brethren of the Old,
have been unfailing in their devotion to their country's cause;
that they have performed an ample part in the conquest of our
liberties and have fully shared in the struggles for the preservation of our institutions. He proves beyond cavil that from an
early stage of our history down to the present day, men of the
Hebrew race and faith have been counted in the van of the
country's progress and in the forefront of its defense, and having proved this fact by historic records and a demonstration of
the truth, his task is done.

That this task was self-imposed but adds to the debt which
the American Jewish community owes to Mr. Wolf for its accomplishment. It was undertaken in the spirit which has animated him throughout a long career of public usefulness, a
spirit of loyalty to the faith that is in him, to his fellow-Israelites
and to the land of his adoption. It has been done with all the
thoroughness that an earnest purpose could impart to it, with a
comprehensiveness in keeping with that purpose, and withal,
in a spirit free from any shadow of sordidness or motive of self-
interest. Mr. Wolf seeks no pecuniary profit from the unstinted

---

* Histoire de Jules César, par Napoleon III, Préface.

labors he has given to this cause, not even the return of the
sums expended by him in the tedious and often costly collection
of his data. Whatever of monetary reward may inure to his
work has been dedicated by him to the orphaned wards of the
B'nai B'rith, whose asylum in Atlanta he helped to found, and
of which he has long been the directing spirit and official head.

The work of gathering the material for this book having been
accomplished by Mr. Wolf, the less onerous task of editing and
collating it has been entrusted by him to the present writer.
In the execution of the work thus outlined for me I have been
guided by the spirit with which the author had imbued it, and
in my introductory references to the successive subjects of the
volume, I have sought to briefly elucidate the author's theme.
In common with him, I have to express my regret that the
army lists compiled herein remain incomplete notwithstanding his unsparing efforts to perfect them. On the other hand,
the more general subject, the place of the Jewish people
in the history of mankind, their influence on the current
of affairs, their attitude before the world and towards it, are
demonstrated by a consensus of many-voiced opinion, gathered
from unquestionable sources, in such abundance and of such
extent that only its necessary curtailment afforded difficulty.
This varied material has been subjected to a careful reconsider-
ation, and in eliminating some portions and including others, I
have sought to render the whole in harmony with the key-note
which Mr. Wolf had sounded.

LOUIS EDWARD LEVY.

Philadelphia, October, 1895.

TABLE OF CONTENTS.

ERRATA.

Page 4, line 20, instead of " Charles RAUM," read "Charles BAUM."

Page 26, line 14 from bottom of page, instead of " Isaac MORRIS," read, " Isaac MOSES."

Page 200, line 2, instead of " WASHINGTON," read " BALTIMORE."

Page 424, under " STATISTICAL," "Other Soldiers (in-dicated in Addenda)," should be " 13 " instead of " 12," making the total " 8258," instead of " 8257."

Page 428, line 25, instead of " 1872 " read " 1870."

B'NAI B'RITH ORPHANS' HOME, ATLANTA, GA.

B'NAI B'RITH ORPHANS' HOME, ATLANTA, GA.

The Orphan Home of the Order of B'nai B'rith at Atlanta, Ga., for the benefit of which Mr. Wolf has devoted the net income of the present publication, was instituted in 1876, under the auspices of District Grand Lodge No. 5, comprising the States of Maryland, Virginia, North and South Carolina and Georgia, and the District of Columbia. The present building was dedicated in 1889. Its benefits are not restricted to the membership of the Order which maintains it, children of all Jews residing within the territory named being admitted to its shelter. There are now sixty children cared for in the institution, and a large number are waiting to be admitted when the new wing now in course of erection is completed. This addition is calculated to cost some $25,000, and when finished will enable this Home to adequately meet the existing requirements and bring it to a foremost rank with institutions of this character. It is managed by a Board of Control consisting of thirteen members, of which Mr. Wolf, to whose efforts the existence of the Home is primarily due, has been chairman since its foundation. The administration of the Home is supervised by a local Board of Managers, of which Hon. Joseph Hirsch is Chairman.

INTRODUCTION.

In December, 1891, there was printed in the *North American Review* a letter in reply to certain statements of a contributor to a previous number of the same magazine regarding the services of American Jewish citizens as soldiers in the Civil War. Under the caption "Jewish Soldiers in the Union Army," the writer, after denying the statement that Generals Rosecrans and Lyon were of Jewish birth, proceeds as follows :—

"I had served in the field about eighteen months before being permanently disabled in action, and was quite familiar with several regiments ; was then transferred to two different recruiting stations, but I cannot remember meeting one Jew in uniform, or hearing of any Jewish soldier. After the war, for twenty-five years, I was constantly engaged in traveling, always among old soldiers, but never found any who remembered serving with Jews. I learned of no place, where they stood, shoulder to shoulder, except in General Sherman's department, and he promptly ordered them out of it for speculating in cotton and carrying information to the Confederates. If so many Jews fought so bravely for their adopted country, surely their champion ought to be able to give the names of the regiments they condescended to accept service in," etc., etc.

A statement of this nature, logically inconclusive and practically absurd as it is, might well, under ordinary conditions have been left unnoticed. Under ordinary conditions a reply of any kind to such a tissue of misstatements, would but have dignified it beyond reason, and but helped, perhaps, to save it and its author from oblivion. But the conditions were not ordinary, but most unfortunately, otherwise.   It was at a time when the public mind throughout the civilized world was wrought to a high pitch of excitement by the flaunting villainy of the Russian government in the outrageous persecution of its Jewish subjects, when the wave of anti-Semitism was at flood-tide in Germany, and was flowing high in France, and when bigots like Stoecker, fools like Ahlwardt, and knaves like Drumont, were finding imitators on both sides of the Atlantic.   Here in our country, public attention was being centered on the Jewish refugees from Russia, and the Jewish people throughout the land were massing their strength to cope with the problems which Muscovite tyranny had set before them.   In the midst of this agitation, the magazine article referred to, slurring the Jewish people as it did, attracted unusual attention, and being widely quoted and commented on by the newspaper press, it attained a degree of publicity out of all proportion to its merits or its authorship.

Under these circumstances I felt myself impelled to reply to the writer in the *North American Review*, and at once sent to that magazine a letter embodying a statement of a few indisputable facts bearing on the subject.   This statement the publishers of the magazine declined to print on the ground that they had received so many articles on the subject that they could not undertake to discriminate in favor of any one of them, and that they would therefore publish none.   My cursorily compiled citations were, however, published at the time in the Washington *Post*, and as germane to my present subject I reprint them in the main, as follows :—

" Has this much-traveled and keen observer, Mr. Rogers, ever heard of General Edward S. Salomon, who enlisted as Lieutenant-Colonel of the 82d Illinois ?   He became Colonel of the regiment after Colonel Frederick Hecker's retirement, was made Brigadier-General, was subsequently appointed by General Grant governor of Washington Territory, and, at present residing in San Francisco, has been Department

Commander of the Grand Army of the Republic, and is recognized as one of the bravest and most gallant officers that ever sat in saddle. This encomium I have from the lips of General Grant himself, and it will be cheerfully endorsed by General O. O. Howard, or by any of the officers yet living who served with him. In the same regiment, as I have learned from General Salomon, were more than one hundred private soldiers and subalterns of Jewish faith. General L. C. Newman, of the city of New York, who was fatally wounded in the first battle of the Rebellion, died in the city of Washington, while President Lincoln, who had brought Newman's commission as Brevet Brigadier-General, was with him at his bedside. General Leopold Blumenberg, of Baltimore, who, as Major of his regiment, was severely wounded at the battle of Antietam, and crippled for life and who was subsequently brevetted for his meritorious services, was one of the most loyal and brave of officers. Colonel M. M. Spiegel, of the 120th Ohio, who was severely wounded before Vicksburg, was entreated to retire from the army, but continued in the service and was killed in the campaign of General Banks, in Louisiana. Lieutenant Sachs, of the 32d Indiana, in command of a company of his regiment at Green River, in 1862, stood single-handed and alone against a company of Texas Rangers, and after killing and wounding eight of his assailants, fell riddled to death. His heroism and bravery had meanwhile given the command time to rally, and they thereupon dispersed the enemy. Captain A. Hart, of the 73d Pennsylvania, now of this city, who was Adjutant of his regiment, was severely wounded in the early part of the war, and is now a pensioner of the United States. Lieutenant Henry Franc, of the Kansas Volunteers, living in this city to-day, did splendid service. Judge. P. J. Joachimson, Lieutenant-Colonel of the 59th New York; Isidore Pinkson, Henry Pinkson and Moses Landauer, of the 110th New York; Captain Lyon and Lieutenant Ababot, of the 5th New York Cavalry; Theodore Wise, of the same regiment; Herman White, and A. T. Gross, of the 2d Maryland, and I. Feldstein, now a member of Koltes Post, New York, acquitted themselves with ample credit in their respective spheres. The 11th New York was more than half composed of men of Jewish faith. In the 2d Pennsylvania Artillery, serving under Captain R. M. Goundy, who lives in this city, there were three Jewish soldiers; Lieutenant Liebschutz, who served throughout the war and was promoted for gallantry on the field, now living in this city to-day ; Leo Karpeles, who is now a clerk in the Post Office Department, to whom a special medal was awarded by Congress for bravery and for the capture with his own hands of rebel flags on the field of battle, and Simon Stern, who died lately in this city and whose widow has been granted a pension. George Stern, who died from disease contracted in the service, also left a widow, now pensioned. Dr. A. Behrend, of this city, who served in our army with great ability, not only as a hospital steward, but as an officer in the field, tells me that in 1863 a general order was issued permitting Jews to be furloughed over their Holy Days, and that at Fairfax Seminary he furloughed eleven on that occasion. Dr. Herman Bendall, of Albany, a prominent citizen of that city, was promoted to the grade of Lieutenant-Colonel in recognition of his meritorious services and was subsequently appointed by General Grant superintendent of Indian affairs of Arizona. Jacob Hirsch, of this city, died from disease contracted in the service and his orphan children are now receiving a pension for their father's sacrifice ; Captain Cohn, of New York City, now connected with the Baron de Hirsch Trust Fund, was as brave an officer as ever did duty. M. L. Peixotto, of the 103 Ohio (a brother of the well-known Benjamin F. Peixotto), died last year in consequence of wounds received and disease contracted in the service. Mr. Bruckheimer, now a practicing physician in this city, Charles Raum, one of our leading merchants, Mr. Hoffa, Sol Livingston, M. Erdman, M. Augenstein, and S. Goodman, all of this city, Edward S. Woog, a clerk in the Interior Department ; Morris Cohen, clerk in the War Department; Henry Blondheim, of Alexandria, Va., were soldiers in the late war. Captain Morris Lewis, of the 18th New York Cavalry, now living in this city, served on General Kearney's staff ; he receives a special pension, having been shot through the body and paralyzed in his lower limbs. August Bruckner was killed at the second battle of Bull Run. Colonel M. Einstein and Colonel M. Friedman, both of Philadelphia, commanded regiments ; Uriah P. Levy was Commodore of the United States Navy. Jacob Hayes, of the city of New York, Mr. Phillips, son of the sexton of the Portuguese congregation of that city, E. J. Russell, of the 19th Indiana, a resident of this city, and so severely wounded as to render him almost incapable of work ; L. Myers, of the same regiment, and Julius Steinmeyer, of the 7th United States Infantry ''stood shoulder to shoulder '' at the front. General William Meyer, editor of several New York papers, served with credit and distinction during the draft riots in the city of New York, and has in his possession an autograph letter from President Lincoln thanking him for his eminent services during those hours of darkness. William Durst, of Philadelphia, is one of the few survivors of the memorable fight between the Monitor and the Merrimac ; when volunteers were called for he went to his duty with death staring him in the face, and Admiral Worden himself told me some months ago that Durst was a man of distinguished bravery, whose services should be specially recognized by Congress. Major Joseph G. Rosengarten, of Philadelphia, is a soldier of national reputation and an author of ability, whose brother Adolph G. Rosengarten was killed at Stone River while acting as staff officer. Quartermaster Rosenfield, of the 13th Kansas, not only discharged the duties of that office with ability, but served also in the ranks. Lieutenant Rosenberg, of this city, is now dead, and his widow is pensioned. Colonel H. A. Seligson, who died some two months ago, led a Vermont regiment during the war, and achieved a high reputation as a soldier. Captain Frederick Leavy, of the 1st New York Infantry; Captain Max Conheim, of New York, and now of San Francisco, and Major H. Kœnigsberger, of Cincinnati, were officers of distinction, and so, too, were David Ezekiel and Lieutenant Louis Blumenthal, of New Hampshire. Sergeant Elias Leon Hyneman, of the 5th Pennsylvania Cavalry, was one of the heroes of the war, in which he served from the beginning. In June, 1864, during a cavalry sortie about Petersburg, while his command was retreating before the main body of the enemy, he hurried to the relief of a dismounted and wounded comrade. He lifted him into his own saddle and enabled him to escape, and started to make his own way on foot. On his way he met another comrade, barefooted and bleeding; he took off his own boots and gave them to the sufferer. But he himself was captured, and after months of agony in Andersonville, he died

Frederick Kneffler, a resident of Indianapolis, attained the rank of Major General; he commanded the 79th Indiana, and was conspicuous for bravery at the battle of Chickamauga. As a further list of officers and privates in the various commands, I may yet add the names of Lieutenant Suldman, 44th New York; Captain Gremitz, 62d Pennsylvania; Corporal Gisner, 142d Pennsylvania; Lieutenant Evan Davis, 115th Pennsylvania; Sergeant Myers, 62d Pennsylvania; Captain A. Goldman, 17th Maine; Lieutenant A. A. Rinehard, 148th Pennsylvania; Lieutenant Nieman, 103d New York; M. S. Asher, 103d New York; Lieutenant George Perdinger, 39th New York; Lieutenant Philip Truffinger, 57th New York; Lieutenant Herman Musschel, 68th New York; Lieutenant Herman Krauth, 103d New York; Lieutenant Julius Frank, 103d New York; Captain H. P. Schwerin, 119th New York; Julius Niebergall, Levi Kuehne and Henry Luterman, all of the New York 3d Artillery, and Lehman Israels, Lieutenant in the 58th New York.

It must be taken into account that when the War of the Rebellion broke out the number of Jews in the United States was quite limited; according to the census taken in 1876 by

Mr. William B. Hackenburg, of Philadelphia, and myself, in behalf of the Union of American Hebrew Congregations, there
were then in the United States, fifteen years after the war commenced, only 250,000 Jews. It is altogether doubtful whether
there were more than 150,000, if that many, when hostilities
commenced. The proportion of Jewish soldiers is, therefore,
only large, but is perhaps larger than that of any other faith in
the United States. I have been told by one of the Jewish soldiers
in this city, one who bears the scars of the war, that there were
at least, as far as he could judge—and he had experience during
the whole conflict—from 6,000 to 8,000 soldiers of the Jewish
faith in the Union Army alone. I am not prepared to assert
this number, but would not be surprised if it were found to be
correct.

The animus of the writer in the *North American Review* is
indicated by the words, "*Except in General Sherman's Department, and he promptly ordered them out of it for speculating in
cotton and conveying information to the Confederates.*" This
statement is made with the same disregard of facts as are others
in the article referred to, for while a few Jews may have
violated the laws of war by running the blockade or furnishing
information to the enemy, it was no more than others of other
races and religious faiths did under like circumstances, even
to a larger degree: and why the Jews as a class should be
held up to the contempt and scorn of the world in consequence of the want of patriotism of a few of their number, is to
me a profound mystery, and can only be explained upon the
theory that inculcated prejudice is stronger than the desire for
fair play or the regard for justice. No one for a moment would
charge a particular class of Christians with want of honesty
because one or more of their number had violated law. The War
Department records and the Treasury files will furnish ample
evidence of the fact that many of the sins that were committed
by others were heaped upon the shoulders of the Jews.   It has
always been an easy thing to strike at the minority and from time
immemorial the prejudice against the Jew has been made a
convenient vehicle for furthering malignant purposes and selfish
ends.

Having enjoyed the friendship of President Grant and of
General Sherman (I was for eight years officially connected with
the former, and for a time on intimate social terms with the
latter), I can state that I had repeated conversations with them
regarding "Order No. 11," which was issued over the signature
of General Grant, but of which he, at the time, had absolutely no
knowledge.   This fact I proved conclusively during the presidential campaign of 1888, when political capital was being made
against General Grant among the Jews. By both generals I

was assured that there had been a great deal of misinformation on the subject, and, that if they could permit themselves to speak of the facts as they were known to them it would not be the Jews who would be shown to have been derelict but a large number of Christians, many of whom had come highly recommended. It was the latter who were abusing the privilige accorded to them by the authorities at Washington and who had given both generals a great amount of trouble and annoyance.

I admit that it is unfortunate that the writer of the earlier article in the *North American Review*, whose statements otherwise deserve the fullest consideration, should have been led into so glaring an error as to name Generals Lyon and Rosecrans as Jewish soldiers. While we would have no objection to classing them among our American citizens of Jewish faith, we can substantiate our case very well without doing so, as the cursory list which I have cited will abundantly show. But while admitting the error of the earlier writer I cannot allow the statement of the latter one, with its implication that there was no one of Jewish faith who battled for the Union, to go unchallenged. The Jewish cemeteries of this city, and of every other large city in the land, contain the remains of brave men of Jewish birth who are not forgotten on Decoration Day by their surviving comrades of Christian faith; and what these men recognize the American people will not ignore.

The armies of every country afford ample proof of Jewish patriotism and valor. Even in benighted and tyrannical Russia, where, to a large extent they are soldiers by compulsion— 50,000 or 60,000 of them — their officers have uniformly admitted that in battle there were no braver men than the Jews. The late Franco-German war afforded instances of distinguished heroism on the part of Jewish officers and soldiers in both armies. The Italian army and the French army to-day contain a large contingent of Jewish officers and privates who are not only respected, but honored by their compatriots. In the Turkish army some of the leading officers are of Jewish faith. Patriotism, however, is not confined to the field of battle; in private life, from time immemorial, acts have been performed of greater service, possibly, than any in the field, showing greater powers of endurance and evincing higher virtues than were ever recorded in the annals of war. During our late conflict many who remained at home made sacrifices of the most heroic character, and did their duty cheerfully and with alacrity, and I know of none who did their part more fully than the citizens of the United States of Jewish faith. In fact, the history of the Jewish people is one long tragedy of personal sacrifice and heroism. But as I wish to trespass no longer on the columns of your valuable paper, I beg leave to close with this simple statement; that it seems to me high time for Americans of all faiths to frown down all attempts that have for their object the lowering and humiliation of any class of our citizens.''

SIMON WOLF.

Finding that my letter had been copied extensively, not only by the Jewish press, but by leading newspapers in the country, and favorably commented on generally, I determined to give to the world, as complete as I might find possible, a list of American citizens of Jewish faith who had "stood shoulder to shoulder" on the field of battle, and to add thereto the record of some typical instances of exceptional energy and public spirit in the civil walks of life.

What I had anticipated and supposed would be an easy task, requiring probably no more than six months at the utmost, has taken more than four years of continuous work, notwithstanding the assistance I received from many quarters, and I am even now compelled to give this work to the public in an inadequate form, with the feeling that it is incomplete and that much more should have been made of it.

The difficulties in the way of completing fully and accurately such a compilation as I have here attempted will scarcely be realized by those who have not undertaken a similar task. The work was begun nearly thirty years after the close of the war, when many of those whose names were to be gathered were dead, and many others dispersed throughout our vast domain and beyond our borders. In response to three successive calls made through the leading newspapers of the country, I received, indeed, a large number of replies, but after all, the great majority even of the survivors failed to respond, and of the data that reached me much could not be classified. Nearly a thousand names are accordingly placed in the unclassified list.

By far the majority of the names herein included were

furnished by the soldiers themselves or their relatives, but a large number of them were sent to me by army comrades of the men referred to. Some of these may be incorrectly quoted both as to their names and the commands with which they were connected, but these errors may scarcely be considered as affecting the general result, so far at least as numbers are concerned. It was naturally impossible to verify all the notices sent to me, and this compilation must therefore, in the very nature of the case, be more or less imperfect and incomplete, but I may say without hesitation that the work is free from all errors which could be eliminated through a patient and cautious scrutiny. Several hundred names of soldiers from Indiana alone were finally excluded from my present lists, notwithstanding their pronounced Jewish character, such as Marks, Abrahams, Isaacs and others of a similar strain, whose owners were ascertained by my correspondents to be non-Jews, while on the other hand many soldiers bearing names of decidedly non-Jewish derivation were authenticated as Jews. If many whose names should be included fail to see them on this "roll of honor" the fault is at all events not mine, and the earnest effort which I have given to this work, wholly a "labor of love" on my part, leaves me free from the necessity of offering apology for whatever errors of omission or of commission may remain in it. The public records could not be utilized, because our army lists, unlike those of foreign powers, make no registry of the religious faith of the enrolled soldiers. I should, in this connection, urge upon my readers to aid me with such corrections of these army lists as they may be able to furnish, with the view to the record being perfected as far as may be, in a future edition of this book.

Unsatisfactory and at times discouraging as has been my task and its outcome, I have yet had at times the pleasure of obtaining and recording data of a most gratifying character. One of the most pleasing results of my labors is the fact that I am able to present a list of fourteen Jewish families that contributed to the Union and Confederate armies no less than fifty-one soldiers. Three, four, five brothers; a father and three sons, a father and four sons, volunteers in a deadly strife, leaving their homes and kindred, breaking their family ties to face privation, disease, wounds and death, sacrificing all to fight with their compatriots for the cause which they deemed right.

My primary purpose has been to show that the Jewish people throughout the land not only took a share in the struggle which has ended so beneficently as to have brought prosperity to both antagonists and dispelled the cause of discord, but that they took their full share, and it is now conclusively shown that the enlistment of Jewish soldiers, north and south, reached proportions considerably in excess of their ratio to the general population. This fact had become apparent before my present work had been systematically begun, as I indicated in my letter to the Washington *Post*, quoted above, but the lists obtained by me, incomplete as they must inevitably be, make up a number that leaves no reasonable doubt on this subject. This fact, in view of statements minimizing the numbers of Jewish soldiers of the late war, or denying the existence of any at all, cannot be too strongly emphasized. To complete, however, my ultimate purpose of presenting a consideration of the Jew as citizen and philanthropist as well as patriot and soldier, I have herein collated a symposium of expressions on this comprehensive subject from sources at once authoritative and unbiased. I have included in this collection of views and reviews, the carefully considered statements of many of the foremost men of modern times, statesmen and soldiers, philosophers, divines, writers and other leaders of public opinion, as widely divergent in locality as they are unanimous in sentiment. Among these I have included only such as are entirely non-Jewish in their origin, men whose thoughts are the expressions of well-disciplined minds, and whose opinions are the deliverances of an impartial judgment.

I gladly record my obligations to the Grand Army of the Republic for the aid afforded me in obtaining information through the machinery of its organization, and to General J. B. Gordon, of the Confederate Memorial Association, for a like co-operation. To the Union of American Hebrew Congregations, to the Independent Order of B'nai B'rith, and to the Jewish Publication Society of America, I am indebted for contributions to the cost of publication and for other aid in the prosecution of my work.

I owe my thanks to Captain Eugene H. Levy, Mr. George Alexander Kohut and Mr. Max J. Kohler, of New York, to Messrs. Lewis Abraham and L. Lichtenstein, of Washington, for their assistance, and especially to Colonel F. C. Ainsworth, of the War Department, for the loan of Records. To Mr. Henry S. Morais' recent historical work on ''The Jews of Philadelphia,'' I am much indebted for valuable data, and other important materials have been gleaned from Mr. Isaac Markens' compendious work on ''The Hebrews in America.'' To the Jewish press I owe acknowledgement for many welcome items of information and for repeated expressions of encouragement.

Finally, among my obligations to numerous correspondents in different parts of the country are those which I owe to many soldiers of Christian faith, some of them officers of distinguished rank, who afforded me much valuable information and who added, in almost every case, some warm expression of their sympathy and good-will.

Washington, D. C., June, 1895.

JEWISH PATRIOTS OF THE REVOLUTIONARY PERIOD.

The keen and responsive sense of duty with which, through Torah and Talmud, the Jewish character is so deeply imbued, has never failed to become manifest when occasion has called it forth. Jews have never been wanting in patriotism and though a peace-loving people, (the very mission of Israel being peace, and good-will towards neighbors a cardinal teaching of Judaism) they have always espoused, eagerly and earnestly, the cause of their countrymen. The heroism and self-devotion which marks the course of Jewish history from the earliest Biblical records, emblazoning the era of the Maccabees, signalizing the Roman period and illuminating the Dark Ages, has found many a worthy example in these modern days. We have here to deal with the records of but one country, yet these records are replete with instances of bravery and undaunted courage, of earnest devotion and of faithful service performed by men of Israel in behalf of this land of their adoption. These records begin at a time before the Revolutionary epoch, when the Jewish settlers in America were very few indeed. At the date of the first census, in 1790, just after the close of the Revolution, when the total population of the country was figured at almost 4,000,000, the number of Jewish inhabitants could scarcely be estimated at 3,000, or only one to 1,330 of the population.*

The dearth of accessible records of a detailed character rendered it practically impossible to present more than a very imperfect list of the Jewish participants in the Revolutionary struggle. However, sufficient data are at hand to prove conclusively that the Jewish colonists of that period, comparatively recent settlers and few in number as they were, furnished, as usual in all struggles for liberty and freedom, more than their

---

* According to a careful estimate by Mr. Isaac Harby, in 1826, there were then, nearly forty years after the Revolution, not over 6,000 Jews in the United States.

proportion of supporters to the colonial cause. They not only risked their lives in the war for independence, but aided materially with their money to equip and maintain the armies of the Revolution. That they took their part in the earliest stages of resistance to the encroachments of the mother country is proved by the signatures to the Non-Importation Resolutions of 1765. Nine Jews were among the signers of these resolutions, the adoption of which was the first organized movement in the agitation which eventually led to the independence of the colonies. The original document is still preserved in Carpenter's Hall, in Philadelphia, and following are the names of the Jews on that early roll of patriots:

Benjamin Levy, Samson Levy, Joseph Jacobs, Hyman Levy, Jr., David Franks, Mathias Bush, Michael Gratz, Barnard Gratz, Moses Mordecai.

With these as worthy precursors of the Jewish patriots of the Revolution we may proceed to note the list of Jews whose names have come to us from the Revolutionary period, through various published sources, as men of special distinction among their fellows. One of the most notable of these was Haym Salomon, a man who, while not the only Jewish patriot that lavished his ample fortune in behalf of liberty and independence, yet stands out as so unique a figure in the history of the American Revolution that the record of his part in the making of that history may well take precedence. Fragmentary presentations of this subject have been made in public documents and in historic essays at various times since the submission by Salomon himself of his memorial to the Continental Congress in August, 1778.* However, as embracing a succint statement and detailed review of the whole matter to the present time, the following paper from the "Publications of the American Jewish Historical Society" (No. 2, 1894) may be quoted in full :—

* See Markens, "The Hebrews in America" (New York, 1888), and Morais, "Jews of Philadelphia" (Philadelphia, 1894).

A SKETCH OF HAYM SALOMON.

FROM AN UNPUBLISHED MS. IN THE PAPERS OF JARED
SPARKS.

[Contributed by HERBERT B. ADAMS, PH. D., Professor in the Johns
Hopkins University. With Notes by J. H. HOLLANDER.]

In the fall of 1841, Jared Sparks, while professor of history
in Harvard College, was delivering a course of lyceum lectures
in New York City upon the American Revolution.   His remarks
upon the services of certain public men of the period excited
deep interest in the mind of a Jewish hearer, Mr. Haym M.
Salomon, who wrote to and afterwards called upon Mr. Sparks
in reference to the patriotic activity of Haym Salomon, a contemporary and associate of Robert Morris, James Madison,
Edmund Randolph and other distinguished publicists of the
Revolutionary period.   At the request of Mr. Sparks, Mr.
Salomon prepared certain memoranda of the eminent services
of his father, Haym Salomon, and this manuscript passed into
the possession of Mr. Sparks.

The interview and the information thus obtained seem to
have made a profound impression upon Mr. Sparks.   He mentioned something of the above matter to Mr. Joshua I. Cohen,
of Baltimore, and almost a quarter of a century after the original interview, under date of October 29, 1865, Mr. Cohen
wrote to Mr. Sparks as follows :

"You may probably recollect a conversation I had with you
many years ago during a visit to Cambridge, in which I mentioned that Judge Noah, of New York, was then engaged in
gathering together the facts and memorials of the part which
our people, the Israelites, took in our Revolutionary struggle,
and you kindly offered to him through me the use of your biographical series for any memoirs he might prepare on the subject.   The death of Judge Noah, not long after, put an end to
the project.   I mentioned to you a military company that was
formed in Charleston, S. C., composed almost exclusively of

Israelites, of which my uncle was a member, and which behaved well during the war. Major Frank, one of Arnold's aids, was spoken of, and also Haym Salomon and others. In connection with Mr. Salomon you expressed yourself very fully, and, in substance (if I recollect correctly), that his association with Robert Morris was very ·close and intimate, and that a great part of the success that Mr. Morris attained in his financial schemes was due to the skill and ability of Haym Salomon. I do not pretend to quote your language, but only the idea. The matter was brought up to my mind recently by the marriage of a great-grandson of Mr. Salomon to a niece of mine, one of the young ladies of our household.'' *

The original sketch of Haym Salomon thus prepared by his son was found in a somewhat mutilated condition by Professor Herbert B. Adams, of the Johns Hopkins University, among the Sparks Papers, which had been entrusted to his care during the preparation of '' The Life and Writings of Jared Sparks,'' published in 1893 by Houghton, Mifflin & Co. The manuscript was stitched to other papers and had been apparently cut down somewhat in order to make it more uniform in size with the smaller sheets. This fact will explain certain tantalizing, but apparently brief omissions in the text. The appended copy of the manuscript is furnished by Professor Adams with the full consent of the Sparks family.

Haym Salomon, who died in Philadelphia, then the metropolis of the United States, January, 1785, was the fellow-countryman and intimate associate of the Polish Generals Pulaski and

* See Adams, Life and Writings of Jared Sparks, Vol. II., p. 564. From the general tenor of the letter, it seems probable that Mr. Sparks, during his extensive researches into the historical records, public and private, of the United States, had encountered other evidence of the services of Haym Salomon. This inference is partially corroborated by a passage in a letter written by Mr. Sparks from Cambridge on May 7, 1845, to Mr. Haym M. Salomon, apparently in connection with the first memorial to Congress : '' Among the numerous papers that have passed under my eye I have seen evidences of his [*Haym Salomon's*] transactions, which convince me that he rendered important services to the United States in their pecuniary affairs.'' See Report on Claim of H. M. Salomon ; Senate Reports, No. 177, 31st Cong., 1st Sess., Vol. I. It is not, however, impossible that only the present manuscript may be here referred to.

Kosciuszko, and was first publicly known in 1778, when he was taken by the British General Sir H. Clinton in New York on charges that he had received orders from General Washington to burn their fleets and destroy their store-houses, which he had attempted to execute to their great injury and damage. He was accordingly imprisoned, treated inhumanly, and ordered to suffer military death. From the sacrifice of his life, with which he was threatened in consequence of the sentence, he escaped by means of a considerable bribe in gold. This is corroborated from his letter to his brother-in-law, Major Franks, dated soon after in Philadelphia, in which his intimacy is stated with the brave General McDougall, who then commanded the American army in the neighborhood of New York, and with whom it appears he must have been in co-operation in order to drive . . . away from the comfortable quarters, which the maritime and military positions of that city so happily promised them after its abandonment by the friends of the Revolution.*

A few days after his escape from the merciless enemy he

---

* It is probable that Haym Salomon's first encounter with the British Government took place several years before 1778. The Senate Report to the 31st Congress (*supra*) states that : " As early as 1775 he became obnoxious to the British Government, and was imprisoned in New York, sharing the privations and horrors of the sufferers confined in a loathsome prison called the Provost." Essentially the same fact is repeated in later Reports, and is specifically presented in certified form in a later part of the present paper.

The Memorial of Haym Salomon to the Continental Congress (see Bibliographical Note, *infra*) is of such immediate interest in connection with the circumstances of his escape from New York as to permit partial citation. It sets forth : " That your Memorialist was some time before the Entry of the British Troops at the said City of New York and soon after taken up as a Spy and by General Robertson committed to the Provost. That by the Interposition of Lieut-General Heister (who wanted him on account of his knowledge in the French, Polish, Russian, Italian &c. Languages) he was given over to the Hessian Commander who appointed him in the Commissary Way as purveyor chiefly for the Officers. That being at New York he has been of great Service to the French and American prisoners and has assisted them with Money and helped them off to make their Escape. That this and his close connexions with such of the Hessian Officers as were inclined to resign and with Monsieur Samuel Demezes has rendered him at last so obnoxious to the British Head Quarters that he was already pursued by the Guards and on Tuesday the 11th inst. he made his happy Escape from thence." The Memorial bears date of August 25, 1778, thus indicating the precise time of Salomon's departure from New York as August 11, 1778.

safely arrived in Philadelphia, where he was welcomed and esteemed as one devoted to the principle . . . [*MS. cut off.*]

We then find him meriting the well-placed confidence and affection of the patriots who had been distinguished in the Revolutionary Congress of 1776 ; also the great men who were famous in those succeeding sessions, 1780, '81, '82, '83 and '84, as furnished us by such circumstantial testimony as yet remains of that immortal body of devoted patriots.

It is seen as soon as the generous monarch of France agreed to furnish the expiring government of that day with means to reanimate their exertions in the glorious cause. It was he who was charged with the negotiation of the entire amount of those munificent grants of pecuniary supplies from the government of France and Holland.*

In 1783–4, after the satisfactory close of these truly confidential services, he is found to have made considerable advances, moneys, loans, &c., to Robert Morris, of the Congress of the Declaration of '76. To General Miflin, to General St. Clair, to General Steuben, to Colonel Shee, to Colonel Morgan, Major McPherson, Major Franks, and many other officers such sums as they required. And as it regarded the deputies to the Continental Congress, [*to*] the amiable Judge Wilson (another member of the session of '76) considerable loans.†

To the immortal delegation from Virginia, namely, Arthur Lee, Theodore Bland, Joseph Jones, John F. Mercer and Edmund Randolph, liberal supplies of timely and pecuniary aid, and we find it declared by one of the most accomplished, most learned and patriotic members of the succeeding sessions of the Revolutionary legislature, James Madison, that when by the . . . [*MS. cut off*] pecuniary resources of the members of Congress, both public and private, were cut off, recourse was

---

* For details see Report to 31st Congress. The exact location of this and other Congressional Reports is given in the Bibliographical Note appended to the paper.

† This is corroborated by a letter from the eminent jurist, Henry Wheaton, to Haym M. Salomon. Among "the patriots of the Revolution who were compelled to sacrifice their private pursuits to the public," Mr. Wheaton mentions Judge Wilson, "who must have retired from public service if he had not been sustained by the timely aid of your father, administered with equal generosity and delicacy." See Report to 31st Congress.

2

had to Mr. Salomon for means to answer their current expenses, and he was always found extending his friendly hand.*

The exalted and surviving delegate of the Revolutionary Congress above alluded to, who has since that period been promoted for two successive terms to the chief magistracy of these States, in his letter on the subject of the character of Mr. Haym Salomon, testifies fully as to the unquestionable uprightness of his transactions, as well as the disinterestedness of his "friendship," and also his "intelligence," and which no doubt from his confidential intercourse with the foreign ambassadors made his communications serviceable to the public safety.† That conferences were sought with him by the great

* Under date of August 27, 1782, Mr. Madison wrote from Philadelphia to Edmund Randolph : " I cannot in any way make you more sensible of the importance of your kind attention to pecuniary remittances for me than by informing you that I have for some time been a pensioner on the favor of Haym Salomon, a Jew Broker." See Gilpin, Madison Papers, I., 163. During the following month Mr. Madison's position seems to have grown more aggravated, for, on September 24, he declared : " I am relapsing fast into distress. The case of my brethren is equally alarming." *Ibid*, p. 176. Assistance in sufficient amount was still not forthcoming, and a week later, September 30, 1782, he acknowledged to Mr. Randolph the local source of his benefactions as follows : " I am almost ashamed to acknowledge my wants so incessantly to you, but they begin to be so urgent that it is impossible to suppress them. The kindness of our little friend in Front street, near the coffee-house, is a fund that will preserve me from extremities, but I never resort to it without great mortification, as he obstinately rejects all recompense. The price of money is so usurious that he thinks it ought to be extorted from none but those who aim at profitable speculations. To a necessitous delegate, he gratuitously spares a supply out of his private stock." *Ibid*, pp. 178–179.

There seems little doubt but that the " little friend in Front street " is meant to indicate Haym Salomon. This view is taken by the Congressional committees and by Madison's biographer ; see Gay, Life of James Madison, p. 25. The fact that the first Philadelphia City Directory was issued in 1785, and that Haym Salomon died on January 6 of that year (*vide infra*), renders direct verification impracticable. Search among the Philadelphia newspapers of the period would probably determine the point once for all.

† The writer of the MS. is probably quoting from memory from a letter written by Mr. Madison from Montpelier, on February 6, 1830, to Mr. Haym M. Salomon, in connection with claims upon Congress for indemnity. The Senate Report to the 31st Congress preserves the following paragraph of this letter : " The transactions shown by the papers you enclosed were the means of effectuating remittances for the support of the delegates [*to Congress*], and the agency of your father therein was solicited, on account of the respectability and confidence he enjoyed among those best acquainted with him."

The Report to the 37th Congress mentions among the various letters

men of the time is proved from the existence of a note in the handwriting of another member of the Congress of Declaration, the incorruptible President Reed.

His services to the cause of his country were not confined to aiding the native agents of our own government, but he was the most confidential friend and timely adviser to the agents, consuls, and ambassadors representing the interests of the kings of those countries then in our alliance, as it appears from the amount of specie granted for the service of the army and hospital of Rochambaud, and large sums appear to have been received from him by Chevalier De La Luzerne, Marbois, consul-general, De La Forest, John . . . [*MS, cut off*], recollected by the elders of the nation as the active agents of the good French king.*

As to the minister of the King of Spain, then the richest of the European monarchs. The amount granted him was expressly to relieve the wants, conveniences and necessities of this ambassador, whose king was then countenancing the Revolution in this country, but with whose European dominions all intercourse was stopped, and in regard to the monies so furnished, whether Mr. S. was ever repaid by Spain is a matter of as much uncertainty as that regarding the considerable sums advanced to other Revolutionary agents.†

received by Haym M. Salomon relative to the justice of his claim, one from James Madison, in 1827, who, among other things, stated: "The transactions shown by the papers you enclose were for the support of the delegates to Congress, and the agency of your father therein was solicited on account of the respect and confidence he enjoyed among those best acquainted with him,' etc., and concludes with the wish that the memorialist might be properly indemnified."

The resemblance between the two paragraphs is so striking as to make it probable, despite the discrepancy in dates, that the same communication is referred to.

* The Report to the 31st Congress states: "On the accession of the Count de la Luzerne to the embassy from France, Mr. Salomon was made the banker of that government. . . . He was also appointed by Monsieur Roquebrune, treasurer of the forces of France in America, to the office of their paymaster-general, which he executed free of charge."

† Details of the assistance so rendered are given in the Report to the 31st Congress. Mr. Salomon, it is said, "maintained from his own private purse Don Francesco Rendon, the secret ambassador of that monarch for nearly two years, or up to the death of Mr. S., during which Rendon's supplies were cut off." A striking passage is quoted in the same Report from a letter said to have been written in 1783 by Rendon to the Governor-General of Cuba, Don José Marie de Navarra:

It appears that the death of Mr. S. after a short and severe illness was quite as unexpected as calamitous to his family, leaving no will nor relatives in this country competent to take charge of his estate, at this difficult period of the unsettled state of the jurisprudence of the country, being four years prior to the formation of the Constitution of the United States.

A letter from him yet exists, dated in New York a few days previous to his return and death, directed to the agent of his house in Philadelphia, in which he speaks of the full competency of his fortune and his intention of retiring from business. An additional inducement no doubt was owing to the impaired state of his health from the great exertions he had made to promote the views of the Revolution, and which letter further declares that he had many claims uncollected due him,[1] and spoke of the quantities of public securities and government papers which . . . [*MS. cut off*]. Of this latter, on examination of a list deposited in the Probate Office, it appears there was upwards of $300,000, more than $160,000 of which were of certificates of the Loan Office of the Treasury and the army.*

" Mr. Salomon has advanced the money for the service of his most Catholic Majesty and I am indebted to his friendship in this particular, for the support of my character as his most Catholic Majesty's agent here, with any degree of credit and reputation ; and without it, I would not have been able to render that protection and assistance to his Majesty's subjects which his Majesty enjoins and my duty requires." The statement is also made that : " Moneys thus advanced to the amount of about 10,000 Spanish dollars remained unpaid, when Mr. Salomon died shortly after."

[1] Mr. Henry S. Morais, in his history of "The Jews of Philadelphia," notes as follows : (p. 24.) "The amount has been variously given at as much as $600,000 and more. Hon. Simon Wolf, of Washington, D. C., in February, 1892, presented a complete and elaborate statement of this question, based upon official documents, in an article (entitled, "Are Republics Ungrateful ?") published in the *Reform Advocate*, of Chicago."

In another note on the same subject Mr. Morais states : " Mr. Salomon's loan and its accruing interest would now (1893) amount to over $3,000,000." Haym M. Salomon, a son of the philanthropist, and who kept a store on Front street, vainly endeavored to obtain payment of his just claim, nothwithstanding that it was favorably reported to the U. S Senate in 1850. In this report it was said : ' Haym Salomon gave great assistance to the government by loans of money and advancing liberally of his means to sustain the men engaged in the struggle for independence at a time when the sinews of war were essential to success.' "

* For a summary of the account see the certificate appended, *infra*. Some few further details of the inventory are given in the Committee Report to the 30th Congress.

At his decease the management of his estate passed into the hands of strangers, all of whom not very long after became either bankrupts or died, as well as Mr. Macrea,* his chief clerk, who had committed suicide about the same period. Consequently the books and papers have nearly been all lost, and the obscurity into which these matters are thrown is increased in consequence of the destruction by the British of many of the public archives of that period, during the invasion of the city of Washington by their army during the last war.† And such were the effects of those unfortunate circumstances to the heirs that when the youngest son became of age nothing was obtained from the personal estate of this munificent and patriotic individual in Philadelphia. And no other inheritance now survives to the offspring except the expectation of the grateful remembrance of a just and generous republic.

It ought not to be forgotten, that although he endorsed a great portion of those bills of exchange for the amount of the loans and subsidies our government obtained in Europe, of which he negotiated the entire sums, and the execution of which duty occupied a great portion of his valuable time from '81 to '83, still there was only charged scarcely a fractional percentage to the United States, although individuals were willing to pay him . . . [*MS. cut off*] for his other negotiations and guarantee. And it is known that he never caused the loss to the government of one cent of those many millions of his negotiations, either by his own mismanagement or from the credit he gave to others on the sales he made of those immense sums of foreign drafts on account of the United States.‡

We find that immediately after the peace of '83, when foreign commerce could securely float again on the ocean, that he resumed his business as a merchant for the few remaining months

---

* "Mr. McCrea," in the Report to the 31st Congress.

† Mr. Joseph Nourse, Register of the Treasury of the United States from 1777 to 1828, wrote from Washington in 1827, to Mr. H. M. Salomon : "I have cast back to those periods when your honored father was agent to Office of Finance ; but the inroads of the British army in 1814 deprived us of every record in relation to the vouchers of the period to which I refer." See for details, Report to 31st Congress ; also Bibliographical Note.

‡ For details, see Report to 31st Congress.

of his life, trading to foreign countries, which may be collected from the few original letters (that are preserved) bearing date [*of*] London, Holland and Spain, and from the return of the large ship Sally from Spain to his consignment a few weeks succeeding his death, on which cargo and hull he was interested in the sum of 40,000 florins; his estate on the expedition sustained almost total loss, owing to the failures and disasters among merchants of those days, to whom the property had been consigned and by whose advice it had been undertaken.

He was most friendly in aiding those other commercial citizens and merchants who recommenced trading after the war had closed. One remarkable instance [*that*] may be noted among others was the case of Mr. Willing's house, the head of which was the presidert of the National Bank, and whose active partner was the Superintendent of Finance. The firm traded under the name of Willing, Morris & Swanick. To them he made a loan of his name to obtain 40,000 dollars in specie in one amount from the bank. A second loan of his name in addition of 24,000 specie dollars also, a few months preceding his death, for both of which considerable accommodations of credit at this eventful period of our commercial history he never charged them one cent of consideration.*

[Copy of an authentic certificate from the Register's Office in Philadelphia shewing the amount of public securities[1] and Revolutionary papers left by the deceased Haym Salomon at

---

* Hon. Simon Wolf, of Washington, D. C., in an article in *The Reform Advocate* of Chicago (see Bibliographical Note), calls attention to the fact that Professor Sumner—the most recent biographer of Robert Morris—in his "The Financier and the Finances of the American Revolution," makes no mention of the services of Haym Salomon. Mr. Wolf adds: "When I called Mr. Sumner's attention to it he answered in a letter which I received to-day, that he had supposed that Mr. Salomon had been paid long since, and was surprised at the statement which I made."

[1] Not a penny of the large sums represented by these securities has ever been repaid to the heirs of the philanthropist and patriot who so generously aided the Revolutionary cause, and the fact is but another instance of the ingratitude of republics. The remissness of the people's representatives in the adjustment of private claims has been but too often flagrantly demonstrated, but there is not to be found on the public records a more signal case of public injustice. When to pay a debt is everybody's business, then it is apparently forever nobody's' business to do so, and thus it happens that popular governments fail utterly in cases of this nature, where a monarchy would hasten to do justice.

his death and from which personal estate mentioned in said certificate not a cent was ever received by any of his heirs.]

" 58 Loan Office Certificates	. .	\$110,233.65.
19 Treasury "	. .	18,259.50.
2 Virginia State "	. .	8,166.48.
70 Commissioners "	. .	17,870.37.
Continental Liquidated	. .	199,214.45.

$$\$353,744.45.$$

" Seal

" I certify that the above writing is a true extract from the original inventory and appraisement of the personal estate of Haym Salomon deceased filed in the register's office Philadelphia on the 15th February, 1785.

   (Signed) JOHN GEYER, *Register.*

Given under my hand and seal of office this 28th May, A. D. 1828."

[EXTRACT FROM A CERTIFICATE.]

The father of Mr. Haym M. Salomon was the deceased Haym Salomon, Esq., who died in Philadelphia, January 6, 1785, and who is found to have exhibited the most ardent personal devotion to the cause of the Revolution.

On investigating such of the memoranda and papers regarding his civil services in that era of our history which have accidentally been preserved and now submitted, I find the following facts.

By an affidavit made in New York, January, 1778, before Alderman Matthews, certified on its back by William Claygen, military secretary to Major-General Horatio Gates, dated at the encampment White Plains, August 15, 1778, it appears that so early as the year 1775, Mr. S. was in controversy with the enemies of the projected Revolution.

New York, May 9, 1828.

   (Signed) WM. H. BELL.

The affidavit further states that it had been alleged against him in New York that he was charged by General Washington to execute an enterprise as hazardous to the safety of his person and life as it was most important to the interests of the Revolutionary army. Supposed to be the enterprise for which he was condemned to death by the British General Clinton, as mentioned in the first part of this memorandum.

The two infant sons which Mr. Salomon (at the age of 45) left at his death were Ezekiel and Haym. Ezekiel was he (the eldest) who in 1807, in charge of a large amount of American property, was (with many other American citizens whose cargoes as well as his own was sequestered at Leghorn by the French) placed in much perplexity, but through the spirited remonstrance which he made to the Tuscan and French Governments, succeeded in procuring its release. He subsequently was charged with the government of the U. S. Branch Bank at New Orleans, and while in the successful application of the duties of his office died in 1821.

Haym M., the youngest son and sole survivor of the male part of the family, has been engaged in commercial pursuits for many years past, for particulars of which see letter from Hon. Johnson, Esq., who for eight years was the representative in Congress from New York, the Empire City of the United States, and now* one of the chief officers in the Custom House of that city.†

BIBLIOGRAPHICAL NOTE.

Little of the mass of original material at one time in existence relative to the life and activity of Haym Salomon can now be located. Mr. William Salomon, of New York, a great-grandson of Haym Salomon, writes in response to a recent inquiry as follows : " I am under the impression that all the papers bearing on the services of Haym Salomon in the cause of the Revolution which were not lost when he died intestate (and a few months before Haym M. Salomon was born) came into Haym M. Salomon's possession, but unfortunately his descendants have been deprived of that valued inheritance by reason of their disappearance while in the custody of the Government. All

---

* *Circa* 1842.

† A third child of Haym Salomon was a daughter, Sallie Salomon, who married Joseph Andrews. Their son, Joseph I. Andrews, married Miriam Nones, of New York, a daughter of Major Benjamin Nones of Revolutionary fame. The daughter of this union, Louisa Andrews, is now Mrs. E. L. Goldbaum, of Memphis, Tenn. Mr. Goldbaum kindly writes me : " We have in our possession life-size oil paintings of Joseph Andrews, son-in-law of Haym Salomon, and of his wife Sallie Andrews, *née* Sallie Salomon. "

I ever discovered among my father's papers was a letter from either President Tyler or Polk (I cannot remember positively which, and the letter is not now within easy reach) stating that papers my grandfather, Haym M. Salomon, desired to have returned could not be found in the Department where they had been placed."

Some further details of the strange negligence to which this unfortunate loss is due may be found in the Senate Committee Report to the 31st Congress on the claim of H. M. Salomon. The timely services rendered by Haym Salomon to James Madison during the sessions of the Constitutional Convention in Philadelphia are specifically indicated in the published letters of Madison; see Gilpin, Madison Papers, Vol. I., pp. 163, 178–9. Mr. Herbert Friedenwald, of Philadelphia, has recently found among the records of the Continental Congress an interesting Memorial of Haym Salomon, submitted to the Congress in August, 1778; see Publications of American Jewish Historical Society, I., 87. The main sources of information relative to the life of Haym Salomon are thus the secondary Congressional Committee Reports upon the claims of his descendants for indemnity for money advanced to the United States Government during the Revolution. These, in the order of their presentation, are as follows:*

1. Report on Claim of Haym M. Salomon. Rep. F. A. Tallmadge. April 26, 1848. 3 pp. House Reports, No. 504, 30th Cong., 1st Sess., Vol. III.

2. Report on Claim of H. M Salomon. Senator J. D. Bright. July 28, 1848. 3 pp. Senate Reports, No. 219, 30th Cong., 1st Sess.

3. Report on Claim of H. M. Salomon. Senator I. P. Walker. August 9, 1850. 7 pp. Senate Reports, No. 177, 31st Cong., 1st Sess., Vol. I.

4. Report on Claim of Haym M. Salomon. Senator Charles Durkee. March 9, 1860. 10 pp. Senate Reports, No. 127, 36th Cong., 1st Sess., Vol. I.

5. Report on Claim of Haym M. Salomon. Senator M. S. Wilkinson. July 2, 1862. 5 pp. Senate Reports, No. 65, 37th Cong., 2d Sess.

6. Report on Petition of Haym M. Salomon. June 24, 1864. 4 pp. Senate Reports, No. 93, 30th Cong., 1st Sess.

The second, third, fifth and sixth of the above reports have been reprinted in pamphlet form, presumably for private circulation. During the first session of the 29th Congress, the Senate Committee of Claims unanimously agreed upon a report similar to that adopted by the House Committee of the 30th Congress, but too late for presentation. Another report was drawn up during the second session of the same Congress, placed on file, but never adopted. It was largely embodied in the Senate Report to the 31st Congress; see Senate Report

* Poore, Descriptive Catalogue of the Government Publications of the United States (Washington, 1885), pp. 558, 565, 593, 762, 807, 828.

to the 31st Congress. The last sentence of the Report to the 38th Congress: "except the report of this committee made at the last session," and several paragraphs inserted in the Report to the 37th Congress as statements of "the committee of the last Congress," indicate the presentation of additional reports. No positive evidence of their existence has, however, been found. At the second session of the 52d Congress (February 24, 1893), a bill was presented to the House, ordering that a gold medal be struck off in recognition of services rendered by Haym Salomon during the Revolutionary War, in consideration of which the Salomon heirs waived their claims upon the United States for indemnity. The measure was reported favorably by the House Committee on the Library, but too late for consideration. The Report (No. 2556; to accompany H. R. 7896) summarizes the efforts made in previous Congresses, and reprints in full the Senate Report to the 37th Congress.

OTHER JEWISH CONTRIBUTORS TO THE COLONIAL TREASURY.

The monetary contribution by Haym Salomon to the successful issue of the Revolutionary struggle was doubtless the largest made by any individual, but while it is the most signal instance of its kind, it does not stand alone. Haym Salomon was not the only Jew who showed his earnestness in behalf of freedom by a jeopardy or sacrifice of fortune. Among the signers of the Bills of Credit for the Continental Congress in 1776 were Benjamin Levy, of Philadelphia and Benjamin Jacobs, of New York ; and Samuel Lyon, of the same city, was among the signers of similar bills in 1779. Isaac Morris, also of Philadelphia, and who, after the Revolutionary War, was one of the incorporators of the Bank of New York, contributed three thousand pounds sterling (£3000) to the colonial treasury, and still another Philadelphian, Hyman Levy, repeatedly advanced considerable sums for the support of the army in the field. A yet more notable instance of patriotic devotion was that of Manuel Mordecai Noah, of South Carolina, who not only served in the army as officer on Washington's staff, and likewise with General Marion, but gave of his fortune twenty thousand pounds (£20,000) to further the cause in which he was enlisted. Many minor cases of a similar order could be cited, but only the more important instances, such as are of public record, have here been adduced.

INCIDENTS ILLUSTRATIVE OF AMERICAN JEWISH PATRIOTISM.

[A paper written for the American Jewish Historical Society by MAX J. KOHLER.]

In the present article, the writer proposes to set forth several incidents in our history not otherwise connected with each other than the above title indicates, but all tending to show that the Jew has ever been ready to battle for the cause of his adopted country, be his domicile where it may. Our subjects herein had differing views as to what patriotism demanded. We shall speak of French Jews battling for France, of English Jewish Colonists championing England's cause, and of American Jews fighting for American liberty and glory, yet all were equally patriots. In selecting the incidents to be set forth herein the writer has confined himself exclusively to matters which he believes are either wholly unknown to the Jewish historian or only partially or imperfectly known ; no treatment of the main subject, other than these incidents may furnish, will be attempted.

I.

COLONEL DAVID S. FRANKS.

Members have no doubt still fresh in mind the interesting items relating to Col. Franks, set forth by Dr. Herbert Friedenwald 'and Prof. M. Jastrow in No. 1 of our "Proceedings." Since then other data have been collected and published in regard to the Franks family, to which I will merely refer ; (see the very interesting article on the History of the Jews of Montreal, prepared for the Montreal *Daily Star*, December 30, 1893, and repeated in the *American Israelite* in January, 1894, which has been attributed to Rev. Dr. Meldola de Sola ; and also an article on Rebecca Franks by the present writer, which appeared in the *American Hebrew*, November 9, 14, 21, and also in pamphlet reprint). In the present paper, Colonel

Franks' early career in Canada will be chiefly dealt with, the documents herein cited demonstrating the correctness of Dr. Friedenwald's theory (p. 76) that Franks was drawn into the Revolutionary contest through pure patriotism and interest in the struggle which was being carried on south of his earlier domicile. A contemporary periodical furnishes the data I refer to ; it is entitled : '' The Remembrancer or Impartial Repository of Public Events.'' Part I, for 1776, London, 1776, pp. 100–6. (The narrative is somewhat condensed herein, but the documents are set forth in their entirety.)

'' On May 2, 1775, the bust of the king at Montreal was found daubed over and indecently ornamented, the words, ' This is the pope of Canada and the fool of England,' being written upon it in French. A reward of 100 guineas was offered for the discovery of the perpetrator, and much indignation was expressed among the French inhabitants, eager to manifest their loyalty to England, one French gentleman even expressing his opinion that the act ought to be punished by hanging. Upon hearing this severe opinion, a young English merchant of the name of Franks, who had settled at Montreal and who at that time happened to be near the speaker, replied to him in these words : ' In England men are not hanged for such small offenses,' which he repeated twice or three times. This provoked M. de B—— (the former speaker) to such a degree, that, after giving the young man much opprobrious language, he at last proceeded to blows, and struck him in the face and pulled him by the nose ; upon which the other gave him a blow that knocked him down. The next day, May the 3d, upon a complaint of M. de B—— to three officers of justice of a new order, called the Conservators of the Peace for the District of Montreal, not of the blow he had received from Franks (for to this he was conscious he had given occasion by striking him first) but of the words pronounced by the latter, ' that in England people were not hanged for such small offenses,' the Conservators issued the warrant hereunder following for committing young Franks to prison. He was accordingly carried thither by a party of soldiers with bayonets fixed, and £10,000 bail, that was offered to procure his liberty, and be security for his appearance to take his trial for the offence, was refused. And there he continued for a week, at the end of which time, the same Conservators of the Peace (by the direction, as it is supposed, of Governor Carleton) ordered him to be discharged without any bail at all.

The following are the official documents, in translation :

" *District of Montreal.*

" By John Fraser, John Marteilhe and Réné Ovide Hertel de Rouville, Esquires, Judges and Conservators of the Peace in the District of Montreal :

" WHEREAS, Francis Mary Picote de Bellestre, Esquire, has made oath on the holy gospels that on Tuesday the second day of this present month of May, as he was standing still in the street to hear a proclamation published, concerning those wretches who had insulted his Majesty's bust, he had openly declared that he thought they deserved to be hanged : and that thereupon one Salisbury Franks had answered with surprise, ' that it was not usual to hang people for such small offences and that it was not worth while to do so,' and that he had repeated those words several times, and with a loud voice.

" We, having regard to the said complaint, and considering that every good subject ought to look upon the said insult to his Majesty's bust as an act of the most atrocious nature, and deserving of the utmost abhorrence, and that therefore all declarations made in conversation that tend to affirm it to be a small offence, ought to be esteemed criminal : Do, for these reasons, authorize and command you to convey the said Salisbury Franks to the prison of the town to be there detained, till he shall be thence discharged according to law.   And for so doing, this warrant shall be your justification.

" Given at Montreal, under our hands and seals, on the third day of May, 1775.

(Signed)	John Fraser, John Marteilhe, Hertel de Rouville."

The warrant to the jailor we omit, but the warrant for his discharge follows :

" *To the keeper of the jail in Montreal :*

Whereas David Salisbury Franks is now in your custody, in virtue of our warrant duly sealed and signed ; these are now to command you to forbear detaining any longer the said David Salisbury Franks, but to suffer him to go at large wherever he pleases and that without fees.   And for so doing, this will be your sufficient warrant.

" Given under our hands and seals at Montreal, on the 9th day of May, 1775."

(Signed as above).

It will be noticed that the warrant of release gives the full name of Franks and leaves it clear that he was the future American patriot. It should also be noticed that he is described as an Englishman, pointing to that country as the common home of the various members of the family of that name in America. (Compare Life of Peter Van Schaack, p. 143, and Kamble Papers, for references to Franks' family home, a mansion near London). Also that the amount of bail offered for young Franks, £10,000, was extraordinarily large for those days.

It is not proposed herein to repeat the interesting incident in the career of Arnold's aide-de-camp which others have set forth so well. Their accounts may, however, be supplemented by the following. It seems that Franks gave testimony to Mrs. Arnold's innocence of all complicity in her husband's treason. This fact is cited in a note in the present writer's sketch of Rebecca Franks (p. 12), but the original authority, the preface to the privately printed Shipper papers, he has thus far been unable to consult. After the inquiry into Frank's conduct,— occasioned by the suspicions aroused against him on account of Arnold's treason—had been held in accordance with his demand, Franks appears to have been sent to Europe with important dispatches to Jay and Franklin, with instructions to await their orders. In a letter from Robert Morris to Franklin, dated Philadelphia, July 13, 1781, we read: "The bearer of the letter, Major Franks, formerly an aide-de-camp to General Arnold, and honorably acquitted of all connection with him after a full and impartial inquiry, will be able to give you our public news more particularly than I could relate them." (*Diplomatic Correspondence*, edited by Sparks, Vol. XI, p. 382). His conduct in France and Spain appears to have been very creditable; Jay speaks very highly about his discretion and tact and he seems to have won the particular regard of the Count of Florida Blanca, the Spanish Minister, with whom Jay was negotiating. (See "Diplomatic Correspondence of the U. S.," edited by F. Wharton, Vol. IV, 752–754, 756–757, 764–784, V, 121. Thompson Papers (N. Y. Hist. Soc. Collections, 1878), p. 183. Accounts of the U. S. during the Administration of the Superintendent of France, 1781–1784). As noted by Dr. Friedenwald, Franks was sent by Congress to Europe again in 1784, this time to deliver a triplicate of the definitive treaty of peace to our ministers plenipotentiary. Further details about this trip are alluded to in "Military Journal of Major E. Denny" (Pa. Hist. Society, Pub. 1860) p. 415, where letters from Frank's associate, Col. Harman, are quoted, and in a letter written by Harman to a Philadelphia merchant, Jonathan Williams, in 1790, wherein he sends his regards to Franks, and alludes to the "gay moments we passed together in France, particularly the civilities received from you at St. Germain, where I dined with you in company with Mr. Barclay and Col. Franks" (p. 461). Not less interesting is the narrative of an encounter with Major Franks in 1787, by Dr. Cutler, on a trip to Philadelphia: "July 12th. Made our next stay at Bristol. Dined in company with the passengers in the stage, among whom were General Armstrong and Col. Franks. General Armstrong is a member of Congress with whom I had a small acquaintance at New York; Franks was an aide of General Arnold at the time of his desertion to the British. Both of them high bucks, and affected, as I conceived, to hold the New England states in contempt. They had repeatedly touched my Yankee blood, in their conversation at the table; but I was much on the reserve until, after we had dined, some severe reflections on the conduct of Rhode Island, and the Insurgency in Massachusetts—placing the two States in the same point of light—induced me to observe that 'I had no doubt but that the conduct of Rhode Island would prove of infinite service to the Union; that the insurgency in Massachusetts would eventually lead to invigorate and establish our government; and that I considered the State of Pennsylvania—divided and distracted as she was then in her Councils, the large County of Luzerne on the eve of an insurrection—to be in as hazardous a situation as any one on the Continent.'

"This instantly brought on a warm fracas indeed. The cudgels were taken up on both sides: the contest as fierce as if the fate of empires depended on the decision. At length victory declared in our favor. Armstrong began to make concessions. Franks, with more reluctance, at length gave up the ground. Both acknowledged the New England States were entitled to an equal share of merit with any in the Union, and declared they had no intention to reflect.   We had the satisfaction to quit the field with an air of triumph, which my little companion enjoyed with a high relish; nor could he forget it, all the way to Philadelphia.   But we parted with our antagonists on terms of perfect good humor and complaisance.   My companion frequently afterwards mentioned the pleasure it gave him to see Armstrong and Franks, "so completely taken down," as he expressed it, which led me to conclude he was of the party opposed to them in the political quarrels of Philadelphia."   (Historical magazine, Third Series, Vol. II, pp. 84–85).

But let us pass from Franks to another Canadian.

II.

CHEVALIER DE LEVIS.

The student of Canadian history is very familiar with the name of Levis, which bids fair to be perpetuatad in several geographical names in that country.   The name was borne by Henri de Levis, Duke of Vontadour, Viceroy of Canada for some time after 1626, but was rendered more famous through the brilliant career of his relative, the Chevalier de Levis, Montcalm's able lieutenant, subsequently his successor as commander of the French forces in Canada, and still later Marshal of France.   Numerous striking illustrations of his gallantry and chivalry are extant, and it is suggestive that Montcalm should have spoken some of his last words, in praise of "his gallant Chevalier de Levis," for whose talents and fitness for command he expressed high esteem.   The writer hereof does not claim that either of these two de Levis' were Jews, but he does believe that they were of Jewish descent, less on account of their family name than on account of the following curious explanation of it: " A family that considered itself to be the oldest in Christendom.   Their chateau contained, it was said, two pictures: one of the Deluge in which Noah is represented going into the Ark, carrying under his arm a trunk on which was written: 'Papiers de la maison de Levis.'   The other was a portrait of the founder of the house, bowing reverently to the Virgin, who is made to say : ' Couvrez-vous, mon cousin.' 'It is for my own pleasure, my cousin,' replied the descendent of Levi."

(Compare Horace Walpole's Letters, Kingsford's History of Canada, Vol. I, p. 77, Parkman's Montcalm and Wolfe, I, 150, 360, 363, 378–379, 455, 478, 466; II, 308, 312, 354).

III.

LOPEZ AND HART, OF NEWPORT.

In the last volume of our "Proceedings" and also in Judge Daly's work, numerous references are to be found to the interesting career of Aaron Lopez, of Newport, whom the present writer has described as probably the richest and most successful Jewish man of affairs who lived in this country before the Revolution. It may be remembered that Lopez was one of a number of Jewish residents of Newport who found it necessary to flee from that city at the beginning of the war, when the British forces moved against the city. Lopez withdrew to Leicester, Massachusetts, with his family, and remained there until May, 1782. (Daly's Jews in North America, p. 86). Short as was his stay there, however, he left a noble memorial of his sojourn behind him, as appears from the following extract from the Diary of a journey from Plymouth to Connecticut by Samuel Davis in 1789. (Mass. Hist. Society Proceedings, 1869–1870, p. 11). "Leicester is situate on very high ground. The Meeting house is a decent edifice, very illy painted. Near it is the Academy, founded by the late Mr. Lopez, a worthy merchant of the Jewish tribe. It is a long building of two stories, with a cupola and bell, and two entrances, fronted by porticos; appears to be decaying. Mr. James observed at Worcester, that he supposed the preceptor and pupils would be removed to a handsome new school house in that town."

But Newport contained many Tories as well as Patriots, many of whom must to-day be regarded as no less patriotic than those whom we designate by that term. It is, therefore, not surprising to find Jewish Tories there, and one of the number appears to have been a martyr to his views, as the following item shows: "Mr. Isaac Hart, of Newport R. I., formerly an eminent merchant and ever a loyal subject, was inhumanly fired upon and bayoneted, wounded in fifteen parts of his body, and beat with their muskets, in the most shocking manner in

3

the very act of imploring quarter, and died of his wounds a few
hours after, universally regretted by every true lover of his
King and country." (Account of the attack on Fort St.
George, Rivington's Gazette, December 2, 1780).

To leave no doubt as to his faith, the following item, (from
Du Simmitiaire, MSS., 1769) accompanies the preceding one in
the Magazine of American History (Vol. III, p. 452): "At
Mr. Isaac Hart's, a Jew, living at the Point, in Newport, R. I.,
there is a portrait of the late Czar, Peter I, done, I believe, by
Sir Godfrey Kneller."

IV.

SOME NEW YORK JEWISH PATRIOTS.

The number of New York Jews who served their country
by risking life or fortune in its behalf is well-nigh legion.
Hundreds upon hundreds of instances have been set forth from
time to time, covering a time from the early colonial period, as
appears particularly from another paper by the present writer,
through the Revolutionary struggle down to our own day.   But
little cause can be assigned for distinguishing a few from the
many in the present article unless it be the probability that the
instances to be referred to herein are but little known.   It
should be of interest to notice, for instance, that the decision
reached in 1770 to make more stringent the Non-Importation
Agreement, which the colonists adopted to bring England to
terms on the taxation question, had among its signers Samuel
Judah, Hayman Levy, Jacob Moses, Jacob Myers, Jonas Phillips, and Isaac Seixas (*New York Gazette* and *Weekly Post Boy*,
July 23, 1770).

The victory won by the Jewish Patriots over the loyalists
in the New York Jewish Congregation at the outbreak of the
Revolution, which induced the majority to determine to dis-
band the congregation for country's sake, has been well described in a former article in our Society's periodicals and the
names of the patriots who, in consequence, fled to Philadelphia
on the approach of the British to New York are known.   In
another paper, the writer hereof enumerates some of the less
known but possibly equally patriotic Jewish Loyalists, who remained in the city.   It appears, however, that even the Jewish

cemetery was to witness the strife and struggles of war, for we read that a battery to overlook the East River and prevent British ships from entering into it "is planned in some forwardness at the foot of the Jews' Burying Ground," in March, 1776. (N. Y. Hist. Soc. Collection Pub. Fund Series, Vol. III, pp. 354, 355).

During the war of 1812, the New York Jews appear to have again manifested their love of country, and one of their number, Col. Nathan Myers, was even in command of a brigade stationed near the City of New York in the beginning of the war. (Guernsey; "New York City during the War of 1812," pp. 86, 436–7). Others manifested their patriotism by bringing pecuniary sacrifices, as did Herman Hendricks in 1813. In February of that year, Congress passed an act authorizing a loan of $16,000.000, but less than $4,000,000 were subscribed. It was then that New York merchants came to the rescue by subscribing for the bonds, in spite of the sacrifices that were made in view of the fact that the government could not obtain money except at a discount of 15 per cent. Hendricks subscribed for $40,000 of the bonds, being one of the largest individual subscribers. (Scoville: The Old Merchant of New York City. First Series, pp. 329–333.)

Among those who served under Col. Myers in this War, was probably Samuel Noah, a cousin of Mordecai M. Noah, who led a most eventful life, which has been chronicled in a very interesting way by Gen. George W. Cullom in his "Biographical Sketches of Deceased Graduates of the United States Military Academy." We quote the account in full:

"SAMUEL NOAH.

"Class of 1807.

"Died March 10, 1871, at Mount Pulaski, Ill., aged 92.

"Samuel Noah, who was born July 19, 1779, in the City of London, died March 10, 1871, at Mount Pulaski, Logan county, Illinois, at the advanced age of nearly 92, he having been for several years the senior surviving graduate of the United States Military Academy. He was of Jewish descent, and was a cousin of Mordecai M. Noah, formerly consul to

Tunis, and for many years the editor of various New York journals.

" When twenty years old he emigrated to this country, and after a residence of several years in New York City, solicited a midshipman's appointment, but not succeeding, accepted, May 5, 1805, that of a cadet in the First Regiment of Artillery. Being intelligent and a good penman, he was often selected as amanuensis to the Superintendent of the Military Academy, and frequently acted as Judge Advocate or Recorder of Courts at West Point. Upon graduation, Dec. 9, 1807, preferring the Infantry arm, he was promoted an ensign in the Second Regiment, which, after a tedious journey, he joined at Cantonment, Columbia Springs, in the rear of Fort Adams, Miss. Here he devoted his leisure hours to the study of the early campaigns of Napoleon, who was then the military prodigy of the world ; but this fascinating occupation was soon interrupted by his having to watch smugglers on the Florida frontier and march from one unhealthy camp to another in the Gulf States. During these migrations he met Captain Winfield Scott just after his duel near Natchez with Dr. Upshur (brother of the Secretary of State blown up on board the Princeton), Lieutenant James Gibson, subsequently killed at the sortie from Fort Erie, Gen. James Wilkinson, Captain Edmond P. Gaines, Gen. Wade Hampton, and other since famous officers of whom he had many anecdotes to relate. Wearied finally with slow promotion, and disgusted that ignorant civilians were appointed to rank him, he resigned March 13, *1811, his commission of First Lieutenant in the Army.

" Soon after this period a Mexican deputation from the Junta of Coahuila, Gen. Bernado Guiteras and Captain Manscac arrived at Natchitoches, where Lieutenant Magee, a graduate of 1809, was stationed, and offered him the command with the rank of Colonel of the combined forces there assembled of Mexicans and Anglo-Americans. After Magee assumed the command, Noah, allured by visions of a golden future, joined, as First Lieutenant, this little undisciplined Falstaffian regiment on the Brazos river, while on its march to Fort Bahia, which it entered Nov. 14, 1812 ; but no sooner was the fort in possession of the Patriot Army than the Spanish royalists besieged it with a force of five times the strength of the garrison. In this struggle poor Col. Magee sickened and died, and was buried with the honors of war during the enemy's cannonade, a six-pounder ball lodging close to the grave. After the siege was raised, March 28, 1813, and the patriots re-inforced, this little army, with Noah in command of its rear guard, pursued and routed the Royalists, April 4, 1813, in a sharp combat near San Antonio, and three days later entered the capital of Texas, Salcido, the governor, surrendering at discretion with his entire force.

" Informed soon after of the declaration of war by the United States against Great Britain, Noah, true to the flag of his adopted country, left Texas, and, escaping through many perils by flood and field, reached the city of Washington, where he was most sadly disappointed in not being re-commissioned by President Madison in the United States Army. Nothing daunted, however, he proceeded to New York, and volunteered his services as a private soldier with Captain Benjamin Dunning's company for the defence of Brooklyn, then being fortified by Gen. Joseph G. Swift, to repel an anticipated descent of the British on Long Island at Sag Harbor. His services here and at Harlem Heights, to the close of the war, in aid of the militia force, were most zealous and untiring, his military education, practical knowledge and quick intelligence proving powerful auxiliaries to his patriotic devotion to duty. After the termination of Noah's military career, he taught school near Goshen, New York, till 1820 ; then for two years was in England, being present at the trial of Queen Caroline and the Coronation of George the Fourth; resumed school teaching and was employed in various academies in Virginia until May 24, 1848 ; and subsequently resided with a faithful friend at Mount Pulaski, Logan county, Ill., where he died. The romantic record of Samuel Noah's early life is full of wild adventure and thrilling incidents; his after history was a curious medley, almost the very counterpart of the vicissitudes to which Gil Blas was exposed; and his declining years were an old age of poverty, with little relief even from sources upon which he confidently counted to ease his weary journey to the grave."

In this connection reference would also seem to be in order to some New York Jews who served in the Mexican War, one of them with particular distinction and honor.   This list includes Sergeant Jacob David, Sergeant Samuel Henry, and Private Abraham Adler (killed); Corporal Jacob Hirshhorn and Private Otto Neubauer, Phillip Myers, and Jacob Lema, Mark Kahn, Alexander Simm, John Myers, James Hart and William Hart, ---- Myers, Marx M. Hart, Henry Phillips, Joseph Henriques, and Jacob C. Somers. (See article by the present writer in *American Hebrew*, February 9, 1894.)

V.

SOME BALTIMORE JEWS.

Turning next to Baltimore, two interesting incidents are in point.   The one carries us back to Revolutionary times, and is to be connected with the name of Jacob Hart, one of a number of patriotic merchants of Baltimore; whether he was the only Jew in the group is unknown.   The incident is briefly referred to as follows, in a letter written by Lafayette to Washington, April 18, 1871.   (Memoirs, Correspondence and Manuscripts of General Lafayette, Vol. I, page 403.)   "To these measures for punishing deserters, I have added one which my feelings for the sufferings of the soldiers and peculiarity of their circumstances have prompted me to adopt.   The merchants of Baltimore lent me a sum of about £2000 which will procure some shirts, linen, overalls, shoes and a few hats ; the ladies will make up the shirts, and the overalls will be made by the detachment, so that our soldiers have a chance of being a little more comfortable.   The money is lent upon my credit, and I become security for the payment of it in two years' time, when, by the French laws, I may better dispose of my estate.   But before that time, I shall use my influence with the French court, in order to have this sum of money added to any loan Congress may have been able to obtain from them."   The following entry "Accounts of the United States with the Superintendent of Finance" (Robert Morris) serves to identify the merchants : "May 27, (1782) Jacob Hart and others for the Repayment of Money Loaned the Marquis de Lafayette at Baltimore — 7256 dollars."   Further details appear from the following passages in the Journals of Congress, Vol. VII p. 86: "Thursday, May 24, 1781. On the report of the committee to whom was referred a letter of April 22 from Maj. Gen. the Marquis de la Fayette:

Resolved, That Congress entertains a just sense of the patriotic and timely exertions of the merchants of Baltimore who so generously supplied the Marquis de la Fayette with about 2000 guineas, to enable him to forward the detachment under his command; That the Marquis de la Fayette be assured that Congress will take proper measures to discharge the engagement he has entered into with the merchants."

Compare with this an article on "Old Maryland Homes and Ways," by John W. Palmer, in the *Century*, December 1894, p. 258. Markens in his "Hebrews in America" (p. 93) briefly refers to the incident, describing Hart as a Hebrew of German birth, who came to this country in 1775; he was the father-in-law of Haym M. Salomon, son of the patriot, Haym Salomon. Certainly not less interesting, though less well known, is the following incident in the Mexican War, which is translated from the "Allgemeine Zeitung des Judenthums," Vol. X p. 508, August 24, 1846 : "The *New York Herald* of July 15, (1846) contains the following item, in reference to the call for 50,000 volunteers to join the army against Mexico: ' Baltimore July 3. Among the companies which have been formed here, a volunteer corps of Jews attracts particular attention. Although composed for the most part of immigrants, they have given, by the raising of this company, to fight with the native militia on behalf of our institutions, a splendid instance of their love and devotion for these and for their new fatherland. Yes, their love for the fame and independence of our country has been displayed all the more pointedly as they have organized their company by selecting one not of their faith as their chief officer, namely, Captain Carroll, who was paymaster of the Fifth regiment, but willingly resigned his position to accept the command of this patriotic company of volunteers. Its other officers are: Mr. Levi Benjamin, first lieutenant; Joseph Simpson, second lieutenant; Samuel G. Goldsmith, third lieutenant; S. Eytinge, first sergeant; Dr. J. Horwitz, surgeon." An examination of the copy of the *Herald* thus referred to, fails to show the English original of the above item ; either the date or the name of the paper is incorrectly cited, though the facts are no doubt correctly given.

VI.

SOUTH CAROLINA JEWISH PATRIOTS.

The following item from an article by Rev. Isaac Leeser, in *The Occident*, Vol. XVI, p. 142 (1858) gives in some little detail a story since then oft repeated ; the primary authorities for the incident are still unknown to the writer thereof: " A company of soldiers who did good service in the defence of Charleston Harbor were nearly all, if not all Jews. The names of Daniel W. Cardozo, Jacob I. Cohen, Sr., and Isaiah Isaacs, we think, must have been on the roll of that company. Relations or descendants of all of these are still to be found among our most respectable families. Sheftall Sheftall, Isaac N. Cardozo, a brother of David, and Colonel Bush, occur to us just now as brave soldiers in the Revolution, and no doubt many others are known to other persons." Compare with this the following passage from a speech of Col. J. W. D. Worthington on the Jew Bill, Maryland, 1824 (Speeches on the Jew Bill, etc., by H. N. Brackenridge, Phila. 1829, p. 115): " Here is another paper which contains the names of a corps of volunteer infantry, in Charleston, South Carolina, in February, 1779. It was composed chiefly of Israelites, residing in King's Street and was commanded by Captain Lushington, and afterward fought under Gen. Moultrie at the Battle of Beaufort." Also Westcott's " Persons Who Took the Oath of Allegiance to Pennsylvania." " Abraham Seixas, formerly an officer in the Militia of Charleston, South Carolina, lately arrived in this city, Philadelphia; Merchant, May 31, 1782."

VII.

MORDECAI SHEFTALL, OF SAVANNAH, GEORGIA.

We may fittingly close this paper with an account of a Jewish patriot of the Revolution who held important and responsible positions under both Congressional and Georgia State control, and who had occasion to find that the Sovereign will often decline to pay even the most bona fide debts, where powerful influence to force bills for their payment through Congress is wanting. One of the witnesses in the Court Martial Proceedings, of Major General Howe, in 1780, (N. Y. Hist. Soc. Collections, 1879, pp. 260–263, 301) was Mordecai Sheftall, who was Deputy Commissary General of Issues to the Continental troops in Georgia during the period of the British invasion of that State, and also Commissary General of Purchase and Issues to the Militia. He testified to various measures he had recommended for removing supplies from positions of danger, to prevent their falling into the hands of the British, and it is very suggestive that these provisions should be referred to in the Index, under the heading: "Jewish Thrift," (Collections, 1880, p. 461). In his defence, General Howe referred to him as follows: "Mr. Sheftall, the Deputy Commissary General of Issues, has been brought by the prosecutors to prove upon me, as I suppose, a neglect of the public stores. I have ever had a favorable opinion of Mr. Sheftall, as an honest man, and from the testimony of such, I know I have nothing to fear; his evidence, therefore, is in my favor. Many measures, however, were pursued that Mr. Sheftall might have had no knowledge of." Mr. Sheftall's was one of the earliest Jewish families in Georgia, and various items in regard to his character and standing are collated in Judge Daly's work (p. 70, et. seq.), where his name is, erroneously, it seems, spelt Sheftail. On page 72 reference is made to Cushman Polack, who was also a witness in the Howe trial, (pp. 264–5) he having been a private in the militia in Georgia at the same time; his name is there spelt "Coshman Pollock"). Markens also adds, on what authority I am unable to state, (p. 49) that when the British took possession of Savannah, December 29, 1778, Mordecai Sheftall, with his son Sheftall Sheftall, endeavored to make his escape, but was compelled to surrender by a body of Highlanders. He was taken to the guard-house, where the officer in charge was instructed to guard him well, as he was "a great rebel." There he was confined with a number of soldiers and negroes without a morsel to eat until a Hessian officer named Zeltman, finding he could speak his language, removed him to his quarters and permitted him to communicate with his wife and son. In an interesting narrative, published many years ago, Mr. Sheftall states that he was treated with abuse by Captain Strarhope of the "Raven" sloop of war, and he and his son were ordered on board the prison ship. His name, with the inscription, "Chairman Rebel Provisional Committee," is enrolled on the list of those who were selected as coming under the Disqualifying Act of July, 1780, and thus rendered "incapable of holding or exercising any office of trust, honor or profit in the Province of Georgia."

The writer hereof believes that, until now, no particulars have been known to the Jewish historian in regard to a claim urged by Sheftall, and afterwards his widow, before Congress. It appears that he presented a petition to the House of Representatives on March 29, 1792, asking for a settlement of his accounts as Deputy Commissary General of Issues for the Southern Department during the Revolutionary War with Great Britain. The claim was referred to the Secretary of the Treasury, who reported it to the next Congress, though the nature of his report is not known to the writer. In the fourth Congress the petition was referred to the Committee on Claims, which reported it back to the House, February 11, 1797. In the House List of Private Claims (Vol. III, p. 305–6), this report is marked "adverse." No authority seems to exist for this statement. In fact, another claim reported at the same time was rejected at once, but the Sheftall claim was referred to the Committee of the Whole on the following Wednesday, but on that day it does not appear to have been considered. In the Seventh Congress, Frances, widow of Mordecai Sheftall, renewed her husband's petition and it was again referred to a committee. This committee's report was read and considered on April 3, 1802, but further consideration was postponed till the 4th Monday of November following, which was practically equivalent to killing the measure, as Congress never meets in ordinary session in November. (Journals of Congress, House, Second, 1st Session, p. 554; Third, 1st Session, pp. 77–8; Fourth, 1st Session, p. 451; Fourth, 2d Session, p. 691; Seventh, 1st Session, 136, 177, Carpenter; American Senator, III, 449–50). No further information as to the claim is at hand. From the persistence in pressing it, it must be concluded that some substantial sum was involved. It may be that it was rejected because the United States declined to assume liability for the acts of the State of Georgia, there having been a series of controversies between the State and General Government as to the liability of the latter for military services and expenditures incurred in behalf of the former. At any rate, the claim does not appear to have been paid, and like the Haym Salomon claim, is another illustration of our country's ingratitude to those who made sacrifices for it of worldly goods and life and limb in its hours of need.

JEWISH SOLDIERS IN THE CONTINENTAL ARMIES.

Scant and unsatisfactory as are the army records of the Revolutionary period, enough of an authentic character has been preserved to fully sustain the statement of Solomon Etting, who, writing in Baltimore in 1824, notes that among the soldiers of the Revolution "were many Hebrews who were always at their post and always foremost in all hazardous enterprises." This almost contemporary notice emanates from a Jew whose father had served in the Continental army from the beginning of the Revolution to the capture of Charleston, and who, through the prominence of his family had been brought in contact with many of the distinguished participants in the momentous struggle.

The active co-operation of Jewish citizens in the non-importation movement of 1763 has already been adverted to, but even before that time we find references to prominent Jewish participants in the public defense. In 1754, during the French and Indian War, Isaac Myers, a Jewish citizen of New York, called a town meeting at the "Rising Sun" Inn and organized a company of bateau men of which he became captain. Two other Jews are named as taking part in the same war, both of whom served in the expedition across the Allegheny mountains in the year above noted. It is altogether probable that these three were not the only Jewish soldiers of that early war, but only these have left traces of their presence. In the following year, 1755, when the colonies were agitated by the disastrous ending of the Braddock campaign and the incipient movement toward federation, we find a Jew, Benjamin Cohen, a member of the Provincial Council of Pennsylvania and Attorney-General of the colony.

The chronicles of the Revolutionary War afford a considerable and in many respects an interesting list of Jewish names. A few of the more prominent of these have already been mentioned

under preceding heads, and others cited on the records are here
added in alphabetical order :

Captain NOAH ABRAHAM
> was called out with the battalion of Cumberland County
> Militia, of Pennsylvania, "by an order from Council, July
> 28, 1777."

AARON BENJAMIN,
> Ensign of 8th Connecticut Regiment, January 1, 1777;
> Second Lieutenant, February 14, 1778; First Lieutenant,
> May 7, 1778; Regimental Adjutant, April 1, 1780, to
> January, 1783; transferred to 5th Connecticut Regiment
> January 1, 1781; transferred to 3rd Connecticut Regi-
> ment January 1, 1783; retained in Swift's Connecticut
> Regiment June, 1783, and served to November 3, 1783;
> Lieutenant-Colonel of 37th United States Infantry March
> 11, 1813; honorably discharged June 15, 1815; died
> January 11, 1829.

SAMUEL BENJAMIN,
> Ensign of 8th Massachusetts Regiment January 1, 1777;
> Second Lieutenant October 3, 1777; First Lieutenant
> March 28, 1779, served to June, 1783.

JOSEPH BLOOMFIELD,
> Captain of 3rd New Jersey Regiment February 9, 1776;
> Deputy Judge Advocate-General November 17, 1776, to
> October 29, 1778; Brigadier-General United States Army
> March 27, 1812; honorably discharged June 15, 1815;
> died October 3, 1823.

MOSES BLOOMFIELD,
> (New Jersey) Hospital Surgeon May 14, 1777; Hospital
> Physician and Surgeon October 6, 1780; resigned De-
> cember 13, 1780; died August 14, 1791.

HENRY PIKE BUSH
> is recorded as a soldier in the "Associators and Flying
> Camp," Pennsylvania.

Colonel SOLOMON BUSH
> was an officer in the Pennsylvania Militia (1777–1778),
> whose record is highly creditable and whose services won

for him a well-deserved promotion. He was appointed Deputy Adjutant General of the Militia of the State on July 5, 1777. As to his subsequent career in the army, no stronger testimony could be desired than that set forth in the resolution adopted by the Supreme Executive Council of Pennsylvania, at its session on Wednesday, October 20, 1779. It reads thus :

"The petition of Major Solomon Bush, in the militia of this State, being read, and due inquiry having been made into the circumstances of his case, it appears that Major Bush has, on many occasions, distinguished himself in the public service, especially in the winter of 1776, when the service was critical and hazardous.

"That he entered again into the said service in the summer of 1777, when General Sir William Howe invaded the State and the militia were called out pursuant to the resolutions of Congress and the requisition of His Excellency, General Washington ; and in the month of September, 1777, acting as Deputy Adjutant General, he was dangerously wounded in a skirmish between the militia and the advance of the British Army, his thigh being broken and he brought off with great difficulty ; that being carried to his father's house, on Chestnut Hill, and incapable of being moved, he fell into the hands of the British Army, when it moved up to Whitemarsh, in December, 1777, who took his parole ; That he has ever since been confined with his wound, and incapable of performing any military duty, or acquiring a livelihood, but on the other hand, his situation attended with much difficulty and expense.

" All which circumstances being considered, and that the said Major Bush being at the time of receiving his wounds in Continental Service and now a prisoner of war.

" Resolved, That he be recommended to the especial notice of the Honourable Board of War, in order to obtain pay and rations equal to his rank ; and that this Board in consideration of the services and sufferings of Major Bush, will permit him to draw from the State store, from time to time, such articles as may be necessary for his comfortable Subsistance and Support.''

That Major Bush had already been promoted to the rank of Lieutenant-Colonel, is evidenced by another resolution, complimentary to him, adopted by the same Council seven days later, when he was "recommended to the Honourable' the Board of War, for pay and rations accordingly." Again on November 5, 1785, the Council, over which Benjamin Franklin then presided, passed an order for the payment of a pension due to Lieutenant-Colonel Bush.

Major LEWIS BUSH

became First Lieutenant of the 6th Pennsylvania Battalion on January 9, 1776 and Captain the following June. He was transferred to Colonel Thomas Hartley's Additional Continental Regiment January 13, 1773 and was commissioned Major, March 12, 1777. That he proved a brave soldier, his efficient service in a number of battles affords ample evidence. At the battle of Brandywine, September 11, 1777, he was fatally wounded, and four days later he died.

JONAS BUSH

was in the roll of revolutionary soldiers, but there is no information given as to his rank or date of enlistment.

JACOB I. COHEN

in 1783 went to Charleston, S. C., and during the campaign which followed, took part as a volunteer soldier in the Continental army, serving under Moultrie and Lincoln. Frequent references to Mr. Cohen are found in the Madison papers, and his valuable services are repeatedly adverted to.

PHILIP JACOB COHEN

became so distinguished for the services he rendered to the Colonies that he was singled out by the British authorities through a special order depriving him of the right of holding or exercising any office of trust, honor or profit in the Province of Georgia.

MORDECAI DAVIS,

Ensign of 2nd Pennsylvania Battery January 5, 1776; died on August 12, 1776.

REUBEN ETTING

was a clerk in Baltimore at the time of the battle at Lexington. Although only 19 years of age, he enlisted in a Maryland company, which hastened north to join the forces of Congress. He served in various battles and was taken prisoner by the British at the surrender of Charleston. When released from imprisonment by exchange he was broken in health from ill treatment in prison and exposure on the field. He was a captain of the Independent Blues in 1798, and Marshal of Maryland, appointed by President Jefferson.

SOLOMON ETTING,

a native of York, Pennsylvania, appears as one of the committee of citizens appointed to forward resolutions to Washington expressive of disapprobation of a proposed treaty with Great Britain. Subsequently settled in Baltimore and became President of the Municipal Council.

Colonel ISAAC FRANKS,

who then lived in Philadelphia, entered the army shortly after the battle of Lexington. He became aid-de-camp to General Washington, holding the rank of colonel, and serving throughout the war. After the Revolution Colonel Franks became the incumbent of various civil offices, among them Prothonotary of the Supreme Court of Pennsylvania, being appointed to that position on February 18, 1819. His residence in Germantown was for some time occupied by President Washington.

Colonel DAVID S. FRANKS, Aide-de-camp. See sketch on p. 27.

MICHAEL GRATZ,

of Philadelphia, aided the Colonists in the Revolutionary war. He was one of the signers of the Non-Importation Resolutions (October 20, 1765), after the passage of the Stamp Act, and was among the most active, patriotic and respected Israelites of Philadelphia, being a conspicuous character in public affairs.

BERNARD HART

was Quartermaster of a brigade of State troops during the Revolution.

MICHAEL HART,

a public spirited and leading citizen of Easton, Pa., of whom it is recorded :

"Let it be remembered that Michael Hart was a Jew, practically pious, a Jew reverencing and strictly observant of the Sabbath and Festivals ; dietary laws were also adhered to. * * * Mark well that he, Washington, the then honored as 'first in peace, first in war, and first in the hearts of his countrymen,' even during a short sojourn, became for the hour the guest of the worthy Jew."

MOSES HAMMER

enlisted as a private in the 1st Pennsylvania Battalion November 15, 1775.

DAVID HAYS, JR.,

was an active participant in the struggle for independence and served with the Colonial Army on Long Island. In retaliation for his patriotic services the Tories burned his house and store. Prior to the Revolution he was one of the Commissioners appointed by the British authorities to lay out public lands. All of his family sided with the Colonists during the War of Independence.

DAVID HAYS and JACOB HAYS,

father and son, fought in various of the battles for independence.

Colonel ISAACS,

of North Carolina Militia ; wounded and taken prisoner at Camden August 16, 1780; exchanged July, 1781.

MOSES ISAACKS,

one of the early settlers of Newport, R. I., was an active supporter of the Army of the Revolution. He had the honor of receiving General Washington as a guest at his house.

SOLOMON ISAAC

enlisted as a private in the 6th Pennsylvania Battalion, company of Capt. Robert Adams, February 6, 1776.

4

ISAAC ISRAEL,

    2nd Lieutenant of 8th Virginia Regiment, February 9, 1776 ; 1st Lieutenant, January, 1777 ; Captain, November 23, 1777 ; transferred to 4th Virginia Regiment, September 14, 1778.

JOSEPH ISRAEL

    volunteered as a soldier during the Revolution.

JACOB LEON

    was an officer on the staff of General Pulaski.

JACOB DE LEON,

    of Charleston, S. C., was a distinguished officer of the War of the Revolution. He served as captain on the staff of General de Kalb, and when the latter was mortally wounded at the battle of Camden, S. C., de Leon in company with Major Benjamin Nones and Captain Jacob de la Motta, of the staff, carried de Kalb from the field.

ASHER LEVY,

    Ensign of 1st New Jersey Regiment, September 12, 1778 ; resigned June 4, 1779.

NATHANIEL LEVY,

    of Baltimore, served under Lafayette during the Revolutionary War.

ISRAEL DE LIEBER

    was a soldier of the Revolutionary War, who rose from the ranks to military positions of honor and trust.

JACOB MOSER,

    Captain of 6th Pennsylvania Regiment, February 15, 1777; retired, July 1, 1778.

BENJAMIN MOSES

    served on the staff of General Pulaski.

ISAAC MOSES,

    of Philadelphia, advanced three thousand pounds when Robert Morris undertook to raise money to prosecute the War of Independence; he was active in the Jewish communities of New York and Philadelphia.

EMANUEL DE LA MOTTA

serve in the Revolution and in the War of 1812. In recognition of his valor as displayed in battle he was promoted from the ranks to a military position of honor.

JACOB DE LA MOTTA

was a captain on the staff of General Pulaski.

MANUEL MORDECAI NOAH,

of South Carolina, (1747–1825) patriot and soldier; heretofore referred to as having contributed twenty thousand pounds to the support of the American army; served with General Marion, also on the staff of General Washington.

MAJOR BENJAMIN NONES,

a native of Bordeaux, France, came to Philadelphia in 1777. He served at various times on the staff of General Lafayette and on that of General Washington. He had previously been a private under General Pulaski, and had, as he writes, "fought in almost every action which took place in Carolina, and in the disastrous affair of Savannah, shared the hardships of that sanguinary day." He became major of a Legion of four hundred men attached to Baron De Kalb's command and composed in part of Hebrews. At the battle of Camden, S. C., on August 16, 1780, when the brave De Kalb fell mortally wounded, Major Nones, Capt. Jacob De la Motta and Capt. Jacob de Leon bore their chief from the battlefield.

Major Nones rendered many conspicuous services, civil and military, to his adopted country.

ABRAHAM R. RIVERA

was a member of the artillery corps of Newport, R. I., in 1790.

PHILIP MOSES RUSSEL

was born 1745, and resided in Germantown, Pa. When the war broke out in the Spring of 1775 he enlisted as surgeon's mate under the command of General Lee, serving about ten months. After the British occupation of Philadelphia, in September, 1777, he became surgeon's mate to Surgeon Norman, of the Second Virginia Regiment.

Russell went into winter quarters with the army at Valley Forge, 1777–1778. An attack of sickness, which impaired both his sight and hearing, forced him to resign in August, 1780. He received a letter of commendation from General Washington, "for his assiduous and faithful attentions to the sick and wounded."

EZEKIEL SAMPSON,
Lieutenant of Baldwin's Artillery, Artificer Regiment, May to December, 1775.

JOSEPH SAMPSON,
2nd Lieutenant of Cotton's Massachusetts Regiment, May to December, 1775.

ABRAHAM SEIXES, was a lieutenant in the Georgia Brigade of the Continental Army.

MORDECAI SHEFTALL. See biographical sketch, p. 40.

CORRESPONDENCE BETWEEN GEORGE WASH-INGTON AND HEBREW CITIZENS.

[Papers collated by LEWIS ABRAHAM, Esq., and presented at the meeting of the American Jewish Historical Society, at Washington, December 27th, 1894.]

When Washington had concluded his labors in the field of war and had attained deserved civic honors, and when laurels were showered upon him from all quarters the Hebrews joined their fellow-citizens in felicitating the hero and statesman.

The following correspondence is collated from *The United States Gazette,* of 1790; a partial file of this paper can be found in the Congressional Library. It is strange that the letters are not all to be found in books in which the Washington correspondence are compiled.

The original letter addressed to the '' Beth Elohim '' congregation of Charleston, S. C., was carefully preserved among the many other valuable records of that city, but was destroyed by the great fire of 1838. The Mayor of Charleston endeavored to obtain a copy from the general government, but after a thorough examination of the records, no such document could be found. After a prolonged search, however, the present writer was enabled to discover the missing document, and was well rewarded with the thanks of the authorities of Charleston. (Year-Book of the City of Charleston for 1884, page 280.)

The '' *Address from the Hebrew Congregation of the City of Savannah, Ga., to George Washington, the First President of the United States,*'' presented by Mr. Jackson, one of the representatives from Georgia.

SIR : We have long been anxious of congratulating you on your appointment, by unanimous approbation, to the Presidential dignity of this country and of testifying our unbounded confidence in your integrity and unblemished virtue. Yet however exalted the station you now fill, it is still not equal to

the merit of your heroic services through an arduous and dangerous conflict which has embosomed you in the hearts of her citizens.

Our eccentric situation, added to a diffidence founded on the most profound respect, has thus long prevented our address, yet the delay has realized anticipation, given us an opportunity of presenting our grateful acknowledgements for the benediction of Heaven through the magnanimity of federal influence and the equity of your administration.

Your unexampled libèrality and extensive philanthropy have dispelled that cloud of bigotry and superstition which has long, as a vail, shaded religion—unrivetted the fetters of enthusiasm —enfranchised us with all the privileges and immunities of free citizens, and initiated us into the grand mass of legislative mechanism. By example you have taught us to endure the ravages of war with manly fortitude, and to enjoy the blessings of peace with reverence to the Deity and with benignity and love to our fellow-creatures.

May the Great Author of the world grant you all happiness —an uninterrupted series of health—addition of years to the number of your days, and a continuance of guardianship to that freedom which under auspices of Heaven your magnanimity and wisdom have given these States.

LEVI SHEFTALL, President.

In behalf of the Hebrew Congregations.

To which the President was pleased to return the following reply : (Printed in Jared Sparks collection, Vol. XII, p. 185).

To the Hebrew Congregations of the City of Savannah, Georgia:

GENTLEMEN: I thank you with great sincerity for your congratulations on my appointment to the office which I have the honor to hold by the unanimous choice of my fellow-citizens, and especially the expressions you are pleased to use in testifying the confidence that is reposed in me by your congregations.

As the delay which has naturally intervened between my election and your address has afforded me an opportunity for appreciating the merits of the Federal Government and for communicating your sentiments of its administration, I have rather to express my satisfaction rather than regret at a circumstance which demonstrates (upon experiment) your attachment to the former as well as approbation of the latter.

I rejoice that a spirit of liberality and philanthropy is much more prevalent than it formerly was among the enlightened nations of the earth, and that your brethren will benefit thereby in proportion as it shall become still more extensive; happily the people of the United States have, in many instances exhibited examples worthy of imitation, the salutary influence of which will doubtless extend much farther if gratefully enjoying those blessings of peace which (under the favor of heaven) have been attained by fortitude in war, they shall conduct themselves with reverence to the Deity and charity toward their fellow-creatures.

May the same wonder-working Deity, who long since delivered the Hebrews from their Egyptian oppressors, planted them in a promised land, *whose providential agency has lately been conspicuous in establishing these United States as an independent nation*, still continue to water them with the dews of heaven and make the inhabitants of every denomination participate in the temporal and spiritual blessings of that people whose God is Jehovah.

G. WASHINGTON.

Address of the Newport Congregation to the President of the United States of America :

SIR: Permit the children of the stock of Abraham to approach you with the most cordial affection and esteem for your person and merit, and to join with our fellow-citizens in welcoming you to Newport.

With pleasure we reflect on those days of difficulty and danger when the God of Israel, who delivered David from the peril of the sword, shielded your head in the day of battle; and we rejoice to think that the same spirit which rested in the bosom of the greatly beloved Daniel, enabling him to preside over the province of the Babylonian Empire, rests and ever will rest upon you, enabling you to discharge the arduous duties of the Chief Magistrate of these States.

Deprived as we hitherto have been of the invaluable rights

of free citizens, we now—with a deep sense of gratitude to the Almighty Disposer of all events—behold a government erected by the majesty of the people, a government which to bigotry gives no sanction, to persecution no assistance, but generously affording to all liberty of conscience and immunities of citizenship, deeming every one of whatever nation, tongue, and language equal parts of the great governmental machine.

This so ample and extensive Federal Union, whose base is philanthropy, mutual confidence and public virtue, we cannot but acknowledge to be the work of the Great God who rules in the armies of the heavens and among the inhabitants of the earth, doing whatever seemeth to Him good.

For all the blessings of civil and religious liberty which we enjoy under an equal benign administration, we desire to send up our thanks to the Ancient days, the great Preserver of men, beseeching Him that the angel who conducted our forefathers through the wilderness into the promised land may graciously conduct you through all the difficulties and dangers of this mortal life; and when, like Joshua, full of days and full of honors, you are gathered to your fathers, may you be admitted into the heavenly paradise to partake of the water of life and the tree of immortality.

Done and signed by order of the Hebrew Congregation in Newport, Rhode Island.

MOSES SEIXES, *Warden*.

Newport, August 17, 1790.

Washington's reply to the Hebrew Congregation in Newport, R. I.:

GENTLEMEN: While I receive with much satisfaction your address replete with expressions of esteem, I rejoice in the opportunity of assuring you that I shall always retain grateful remembrance of the cordial welcome I experienced on my visit to Newport, from all classes of citizens.

The reflection on the days of difficulty and danger, which are past, is rendered the more sweet from a consciousness that they are succeeded by days of uncommon prosperity and security.

If we have wisdom to make the best use of the advantages with which we are now favored, we cannot fail, under the just administration of a good government, to become a great and happy people.

The citizens of the United States of America have a right to applaud themselves for having given to mankind examples of an enlarged and liberal policy, a policy worthy of imitation. All possess alike liberty of conscience and immunities of citizenship.

It is now no more that toleration is spoken of as if it were by the indulgence of one class of people that another enjoyed the exercise of their inherent natural rights, for, happily, the Government of the United States, which gives to bigotry no sanction, to persecution no assistance, requires only that they who live under its protection should demean themselves as good citizens in giving it on all occasions their effectual support.

It would be inconsistent with the frankness of my character not to avow that I am pleased with your favorable opinion of my administration, and fervent wishes for my felicity.

May the children of the stock of Abraham who dwell in this land continue to merit and enjoy the good will of the other inhabitants, while every one shall sit in safety under his own vine and fig tree, and there shall be none to make him afraid.

May the Father of all mercies scatter light, and not darkness, upon our paths and make us all in our several vocations useful here, and in his own due time and way everlastingly happy.

G. WASHINGTON.

The address of the Hebrew Congregations in the cities of Philadelphia, New York, Richmond, and Charleston, to the President of the United States:

SIR: It is reserved for you to unite in affection for your character and person every political and religious denomination of men, and in this will the Hebrew congregations aforesaid yield to no class of their fellow-citizens.

We have hitherto been prevented by various circumstances peculiar to our situation from adding our congratulations to those which the rest of America have offered on your elevation to the chair of the Federal Government. Deign, then, illustrious sir, to accept this our homage.

The wonders which the Lord of Hosts hath worked in the

days of our forefathers have taught us to observe the greatness of His wisdom and His might throught the events of the
late glorious Revolution; and, while we humble ourselves at His
footstool in thanksgiving and praise for the blessing of His deliverance, we acknowledge you, the leader of American armies,
as His chosen and beloved servant.   But not to your sword
alone is present happiness to be ascribed; that, indeed, opened
the way to the reign of freedom, but never was it perfectly secure
until your hand gave birth to the Federal Constitution and you
renounced the joys of retirement to seal by your administration
in peace what you had achieved in war.

To The Eternal God, who is thy refuge, we commit in our
prayers the care of thy precious life; and when, full of years,
thou shalt be gathered unto thy people, 'thy righteousness shall
go before thee,' and we shall remember, amidst our regret,
"that the Lord hath set apart the godly for Himself," whilst
thy name and thy virtues will remain an indelible memorial on
our minds.

MANUEL JOSEPHSON.

For and in behalf and under the authority of the several congregations aforesaid.

Philadelphia, December 13, 1790.

The President was pleased to reply to the foregoing as follows:

*Answer—To the Hebrew Congregations in the cities of Phila-
delphia, New York, Charleston, and Richmond:*

GENTLEMEN: The liberality of sentiment toward each other,
which marks every political and religious denomination of men
in this country, stands unparalleled in the history of nations.

The affection of such a people is a treasure beyond the reach
of calculation, and the repeated proofs which my fellow-citizens
have given of their attachment to me and approbation of my
doings, form the purest source of my temporal felicity.   The
affectionate expressions of your address again excite my gratitude and receive my warmest acknowledgement.

The power and goodness of The Almighty, so strongly manifested in the events of our late glorious revolution, and His

kind interposition in our behalf, have been no less visible in the establishment of our present equal government. In war He directed the sword, and in peace He has ruled in our councils. My agency in both has been guided by the best intentions and a sense of duty I owe to my country.

And as my exertions have hitherto been amply rewarded by the approbation of my fellow-citizens, I shall endeavor to deserve a continuance of it by my future conduct.

May the same temporal and eternal blessings which you implore for me, rest upon your congregations.

G. WASHINGTON.

The foregoing expressions of the father of his country to his Hebrew fellow-citizens may be appropriately supplemented by the following correspondence of patriots of the early days of the United States.

In 1818 the Mill Street Synagogue was consecrated. Mordecai M. Noah delivered an eloquent address on the occasion, and sent copies thereof to distinguished statesmen. Among the replies received were the following, which are worthy of preservation:

COPY OF A LETTER FROM THOMAS JEFFERSON.*

MONTICELLO, May 28, 1818.

Sir :—I thank you for the discourse on the consecration of the Synagogue in your city, with which you have been pleased to favor me. I have read it with pleasure and instruction, having learnt from it some valuable facts in Jewish history which I did not know before. Your sect by sufferings has furnished a remarkable proof of the universal spirit of religious intolerance inherent in every sect, disclaimed by all while feeble, and practiced by all when in power. Our laws have applied the only antidote to this vice, protecting our religious, as they do our civil rights, by putting all on an equal footing. But more remains to be done, for although we are free by the law, we are

---

* *Travels in England, France, Spain and the Barbary States in the years* 1813–14 *and* 15. By Mordecai M. Noah; New York and London, 1819. Appendix, pp. xxv and xxvi.

not so in practice; public opinion erects itself into an Inquisition, and exercises its office with as much fanaticism as fans the flames of an *Auto-de-fe*.

The prejudice still scowling on your section of our religion, although the elder one, cannot be unfelt by yourselves; it is to be hoped that individual dispositions will at length mould themselves to the model of the law, and consider the moral basis, on which all our religions rest, as the rallying point which unites them in a common interest; while the peculiar dogmas branching from it are the exclusive concern of the respective sects embracing them, and no rightful subject of notice to any other; public opinion needs reformation on that point, which would have the further happy effect of doing away the hypocritical maxim of *" intus et lubet, foris ut moris."* Nothing, I think, would be so likely to effect this, as to your sect particularly, as the more careful attention to education, which you recommend, and which, placing its members on the equal and commanding benches of science, will exhibit them as equal objects of respect and favor. I salute you with great respect and esteem.

(Signed)   THOMAS JEFFERSON.

M. M. NOAH, Esq."

COPY OF A LETTER FROM JAMES MADISON, ESQ., ON THE SAME SUBJECT.

MONTPELIER, May, 15, 1818.

Sir :—I have received your letter of the 6th, with the eloquent discourse delivered at the consecration of the Synagogue. Having ever regarded the freedom of religious opinions and worship as equally belonging to every sect, and the secure enjoyment of it as the best human provision for bringing all, either into the same way of thinking, or into that mutual charity which is the only proper substitute, I observe with pleasure the view you give of the spirit in which your sect partake of the common blessings afforded by our Government and laws.

As your foreign mission took place whilst I was in the administration, it cannot but be agreeable to me to learn that your accounts have been closed in a manner so favorable to you.

(Signed)   JAMES MADISON.

Copy of a Letter from John Adams, Esq.

QUINCY, July 31, 1818.

Sir :—Accept my best thanks for your polite and obliging favor of the 24th, and especially for the discourse inclosed. I know not when I have read a more liberal or more elegant composition.

You have not extended your ideas of the right of private judgment and the liberty of conscience, both in religion and philosophy, farther than I do. Mine are limited only by morals and propriety.

I have had occasion to be acquainted with several gentlemen of your nation, and to transact business with some of them, whom I found to be men of as liberal minds, as much honor, probity, generosity ond good breeding, as any I have known in any sect of religion or philosophy.

I wish your nation may be admitted to all privileges of citizens in every country of the world. This country has done much. I wish it may do more; and annul every narrow idea in religion, government, and commerce. Let the wits joke; the philosopher sneer ! What then? It has pleased the Provident of the 'first cause,' the universal cause, that Abraham should give religion, not only to Hebrews, but to Christians and Mahometans, the greatest part of the modern civilized world.

      (Signed)   JOHN ADAMS.

EXEGI *MONUMENTUM* ÆRE PERENNIUS.

THE STATUE OF JEFFERSON.

[A paper read before the Jewish Historical Society, December 27, 1894, by LEWIS ABRAHAM, Esq.]

In accordance with a resolution offered by Senator Justin S. Morrill, of Vermont, while he was a member of the House of Representatives, in 1864, "that each State should be permitted to send the effigies of two of her chosen sons, in marble or bronze, to be placed permanently here," the old Hall of Representatives is fast becoming an American memorial chamber.

Several statues, purchased by the United States, have been deposited there, and many of the States have taken advantage of the privilege and have honored their distinguished dead in the manner suggested by the resolution of Congress.

There is, however, one splendid work of art in the corridor that has a peculiar history. It was a gift to the Government. All the others have been paid for by Congress or the several State Legislatures. The bronze statue of Thomas Jefferson, by David d'Angers, a French sculptor, was presented to Congress by an Israelite, Lieutenant (afterward Commodore) Uriah Phillips Levy, of the United States Navy, in 1833, but was not formally accepted until forty years thereafter.

Originally it stood in the rotunda, but was removed from there and for many years remained in the grounds in front of the Presidential Mansion. After its acceptance in 1874, upon motion of Senator Sumner, it was finally located in its present position. It represents the author of the Declaration of Independence as just having signed that instrument of American Liberty. The pedestal is a superb piece of work, executed by Struthers, of Philadelphia, in four varieties of marble. It was the first piece of statuary ever owned by the Government, and is dedicated by the donor to his fellow citizens. Upon the scroll which Jefferson holds in his hand is engraved a verbatim copy of the Declaration of Independence, with fac-simile signatures of John Hancock and Thomas Jefferson.

The Levy famliy were intimate personal friends of the great framer of our *Magna Charta* and second President, and after his death became the owners of his old family seat, Monticello. There is a special significance in the gift and in the sentiment it conveys, and the co-religionists of Levy remember with pardonable pride that this piece of statuary, symbolizing the grand declaration of human equality and honoring one of the greatest of the men who erected the fabric of American Liberty, was the free-will offering of one of their people.

Bunker Hill Monument.

The commemoration of the first battle field of the Revolutionary War by a monument was made possible through a liberal contribution by Judah Touro. The proceedings of the Committee charged with the erection on Bunker Hill of a memorial to the patriots and heroes who laid the foundation of the Union, include a grateful acknowledgment of Touro's assistance.

The history of the monument, published by George Washington Warren, contains the following statement (page 283): " It was confidentially communicated to the Directors by Mr. William Appleton that whenever the Association, in addition to a like offer of Mr. Lawrence, should have money enough within ten thousand dollars ($10,000) to finish their work, Judah Touro would give that sum. It was a noble offer, and coming from a resident of a distant State, curiosity was excited.''

Then follows a biographical sketch of this eminent citizen, concluding as follows: " He was one of that smallest of all classes into which mankind can be divided—of men who accumulate wealth without even doing a wrong, taking an advantage, or making an enemy; who become rich without being avaricious: who deny themselves the comforts of life, that they may acquire the means of promoting the comfort and elevating the condition of their fellow-men.''

To complete the monument a fair (at which delegates from all the States attended) was held in Boston by ladies in aid of the building fund. The delegation from Louisiana, in their capacity as representatives of that State, purchased the fine model of the monument which adorned the Charleston table and they caused it to be transported to New Orleans and to be placed, in honor of Judah Touro, in one of the public buildings where it remained until it was destroyed with the building by fire.

In the abstract of donations (page 311) received from private sources, the gross sum is stated as $55,153.27, of which Judah Touro donated $10,000.

At a meeting of the Board of Directors the following resolutions were unanimously adopted:

" RESOLVED, That the Directors receive the contribution of Mr. Touro with sentiments of deep and grateful respect, considering it as a testimonial of his regard for the principles and the contest for which, and its successful issue, the monument is intended to commemorate, and his affectionate recollection of the friends of his youth and the place of his early residence.

" RESOLVED, That John Quincy Adams, Daniel Webster, Joseph Story, Edward Everett and Franklin Dexter be appointed a committee to prepare an inscription for a tablet to be placed in the monument stating the object for which it is erected and recording the liberality of Judah Touro and Amos Lawrence, and the successful exertions of the daughters of those patriots whose memory we would perpetuate — donations and labor which have placed in the possession of the Directors a fund sufficient to complete this memorial of one of the most important events in the history of our country." (Page 312.)

On June 17, 1843, a banquet was held in Fanueil Hall to celebrate the completion of the monument. Governor Marcus Morton, who was suffering from indisposition, was unable to attend, but sent a letter which was read. The two great benefactors of the Association were remembered by the following: (Page 330.)

> " Amos and Judah, venerated names,
> Patriarch and Prophet press their equal claims,
> Like generous coursers running ' neck and neck,'
> Each aids the work by giving it a *check*.
> Christian and Jew, they carry out one plan,
> For though of different faiths each is in heart a MAN."

STATUE OF RELIGIOUS LIBERTY, CENTENNIAL CELEBRATION,
1876.

One hundred years elapse, with their cares and joys, jeopardy and success, and America celebrates the centennial year of its existence by a grand exhibition in the city where is deposited the liberty bell that proclaimed "liberty throughout the land unto all the inhabitants thereof." The massive engine that moves obedient machinery sings a pæan to the Republic!

The nimble shuttle and the agile loom weave chaplets and trophies! Lightning-flashes leap from fathomless seas and speak with living fire congratulations of emperors, kings, and potentates! Human handicrafts, from Occident to Orient, delve and build, and fuse and shape tributes of felicitation to the glory and honor of praise, aye, even worship, of the land of Washington!

Fairmount Park blazes with the light of human advancement in science and art, literature, education and religion; and, with humility be it stated, no portion of God's footstool is more to be credited with aiding and nurturing the progress of the century than the land of Washington and Jefferson and Franklin.

There, on the Centennial grounds, the Israelites of the United States, through one of their organizations, "the Sons of the Covenant," placed their homage. It is in the shape of a group of statuary in Carrara marble styled

RELIGIOUS LIBERTY.

It was executed in Rome, by one of their own people, Moses Ezekiel, a native of Richmond, Virginia. Upon the pedestal is an inscription, neither narrow in scope nor sectarian in spirit. The promoters of this tribute felt the eloquence of the Bill of Human Rights they desired to typify, and simply transcribed the clause of the Constitution which reads:

CONGRESS SHALL MAKE NO LAW RESPECTING
AN ESTABLISHMENT OF RELIGION OR PRO-
HIBITING THE FREE EXERCISE THEREOF.

An eminent and thoughtful foreigner, a statesman of worldwide fame, passing through Fairmount Park, earnestly gazed

5

at the marble group, and exclaimed: "If the Centennial Exhibition of 1876 resulted in this work of art and did nothing else, the American people should be satisfied. I, the subject of a monarch, salute the Nation that makes this creation possible."*

* The statue of Religious Liberty was erected by the Independent Order of B'nai B'rith, pursuant to the resolution to that effect, adopted by the General Convention of the Order at Chicago in 1874. Of that Convention Hon. Simon Wolf was President, and the adoption of the measure by the Convention, as well as the eventual success of the undertaking through the active support of the various lodges, were due mainly to Mr. Wolf's indefatigable efforts.—*Ed.*

JEWISH SOLDIERS IN THE WAR OF 1812, AND IN THE MEXICAN WAR.

It is questionable whether the Jewish population of the American Union kept pace with the general increase during the time from the close of the Revolutionary struggle to the middle of the present century. Certain it is that at a comparatively developed period, in 1824, Solomon Etting estimated the Jewish population of Maryland as "at least 150," and that of the United States as "at least 6000,"* while another experienced publicist, Isaac Harby, estimates it, as we have seen, (note, page 12), at "not over 6000" in 1826. Up to the close of the Eighteenth Century the Jewish immigrants to this side of the Atlantic were derived almost entirely from the Sephardic stock, mainly indeed from England and Holland and their colonial dependencies, and these, from the comparative paucity of numbers at their source, could not, in the very nature of things, have been very numerous. Of the Jewish colonists of the time of the Revolution, some, who had remained loyal to the mother country, went back to England or to the West Indies after the war was over, and the number of these, though quite limited, was but little overbalanced by the new arrivals. The emigration of the German Jews remained altogether sporadic throughout the period of the Napoleonic wars, because of the almost insuperable obstacles which hindered their departure, and for a time thereafter they were content to remain at home in view of the great political concessions which they had gained from the German rulers in return for their valor and heroic sacrifices in defense of the fatherland. The increase of the Jewish population in this country was thus limited

---

* Replies to inquiries of Colonel W. G. Worthington, quoted by the latter in his advocacy of the enfranchisement of the Jews of Maryland. ("*Speeches on the Jew Bill in the House of Delegates of Maryland*," by *H. M. Brackenridge, Philadelphia, 1829*).

mainly to the surplus of births over deaths until some time after the close of the War of 1812. In the course of the reaction against the innovations of liberalism which ensued after 1820, the hardly-gained political rights of the German Jews were gradually curtailed or entirely withdrawn, and at this time the Jews of the German maritime cities began to emigrate to the United States in increasing numbers. It was not, however, until after the revolution of 1848 and the beginning of steam navigation on the Atlantic, that any considerable exodus took place. At the time of the Mexican War, in 1846, the Jewish population of the United States was probably not greater in proportion than that estimated for the period of the Revolutionary War. In point of fact, at the time of the second war with Great Britain, and likewise also at the date of the Mexican War, the Jewish element composed as yet only a minute fraction of the general population, and no very considerable number of Jewish names are to be looked for in the army lists of those two wars. At the same time it remains to be added that the lists here given for both the wars referred to are not at all complete, comprising for the most part only the names of such individuals as left notable evidence of their presence in the ranks.

WAR OF 1812.

Private JACOB APPEL
> served in Captain Samuel Borden's Company, 4th Detachment, Pennsylvania.

Private JACOB BACHMAN and

Private SAMUEL BACHMAN,
> served in Captain Peter Nungesser's Company, 2nd Regiment, Volunteer Light Infantry, Pennsylvania.

Brigadier-General JOSEPH BLOOMFIELD,
> in command of Military District No. 4, embracing Pennsylvania, Delaware and Western New Jersey.
> [*His military record is included in the list of Jewish soldiers in the American Revolutionary War*].

ISRAEL I. COHEN
    was a member of Captain Nicholson's Company of Maryland Fencibles, and served in the defense of Fort McHenry.

MENDES I. COHEN,
    brother of the above, volunteered for the defense of Baltimore and also served at Fort McHenry during the memorable bombardment.

Sergeant SAMUEL GOODMAN,
    served in Captain George Zieber's Company, 1st Regiment, 2nd Brigade, Pennsylvania, under Lieutenant-Colonel Jeremiah Shappel.

Second Lieutenant BENJAMIN GRATZ
    served in company of Pennsylvania Volunteers commanded by Captain John Swift, 1813.

Corporal ABRAHAM GUNSENHOUSER,
    served in Captain Jacob Wentz's Company—3d Company, 52d Regiment, Pennsylvania.

Private JACOB HAAS
    served in Captain George Dinckey's Company, 18th Section of Riflemen from Pennsylvania.

JACOB HAYS,
BENJAMIN HAYS, } father and son served in N. Y. commands.

Private EZEKIEL JACOBS
    served in Captain Florence Cotter's Company, 1st Detachment, 1st Brigade, Pennsylvania.

Private HENRY LOEB
    served in Captain Jacob Ashey's Company, 1st Regiment of Pennsylvania.

First Lieutenant ISAAC MERTZ
    served in Captain Middleswarth's Company, Battalion of Riflemen from Pennsylvania.

Lieutenant DAVID METZLER

Corporal DANIEL METZLER
    served in Captain Nicholas Beckwith's (Fifth Battalion) Company from Pennsylvania.

Private JOSEPH METZGAR
　　served in Captain Adam Diller's Company, 2nd Brigade,
　　Pennsylvania.

Ensign SAMUEL MEYER
　　served in Captain George Hess's Company of Riflemen
　　from Northampton County, Pennsylvania.

Private JACOB MILLER
　　served in Captain Nickolaus Derr's Company, 101st Regi-
　　ment, from Pennsylvania.

Private JACOB MILLER
　　served in Captain John Christian's Company, 2nd Regi-
　　ment from Pennsylvania.

Private ABRAHAM MITCHELL
　　served in the Pennsylvania line.

MYER MORDECAI
　　served among Pennsylvania Volunteers.

Private ISAAC MOSER
　　served in Captain John Christian's Company, 2nd Regi-
　　ment from Pennsylvania.

Sergeant JACOB MOSER
　　served in Captain J. Bakeoven's Company, 2nd Brigade,
　　from Pennsylvania.

Captain MYER MOSES
　　was commissioned from South Carolina.

Captain MORDECAI MYERS,
　　13th Pennsylvania Infantry; wounded at Chrysler's
　　Field.

Colonel NATHAN MYERS
　　was in command of a brigade stationed near the City of
　　New York.

Adjutant ISAAC MYERS
　　served in 1st Regiment of Pennsylvania.

JONAS PHILLIPS
　　served in Captain John Linton's Company in the Battalion
　　of Philadelphia Militia, under Colonel William Bradford,
　　Pennsylvania.

JOSEPH PHILLIPS
> served in the Pennsylvania line.

Private SAMUEL PHILLIPS
> served in Captain Florence Cotter's Company, 1st Detachment of 1st Brigade, Pennsylvania.

Private JACOB ROSENSTEEL
> served in Captain John Williamson's Company, 2nd Brigade, Pennsylvania Militia, under Brigadier-General Richard Crooks.

DAVID G. SEIXAS
> served from Pennsylvania. He was instrumental in founding the Pennsylvania Institution for the Deaf and Dumb, and won esteem by his philanthropy. [*A sketch of his career is published elsewhere in this work.*]

Private ABRAHAM SHATZ
> served in Captain George Zieber's Company, 1st Regiment, 2nd Brigade, Pennsylvania, under Lieutenant-Colonel Jeremiah Shappel.

Private SIGFRIED SOLOMON
> served in Captain George Dinckey's Company, 18th Section of Riflemen, from Pennsylvania.

JUDAH TOURO
> enlisted as a volunteer in the American Army, under General Andrew Jackson; was severely wounded in the battle of New Orleans, January 1, 1815; rendered many services as patriot and philanthropist, as detailed elsewhere in this work.

Private SAMUEL WAMSER and Private MICHAEL WOLF
> served in Captain George Zieber's Company, 1st Regiment, 2nd Brigade, Pennsylvania, under Lieutenant-Colonel Jeremiah Shappel.

Corporal SAMUEL WEISS
> served in Captain John M. Buckius's Company, 2nd Brigade, Pennsylvania.

Private JACOB WOLF
> served in Captain Samuel Wilson's Company of Militia, from Buck's County, Pennsylvania.

Private JACOB WOLF
> served in Captain John Christian's Company, 2nd Regiment, from Pennsylvania.

ISAAC DE YOUNG
> Company A, 3d New Jersey Artillery, enlisted when only a boy ; wounded in the groin at Lundy's Lane in a bayonet charge.

Private ABRAHAM YUXSHEIMER
> served in Captain Nickolaus Derr's Company, 101st Regiment, from Pennsylvania.

MEXICAN WAR.

Sergeant ABRAHAM ADLER,
> New York Volunteers; killed in action.

SAMUEL BEIN.

First Lieutenant LEVI BENJAMIN, Maryland Militia, 1846.

EUGENE JOSEPH CHIMÉNE,
> served with Sam Houston, in the Texan War.

Sergeant JACOB DAVID, New York Volunteers.

JOSEPH DAVIS, Co. D, 12th Regiment.

General DAVID DE LEON
> was born in South Carolina in 1822. In the Mexican War he twice took the places of commanding officers who had been killed or disabled by wounds. He acted with such gallantry and ability as to twice receive the thanks of the United States Congress. In February, 1861, he resigned his rank as Surgeon and Major in the United States Army and was appointed first Surgeon General of the Armies of the Confederacy.

Colonel LEON DYER,
 Quartermaster-General of the State of Louisiana; sub-
 sequently held the same rank under General Winfield
 Scott.

GABRIEL DROPSIE, Co. E, 1st Pennsylvania Regiment.

HERMAN EHRENBERG
 fought under Fannin at Goliad.

ALBERT EMANUEL,
 in Captain Kimball's Company, 2d Regiment of Texas
 Volunteer Cavalry.

S. EYTINGE, Maryland Militia, 1846.

MARCUS FLENDROWITZ,
 wounded in action.

DAVID FRIEDMAN.

Third Lieutenant —— GOLDSMITH, Maryland Militia, 1846.

JAMES HART, New York Volunteers.

WILLIAM HART, New York Volunteers;
 lost a leg at Cherubusco.

Sergeant MARX M. HART, New York Volunteers.

Sergeant JOSEPH HENRIQUES, New York Volunteers.

Sergeant SAMUEL HENRY, New York Volunteers.

Corporal JACOB HIRSCHHORN, 1st New York Volunteers.

Surgeon J. HORWITZ, Maryland Militia, 1846.

PHILIP HORWITZ.

Colonel S. M. HYAMS.

SAMUEL ISAACS, Texas Army, 1836–1837 (Co. D, 10th
 Infantry.)

EDWARD J. JOHNSON
 volunteered in Captain King's Company during Texas
 revolution; killed at Goliad, March 27, 1836.

MARK KAHN, New York Volunteers.

DAVIS S. KAUFFMAN,
> aide to General Douglas, wounded at the battle of Neches ; was Speaker of the Texas Assembly and advocated its annexation; was member of Congress from Texas from date of annexation (1846) to his death in 1851.

NATHAN KLUGAN.

—— KOHN, Texas Spy Company (at San Jacinto).

D. I. KOKERNOT
> fought at Anahuac; also at the Grass battles, 1835, and in Texan War, 1836.

JACOB LEVA, New York Volunteers.

WILLIAM MALLOY LEVI.

Surgeon-General MOSES ALBERT LEVY,
> in Sam Houston's Army, in service throughout the Texas-Mexican War. Colonel Johnson's report of the capture of San Antonio, December 15, 1835, stated: "Doctors Levy and Pollard deserve my warmest praise for their unremitted attention and assiduity."

Doctor ISAAC LYONS,
> of Charleston, served as Surgeon-General under General Tom Green, in the Texan War of 1836.

BENJAMIN H. MORDECAI
> served under General Fannin.

Lieutenant-Colonel ISRAEL MOSES,
> promoted from Assistant Surgeon; served also in Civil War.

M. K. MOSES
> served under General Fannin.

JOHN MYERS, New York Volunteers.

PHILIP MYERS, New York Volunteers.

SOPPHE MYERS, New York Volunteers.

OTTO NEUBAUER, New York Volunteers.

HENRY PHILLIPS, New York Volunteers.

GEORGE RIELL, New York Volunteers.

ELIAS SCHOENBERG.

Lieutenant HENRY SEELIGSON,

> Galveston Cadets, was appointed First Lieutenant of that Company when the Mexican invasion of Galveston was threatened. In the Mexican War of 1846 he enlisted in Captain McLean's Company, and subsequently volunteered in Captain Bell's Regiment, which was ordered to join the command of General Taylor, en route for Monterey. He bore so conspicuous a part in the battle at that point that he was sent for by General Taylor and highly complimented; being offered a Lieutenancy in the 2d Dragoons. At the outbreak of the Civil War, he enlisted in the Confederate Army, joining a Cavalry Company commanded by Captain Woodward.

HENRY SIESEL.

ALEXANDER SIMM, New York Volunteers.

Second Lieutenant JOSEPH SIMPSON, Maryland Militia, 1846.

JACOB C. SOMERS, New York Volunteers.

Assistant Surgeon HENRY H. STEINER,

> with rank of Captain.

ADOLPHUS STERNE

> joined the American settlers in their early struggles against the Mexicans; took part in the Fredonian War; he was captured by the Mexicans and sentenced to be shot, but was subsequently released. He served in both lower and upper Houses of the Texas Legislature, previous to annexation.

SELIGMAN STRAUSS.

Captain MICHAEL SZTYFFT

> served on the staff of General Zachary Taylor.

J. VALENTINE, Palmetto Regiment, South Carolina.

Sergeant ALEXANDER B. WEINBERG, New Jersey Battalion.

HENRY WIENER

> fought in the battle of Buena Vista.

A. WOLF,

> killed at the storming of the Alamo, in the Texan War, December, 1835.

UNITED STATES REGULAR ARMY.

The following list comprises names of Jewish soldiers on the rolls of the standing army of the United States, from the earliest period of the Republic to our present time. It is more or less incomplete, as only those have been included whose identity has been sufficiently established.

The roster includes the names of men in every branch of the service, many with a distinguished and all of them with honorable records.

E. ABRAHAM, Co. H, 16th Regiment.

Surgeon MORRIS JOSEPH ASCH,
    brevetted Captain and Major for meritorious services; served in all from August 5, 1861 to March 31, 1873.

Post Surgeon DANIEL M. APPEL,
    with rank of Captain; entered army in 1876, and now in service.

Assistant Surgeon AARON H. APPEL,
    with rank of Captain; entered army in 1887.

J. BERGMAN, Co. B, 1st Dragoons.

DAVID BEHRENBERG, 18th Infantry;
    served five years.

Assistant Surgeon M. BLOCK, 14th Infantry.

W. BLONDHEIM, Co. B, 14th Infantry.

WILLIAM HARRIS BOAS, Co. I, 3d Infantry.

ALEXANDER BORG, 2d Infantry.

ISAAC H. BRANDON, 12th Infantry.

I. M. BRANDON, 12th Infantry.

—— CHAPPELL, Co. C, 10th Infantry.

A. E. COHEN, Co. G, 17th Infantry.

GEORGE COHEN, 7th Infantry.

HERMAN COHEN, 13th Infantry.

Lieutenant HYMAN COHEN.

JOSEPH COHEN, Co. F, 1st Artillery.

LEOPOLD COHEN, general service.

MORRIS COHEN, War Department.

Sergeant MORRIS COHEN, 3d Dragoons,
   enlisted as Private.

R. P. COHEN, 5th Infantry.

BENJAMIN DAVID, Co. I, 2nd Artillery.

HENRY M. DAVIS, 2nd Battalion, 18th Infantry.

Surgeon ABRAHAM DELEON.

SIMON H. DE YOUNG, 4th Infantry.

Brevet Lieutenant-Colonel FRANX MARK ETTING
   served from 1861 to 1868.   Chief Paymaster of the Army
   from 1864 to 1867.

Brevet Captain D. I. EZEKIEL, 4th Infantry.
   Promoted from private on account of bravery displayed
   in battle ; was seriously wounded.

MAX FELDMAN, 2nd Artillery.

JACOB GABRIEL, 5th Artillery,
   killed at Cedar Mountain.

S. GERSTMAN,
   served five years.

N. GLEISER, Co. G, 10th Infantry.

CHARLES GOLDSMITH, 8th Infantry.

ELLIS M. GOTTHOLD,
   1st Artillery.   Served five years ; mustered out as Corporal ; the recipient of a medal from the Chamber of Commerce, New York City.

Lieutenant HARRY J. HIRSCH
   entered army in 1891 ; now in service.

THEODORE JOSEPH, Co. H, 10th Infantry.

C. G. JACOBS, 13th Infantry.

JACOB JACOBSON.

MICHAEL JACOBSON, Ordnance Corps.

OSCAR JACOBY, 2nd Artillery.

———— KOSMINSKI.

MAX LEPPOWITZ, Co. B, 14th Artillery.

BENJAMIN LEVI, Co. B, 14th Artillery.

Captain CHAPMAN LEVY.

HENRY J. LEVY, Hospital Steward.

JOHN LEVY, 19th Infantry.

ALBERT LIEBER, 10th Infantry.

AARON LIVINGSTIN, 2nd Infantry.

A. MANTNER, 4th Artillery.

SIMON MARKS
    served in General Custer's Cavalry Division.

Major ABRAHAM A. MASSIAS,
    1st Lieutenant of Riflemen, 1808; Captain, 1809, after-
    wards Major; promoted Paymaster in United States Army
    in 1820.

H. MENDEL, Co. A, 4th Cavalry.

M. MENDEL
    served thirty years in the United States Army, retiring
    as Quartermaster Sergeant.

HEINRICH MEERHOLZ, Co. D, 10th Infantry.

Captain OTTO E. MICHAELES, Ordnance Department.

C. MILTENBERGER, Co. B, 9th Infantry.

Surgeon PHILIP MINIS.

Major ALFRED MORDECAI,
    a recognized authority in the military world in the field of
    scientific research, and in the practical application of me-
    chanical science to the art of war; he served in the Mexi-
    can War, and was sent by our Government, together with

General George B. McClellan, and Major Richard Dela-
field, to witness and report upon the operations in the
Crimea.   Major Mordecai was the author of " Reports of
Experiments on Gunpowder," an " Ordnance Manual,"
and other works.

Colonel ALFRED MORDECAI, JR.,

entered the army as Lieutenant in 1861 ; served in Civil
War in various capacities; has been an instructor at the
Military Academy, West Point; promoted for meritorious
and faithful services; is now in command of National
Armory, at Springfield, Massachusetts.

J. F. MOSES, Battery A, 4th U. S. Artillery.

A. S. NELSON, Co. G, 15th Infantry.

1st Lieutant GEORGE J. NEWGARDEN, M. D., now in service.

MICHAEL NEWMAN, 5th Cavalry.

MOSES NEWMAN, 13th Infantry.

Cadet SAMUEL NOAH, 1st Artillery.

JULIUS OPPENHEIMER, F, 5th Artillery.

Lieutenant LOUIS OSTHEIM

entered army in 1883 ; has been in command of various
forts and now in service.

Sergeant OSCAR POLLACK, 2nd Cavalry,

served nine years ; enlisted as private ; wounded ; killed
in the fight with the Sioux at Wounded Knee.

Sergeant —— POLLOCK, 7th Cavalry.

Killed at Wounded Knee.

GEORGE POPPERS, 3d Infantry.

MAX REECE, Co. B, 4th Artillery.

A note attached to his discharge reads : "A sober, faithful, intelligent, brave and excellent soldier."

1st Sergeant SAMUEL REIS, Company C, U. S. Cavalry.

Served ten years.   Discharged for disability to serve any
longer.

ADOLPH RESSIE, Co. K, 10th Infantry.

Isaac Rice, 10th Infantry.

D. S. Rœdelsheimer.

E. Rose, 10th Infantry.

—— Rosenfeld, Co. C, 10th Infantry.

David Rosenheim, 1st Infantry.

John Rosenthal, Ordnance Corps.

Nathan Schœnfarber, Co. G, 14th Infantry.

Elias Schumacher, Co. C, 2nd Infantry.

Isaac Smith, Co. H, 11th Infantry.

J. Sommer, Co. E, 4th Infantry.

Major and Paymaster Justus Steinberger.
   [See *Record in Civil War List.*]

Julius Steinmeyer, 7th Infantry.

Joseph Sturmer, Co. G, 10th Infantry.

Surgeon G. Waage.

Israel Waterman,
   in Civil War ; transferred from ranks of 40th Regiment of
   Pennsylvania Volunteers November 9, 1862.

Meyer Weiler, Co. A, 13th Infantry.

Marcus Weiler, Co. F, 13th Infantry,
   wounded at Vicksburg.

Joseph Wenk, —— Cavalry.

Wilem West, Fort Lyon, Colorado.
   discharged for disability incurred in service—(1882–1884).

Emanuel Wodick, Co. K, 10th Infantry.

Adam Wolf, 2nd Infantry.

Isaac Wolf.

L. W. Worstman,
   Chief Telegraph Operator, Military Department.

UNITED STATES NAVY.

The spirit of devotion to this country and its interests always manifested by its Jewish inhabitants has not failed to leave its impress on the rolls of the United States Navy. From the time of the organization of that branch of the national defense many Jews have been present in the service. That they did their full duty the records indisputably show, and from the man before the mast to flag officer, from stoker to chief engineer, sons of Israel have given their efforts in behalf of the American cause. At the time of our Civil War their ranks were especially reinforced, and at the present day a considerable number of Jews are at posts of duty on the vessels of our navy.

Instances of personal distinction on the part of these defenders are numerous, but specific reference need here be made only to the great advance accomplished by Uriah Phillips Levy in behalf at once of the Navy and of humanity at large, by the abolition through his influence of the degrading practice of corporal punishment in the navy of the United States. He had long opposed the brutal system of flogging, and when promoted to the position of Flag Officer—the highest rank registered before the Civil War—he used his authority to promote the self-respect and well being of the sailors of his fleet. The records of others besides Commodore Levy are creditable in a high degree, and all comprised in the list are examples of men who devote to the cause in which they are enlisted "their lives, their fortunes and their sacred honor."

S. AMERICAN, U. S. Gunboat Seneca.

BENJAMIN ABRAHAMS, Acting Assistant Paymaster.

SIMON ARNBACH, Mexican War.

SOLOMON ASHER, U. S. Gunboat Wissahickon,
      promoted to Acting Assistant Yeoman (1862–1863).

Paymaster JONAS BARNETT, U. S. Steamer Essex,
      lost his life by falling from the rigging of his vessel while
      at sea.

Lieutenant HENRY BARNETT.

6

Major DAVID M. COHEN,
>   fourteen years an officer of the U. S. Marine Corps;
>   appointed Lieutenant, 1855, subsequently appointed Major
>   and placed on retired list on account of physical disability.

JACOB DA SILVA SOLIS COHEN,
>   Acting Assistant Surgeon under Rear-Admiral S. F.
>   Du Pont (1861–1864).

Midshipman JOSEPH COHEN (1826).

GUSTAVE DUVAL, U. S. Steamer Pawnee.

WILLIAM DURST, U. S. Monitor,
>   one of the few survivors of the memorable fight between
>   the Monitor and the Merrimac. Admiral Worden expressed
>   himself that Durst was not only a brave, fearless and
>   patriotic man, but eminently worthy to be recognized by
>   some action on the part of Congress (1862–1864).

CHARLES EDELMAN, U. S. Steamer Ohio.

JONATHAN MANLY EMANUEL,
>   Past Assistant Engineer, served under Commodore Mead.
>   Twice shipwrecked (1862–1891).

Purser GRATZ ETTING.

Captain HENRY ETTING
>   entered as Midshipman, promoted to Purser, Navy Pay-
>   master and retired with the rank of Captain — 1818–1861.

Lieutenant THEODORE MINIS ETTING
>   was appointed Acting Midshipman when a little over
>   sixteen years old, promoted Midshipman, Ensign, Navy
>   Paymaster, Lieutenant (1862–1877).

Acting Ensign ISAAC N. GOLDSMITH,
>   Mate, Acting Ensign (1863–1865).

Mate NATHAN A. GOLDSMITH,
>   (1864–1866).

JEROME HAAS.

Lieutenant E. C. HAMBURGER;
>   promoted step by step, finally commissioned Lieutenant.

Captain LEVI MYERS HARBY (1793–1870).

At the age of fourteen he was Midshipman in the U. S. Navy. During the War of 1812–1814, he was captured by the British and confined for eighteen months in "Dartmoor Prison," from which he finally escaped by swimming. In December, 1823, he served as sailing-master on the U. S. Vessel Beagle. He served for fifty-two years under the U. S. flag and rose to the rank of Captain. He participated in the Texan War of Independence and in the Mexican War. He also served in the Seminole War of Florida, and had command of a vessel in the expedition against the pirates of Algiers and Tripoli. On leave of absence he also fought in the Bolivian War of Independence. In 1861 he resigned his commission and entered the Confederate service with the rank of Commodore, distinguishing himself as Commander of the Neptune, capturing the Harriet Lane at Galveston, Texas. He was subsequently in command of a fleet of Confederate gunboats on the Sabine River.

SOLOMON HARBY

died in the service.

J. HARRISON, U. S. Steamer North Carolina.

SAMUEL HERFORD, U. S. Steamers Richmond and Wyoming.

FREDERIC D. HENRIQUES;

Acting Second Assistant Engineer (1864–1865).

Midshipman ISRAEL ISRAEL,

midshipman (1813–1818).

Midshipman JOSEPH ISRAEL,

distinguished himself, died in the service (1801–1804).

JACOB JACOBS, U. S. Steamer Portsmouth,

was on board the Ida when she was blown up by a torpedo.

AUGUSTUS JACOBSON,

transferred from Twenty-seventh Pennsylvania Regiment.

Midshipman and Master HENRY M. JACOBY, Shenandoah, Wachusett, Worcester, Yantic, Lackawanna (1866–1883).

Surgeon GERSHOM R. JACQUES,
   promoted from Surgeon's Mate to Surgeon (1800–1808).

Mate SAMUEL JESSURUN (1863–1864).

S. S. KRAUSS, U. S. Steamer Raritan,
   served four years.

C. C. KEANE.

DAVID J. KING, U. S. Steamer Wissahickon.

ISAAC M. KING.

NATHAN LANG.

ALEXANDER A. LAZARUS U. S. Steamer Horace Beals, also
   Rhode Island.

HENRY LEVI, U. S. Steamer Princeton,
   transferred to New Ironsides, Vandalia, etc. (1862–1865).

Master MEARS LEVY (1812–1813).

Second Assistant Engineer CHARLES H. LEVY (1857–1861).

Mate CHARLES LEVIN (1870–1874),
   died during his service.

M. LINDHEIM, Pocahontas.

HENRY LYONS.

Commodore URIAH PHILLIPS LEVY,
   one of the best known American naval officers of former
   days. At the time of his death, 1862, he was the highest
   ranking officer in the U. S. Navy. He served in the War of
   1812, being the master of the brig of war Argus, which ran
   the blockade to France with Mr. Crawford, the American
   Minister to that country, on board. The Argus destroyed
   twenty-one British merchantmen. In recognition of his
   valuable services to the nation the Common Council of
   New York City honored him with "the freedom of the
   city." Commodore Levy vigorously opposed the application of the lash to seamen. Upon his tombstone at Cypress
   Hill is recorded the fact that "he was the father of the
   law for the abolition of the barbarous practice of corporal
   punishment in the U. S. Navy."

Captain JONAS P. LEVY
> commanded the U. S. Steamer America during the Mexican War and was active in the transportation of U. S. troops to Vera Cruz. At the surrender of that port he was appointed its captain by General Winfield Scott.

MARX MAAS, U. S. Gunboat No. 29.

JACOB MAAS, Gunboat.

A. MEYER.

HORACE MOSES
> served in the U. S. fleet during the Mexican War and was Secretary to Captain (afterwards Admiral) S. P. Lee.

FLORIAN MOSS,
> on Commodore S. F. Du Pont's blockading squadron Vermont and Massachusetts (1862–1865).

Midshipman PHILIP MOSES.

JOSEPH MOSS,
> Mate and Acting Ensign, (1861–1863).

Acting Master EDWARD MOSES,
> (1862–1864); died while in service.

WILLIAM NOAH.

LOUIS NEWBERGER, U. S. Gunboat Pawpaw.

JOSEPH B. NONES, Guerriere.
> In 1814, when seventeen years of age, he accompanied Henry Clay, Gallatin and John Quincy Adams on the Frigate John Adams to Europe on the Ghent Mission ; severely wounded and obliged to resign from the service (1812–1822).

Master NEWMAN MORRIS (1801–1803).

Captain HENRY BENJAMIN NONES, Revenue Marine,
> promoted from 3d Lieutenant ; served from 1831 ; died in 1868.

Chief Engineer HENRY BEAUCHAMP NONES,
> served on various vessels ; rose from Second Assistant Engineer ; has served since 1853.

Midshipman JEFFERSON H. NONES, 1840–1846.

Second Assistant Engineer WASHINGTON H. NONES (1850–1853); died while in service.

Midshipman ABRAM PHILLIPS (1812–1813).
Drowned, 1813.

Paymaster EMANUEL J. PHILLIPS.

Captain ISAAC PHILLIPS (1798–1799).

Assistant Surgeon MANUEL PHILLIPS (1809–1824).

SOLOMON PINHEIRO, Juniata.
Wounded in the attack on Fort Fisher (1863–1866).

MILTON JOSEPH ROSENAU,
Past Assistant Surgeon in the Marine Hospital Service.

Acting Ensign ALBERT P. SAMPSON (1862–1865).

Acting Ensign ISAAC P. SAMPSON (1863–1865).

J. SCHLESINGER, U. S. Steamer Pocahontas.

M. J. SIESEL, U. S. Steamer Hartford.

Sergeant SIEGMUND SILVERBURG, U. S. Marine Corps.

Midshipman BENJAMIN SOLOMON (1809–1810).

Purser EZEKIEL SOLOMON (1814–1816).

CHARLES STEIN, Marine Corps,
Died of exposure in the service.

Lieutenant EDWARD TAUSSIG,
served fourteen years on sea and did seven years' duty on land.

CHARLES WIENER
served four years.

LEO WISE, U. S. Steamer Springfield.

A PAGE FROM THE SECRET HISTORY OF THE CIVIL WAR.

As a fitting prelude to the record of Jewish activity in the War of the Rebellion, there may be cited here an episode in its history which has had no counterpart in the course of the world's affairs. Recondite and romantic incidents are present in the annals of all nations, and the history of the Jewish people especially is fraught with many striking instances of unhoped and unexpected deliverance from impending calamity, but they were largely the outcome of times and conditions widely at variance with those of the present day. The narrative of Haym Salomon's sacrifice in behalf of American freedom and the cause of human liberty forms a singular chapter in the annals of the American Revolution. But a yet more remarkable incident, one that appears wholly foreign to the *laisser-faire* spirit of our modern time, and which is likely in the future to centre a much greater degree of attention than it has yet received, is a transaction that has but lately become part of the history of the Civil War.

On October 2, 1863, the British Government seized in the shipyard of the Lairds, at Birkenhead, two armored vessels which had ostensibly been built for the government of China, but which, according to constantly reiterated reports, had been built for the Southern Confederacy in rebellion against the United States. The contemporary chronicles of the Civil War contain at most only such reports of that incident as became public in the course of the controversy over the subject, but the inner details of the occurrence, notable enough even in its most obvious features, remained for many years a diplomatic secret until revealed by the then Register of the Treasury, Mr. L. E. Chittenden, in his "Recollections of President Lincoln."

The two vessels had indeed been embargoed by the British Government, but under conditions which had been settled upon by the advisers of the Crown with the almost clearly manifest purpose of permitting the vessels to escape, while at

the same time apparently complying with the requirements
of international law and the representations of the American Minister. The sympathies of the ruling powers in Great
Britain were strongly with the Southern cause ; the fact that
the success of that cause meant the perpetuation of negro
slavery, against which the English people had constantly in-
veighed, was held by many of the leaders of the party in
power to be of small moment in comparison with the advancement of British interests, which these leaders believed would
result from the disruption of the American Republic. They
were accordingly ready to take advantage of a virtual breach
of international comity and law, under cover of a technical
compliance with its provisions, and incur the risk of all the
terrible outcome of a war between the two great Anglo-
Saxon nations of the world. That such a war would surely
have resulted if the two armored corsairs had eventually been
let loose upon this country, no student of history can doubt.
It was being busily fomented by that arch enemy, both of
England and America, Napoleon III., who had assiduously
been seeking an adequate pretext to recognize the independence
of the Confederate States. He was actively conferring with
British parliamentary leaders with the purpose of a joint intervention in our struggle, and if these ships were liberated to
prey upon our commerce, lift the blockade of the Confederate
ports, weaken the Federal power and strengthen that of the
Rebellion, he would then assuredly be able to build up his empire in Mexico. That empire was already planted on the soil
of the Mexican Republic, and the triumph of the Southern
cause meant the success of the foolhardy and villainous undertaking which Napoleon III. had established under Maximilian.
If the outcome of British co-operation for the disruption of the
American Union were eventually to be a war between England
and the United States, it would but be further grist for the mill
of the French usurper.

From all of this procession of possible and unmeasured evils
it appears that the world was saved through the timely and
powerful interposition of a single will. It was the will of a
man who was manifestly near enough to the mainspring of
affairs to be aware of its primary movements, who was yet so

hidden from public view that his action would remain as secret as he himself determined it to be; whose purpose was clearly in opposition to the motives of the ruling powers, and who possessed the means with which to effect his purpose.

Who was it that so signally changed the current of the world's affairs? whose influence yet remains as mysterious as it was far-reaching? The question has been often asked and still remains unanswered. He still remains unnamed on the page of history. His position, his motive and his means of action appear to be defined, and it was clearly with these considerations in view that Mr. Chittenden wrote the letter which is here subjoined. The "process of exclusion" to which he so pointedly adverts leaves but very few among whom he is to be sought, and to the almost unerring indication which Mr. Chittenden has given is to be added a still nearer one which the author of the present work obtained from another source. Miss Kate Chase, daughter of Salmon P. Chase, the then Secretary of the Treasury, while assuring Mr. Wolf that the name of the mysterious personage was unknown to her, was yet able to inform him that the man was a Jew. That it was a Jew, one well known for his outspoken admiration and love for our country as the home of religious liberty, a man who was not of the unsympathetic government, nor of the hostile aristocracy, nor of the jealous manufacturing class, might well be surmised from all the circumstances of this remarkable occasion, and his identity can scarcely be misinterpreted in the light of Mr. Chittenden's indications.

The following is a copy of Mr. Chittenden's letter, which may well serve as an author's preface to the chapter of his "Recollections" to which it refers, in which the incident is narrated in detail, and which we shall quote in full:

11 PINE ST., NEW YORK, May 7, 1892.

DEAR SIR :—

It would give me great pleasure to answer your letter of April 26th and a large number of others on the same subject. You will readily see that the name may be reached by a process of exclusion as definitely as by its direct statement. The extraordinary character of the incident did not occur to me at the time, or I should have probably suppressed it. As it is I have no alternative but silence.

However, it gives me pleasure to say one thing. The experience of an active life now drawing to its close has taught me that race prejudices have no place in the heart of a true American, and I am certainly not conscious tnat I have ever entertained a shadow of them against any one of Hebrew origin. On the contrary I have found much in the history of that persecuted race to respect and admire. Illness has delayed this reply to your note.

Yours truly,
L. E. CHITTENDEN.

Mr. SIMON WOLF,
      Washington, D. C.

A REMARKABLE EPISODE.

EXTRACT FROM "RECOLLECTIONS OF PRESIDENT LINCOLN
AND HIS ADMINISTRATION," BY L. E. CHITTENDEN,
HIS REGISTER OF THE TREASURY.

(Chapter XXV, Pages 197—203. N. Y., Harper & Brothers, 1891.)

Mr. Charles Francis Adams (our minister) had for several
weeks been aware, and had communicated the fact to his government, that the Messrs. Laird, extensive ship builders, were
building at their yards in Birkenhead, near Liverpool, two
armored vessels for the Confederate government. They were
to be furnished with powerful engines, and cabable of great
speed. When completed they were to proceed to a small un-
frequented British island in the West Indies, where they were
to be delivered to the agents of the Confederacy. They were
then to receive their armament, previously sent thither, take
their crews on board, and then set forth on their piratical
cruises, after the example of the *Alabama*. After sweeping our
remaining commerce from the seas, by burning and sinking
every merchantship bearing our flag, they were to come upon
our own coast, scatter our blockading fleet, and open all the
Southern ports to British commerce, which would no longer
be required to take the great risk of breaking the blockade.
This feat was to be accomplished by vessels which had never
entered a Confederate port, nor, indeed, any harbor which was
not covered by the British or some other flag which protected
the ironclads against pursuit or capture by vessels of the United
States Navy.

Greater danger than these vessels never threatened the safety
of the Union. In tonnage, armament and speed, they were
intended to be superior to the *Kearsarge*, and every other vessel
of our navy. Their armor was supposed to render them invul-
nerable. If the blockade was not maintained, an immediate
recognition of the belligerent character of the rebels by Great

Britain was anticipated. Even if that did not take place, all the cotton gathered in Confaderate ports would be released and find a profitable market, while the old wooden vessels, now principally constituting the blockading fleet, would not resist one of these iron-clad vessels long enough for a second broadside.

The impending danger was fully appreciated by Mr. Adams. With his accustomed energy, notwithstanding the secrecy in which all the Confederate movements in Great Britain were shrouded, he had collected and laid before the English authorities clear proofs of the rebel ownership, and intended unlawful purpose of these vessels. He had even procured copies of the contracts under which the Messrs. Laird were building them, and had ascertained that payments on their account had been made from proceeds of cotton owned by the Confederacy. He had represented that the evidence furnished by him, verified by the oaths of credible witnesses, was sufficient not only to justify their seizure, but to secure their condemnation in the courts, and he had insisted with a force apparently unanswerable, that it was the duty of Great Britain to prevent the vessels from leaving the Mersey and setting forth upon their piratical career.

But, unfortunately, the sympathies of the party in power in England were not with the Union cause. It suited the view of of the law-officers of the Crown not to interfere, and to excuse their inaction by raising objections to the legal sufficiency of the evidence. The situation was perfectly comprehended by the President and his Cabinet, but remonstrance appeared to be unavailing, and the departure of the vessels was expected at an early day.

Hopeless as the task appeared to be, neither Mr. Adams nor his active agents relaxed their efforts for a moment. Their recent investigations had been prosecuted with such energy that the minister had finally been able to furnish the British premier with the sworn affidavits of some of the officers and men actually enlisted in Liverpool, and other English cities, for service on these vessels; that the advance payments to these men had been made by Confederate agents, that the ships were to leave the Mersey at an early appointed date for an island near Bermuda; that their guns and ammunition had already been sent thither. Mr. Adams had also secured the names of the ships' officers, with copies of their commissions, bearing the signature of President Davis and the seal of the Confederacy.

The last instalment of affidavits forwarded by our minister proved to be more than the crown lawyers could digest. They covered every defect named in their former objections; they could not be answered even by a special demurrer. They were reinforced by the caustic pen of Mr. Adams, whose arguments so clearly pointed out the duty of the English government in the premises that it would obviously be regarded as conclusive by every one but these lawyers, who possessed the exclusive power to move the slow authorities of the customs to action. The crown lawyers finally decided that the demand of Mr. Adams must be complied with, and that an order must issue, prohibiting the departure of these vessels from the Mersey until the charges of the American minister had been judicially investigated.

There were, however, some incidents attending this most important decision, which prevented its communication from giving to Mr. Adams a satisfaction wholly unalloyed. The decision had been withheld until the vessels were on the very eve of departure. The order must be immediately served, and possession taken by the customs authorities, or the vessels would escape. The crown lawyers, properly enough, observed that the affidavits furnished by Mr. Adams were *ex-parte*—the witnesses had not been cross-examined. If Mr. Adams should fail to prove his charges by evidence which would satisfy the judicial mind, and the vessels be released, the damages caused by arresting them might be very heavy. It was a settled rule of procedure in the courts in such cases to secure the payment of such damages beyond any peradventure. The restraining order would, therefore, be issued, but it would not be enforced against the vessels until these damages had been secured by a deposit of £1,000,000 sterling *in gold coin*.

The situation was well known to be critical. Within three days the vessels were to sail for their destination ; if necessary, they might sail forthwith. The cable was useless, broken or disabled—and Mr. Adams could not communicate with his own government. Without such communication he had no authority to bind his government as an indemnitor, or to repay the money if he could borrow it. Even if he had the fullest authority, where was the patriotic Briton who would furnish a million pounds on the spur of the moment to a government which was believed by the party in power in Great Britain to be *in articulo mortis ?* Unless, therefore, the crown lawyers supposed our minister to have anticipated their decision by providing himself with this money, they must have known that this condition could not be complied with, and that they might just as well have declined to interfere. If they had intended that these ships should not be prevented from making their intended crusade against our commerce and our cause, no better arrangement could possibly have been devised. It is not to be denied that suspicions existed that such was their purpose.

But the unexpected sometimes happens. The event which prevented these floating engines of destruction from entering upon their intended work was as unanticipated as a miracle. It constituted, possibly, the most signal service ever rendered by a citizen of one country to the government of another. It was all the more noble, because it was intended to be anony-mous. The eminently unselfish man who performed it made a positive condition that it should not be made public, that not so much as his name should be disclosed, except to the officers of our government, whose co-operation was required in order to transact the business in a proper manner and upon correct principles. So earnest was his injunction of secrecy that his identity will not even now be disclosed, although he has long since gone to his reward.

Within the hour after the crown lawyers' decision, with its conditions, had been made known to Mr. Adams, and when he had given up all hope of arresting these vessels, a quiet gentle-man called upon him and asked if he might be favored with the opportunity of making the deposit of coin required by the order ? He observed "that it had occurred to him that if the United States had that amount to its credit in London, some question of authority might arise, or Mr. Adams might otherwise be embarrassed in complying with the condition, especially as communication with his government might involve delay ; so that the shortest way to avoid all difficulty would be for him to deposit the coin, which he was quite prepared to do.''

Had a messenger descended from the skies in a chariot of fire, with $5,000,000 in gold in his hands, and offered to leave it at the embassy without any security, Mr. Adams could not have been more profoundly surprised. He had accepted the condition as fatal to his efforts ; he had concluded that nothing short of a miracle could prevent the departure of the vessels ; and here, if not a miracle, was something much like one. He made no secret of the pleasure with which he accepted the munificent offer, provided some method of securing the liberal Englishman could be found. The latter seemed indisposed to make any suggestion on the subject. '' It might be proper,'' he said, ''that some obligation might be entered into, showing that the American government recognized the deposit as made on its account ; beyond that he should leave the matter wholly in the hands of Mr. Adams.''

The existing premium on gold was then about sixty per cent. in the United States. It would have been largely increased by the departure of these ironclads. The '' five-twenties '' or '' sixes '' of 1861, as they were popularly called, were then being issued, and were the only securities upon '' long time '' then authorized by Congress. The best arrangement that occurred to Mr. Adams, and which he then proposed, was that $10,000,000, or £2,000,000, in these bonds, to be held as collateral security for the loan of £1,000,000 in gold, should be delivered to the lender, to be returned when the loan was paid or the order itself was discharged and the coin returned to the depositor. The proposition of Mr. Adams was satisfactory to the gentleman, but he said that to prevent the disclosure of his name the deposit should be made in coupon and not in registered bonds. The coupons were payable to bearer; the registed were required to be inscribed on the books of the Treasury in the owner's name.

Mr. Adams then volunteered the assurance that these bonds, to the amount of $10,000,000, should be transmitted to London by the first steamer which left New York after his despatch concerning the transaction was received at the State Department at Washington.

It was this assurance of Mr. Adams which the President and both of the Secretaries desired should be made good. They regarded the faith of the government as pledged for its performance, and that faith they proposed should not be violated.

All the details of this transaction were not then disclosed. They reached the government in private, confidential despatches from Mr. Adams, some of them long afterwards. The despatch in question was understood to be confidential; certainly that part of it which related to the deposit and security proposed. It was necessarily brief, for in order to reach the steamer the special messenger had to leave London within a very few hours after the proposition of the deposit was made. There was enough in it to show that an inestimable service had been rendered to the country by some one to whom Mr. Adams had pledged the faith of the nation for the transmission of these bonds by the next steamer which left New York. There was no dissent from the conclusion that the pledge of Mr. Adams, if it were in the power of the government, must be performed.

Since the publication of the foregoing facts in *Harper's Magazine* for May, 1890, I have been solicited by many correspondents to give the name of the gentleman who offered to perform such a signal service to our country. It must be obvious that nothing could give greater pleasure than to publish his name, and to secure for him the enduring gratitude of the American people. I have, however, a special reason for my present determination not to disclose it, nor to permit myself to speculate upon the consequences of the disclosure. When we were informed that the emergency had passed, it became necessary to make a change in the entries of this large amount upon the books of the register. This was found to be a difficult matter, unless a plain statement of the issue, to the gentleman in question, and its purpose was made with its subsequent cancellation. This course I proposed to Secretary

Chase. He was decided in his opinion that the value of the service would not have been enhanced if an actual deposit of the money had been required, and that, as the gentleman himself had imposed the obligation, he was the only authority who could possibly release it. While I regarded his conclusion as incontrovertible, I did suggest that our first duty was the official one, to our own obligation to conceal nothing, and to make our official records strictly conform to the fact.

"We should have thought of that at the time," said the Secretary. "We might have declined his offer, coupled as it was with the obligation to conceal his name, but I do not remember that we considered that question. Do you?"

"No," I said. "Nothing was discussed in my presence except the possibility of compliance with his conditions to the letter."

"Then, I think, we must continue to keep his secret whatever the consequences may be, until he releases us from the obligation," was the final conclusion of the Secretary.

I am, I believe, the only survivor of those to whom this gentleman's name was known. I have hitherto declined to discuss the question of his name or its disclosure. I depart from my practice far enough to say that I do not believe he was interested in the price of cotton, or that he was moved in the slightest degree by pecuniary motives in making his offer. More than this, at present, I do not think I have the moral right to say. If I should at any time hereafter see my way clear to a different conclusion, I shall leave his name to be communicated to the Secretary of Treasury, who will determine for himself the propriety of its disclosure.

7

JEWISH SOLDIERS IN THE CIVIL WAR.

The consciousness of the imperfect nature of the several rosters included under our present head has been the only influence that has detracted from the satisfaction which the preparation of this work in general has afforded the author. This feeling has already been adverted to in the introduction to this work and will not further be dwelt upon beyond the hope that the present volume may become the forerunner of a more complete and perfected result in the future.*

The unquestionably large proportion of Jewish soldiers in both the Union and Confederate armies is vouched for by such statistics as have been thoroughly verified and by the statement of many individual observers. In this connection the following communications to the author may well be quoted as having a definite bearing on this subject, and as coming from sources whose authority is beyond question :

120 BROADWAY, NEW YORK,
December 30th, '91.

MY DEAR JUDGE :

I have your favor of the 22nd instant, asking for some expression of opinion from me regarding the bravery and faithfulness of Hebrew soldiers in the War of the Rebellion. There were many Hebrews under me while serving as Brigade and Division Commander ; and, while the great lapse of time renders it impossible for me to recall names or recount specific acts of gallantry, I take pleasure in saying that I always found the soldiers of Jewish faith as firm in their devotion to the

---

* The numerous communications from correspondents in various parts of the country, which are being received while this volume is in course of completion by the printer, renders it altogether probable that the author's hope will be realized. The information conveyed by these correspondents, frequently too late for incorporation in the present work, will be collated with the view to its eventual publication, and all who feel an interest in our present subject, and who can contribute such data as will further the correction of these records, are earnestly requested to communicate their information to the author.

cause of the country they were serving as any others, and ever ready to perform any duty to which they might be assigned.

Yours very truly,

J. STAHEL.

TO HON. SIMON WOLF,
Washington, D. C.

HEADQUARTERS DEPARTMENT OF THE EAST,
GOVERNOR'S ISLAND, NEW YORK.

January 2d, 1892.

DEAR MR. WOLF :

It is impossible for me to do justice to those who served with me under my command who are known to be of Hebrew extraction. I would hardly be justified without their permission to give their names. I had a Jewish Aide-de-Camp, one of the bravest and best, in the first battle of Bull Run ; he is now a distinguished officer of the army, a man of high scientific attainment. I had another aide who was killed at the battle of Chancellorsville, a true friend and a brave officer. Two of my brigade commanders, who answer to the above description, one of whom you have mentioned, served ably and faithfully at Gettysburg and in other great battles of the war. So many of the German officers and men, the Poles and the Hungarians, were of Jewish lineage that I am unable to designate them. I can assure you, my dear sir, that, intrinsically, there are no more patriotic men to be found in the country than those who claim to be of Hebrew descent, and who served with me in parallel commands or more directly under my instructions. I have always greatly esteemed the Jewish people, and in fact, the highest hopes I have in the great future are derived from him whom I think justly claimed to be the spiritual king of the Jews. So far as bravery is concerned, bravery often carries to rashness. History affords no example superior to those of the Maccabees and other leaders of the Jews, back to the time of Jacob, the prince, who prevailed with God.

Very truly yours.

OLIVER O. HOWARD,
Major General U. S. Army.

SIMON WOLF, ESQ.,
Washington, D. C.

Further testimony of a like character with reference to the Jews in the Union Army might be adduced from numerous sources if space limits would permit, but the following citations regarding the Jewish soldiers in the Southern Armies are not only warranted by the occasion but by the exceptionally interesting data which they contain.

[*From the Nashville American, May 25, 1894.*]

"Among the delegates to the recent Convention of the Bn'ai B'rith there were thirty who were old enough to take up arms during the late war. Of this number twenty-five had shouldered their muskets in defence of their country, twenty-four belonging to the Confederate and one to the Federal Army. This shows that the Israelite is as much of a patriot as any other man when the liberties of his country are endangered. In this connection the following letter will be read with interest."

"*Galveston, Texas, May 17, 1894.*

LEO N. LEVI, ESQ., *Galveston.*

DEAR SIR:—

"My attention having been called by you to the published remarks of a writer in disparagement of the patriotism and gallantry of the Jew as a soldier, and having had the honor to command a force composed to a considerable extent of Israelites, I feel impelled by this attempted injustice to the race to give my experience with them as soldiers.

"Under a commission from the Government I organized 'Waul's Texas Legion,' upon the express terms that they were to leave the State, cross the Mississippi River and join in the fray where the blows fell heaviest and thickest. The Legion consisted of ten companies of infantry, five companies of cavalry and two companies of artillery. Two of the infantry companies had a large number of Jews in their ranks, and the largest company in the command—120 men—was officered by Jews, and three-fourths of the rank and file were of that faith. There were also a number of Jews scattered through the command in the other companies.

" They were all volunteers, and I know there was not a Jew conscript in the Legion. As soldiers they were brave, orderly and well-disciplined and in no respect inferior to the gallant body of which they formed a prominent part. Their behavior in the camp, as in the field, was exemplary. No Jew in the command was arraigned before a court-martial, and, in proportion to their numbers, there were fewer applications for leaves of absence, and their regular habits caused very few of their names to appear on the hospital rolls.

" In battle, without distinction of race or religion, all were apparently willing and eager for the contest. I will say, however, I neither saw nor heard of any Jew shrinking or failing to answer to any call of duty or danger.

" I regret I cannot go more in details, but am unwilling to permit an aspersion that remotely may affect the Jews who served with me to pass unnoticed, as, to a considerable extent, the reputation won by the command and personally obtained by myself was acquired by their conduct, courage and soldierly qualities. I state without hesitation that in no atttribute suited to the soldier, whether as an officer or in the ranks, will the Jew suffer by comparison with the best and bravest of our army.

" As these happenings were before your time, I jot down these recollections that you may have the testimony of one Gentile to attest the courage, endurance and patriotism of the Jew as a soldier.

Yours sincerely,

T. N. WAUL.

The discussion of the question of Jewish participation in the Civil War elicited the following expression from a Charleston newspaper:

"The list of South Carolina Jews who remained true to their country and to their country's cause in the darkest hours and who proved their fidelity and patriotism by laying down their lives upon the field of battle could be greatly extended. Their names are graven upon many a monument throughout the land, and their prowess in arms is a part of the military glory of the country. As Montaigne says, the virtue and valor of a man consist in the heart and in the will, and by this rule the Hebrew soldiers of South Carolina may be fairly judged. What they had they gave freely to the State and on many a bloody field did they prove the high quality of their courage. They possessed, what Napoleon called "the two o'clock in the morning courage" and they followed the flag with superb loyalty to victory and defeat. When the history of South Carolina's part in the great struggle is written and the books are finally posted, we are sure that the Hebrew soldiers of this State, who wore the grey will have their full meed of praise."

Another communication which is at hand, originally made to one of our Jewish weeklies, may also be quoted as affording an effective side light on our present subject:

"From the beginning of the late war until its close I was connected with the War and Navy Departments of the Confederate States as a contractor for side arms and accoutrements. In this capacity I became acquainted with the organization and direction of the Army and Navy and also became well acquainted with the governing officials of the State, War and Navy Departments.

"Shortly before the Fall Festivals of our Jewish observance in 1864 I came to Richmond, Va., and as usual, met my late old friend, the Rev. Mr. Michelbacher. After receiving an assurance of my readiness to aid him in the purpose which he outlined to me, he detailed his request as follows:

"'There are right around here and in our other armies many Jewish soldiers who would like to keep *Rosh Hashanah* but especially *Yom Kippur* according to our law and ritual. I am trying to get a furlough for these soldiers over these Holy Days, but do not know how to go about it. Here is a petition to the Secretary of War; you know him well; will you present it or will you go with me to introduce me? or will you get Mr. Benjamin to recommend it?' I informed Mr. Michelbacher that as far as Mr. Benjamin was concerned it did not come within the scope of his special office; that if his recommendation was needed I could pledge it, and that the whole matter was for Mr. Seddon to decide. Next morning Mr. Michelbacher and myself went to Mr. Seddon, who received us, as he did all his petitioners, with kindness. He read the petition quietly and talked the matter over with us for some time, even at more length than the pressing duties upon him seemed to warrant. After mature deliberation he spoke about as follows: 'Well, gentlemen, as far as I am concerned I will give my consent, but must refer the matter to the Adjutant and Inspector-General. Whatever he does, I will sanction.' He thereupon wrote his endorsement on the petition and Mr. Michelbacher and I took it up to General Cooper, who, like Mr. Seddon, received us kindly, and with great interest discussed the proposition with us. He would gladly, he said, grant the furloughs, but, 'gentlemen,' he added, 'look, we have here a roster of all our soldiers and we know, as far as possible from their names, how many of them belong to your religious denomination, and astonishing it is that we count about 10,000 to 12,000 Jews who are serving in our Army. Now should I grant the furloughs you request, you will readily see, that for the time being, it would perhaps disintegrate certain commands in the field and might work to a bad effect; besides, the commanders of the different army corps should certainly be consulted. On the whole it would be impracticable, as you, Goldsmith (turning to me) will readily acknowledge. In fact,' he pleasantly added, 'you will admit that if your forefathers had fought Titus on the Sabbath day, during the siege of Jerusalem they most certainly would have beaten him. You see, therefore, I cannot conscientiously grant your request ' So it ended, but we had the satisfaction of having learned that out of the small number of Jews then living in the South, it was believed that over 10,000 were serving in the Confederate Army. Those who would not serve left the country. For many of these latter I myself procured passports and permits, deeming it better that they should leave quietly and unmolested than that they should be forced into the ranks where they would have made unwilling defenders of the country.

"I am still a living witness and can, from my own memory, give you many names of gallant Jewish soldiers of the Confederate army. I had ample opportunity to see and to know.

Many a wounded Jew have I met in the hospitals of Richmond
and administered to his wants, and many a Jewish soldier have
I seen walking on his crutch or having his arm in a sling,
travelling to and from his command during the war. And I
know further that it was simply a sense of loyalty to their
homes and their neighbors that prompted them to fight for
the South. If not, they could readily have left this country at
any time as well as I myself could have done, had I so chosen.
But love for our adopted country kept us here and we offered
all we had in its behalf.

M. GOLDSMITH.''

The closing paragraph of Mr. Goldsmith's letter is truly
expressive of Jewish sentiment. It emphasizes the fact that
the Jew, while retaining his racial and religious distinctiveness,
identifies himself with the people among whom he dwells, if he
is not deliberately excluded from the possibility of doing so.
Were further evidence of this required beyond the records of
earlier times, a convincing proof can be found in the presence
of large numbers of Jews in both the Union and Confederate
armies throughout the Civil War.

It should not be overlooked that the profession of arms
for its own sake is not distinctively a Jewish trait; the busi-
nesss of war having always been taken up as the means to
an end rather than the end itself. This phase of the Jewish
character finds a significant expression in the large proportion
of Jewish combatants in both the Revolutionary and Civil
Wars. In both cases the issue was one in which they felt a
deep and abiding interest, and they manifested their earnestness in the most positive manner by taking an active and
determined part in the decision of the issue. That interest was
far from being prevalent during the War of 1812 and the subsequent war with Mexico. The former lacked the support of a
large fraction of the people, being held by the Federal party of
that time to be a heedless and needless undertaking, which in
many respects it was, and the latter, the Mexican War, was
regarded by the anti-slavery Whigs as tending to aggrandize
the slave power by an extension of its territory. Both these
wars were party measures, and in both a decidedly smaller

proportion of Jewish combatants took part than otherwise have been the case. Where home, or liberty or law is at stake the Jewish people have never been chary of the uttermost sacrifice, and the muster rolls of the armies in the great war between the States afford the fullest evidence of their ample share in its burdens and its sufferings.

MEDALS OF HONOR.

(From a paper read by the present author before the American Jewish
Historical Society, Washington, D. C., December 26, 1894.)

On the 12th day of July, 1862, President Lincoln gave his
approval to an Act of Congress, authorizing the President to
cause to be prepared 2,000 "Medals of Honor," to be presented
to such non-commissioned officers and privates as would
especially distinguish themselves by their gallantry in action,
and by other soldierly qualities during the war then in progress.

While I am not prepared to say how many soldiers of Hebrew
faith were honored with such medals, I can mention seven who
have come under my notice.

First, LEOPOLD KARPELES, Color Sergeant, of the 57th
Massachusetts Infantry, at the Battle of North Anna, distinguished himself by a noble defence of the flag under a terrific
fire from the enemy. Although seriously wounded, he held
the colors aloft until through weakness from loss of blood he
had at last to give them to a comrade. Sergeant Karpeles has
high testimonials from his superior officers for bravery, daring
and discipline, and is at present a clerk in the General Post-
Office Department.

Second, BENJAMIN B. LEVY, who enlisted at the age of sixteen as a drummer boy, in the 1st New York Volunteers. He
was detailed as Orderly to General Mansfield. While on board
the steamer "Express," carrying dispatches to General Wool
at Fortress Monroe, the vessel was attacked by the Confederate
gunboat, "Seabird." The "Express" with all on board, was in
imminent danger of capture, when young Levy saved the steamer
by cutting loose a water schooner which was in tow. For his
prompt action, Levy was highly complimented by Generals
Mansfield and Wool. At Charles City Cross Roads, two of the
colors of his regiment were saved by him from capture, for
which act he was promoted on the field by General Kearney to

Color Sergeant of his regiment. At the expiration of his term, he re-enlisted in the 40th New York (Mozart) regiment, and was seriously wounded at the battle of the Wilderness. He was appointed by President Lincoln to the New York Custom House.

Third, Sergeant Major and Adjutant ABRAHAM COHN, who enlisted as private in the 6th New Hamshire Infantry. For distinguished services he was gradually promoted to Adjutant; he served until the close of the war. Some time after Adjutant Cohn received the "Medal of Honor," from the Assistant Adjutant General's office, he was addresesd the following highly complimentary communication:

ADJUTANT GENERAL'S OFFICE,
Washington, August 14, 1879.

The Medal, mentioned within, was given for conspicuous gallantry displayed in the battle of the Wilderness, in rallying and forming disorganized troops, under heavy fire; also for bravery and coolness in carrying orders to the advance lines under murderous fire in the battle of the Mine, July 30, 1864.

(Signed)   S. N. BENJAMIN,
Assistant Adjutant General.

Adjutant Cohn has the most gratifying testimonials from his superior officers. Before enlisting in the 6th New Hamshire he had served in the 68th New York as a private and rose gradually to be captain. Owing to sickness he was honorably discharged, being then, in the opinion of the surgeons, unfit for further duty. Notwithstanding his discharge as Captain, when strong and able again, he re-enlisted as Private, in the 6th New Hampshire, and rose to the rank of Adjutant.

Fourth, DAVID OBRANSKI, of the 58th Ohio Infantry, who received a Medal of Honor for distinguished bravery and coolness under heavy fire at Shiloh, Tennessee, and at Vicksburg, Mississippi.

Fifth, HENRY HELLER, of Company A, 66th Ohio Infantry. He earned the Medal of Honor for daring bravery at Chancellorsville.

Sixth, ABRAHAM GRUNWALT, of Company G, 104th Ohio Infantry, who earned his Medal of Honor, at Franklin, Tennessee, November 30, 1864 in the capture of Corps headquarters' flag.

Seventh, Corporal ISAAC GANS, of the 2nd Ohio Cavalry, who for bravery displayed on the battle-field was apppointed escort to the colors captured by the Third Division.

FAMILIES OF "BROTHERS-IN-ARMS."

[Compiled from a paper read by the present author before the
American Jewish Historical Society, Washington, D. C.,
December 26, 1894.]

One of the most remarkable facts developed by the records of
our Civil War, and especially gratifying because unsurpassed,
if equalled, is the spontaneous and cheerful alacrity with which
our citizens of Hebrew faith entered their country's service in
the hour of its need. In a number of families all the male
members able to bear arms were enrolled in the army. My
list of these may not be complete, and there may be other
equally notable examples, but I here name only those which
have been definitely reported to me.

North Carolina is to the fore with a host of six militant
brothers, united in the cause which they held at heart as well
as by the ties of blood. They bear the titular name of the
priestly brother of Moses, and their devotion lends it new
lustre. The list of these six brothers-in-arms is as follows:

AARON COHEN,	EDWARD COHEN,
JACOB H. COHEN,	GUSTAVUS A. COHEN,
JULIUS COHEN,	HENRY M. COHEN.

Mississippi claims a set of five brothers in the field, but,
remarkable enough, one of these was arrayed on the side of the
Union against his four Confederate brothers, a fair example of
the Jewish spirit of loyalty to conviction. The following is the
list:

EDWARD JONAS, 50th Illinois Infantry.	JULIAN JONAS,
	Major CHARLES H. JONAS,
S. A. JONAS,	HON. BENJAMIN F. JONAS (of Louisiana).

South Carolina also had five brothers enrolled in the Confederate army. Their names are:

PERCY MOSES, JR.,	HORACE MOSES,
JOSHUA L. MOSES,	J. HARBY MOSES,
A. JACKSON MOSES.	

Georgia mustered a family of four, a father and three sons, bearing the same historic name as their South Carolina comrades:

RAPHAEL MOSES, SR.,	ISRAEL N. MOSES,
RAPHAEL MOSES, JR.,	A. L. MOSES,

Arkansas furnishes an instance of three brothers, namely:

PETER COHEN,	JACOB COHEN,
PO'EL COHEN.	

Another trio hail from the South, two from Georgia and one from South Carolina:

ISAAC A. GOLDSMITH,	A. A. GOLDSMITH,
M. M. GOLDSMITH.	

Virginia sent out another three:

LEOPOLD LEVY,	SAMSON LEVY,
SOLOMON LEVY.	

Louisiana has also a list of three brothers on her muster rolls:

EUGENE H. LEVY,	JULIUS H. LEVY,
JOSEPH C. LEVY.	

And yet another trio went forth from Alabama:

MORDECAI MOSES,	HENRY C. MOSES,
ALFRED MOSES.	

This makes a total of nine families on the Southern side, embracing a membership numbering thirty-five, of whom one was enrolled in the Union army.

The preponderance of such instances in the ranks of the Confederates is due to the fact that the Jews of the Southern States were, in a much larger proportion than those of the North, natives of the soil or residents of long standing. While the Jews were doubtless more numerous at the North than at the South, they were, for the most part, immigrants of a comparatively recent date, and therefore less intensely imbued with the spirit of the conflict.

On the Union side, New York, the nucleus of the Jewish population of this country, naturally furnished the largest quota of Jewish soldiers, and among them were three bands of brothers; one of the families being reinforced by the presence of the father. The roll is as follows;

First, a family of five:

LEOPOLD WENK,	JOSEPH WENK,
AUGUST WENK,	JULIUS WENK,

AARON WENK.

Second, a father and his three sons:

SIMON LEVY,   BENJAMIN C. LEVY.   ALBERT LEVY,
Hon. FERDINAND LEVY, Ex-Coroner and present Register of New York City.

Third, a trio of brothers:

ABRAHAM FEDER,	HENRY FEDER,

ADOLPH FEDER.

Pennsylvania also sent three Jewish brothers to the front:

LYON L. EMANUEL,   LOUIS M. EMANUEL,
JONATHAN M. EMANUEL.

From Ohio we have another list of three brothers who together took part in the War for the Union:

HERMAN KOCH,   MOSES KOCH,
JOSEPH KOCH.

We have thus a list of five families on the Union side, containing eighteen men, a total for both the Confederate and Union sides of fourteen families sending fifty-three men to the war.

JEWISH STAFF OFFICERS IN THE UNION ARMY.

Assistant Adjutant-General MYER ASCH
> entered the service September 19, 1861, as 2d Lieutenant Company H, 1st New Jersey Cavalry Volunteers; promoted to 1st Lieutenant and Adjutant, December 29, 1861, and Captain, March 24, 1862; served on staff of Major-General John Pope, subsequently appointed Assistant Adjutant-General to Major-General Kautz; also distinguished in other ways; held civic honors, particularly during the Centennial Exhibition of 1876 at Philadelphia.

Doctor MORRIS J. ASCH,
> on staff of Major-General Philip H. Sheridan.

Major NEWMAN BORCHARDT
> enlisted as Private in Company K, 6th New York Volunteers; promoted to serve on staff of Major-General Oliver O. Howard.

Captain ISIDORE BUSH, aide-de-camp to General Fremont.

Captain MAX COHNHEIM
> enlisted in the 41st New York; promoted with rank of Captain on the staff of General Sigel.

Captain —— DESSAUER,
> on staff of Major-General Oliver O. Howard; killed at Chancellorsville.

Rev. JACOB FRANKEL,
> of Philadelphia, served as Chaplain of United States Hospitals during the Civil War, by appointment of President Lincoln.

Captain EDWARD JONAS
> enlisted in Illinois on staff of Major-General Prentice.

Major M. LULLEY,
> formerly on staff of Louis Kossuth, during the Hungarian Revolution of 1848; rendered valuable services during the Civil War, under direction of Secretary of War.

Colonel ISAAC MAY, aide-de-camp to Governor Andrew G. Curtin, of Pennsylvania.

Sergeant LOUIS H. MAYER
> enlisted in the 27th Ohio Regiment, served on staff of General Pope; also with Generals Rosecrans and Grant, taking part in various campaigns.

Captain NATHAN D. MENKEN,
> on staff of Major-General John Pope, as Commander of his body-guard; he sacrificed his life by remaining in Memphis, Tennessee, and tending to the suffering during a terrible visitation of Yellow fever in 1878.

ISAAC MOSES, Adjutant-General 3d Army Corps, staff of Major General Heintzelman; subsequently under General Banks.

Captain JÚLIUS SPRING,
> on staff of General Van Buren.

Lieutenant M. SZEGELY,
> on staff of General Sigel.

Major JOSEPH FRANKLIN TOBIAS, aide-de-camp with rank of Major to Major-General D. B. Birney (April 14, 1862 — May 16, 1864).

8

JEWISH STAFF OFFICERS IN THE CON-FEDERATE ARMY.

JACOB ABRAMS,
>   on staff of General Elzey.

Doctor I. BARUCH, Assistant Surgeon-General.

MARCUS BAUM,
>   on the staff of General Kershaw; enlisted as private; wounded at first Battle of Manassas; mentioned in general orders for distinguished bravery; killed at the Battle of the Wilderness.

Captain H. L. BENJAMIN, General Staff.

Honorable JUDAH P. BENJAMIN, Secretary of War.

General DAVID DE LEON, Surgeon-General.
>   The first surgeon-general of the Confederate Army. He was born in South Carolina in 1822. In the Mexican War he twice took the place of commanding officers, who had been killed or wounded and acted with such gallantry and ability as to receive twice the thanks of the United States Congress. In February, 1861, he resigned his rank as Surgeon and Major in the United States Army and was appointed Surgeon-General of the Armies of the Confederacy.

Honorable EDWIN DE LEON,
>   Special Confederate States Envoy to Court of Napoleon III.

Captain JOSEPH FRANKLAND,
>   on Staff of General Wheeler, 1st Tennessee Battalion of Cavalry; entered as private; promoted step by step; Assistant Provost Marshal.

Orderly EDWARD KAUFFMAN, Staff of General Bagly, Green's Brigade.

N. KRAUS, Staff of General Miller.

Lieutenant ALEXANDER LEVY, Richmond, Virginia; Staff of General Magruder; wounded at Big Bethel.

Captain M. LEVY, 6th Arkansas, Staff of General Baxton Bragg; Enlisted Co. E, 6th Arkansas.

Lieutenant M. J. MARCUS, Staff of General Benning.

VICTOR MEYER, Staff of General Barksdale.

Assistant-Adjutant-General J. RANDOLPH MORDECAI
entered the service of the Confederate States as private in the Washington Artillery, South Carolina, December 19, 1860; shortly afterwards was appointed 2nd Lieutenant, when transferred to the C. S. Army, afterward assigneds to duty as Assistant-Adjutant-General to General White's Brigade Light Artillery until July, 1863, to A. A. M., C. S. Army, and assigned to General Taliaford's Division.

Captain A. J. MOSES, Staff of General Hannon.

Major ALFRED T. MOSES, Staff of General R. Taylor; enlisted Co. E, 6th Arkansas.

ALTAMONT MOSES, Military Telegraph Service.

F. J. MOSES, Assistant Surgeon.

Colonel RAPHAEL J. MOSES, Staff of General Longstreet.
Appointed chief commissary for the State of Georgia. Known to Generals Lee and Longstreet as the "honest commissary." He turned over thirty thousand dollars in gold to General Molyneux at the close of the war on condition that it should be used for the benefit of the Confederate soldiers and Confederate hospitals, which was done.

General A. C. MYERS, Quartermaster General C. S. A.

Major J. M. NANEZ, Staff of General Longstreet.

Major ISAAC SCHERCK, Staff of General Hardee; enlisted in Mississippi.

MORRIS STRAUS, Staff of General Jenkins; enlisted in South Carolina.

JEWISH OFFICERS IN THE CONFEDERATE NAVY.

Lieutenant BARNHAM.

PERRY DE LEON, South Carolina.

Captain L. C. HARBY, South Carolina.
     When South Carolina seceded he resigned his commission in the United States Navy and entered the Confederate service with the rank of Commodore in the Navy and afterwards distinguished himself in the defence of Galveston, when he commanded the Neptune at the capture of the Harriet Lane, and later on when in command of a fleet of gunboats on the Sabine river.

LOUIS P. LEVY, Gunboat Chicora, Virginia;
     A midshipman at the age of fifteen.

Midshipman RANDOLPH LYONS;
     detailed as Signal Officer on blockade running.

LAZARUS WEIL, C. S. Navy.

SIMON WEIL, C. S. Navy.

ISAAC MOISE, C. S. Navy.

Paymaster I. C. MOSES, Navy.

Lieutenant R. J. MOSES, Jr., C. S. S. Merrimac, Georgia.

Z. P. MOSES, Navy Department.

LISTS OF JEWISH SOLDIERS IN THE UNION AND CONFEDERATE ARMIES DURING THE CIVIL WAR, CLASSIFIED ACCORDING TO STATES AND ALPHABETICALLY ARRANGED.

ALABAMA.

NAME.	RANK.	COMPANY.	REGIMENT.
ABRAHAM, JACOB			3d Infantry.
ABRAHAM, ISAAC			1st Artillery.
ABRAHAM, JOSEPH		B	2d Cavalry.
ALTEMOUNT, SIMON		C	12th Infantry.
ABRAHAM, D.		B	1st Cavalry.
ALTMAN, ——			12th Infantry.
ABRAHAM, A.		G	6th Infantry.

BLOCK, MAURICE			27th Infantry.

Killed at Seven Pines.

BEAN, LEWIS			33d Infantry.
BAMBURGER, SOLOMON S., Major			6th Infantry.

Wounded at Seven Pines ; after which General Johnston appointed him Private Secretary.

BLUM, ELIAS			10th Infantry.

Wounded at Frazier's Farm.

BENEDICK, F.			3d Infantry.
BERNSTEIN, P.			Eufala Light Artillery.
BARWALD, M.		G	6th Infantry.
BARWALD, D.			3d Infantry.

COHN, L. J.			3d Infantry.
COHEN, LOUIS			4th Infantry.
COLEMAN, ——	Sergeant		6th Infantry.

NAME.	RANK.	COMPANY.	REGIMENT.
CAHN, JACOB		B	4th Infantry.
COLLING, WILLIAM		B	4th Infantry.
CAHN, S.			3d Infantry.
DANIEL, WILLIAM		A	1st Infantry.

Captured; died and buried at Woodlawn Cemetery, Elmira, New York.

DREYFUS, SAMUEL		B	1st Artillery.
DRYFUS, L.		B	4th Infantry.
EINHORN, AARON		B	4th Infantry.
EHLBERT, M.			21st Infantry.
FALK, L. M.		D	5th Cavalry.
FISCHER, E.	Captain	A	12th Infantry.

Promoted from private.

GOODMAN, HENRY		A	10th Infantry.
GOLDSTEIN, ISIDORE		E	4th Infantry.
GERSON, M. L.			3d Infantry.
GERSON, A.			3d Infantry.
GOLDSTEIN, I.		B	1st Cavalry.
GUTMAN, JOSEPH		B	1st Cavalry.
GRIEL, LOUIS			14th Infantry.
GUTMAN, EMANUEL		G	10th Infantry.
HIRSCHFELD, JACOB		E	14th Infantry.

Killed at Sharpsburg.

HEYMAN, S.		A	18th Cavalry.

Wounded at New Hope Church; disabled from field duty; on detached service until surrender.

HERZBERG, H.	Lieutenant	J	18th Cavalry.

Killed at New Hope Church.

HEYMAN, ISAAC		J	18th Cavalry.

Wounded seven times; promoted on the field of battle for bravery.

HAAS, SIEGMUND		C	12th Cavalry.
HARTMAN, JOSEPH			3d Cavalry.

NAME.	RANK.	COMPANY.	REGIMENT.
HIRSCHFIELDER, JACOB			5th Cavalry.

Killed at Gettysburg.

HOFHEIMER, HENRY			Washington Light Artillery.
HIRSCHER, E.			3d Infantry.
HENLEIN, A.		B	4th Infantry.
HARRISON, JOSEPH		A	1st Infantry.

Captured ; died and buried at Woodlawn Cemetery, Elmira, New York.

ISRAEL, I.		D	60th Infantry

Captured ; died and buried at Woodlawn Cemetery, Elmira, New York.

JACOBSON, JOSEPH		A	42d Infantry
JONAS, ISRAEL			3d Infantry

Killed in action.

JACOBSON, ADOLPH		B	20th Infantry

Wounded at Vicksburg, June 14, 1863 ; served balance of time in hospital.

JOSEPH, LEONCE G.		H	Temple's Battery and 7th Cavalry
JOSEPH, J.			Lafayette Guard
JARETZKY, MORRIS		G	6th Infantry
JACKSON, ——		G	6th Infantry
KOHN, SOLOMON		D	14th Infantry
KRAUS, LEE		D	7th Infantry
KOHN, JACOB		B	1st Infantry
KULEMAN, E.			3d Infantry
KARCHER, E.	Captain	A	12th Infantry

Promoted from private.

KOFFSKY, S.	Lieutenant	A	12th Infantry

Killed at Seven Pines.

KERN, SIMEON		K	17th Infantry
KLEIN, LOUIS		E	State Reserves
KAISER, LAZARUS M.		E	State Reserves
KAHN, KARL			23d Infantry
KLEIN, ABRAHAM		A	42d Infantry

NAME.	RANK.	COMPANY.	REGIMENT.
LEVEY, ——			3d Infantry

Lost a leg ; subsequently killed.

L'ETONDAL, E.		A	12th Infantry
LEVIS, LAZARUS			24th Infantry
LOEWI, HENRY		E	State Reserves
L'ETONDAL, F.	Captain		12th Infantry

Promoted for bravery.

LOWENTHAL, JACOB			12th Infantry
LEWY, HENRY			3d Infantry
LEVY, B. M.			3d Infantry
LOBMAN, H.			3d Infantry
LEVY, SAMUEL			3d Infantry

Wounded at Gettysburg.

LOEWI, SAMUEL		E	State Reserves
LEMLO, L.		B	1st Cavalry
LEITER, I.		B	1st Cavalry
LEVY, JULIAN C.		E	3d Infantry

Killed at battle of Malvern Hill.

LEVY, SOLOMON			3d Infantry,
			(Montgomery Blues.)

MOSES, MONTEFIORE, Surgeon			
MOSES, MORDECAI			
MOSES, HENRY C. } Brothers			Infantry
MOSES, ALFRED			
MEYER, HERMAN		A	42d Infantry
MEETIF, S. A.			3d Infantry
MARKS, SAMUEL	Lieutenant		3d Infantry
MYER, MOSES		B	1st Artilery
MYER, CHARLES		A	42d Infantry
MYER, HENRY		B	4th Infantry
MOOK, A.		K	11th Infantry
MEYERBERG, L.			3d Infantry
MARKSTEIN, MAX		C	5th Infantry
NEUBRIK, F.			12th Infantry
PEPPERMAN, MARX		B	1st Cavalry

NAME.	RANK.	COMPANY.	REGIMENT.
PICKARD, SAMUEL		C	12th Infantry
PROSKAUER, ADOLPH	Captain	A	12th Infantry

Entered the Confederate Army as private ; was appointed Color Sergeant ; rose to be Captain ; was wounded four times.

RICHMOND, CHARLES		B	2d Cavalry
RICHARDS, JULIUS		K	44th Infantry

Discharged 1862 for disability.

RAUFMAN, S.			11th Infantry
ROHOTSCH, ——			3d Infantry
RICHARD, J.		G	3d Infantry
RICHARD, AARON		A	44th Infantry

SOLOMON, DAVID	Colonel		

Appointed by the Governor of Alabama, as Aide-de-Camp, with the rank of Colonel.

STEINER, L.			3d Infantry
SUSSMAN, DAVID			27th Infantry

Killed at Seven Pines.

STEINER, M.			3d Infantry
STRASSBURGER, H.	Lieutenant		3d Infantry
SUSSMAN, H.		B	4th Infantry
SCHOENBACHER, H.		B	1st Infantry
STRAUS, I.		B	1st Infantry

Served until disabled.

SCHARF, E.		B	1st Cavalry
SOLOMON, JOSEPH		B	1st Cavalry
SULSBACHER, A.			4th Infantry
SCHALHOFER, PHILIP		K	8th Infantry
STERNE, SAMUEL			Eufala Artillery

Wounded at Atlanta.

STERN, JOSEPH			12th Infantry
STRAUSS, LEOPOLD			Cavalry

Served three years until disabled by wounds.

SIEGEL, MOSES		C	12th Infantry

Killed in action.

NAME.	RANK.	COMPANY.	REGIMENT.
SOMENTHEIL, JACOB		C	12th Infantry
SCHIFFMAN, JACOB		{ G	3d Infantry
		{ A	44th Infantry

Killed at Seven Pines.

SIEGLE, ——			3d Infantry

TURGUEIM, DAVID			3d Infantry
TANHAUSER, GUSTAV			23d Infantry

Killed in action.

ULFELDER, M.			3d Infantry
ULLMAN, WILLIAM		A	8th Wheeler Cavalry
WALDMAN, L.			3d Infantry
WEIL, D.			3d Infantry
WEIL, H.			3d Infantry
WAMBACHER, LOUIS		B	20th Infantry

Killed at Vicksburg, June 14, 1863.

WOLF, MAX		C	2nd Infantyy

YOUNG, L.			3d Infantry
YARETSKI, JULIUS	Lieutenant	A	33d Infantry

Served four years; promoted from private.

ZADICK, ABRAHAM		C	2d Cavalry

ARKANSAS.

NAME.	RANK.	COMPANY.	REGIMENT.
AUERBACH, A. K.			8th Cavalry
BURGAUER, I.			Woodruff Battery
BURGAUER, E.			Woodruff Battery
BAUM, HENRY			Woodruff Battery
COHN, WOLF			West's Artillery
COHEN, ALBERT			6th Infantry
DANIEL, DAVID			1st Infantry
DRYFUS, MARCUS			1st Cavalry
DRYFUS, THEO.			1st Cavalry
ERB, JACOB			1st Cavalry
ERB, S.			1st Mounted Rifles
FRANK, ISAAC			1st Cavalry
FLECHTER, J. G.	Captain	A	6th Infantry
FRANKLIN, SAMUEL			1st Cavalry
FOX, W.		B	2nd Cavalry
FEBS, E.			6th Infantry
FRANK, I.			4th Cavalry
GANS, MORRIS			Parson's Cavalry
GATES, DAVID		A	Woodruff Battery
Served four years.			
GATES, FERDINAND		A	Marmaduke
Served four years.			Command
GATES, ISAAC			Ross Arkansas
Served four years.			Battalion
GOODMAN, HERMAN			1st Infantry
HIRSCHFIELD, HENRY		A	5th Infantry
HINEMAN, M. L.		A	6th Infantry

Name.	Rank.	Company.	Regiment.
Heilbroner, Henry			3d Infantry
Hoover, E.			West's Artillery
Kempner, Jacob			3d Cavalry
Kalischer, S,			1st Cavalry
Klein, Abraham			3d Cavalry
Kuhn, Sigismund			West's Artillery
Kempner, Jacob			3d Cavalry
Levy, Julius		A	6th Infantry
Killed at Shiloh.			
Lewis, L.		B	4th Infantry
Meyer, Henry			34th Infantry
Meyer, Gabriel			4th Infantry
Mock, Moses		E	6th Infantry
Mook, Samuel			6th Infantry
Newman, Myer			19th Infantry
Ottenheimer, Philip			1st Infantry
Ottenheimer, Abraham			1st Infantry
Pfarffer, Philip			4th Cavalry
Pollock, Abraham			3d Cavalry
Pollock, M.			3d Cavalry
Pollock, Leo			Woodruff's Battery
Pfeifer, Philip			1st Cavalry
Rich, Rudolph			6th Infantry
Simmons, Jacob			1st Infantry
Stern, Solomon			1st Cavalry
Samuels, J.			3d Cavalry
Simmons, Harvey			1st Infantry
Vollener, Louis			4th Infantry
Winters, Samuel		H	6th Infantry
Winters, Moses		H	6th Infantry

CALIFORNIA.

NAME.	RANK.	COMPANY.	REGIMENT.
ALEXANDER, A.		A	2nd Infantry
ADLER, L.			6th Infantry
BACHARACH, JOSEPH		A	2nd Infantry
COHN, S. B.		F	6th Infantry
COHEN, SOLOMON	Corporal	C	3d Infantry

Served three years.

DAVIDSON, SOLOMON   1st Cavalry

An officer of distinction made the following remarks concerning this gallant soldier:

"Personally I know several Hebrews who served in the California regiments known as the 'California Column' but in the long years that have elapsed I have forgotten their names. They were all good, faithful soldiers to the flag they enlisted to defend. One I remember, by name, Solomon Davidson. Comrade Davidson belonged to a cavalry regiment; I think it was the 1st California, ordered for service in Arizona, Texas and New Mexico. That regiment has seen more hard service in the saddle than any other I know of wearing Uncle Sam's uniform. Comrade Davidson was a brave man, carrying dispatches and orders from one part of the command to another, regardless of storms and dangers of Indian ambush so often to be encountered in the Territories. Davidson was a loyal, gallant soldier, and I am glad to be able to say this much for our old Jewish comrades in arms. We knew no distinction on account of birth or religion in the army, but we loved all loyal men who gave their lives to the government in the hour of its need. Let me in conclusion express my conviction that a comparison of services will not be determined detrimentally to our Hebrew comrades."

NAME.	RANK.	COMPANY.	REGIMENT.
FAUGHT, SOLOMON			1st Infantry
FOX, A.		H	1st Infantry
FRANK, M.		F	Ist Cavalry
GUGGENHEIM, SOLOMON		E	6th Infantry
HARRIS, DAVID		M	1st Cavalry
Served three years.			
HOFFMAN, J.		D	1st Cavalry
HESS, LOUIS		C	2nd Cavalry
HEUBSMAN, J. B.		C	4th Infantry
KLAUS, MOSES		B	2nd Infantry
LAMBERT, F. H.		H	1st Infantry
LEVICK, L.		H	1st Infantry
MILLER, LOUIS			6th Infantry
MEYERS, OTTO		H	1st Infantry
MEYER, A.		I	6th Cavalry
SOLOMON, E.		H	1st Infantry
SIMON, EMIL		A	2nd Infantry
SICHEL, EUGENE		H	2nd Cavalry
SIMON, ISADORE		G	6th Cavalry
SCHILLER, HENRY	Sergeant	A	2nd Cavalry
Entered as private.			
TOKLAS, JACOB W.	2nd Lieutenant	K	6th Cavalry
Enlisted as private; promoted for bravery.			
TOKLAS, FERDINAND		K	6th Infantry
Served three years.			
ZACHARIAS, JACOB		K	6th Infantry

Protecting United States Mail overland from Indian and
Mormon attacks and riot at San Francisco.

CONNECTICUT.

NAME.	RANK.	COMPANY.	REGIMENT.
COHEN, HENRY			7th Infantry
CLINE, SAMUEL		E	26th Infantry
CANTROWITZ, SAMUEL		D	10th Infantry
DETTELBACH, HARRY		D	10th Infantry
DRYFUSS, CHARLES		D	10th Infantry
HOSHLAND, NATHAN		I	7th Infantry
HARRIS, HENRY		D	10th Infantry
ISAAC, JULIUS		D	10th Infantry
LAUBER, LOUIS		D	10th Infantry
MORRIS, SIMON		I	20th Infantry
NEWMAN, LEON		B	3d Infantry
ROSENTHAL, SAMUEL			10th Infantry
ROSENTHAL, SIMON		C	10th Infantry
STRAUS, MOSES			10th Infantry
SCHIFF, LUDWIG		D	10th Infantry
WOLFSOHN, S.		E	7th Infantry
WERTHEIMER, ——		D	10th Infantry

DISTRICT OF COLUMBIA.

NAME.	RANK.	COMPANY.	REGIMENT.

BEHREND, A., Doctor.
  entered as Private, transferred to 2nd U. S. Regulars,
  promoted to Hospital Steward, Army of the Potomac.

FREIRICK, CHARLES   { B   Turner Rifles
                                               8th Battalion

MUNDHEIM, LEWIS   8th Artillery
  Junior Vice Commander Garfield Post No. 7, G. A. R.

FLORIDA.

NAME.	RANK.	COMPANY.	REGIMENT.

COHEN, GUS   Milton Artillery

DANIEL, M.   A   1st Infantry
  Captured; died and buried in Woodlawn Cemetery,
  Elmira, New York.

GEORGIA.

NAME.	RANK.	COMPANY.	REGIMENT.
AARONHEIM, D.		D	49th Infantry
ABRAMS, J. J.			1st Infantry
ABRAHAMS, J. M.			49th Infantry

BAER, SAMUEL   6th Infantry
Served until close of war.

BENJAMIN, S.			51st Infantry
BROWN, M.		D	2nd Battalion
BRANDT, ADOLPH			5th Infantry
BLOOMFIELD, ISAAC		A	10th Infantry

BEAR, SAMUEL
Killed; buried in Jewish cemetery at Richmond, Virginia.

COLEMAN, ——			51st Infantry
COHEN, SOLOMON			51st Infantry
CRONE, HERMAN		A	20th Infantry

Sixteen years old when enlisted; taken prisoner at Williamsburg.

COHEN, PHILIP   A   8th Infantry

DREYER, LOUIS A.			1st and 63d Infantry
DE YOUNG, HARRY			2nd Battalion
DAVISSON, D.			2nd Battalion
DAVIDSON, DAVID	Captain		50th Infantry

EICHBAUM, JOSEPH   44th Infantry
Wounded several times.

ELKAN, M.   63d Infantry
EHRLICH, A.   1st Infantry
Wounded in action.

EBERHART, JACOB   G   7th Cavalry
Captured; died and buried at Woodlawn Cemetery, Elmira, New York.

9

Name.	Rank.	Company.	Regiment.
Falkner, C.		B	4th Infantry

Died of wounds received at Hanover Court House.

Friedenthal, L.			1st Cavalry
Feuchtwanger, ——			2nd Battalion
Foote, Abraham			14th Infantry
Frieslehen, Jacob		D	4th Infantry
Frank, J.			

Killed; buried at Jewish cemetery at Richmond, Virginia.

| Goldsmith, M. M. | Lieutenant | | Home Guards |

Killed near Macon, Georgia.

Green, William			57th Infantry
Goodman, Charles			2nd Battalion
Gans, Jacob		A	4th Infantry
Greenbaum, Jacob			51st Infantry

Killed at Gettysburg.

| Goodman, Isaac | | | 3rd Battalion |
| Goldman, Edward | | A | 2nd Battalion |

Subsequently Drill Officer of 38th North Carolina Infantry.

| Geisenheimer, M. | | B | 1st Infantry |
| Goodman, Henry | Sergeant | B | 14th Infantry |

Enlisted as private; wounded in three actions—Harper's Ferry, Chancellorsville and the Wilderness.

| Goldstein, —— | | | 18th Infantry |

Killed in action.

| Goldsmith, I. | | | Wellington Ranger |

Died of fever contracted in camp.

| Haas, Solomon | | A | 1st Infantry |

Enlisted, 1861; when mustered out, re-enlisted in 12th Artillery.

Hertz, J. H.		I	2nd Infantry
Hirschler, I.		D	2nd Infantry
Harris, Elisha			Cobb's Legion

Captured; died and buried at Woodlawn Cemetery, Elmira, New York.

NAME.	RANK.	COMPANY.	REGIMENT.
HEYMAN, ISAAC		D	4th Infantry

Wounded at Malvern Hill.

HAYMAN, CHARLES   D   4th Infantry

General Phil. Cook introduced this soldier to General Gordon at the reunion of the old brigade with the words: "General, this was one of the bravest men in my brigade."

HEYMAN, A.

Killed; buried at Jewish cemetery at Richmond, Virginia.

ISAACS, A.   46th Regiment
ISAACS, EMANUEL   2nd Battery
ISAACS, ISAAC   2nd Battalion
ISAACS, M.   13th Battalion
JONAS, SIEGFRIED   I   8th Infantry
JACOBUS, JACOB H.   Lieutenant   5th Infantry

Killed at Shiloh.

JACKSON, I.   51st Infantry
JACOBS, WILLIAM M.   5th Infantry

KOPPEL, JACOB   5th Infantry

Killed at Shiloh.

KAHN, MOSES   5th Infantry
KOHN, BERNARD   Cherokee Artillery
KAUFMAN, SELIG   A   8th Infantry
KOHN, JACOB   63d Infantry

LIPPMAN, JULIUS   E   12th Infantry
LEVY, JACOB   Sergeant   22d Infantry

Wounded ; served until close of war.

LEVY, MORRIS   4th Infantry
LIPPMAN, LOUIS   8th Infantry

Wounded at Bull Run.

LEHMAN, A.   63d Infantry
LIPPMAN, JACOB   63d Infantry
LEVY, SIMON   6th Infantry

Served three years.

NAME.	RANK.	COMPANY.	REGIMENT.
LEVY, NATHAN	Lieutenant		5th Infantry

Promoted from the ranks ; killed.

LEVY, JACOB   Lieutenant   5th Infantry
Enlisted as private ; killed at Petersburg.

LEON, MORRIS   44th Infantry
Promoted from private.

LEVY, DICK   10th Infantry
LEVY, M. D.   1st Infantry
LEISSER, L.   A   4th Infantry
Wounded at the Wilderness.

LYON, LEONAREANDE, Colonel
LYONS, JAMES DE
       Graduate of West Point; Adjutant of State Troops.

MOUNT, SAMUEL B., Lieutenant   9th Infantry
Promoted from the ranks.

MARCUS, ——   63d Infantry
MEINHART, ISAAC   63d Infantry
MEINHART, SAMUEL   63d Infantry
MORRIS, W.   C   3d Battery
Captured ; died and buried at Woodlawn Cemetery,
Elmira, New York.

MEHLINGER, J.   C   2d Battalion
METZGER, ISAAC   A   2d Battalion
MAYER, GABRIEL   4th Infantry
MOSS, L. A.   4th Infantry
MARCUS, M.   Captain   15th Infantry
Killed, October 13th, 1864 ; buried in Jewish Ceme-
tery at Richmond, Virginia.

MAGNUS, SOLOMON   Cherokee Artillery
Killed at Resaca, Georgia.

MANNERS, JACOB   I   8th Infantry
MEYER, BERNARD   A   1st Infantry
Killed at Manassas.

MANES, E,   H   8th Infantry
Color-bearer at 2nd battle of Manassas, and at Sharpsburg.

NAME.	RANK.	COMPANY.	REGIMENT.
MEYER, SIMEON			5th Infantry
MAYERS, AARON			Silver Grays
MORRIS, PHILIP			Silver Grays
MAYER, ISAAC	Major		5th Infantry
MEYER, LAZARUS			3d Infantry
MOSES, ——	Lieutenant	C	2d Battery
MOSES, I. CLIFTON		A	10th Infantry
MOSES, MONTEFIORE J.			2d Infantry

Promoted Surgeon.

MOSES, WILLIAM MOULTRIE			2d Infantry
MEHLINGER, M		B	4th Infantry
MYERS, BERNARD			1st Infantry

Killed at Rich Mountain.

MERZ, LOUIS		D	4th Infantry

Killed at Sharpsburg

MOISE, EDWARD M.	Captain	A	10th Infantry

Enlisted in 7th Cavalry; served until surrender;
commanded the 10th; had three horses shot from
under him in one day; commanded the advance in
the Hampton cattle raid; captured 2785 head of
cattle in the rear of General Grant's army in the fall
of 1864.

MOISE, A. W.	Lieutenant	H	24th Infantry

Enlisted at the age of sixteen years as private in first
battalion of Maryland Cavalry; transferred to 24th
Regiment; wounded at the Wilderness carrying the
colors until disabled; promoted from the ranks.

NEWMAN, C.			49th Infantry
POPPER, I.			63d Infantry
ROSENBERG, I.			3d Infantry

Killed; buried at Jewish Cemetery at Richmond, Virginia.

RUSH, GEORGE W.	Captain		22d Infantry

Killed at Petersburg.

NAME.	RANK.	COMPANY.	REGIMENT.
ROBINSON, A.			15th Infantry

Killed in action June 26th, 1863; buried at Jewish
Cemetery, Richmond, Virginia.

ROSENWALT, LAZARUS			3d Infantry
RUSSELL, PHILIP M.			1st Infantry
SHERLEIN, LEOPOLD			5th Infantry
STERN, ISAAC		A	2d Battalion

Wounded at Gettysburg.

SCHIFF, JOSEPH		C	2d Infantry
STERNE, LEVI		D	4th Infantry
STERNE, ANSELM		D	4th Infantry

Wounded by a shell.

SIMON, N.			51st Infantry
SEGAL, M.			50th Infantry
SYLVESTER, L.			5th Infantry
SARLING, SOLOMON			5th Infantry
SCHIFF, JONAS			44th Infantry
SCHIFF, P.			44th Infantry
STERN, JACOB			63d Infantry
TRIEST, JACOB			13th Battalion
WALLERSTEIN, H.			44th Infantry
WERTHEIMER, SAMUEL		K	2nd Infantry
WEIL, JACOB			3d Infantry
WITTKOWSKY, DAVID			51st Infantry
WITTKOWSKY, ALEXANDER	Lieutenant		19th Infantry
WARNER, L.			Silver Grays
WERTHEIMER, HARRIS			Carten Battalion Artillery
WERTHEIMER, HENRY		B	4th Regiment
WEISS, L.			

Killed; buried in Jewish cemetery at Richmond, Virginia.

ZITTERBART, ——			4th Infantry

MACON, GEORGIA, GERMAN ARTILLERY.

At the outbreak of the Civil War there existed in Macon, Georgia, an Artillery Company named "The Macon, Georgia, German Artillery," composed entirely of American citizens of German birth, about one-third being of Hebrew faith. We give the names and positions of a few only, remembered by a survivor.

NAME.	RANK.
BINSWANGER, NATHAN	2nd Lieutenant
BINSWANGER, J.	Corporal
BINSWANGER, G.	Private
BINSWANGER, MOSES	"
EINSTEIN, ——	"
FENDIG, ——	"
HOCHSER, ——	"
KAHN, ——	Orderly-Sergeant
MILLER, H.	Private
NORDLINGER, B.	Bugler
NORDWALT, A.	Private
SANGER, A.	"
SANGER, R.	"

1st Camp, Harrison, between Savannah and Brunswick.
2nd Camp, Satilla, near Brunswick, Georgia.
3d Camp, Failfair, near Savannah, Georgia.
Under Brigadier-General Capers. The Company was subsequently transferred to General Walker.

ILLINOIS.

NAME.	RANK.	COMPANY.	REGIMENT.
ALEXANDER, ISAAC			8th Infantry
ASHER, JULIUS	Sergeant	B	9th Infantry
AUERBACH, SALOMON			{ 10th Infantry { 31st Infantry
Served until the close of the war.			
ABRAHAMSON, OTTO		E	10th Infantry
ARNOLD, AARON		B	12th Infantry
ADLER, CHARLES		G	14th Infantry
ABRAHAM, AUGUST		B	20th Infantry
ABRAHAM, WILLIAM			21st Infantry
Wounded at Stone River.			
ADLER, W.		C	30th Infantry
ABRAMS, SAMUEL			34th Infantry
ASH, DAVID L.	1st Lieutenant	B	37th Infantry
Promoted from the ranks.			
ABRAMS, FRANK		A	39th Infantry
ABRAHAMS, FREDERICK	Lieutenant		44th Infantry
ADOLPH, JACOB			44th Infantry
ARNOLD, ISAAC A.	Captain	A	46th Infantry
Promoted from 2nd Lieutenant.			
ARNOLD, DAVID	Captain		57th Infantry
Promoted from Lieutenant.			
ABRAHAM, JACOB			67th Infantry
ASH, NATHAN			81st Infantry
AARON, G.		A	83d Infantry
ABRAHAMSON, WILLIAM		K	84th Infantry
ARNOLD, SIMON			92d Infantry
AARONS, GEORGE			120th Infantry
ARNOLD, JACOB			130th Infantry
ARNOLD, REUBEN		E	131st Infantry
ADLER, FERDINAND			153d Infantry
ASHER, SAMUEL		E	154th Infantry

NAME.	RANK.	COMPANY.	REGIMENT.
AARON, JULIUS			156th Infantry
ADLER, HENRY			3d Cavalry
ARNOLD, ISRAEL		M	3d Cavalry
Died in service.			
ALEXANDER, W.			4th Cavalry
Died in camp.			
ABRAMS, HENRY	Sergeant		4th Cavalry
Enlisted as private			
ABRAHAM, ALEXANDER			5th Cavalry
AARON, WILLIAM			10th Cavalry
ABRAMS, H.		C	11th Cavalry
ACKERMAN, JACOB		H	11th Cavalry
ARNOLD, BENJAMIN,	Lieutenant		12th Cavalry
ARNOLD, ABRAHAM			17th Cavalry
ABRAHAMSON, J.			1st Artillery
ADLER, DANIEL	Corporal		Hershaw Artillery
ADLER, DANKMAR	Corporal		——— Artillery
BEHRENS, A.			8th Infantry
BERLIN, DAVID		B	8th Infantry
BLIND, PHILIP		K	8th Infantry
BACHMAN, JACOB			8th Infantry
BENJAMIN, CHARLES A.			13th Infantry
BERNARD, GEORGE		K	13th Infantry
BENJAMIN, W.		A	13th Infantry
BRESLAUER, MORRIS		K	19th Infantry
BRESLAUER, JOSEPH			19th Infantry
BEHRENDS, BERNHART			21st Infantry
BENJAMIN, JOHN		K	22d Infantry
Served three years.			
BLUMENTHAL, ISIDORE	Corporal	K	24th Infantry
Enlisted as private ; served three years.			
BLUMENTHAL, EDWARD		K	24th Infantry
BAMBERGER, ALEXANDER		K	24th Infantry
BAUM, BENJAMIN	Corporal		25th Infantry
Enlisted as private.			
BENJAMIN, JACOB,			25th Infantry

NAME.	RANK.	COMPANY.	REGIMENT.
BRUCKER, S. S.	Lieutenant	C	39th Infantry
Enlisted as private.			
BAER, JOSEPH		C	39th Infantry
BIEN, FREDERICK		G	39th Infantry
BIEN, DAVID C.			42d Infantry
BAUM, HENRY			44th Infantry
BAMBERGER, V.			49th Infantry
BAUM, GEORGE			49th Infantry
BLUM, GUSTAV			57th Infantry
BAUER, FERDINAND		E	58th Infantry
BERNHARD, JACOB			63d Infantry
Killed in battle.			
BAMBERGER, SALOMON		A	65th Infantry
BERNSTEIN, SAMUEL	Sergeant	K	67th Infantry
Enlisted as private.			
BRUM, SAMUEL	Captain		81st Infantry
Wounded at Guntown ; promoted to Captain for brav- ery on the battlefield ; served three years.			
BAUM, GEORGE	Sergeant	B	82d Infantry
BLUM, LOUIS			82d Infantry
BAUER, JACOB		H	82d Infantry
BRAND, JACOB			82d Infantry
BREDE, CHARLES		C	82d Infantry
Killed at Chancellorsville.			
BURGHEIM, HERMAN		C	82d Infantry
BAUM, CHARLES			112th Infantry
BEHRENS, FERDINAND		E	113th Infantry
BIEN, JACOB		B	126th Infantry
BAUM, SAMUEL			142d Infantry
BRESLAUER, MORITZ	Sergeant		147th Infantry
BAER, REUBEN B.		D	4th Cavalry
BAUM, FRANKLIN			4th Cavalry
BAER, DANIEL		M	7th Cavalry
BAUER, HERMAN			9th Cavalry
BLUM, CHARLES			16th Cavalry
Died of wounds.			
BEHRENS, HEINRICH			16th Cavalry
BLUM, LOUIS			16th Cavalry

NAME.	RANK.	COMPANY.	REGIMENT.
BLUMENBERG, LEWIS			2d Artillery

COLEMAN, ALEXANDER			8th Infantry
CORNELIUS, ADOLPH			9th Infantry

Re-enlisted as Veteran; died of wounds.

CERFF, GEORGE			13th Infantry

Killed at Little Rock, Arkansas.

COLEMAN, ISAAC			15th Infantry

Re-enlisted after expiration of term.

COHN, J.		E	18th Infantry
COLEMAN, HENRY			18th Infantry
CORNELIUS, SAMUEL		B	26th Infantry
CAUFFMAN, ALBERT	Lieutenant	E	33d Infantry
COLEMAN, ISAAC		D	42nd Infantry
COHEN, A.		H	46th Infantry
COLEMAN, J.			56th Infantry
COHN, FRIEDRICH		C	82nd Infantry
COHEN, HENRY		K	82nd Infantry
COHEN, JACOB		H	147th Infantry
COHEN, LOUIS			7th Cavalry
COHEN, WILLIAM	1st Lieutenant	B	12th Cavalry

Promoted from Corporal.

DARMSTADTER, JACOB		A	8th Infantry
DAVIDSON, HENRY			12th Infantry

Died from wounds.

DAVIDSON, SAMUEL,	Assistant-Surgeon		14th Infantry
DE WOLF, HENRY		A	15th Infantry
DAVID, DANIEL			18th Infantry
DANIELS, ABRAHAM		H	29th Infantry
DAVIDSON, MARCUS L.		G	35th Infantry
DANIELS, JOSEPH			35th Infantry
DAVIDSON, DAVID J.		F	38th Infantry

Killed in action.

DAVIDSON, BENJAMIN T.	Sergeant	B	40th Infantry
DE WOLF, DAVID	Captain		47th Infantry

Killed at the battle of Corinth.

NAME.	RANK.	COMPANY.	REGIMENT.
DANIEL, JOSEPH			49th Infantry
DURST, JACOB		G	57th Infantry
DANIELS, ALEXANDER			65th Infantry
DAVID, E.			65th Infantry
DAVID, LEASER		A	65th Infantry
DANIEL, JACOB		K	87th Infantry
DAVID, JACOB			97th Infantry
DAVID, ISAAC		B	132nd Infantry
DANIELSON, ELOF		I	132nd Infantry
DAVID, ISAAC	Captain		151st Infantry
DAVIDSON, DAVID			5th Cavalry
DANIELSON, GUSTAV		B	9th Cavalry
DE WOLF, WILLIAM		B	1st Artillery
DANIELSON, AUGUST			1st Artillery
ERLACHER, MAX		D	24th Infantry
ESSLINGER, JOSEPH			30th Infantry
ENGEL, FERDINAND		H	43d Infantry
ENGEL, ASA			72nd Infantry
Wounded.			
ENGEL, FRANK		B	132nd Infantry
ECKSTEIN, LEWIS			3d Cavalry
EINDEN, SALOMON	Lieutenant		12th Cavalry
Enlisted as private.			
EHRLICH, WILLIAM			12th Cavalry
ENGEL, MORITZ			12th Cavalry
FRANKS, WILLIAM		F	8th Infantry
FRANK, JOSEPH			10th Infantry
Re-enlisted as Veteran.			
FRANK, PHILIP			12th Infantry
FREEMAN, JOSEPH		H	14th Infantry
FRANK, DAVID E.			21st Infantry
FRANK, FREDERICK			28th Infantry
FREEMAN, MOSES		C	32nd Infantry
FRANKS, E. S.			39th Infantry
FRANK, CARL		D	43d Infantry
Killed in action.			

Name.	Rank.	Company.	Regiment.
Frank, Herman			43d Infantry

Badly wounded.

Frankenberg, Eli			46th Infantry
Frank, Simon		C	57th Infantry
Freeman, J.		A	66th Infantry
Falkenthal, Adolph		D	70th Infantry
Friedenberg, Isaac			75th Infantry
Frank, Jacob			76th Infantry
Frank, I.		A	82nd Infantry
Frank, Meier	Captain	C	82nd Infantry
Frank, Moritz		C	82nd Infantry
Frank, Mayer	Captain	C	82nd Infantry

Enlisted at Chicago; was elected Lieutenant of Company C of the 82nd Regiment, in which he served about two years, when he was promoted to Captain. He was at Chancellorsville and Gettysburg from first to last. Subsequently he was apppointed Brigade Inspector and ordered West. He took part in the battle of Wauhatchie and at Missionary Ridge, commanding the 80th. He went with Sherman to Knoxville to relieve Burnside. Captain Frank's deeds entitle him to a place among the bravest Captains in the service of the United States. When Captain Frank volunteered to dislodge Confederate sharpshooters, his whole Company to a man followed him. It was subsequent to this act that he was appointed Brigade Inspector. Two horses were shot from under him at the first days battle at Gettysburg. He scouted for some time in Georgia, Tennessee and Alabama against guerilla chief "Roddy."

Frank, Jesse			86th Infantry
Frank, Isaac			104th Infantry
Frank, David	Sergeant	I	105th Infantry
Franks, William	1st Lieutenant	B	168th Infantry

Promoted from Corporal.

Frank, Isaac			118th Infantry
Frankenberg, Benjamin			119th Infantry

Died of wounds received in battle.

NAME.	RANK.	COMPANY.	REGIMENT.
FRANK, EMANUEL			130th Infantry
FISHEL, SAMUEL			135th Infantry
FISHEL, DANIEL			135th Infantry
FRANKENBERGER, DAVID			150th Infantry
FRANKENBERGER, EPHRAIM			150th Infantry
FRANK, ISRAEL		B	2nd Cavalry
FRANK, NOAH			3d Infantry

Died in the service.

FREEMAN, MARCUS			7th Infantry
FRANK, HENRY		B	9th Infantry
FREUND, LUDWIG			13th Infantry

Died in the service.

FRANK, PHILIP			2nd Artillery

GOLDSMITH, DAVID		H	7th Infanrty
GREENWALL, DAVID		A	8th Infantry
GOTTLOB, THEO.	Lieutenant		9th Infantry
GLEISER, N.		G	10th Infantry
GOLDSMITH, J.	Corporal		14th Infantry

At expiration of term re-enlisted as a veteran.

GOTTLOB, ADOLPH		G	14th Infantry
GOLDSMITH, GEROGE			14th Infantry
GOLDSMITH, ALEXANDER			10th Infantry

Re-enlisted after being honorably discharged.
Wounded in action at Stone River.

GOLDSMITH, ALEXANDER	Corporal	F	19th Infantry

Wounded at Stone River, Kentucky.

GOLDSMITH, JONAS		F	19th Infantry

Enlisted as private; re enlisted after being honorably
discharged. Killed at Stone River, Kentucky.

GOLDSMITH, ABRAHAM			24th Infantry
GOODMAN, DANIEL		E	27th Infantry
GOLDSMITH, HENRY		K	28th Infantry
GOTTLIEB, JOSEPH		G	28th Infantry
GOTTSHALK, EMANUEL		H	37th Infantry
GOLDSMITH, JACOB		I	37th Infantry
GREENEBAUM, SAMUEL		C	39th Infantry
GREEN, S. W.			42nd Infantry

NAME.	RANK.	COMPANY.	REGIMENT.
GREENWALT, SAMUEL			49th Infantry
GOLDSMITH, BEUJAMIN		F	70th Infantry
GOLDMAN, E.			71st Infantry
GOTTLOB, JOSEPH	Captain	I	82nd Infantry

Promoted from Lieutenant.

GREENHUT, JOSEPH B.   Captain   K   82nd Infantry

Enlisted as a private at Chicago, April, 1861, in 12th Illinois Infantry, being the second man on the enrollment list of those who enlisted in Chicago for the war. He was promoted to Sergeant, August, 1861; was with the 12th Illinois Regiment through all the campaigns under General Grant, in Kentucky and Tennessee, up to and including the Battle of Fort Donaldson, in February, 1862, at which battle, while storming the Fort and just before its surrender, he was badly shot in the right arm which caused his retirement from the 12th Illinois shortly thereafter. In August, 1862 he was appointed Captain of Company K, 82nd Illinois Infantry, in which Regiment he passed through the various campaigns and battles in Virginia, under Generals Burnside, Hooker and Meade. Captain Greenhut participated in the memorable Battle of Gettysburg, July 1st, 2nd and 3d, 1863. He was then transferred to the staff of Brigade Commander Hecker, being appointed Adjutant-General of the brigade. This brigade, after the Gettysburg Battle, Rosecrans who, with his army, was surrounded at was transferred to the Western army to relieve General Chattanooga, Tennessee. The brigade had a severe battle at Wauhatchie, near Chattanooga, in opening communications with Rosecrans. The same brigade also took a prominent part in the battles of Mission Ridge and Lookout Mountain, as well as shortly thereafter of that of Knoxville, Tennessee. On the retirement of General Hecker, in February, 1864, Captain Greenhut also resigned his position in the army; the following communication being handed him on his

retirement, by General McGroarty, who succeeded in
the command of the brigade:

"Headquarters 3d Brigade, 3d Division, 11th Corps.
          WHITESIDE, TENN., February 28th, 1864.

General order No. 9.

Captain Joseph B. Greenhut, of the 82nd Regiment Illinois
Volunteers, having tendered his resignation, is, in pursuance of
special order, No. 55, Headquarters Department of the Cumberland, February 24, 1864, relieved from duty as Assistant
Adjutant-General of this Brigade, and Lieutenant Rudolph
Muller is announced as his successor. In parting with Captain
Greenhut, the Colonel commanding feels it both a duty and a
pleasure to bear testimony to his diligence, zeal and fidelity in
the performance of his duty in the office, as well as in the field,
and he regrets to see so excellent and brave an officer as Captain Greenhut leave his command.

Matters of important character only could induce Captain
Greenhut to leave the army in which he served three long and
hard years, taking active part in all the most decisive battles
east and west.

To be read on dress parade to the troops to-day.

     By order of Colonel McGROARTY,
                    Commanding Brigade and Post.
     RUDOLPH MULLER,
               1st Lieutenant and A. A. A. General.

Captain JOSEPH B. GREENHUT,
               Assistant Adjutant-General, 3d Brigade."

In recent years Captain Greenhut was appointed by Governor
Fifer one of the three commissioners to erect a monument on
the battle-field of Gettysburg, in honor of the Illinois soldiers
who participated in that battle. He delivered the dedicatory
address at the unveiling of the monument, September 3, 1891,
in the presence of Governor Fifer, and a large multitude of
veterans and representative citizens of the State of Illinois, who
visited the battle-field on that occasion.

The *Chicago Tribune*, of September 4, 1891, prints Captain Greenhut's speech, as follows:

"Friends and Comrades: We are assembled here to-day on the spot where, on the first day of July, 1863, our regiment stood in line, at the beginning of the first day's memorable Battle of Gettysburg. More than twenty-eight years have passed since that eventful struggle, but our memory is re-freshed and brightened when we cast our eyes about us and view these familiar surroundings, and we are impressed in part with the feelings which raged in our breasts when we were formed into line on this field to stem the advance of the Rebel Army. It was an herculean task to perform when we consider that only a small portion of our army was in the field on the first day of the battle, while the larger portion of Lee's Army was concentrated on our front and right.

"None of us knew what a hot day's fight was before us when we broke camp at Emmetsburg early on the morning of July 1st, and began our march towards Gettysburg. We had not gone far when orders came to move faster and to be prepared for an engagement. As we approached the town of Gettysburg on the Emmetsburg road, we could hear the first shots that were being fired on the cavalry skirmish lines and soon there-after received word that the First Corps, which was ahead of us, was already engaging the enemy, and then came the sad news that General Reynolds had been killed. We then moved double-quick through the town to this field where our batteries were placed in position, and at once opened fire on the advancing enemy. I was detailed in command of two companies of our regiment to support Dilger's battery, and I can bear witness to the effective work done by that gallant battery in holding the enemy in check. We were exposed to the fearful cannonade fire which the enemy opened in our front, and by which we had several of our men wounded. We held our ground for a long time against the large force in our front, but later in the after-noon Ewell's corps flanked us on the right, and as our numbers were still entirely too small to combat with the overwhelming forces of the approaching enemy on our right, there was no alternative for us but to retreat through the town and take up a

10

position on Cemetery Hill. It was in this retreat through the
town that our regiment suffered most severely, the rebels coming in through the side streets, which compelled us to fight our
way through the entire town.

" Besides the killed and wounded we suffered in this street
conflict, a number of our officers were cut off and captured by
the enemy. It was a fearful struggle against great odds, and
as our regiment covered the rear of our brigade in that retreat
it has been a surprise to me that we were not entirely annihilated
in our endeavors to force our way through the town up to
Cemetery Hill. Each one of us can, however, vividly recollect
the hair-breadth escapes experienced on that occasion without
any allusions on my part. From Colonel Salomon, who had
his horse shot from under him in the street, down through the
entire rank of officers and men, none will ever forget that
terrible day. As soon as we reached Cemetery Hill, we felt
that we were in a better position and could resist any further
attacks, if they should be made, and the rebels evidently came
to that conclusion, as they did not make any further attempt
that day.

" During the night we were reinforced by the remainder of
our army, which reached Gettysburg from different points and
which brought confidence and encouragement to us who had
withstood the hardships of the engagement of the first day's
battle. When daylight appeared July 2nd, we were prepared
and ready for the second day's struggle.

" Early morning hours on the second day were spent in comparative quiet, each army in full view of the other, and each
waiting for the other to begin the fight. The rebels, however,
who had possession of the town, had filled the houses standing
on the outskirts of the town, just below Cemetery Hill, with
sharpshooters for the purpose of picking off our officers, whom
they could easily spy standing or walking about on the hill.
This had become quite troublesome and General Schurz requested Colonel Salomon to send a detail of about one hundred
men to dislodge the sharpshooters. I had the honor to command that detail, which was made up of volunteers, and
stormed those houses, driving out the sharpshooters and keeping possession of the houses the balance of the day. In

making up this detail an incident happened which I shall surely remember as long as I live, and I cannot refrain from referring to it at this time.   Brave John Ackerman, a private in my company, who on every previous occasion was the first to respond when volunteers were asked for to engage in some daring work, did not come to the front on this occasion.   I was much surprised at his action, and stepped over to speak to him about it.   He said to me:

" 'Captain, I cannot go with you this time; I feel as though something terrible was going to happen to me to-day.'

" He looked pale and despondent.   Believing that he did not feel well, I left him, after saying a few encouraging words to him.   Within an hour after I left him, Ackerman was killed, a rebel shell cutting off more than half his head.   His remains were buried on Cemetery Hill, close to where he was killed. It is singular, that he is the only one of our regiment killed at Gettysburg whose name appears on any headstone in the National Cemetery.

"The great artillery duel, consisting of the firing of more than 200 cannon, which was the beginning of the second day's battle, was especially severe on the exposed position occupied by the Eleventh Corps on Cemetery Hill, and the rebels seemed determined to dislodge us from our position, but were unsuccessful in their efforts.   All of us can recollect the myriads of shells and bombs that flew in our midst and over our heads, dealing out death wherever they struck in our ranks, and few of the headstones which marked the graves in the old cemetery were left unbroken after that shower of shells.

" The terrible charge the rebels made in the evening of the second day to force us from our position on Cemetery Hill has passed into history as one of the most desperate and bloody of this memorable battle.   The charge was made from the streets of the town by the rebel brigade known as the ' Louisiana Tigers,' and it is officially stated that out of 1700 men in that brigade less than 300 ' Tigers ' returned to the town after that charge.   The third day's battle was nearly a duplicate of the day previous, our regiment holding the same position on Cemtery Hill and standing the terrible fire of the enemy with the same bravery and gallantry that had characterized our organization from the beginning. We can all recollect how with frantic desperation the rebels tried to dislodge us from the position we occupied, but all their attempts were unavailing, and when the radiant sun sank behind the western horizon after the third day's fight, the rebels signalized their defeat by a hasty retreat southward. We can also vividly remember how light-hearted and joyous we felt on that early Fourth of July morning when we gazed on those fields and hills in our front which only the evening before were full of life, covered with rebel soldiers and cannon, and now looked deserted and forsaken. We then first began to realize the great victory we had won, a victory which I confidently believe was the turning point for the salvation of this country. But while the face of every Union soldier on that morning was glowing with the flush of heroism, there were but few, however, who could pass without sad emotions over the fields which were so thickly strewn with dead and dying that in some places it was impossible to walk without stepping on some of the dead bodies. But these are the consequences of war, and I sincerely hope it may never again become necessary in this glorious country to call out large armies and to bring such great sacrifices in order to perpetuate our liberties and freedom. (Cheers.)

" It is not necessary to-day to eulogize the many brave deeds of the officers and men of our regiment on this battle-field, as the official records bear ample testimony on that subject, and I doubt whether any regiment can show a better record for bravery than the old 82nd Illinois. (Applause.)

" This monument which has been erected through the generosity of the State of Illinois to commemorate the noble deeds of the 82nd Regiment will stand for ages as a tribute of a grateful people to her sons, now living or dead, who participated in this, the greatest battle which was fought during the war for the preservation of the Union. (Cheers.)

" We, the surviving members of the 82nd Regiment, fully appreciate this token erected in our honor by the State of Illinois and in behalf of our comrades I desire to express through his excellency, Governor Fifer, our sincere thankfulness for the same." (Applause.)

*   *   *   *   *   *   *   *

"Mr. Greenhut concluded by paying a handsome compliment to the old Colonel of the 82nd, Colonel E. S. Salomon, and the ceremonies closed with the recitation of a short poem in German by Lieutenant John Baus, of Chicago."

NAME.	RANK.	COMPANY.	REGIMENT.
GOODMAN, ABRAHAM			83d Infantry
GOODMAN, LEWIS			87th Infantry
GOLDSMITH, W.			93d Infantry

Wounded in battle.

NAME.	RANK.	COMPANY.	REGIMENT.
GOLDSMITH, J.			103d Infantry
GOODMAN, MOSES	Lieutenant		109th Infantry
GOODMAN, JACOB			116th Infantry
GOLDSMITH, JOSEPH		D	118th Infantry
GOODMAN, E.			120th Infantry
GOLDSMITH, DAVID			155th Infantry
GANS, HENRY		C	2d Cavalry
GOLDSMITH, J.	Corporal		4th Cavalry
GANS, LEVI			10th Cavalry
GOLDSMITH, WILLIAM			10th Cavalry
GOLDSMITH, G. W.		I	14th Cavalry
GOTTHELF, JOSEPH	Adjutant		16th Cavalry

Enlisted as private ; promoted for bravery to 1st Lieutenant and Adjutant. After being mustered out re-enlisted in 4th Regiment, Hancock's Veteran Corps; served as Quartermaster Sergeant.

NAME.	RANK.	COMPANY.	REGIMENT.
GOTTHART, MORITZ		E	2d Artillery
HAYS, BENJAMIN		B	7th Infantry
HESS, JOSEPH		A	8th Infantry

Severely wounded at Fort Donelson.

NAME.	RANK.	COMPANY.	REGIMENT.
HAHN, MARTIN		D	8th Infantry
HEINEMAN, HENRY		A	9th Infantry
HAAS, FERDINAND		A	9th Infantry
HEINEMAN, J.		A	9th Infantry
HERRMAN, FRANK		B	9th Infantry
HESS, ALEXANDER		B	11th Infantry
HEINEMAN, WILLIAM		A	12th Infantry

Killed at Fort Donelson.

NAME.	RANK.	COMPANY.	REGIMENT.
HAYS, MOSES			18th Infantry
HESS, ABRAHAM			19th Infantry

Re-enlisted as a veteran.

HELLER, ADOLPH			19th Infantry
HERRICK, C. K.			19th Infantry

Died from wounds received at Elizabethtown, Kentucky.

HELLER, ALBERT			19th Infantry
HAHN, CHARLES			22nd Infantry
HAYS, ABRAHAM	Corporal	C	25th Infantry

Mustered out as Sergeant.

HAYS, FRANKLIN		C	25th Infantry
HAYS, DAVID		C	25th Infantry
HAYS, HENRY			25th Infantry
HESS, JACOB	Corporal	A	20th Infantry
HAYS, MORRIS			33d Infantry
HAYS, LEVI			34th Infantry
HART, AARON			34th Infantry
HAYS, DANIEL			35th Infantry
HOFFMAN, ADOLPH	Captain		39th Infantry

Promoted from 2nd Lieutenant.

HERRMAN, M. } 2 Brothers			41st Infantry
HERRMAN, HENRY }			41st Infantry
HEINEMAN, GEORGE		A	43d Infantry
HERRMAN, LOUIS		B	43d Infantry
HESS, JACOB		G	43d Infantry
HEINEMAN, HENRY		K	43d Infantry
HEILBRUN, JOSEPH			43d Infantry
HAHN, DANIEL			44th Infantry

Wounded and captured.

HESS, AARON		B	46th Infantry
HAYS, MORRIS		C	47th Infantry
HAYS, B		B	54th Infantry
HAYS, LEVI			55th Infantry
HAYMAN, A.		F	57th Infantry
HEINEMAN, JOSEPH		A	58th Infantry
HEINEMAN, JACOB		F	58th Infantry

NAME.	RANK.	COMPANY.	REGIMENT.
HERRMAN, FRANK			59th Infantry
HART, ISAAC			63d Infantry
HIRSCH, JOSEPH		F	64th Infantry
HIRSCH, JULIUS			64th Infantry
HAYS, JOSEPH			65th Infantry
HAAS, JOSEPH		F	65th Infantry
HARRIS, CHARLES			66th Infantry
HAYS, ISAAC			66th Infantry
HEINEMAN, WILLIAM		E	67th Infantry
HAAS, MORRIS			72nd Infantry
HESS, ALEXANDER			79th Infantry
HIRSCHBERG, LOUIS			80th Infantry
HERRMAN, JULIUS		A	82nd Infantry
HERRMAN, JACOB		C	82nd Infantry
HESSBERGER, LEOPOLD		C	82nd Infantry
HENSHALL, ALEXANDER		C	82nd Infantry
HEYMAN, JACOB		C	82nd Infantry
HIRSCHLEIN, LEOPOLD		C	82nd Infantry
HIRSCH, L.		C	82nd Infantry
Wounded at Gettysburg.			
HESSLEIN, ISIDORE		C	82nd Infantry
HAHN, ISAAC			93d Infantry
HAHN, JACOB			93d Infantry
HIRSCH, AUGUST	Lieutenant	C	100th Infantry
HIRSCHBERGER, AARON	Lieutenant		107th Infantry
HIRSCH, BENJAMIN			108th Infantry
HIRSCHBERGER, HERMAN			111th Infantry
HIRSCHMAN, JACOB		H	117th Infantry
HERZBERGER, F.			117th Infantry
HEINEMAN, HENRY			120th Infantry
HESS, JACOB			120th Infantry
HARRIS, JACOB			130th Infantry
HARRIS, CHARLES		K	134th Infantry
Served four years.			
HOLZMAN, S. L.		A	140th Infantry
HAYS, JACOB	Captain		142nd Infantry
HARRIS, BENJAMIN	Lieutenant		143d Infantry
HERRMAN, GOTTLIEB		K	144th Infantry

NAME.	RANK.	COMPANY.	REGIMENT.
HIRSCH, HENRY			152nd Infantry
HERZ, DAVID			156th Infantry
HART, AARON			1st Cavalry
HERRMAN, HERMAN			3d Cavalry
HIRSCHMAN, JOSEPH			3d Cavalry
HERRMAN, JACOB		G	5th Cavalry
HAHN, HENRY		K	7th Cavalry
HEROLD, HERMAN	Lieutenant		11th Cavalry

Enlisted as private; promoted for gallant conduct.

| HAHN, SAMUEL | | | 1st Artillery |
| HART, LEVI | Captain | | 1st Artillery |

Promoted from 2nd Lieutenant.

HERMAN, GOTTLIEB			2nd Artillery
HESS, HENRY			2nd Artillery
HYMAN, L.		Chicago Board of Trade Battery	

ISAACS, JOSEPH		F	8th Infantry
ISRAEL, SAMUEL			18th Infantry
ISRAEL, AARON	Sergeant	K	23d Infantry
ISENSTEIN, GEORGE	Captain		24th Infantry
ISAACS, AARON			42nd Infantry
ISAAC, CHARLES			59th Infantry
ISAACSON, ISAAC			92nd Infantry
ISAACS, W. A.			117th Infantry
ISAAC, DAVID			119th Infantry
ISRAEL, W.			12th Cavalry

| JACOBS, C. | | | 8th Infantry |
| JACOBS, BENJAMIN | Corporal | G | 9th Infantry |

Killed at Fort Donelson.

JOSEPH, JOSEPH		H	10th Infantry
JACOBS, JAMES		A	12th Infantry
JACOBSON, FR.		D	12th Infantry
JACOBS, G.			18th Infantry
JACOBS, DANIEL	Corporal	H	25th Infantry
JACOBS, JOSEPH N.		A	26th Infantry
JACOBS, SAMUEL			30th Infantry
JACOBS, FR.			37th Infantry

NAME.	RANK.	COMPANY.	REGIMENT.
JACOBS, ELIAS		D	38th Infantry
JACOBS, J. B.			38th Infantry
JACOBS, BERNHART			39th Infantry
JACOB, PHILIP		K	43d Infantry
JACOBSON, JACOB			44th Infantry
JACOBS, HENRY		K	47th Infantry
JACOBSON, JACOB			53d Infantry
JACOBS, ABRAHAM			53d Infantry
JACOBS, E.			56th Infantry
JACOBS, BENJAMIN			57th Infantry
JACOBS, SAMUEL.		C	59th Infantry
JACOBS, S.			62nd Infantry

Died in the service.

NAME.	RANK.	COMPANY.	REGIMENT.
JACOBS, HENRY		H	65th Infantry
JACOB, AARON			66th Infantry
JACOBS, SAMUEL		F	78th Infantry
JACOBSON, A.		I	82nd Infantry
JACOBS, WILLIAM			93d Infantry

Died in the field.

NAME.	RANK.	COMPANY.	REGIMENT.
JACOBSON, CHARLES			94th Infantry
JACOBS, JOSEPH		C	98th Infantry
JACOBS, AARON			98th Infantry
JACOBS, SAMUEL		E	98th Infantry
JACOBS, W.	Corporal		103d Infantry
JACOBS, JOSEPH			133d Infantry
JACOBS, HENRY C.		C	134th Infantry
JACOBS, JOSEPH E.			143d Infantry
JONAS, EDWARD	Captain		149th Infantry
JULIAN, DAVID			153d Infantry
JACOBS, CHARLES			2nd Cavalry
JACOBS, J.			3d Cavalry
JACOBS, JOSEPH, JR.		H	9th Cavalry
JACOBSON, J.			9th Cavalry
JACOBS, CHARLES		H	11th Cavalry
JACOBS, CHARLES	Corporal	F	11th Cavalry
JACOBS, HENRY			11th Cavalry
JACOBS, ALEXANDER			12th Cavalry
JACOBS, BERNHARD			12th Cavalry

NAME.	RANK.	COMPANY.	REGIMENT.
JACOBS, A.			15th Cavalry
JACOBS, DAVID F.		A	1st Artillery
JACOBS, JACOB		G	1st Artillery
JACOBS, DAVID M.			2nd Artillery
JACOBS, DANIEL W.			2nd Artillery
JACOBS' DANIEL			Chicago Mercantile Artillery
JACOBS, C. G.			13th United States Infantry
JONAS, EDWARD	Major		50th Infantry

Enlisted as private; promoted to 2nd Lieutenant, Captain and Major; captured at Shiloh.

NAME.	RANK.	COMPANY.	REGIMENT.
KAHN, MOSES		D	9th Infantry
KOHN, EDWARD		H	12th Infantry
KURZ, ELIAS		C	14th Infantry
KATZ, ELIAS		C	14th Infantry
KUHN, GEORGE			16th Infantry
KAHN, HENRY			20th Infantry
KOHN, HENRY			24th Infantry
KAUFMAN, MORITZ	1st Lieutenant	H	24th Infantry

Promoted from Corporal.

NAME.	RANK.	COMPANY.	REGIMENT.
KAUFMAN, JACOB		K	24th Infantry
KRAUSKOPF, G.	Sergeant	A	39th Imfantry
KAUFMAN, ISAAC	Corporal		47th Infantry
KAUFMAN, REUBEN	Corporal		54th Infantry
KING, LOUIS		H	57th Infantry
KAUFMAN, JOSEPH			58th Infantry
KAUFMAN, LEVI	Corporal	I	68th Infantry
KOCH, HERMAN	Sergeant	F	82nd Infantry
KOCH, FRANK		F	82nd Infantry
KOCH, GUSTAV		H	82nd Infantry
KRAMER, SAMUEL		C	82nd Infantry
KARMINSKI, JACOB		G	88th Infantry

Wounded at Stone River.

NAME.	RANK.	COMPANY.	REGIMENT.
KOHN, JACOB			95th Infantry
KAUFMAN, LEVI			106th Infantry
KAUFMAN, ISAAC			106th Infantry
KAUFMAN, ISAAC C.		F	115th Infantry
KONIG, JACOB			132nd Infantry

NAME.	RANK.	COMPANY.	REGIMENT.
KAUFMAN, JACOB			149th Infantry
KAUFMAN, PHILIP		I	1st Cavalry
KAUFMAN, E. B.		C	2nd Cavalry
KOHN, N.			3d Cavalry
KAUFMAN, PHILIP		E	7th Cavalry
KONIGSTEIN, JACOB	Corporal		7th Cavalry
Wounded in action			
KOHN, FREDERICK			8th Cavalry
KOHN, CHARLES			9th Cavalry
KAHN, FRIEDRICH		H	13th Cavalry
KAUFMAN, BENJAMIN	Sergeant		14th Cavalry
Died in the service.			
KOCH, LOUIS		C	16th Cavalry
KAUFMAN, MICHAEL			1st Artillery
KAUFMAN, MARTIN,			2nd Artillery
KOCH, JOSEPH M.		2nd United States Veteran Volunteers	
KOCH, LEWIS		2nd United States Veteran Volunteers	
LEAVIT, LEVI		G	3d Infantry
LESSER, SAMUEL B.		I	8th Infantry
LEIB, HERMAN	Major		8th Infantry
LEHMAN, JACOB	Corporal		8th Infantry
Enlisted as private.			
LEHMAN, REUBEN		F	10th Infantry
LOESER, LEVI		H	14th Infantry
LEVIN, CHARLES		E	17th Infantry
LEVY, MICHAEL			19th Infantry
LANG, Adolph			19th Infantry
LEHMAN, ERNST		A	20th Infantry
LUDWIG, OSCAR	Captain		20th Infantry
Promoted from Sergeant.			
LEHMAN, FRANK			20th Infantry
Died in the service.			
LEHMAN, JACOB			20th Infantry
LIEBERMAN, MARTIN			21st Infantry
Died of wounds.			
LEVY, JOSEPH		A	24th Infantry

NAME.	RANK.	COMPANY.	REGIMENT.
LEOPOLD, WILLIAM			45th Infantry
LORCH, ALEXANDER			46th Infantry
LEHMAN, JOSEPH		B	47th Infantry
LEHMAN, HENRY		B	47th Infantry
LOEB, PHILIP			49th Infantry
LYON, JACOB F.			50th Infantry
LOUIS, LEVI			50th Infantry
LEHMAN, HENRY L.	1st Lieutenant	A	59th Infantry
LEHMAN, HENRY	Corporal		59th Infantry
LEDERMAN, DAVID		E	59th Infantry
LEDERMAN, DANIEL		E	59th Infantry
LEHMAN, J.			70th Infantry
LOEB, WILLIAM	2nd Lieutenant	C	82nd Infantry
LEVY, LOUIS		C	82nd Infantry
LAMMFROMM, JACOB		C	82nd Infantry
LASALLE, JACOB	Captain	C	82nd Infantry
LOEB, WILLIAM	Captain	C	82nd Infantry

Entered as private; promoted for gallant conduct.

LEHMAN, LEWIS		B	86th Infantry
LICHTENBERG, JACOB			87th Infantry
LISTNER, LOUIS			93d Infantry
LEDERMAN, ABRAHAM		F	113th Infantry
LEDERMAN, A.			130th Infantry
LANDENBURG, ABRAHAM			137th Infantry
LYON, DAVID M.	Captain		138th Infantry
LORCH, JACOB			144th Infantry
LEIB, LEVI H.			2nd Cavalry

Died of wounds.

LUDWIG, DANIEL			3d Cavalry
LICHTENBERGER, ALFRED			3d Cavalry
LEHMAN, FREDERICK			4th Cavalry
LEOPOLD, WILIAM			8th Cavalry
LOESER, JACOB			9th Cavalry
LIEBMAN, DANIEL			10th Cavalry

Died of disease contracted in camp.

LEHMAN, JACOB			12th Cavalry
LEVI, R.		B	13th Cavalry
LEHMAN, FREDERICK		F	13th Cavalry

NAME.	RANK.	COMPANY.	REGIMENT.
LEHMAN, MICHAEL	2nd Lieutenant		13th Cavalry
LEHMAN, MAX	1st Lieutenant		16th Cavalry

Promoted from 2nd Lieutenant.

LEOPOLD, WILLIAM   1st Artillery

MENDEL, NOAH E. Captain   7th Infantry

Promoted from 2nd Lieutenant; killed at Fort Donelson.

MYERS, LEO W. 1st Lieutenant   7th Infantry

Killed at Shiloh.

MORRISON, SAMUEL			8th Infantry
MEYER, LEO			9th Infantry
MAYER, CHARLES		G	12th Infantry

Enlisted as private.

MEYERS, HERMAN			12th Infantry
MEYERS, DAVID			7th Infantry
MEYERS, HENRY			8th Infantry
MEYER, JACOB			9th Infantry

Died in the service.

| MOSES, FRANK | | C | 9th Infantry |
| MEYER, MOSES | | | 9th Infantry |

Died in the service.

MEYERS, AARON		H	9th Infantry
MYERS, DANIEL			9th Infantry
MEERHOLZ, HEINRICH		D	10th Infantry
MARKS, A. L.		K	13th Infantry

Served four years under the name of Charles Harris.

MORRIS, LEVI		C	14th Infantry
MYERS, FRANK			14th Infantry
MOSES, GEORGE			15th Infantry
MENKEN, HERMAN			16th Infantry
MEYERS, DAVID			19th Infantry
MAYER, JACOB		A	20th Infantry
MEYERS, SAMUEL			20th Infantry
MYER, ALEXANDER			20th Infantry
MYER, JONAS		G	22nd Infantry
MAYER, A.	Sergeant	A	24th Infantry

NAME.	RANK.	COMPANY.	REGIMENT.
MEYER, SAMUEL	Sergeant		24th Infantry
MEIER, JACOB		E	25th Infantry
MAYER, CHARLES	Corporal	F	24th Infantry

Captured; died in Andersonville Prison.

MEIER, ISIDORE		K	24th Infantry

Captured; died in Andersonville Prison.

MEIER, LOUIS			26th Infantry
MYERS, JOSEPH			26th Infantry

Died of wounds.

MANUEL, JOSEPH		G	27th Infantry

Killed in action.

MOSES, ALBERT	Major		28th Infantry

Promoted from Sergeant.

MEIER, CHARLES			28th Infantry
MANN, ISAAC	Corporal	B	30th Infantry

Promoted to 1st Lieutenant.

MARKS, ISAAC	Corporal		30th Infantry
MEIER, JACOB			31st Infantry
MORRIS, SIMEON			31st Infantry
MORRIS, LEVI E.			31st Infantry
MEYERS, ABARAHM		A	33d Infantry

Killed at Vicksburg.

MYERS, JOSEPH	Captain		34th Infantry

Promoted from 2nd Lieutenant.

MARCUS, FREDERIC			36th Infantry
MORRIS, SOLOMON			37th Infantry
MYERS, ABRAHAM		G	40th Infantry
MANN, CHARLES		B	43d Infantry
MEIER, FRANK			43d Infantry
MEYER' LOUIS		K	43d Infantry
MANN, GUSTAV			44th Infantry
MEIER, LEWIS			44th Infantry
MEYERS, JOSEPH	1st Lieutenant		44th Infantry

Promoted from Sergeant.

MOSES, LEWIS			46th Infantry
MOSES, WILLIAM			46th Infantry
MAYER, ISAAC		H	46th Infantry

NAME.	RANK,	COMPANY.	REGIMENT.
MYERS, JACOB			47th Infantry
MENDEL, DAVID		H	47th Infantry
MORITZ, WILLIAM			48th Infantry
MAY, CHARLES	Lieutenant		50th Infantry
MYERS, LOUIS			54th Infantry
MAYER, CHARLES	Adjutant		58th Infantry

Promoted from private.

MEYERS, HENRY		E	58th Infantry
MOSES, CHARLES		F	58th Infantry
MAYER, BENJAMIN			59th Infantry
MAYER, ABRAHAM			62nd Infantry
MEYER, FREDERICK			63d Infantry
MEYERS, SIMEON	2nd Lieutenant		63d Infantry
MAY, AARON E.	Adjutant		64th Infantry
MEYER, CHARLES	Sergeant		65th Infantry
MEIER, CHARLES E.	Corporal	G	65th Infantry
MEIER, SAMUEL		G	65th Infantry
MANN, MARTIN	Captain		65th Infantry
MANTEL, A.		E	69th Infantry
MEYER, CHARLES			69th Infantry
MEYERS, WILLIAM			69th Infantry
MEYERS, ALEXANDER			70th Infantry
MEYER, GUSTAV			72nd Infantry
MEIER, FERDINAND			72nd Infantry
MANTEL, CHARLES			73d Infantry

Killed in action.

MAYER, SAMUEL			76th Infantry
MARX, C. H.		G	80th Infantry
MARKS, NATHAN		C	82nd Infantry
MEIER, DANIEL		C	82nd Infantry
MEIER, PHILIP		C	82nd Infantry
MANNHEIM, E.		C	82nd Infantry
MEIER, GOTTLIEB		D	82nd Infantry
MAYER, WILLIAM		D	82nd Infantry
MEIER, JACOB	Corporal	K	82nd Infantry

Killed at Chancellorsville.

MEYERS, DAVID		I	82nd Infantry

Name.	Rank.	Company.	Regiment.
Manheimer, Godfrey		C	82nd Infantry
Wounded at Atlanta.			
Meyers, Isaac			83d Infantry
Mann, Isaac	Corporal		85th Infantry
Meyers, Solomon			85th Infantry
Mayer, Jacob			87th Infantry
Meyer, Joseph		F	87th Infantry
Meyers, Frank			89th Infantry
Mayers, W.	Lieutenant		92nd Infantry
Myers, Isaac			103d Infantry
Myers, Henry			111th Infantry
Morgenthal, Jacob			116th Infantry
Mayer, Charles			118th Infantry
May, Abraham	Lieutenant		130th Infantry
Myers, Lewis			131st Infantry
Morris, Nathan		D	131st Infantry
Meyer, Gustav		D	134th Infantry
Mayer, Henry			142d Infantry
Meier, Joseph			142d Infantry
Moses, Reuben	Lieutenant		146th Infantry
Promoted from the ranks.			
Moses, Aaron	Sergeant		1st Cavalry
Moses, Reuben	Sergeant		1st Cavalry
Meyers, Henry			2nd Cavalry
Mann, Levi			7th Cavalry
Meyers, Morris		G	7th Cavalry
Meier, Henry			7th Cavalry
Meyers, Daniel			8th Cavalry
May, Oscar			9th Cavalry
Meier, Herman			9th Cavalry
Died of wounds.			
Meier, William			9th Cavalry
Meier, Herman			10th Cavalry
Meier, August	Lieutenant		10th Cavalry
Enlisted as private.			
Mayer, Moses		A	12th Cavalry
Marks, Samuel		L	12th Cavalry
Meyers, Henry			13th Cavalry

NAME.	RANK.	COMPANY.	REGIMENT.
MEYER, FERDINAND			13th Cavalry
MARX, FELIX	Captain		13th Cavalry

Promoted from Lieutenant.

MEIER, MOSES		B	15th Cavalry
MANN, EUGENE	Corporal	H	15th Cavalry
MEYERS, CHARLES		A	16th Cavalry
MAYER, J.		B	16th Cavalry
MEIER, HERMAN			16th Cavalry
MARX, JOHN F.	Lieutenant		16th Cavalry
MEIERS, NATHAN			17th Cavalry
MEYERS, DAVID		C	1st Artillery
MEIERS, FRANK		G	1st Artillery
MEYERS, HENRY	Sergeant		1st Artillery

Enlisted as private.

MARX, LOUIS		A	2nd Artillery
MOSES, FERDINAND		K	2nd Artillery
MANN, LEWIS		Chicago Mercantile Artillery	
MEYER, HENRY		Elgin Artillery	

NEUMAN, ALBERT		C	9th Infantry

At expiration of term re-enlisted in Company B; was killed at Fort Donelson.

NATHAN, G. M.		B	24th Infantry
NATHAN, MORRIS			24th Infantry
NEWMAN, JOSEPH		F	42nd Infantry
NEWMAN, J.			66th Infantry
NIEMAN, MORITZ		A	82d Infantry
NEWMAN, BENJAMIN			91st Infantry
NEWMAN, JACOB		F	82nd Infantry
NATTINGER, S. L.		E	104th Infantry
NEWMAN, JESSE			112th Infantry
NEWMAN, SIMON	Captain		145th Infantry
NEWMAN, J.			4th Cavalry
NEWMAN, DAVID			13th Cavalry

Died of wounds.

NEWMAN, JACOB	Corporal		Springfield Artillery

11

NAME.	RANK.	COMPANY.	REGIMENT.
OCHS, GEORGE		C	9th Infantry
OCHS, FERDINAND		H	24th Infantry
OPPERMAN, JULIUS			24th Infantry
OCHS, MARTIN			27th Infantry
OCHS, CHARLES	Corporal	B	71st Infantry
OCHS, FRIEDRICH			72nd Infantry
OPPENHEIMER, ABRAHAM			17th Cavalry
PHILLIPSON, AARON		D	3d Cavalry
ROSE, E.		E	10th Infantry
RESSIE, ADOLPH		K	10th Infantry
ROSENBACH, MOSES		G	10th Infantry
ROSE, DANIEL		H	12th Infantry
ROSENTHAL, HENRY			21st Infantry
ROSENFELD, FRANK		K	23d Infantry
ROSENTHAL, M.		K	43d Infantry
ROSENTHAL, CHARLES			49th Infantry
ROSENTHAL, C. W.	Lieutenant		57th Infantry
ROSE, DANIEL			58th Infantry

Mortally wounded at Shiloh.

RICE, JOSEPH			58th Infantry
ROSENBAUM, ALEXANDER		A	75th Infantry
ROSENBAUM, WILLIAM			76th Infantry
ROSENTHAL, SAMPSON			82nd Infantry
ROSENHAUPT, JOSEPH			107th Infantry
ROSENBERG, S.			118th Infantry
ROSENHAUPT, SIMON		I	142nd Infantry
RAPP, JACOB			146th Infantry
ROSENBERG, J.			3d Cavalry
RUBEN, FREDERICK			12th Cavalry
SIMPSON, ELIAS			7th Infantry
SIMPSON, DAVID		K	7th Infantry
SIMONSON, ISAAC		E	8th Infantry

At expiration of term re-enlisted as veteran; promoted
to Sergeant; killed at Fort Blakely.

STURMER, JOSEPH		G	10th Infantry
SANDERS, FRANK			16th Infantry

NAME.	RANK.	COMPANY.	REGIMENT.
SAMUELS, CHARLES		H	19th Infantry
SIMON, JOSEPH		G	24th Infantry
SUMMERFIELD, ELIAS			24th Infantry
SIMON, ADAM	Corporal		24th Infantry
SANDERS, JACOB			25th Infantry
SOLOMON, F.		A	25th Infantry
STERN, JACOB			30th Infantry
SIMPSON, ISAAC		I	31st Infantry
SIMPSON, WILLIAM		I	31st Infantry
STERN, JOSEPH			35th Infantry
SIMONS, ADOLPH		C	37th Infantry
SIMONS, MARCUS		C	37th Infantry
SIMONS, LEVI	Corporal	F	37th Infantry
SIMPSON, JOSEPH			38th Infantry
SIMPSON, DANIEL			40th Infantry
SAMUELSON, ALEXANDER		C	43d Infantry
SAMUELSON, CHARLES		C	43d Infantry
SAMUELSON, CHARLES A.		C	43d Infantry
SANGER, LOUIS			47th Infantry
SOLOMON, HENRY		D	48th Infantry
SIMON, LEWIS			51st Infantry
SOLOMON, DAVID			52nd Infantry
SAMPSON, SAMUEL			53d Infantry
SIMPSON, SAMUEL	Corporal		55th Infantry
SAMUELSON, CHARLES			55th Infantry
Killed at Kenesaw Mountain			
SOLOMON, D.			58th Infantry
STRAUSS, CHARLES		E	59th Infantry
STINE, ISAAC			68th Infantry
SIMONS, ALEXANDER			78th Infantry
SOMMER, FRANK	Corporal	B	82nd Infantry.
SALOMON, A.		C	82nd Infantry
SIMON, GUSTAV		C	82nd Infantry
STEINBACH, M. JOSEPH			82nd Infantry
SIMPSON, HERMAN	Corporal		82nd Infantry
Killed at Chancellorsville			
SHOENWALT, FRANK	Lieutenant	K	82nd Infantry
SALOMON, ABRAHAM		C	82nd Infantry

Name.	Rank.	Company.	Regiment.
SIESEL, SIEGMUND		C	82nd Infantry
SALOMON, EDWARD S.	Brigadier-General		82nd Infantry

Joined the 24th Illinois as 2nd Lieutenant, participating in the battles of Frederickton and Mainfordsville, Kentucky. His gallantry in action and general proficiency in tactics were the cause of successive promotions till in 1862 Lieutenant Salomon was gazetted Major of the regiment. Owing to disagreement among the officers of the command of Colonel Hecker, Major Salomon and other officers resigned and organized another regiment under the official designation of the 82nd Illinois Infantry, of which Major Saloman ultimately became Colonel. As a member of the 11th Army Corps under General Howard, he participated in the campaign of which the actions at Chancellorsville and Gettysburg were salient features. He also took part in the battles round Chattanooga, Lookout Mountain, and Missionary Ridge; fought in fact throughout all the campaign in the Southwest and was ultimately brevetted to the rank of Brigadier-General.

President Grant appointed General Salomon to the Governorship of Washington Territory which position he held four years to the satisfaction of the citizens and to the increased industrial prosperity of the Northwest.

As the subject of this sketch has also been prominent in politics on the Republican side, his military service .has frequently been attacked by political enemies. To show with what little justice these attacks have been made, we publish a few of the opinions entertained by prominent Generals of the army:

"HEADQUARTERS 3D DIVISION,
August 20, 1863.

MAJOR GENERAL HOWARD,
            Commanding 11th Corps.

GENERAL:

Of the part taken by my Division in the actions of July 2 and 3 at Gettysburg, I have the honor to submit the following report: One of the five regiments of the 1st Brigade, the 74th Pennsylvania, was left with General Ames to strengthen his right wing; the remaining four were directed towards a strip of woods on the right of the Division, in which the firing had become very heavy, and where, according to a report of some staff officers of the 1st Corps, immediate aid was needed. Two regiments, the 157th New York and the 61st Ohio, were guided by one of their officers, while the other two, the 82nd Illinois and the 45th New York, were led by my Chief of Staff, Lieutenant-Colonel Otto, of the 50th New York.

It had meanwhile become quite dark, the direction of the fight being indicated by nothing but the sound of musketry. The regiment entered the woods with the greatest determination, and drove the enemy from our rifle pits.

It is my pleasant duty to mention as especially deserving, the names of Lieutenant-Colonel Otto, who superintended this operation with great judgment and courage, and Lieutenant Colonel Salomon, of the 82nd Illinois, who displayed the highest order of coolness and determination under very trying circumstances.

I am, General,

Very respectfully yours,
(Signed)   C. SCHURZ,
Major-General Commanding Division.

HEADQUARTERS 3D BRIGADE, 1ST DIVISION, 20TH
ARMY CORPS.

NEAR KENESAW MOUNTAIN, GA.

June 26th, 1864.

ALLEN FULLER,
Adjutant-General, State of Illinois.

SIR :

I have the honor to respectfully request that you issue a Colonel's commission to Lieutenant-Colonel Edward S. Salomon, commanding the 82nd Regiment Illinois Volunteer Infantry, belonging to his brigade. I take pleasure in saying that it is my sincere belief that Lieutenant-Colonel Salomon fully deserves this favor, not only by his inherent ability and merit as an officer, but more particularly by the gallantry and efficiency he has displayed during this campaign. The regiment he commands is his best recommendation, it being soldierly, gallant and thoroughly disciplined. It will be accepted as a personal favor if you will make special effort to obtain the approval of Lieutenant-Colonel Salomon's commission as Colonel, and his muster as such by the War Department.

Respectfully, your obedient servant,

J. S. ROBINSON,

Colonel Commanding 3d Brigade,
1st Division 20th Army Corps.

HEADQUARTERS 1ST DIVISION, 20TH ARMY CORPS.

June 28th, 1864.

Respectfully forwarded, heartily concurring with the within recommendation.

(Signed)   A. S. WILLIAMS,
Brig. Gen. Commanding Division.

HEADQUARTERS 20TH ARMY CORPS.

June 28th, 1864.

Respecfully forwarded. I fully concur in the within recommendation Lieutenant Colonel Solomon has won the good opinion of all his comrades by his great gallantry and good conduct, and it will be but a just and grateful appreciation of his services to confer the preferment upon him.

(Signed)   JOSEPH HOOKER,
Major-General Commanding.

HEADQUARTERS 3D BRIGADE, 1ST DIVISION, 20TH
ARMY CORPS.

GOLDSBORO, N. C., April 2nd, 1865.

HON. E. M. STANTON,
Secretary of War.

SIR :

I have the honor to recommend and earnestly request the appointment of Colonel Edward S. Salomon, of the 82nd Regiment, Illinois Volunteers, as Brevet Brigadier-General for gallant and meritorious services.

Colonel Salomon joined this brigade with his regiment at the opening of the campaign against Atlanta in the spring of 1864. During the fighting before Resaca, Georgia, on the 14th and 15th of May, this regiment behaved with great gallantry.

Again, at New Hope, Georgia, on the 25th of the same month, Colonel Salomon led his command with admirable coolness and courage against the enemy. After having advanced under a severe fire of musketry and artillery more than a mile, he held his line close to the entrenched position of the enemy, without a breastwork, and with a scanty supply of ammunition.

At the battle near Peach Tree Creek, before Atlanta, Georgia, on the 20th of July, 1864, Colonel Salomon performed a most gallant and meritorious part in repulsing the repeated onslaughts made by the enemy. In the face of a furious raking fire, he held his line for four hours, when the enemy withdrew from his front with great loss.

During the siege of Atlanta, Colonel Salomon was ever prominent for his energy, coolness and judgment.

In the fight near Averysboro, North Carolina, on the 16th of March, 1865, Colonel Salomon, as usual, led his regiment into action with great gallantry and skill.

At the battle of Bentonville, on the 19th of March, 1865, Colonel Salomon and his command drew the unqualified admiration of all who witnessed their coolness and discipline

un-ler fire, and their effectual services in repulsing several determined attacks of the enemy.

Colonel Salomon has distinguished himself in other engagements besides those which have been mentioned. At Gettysburg and Missouri Ridge his gallantry was conspicuous and
challenged the highest admiration.

I consider Colonel Salomon one of the most deserving officers of my acquaintance. His regiment is his highest praise.
In point of drill and discipline it is second to none in this
corps. Its record will bear safe comparison with any other of
the same age in the army.

Colonel Salomon has had a commission as Colonel since
April, 1864, but his regiment not containing the requisite
number of men he has been unable to get mustered.

Earnestly hoping that his claims will meet your favorable
attention.

I remain, sir, very respectfully, your obedient servant,

(Signed)   J. S. ROBINSON,

Brig. Gen. U. S. V., Commanding 3d Brigade,
1st Division, 20th Army Corps.

HEADQUARTERS 20TH ARMY CORPS.

GOLDSBORO, April 2, 1865.

I cordially concur in the recommendation of General Robinson. The officer (Colonel Salomon) has just merits. He is
intelligent, gallant, brave and faithful. I have had several
occasions to mark his distinguished merit. There can be no
promotion more deserved.

A. S. WILLIAMS,
Brevet Maj. Gen. Commanding.

WAR DEPARTMENT,

WASHINGTON, June 15, 1865.

SIR :

You are hereby informed that the President of the United
States has appointed you for distinguished gallantry and meritorious services during the war, a Brigadier General of Volunteers, by brevet in the service of the United States, to rank as
such from the thirteeenth day of March, one thousand eight

hundred and sixty-five. Should the Senate at the next session advise and consent thereto, you will be commissioned accordingly.

EDWIN M. STANTON,
Secretary of War.

TO BREVET BRIGADIER-GENERAL EDWARD S. SALOMON,
U. S. VOLUNTEERS.

What was thought of General Salomon and his administration as Governor by the people of Washington Territory is best explained by quoting the following article from the *Pacific Tribune*, published at the time he resigned his office of Governor:

" RESIGNATION OF GOVERNOR SALOMON.

" The acceptance of Governor Salomon's resignation by the President is universally regretted by our people. He was honest, fearless and capable. He mingled freely with the people, identified himself with their interests and generously expended his time and means to bring hither population and to promote our material interests. He has established a reputation in the office which will make his administration a source of pride to his fellow-citizens, and he carries into his retirement the consolation that the good and true of all parties regard it fortunate that he should have been called to preside over our destinies. We speak the sentiment of our people when we express unfeigned regret that he felt it his duty to resign his office. His official acts are his best records; they have all met with the heartiest commendation of our people.

" A thorough and consistent Republican, baptized in the fire of battle, when gallantly sustaining the flags, he has always been true and steadfast to the principles of the party of which he was so distinguished a member. While ever ready with purse, pen and tongue to maintain his partisan principles, he was singularly free from a partisan bigotry in the exercise of official functions. He governed the Territory. Party behests never made him swerve from official integrity or duty to the whole people. How proudly can he look to this episode of his life. He governed well. He satisfied all, for the welfare of the whole was constantly in his eye; he was true to the position he so happily filled.

"But his successor is soon to come among us. We are ready to accord to the new Executive a cordial welcome. We can wish him, however, no higher or better aspiration than that he may prove worthy to be the successor of one who so faithfully and well performed all his duties as Edward S. Salomon."

NAME.	RANK.	COMPANY.	REGIMENT.
SHANWALT, JACOB			91st Infantry
SAMUELSON, G.			105th Infantry
STINE, ABRAHAM			111th Infantry
SIMON, JOSEPH			117th Infantry
SWITZER, MOSES			118th Infantry
SALOMON, TOBIAS			122nd Infantry
SALOMON, LEVI		C	123d Infantry
SALOMON, SAMUEL		C	123d Infantry
STRAUSS, DAVID			124th Infantry
SIMONS, SAMUEL			132nd Infantry
STRAUSS, ALBERT			156th Infantry
SIMON, DAVID S.			2nd Cavalry
STERNBERG, H.			2nd Cavalry
SIMONS, DANIEL			4th Cavalry
STRAUSS, CHARLES			4th Cavalry
SCHIFF, GOTTLIEB			8th Cavalry
STRAUSS, LEWIS			8th Cavalry
SAMUELSON, DAVID	Corporal		10th Cavalry
SALOMON, HENRY, Enlisted as private.	1st Lieutenant		10th Cavalry
SAMPSON, SIMON Died of wounds.			10th Cavalry
SOLOMON, H. J.	2nd Lieutenant		10th Cavalry
STROUSE; CHARLES			12th Cavalry
SACHS, ADAM Promoted from 2nd Lieutenant.	Captain		13th Cavalry
SIMON, HENRY		A	17th Cavalry
SCHONEMAN, JACOB			2nd Artillery
ULMAN, A.			58th Infantry
VOGEL, BERNHARD		D	9th Infantry
VOGEL, LOUIS Veteran.		D	43d Infantry

NAME.	RANK.	COMPANY.	REGIMENT.
VOGEL, LOUIS			44th Infantry
VOGEL, JACOB			67th Infantry
VOGEL, GOTTLIEB			72nd Infantry
VOGEL, JACOB			93d Infantry
VOGEL, CHARLES	Captain	B	132nd Infantry
VOGEL, LEWIS,			2nd Cavalry
WOLF, JULIUS		K	7th Infantry

At expiration of term re-enlisted as Veteran.

WOLF, LOUIS		A	9th Infantry
WEIL, LOUIS		E	9th Infantry
WODIC, EMANUEL		K	10th Infantry

Has testimonies from his superior officers, speaking in
the highest terms of his devotion and courage.

WEISE, SIMON		G	11th Infantry
WOLF, M. P.		G	12th Infantry
WOLFSON, R.			16th Infantry
WOLF, G. W.			16th Infantry
WOLF, CHARLES		K	18th Infantry
WOLF, JOSEPH			21st Infantry
WOLF, HENRY		G	21st Infantry
WELLNER, JACOB		A	23d Infantry
WOLLNER, JACOB		B	23d Infantry

Served three years.

WOLF, CHARLES			24th Infantry
WOLF, JACOB		F	25th Infantry
WISE, SIMON		A	26th Infantry
WISE, ISAAC			31st Infantry
WURZBURGER, ABRAHAM		A	82nd Infantry
WOLF, MOSES		C	82nd Infantry
WEISS, JOSEPH		H	82nd Infantry
WATERMAN, ALFRED	Surgeon		105th Infantry

Promoted from Assistant Surgeon

DE WOLF, HENRY	Sergeant	D	134th Infantry
WATERMAN, DAVID			9th Cavalry
WEIL, SAMUEL			1st Artillery
ZUCKER, SIMON		F	10th Infantry
ZAELLNER, LOUIS		C	82nd Infantry

INDIANA.

NAME.	RANK.	COMPANY.	REGIMENT.
ADLER, HENRY	Corporal	I	15th Infantry
ADOLPH, JACOB		A	22nd Infantry
AARON, ALLEN			33d Infantry
ASHER, W. H.		E	33d Infantry
ASHER, H. C.			33d Infantry
ASH, ISAAC		B	37th Infantry
APPEL, MOSES		A	38th Infantry

Died of wounds received at Stone River.

APPEL, JOSEPH		A	38th Infantry
ASHER, S.			54th Infantry
ASCHER, DAVID		E	57th Infantry
ASH, JOSEPH		H	67th Infantry
ABRAHAM, BENJAMIN		C	68th Infantry
ASH, C. M.		E	70th Infantry
ABRAHAM, EZEKIEL		B	83d Infantry
AARON, DANIEL			90th Infantry
ASH, DANIEL	Captain		99th Infantry
ARNOLD, MOSES		D	99th Infantry
ASH, SALOMON		E	99th Infantry
ALBERT, LEVI			106th Infantry
AARON, ADOLPH		H	107th Infantry
ASHER, NOAH	Corporal	E	128th Infantry

Mustered out as Sergeant.

ASHER, SIMPSON		F	133d Infantry
ASH, HENRY		E	144th Infantry
ABRAHAMSON, EUGENE		K	152nd Infantry
ALEXANDER, LEVI			13th Battery

BAER, SAMUEL A.		I	7th Infantry

Died of wounds received at the Wilderness.

BERLIN, JACOB		C	9th Infantry

Killed at Shiloh.

NAME.	RANK.	COMPANY.	REGIMENT.
BENJAMIN, ABRAHAM	Corporal	C	10th Infantry
Enlisted as private.			
BENJAMIN, THEODORE		F	6th Infantry
BAIR, MANASSEH		K	8th Infantry
BARNETT, ISAAC		D	9th Infantry
BARNETT, LEWIS		D	11th Infantry
BACHMAN, BENJAMIN		A	13th Infantry
BENJAMIN, JULIUS		F	13th Infantry
BARNETT, S.			18th Infantry
BENJAMIN, DAVID		B	20th Infantry
BERNARD, JACOB	Corporal	D	20th Infantry
BERNARD, M.			1st Heavy Artillery
BAIR, SIMON		E	26th Infantry
BERNARD, HENRY		K	1st Cavalry
BENJAMIN, DAVID J.		G	29th Infantry
BERNARD, WILLIAM		E	32nd Infantry
BLUM, MARCUS		H	32nd Infantry
BERNARD, A.			32nd Infantry
BARNHARD, DAVID		G	33d Infantry
BENSON, DAVID S.			3d Cavalry
BERNARD, L.			38th Infantry
BARNHARD, JACOB		F	40th Infantry
BEERS, MARCUS		G	40th Infantry
BACHMAN, L.			42nd Infantry
BEAN, SOLOMON		G	44th Infantry
BEAR, LEVI		E	46th Infantry
BAUM, C.			46th Infantry
BENJAMIN, ABEL		G	46th Infantry
BENJAMIN, PHILIP M.		G	46th Infantry
BAER, MANASSEH N.	Corporal	B	47th Infantry
BAER, DANIEL		B	47th Infantry
BAER, DAVID		G	72nd Infantry
BAER, AARON		I	74th Infantry
Mustered out as Quartermaster.Sergeant.			
BLUM, B.			77th Infantry
BAIER, J.			89th Infantry
BAMBERGER, HERMAN J.		A	107th Infantry
BEAR, MANASSEH		B	116th Infantry

Name.	Rank.	Company.	Regiment.
Baum, Adam E.		E	116th Infantry
Baum, Zachariah		E	116th Infantry
Bernheimer, Leopold		A	136th Infantry
Coffman, Marcus		F	11th Infantry
Cahn, Ad.			32nd Infantry
Cahn, Julius			32nd Infantry
Coffman, Isaac		D	40th Infantry
Coffman, Samuel L.		B	2nd Cavalry
Coffman, Levi		A	8th Cavalry
Coffman, Nathan		B	43d Infantry
Captured; died in Rebel prison.			
Coffman, Levi	Sergeant	L	3d Cavalry
Cornelius, Abraham		B	51st Infantry
Cohn, Gabriel	Sergeant	C	68th Infantry
Coffman, Jacob		E	75th Infantry
Coffman, Jonas			75th Infantry
Coffman, Isaac		D	81st Infantry
Coffman, Isaac		D	97th Infantry
Cohen, Charles, Jr.			110th Infantry
Coffman, Joseph		F	116th Infantry
Cohen, Charles		F	116th Infantry
Coffman, Joseph		K	128th Infantry
Cohen, Isaac		B	13th Cavalry
Coffman, Jacob			8th Battery
Cahn, Albert	Lieutenant		135th Infantry
Cohen, Max			3d Cavalry
Cohn, A. J.	Captain		Pleasanton's Cavalry
David, Daniel		C	6th Infantry
David, Levi		F	7th Infantry
David, Ephraim	Corporal	H	7th Infantry
Davidson, Mordecai		A	17th Infantry
Davidson, David		G	20th Infantry
Dryfus, Jacob		I	32nd Infantry
Daniel, J			44th Infantry
De Witt John			52nd Infantry
Desar, David	Lieutenant		107th Infantry

NAME.	RANK.	COMPANY.	REGIMENT.
EPSTEIN, FRANK		D	7th Infantry
ESLINGER, ISIDOR	Captain	E	32nd Infantry
EMANUEL, BENJAMIN		E	50th Infantry
ELLINGER, JACOB S.		D	53d Infantry
ESLINGER, A.			59th Infantry
ENGEL, ELIAS (Minute Men)		D	105th Infantry
ENGEL, N. (Minute Men)		A	106th Infantry
EMANUEL, DANIEL		A	116th Infantry
ENGELHART, H. D.		C	83d Infantry
ELLINGER, REUBEN			25th Battery
FRANKS, ERNST		K	17th Infantry
FRIEDLEIN, ADAM		K	19th Infantry
FRANK, SAMUEL		F	1st Cavalry
FREUND, HENRY		I	32nd Infantry
FRED, EPHRAIM		H	53d Infantry
FRED, JACOB		H	53d Infantry
FRYBERGER, A. J.		I	54th Infantry
FRANK, MOSES		H	59th Infantry
FISHEL, SOLOMON		K	99th Infantry
FISHEL, DAVID		K	99th Infantry
FALK, ISAAC W.		F	100th Infantry
FALK, JOSEPH		B	100th Infantry
FRIEDLEIN, MICHAEL		C	118th Infantry
FRANKFODER, D.	Lieutenant		142nd Infantry
FRIEDLEIN, JOSEPH		E	147th Infantry
FRIEDLEIN, EMANUEL		E	147th Infantry
FRANK, ADAM	Lieutenant		6th Battery
FRANK, JOSEPH			10th Battery
FRANK, MORRIS F.			25th Battery
GRUNBURG, MARKS			8th Infantry
GOLDSMITH, JOSEPH		F	11th Infantry
GOLDSMITH, J. L.		K	15th Infantry
GOLDSMITH, JOEL L.		E	18th Infantry
Wounded at Pea Ridge.			
GOODMAN, C.	Corporal		23d Infantry
GOLDMAN, W. H.		A	23d Infantry

NAME.	RANK.	COMPANY.	REGIMENT.
GOODMAN, BENJAMIN S.		B	24th Infantry
GOODMAN, D.			26th Infantry
GOLDSMITH, FREDERICK		H	26th Infantry
GOODMAN, JACOB		D	30th Infantry
GOLDSMITH, G. B.		A	31st Infantry
GOLDSMITH, J. L.		G	33d Infantry
GOLDSMITH, JOHN		F	34th Infantry
GOLDSMITH, M.		B	38th Infantry
GOODMAN, J.			38th Infantry
GOODMAN, MAIER		E	38th Infantry
GREENFIELD, HENRY		G	2nd Cavalry
GOLDSMITH, HENRY		B	44th Infantry
GOLDSMITH, J. W.		F	44th Infantry
GREEN, SOLOMON A.		A	54th Infantry
GOODMAN, CHARLES B.		B	54th Infantry
GOLDSMITH, GEORGE W.		B	57th Infantry
GOODMAN, A.			58th Infantry
Killed at Stone River.			
GOLDMAN, JESSE		I	60th Infantry
GOLDSMITH, M. H.		K	67th Infantry
GOLDSMITH, W. H.		I	68th Infantry
GOLDSMITH, JAMES		D	80th Infantry
GOLDMAN, ALEXANDER		I	80th Infantry
GOLDSMITH, JOSEPH		K	103d Infantry
GOLDSTEIN, SAMUEL (Minute Men)		E	107th Infantry
GOODMAN, ABRAHAM (Minute Men)		A	113th Infantry
GOLDSMITH, BERNARD		D	136th Infantry
GOLDMAN, JONATHAN		I	142nd Infantry
GOLDMAN, P.		D	144th Infantry
GOLDSMITH, J. G.	Corporal		9th Battery
GOLDSMITH, EDWIN	Adjutant		100th Infantry
HAYMAN, LOUIS	Corporal	K	18th Infantry
HARRIS, SIMON		H	20th Infantry
Killed at Gettysburg.			
HESS, LEOPOLD		B	23d Infantry
HIRSCH, PHILIP		K	26th Infantry

NAME.	RANK.	COMPANY.	REGIMENT.
HESS, LEVI M.	Lieutenant	B	29th Infantry

Promoted from Sergeant.

HESS, JOSEPH		H	31st Infantry
HAHN, C			32nd Infantry
HAHN, J.			32nd Infantry
HIRSCH, JACOB		C	37th Infantry
HINNEMAN, DAVID		B	8th Cavalry
HINNEMAN, JOSEPH		B	8th Cavalry
HOFFMAN, SOLOMON		A	2nd Cavalry
HESS, ALEXANDER	Lieutenant	F	2nd Cavalry

Promoted from Sergeant.

HOFFMAN, EMANUEL L.		E	42nd Infantry
HERSH, J. W.		C	44th Infantry
HOFFMAN, AARON	Corporal	D	3d Cavalry
HERRMAN, ABRAHAM B.		D	46th Infantry
HERMAN, JOSEPH	Corporal	F	46th Infantry
HESS, J.			46th Infantry
HOFFMAN, JACOB		D	47th Infantry
HUFFMAN, SIMON		D	47th Infantry
HESS, JACOB	Captain	K	21st Infantry
HERSCHMAN, G. W.		B	51st Infantry
HELLER, DANIEL		H	51st Infantry
HOCHSTETTER, JOSEPH		A	52nd Infantry

Killed by guerillas.

HOCHSTETTER, JACOB		C	52nd Infantry
HEACHBURGER, LEVI		C	63d Infantry
HERZOG, ISAAC		D	63d Infantry
HOCHSTETTER, BENJAMIN	Lieutenant		67th Infantry
HIRSCHBERGER, ABRAHAM		D	72nd Infantry
HIRSCHBERGER, NOAH		D	72nd Infantry
HYNEMAN, J.		E	80th Infantry
HYNEMAN, LEWIS		D	83d Infantry
HIRSCH, WOLF		C	86nd Infantry

Wounded at Chickamauga and taken prisoner; he served throughout the Civil War.

HIRSCHMAN, EZEKIEL		G	100th Infantry
HART, AARON	Corporal	D	103d Infantry

12

NAME.	RANK.	COMPANY.	REGIMENT.
HAHN, Joseph (Minute Men)		G	106th Infantry
HERRMAN, A. (Minute Men)			107th Infantry
HART, AARON		I	9th Cavalry
HERMAN, REUBEN		H	12th Infantry
HIRSCH, GEORGE		G	135th Infantry
HIRSCH, JACOB		A	136th Infantry
HAHN, JACOB		A	136th Infantry
HESS, L.			136th Infantry
HIRSCH, AUGUST		A	142nd Infantry
HEINEMAN, WILLIAM	Corporal	F	146th Infantry
HERMAN, JACOB		F	149th Infantry
HERZOG, JACOB C.		D	154th Infantry
HELLER, ABRAHAM		H	155th Infantry
HIRSCH, FERDINAND			6th Battery
HIRSCHLER, ABRAHAM		M	4th Cavalry
Died in Libby Prison.			
ISAACSON, J. A.		H	15th Infantry
JOSEPHS, ABRAHAM C.	Sergeant	K	11th Infantry
JOSEPH, MARK P.	Captain	K	11th Infantry
Enlisted as private; wounded.			
JACOBS, NATHAN		G	13th Infantry
JUDAH, SAMUEL		K	20th Infantry
JOSEPH, MARX			1st Heavy Artillery
JACOBS, ELIAS		K	30th Infantry
JUDAH, ISRAEL		F	31st Infantry
JACOBY, S.			48th Infantry
Died of wounds.			
JUDAH, H.			90th Infantry
JACOBS, A. M.		E	114th Infantry
JUDAH, TH. O.		D	117th Infantry
JOSEPH, JOHN,		A	3d Cavalry
JACOBSON, SAMUEL			14th Battery
KAUFMAN, JACOB C.		G	20th Infantry
KAUFMAN, ADOLPH		F	32nd Infantry
KOCH, JOSEPH		A	60th Infantry

NAME.	RANK.	COMPANY.	REGIMENT.
KOCH, L.	Corporal		60th Infantry
KOCH, P.			60th Infantry
KAHN, JULIUS		I	76th Infantry
KING, ISAAC		B	88th Infantry
KISER, MOSES		B	88th Infantry
KAUFMAN, JACOB	Corporal	A	89th Infantry
KAHN, ELI (Minute Men)		D	110th Infantry
KAUFFMAN, BENJAMIN		A	118th Infantry
KAUFFMAN, ABRAHAM		G	11th Cavalry
KUHN, LEO		B	136th Infantry
KAUFFMAN, BENJAMIN		E	139th Infantry
KAUFFMAN, ABRAHAM		G	149th Infantry
KUHN, S.			3d Battery
KIRSCHLER, A.	Sergeant	M	4th Cavalry

Captured; died in Andersonville Prison.

KUBITSHEK, MICHEL		I	88th Infantry
KUBITSHEK, HENRY	Lieutenant	G	48th Infantry

Promoted from ranks.

KNEFLER, FREDERICK   Brigadier-General   79th Infantry
Attained the highest rank of any Israelite who served
during the Civil War.   He enlisted as a private in the
79th Regiment, Indiana Volunteers, and rose step by
step until he was promoted to the Colonelcy of his
Regiment.   Subsequently he was appointed Brigadier-
General, then Brevet Major-General for meritorious
conduct at Chickamauga.   He participated in the
principal battles of the Army of the Cumberland under
Generals Rosecrans, Thomas, Sherman, and Grant,
and took part in the engagements under Sherman in
the march to the sea.   General Knefler has the reputation of having been one of the most gallant soldiers.
He is now living in Indianapolis, honored and
respected.

LICHTENBERGER, LOUIS		G	6th Infantry
LILIENTHAL, HENRY		H	11th Infantry
LIPPMAN, FR. L.		A	12th Infantry
LOWENTHAL, ISIDOR S.	Corporal	G	18th Infantry
LEHMAN, SIMON	Corporal	C	21st Infantry

Name.	Rank.	Company.	Regiment.
Lehman, C.		C	21st Infantry
Lehman, Rudolph			23d Infantry
Levi, J. S.		E	23d Infantry
Lazarus, Henry		C	24th Infantry
Lowenthal, Adam S.	Captain	H	29th Infantry

Enlisted as private; promoted at the battle of Stone
River.

Lehman, Henry		F	31st Infantry
Lehman, H. D.		F	31st Infantry
Levi, Nathan		H	32nd Infantry
Levy, Nathan	Lieutenant		32nd Infantry
Levy, Abraham		K	32nd Infantry
Leopold, W. W.			8th Cavalry
Lichtenwater, David		B	44th Infantry
Lorsch, David C.		K	44th Infantry
Levi, Morris		I	52nd Infantry
Lehman, Samuel J.		K	57th Infantry
Lippold, Julius		G	58th Infantry
Leavit, Samuel			44th Infantry
Levi, J. S.	Corporal	G	66th Infantry

Killed at Richmond, Kentucky.

Levi, Washington		G	123d Infantry
Letterman, Joseph		M	10th Cavalry
Lowenthal, Theodore		D	135th Infantry
Loeb, Isaac		G	138th Infantry
Ludwig, Herman	Lieutenant		20th Battery
Loeb, Jacob			1st Battery

May, Frank			2nd Infantry
Myers, Levi D,			7th Infantry
Meyer, Jacob		D	7th Infantry
Mayer, Ferdinand	Corporal		10th Infantry

Promoted to Lieutenant.

Marx, Isaac I.		I	11th Infantry
Manuel, Julius P.		B	12th Infantry
Meyer, Abraham		K	12th Infantry
Marks, Samuel		D	13th Infantry

Died of wounds.

NAME.	RANK.	COMPANY.	REGIMENT.
MEYER, ADOLPH	Lieutenant	K	14th Infantry
MENDEL, G. W.	Corporal	E	16th Infantry
MEYERS, DAVID R.			17th Infantry
MAY, ISAAC M.	Major		19th Infantry
MEYERS, L.		F	19th Infantry
MORITZ, JACOB		B	22nd Infantry
MORITZ, FREDERICK		B	22nd Infantry
MARCUS, ALEXANDER B.		G	24th Infantry
MEYER, JOSEPH		K	27th Infantry
MANUEL, SIMON		E	29th Infantry
MORITZ, CHARLES		F	29th Infantry
MARKS, JESSE N.		I	29th Infantry
MEYER, ERNST	Lieutenant		32nd Infantry
MAIER, HENRY		F	30th Infantry
MAYER, LEOPOLD		B	32nd Infantry
MAIER, JACOB		E	32nd Infantry
MEIER, FERDINAND C.	Sergeant	K	32nd Infantry
MEYER, HENRY		G	33d Infantry
MAY, LEWIS		K	34th Infantry
MEYER, JACOB	Sergeant	I	37th Infantry
Promoted from the ranks.			
MAYER, HERMAN L.		C	44th Infantry
MAYER, JULIUS		I	46th Infantry
MAYER, SAMUEL		D	48th Infantry
MORITZ, DANIEL		C	54th Infantry
MAY, SIMON		F	58th Infantry
MAYER, J. G.	Lieutenant		7th Cavalry
MAYER, ABRAHAM		I	59th Infantry
MAYER, HENRY		D	60th Infantry
MYER, ISAAC F.	Corporal	C	63d Infantry
MOSES, SAMUEL		D	63d Infantry
MAAS, ISAAC	Captain		65th Infantry
MOSES, ISAAC		A	66th Infantry
MAIER, JOSEPH		C	67th Infantry
MAYER, HENRY		D	69th Infantry
MANN, DAVID		E	69th Infantry
MANN, ISAAC		E	69th Infantry
MAYER, HENRY F.		G	76th Infantry

NAME.	RANK.	COMPANY.	REGIMENT.
MANN, DANIEL		A	79th Infantry
MOSES, JAMES		K	80th Infantry
MAY, ABRAHAM		F	82nd Infantry
MAY, JACOB		F	82nd Infantry
MEYER, JACOB		K	89th Infantry
MARKS, JACOB		A	90th Infantry
MANN, SAMUEL		C	90th Infantry
MARKS, HENRY		A	91st Infantry
MANUEL, JACOB		D	93d Infantry
MOSS, LEWIS	Lieutenant		107th Infantry
MAYER, LOUIS	(Minute Men)	B	107th Infantry
MEYER, JOSEPH	(Minute Men)	I	107th Infantry
MARKS, ISAAC H.	(Minute Men)	C	108th Infantry
MAY, FRANK	(Minute Men)	K	108th Infantry
MAY, ELI	(Minute Men)	D	110th Infantry
MARKS, ABRAHAM		F	138th Infantry
MORRIS, MORDECAI		B	138th Infantry
MYERS, SOLOMON		D	147th Infantry
MYERS, ISAAC		A	148th Infantry
MYERS, JACOB		D	151st Infantry
MYERS, BENJAMIN		H	151st Infantry
MEYER, HERMAN H.		B	156th Infantry
MEIER, ADOLPH H.		D	156th Infantry

Mustered out as Sergeant

| MAYER, JULIUS | Corporal | | 1st Battery |

NATHAN, HARRIS		H	7th Infantry
NEUMAN, REUBEN		C	33d Infantry
NUSSBAUM, JOSIAH		B	47th Infantry
NUSSBAUM, HENRY		B	47th Infantry
NUSSBAUM, JOEL		F	53d Infantry
NEWMAN, JOSEPH		G	58th Infantry
NEWMAN, SIMON		C	60th Infantry
NUSSBAUM, JOSEPH		A	89th Infantry
NEWBERGER, SYLVESTER		G	138th Infantry
NUSSBAUM, JACOB			13th Battery

NAME.	RANK.	COMPANY.	REGIMENT.
OCHS, LEWIS		G	11th Infantry
OCHS, FRIEDRICH		F	32nd Infantry
Killed at Chickamauga.			
OSCAR, MARCUS		D	59th Infantry
RUSSELL, E. J.		F	19th Infantry
Severely wounded.			
ROSENBAUM, WILLIAM		C	26th Infantry
ROSE, JOSEPH		E	38th Infantry
ROSE, SOLOMON		E	38th Infantry
ROSENTHALER, J. G.		E	46th Infantry
ROSCHILD, ALBERT		I	53d Infantry
RICH, DAVID		E	67th Infantry
RICH, JONAH		E	67th Infantry
ROSENBERG, PHILIP		A	81st Infantry
ROSENGARTEN, LEON T.		I	104th Infantry
ROSENTHAL, MOSES (Minute Men)		H	106th Infantry
ROSENTHAL, SAMUEL (Minute Men)		E	107th Infantry
ROSENTHAL, WILLIAM (Minute Men)		H	110th Infantry
ROSENBERG, JOHN		B	129th Infantry
RICH, NATHAN		C	137th Infantry
SALMON, ENOCH C.		K	10th Infantry
SALOMON, ISAAC		D	10th Infantry
SCHLESSINGER, LEWIS		E	10th Infantry
STERN, HENRY	Lieutenant		13th Infantry
Enlisted as private.			
STETTNER, HENRY		K	11th Infantry
SPEYER, JOSEPH		K	13th Infantry
SAMUELSON, AUGUST		B	17th Infantry
STROUSE, W. H.		G	18th Infantry
SIMON, ISAAC D.		K	18th Infantry
SOLOMON, WILLIAM		D	21st Infantry
STEINER, JACOB			24th Infantry
SEGALL, BERNHARD		F	29th Infantry
Wounded at Shiloh and at Grand Gulf.			
STROUSE, MARTIN		A	30th Infantry
SOLOMON, JACOB		C	31st Infantry

NAME.	RANK.	COMPANY.	REGIMENT.
STEIN, EMIL		H	32nd Infantry
SACHS, MAX	Lieutenant	C	32nd Infantry

Killed at Bowling Green, Kentucky. He had refused to surrender to the rebels surrounding him, but succeeded in retarding the enemy's progress long enough to enable his comrades to obtain support and disperse the enemy—one of the most heroic feats during the war.

NAME.	RANK.	COMPANY.	REGIMENT.
SELIG, SIEGMUND	Lieutenant	K	32nd Infantry
SIMON, LEVY		B	34th Infantry
STROUSE, SIMON		K	34th Infantry
SCHOTT, EZEKIEL		F	37th Infantry
SANDERS, AARON		A	38th Infantry
SOLOMON, MICHAEL		B	2nd Cavalry
STROUSS, LEWIS		H	42nd Infantry
STROUSE, JOSEPH		A	44th Infantry
STROUSE, FREDERICK		D	3d Cavalry
STROUSE, DANIEL		B	47th Infantry
SULZER, JACOB		G	53d Infantry
SALMON, WILLIAM C.		C	54th Infantry
STEINER, JACOB		B	58th Infantry
STERN, SAMUEL	Quartermaster		58th Infantry
SIMON, JOSEPH		F	59th Infantry
SCHOENFELD, JACOB		F	60th Infantry
SWARZ, ISAAC		H	60th Infantry
SWARZ, LEVI		H	60th Infantry
SIMON, LOUIS		D	65th Infantry
STEIN, JOSEPH L.		C	69th Infantry
SIMON, JOSEPH, JR.		F	69th Infantry
SIGMONDS, JOEL		I	69th Infantry
SPIEGEL, DANIEL		A	70th Infantry
SOLOMON, JAMES		H	71st Infantry
SCHILLER, DANIEL		C	73d Infantry
SCHILLER, I.			73d Infantry
SAMUELSON, SAMUEL		E	73d Infantry
SOLOMON, LEWIS		C	80th Infantry
SALMON, JACOB N.		I	81st Infantry
SOLOMON, DAVID N.		E	85th Infantry
STERN, JACOB		C	90th Infantry

NAME.	RANK.	COMPANY.	REGIMENT.
SOLOMON, LEVI		D	91st Infantry
SOMMERS, AARON		I	91st Infantry
SHOEMAKER, AARON	Lieutenant		101st Infantry
SPIEGEL, EDWARD	(Minute Men)	A	107th Infantry
SOLOMON, CHARLES	(Minute Men)	I	107th Infantry
SOLOMON JAMES	(Minute Men)	F	112th Infantry
SCHOEN, MAX	Sergeant	G	7th Cavalry
SCHELT, WILLIAM		B	132nd Infantry

Mustered out as Sergeant.

STROUSE, DAVID		G	133d Infantry
STERNS, ISAAC		A	137th Infantry
SHOTT, EZEKIEL	Lieutenant	I	139th Infantry
STEIN, HERMAN		E	142nd Infantry
SOLOMON, PHILIP	Corporal	G	149th Infantry
SIMONS, SOLOMON			5th Battery
SEIXAS, EUGENE			21st Battery
SAMPSON, JOSEPH	Lieutenant		154th Infantry

WATERMAN, SOLOMON	Captain	I	7th Infantry

Promoted for gallantry; killed at the Battle of Port Republic, Virginia, while at the head of his Company.

WOLF, JACOB		C	9th Infantry
WATERMAN, MOSES		I	11th Infantry
WOLF, SAMUEL		K	11th Infantry
WOLF, SAMUEL		M	11th Infantry
WOLF, JOEL	Lieutenant-Colonel		16th Infantry

Lilled at Richmond, Kentucky.

WOLF, DAVID		C	21st Infantry
WIENER, SIMON		F	30th Infantry
WEILER, AARON		G	32nd Infantry
WEIL, BERNARD		K	32nd Infantry
WOLF, SAMUEL		L	8th Cavalry
WOLF, SAMUEL		H	42nd Infantry
WOLF, DAVID		G	48th Infantry
WOLF, AARON		I	53d Infantry
WOLF, LEVI		K	54th Infantry
WISE, ABRAHAM C.		I	65th Infantry

NAME.	RANK.	COMPANY.	REGIMENT.
WOLF, SAMUEL	Lieutenant		73d Infantry
WOLF, LEWIS		F	74th Infantry
WOLF, REUBEN		K	74th Infantry
Killed at Murfordsville.			
WOLF, JACOB		C	87th Infantry
WOLF, LEVI		B	97th Infantry
WATERMAN, HENRY		C	100th Infantry
WOLF, JOSEPH		I	100th Infantry
WATERMAN, HENRY F.	Lieutenant		101st Infantry
Killed at Mission Ridge.			
WOLF, LEVI (Minute Men)		A	106th Infantry
WOLF, MOSES (Minute Men)		E	107th Infantry
WOLF, ISAAC (Minute Men)			107th Infantry
WISE, EMANUEL D.		G	118th Infantry
WOLF, MOSES A.		I	118th Infantry
WOLF, LEVI	Lieutenant		124th Infantry
WOLF, SOLOMON		C	124th Infantry
WOLF, ADAM	Lieutenant		130th Infantry
WOLF, EMANUEL	Corporal	G	138th Infantry
Enlisted as private.			
WISE, ABRAHAM B.		B	10th Cavalry
WOLF, JACOB		A	152nd Infantry
WIESENTHAL, LOUIS	Lieutenant		7th Battery
WOLF, JOSEPH			9th Battery
WATERHOUSE, CHARLES			Brigade Band

IOWA.

NAME.	RANK.	COMPANY.	REGIMENT.

APPEL, ALEXANDER M. Sergeant Major 16th Infantry
Distinguished for saving regimental colors at· Pittsburg Landing; enlisted as private; promoted for gallantry. For fifteen years a member of George G. Meade Post, of the Grand Army of the Republic, honored with the election as Post Commander and in 1893 appointed Assistant Inspector of G. A. R. Posts.

BENNY, WILLIAM B.   C   4th Infantry.
Wounded at Pea Ridge.

BOEHM, S.   Corporal   F   6th Infantry
Enlisted as private.

ELLER, JACOB   I   34th Infantry.

GERSON, N.   6th Cavalry

KLEIN, MAX   1st Cavalry

MEYERS, JACOB   D   10th Infantry
MELLER, ISAAC   D   24th Infantry
MAY, VICTOR
Answered first call for 75,000 men; subsequently enlisted for the war.

NEWBOLD, H.   Colonel   14th Infantry
Killed at Red River.

SANDERS, LEOPOLD   4th Infantry
STRAUSS, CHARLES   C   24th Infantry

KANSAS.

NAME.	RANK.	COMPANY.	REGIMENT.
BONDI, AUGUST	Sergeant	K	5th Cavalry

Wounded three times; discharged; disabled.

FRANK, HENRY			Infantry

LIEBSCHUTZ, ADOLPH		K	9th Cavalry
	Brevet 1st Lieutenant		

Enlisted as private; brevetted for meritorious conduct; wounded at Prairie Grove, Arkansas.

ROSENFELD, ——	Quartermaster		13th Infantry

ULMER, J.		C	8th Cavalry

WITTENBERG, ARNOLD		H	2nd Infantry
WITTENBERG, MARCUS		H	5th Cavalry

Killed on the battlefield.

WOLF, EUGENE			5th Cavalry

Seriously wounded.

WITTENBERG, MORITZ		B	12th Infantry

KENTUCKY.

NAME.	RANK.	COMPANY.	REGIMENT.
DAVIS, HENRY		B	16th Infantry
DAVID, JOSEPH		E	1st Cavalry

FEIST, JACOB	Sergeant	G	1st Infantry

Promoted from private; four years' service.

NAME.	RANK.	COMPANY.	REGIMENT.
HOFFMAN, LAZARUS		B	15th Infantry

Three years' service; wounded at Chickamauga.

HECHT, NOAH		D	23d Infantry
HILP, JACOB			1st Cavalry

LOWENSTEIN, SAMUEL B.		K	1st Cavalry
LEVI, HENRY			{ 23d Infantry and { 2nd United States Cavalry

POLLOCK, ABRAHAM	Quartermaster		21st Infantry
PFEIFER, JOSEPH			21st Infantry

ROTHSCHILD, A	Captain	B	15th Infantry

Enlisted as private; promoted for bravery at Stone River; wounded.

ROSENTHAL, SAMUEL		D	34th Infantry

STRAUS, LOUIS		E	6th Infantry
SCHOENBERG, ELIAS		C	16th Infantry
SPITZER, JOSEPH		C	16th Infantry
SPEYER, HENRY	Captain	D	23d Infantry
SEESSEL, HENRY		I	1st Cavalry
SLAUGHTER, JOSEPH		K	1st Cavalry

TRAUERMAN, BERNARD		F	1st Infantry

ULMAN, GUS.			3d Infantry

WEIL, MOSES			2nd Infantry
WEIL, BERNARD			3d Infantry

LOUISIANA.

NAME.	RANK.	COMPANY.	REGIMENT.
ADLER, ADOLPH			5th Infantry
AARON, MOSES		B	11th Infantry
ABRAHAM, JOSEPH		B	11th Infantry
ASHER, I.		K	11th Infantry
ALEXANDER, J.		K	11th Infantry
ANSELM, JACOB			18th Infantry
Died on the field of battle.			
ASSENHEIMER, DAVID	Captain	F	22nd Infantry
Promoted from the ranks.			
ALBRECHT, ADOLPH		Crescent Heavy Artillery	
ARONSTEIN, JULIUS		Colonel Wingfield's Battery	
BRANDT, J. R.		B	1st Infantry
Served during the war.			
BAUM, G. A.		C	2nd Infantry
BENSON, F.	Corporal	C	3d Infantry
BRANDENSTEIN, M.		K	3d Infantry
Killed at Vicksburg.			
BADT, W.			3d Infantry
BATH, H.			6th Infantry
BENJAMIN, MICHAEL		B	11th Infantry
BARD, JACOB		B	11th Infantry
BLOOM, ABRAHAM		K	11th Infantry
BROWN, LOUIS		K	11th Infantry
BLOOMENSTEIL, ISAAC		K	11th Infantry
BAER, M.		K	11th Infantry
BODENHEIMER, LAZARUS		K	11th Infantry
BLUM, M.		K	11th Infantry
BERNSTEIN, JACOB		K	11th Infantry
BROWN, HERMAN		Washington Artillery	
BLUM, SAMUEL P.	Lieutenant	D	22nd Infantry

NAME.	RANK.	COMPANY.	REGIMENT.
COHN, M.		D	3d Infantry
CASPARI, L.	Captain	G	3d Infantry

Promoted from the ranks.

CALINSKI, P.		H	3d Infantry
COHN, I.		A	5th Infantry
COHEN, J. C.	Captain		5th Infantry

Killed at Chancellorsville.

COHEN, JACOB A.		A	15th Infantry

Killed at Manassas, August 30th, 1862; buried in Jewish cemetery, Richmond, Virginia.

DANZIGER, ISADORE		B	Orleans Guards
DALSHEIMER, ALEXANDER		K	3d Infantry

Taken prisoner at Corinth.

DE MEZA, J. H.			Washington Artillery
ELLIS, LEWIS C. L.			22nd Infantry
FRANKEL FELIX		K	3d Infantry
FLORENCE, HENRY C.			Washington Artillery
FISCHEL, CHARLES		F	8th Infantry
FALK, S.			11th Infantry
FALK, FERDINAND		K	11th Infantry
FRIEDLIENER, BENJAMIN			12th Infantry

Served three years.

FRIEDHEIM, HERMAN		F	12th Infantry

"Joined a company of Confederate soldiers which became Company F of 12th Infantry. No braver man ever fired a gun. At the Battle of Franklin, Tennessee, when there was not a commissioned officer to lead, he as Sergeant, led his company, and passed over the parapet into the Federal intrenchments, and with James A. Platt, a comrade, he was captured and sent to Camp Douglas, in Illinois, and was kept a prisoner until the expiration of the war."—*From a newspaper clipping*.

FLORENCE, LEWIS			Under Colonel Thomas

Killed at Vicksburg.

NAME.	RANK.	COMPANY.	REGIMENT.
GERSHOLT, WILLIAM		B	1st Infantry
GODCHEAUSE, J.		D	11th Infantry
GALT, JACOB		K	11th Infantry
GUSDOFER, MORRIS		K	11th Infantry
GROSS, CHARLES			17th Infantry

HARBY, I. K.   Washington Artillery

HAAS, A. M.   G   1st Infantry

HABER, FERDINAND A.   1st Infantry

HYAMS, S. M.   Lieutenant-Colonel   3d Infantry
Promoted for bravery.   Colonel of Cavalry.

HAAS, HENRY   3d Infantry
Enlisted 1861; served until close of war.

HIRSCH, B.   A   3d Infantry
Killed at battle of Iuka.

HOCHINSKI, W.   D   3d Infantry

HYAMS; J. P.   G   3d Infantry
Promoted for gallant conduct at the battle of Elk Horn.

HIRSCH, H.   K   3d Infantry
Killed at the battle of Iuka.

HELLMAN, H.   A   5th Infantry

HART, ALEXANDER   Major   5th Infantry
Promoted from Non-Commissioned Officer, from 1863,
Colonel, being wounded; commanded regiment; taken
prisoner at Sharpsburg; seriously wounded at Sharpsburg, again at Gettysburg.

HAAS, ISIDORE   E   8th Infantry
Enlisted 1861; served until close of war.

HIRSCHFIELD, BENJAMIN		C	11th Infantry
HIRSCHBERG, FREDERICK		D	11th Infantry
HOLZMAN, BENJAMIN		K	11th Infantry
HYMES, I.	Lieutenant	K	11th Infantry
HYMES, P.		K	11th Infantry
HERZOG, S.		K	11th Infantry
HART, SIDNEY A.			13th Infantry
HIRSCH, N.			18th Infantry

NAME.	RANK.	COMPANY.	REGIMENT.
HERTZ, SOLOMON			22nd Infantry
HERRMANN, H.			41st Infantry
ISAACSON, H. M.	Captain		22nd Washington Artillery
ISRAEL, E. L.			5th Infantry
JACOBS, ——			5th Infantry
JASTRENSKI, LEON			10th Infantry

Promoted for gallantry and daring.

JACOBS, JULIUS A		K	11th Infantry
JACOBS, AARON		B	11th Infantry
JACOBS, ISAAC			22nd Infantry
JONAS, BENJAMIN F.			Fenner's Battery

Served as private until close of war; afterwards United States Senator from Louisiana.

KURSHEEDT, E. I.   2nd Washington Artillery

Promoted for bravery.

KOHLMAN, S.   Watson's Battery

Enlisted at eighteen and served from 1861 until the close of the war.

KLOTZ, ABRAHAM   Donaldsonville Artillery

Served four years.

KLING, GABRIEL   Donaldsonville Artillery

Served four years.

KAHN, GABRIEL		E	2nd Infantry
KAHN, SELIG		A	3d Infantry

Wounded at Vicksburg; served four years.

KAHN, ABRAHAM			8th Infantry
KAHN, MOSES		B	9th Infantry
KAUFMAN, S.			11th Infantry
KAUFMAN, MOSES		K	11th Infantry
KAHN, ISAAC	Sergeant	K	11th Infantry
KAHN, A.		K	11th Infantry
KAHN, JULIUS		K	11th Infantry
KUHN, SAMUEL			20th Infantry

13

NAME.	RANK.	COMPANY.	REGIMENT.
LEVY, EDGAR			1st Washington Artillery
LEVY, LIONEL L.			5th Washington Artillery
LEVY, SIMON			5th Washington Artillery
LOEB, HENRY			Donaldsonville Artillery

Served through the war.

LEVY, EUGENE H.   C   Dreux Battery
  Wounded at Petersburg;
  served through the war.

LEVY, JULIUS H.   (3 brothers) C Dreux Battery
  Served through the war.

LEVY, JOSEPH C.   Lieutenant   1st Infantry
  Killed in leading charge
  at Shiloh.

LEVY, LIONEL C., JR.   Fenner's Battery
Enlisted at fifteen and served until the close of the war.

LEVY, D. C.   1st Infantry
  Killed at Franklin.

LEVY, DAVID C.   1st Infantry
  Distinguished for courage; killed at Shiloh.

LISSO, JULIUS			1st Infantry
LISSO, MARX			1st Infantry
LEVY, JULIAN S.		B	1st Infantry
LABAT, JACOB C.			2nd Infantry
LICHTENSTEIN, WOLF		A	2nd Infantry
LEVY, D.		D	2nd Infantry

LIPMAN, JOSHUA   Orderly Sergeant { G   2nd Infantry / H   5th Infantry
  Wounded at Winchester; subsequently Lieutenant.

LEVY, WILLIAM	Colonel		2nd Infantry
LEVY, HENRY M.			2nd Infantry
LEVY, L.		I	3d Infantry

Enlisted 1861; served until the close of the war;
wounded at Oak Hill.

LYONS, ISAAC L.   Captain   5th Infantry
  Seriously wounded at Malvern Hill, yet served until
  the close of the war.

NAME.	RANK.	COMPANY.	REGIMENT.

LIPPMAN, LEWIS P.　　Captain　　E　　5th Infantry
Enlisted as private; promoted for bravery; killed at
Fredericksburg.

LABAT, DAVID COHEN　　Captain　　5th Infantry
When, in consequence of severe illness, contracted in
the service, resulting in chronic asthma, Captain
Labat was compelled to resign his commission, J.
Bankhead Magruder, the General commanding, endorsed the Captain's letter of resignation with the
words: "Captain Labat's resignation is a loss to the
public service."

LIPPMAN, L. S.　　Lieutenant　　5th Infantry
Killed May 9, 1863; buried at Jewish Cemetery,
Richmond, Virginia.

LEVY, JULIEN　　5th Infantry
Subsequently with "Stonewall" Jackson.

LABAT, JACKSON E.　　5th Infantry
Captured at Vicksburg.

LIPPMAN, LOUIS C.　　E　　5th Infantry

LEVY, ISAAC　　Point Cooper Artillery
Served through the war with a surgeon's discharge in
his pocket; displayed notable bravery at the battle of
Baker's Creek. His willingness, skill and undaunted
courage combined to render him in every respect an
efficient soldier.

LEVY, ALBERT　　Louisiana Guards Artillery
LION, SYLVAIN　　Donaldsonville Artillery
LEVY, E.　　Donaldsville Artillery
LICHTENSTEIN, WILLIAM　　Louisiana Reserves
LANDMAN, BENJAMIN　　K　　11th Reserves
LEVY, DANIEL　　K　　11th Reserves
LOEB, SOLOMON　　E　　11th Infantry
LEVY, H.　　K　　11th Infantry
LEVY, S., JR.　　K　　11th Infantry
LEVY, DAVID C., JR.　　Lieutenant　　H　　13th Infantry
Promoted from private ; Acting Adjutant ; twice
wounded ; killed at Murfreesboro.

LIPPMAN, ASHER　　22d Infantry

NAME.	RANK.	COMPANY.	REGIMENT.
LYONS, DAVID			22nd Infantry
LEVY, AARON	Sergeant	D	30th Infantry

MARKS, HARRY H.   1st Washington Artillery
Fell in charge at Malvern Hill.

MARKS, EDWIN   National Guards Battery
MEERTIF, SAMUEL   1st Infantry
MARCUSS, M.   2d Infantry
MEYER, ADOLPH   3d Infantry
MAYER, J. P.   Corporal   E   3d Infantry
Wounded at Iuka and again at Vicksburg.

MARCH, ——   3d Infantry
MARCH, HENRY   5th Infantry
Promoted to Assistant Quartermaster.

MAAS, MAX   A   5th Infantry
MOSES, PHILIP   5th Infantry
MARKS, HENRY CLAY   Lieutenant   10th Infantry
Killed at Malvern Hill.

MEYER, LEO W.   B   11th Infantry
MEYER, E. H.   E   11th Infantry
MANNHEIMER, B.   G   11th Infantry
MEYER, E.   K   11th Infantry
MOCH, HENRY   K   11th Infantry
Killed in battle.

MEYER, SIEGMUND   17th Infantry
MAGNER, BERNARD   Fenner's Battery
Served through war.

MARKS, WASHINGTON   Major   22nd Infantry
Promoted.

MARKS, D. H.   Captain   22nd Infantry
MARKS, MARION   Lieutenant   22nd Infantry
Promoted from the ranks.

MARKS, HILLEL   E   22nd Infantry
MARKS, LEON R.   Colonel   27th Infantry
Killed at Vicksburg.

MARKS, I.   Boone's Battery

NAME.	RANK.	COMPANY.	REGIMENT.
MILLED, CHARLES D.			Dreux Battalion
MARKS, FREDERICK			Louisiana Guard Artillery
MOOSE, CHARLES			Donaldsonville Artillery
MEYER, ADOLPH	Hon. General		

NEWMAN, A.		C	3d Infantry

Captured at Corinth.

NATHAN, WOLF			8th Infantry
NATHAN, M.		B	9th Infantry
NEWMAN, HENRY		G	11th Infantry

Wounded at Murfreesboro

NEWMAN, ——	Major		14th Infantry
NATHAN, SAMUEL			22d Infantry

OCHS, LOUIS		B	9th Infantry
OPPENHEIMER, BENJAMIN			22d Infantry

PHILLIPS, EDWARD			3d Infantry

ROSENFIELD, JULIUS			7th Infantry
ROSENSTEIN, MATHIAS			8th Infantry
REISS, ALEXANDER		G	11th Infantry
REISS, GUSTAVE		G	11th Infantry
ROSE, EMANUEL			27th Infantry
REESE, ABRAHAM	Sergeant		Crescent Infantry

Served four years.

SAMUEL, M.		E	2d Infantry

Enlisted 1861; served until close of war.

SILBANAGEL, BENJAMIN		B	3d Infantry
SINGER, LOUIS		F	3d Infantry

Killed at Vicksburg.

SAMPSON, ED.			5th Infantry

Killed at Gaines' Mills.

SEIXAS, J. MADISON			5th Washington Artillery

Served through war.

STRAUS, JOSEPH	Lieutenant	B	11th Infantry
STRASSER, EPHRAIM		B	11th Infantry

NAME.	RANK.	COMPANY.	REGIMENT.
SELIGMAN, J.	Sergeant	K	11th Infantry
SELIGMAN, I.		K	11th Infantry
SIMON, HENRY		K	11th Infantry
STRAUSS, I.		K	11th Infantry
STERN, ——	Captain	B	14th Infantry
SARTARIUS, PHILIP			14th Infantry
SCHLENKER, JACOB			17th Infantry
STEIN, DANIEL			17th Infantry
STRAUSS, NAGEL			21st Artillery
SCHLENKER, ALEXANDER	Quartermaster's Department North		
STROMEYER, GEORGE		F	22nd Infantry
SCHEUER, JONATHAN		Donaldsonville Artillery	

Wounded; died at Richmond during the war; buried
in Jewish Cemetery, Richmond, Virginia.

TAYLOR, RICHARD (DICK)			"Louisiana Tigers"

UNGER, MEYER		F	1st Infantry
UNGER, EMANUEL		E	11th Infantry

WEIL, ALEXANDER		I	2d Infantry

Wounded at Antietam while trying to recover the
regiment's flag; wounded seriously at Gettysburg and
captured.

WINNER, MARKS		C	3d Infantry
WOLF, JOSEPH		D	3d Infantry
WEIL, SAMUEL			3d Cavalry
WEINBERG, SELIG			5th Infantry
WEINBERG, SOLOMON			6th Infantry
WAGNER, G			8th Infantry
WITKOWSKY, LOUIS		B	9th Infantry
WEISS, B.		B	9th Infantry
WAGNER, LOUIS		B	9th Infantry
WILCUISKI, BENJAMIN		B	11th Infantry
WOLFSOHN, ELIAS		B	11th Infantry
WOLFF, LEON		B	11th Infantry
WEISS, SOLOMON		B	11th Infantry
WECHSLER, A.		K	11th Infantry
WEIL, NATHAN		K	11th Infantry

NAME.	RANK.	COMPANY.	REGIMENT.
WOLFF, ISAAC		K	11th Infantry
WECHLER, S.		K	11th Infantry

Killed in battle.

NAME.	RANK.	COMPANY.	REGIMENT.
WEIL, GABRIEL		K	11th Infantry
WORKUM, DAVID J.			13th Infantry
WEIL, ——	Major		14th Infantry
WOLFF, MOSES			Washington Artillery
WOLFF, C.			Pouinte Coupee Infantry

ZARK, JULIUS			7th Infantry

Killed in skirmish,; buried at Jewish Cemetery, Richmond, Virginia.

ZIMMERN, J.		F	22nd Infantry

MAINE.

NAME.	RANK.	COMPANY.	REGIMENT.
GOLDMAN, A.	Captain		17th Infantry

MARYLAND.

NAME.	RANK.	COMPANY.	REGIMENT.

BLUMENBERG, LEOPOLD, Brevet Brigadier-General, U. S. V.

5th Maryland Infantry

After the attack on Fort Sumter he helped to organize the 5th regiment, Maryland Volunteers, of which he was appointed Major. He served near Hampton Roads after which he was attached to Mansfield's Corps and participated in the Peninsular Campaign, and subsequently in Maryland, where his regiment was engaged in the battle of Antietam, under his command. Here he was shot in the thigh and confined to his bed for many months. Being disabled for further military duty President Lincoln appointed him Provost Marshal of the 3d Maryland District. President Johnson subsequently promoted him to the rank of Brevet Brigadier-General, U. S. Volunteers.

It may not prove inappropriate to mention here the remarks made by William P. Wood, Esq., one of Washington's best known gentlemen, with reference to the late General Blumenberg in a communication to the present writer:

" I was intimate with General Leopold Blumenberg, who commanded in person the 5th Regiment, Maryland Volunteers; you and others of his friends are familiar with the deserved encomiums passed upon that gallant and kind-hearted American Jew, who received terrible wounds in leading his regiment on the battle-field of Antietam, and of which wounds he died after having served in several important positions in Baltimore.

"Without being either Christian or Jew, I am familiar with many heroes of your faith, and believe in according honor to whom honor is due. Hoping your work will meet with the success which I believe the subject-matter warrants, I am

Yours truly,

(Signed)   WILLIAM P. WOOD."

NAME.	RANK.	COMPANY.	REGIMENT.
FELDSTEIN, S.			2nd Infantry
GROSS, A. F.			2nd Infantry
SEEMAN, JULIUS D.		A	2nd Infantry
STERN, LIL.			1st Cavalry
UHLFELDER, SAMUEL		G	3d Cavalry

Wounded at Gettysburg.

WHITE, HARMAN   2nd Cavalry

Ordered on detailed service on staff of General Siegel.

MASSACHUSETTS.

NAME.	RANK.	COMPANY.	REGIMENT.
ASH, WILLIAM	Corporal	D	5th Infantry
ADLER, JOSEPH			2nd Cavalry

Served three years.

NAME.	RANK.	COMPANY.	REGIMENT.
ABRAHAM, CHARLES		B	19th Infantry
ASH, DAVID B.		B	19th Infantry
ABRAHAM, BENJAMIN		I	21st Infantry
ABRAHAMS, DAVID		F	22nd Infantry
ASH, JACOB		K	55th Infantry
BOERNSTEIN, HENRY		B	42nd Infantry
BLOOM, JULIUS R.		A	44th Infantry
BLUMENTHAL, ROBERT		B	3d Cavalry
BAUMGARTEN, MORRIS		L	4th Cavalry
BOERNSTEIN, MAYER			21st Infantry
BLUMENTHAL, HENRY		H	30th Infantry
BRAND, FREDERICK		F	35th Infantry
BLOOM, JOSEPH		Veteran Reserve Corps	
COHN, JULIUS		K	1st Infantry
COHEN, ABRAHAM			20th Infantry
COHEN, JOSEPH			2qth Infantry
COHEN, WILLIAM		B	21st Infantry
COHN, DAVID		F	29th Infantry
COHN, WILLIAM	Corporal	B	56th Infantry
DESSAUER, JOHN	Corporal		3d Cavalry
DIAS, DAVID		G	22nd Infantry
DIAS, EMANUEL		G	22nd Infantry
DIAS, SAMUEL A.		A	38th Infantry

Served three years.

NAME.	RANK.	COMPANY.	REGIMENT.
DIAS, EMANUEL	Corporal	C	3d Heavy Artillery

NAME.	RANK.	COMPANY.	REGIMENT.
EPHRAIM, JOSEPH H.		K	31st Infantry
Served four years.			
EMANUEL, MICHAEL.		K	32nd Infantry
FRIEND, JOEL M.		A	50th Infantry
FRIEND, ELLIS A.			10th Battalion
FRANKLE, JONAS	Brevet Brigadier-General		17th Infantry
Promoted from Major.			
FELDMAN, JULIUS	Sergeant	F	2nd Cavalry
FRANK ERNST			2nd Cavalry
FRIEDMAN, LEWIS		I	30th Infantry
FRIEND, SOLOMON		K	30th Infantry
FRIEDMAN, GOTTLIEB			4th Cavalry
GANS, CHARLES		K	4th Cavalry
GUGGENHEIMER, SAMUEL		A	13th Infantry
GOLDBERG, JACOB		C	20th Infantry
Died in the service.			
GLAZIER, JAMES E.		F	23d Infantry
Served three years.			
GOLDSMITH, ALBERT	Corporal	C	30th Infantry
GUGGENHEIMER, SAMUEL			32nd Infantry
GERSHEL, MANHEIM	Corporal	G	34th Infantry
GOLDSMITH, BENJAMIN F.		A	59th Infantry
GOTTLIEB, JOSEPH		F	4th Infantry
GOLDSMITH, DANIEL, JR.		27th unattached company	
GOLDSMITH, DANIEL			1st Heavy Artillery
HESS, HENRY		K	1st Infantry
HART, ISAAC C.		L	4th Infantry
HART, SAMUEL S.		D	1st Heavy Artillery
Served three years.			
HERRMAN, JULIUS		C	3d Heavy Artillery
HAMMERSLOUGH, EDWARD			1st Cavalry
HART, DANIEL C.		F	1st Cavalry
HARTMAN, I.		M	3d Cavalry
HERZ, JOSEPH		B	20th Infantry
HELLER, LOUIS		B	20th Infantry

NAME.	RANK.	COMPANY.	REGIMENT.
HART, ISAAC C.		D	23d Infantry
HART, DAVID		D	27th Infantry
Served three years.			
HART, BERNARD		D	28th Infantry
HIRSCH, JACOB		A	35th Infantry
HARRIS, MOSES		F	54th Infantry
HART, JOSEPH		A	56th Infantry
HART, DAVID A.		K	57th Infantry
Died in the service.			
HART, DANIEL			Veteran Reserve Corps
HOFMAN, JACOB			Veteran Reserve Corps
HOFMAN, JOSEPH			Veteran Reserve Corps
HERZBERG, ADOLPH			
ISAACS, CHARLES E.		B	6th Infantry
ISAACS, JOSEPH		K	4th Heavy Artillery
ISAACS, JOHN		E	11th Infantry
ISAAC, ALEXANDER		B	12th Infantry
Killed at Antietam.			
ISAAC, W. H.			Veteran Reserve Corps
JACOBS, GUSTAV		G	18th Infantry
Died in the service.			
JOSEPH, EMANUEL		C	20th Infantry
JACOBY, FERDINAND		G	25th Infantry
JACOBSON, HENRY		H	29th Infantry
JOSEPH, JOSEPH M.			Veteran Reserve Corps
JOEL, HENRY			3d Heavy Artillery
JACOB, JOSEPH		M	3d Cavalry
JOSEPH, HENRY			6th Battery
JACOBS, HENRY	Corporal		35th Infantry
JACOBS, JACOB			59th Infantry
KOHN, HENRY	Corporal	F	3d Infantry
KAUFMAN, LEOPOLD			6th Battalion
Served three years.			
KUHN, ISRAEL		D	26th Infantry
Served three years.			

NAME.	RANK.	COMPANY.	REGIMENT.
KUHN, FREDERICK		C	32nd Infantry
KLEIN, JULIUS		G	32nd Infantry
KOWALTZKI, LUDWIG		H	35th Infantry
KOHLER, JACOB		Veteran Reserve Corps	
KARPELES, LEOPOLD	Color Sergeant	E	57th Infantry

Enlisted September, 1862 in Company A, 46th Regiment. After expiration of service re-enlisted in Company E, 57th Massachusetts, 1865. He was wounded at the Battle of North Anna River (Wilderness), but rejoined his regiment after a short time, though unable to walk without the aid of a cane, and was finally disabled, totally, in December, 1864, at Petersburg.

Sergeant Karpeles received a medal of honor from Congress for distinguished services in the Battle of the Wilderness, May 8, 1864, he having saved a part of the army from being captured during a retreat in disorder by rallying troops around his colors, thereby checking the enemy's pursuit."

> PITTSFIELD, MASS.,
> April 10, 1870.

This is to certify that Leopold Karpeles was a soldier under my command during part of the late war. My estimation of his good qualities may be judged from the fact that I entrusted him the *colors* of the 57th Massachusetts Infantry.

He was always faithful in the discharge of his duties as a soldier, and if my certificate to that effect can assist him in getting employment in some position for which he is qualified, I very gladly give it.

> W. F. BARTLETT,
> Late Brigadier-General, U. S. V.,
> Brevet Major-General.

> CAMP OF THE 46TH REGIMENT M. V. M.
> • New Berne, N. C., May 17, 1863.

This is to certify that Mr. Leopold Karpeles is a Corporal of Company A of this regiment. * * * * In the battles of Kingston, Whitehall and Goldsborough he bore the State colors. The promptness with which he came upon the line of battle, and the firmness with which he stood his ground, though his flag was several times pierced by the bullets of the enemy, were so conspicuous as to be the subject of remark and commendation.

I have no hesitation in endorsing him as a man who in any position would only have to know his duty, and he would discharge it to the best of his ability.

(Signed)   S. B. SPOONER,
Major 46th Regiment, Massachusetts V. M.

I very readily give my testimonial to the efficiency and soldierly qualities of L. Karpeles, within named, having frequently remarked and observed his alertness, promptness and faithfulness to duty.

(Signed)   W. S. SHURTLESS.
Colonel Commanding.

I cheerfully concur in the above.

(Signed)   S. B. WALKLEY,
Lieutenant-Colonel 46th Regiment, M. V. M.

FORT GIBSON, INDIAN TERRITORY.
June 1, 1888.

MY DEAR OLD COMRADE AND FRIEND:

Your letter of the 13th of May just received, and I hasten to reply. I was glad to hear from you and glad to find you still on the shores of mortality, where our numbers are fast diminishing. Our duty now lies in planting the principles and memory of the great struggle in the hearts of generations to follow us, endear to them the old flag that you carried from the Wilderness to North Anna, so gallantly and faithfully, and teach them to love their country which was saved at such a sacrifice.

Yes, Karpeles, I well remember you at the Battle of North Anna; I remember that you carried the colors of the glorious old "57th," far beyond any other colors; your bravery was conspicuous. I remember that you fell, badly wounded; another Sergeant was sent to take the colors from you but you refused to give them up but carried them forward until loss of blood, or another wound, I have forgotten which, compelled you to give them into the hands of another. I remember all of this distinctly as I felt justly proud of you as a Sergeant of Company ''E.'' *   *   *   *

Please write me and accept my very best wishes.

Sincerely and fraternally yours,

JOHN ANDERSON,

1st Lieutenant, 18th Infantry,

U. S. Army.

NAME.	RANK.	COMPANY.	REGIMENT.
LEVY, WILLIAM		A	10th Infantry
LEHMIER, LOUIS		E	11th Infantry
Served three years.			
LIPPMAN, JOHN W.		E	11th Infantry
Died in service.			
LEHMAN, AARON W.		K	11th Infantry
LOESTEIN, SIMON		B	20th Infantry
LEON, ALEXANDER		C	20th Infantry
LOWENTHAL, LOUIS		F	20th Infantry
LYON, MARCUS E.		I	24th Infantry
Killed at Deep Run, Virginia.			
LEVY, DAVID		H	26th Infantry
LIPPMAN, CARL N.		K	27th Infantry
LEHMAN, ALBERT		E	28th Infantry
LEVIN, SIMON	Corporal	H	30th Infantry
LEVI, RAPHAEL		I	30th Infantry
LEO, LOUIS	Corporal		35th Infantry
LEVY, JOSEPH			35th Infantry
LEVY, ADOLPH M.		F	38th Infantry
Served three years.			
LEVINS, MORRIS		E	39th Infantry
Served three years.			
LYON, JULIUS M.	Lieutenant	H	42nd Infantry
LYON, CHARLES F		F	42nd Infantry
LEVY, MORRIS		C	43d Infantry
LEO, EUGENE		A	44th Infantry

NAME.	RANK.	COMPANY.	REGIMENT.
LEVY, DAVID			13th Battalion
LEVI, SAMUEL			2nd Heavy Artillery
LEOPOLD, HENRY A.	Corporal	H	1st Cavalry
LYON, DANIEL		L	4th Cavalry
LEVI, SAMUEL		F	56th Infantry
Killed at Spottsylvania.			
LEWIN, W. H.		F	58th Infantry
Died in the service.			
LEOPOLD, AUGUST			Veteran Reserve Corps
LEVY, BERNARD H.			Veteran Reserve Corps
LOEBS, JACOB			Veteran Reserve Corps
MARKS, EDWARD			11th Infantry
MAY, SIMON	Sergeant	D	21st Infantry
MARCUS, HERMAN		H	30th Infantry
MEIER, JACOB		C	20th Infantry
MAYER, CHARLES		A	30th Infantry
MARKS, HENRY			1st Heavy Artillery
MAIER, ADOLPH			Veteran Reserve Corps
NUSSBAUM, LEVI		D	47th Infantry
NATHAN, JOSEPH		B	5th Cavalry
OCHS, JOSEPH A.		B	45th Infantry
ROSE, BENJAMIN		C	8th Infantry
ROSE, ELI		18th	Unattached company
ROSE, BENJAMIN, JR.		27th	Unattached company
ROSENAU, HENRY			3d Cavalry
Died in the service.			
ROSENTHAL, JACOB		L	4th Cavalry
ROSE, ARNOLD			13th Infantry
ROSENTHAL, JOHN	Corporal	B	40th Infantry
RICH, REUBEN		H	56th Infantry
ROSE, SAMUEL			Veteran Reserve Corps
ROSE, ABRAHAM			Veteran Reserve Corps

NAME.	RANK.	COMPANY.	REGIMENT.
SPIEGEL, CHARLES			2nd Infantry
SOLOMON, MORRIS	Sergeant	A	2nd Infantry
SOLOMON, HENRY	Sergeant	K	10th Infantry
SIMONS, WOLF			10th Infantry
SIMON, FREDERICK		E	29th Infantry
SOMMER, ADOLPH			35th Infantry
STEINER, FERDINAND	Corporal	I	35th Infantry
STEINGARDT, BENJAMIN			38th Infantry
STEINGARDT, DANIEL			38th Infantry
STEINGARDT, JOSEPH			38th Infantry
SAMUELS, SAMUEL D.			7th unattached Company
SAMUEL, JOSEPH			7th unattached Company
SILBERMAN, BARNEY		A	47th Infantry
SIMON, JOHN T.	Corporal	A	50th Infantry
Died in the service.			
STEINMAN, LOUIS		B	2nd Heavy Artillery
SAMUEL, JOSEPH	Sergeant	K	4th Heavy Artillery
SAMUELS, SAMUEL D.		K	4th Heavy Artillery
SOLOMON, JOSEPH A.		D	5th Cavalry
SIMON, DANIEL J.	Sergeant	B	57th Infantry
SAMUEL, SOLOMON			8th Battalion Light Artillery
VOGEL, HENRY		C	20th Infantry
VOGEL, LOUIS		I	35th Infantry
VOGEL, FERDINAND		K	47th Infantry
WATERMAN, FRANK		H	5th Infantry
WOLF, SAMUEL		C	3d Cavalry
WATERMAN, FRANKLIN		H	15th Infantry
Died in the service.			
WOLF, JOSEPH	Sergeant	C	20th Infantry
Died of wounds.			
WOLF, MICHAEL			20th Infantry
Killed at Cold Harbor.			
WATERMAN, BENJAMIN		A	24th Infantry
WEISS, JACOB		C	24th Infantry
Served four years.			

NAME.	RANK.	COMPANY.	REGIMENT.
WEISS, JOSEPH		D	24th Infantry
WATERMAN, CHARLES	Sergeant	D	28th Infantry
WATERMAN, FRANKLIN		F	34th Infantry
WEISS, REUBEN		Veteran Reserve Corps	

MICHIGAN.

NAME.	RANK.	COMPANY.	REGIMENT.
ASH, MICHAEL		I	1st Infantry
BENJAMIN, H.		C	4th Cavalry
Died in the service.			
BARLOW, ADOLPH		C	5th Infantry
BROWN, MOSES		E	8th Infantry
Served three years.			
BUSH, LEVI		K	9th Cavalry
Died in the service.			
BUSH, SIMEON		M	9th Cavalry
Died in the service.			
BLUM, SIMEON			14th Battery
COHEN, CHARLES		I	10th Cavalry
FUCHS, DAVID		C	1st Infantry
FRANK, SIMEON H.	Lieutenant	K	1st Infantry
FREUND, JOSEPH		A	2nd Infantry
Transferred to Veteran Reserve Corps.			
FRIEDENBERG, JOSEPH		H	6th Infantry
Died in the service.			
FRIEDENBERG, CHARLES A.		E	8th Infantry
Re-enlisted as Veteran.			
FOX, J. H.		E	11th Infantry
FRIEDENBURG, ELYAH		I	22nd Infantry
FRANK, A.			1st Cavalry

14

NAME.	RANK.	COMPANY.	REGIMENT.
FRIEDENBERG, ALBERT		G	5th Cavalry
FRIEDENBERG, BENJAMIN		C	7th Cavalry

Died in the service.

| FRANK, SIMON H. | 1st Lieutenant | G | 1st Light Artillery |

Enlisted as private in K 1st Infantry; re-enlisted in Battery G; served as non-commissioned officer until promoted to 1st Lieutenant.

| FRIEDLANDER, CHARLES | | H | 1st Light Artillery |
| FRIEDLANDER, CHARLES | | H | 1st Light Artillery |

| GOLDSMITH, GUSTAV | | F | 1st Infantry |
| GOODMAN, DAVID | | H | 8th Infantry |

Re-enlisted as Veteran.

GOODHEART, JACOB		A	9th Infantry
GOLDSMITH, ——	Captain	17th Infantry Reserve
GANS, JACOB		D	8th Cavalry
GOODMAN, FRANK		I	8th Cavalry

| HOFMAN, MOSES | | A | 1st Infantry |

Died of wounds.

HOFMAN, MOSES		G	1st Infantry
HOFMAN, JACOB		K	1st Infantry
HEINE, JULIUS		F	2nd Infantry
HOFMAN, S.			4th Infantry
HOFMAN, S.			4th Infantry
HOFMAN, F.		F	4th Infantry
HERRMAN, MARK		G	9th Infantry
HARRIS, LIONEL W.		B	10th Infantry
HELLER, EMIL		A	14th Infantry
HESS, JOSEPH		D	16th Infantry

Served three years.

HOFMAN, D.			17th Infantry
HATTENDORF, CHARLES		C	3d Cavalry
HAMBURG, FREDERICK		L	11th Cavalry

| JONAS, H. | | G | 22d Infantry |
| JONAS, JULIUS | | G | 22d Infantry |

NAME.	RANK.	COMPANY.	REGIMENT.
KATZ, ISAAC		E	1st Infantry
KLEIN, SAMUEL		C	2nd Infantry
KLEIN, JACOB		C	3d Infantry
KLEIN, JACOB		I	5th Infantry
KLEIN, H.			8th Infantry

Killed in action.

KAUFMAN, SIMPSON		E	8th Infantry
KING, JOSEPH		I	10th Infantry
KLEIN, DAVID		E	26th Infantry

Died in the service.

KLEIN, LOUIS		F	9th Cavalry
KRONBERG, AUGUST		B	10th Cavalry

Transferred to Veteran Reserve Corps.

KOHN, WILLIAM		G	1st Light Artillery
KOHN, M.		L	1st Light Artillery
KLEIN, EMANUEL			14th Battery

LAZARUS, DANIEL		E	3d Infantry
LEVINGSTON, MEYER		F	3d Infantry

Killed on the field of battle.

LIMBERGER, WILLIAM E.		F	4th Infantry
LYON, SOLOMON T.	Captain		5th Infantry
LYON, EPHRAIM W.	Major		8th Infantry
LYON, ISAAC C.		A	9th Infantry

Transferred to Veteran Reserve Corps.

LEVY, NATHAN	1st Lieutenant		10th Infantry

Promoted from 2nd Lieutenant.

LYONS, ISAAC B.		G	11th Infantry
LYON, ASHER		G	13th Infantry
LEVY, D.		E	16th Infantry
LYON, DAVID		H	22nd Infantry

Died in the service.

LYON, HENRY J.		H	22nd Infantry

Died in the service.

LYON, DAVID		L	1st Light Artillery

Died in the service.

LEWIS, LEVI		K	2nd Cavalry

NAME.	RANK.	COMPANY.	REGIMENT.
LEVY, NATHAN	Lieutenant		3d Cavalry
LYON, AARON D.		F	5th Cavalry

Captured; died in Andersonville Prison.

LEWIS, ABRAHAM		K	5th Cavalry
LYON, D.			8th Cavalry
LEVY, JOHN C.		H	10th Cavalry
LYON, MOSES F.		I	10th Cavalry

MOSES, HENRY		F	4th Infantry
MEYER, JOSEPH		I	7th Infantry
MARK, LEOPOLD			9th Infantry
MARK, ISAAC		C	12th Infantry

Re-enlisted as veteran.

MANDEL, AUGUST		G	22nd Infantry

Transferred to Veteran Reserve Corps.

MANDEL, JULIUS		G	22nd Infantry
MANDEL, LOUIS		G	22nd Infantry

Died in the service.

MANN, JOSEPH			27th Infantry

Killed at Cold Harbor.

MANDEL, CHARLES			1st Engineers

Served three years.

MAYER, SIMON			1st Engineers
MANN, SOLOMON		A	1st Light Artillery
MANN, ELI		G	1st Light Artillery
MEYERS, ELISHA		G	1st Light Artillery
MAYER, FREDERICK		G	1st Light Artillery
MAYER, BENJAMIN		K	1st Light Artillery
MEYER, JOSEPH		A	8th Cavalry

Transferred to Veteran Reserve Corps.

MOCK, LEOPOLD			9th Cavalry
MANN, S.			10th Cavalry
MANN, DAVID		M	82nd Cavalry

Died in the service.

NATHAM, LEWIS W.		B	9th Infantry
NATHAN, C.		E	7th Cavalry

NAME.	RANK.	COMPANY.	REGIMENT.
NATHANS, LEWIS		B	9th Cavalry
Re-enlisted as Veteran.			
NATHAN, CHARLES W.			16th Cavalry
Killed at Bull Run.			
ROTHSCHILD, LEVI		I	2nd Infantry
Killed at Petersburg, Virginia.			
ROSENFELD, JOHN		H	3d Infantry
Died in the service.			
ROSE, MOSES		C	4th Infantry
Died in the service.			
RICE, NATHAN H.		K	5th Infantry
ROSENBERG, CORNELIUS		C	10th Infantry
Died in the service.			
RICH, ANSCHEL		B	11th Infantry
RICH, HENRY		K	27th Infantry
Killed at Petersburg, Virginia.			
RICH, DAVID		A	1st Cavalry
Served three years.			
RICH, DAVID		H	1st Cavalry
Died in the service.			
ROSENBERG, C.		C	5th Cavalry
STERNBERG, NATHAN		K	1st Infantry
STRAUS, LEVI		B	5th Infantry
SCHWAB, FRANK		K	5th Infantry
STEIN, FREDERICK		K	5th Infantry
Re-enlisted as Veteran.			
STRAUS, JACOB		E	9th Infantry
STEIN, JOSEPH		H	9th Infantry
Re-enlisted as Veteran.			
SOLOMON, JOHN		G	13th Infantry
STEIN, DANIEL		G	17th Infantry
Killed at Spottsylvania.			
STERN, ADAM		B	1st Light Artillery
STEIN, JACOB C.		A	2nd Cavalry
Died in the service.			

NAME.	RANK.	COMPANY.	REGIMENT.
SOLOMON, JOSHUA		K	3d Cavalry

Transferred to Veteran Reserve Corps.

SACHS, HENRY		F	4th Cavalry
SOMMERS, JOSEPH		K	8th Cavalry
SCHONEMAN, SAMUEL		K	8th Cavalry
SAMPSON, JOEL		K	9th Cavalry
SAMPSON A.		K	9th Cavalry
VOGEL, JACOB		G	27th Infantry
WERTHEIMER, SIMON			1st Infantry
WEINBERG, REUBEN		E	11th Infantry
WEINBERG, WILLIAM		E	11th Infantry
WEILER, FRANK J.		I	6th Cavalry

MISSISSIPPI.

NAME.	RANK.	COMPANY.	REGIMENT.
ADLER, MOSES		A	10th Infantry
ADAMS, ——	Colonel		2d Cavalry
ASH, JULIUS		D	28th Cavalry
AXMAN, ——			Kit Mott's Regiment
AUERBACH, MORRIS			17th Drum Corps
BRADINSKY, ——	Lieutenant		1st Infantry

Served until close of war.

BAUM, DANIEL		I	13th Infantry
BLOOM, RAPHAEL		G	16th Infantry
BERNHEIM, MORRIS F.	Quartermaster Sergeant		17th Infantry

Promoted from private.

BRUNN, ADOLPH		C	18th Infantry
BARUCH, SIMON, DR., Brigade Surgeon			21st Infantry

Appointed to General Barkdale's Division; subsequently Chief Surgeon of Confederate Hospitals in North Carolina.

NAME.	RANK.	COMPANY.	REGIMENT.

BERKSON, THEODORE   A   1st Artillery
    Captured; when exchanged rejoined his regiment.

BLYTH, ——   Mississippi Battalion

CAHN, WILLIAM   G   16th Infantry

DREYFUS, H.   4th Infantry
    Enlisted 1861.

DE YOUNG, SIMON H.   4th Infantry

DRYER, H.   Sergeant-Major   33d Infantry
    Served until close of war.

ETTINGER, JOSEPH   2nd Infantry
    Died from wounds received at Murfreesboro.

EISEMAN, GUS.   Corporal   12th Infantry
    Killed; buried at Jewish Cemetery, Richmond, Virginia.

EICHEL, AARON   G   16th Infantry

EISENMAN, C.   18th Infantry
    Killed at Gaines' Mills, Virginia.

ELSON, JULIUS   Mississippi Sharp-shooters

FRANK, SA.   Major   12th Infantry
    Promoted from the ranks.

FOLTZ, F.   16th Infantry
    Killed; buried at Jewish Cemetery, Richmond, Virginia.

FRANKENTHAL, MAX   A   16th Infantry

FOLTZ, S.   A   16th Infantry

FOLTZ, THEO.   16th Infantry
    Killed at Sharpsburg.

FRAUENHELD, ——   A   16th Infantry

FORSCHHEIMER, B.   Warden Artillery

FRANK, THEODORE   Steward's Cavalry

FARBUSH, ——   Washington Cavalry

GROSS, CHARLES L.   K   13th Infantry

GATTMAN, JACOB   C   18th Infantry

NAME.	RANK.	COMPANY.	REGIMENT.
GOODMAN, LOUIS		H	38th Infantry

Served two years.

GERSON, A.		K	44th Infantry
GROSS, EMIL.		K	44th Infantry

Lost a leg at Shiloh.

GUSDOFER, MARX			Warren's Dragoons
GUSDOFER, I.			Warren's Dragoons

HIRSCH, LEOPOLD			9th Infantry
HOLBERG, L.		F	11th Infantry

Wounded at Manassas.

HANSMAN, M.		I	11th Infantry
HORATMEL, LOUIS			12th Infantry
HESSER, LOUIS		H	15th Infantry

Wounded at Corinth.

HYMAN, JACOB		A	16th Infantry
HILLER, JONAS		A	16th Infantry
HERMAN, J.		A	16th Infantry
HILLER, WILLIAM		A	16th Infantry
HILLER, MAX.		A	16th Infantry
HAZEN, HYMAN		I	16th Infantry

Killed at Fredericksburg.

HART, M.		A	16th Infantry
HART, P.		A	16th Infantry
HILL, NATHAN		A	16th Infantry
HILLER, NATHAN		A	17th Infantry
HAAS, SAMUEL			18th Infantry

Killed at Shiloh.

HART, JOSEPH		K	18th Infantry
HAVERMAN, GABRIEL		K	44th Infantry
HIRSCH, JOSEPH			Barnes' Battery
HAYES, E. P.		H	Conner Battery
HESSER, LEO	Captain		Blight's Battery Sharpshooters

Promoted at battle of Chickamauga from private.

HOLBERG, JACOB			1st Cavalry
HAAS, S.			2nd Cavalry
HILBORN, B.		A	16th Cavalry

NAME.	RANK.	COMPANY.	REGIMENT.
HYMAN, B.		A	16th Cavalry
HILLER, M.		A	16th Cavalry
JACOBS, VICTOR			11th Infantry
JOEL, MORDECAI			18th Infantry
JOEL, MOSES		K	18th Infantry
JONAS, CHARLES H.			Barksdale Infantry
JONAS, JULIAN			Barksdale Infantry
JONAS, HON. B. F.	(Five brothers)		Louisiana Infantry
JONAS, S. A.	Major		Barksdale Infantry
JONAS, EDWARD			(*50th Illinois Infantry*)
KLAUS, A.		C	11th Infantry
KRAUS, FREDERICK		A	12th Infantry
KAHN, C. J.		G	16th Infantry
KAUFMAN, W. M.		G	16th Infantry
KAUFMAN, W.		G	16th Infantry
KAHN, GABRIEL		K	16th Infantry
KAUFMAN, I.		A	16th Infantry
KAHN, GUSTAVUS			16th Infantry

Killed; buried in Jewish cemetery, Richmond, Virginia.

NAME.	RANK.	COMPANY.	REGIMENT.
KAUFMAN, HERMAN		C	18th Infantry
KUHN, J.		D	38th Infantry
LOWENSTEIN, LEOPOLD			8th Infantry
LOWENSTEIN, M.		C	8th Infantry
LEVY, OSCAR S.			10th Infantry

Enlisted 1861; subsequently attached to Army Signal Corps.

NAME.	RANK.	COMPANY.	REGIMENT.
LEVENS, LOUIS			11th Infantry
LEVY, ED.			12th Infantry
LOEB, ISIDORE			12th Infantry
LINCOLN, S.			12th Infantry
LOEB, SAMUEL			13th Infantry
LEVY, SOLOMON		D	13th Infantry
LOEB, SAMUEL		K	13th Infantry
LEVY, ABRAHAM			14th Infantry
LICHENSTEIN, ISAAC		A	16th Infantry

NAME.	RANK.	COMPANY.	REGIMENT.
LICHENSTEIN, SIMON		A	16th Infantry
LEVY, MOSES		G	16th Infantry

Killed May 31, 1862; buried in Jewish cemetery, Richmond, Virginia.

LONETHEIM, A. J.		G	17th Infantry

Discharged for disability.

LEVY, S.		K	18th Infantry
LOEB, A		D	38th Infantry
LORSCH, ADOLPH		K	44th Infantry
LOWENHAUPT, BENJAMIN			28th Cavalry
LEHMAN, H. F.		D	28th Cavalry
LECINSKI, E. L.		H	28th Cavalry
LEE, SEYMOUR			Washington Cavalry
LEVY, DANIEL S.		G	1st Light Artillery
LOWENSTEIN, MARX		C	8th Reserves
LEVY, ISRAEL		B	Ward's Legion
LEVINSON, A.		B	Ward's Legion
LEVINSON, PAUL		B	Ward's Legion
LOTTERHOSS, PHILIP		F	Wither's Artillery

Enlisted at eighteen years of age; served with conspicuous bravery; killed at Kenesaw Mountain.

LOUCHEIM, ABRAHAM			17th Regiment Drum Corps
LEVY, J. C.			17th Drum Corps

MOSES, I. O.		G	2nd Infantry
MANSBACH, H. H.			9th Infantry

Enlisted 1861; promoted at Greensboro.

MAYER, D.			10th Infantry
MYERS, ——	Captain		14th Infantry

Promoted from the ranks.

MOOSER, ABRAHAM		H	15th Infantry

Wounded four times at Shiloh.

MOCH, ABRAHAM		A	16th Infantry
MOAK, C.		A	16th Infantry
MOYSE, ISIDORE		A	16th Infantry
MYERS, JOHN		A	16th Infantry
MEYER, ALEXANDER		E	36th Infantry

NAME.	RANK.	COMPANY.	REGIMENT.

MOOSER, ISAAC   Adjutant   Wheeler's Cavalry
    Promoted from the ranks.

MEYER, BLUM   H   Conner's Battery
MYERS, —— Major, Quartermaster-General Price's Command

NATUTIOUS, OTTO   Captain   B   Wand's Legion

OURY, S.   10th Infantry
    Killed June 16, 1864; buried in Jewish Cemetery,
    Richmond, Virginia.

PICKARD, M.   Warren Guards
PORODAR, SOLOMON   Warren Guards

RUBEL, EMANUEL,   D   19th Infantry
REINACH, DAVID   Bolivar Troop Cavalry
ROTH, CHARLES   Lieutenant   Swamp Ranger
    Killed in action.

SCHAEFER, EMILE   A   3d Infantry
    Appointed Orderly Sergeant; subsequently detached
    and served in the Quartermaster's Department.

STONE, E. S.   Sergeant   D   7th Infantry
SHARP, BENJAMIN   F   12th Infantry
SHERCK, LOUIS   A   16th Infantry
SAMUELS, A.   17th Infantry
SCHÄRFF, B.   17th Infantry
STINE, S. E.   17th Infantry
STORM, E.   D   28th Cavalry
SHRINSKI, ——   D   28th Cavalry
SULSPACHER, AARON   Kit Mott's Regiment

UNGER, SOLOMON   H   9th Infantry
ULLMAN, SAMUEL   C   16th Infantry
    Wounded at Cross Keys, and again at Sharpsburg;
    served gallantly through the war; now Rabbi at Bir-
    mingham, Alabama.

URIC, SOLOMON   H   16th Infantry
    Killed at Cold Harbor, Virginia.

NAME.	RANK.	COMPANY.	REGIMENT.
VAN RONKEL, ISAAC			18th Infantry
WILE, M. Served four years.		A	16th Infantry
WEINER, SAMUEL		A	16th Infantry
WEIL, CHARLES		D	16th Infantry
WEINBERG, JONAS			19th Infantry
WOLFE, M.		G	Vicksburg Sharpshooters
WEINER, SAMUEL			Mississippi Artillery
WATERMAN, LOUIS		D	28th Cavalry
WESTHEIMER, MORRIS Served through war.			Jefferson Artillery
WEXLER, PHILIP		A	1st Cavalry
WIENER, SOLOMON			Carrol Rangers
WILE, SIMON Promoted from ranks.	Sergeant		Stanford's Battery
WATERMAN, LEOPOLD			Washington Cavalry

MISSOURI.

NAME.	RANK.	COMPANY.	REGIMENT.
ANSELM, ALBERT	Lieutenant-Colonel		3d Infantry
BENDER, SAMUEL			3d Infantry
BERKSON, S.			3d Infantry
BOHN, HERMAN G.			5th Cavalry
BOHN, ISAAC G.	2nd Lieutenant		11th Cavalry
BENDEL, HERMAN	Captain		12th Infantry
BOERNSTEIN, GUSTAV Promoted from Lieutenant.	Captain		41st Infantry
CARSE, LEVI		I	7th Infantry
COHEN, ALBERT B.	Captain		11th Cavalry
COHN, L.			Home Guard
DARMSTADER, LOUIS Promoted from 2nd Lieutenant.	Captain		17th Infantry

NAME.	RANK.	COMPANY.	REGIMENT.
EPSTEIN, MAX.			1st Infantry
EISEMAN, ANTHONY	Captain		12th Infantry

Promoted from 2nd Lieutenant.

ERDMAN, ADOLPH	Quartermaster		15th Infantry

Promoted from 2nd Lieutenant.

EPPSTEIN, FRANCIS	2nd Lieutenant		48th Infantry
EPPSTEIN, JOSEPH A.	Lieutenant-Colonel		5th Cavalry
EDEMAN, MICHAEL S.	1st Lieutenant		{ 5th Cavalry { 12th Cavalry

FRIEDLEIN, GEORGE D.	Captain		3d Infantry
FALK, HENRY	2nd Lieutenant		48th Infantry
FRANK, PHILIP	Captain		4th Cavalry

Promoted from 2nd Lieutenant.

FRANK, CHARLES	2nd Lieutenant		2d U. S. R. C.
FRIEDLEIN, GEORGE G.	1st Lieutenant		4th Cavalry
FURTH, SAMUEL			Home Guard

GUTMAN, LOUIS		E	3d Infantry

Served three years.

GREENBAUM, SIMON		D	7th Infantry

HARTMAN, J.			1st Infantry
HOLZMAN, SAMUEL		I	1st Infantry
HOMBURG, S.	Adjutant		4th Infantry
HERRMAN, THEODORE	Captain		12th Infantry

Promoted from 2nd Lieutenant.

HESS, FERDINAND	1st Lieutenant		4th Cavalry

Promoted from 2nd Lieutenant; also Adjutant 1st Battery

HAMBURGER, HENRY	2nd Lieutenant		13th Cavalry
HOFMAN, JOSEPH	1st Lieutenant		1st Artillery
HURWITZ, HARMAN			General Lyon's Body-guard

JACOBS, PHILIP		H	1st Infantry

Received Medal of Honor.

JACOBS, EMIL		K	8th Infantry
JACOBY, MORRIS	2nd Lieutenant		17th Infantry

NAME.	RANK.	COMPANY,	REGIMENT.
KLEIN, MOSES	Captain		13th Infantry
KEMPINSKI, A.	Captain		49th Infantry

Served four years.

KEMPINSKI, LEO		F	49th Infantry
KAUFMAN, ALBERT B.	{ Captain { Major		{ 11th Cavalry { 10th Cavalry
KLEIN, BERNHART	1st Lieutenant		2nd U. S. R. C.
KOCH, JULIUS	1st Lieutenant		4th U. S. R. C.

LIEBSCHUTZ, A.		C	2nd Infantry
LIPMAN, LOUIS	1st Lieutenant		8th Infantry
LOWENTHAL, I. S.		G	18th Infantry
LOWENSTEIN, CHARLES	2nd Lieutenant		2nd Artillery
LEVISTEINE, ISAAC M.	Lieutenant	L	2nd Artillery

Died from wounds received in action.

LEVI, SOLOMON I.   Captain   1st Cavalry
Appointed by Governor Clark, of Missouri (1839), of
the 1st Militia.

LEVI, JACOB J.			6th Cavalry
LIEBERMAN, LORENZO	1st Lieutenant		1st U. S. R. C.

MONTZHEIM, JULIUS   1st Lieutenant   17th Infantry
Promoted from 2nd Lieutenant.

MEYER, B. F.			24th Infantry
MOHSBERG, A.		G	41st Infantry
MEYER, LOUIS		F	49th Infantry
MANN, CHARLES	{ 2nd Lieutenant { Major		{ 11th Cavalry { 1st Artillery
MOSES, T. W.	Quartermaster		14th Cavalry

Promoted from Lieutenant.

MANDELBAUM, FRANK			Home Guards
MANDELBAUM, JOHN W.			Home Guards
MANDELBAUM, S. E.			Home Guards

NEWDORF, JULIUS   1st Lieutenant   2nd Infantry
Promoted from 2nd Lieutenant.

ROSENSTEIN, D. W.	Captain		1st Infantry
RINDSKOPF, T.			1st Cavalry

NAME.	RANK.	COMPANY.	REGIMENT.
RINDSKOPF, I.		A	1st Cavalry
ROSENBAUM, H. A.	1st Lieutenant		29th Infantry
RAPHAEL, JACOB			1st Light Artillery

Served three years.

SINGER, DAVID		D	1st Infantry

Served three years.

SICHER, WILLIAM		C	2nd Infantry
SIMON, JOSEPH		G	2nd Infantry
SOLOMON, CHARLES E.	Colonel		5th Infantry
SOLOMON, FREDERICK	Captain		5th Infantry
SCHWERINER, THEODORE		H	8th Infantry

Wounded in Arkansas; totally disabled at Vicksburg.

STEINBERG, O.	Captain		12th Infantry

Promoted from Lieutenant.

STERNBERG, E.		F	17th Infantry
STEIN, GEORGE W.	1st Lieutenant		21st Infantry

Promoted from 2nd Lieutenant.

STEINAN, EMANUEL			21st Infantry

Not being of sufficient measurement his offer to enlist
was refused; but determined to fight for his adopted
country, he followed his regiment in which many
personal friends had enlisted, until finally he was
mustered in.

SOMMERS, HERMAN	1st Lieutenant		41st Infantry

Promoted from 2nd Lieutenant.

SLINSKY, LOUIS		F	49th Infantry
SIMONS, A.		A	2nd Cavalry
SINSHEIMER, A. H.		G	2nd Cavalry

Enlisted at eighteen years of age.

STEINMAN, E. H.	Captain		5th Cavalry
SANDERS, FRANK	2nd Lieutenant		7th Cavalry
SOLOMON, G. A. M.	1st Lieutenant		8th Cavalry
SALTZMAN, GUSTAV	2nd Lieutenant		1st Engineers
SALTZMAN, SIEGMUND	2nd Lieutenant		1st Artillery
STUGER, DAVID		D	Bender Cadets
TAKRZEWSKI, HERMAN	Captain		2nd U. S. R. C.

NEVADA.

NAME.	RANK.	COMPANY.	REGIMENT.
ISSERMAN, T. W.		A	1st Cavalry
JACOBS, SIMON L.		A	1st Cavalry
MANHEIM, DAVID	Colonel		1st Cavalry

Enlisted as private; promoted step by step.

NEW HAMPSHIRE.

NAME.	RANK.	COMPANY.	REGIMENT.
COHN, ABRAHAM	Adjutant		6th Infantry

enlisted as private; promoted for efficiency and distinguished bravery to Sergeant and Adjutant; wounded at Petersburg; the recipient of the Congressional "Medal of Honor;" served until the close of the war.

WAR DEPARTMENT, ADJUTANT GENERAL'S OFFICE,
WASHINGTON, August 24, 1865.

SIR:

Herewith I enclose the "Medal of Honor" which has been awarded to you by the Secretary of War, under the resolution of Congress, approved July 12, 1862. To provide for the presentation of "Medals of Honor" to the enlisted men of the army and volunteer forces who have distinguished or may distinguish themselves in battle during the present rebellion.

Very Respectfully,
Your obedient servant,
(Signed)   E. D. TOWNSEND,
Assistant Adjutant General.

To Sergeant-Major ABRAHAM COHN,
6th N. H. Veteran Volunteers,
439, 8th Avenue, New York.

ADJUTANT GENERAL'S OFFICE,
WASHINGTON, August 14, 1879.

The medal mentioned within was given for conspicuous gallantry displayed in the battle of the Wilderness, Virginia, in rallying and forming under heavy fire disorganized troops; also for bravery and coolness in carrying orders to the advance lines under murderous fire in the battle of the Mine, July 20, 1864.

(Signed)   S. N. BENJAMIN,
Assistant Adjutant-General.

GENERAL HEADQUARTERS, STATE OF NEW HAMPSHIRE.
ADJUTANT-GENERAL'S OFFICE,

CONCORD, August 17, 1865.

TO WHOM IT MAY CONCERN.

I take great pleasure in bearing testimony to the faithful services of Adjutant Abraham Cohn, both as a private and as an officer in the late 6th Regiment of New Hampshire Volunteers Infantry. His record in connection with this regiment has been one of great fidelity and ability and his successive promotions have been well merited rewards. I am also happy to bear testimony to the untiring industry and literary ability which Adjutant Cohn has displayed in collecting data for an official history of the Sixth Regiment, New Hampshire Volunteer Infantry.

Very Respectfully,
(Signed)   NATT HEAD.

(NATT HEAD, subsequently Adjutant, Inspector and Quartermaster, became Governor of the State of New Hampshire.)

KEENE, N. H., November 23, 1865.

This certifies that Abraham Cohn enlisted in the 6th New Hampshire Volunteers, of which regiment I was the Colonel, on the 5th day of January, 1864, and very soon after joined the command in the State of Kentucky. He at once attracted the attention and won the approbation of his officers by his soldierly bearing and faithful performance of duty, as well as

15

by his accomplishments in being able to communicate with recruits from European countries in their own various languages.

On the 28th day of March, 1864, he was promoted to the position of Sergeant-Major of the regiment, and throughout the great campaign that followed—from the Rapidan to the capture of Petersburg and Richmond—displayed remarkable bravery and coolness in action, endurance in the field and efficiency in his office.

He was wounded at the "battle of the Mine" in front of Petersburg, July 30, 1864, where he won a "Medal of Honor" for his distinguished bravery awarded by the War Department.

In appreciation of his meritorious services during this campaign he was promoted to the rank of Adjutant of his regiment, in which capacity he remained until the close of the war, winning the esteem and admiration of all who knew him by his gentlemanly and officer-like deportment, his sobriety and integrity, and by his noble devotion to the cause of the country of his adoption.

(Signed) S. G. GRIFFIN.

Late Brigadier-General and Brevet Major-General U. S. Volunteers.

S. G. GRIFFIN was subsequently elected Speaker of the House of Representatives of New Hampshire.

ROME, C. M.   E   4th Infantry

NEW JERSEY.

NAME.	RANK.	COMPANY.	REGIMENT.
ASH, JOSEPH W.		K	1st Infantry
ABRAHAM, C. S.	2nd Lieutenant	B	1st Infantry
Enlisted as private.			
ABRAHAM, AARON		K	1st Infantry
AARONSON, NAPOLEON		B	4th Infantry
AARONSON, FREDERICK	2nd Lieutenant	B	4th Infantry
ADLER, HERMAN		C	5th Infantry
ABRAMS, ISAAC N.		K	7th Infantry

NAME.	RANK.	COMPANY.	REGIMENT.
ABRAHAMS, JOSEPH	Corporal	B	10th Infantry

Wounded in action.

ADLER, MORRIS		G	15th Infantry
AARONSON, BENJAMIN	Corporal	I	23d Infantry
ADLER, HENRY		B	24th Infantry

Died of wounds received at Fredericksburg.

ASH, W. H.		C	26th Infantry
ABRAHAM, BENJAMIN		E	33d Infantry
ALEXANDER, DAVID		D	34th Infantry
ARNOLD, JOSEPH		K	34th Infantry

Died in the service.

ASCH, MYER	Brevet Major		1st Cavalry

Promoted from Adjutant for gallant and meritorious conduct.

ADLER, LEOPOLD			Veteran Reserve Corps
ADLER, ISIDOR			Battery A

BUXBAUM, WILLIAM		D	2nd Infantry
BLANKENSTEIN, LEVI		D	10th Infantry
BAUM, JACOB		I	11th Infantry
BALL, ABRAHAM S.		C	13th Infantry

Served three years.

BACHMAN, SAMUEL		D	13th Infantry
BUSH, AARON	Corporal	E	22nd Infantry
BALL, ISAAC		K	26th Infantry
BAER, FREDERICK		E	29th Infantry
BERNHEIM, WILLIAM		C	30th Infantry
BACHMAN, WILLIAM H.		A	31st Infantry
BLOOM, ISAAC		F	31st Infantry
BACHMAN, SAMUEL		I	31st Infantry
BALL, AARON		I	35th Infantry

Died in the service.

BLUHM, JACOB		B	35th Infantry

Transferred to Veteran Reserve Corps.

BIEN, ALPHONSE		I	39th Infantry
BAUM; FREDERICK		B	40th Infantry
BAUER, JACOB		B	3d Cavalry

NAME.	RANK.	COMPANY.	REGIMENT.
BACHMAN, SAMUEL		F	3d Cavalry
BAER, AUGUST			Battery C
BAER, MAX			Veteran Reserve Corps
BARNETT, MORRIS		C	66th Infantry
COHEN, THOMAS		D	10th Infantry
COHN, HARRIS		G	10th Infantry
COHN, GEORGE		H	13th Infantry
COHEN, EDWARD		C	34th Infantry
COHEN, ISAAC		E	1st Cavalry.
DANNENBERGER, JOSEPH	Corporal	A	2nd Infantry
Enlisted as private.			
DAVIDSON, DAVID	Sergeant	G	38th Infantry
ECKSTEIN, SIEGMUND		C	8th Infantry
Died of wounds received at Petersburg.			
ENGEL, JACOB		K	13th Infantry
ERDMAN, LOUIS		B	33d Infantry
EPPSTEIN, DANIEL	Sergeant	A	34th Infantry
Enlisted as private.			
ELLINGER, EMANUEL		F	34th Infantry
ETTINGER, MARK		F	34th Infantry
ELSAS, JACOB		D	3d Cavalry
Wounded at Mount Jackson, Virginia.			
ERDMAN, HENRY	Corporal	K	3d Cavalry
Enlisted as private.			
FRANK, CHARLES		F	1st Infantry
FOX, SOLOMON J.		C	2nd Infantry
Served three years.			
FOX, JACOB		A	4th Infantry
FEEDER, HENRY		K	7th Infantry
FOX, ISAAC	Corporal	I	12th Infantry
Killed near Petersburg.			
FRIEBERG, HENRY		F	15th Infantry
FEEDER, MORRIS		C	22nd Infantry
FRANK, FREDERICK		K	35th Infantry

NAME.	RANK.	COMPANY.	REGIMENT.
FREUND, GUSTAV		A	39th Infantry
FRANK, JACOB,	Sergeant	B	39th Infantry
FALK, JACOB		B	39th Infantry
FREUND, AUGUST		B	39th Infantry
FREUND, THEODORE		F	1st Cavalry
FRIEDLANDER, CHARLES		B	2nd Cavalry
Captured; died in Andersonville.			
FUCHS, EUGENE	Sergeant	D	3d Cavalry
Enlisted as private.			
FRIEDMAN, WILLIAM			Battery A
GOLDSMITH, WILLIAM		G	2nd Infantry
Captured; died at Andersonville.			
GREEN, JACOB		I	5th Infantry
GLUCKAUL, JACOB		A	8th Infantry
GOLDBERG, CHARLES		F	1st Cavalry
GOLDSMITH, CHARLES		G	2nd Cavalry
Died in service.			
GOLDMAN, CHARLES		I	2nd Cavalry
HAAS, BERNHARD			1st Infantry
HERZOG, LOUIS		K	1st Infantry
HOFMAN, JACOB H.	2nd Lieutenant	B	2nd Infantry
HAHN, MORRIS S.	2nd Lieutenant	D	2nd Infantry
HERMAN, CHARLES		B	2nd Infantry
HART, DAVID		B	2nd Infantry
HERRMAN, EMIL		E	2nd Infantry
HOFMAN, JACOB		E	2nd Infantry
HEINEMAN, HERMAN		{ H	2nd Infantry
		{ K	15th Infantry
HIRSCHFELD, ALFRED		{ K	2d Infantry
		{ K	14th Infantry
HIRSCH, JACOB		A	4th Infantry
Served three years.			
HOFMAN, SAMUEL		H	4th Infantry
HOFMAN, JACOB		I	4th Infantry
HOFMAN, LEVI W.		I	7th Infantry

NAME.	RANK.	COMPANY.	REGIMENT.
HOFMAN, AARON	Sergeant	H	8th Infantry
Promoted from Corporal.			
HOFMAN, ABRAHAM		H	8th Infantry
HOFMAN, ELIAS		H	8th Infantry
HAYS, DAVID		I	10th Infantry
HAAS, JACOB		G	10th Infantry
HARRIS, ABRAHAM M.	Corporal	D	13th Infantry
Enlisted as private.			
HELLER, JOSEPH		C	13th Infantry
HARTMAN, REUBEN	Sergeant	H	23d Infantry
HOFMAN, BENJAMIN		D	24th Infantry
HELLER, ADOLPH		D	24th Infantry
HAHN, HENRY		B	26th Infantry
HART, JOSEPH S.		B	27th Infantry
HART, NOAH L.		B	28th Infantry
HARRIS, ABRAHAM C.		H	30th Infantry
HART, ABRAHAM		K	30th Infantry
HOFMAN, DAVID		A	31st Infantry
HAMBURG, AUGUST		E	33d Infantry
HIRSCH, FERDINAND		F	33d Infantry
HEYMAN, HENRY		I	35th Infantry
HENMAN, JOSEPH		K	35th Infantry
HESS, JOSEPH		I	40th Infantry
HART, JACOB		A	1st Cavalry
HART, DAVID		H	1st Cavalry
HARRIS, ABRAHAM	Sergeant	I	1st Cavalry
Enlisted as Private; served four years.			
HARRIS, BENJAMIN		C	2nd Cavalry
HIRSCH, FREDERICK		E	2nd Cavalry
HART, SAMUEL		I	2nd Cavalry
HARRIS, ELIAS		M	2nd Cavalry
HOFMAN, AARON		A	3d Cavalry
HERRMAN, GUSTAV		C	3d Cavalry
HARRIS, DAVID		G	3d Cavalry
HARRIS, SAMUEL		H	3d Cavalry
HERZBERG, ALBERT	Captain	I	3d Cavalry
HIRSCH, LOUIS		K	3d Cavalry

NAME.	RANK.	COMPANY.	REGIMENT.
ISAAC, HENRY		H	3d Infantry
JACOBY, AUGUST		D	2nd Infantry
Served three years.			
JACOBY, FRITZ			4th Infantry
JACOBSON, CHARLES		A	4th Infantry
JOSEFF, EMANUEL		E	4th Infantry
JOSEFF, PHILIP		E	4th Infantry
JACOBSON, WILLIAM E.		B	8th Infantry
Served three years.			
JACOBSON, ISRAEL J.		K	11th Infantry
Captured; died at Libby Prison.			
JACOBUS, ABRAHAM		F	15th Infantry
JACOBY, SAMUEL		I	28th Infantry
Died of wounds.			
JACOBSON, W. E.	Corporal	D	38th Infantry
Enlisted as Private.			
JACOBSON, LOUIS		D	40th Infantry
JACOB, D.		A	1st Artillery
KING, MOSES W.		G	1st Infantry
KAUFMAN, ADOLPH		K	1st Infantry
KAUFMAN, FREDERICK		C	2nd Infantry
KAMINZKY, JOSEPH		D	2nd Infantry
KATZENBERG, JOSEPH		B	4th Infantry
KOCH, JACOB		K	7th Infantry
KING, ASHER	Corporal	C	8th Infantry
Enlisted as private.			
KLEIN, MANUEL	2nd Lieutenant	A	15th Infantry
Enlisted as Private.			
KING, ABRAHAM G.		B	15th Infantry
Killed at Spottsylvania.			
KLEIN, JULIUS		A	21st Infantry
KING, AARON		A	25th Infantry
KING, JACOB		C	25th Infantry
KOHN, LEIB		I	35th Infantry

NAME.	RANK	COMPANY.	REGIMENT.
KLEIN, BENJAMIN		G	38th Infantry
KAUFMAN, JACOB		B	40th Infantry
KAUFMAN, SAMUEL		5th	Hancock's Corps
KATZ, JACOB		D	2nd Cavalry
KOCH, GOTTLIEB		I	3d Cavalry
KOEHLER, ELIAS		K	3d Cavalry
KOCH, HERMAN			Battery C
LYON, BENJAMIN		D	1st Infantry
LINDEMAN, ADOLPH		K	1st Infantry
LOWENTHAL, GEORGE		K	1st,Infantry
LILIENDALL, GUSTAV	Captain	D	2nd Infantry
LOEB, LOUIS		I	3d Infantry
Leg amputated.			
LEO, CHARLES		C	4th Infantry
LEOPOLD, WILLIAM		B	5th Infantry
LIMBURGER, ALBERT		H	5th Infantry
Died in the service.			
LOEB, JOHN E.	Sergeant	I	6th Infantry
LOEB, W. W.		I	6th Infantry
LYON, SAMUEL		C	7th Infantry
LEVY, JOSEPH		I	8th Infantry
LEAVY, CHARLES M.			9th Infantry
LEVY, WILLIAM P.		K	9th Infantry
LICHTENFELZ, LUDWIG		I	12th Infantry
LANGENDORF, JACOB		A	13th Infantry
LEVI, DAVID		B	13th Infantry
Served four years.			
LEHMAN, CHARLES		F	14th Infantry
LOWENTHAL, LEWIS		C	22nd Infantry
LEVI, MARCUS		C	26th Infantry
LEVI, MORRIS		I	30th Infantry
LEVI, HERMAN J.		G	34th Infantry
LYON, SAMUEL		C	35th Infantry
LIMBURGER, DAVID		K	35th Infantry
LIMBURGER, W. H.		K	35th Infantry
LEVINE, WILLIAM		F	40th Infantry

NAME.	RANK.	COMPANY.	REGIMENT.
LEVI, MAX		C	1st Cavalry
LEVI, MORRIS		D	1st Cavalry
Died in the service.			
MENDEL, JACOB		K	1st Infantry
MARX, CHARLES		E	2nd Infantry
MAYER, JACOB		G	2nd Infantry
MARX, AUGUST		F	3d Infantry
MAYER, FRANK		D	7th Infantry
Died in the service.			
MARX, MARTIN	Corporal	B	7th Infantry
Enlisted as private.			
MEYER, JACOB	Corporal	H	9th Infantry
Served three years.			
MARKS, EMANUEL		B	10th Infantry
MEIER, HENRY		C	11th Infantry
MEYERS, JACOB	Sergeant	G	11th Infantry
Wounded at Chancellorsville.			
MAYERS, JACOB		E	15th Infantry
MAAS, FREDERICK W.		E	22nd Infantry
MARKS, JOSEPH		D	29th Infantry
Died in the service.			
MAYER, SAMUEL		E	29th Infantry
MENDEL, WILLIAM		B	30th Infantry
MARKS, JOSEPH C.		F	38th Infantry
MAYER, JACOB		I	40th Infantry
MAYER, AUGUST			Battery A
MANN, FERDINAND			Battery C
MEYER, ADOLPH	2nd Lieutenant		1st Regiment, Hancock's Corps
Promoted from Sergeant.			
MARKS, FREDERICK			1st Regiment, Hancock's Corps
NAUMAN, GUSTAV		F	9th Infantry
NUSSBAUM, MICHAEL		H	10th Infantry
NEWMAN, DAVID M.	Corporal	I	29th Infantry
NAUMAN, JULIUS	Corporal	I	31st Infantry
Enlisted as private.			

NAME.	RANK.	COMPANY.	REGIMENT.
NAUMAN, JULIUS		I	35th Infantry
NEUSTADT, MAX		C	66th Infantry
OPPENHEIM, DAVID		K	1st Infantry
OPPENHEIMER, JACOB			Battery C
PINCUS, ADOLPH		K	7th Infantry
PINCUS, SIMON		C	66th Infantry
ROSE, ELIAS M.		C	1st Infantry
ROSENBORGER, JOHN		D	4th Infantry
Captured; died at Andersonville.			
RICE, DAVID S.		B	5th Infantry
Captured.			
RAPHAEL, WILLIAM		I	8th Infantry
Died in the service.			
ROSE, DANIEL M.		I	8th Infantry
ROSE, ABRAHAM H.		F	9th Infantry
ROSE, SAMUEL		E	11th Infantry
ROSE, HENRY		D	14th Infantry
ROSE, SAMUEL B.		F	14th Infantry
Died in the service.			
RICE, DAVID		A	21st Infantry
ROSENDALE, GEORGE		B	30th Infantry
ROSENDALE, GEORGE		A	35th Infantry
RUBENSTEIN, SAMUEL		K	1st Cavalry
ROSENBERG, JOHN		G	2nd Cavalry
ROSE, BENJAMIN		A	3d Cavalry
RICE, JACOB		D	2nd Cavalry
ROSENBERG, BENJAMIN		Veteran Reserve Corps	
SOLOMON, CHARLES		A	1st Infantry
SAMPSON, DAVID		A	2nd Infantry
Transferred to Veteran Reserve Corps.			
STEIN, GUSTAV		H	2nd Infantry
SALMON, ABRAHAM	1st Lieutenant	A	3d Infantry
Promoted from Sergeant.			
SOLOMON, SAMUEL D.		G	3d Infantry

NAME.	RANK.	COMPANY.	REGIMENT.
SALZMAN, LOUIS		K	3d Infantry
SACHS, HENRY		H	5th Infantry
STRAUS, CHARLES		H	5th Infantry
STRAUSS, JONATHAN		G	6th Infantry
STERN, JOSEPH		H	7th Infantry
SPANNENGBERG, MOSES		I	7th Infantry
SPANNENGBERG, WILLIAM		I	7th Infantry
SICKLES, SOLOMON		H	14th Infantry
STEIN, JACOB		A	14th Infantry
SALMON, LEWIS A.	Sergeant	F	15th Infantry

Enlisted as Private.

SIMON, ADOLPH		G	21st Infantry
STRAUSS, WILLIAM		C	22nd Infantry
STINE, ISAAC		K	27th Infantry
STEINFELD, HARRY		C	34th Infantry
SIMONS, LEWIS		I	34th Infantry

Enlisted as Private.

SOLINGER, LEE		K	35th Infantry
SACHS, ABRAHAM		B	40th Infantry
SACHS, NOAH		B	40th Infantry
STRAUSS, NATHANIEL		E	40th Infantry
STEIN, HERMAN			Veteran Reserve Corps
SACKS, DAVID			Battery A

Died in the service.

STEIN, HERMAN	Sergeant		Battery C

Entered as Private.

WOLF, NATHANIEL		D	1st Infantry
WEISS, ADOLPH	Captain	A	2nd Infantry

Promoted from Sergeant.

WOLF, CHARLES		I	4th Infantry
WOLF, HERMAN		F	8th Infantry
WOLF, HENRY		A	9th Infantry
WOLF, JOSEPH	Corporal	I	9th Infantry
WOLF, SAMUEL		B	27th Infantry
WOLF, FERDINAND	Lieutenant	C	27th Infantry
WOLF, DAVID	Corporal	A	33d Infantry

Enlisted as Private.

NAME.	RANK.	COMPANY.	REGIMENT.
WEIL, JOSEPH		I	33d Infantry
WOLF, SELIG		B	39th Infantry
WEILER, JOSEPH		F	39th Infantry
WOLF, JOSEPH		K	40th Infantry
WEISS, AARON		I	1st Cavalry
WOLF, GUSTAV		I	3d Cavalry
WOLF, FREDERICK		I	3d Cavalry
WOLF, DAVID			Militia

NEW MEXICO.

NAME.	RANK.	COMPANY.	REGIMENT.
KAHN, EMIL M.		F	7th Infantry

Killed at Fort Laramie by Indians.

MAYER, ADOLPH A.   Inspector-General   4th Infantry
Promoted for efficiency Inspector-General, and by
special appointment of President Lincoln assigned to
Pennsylvania.

NEW YORK.

NAME.	RANK.	COMPANY.	REGIMENT.
ABRAHAM, EDWARD		I	1st Infantry
ASHER, WILLIAM		G	3d Infantry
ASSENHEIMER, O. C.		B	5th Infantry
ADLER, HEINRICH		I	8th Infantry
ARENSON, DANIEL		D	9th Infantry
ASH, JACOB		B	13th Infantry
APPLE, SALOMON		D	20th Infantry
AUGUST, SIMON		A	24th Infantry
ADLER, SIMON		E	25th Infantry
ABRAMS, WILLIAM H.		H	27th Infantry

NAME.	RANK.	COMPANY.	REGIMENT.
ARNHEIM, JULIUS		I	29th Infantry
ABRAMS, ANDREW		K	30th Infantry
ABRAMS, JOHN		K	30th Infantry
ADLER, ISIDOR		C	31st Infantry
ARNOLD, DAVID			35th Infantry
ARNOLD, EPHRAIM		H	36th Infantry
AARON, LEWIS		B	38th Infantry
ARNZ, J.			39th Infantry
ALEXANDER, SAMUEL		H	39th Infantry
ABRAHAMS, ABRAHAM		D	40th Infantry
ARNOLD, H.		C	41st Infantry
ARNOLD, GUSTAVE		G	41st Infantry
ALEXANDER, JOSEPH		I	41st Infantry
ASHER, JACOB H.		C	44th Infantry
ARNOLD, LOUIS		G	45th Infantry
ANSEL, JACOB		H	45th Infantry
ALTMAN, JOSEPH		I	46th Infantry
AARON, GABRIEL		B	47th Infantry
ABRAMS, AUGUST		B	48th Infantry
ALEXANDER, EPHRAIM		R	50th Infantry
AARONS, GEORGE		H	53d Infantry
ADLER, JOSEPH,		F	54th Infantry
AUFANGER, SIEGMUND		H	54th Infantry
ASCHER, SAMUEL	Lieutenant	H	54th Infantry

Promoted from the ranks.

AUERBACH, JOSEPH			5th Cavalry

Killed at Fredericksburg.

ABRAHAMS, EDWARD		F	57th Infantry
ARNOLD, JACOB		G	64th Infantry
ALTENBURG, MORRIS		H	64th Infantry
ABRAHAMS, HENRY		F	67th Infantry
ASHER, PHILIP	Sergeant	I	68th Infantry
ASHER, ADOLPH	Sergeant	K	68th Infantry
ASHER, LOUIS	Sergeant	K	68th Infantry
AUERBACH, J.			68th Infantry
ABRAMS, JAMES		C	70th Infantry
ARNOLD, AARON		B	72nd Infantry
ACKERMAN, JOSEPH		G	73d Infantry

NAME.	RANK.	COMPANY.	REGIMENT.
ARNOLD, FRANK		A	76th Infantry
ARNOLD, DAVID W.		A	76th Infantry
ACKERMAN, JACOB		B	78th Infantry
ARNOLD, NATHAN K.	Lieutenant		79th Infantry
ACKERMAN, A.		A	83d Infantry
ABRAMS, GEORGE		K	88th Infantry
ABRAMS, EDWARD	Corporal	A	95th Infantry
ABRAMS, W. B.		F	97th Infantry
ARNOLD, NATHAN J.		A	100th Infantry
ALEXANDER, JACOB		F	100th Infantry
ASHER, M. S.			103d Infantry
ABRAHAM, JOSEPH		A	112th Infantry
ALEXANDER, OSCAR		I	115th Infantry
ABRAHAM, MOSES		E	119th Infantry
ABRAMS, DANIEL		H	122nd Infantry
ANTHONY, A.			131st Infantry
ASH, MORRIS		C	132nd Infantry
ASH, DAVID		K	142nd Infantry
ARNOLD, MARCUS		I	146th Infantry
ARNOLD, DNNIEL W.	Sergeant	A	151st Infantry
ABRAMS, LEVI		D	158th Infantry
ABRAHAM, LEVY	Lieutenant	H	164th Infantry
ABRAHAMS, JOSEPH S.	Lieutenant		164th Infantry
Killed at Cold Harbor.			
ACKERMAN, ABRAHAM		K	170th Infantry
ADLER, ALBERT	Corporal	G	178th Infantry
ACKERMAN, LEWIS	Lieutenant	I	189th Infantry
ADELMAN, EUGENE		B	5th S. V.
ABRAHAM, HENRY		F	5th S. V.
ASH, SAMUEL		B	7th S. V.
ABRAHAM, THEO.		A	25th S. M.
ACKERMAN, GUSTAVE	Corporal	A	4th Cavalry
ABABOT, DAVID	Lieutenant	B	5th Cavalry
ABRAHAM, AARON		B	7th Cavalry
ABRAMS, W. H.	Sergeant	G	9th Cavalry
ACKERMAN, DAVID R.	Corporal	C	11th Cavalry
ADLER, ISIDOR	Corporal	F	14th Cavalry
ALEXANDER, EPHRAIM		D	15th Cavalry

NAME.	RANK.	COMPANY.	REGIMENT.
ARNOLD, JACOB		D	20th Cavalry
ARNDT, ALBERT	Major		1st Battalion Artillery

Killed at Sharpsburg.

ABRAMS, SAMUEL		A	1st Mounted Rifles
ARNOLD, BENJAMIN		E	9th Artillery
ABRAMS, MAURICE		A	16th Artillery
ABRAHAM, MOSES			3d Independent Artillery
ADLER, SAMUEL			9th Independent Artillery
ANSBACHER, MOSES			24th Independent Artillery

BARNARD, LEON	Captain	G	1st Infantry

Promoted from Lieutenant; transferred 9th Infantry.

BLUMENSTEIN, J.			4th Infantry
BLUMENTHAL, J.			4th Infantry
BENJAMIN, EMANUEL		A	4th Infantry
BENJAMIN, LEVY		B	4th Infantry
BERNSTEIN, JACOB		D	4th Infantry
BERNSTEIN, MARK		G	4th Infantry
BARNETT, SAMUEL		K	4th Infantry
BACHARACH, JULIUS			6th Infantry
BORCHARD, NEWMAN		K	6th Infantry
BEHREND, WILLIAM	Captain	A	7th Infantry

Promoted from Sergeant.

BERNHARD, FRANK		C	7th Infantry
BADER, ADOLPH		D	7th Infantry
BERNHARD, MORITZ		F	7th Infantry
BLUM, JACOB		I	7th Infantry
BARUCH, BERNHARD		K	7th Infantry
BEISHEIM, THEODORE	1st Lieutenant		8th Infantry
BEHREND, M.		C	8th Infantry
BERNHARD, EDWARD	1st Lieutenant		11th Infantry
BAHR, FRANK		B	12th Infantry
BERNHARDT, ALEXANDER		F	16th Infantry
BALL, FELIX		F	18th Infantry
BACHMAN, JOSEPH		C	20th Infantry
BEHRENS, GUSTAVE		H	20th Infantry
BIEN, MARTIN		F	23d Infantry

NAME.	RANK.	COMPANY.	REGIMENT.
BENJAMIN, DAVID W.		G	26th Infantry
BACHMAN, SIEGMUND		E	27th Infantry
BERNE, MAX	Lieutenant		29th Infantry
BRANDEIS, H.			38th Infantry
BLUHM, JACOB		B	39th Infantry
BERLINER, SIEGMUND		F	39th Infantry
BAER, BERNHARD	Captain	H	39th Infantry

Promoted from Lieutenant.

BEHRENS, AUGUST		H	39th Infantry
BERNHARD, ADAM		H	39th Infantry
BROD, HERMAN			39th Infantry
BARNETT, DANIEL		B	40th Infantry
BEHRENDS, HERMAN		D	41st Infantry
BRESLAUER, CHARLES		D	41st Infantry

Wounded in the head and abdomen, killed in action
at 2nd Battle Bull Run.

BERNSTEIN, LOUIS	Corporal	I	41st Infantry
BEER, JACOB		B	42nd Infantry
BARNETT, SAMUEL		C	42nd Infantry
BAEHR, WILLIAM			45th Infantry
BAUM, JOSEPH		B	45th Infantry
BLUM, JACOB		H	45th Infantry
BERNHARD, JOSEPH		A	52nd Infantry
BLOCK, JULIUS		G	52nd Infantry
BLOCK, LOUIS		G	52nd Infantry
BERNHARD, JOSEPH		E	53d Infantry
BERNSTEIN, JOSEPH		G	54th Infantry
BLOCK, EMIL		C	55th Infantry
BRUCKHEIMER, MOSES		{	6th Infantry
		{ D	55th Infantry

Disabled in the service.

BENJAMIN, CHARLES		G	55th Infantry
BOSCOWITZ, C. J.		D	56th Infantry
BASH, ADOLPH	Lieutenant		58th Infantry
BAUM, ADOLPH		C	58th Infantry
BLUMENTHAL, WILLIAM		I	58th Infantry
BERNHARD, ISIDOR		A	62nd Infantry

NAME.	RANK.	COMPANY.	REGIMENT.
BAACH, JACOB	Corporal	F	62nd Infantry
			(Anderson's Zouaves)

Wounded at Fredericksburg and at the Wilderness.

BERLINER, SOLOMON		K	62nd Infantry
BACHARACH, MAX.		D	63d Infantry
BARNETT, MORRIS			66th Infantry
BAMBERGER, JOSEPH		E	66th Infantry
BIRNBAUM, ADOLPH	Lieutenant		68th Infantry
BENJAMIN, GOTTLIEB		K	68th Infantry
BRUNN, JACOB	Captain	E	70th Infantry

Killed at Williamsburg.

BEHREND, A.			72nd Infantry
BENJAMIN, ISAAC, JR.		B	75th Infantry
BENJAMIN, ISAAC		B	78th Infantry
BENJAMIN, OSCAR A.		I	81st Infantry
BENJAMIN, HENRY		C	87th Infantry
BARNETT, ISAAC			90th Infantry

Severely wounded.

BUXBAUM, JULIUS		D	91st Infantry
BENJAMIN, DANIEL H.		E	92nd Infantry
BENJAMIN, DANIEL		A	93d Infantry
BENJAMIN, JOEL		A	93d Infantry
BASH, J.			98th Infantry
BARNHART, BENJAMIN			98th Infantry
BLOOMINGDALE, ALEXANDER		C	102nd Infantry
BAER, LEOPOLD		C	103d Infantry
BERLINER, MEIER	Sergeant	F	103d Infantry
BERKENMEYER, A.		G	103d Infantry
BEAR, FRANK	Sergeant	G	110th Infantry
BENJAMIN, JOSEPH W		H	117th Infantry
BEHRENS, L.			119th Infantry
BACHMAN, ADOLPH		H	119th Infantry
BLOOMINGTON, EMIL		K	119th Infantry
BENJAMIN, FRANK L.		F	121st Infantry
BENJAMIN, ELISHA		B	124th Infantry
BLOOMINGDALE, JOSEPH		D	125th Infantry
BACHMAN, JACOB H.	Corporal	I	126th Infantry

16

NAME.	RANK.	COMPANY.	REGIMENT.
BENJAMIN, MARCUS		K	126th Infantry
BENJAMIN, A.	Lieutenant	D	131st Infantry

Killed at Port Hudson.

BLUM, ABRAHAM		A	132nd Infantry
BEHRENS, JOSEPH			135th Infantry
BENJAMIN, DAVID		K	138th Infantry
BERNHARD, HERMAN		C	143d Infantry
BAER, FRANK	Lieutenant	G	147th Infantry

Promoted from Sergeant.

BRONNER, SAMUEL	Lieutenant	A	149th Infantry
BAMBERG, FREDERICK		C	178th Infantry
BENJAMIN, DAVID		C	179th Infantry
BACHMAN, JACOB		E	187th Infantry
BERNARD, JOSEPH E.		I	188th Infantry
BERNHEIM, JULIUS		K	1st Independent
BLUM, JACOB		K	5th S. V.
BEHR, ISAAC		F	7th S. V.
BERLINER, SIEGMUND M. I., 1st Lieutenant			
			17th S. V. re-organized
BERNSTEIN, MORRIS		F	22nd S. M.
BACHMAN, JOSEPH	Corporal	G	1st Cavalry
BERLINER, EMIL		I	1st Cavalry
BEHREND, MORITZ	Battalion Quartermaster		4th Cavalry
BAUER, MORITZ		M	4th Cavalry
BLANK, SIMON		H	6th Cavalry
BACHMAN, FREDERICK		H	8th Cavalry
BERKOWITZ, LEON		B	13th Cavalry
BERKOWITZ, ISIDOR	Corporal	D	13th Cavalry
BLOOMINGDALE, DAVID		D	21st Cavalry
BACHMAN, FREDERICK		F	22nd Cavalry
BLUM, E.			25th Cavalry
BAER, JACOB		I	1st Artillery
BERNHARD, SIMON		K	13th Artillery
BLANKENBERGER, A.		K	15th Artillery
BENJAMIN, AARON		H	16th Artillery
BENJAMIN, FERDINAND		B	Marine Artillery
BEHRENS, AUGUST			2nd Independent Artillery
BRILL, JOSEPH			25th Independent Artillery

NAME.	RANK.	COMPANY.	REGIMENT.
BAER, SIMON			30th Independent Artillery
BENDELL, HERMAN	} Assistant Surgeon } Surgeon		} 6th Heavy Artillery } 86th Infantry

Brevetted Lieutenant-Colonel for meritorious and honorable conduct; afterwards Superintendent of Indian affairs for Arizona.

BRUN, SAMUEL

NAME	RANK	COMPANY	REGIMENT
CALISH, ARNOLD H.		I	1st Infantry
COHEN, HENRY E.	Corporal	H	5th Infantry
COHEN, HERMAN		K	6th Infantry
CORPEL, BENJAMIN		K	6th Infantry
COHN, ALBERT			8th Infantry
COHEN, LEWIS		H	8th Infantry
COHEN, ISAAC		H	10th Infantry
COHEN, THOMAS		G	11th Infantry
CANTER, LEON A.			12th State Militia

Captured at Harper's Ferry; exchanged; re-enlisted after being discharged at expiration of term (May 21, 1862—July 20, 1863).

NAME	RANK	COMPANY	REGIMENT
COHEN, SAMUEL			20th Infantry
CONHEIM, JULIUS		D	20th Infantry
CHAPMAN, HARRIS A.		A	24th Infantry
COLEMAN, F.			27th Infantry
COHEN, HARRIS		C	31st Infantry
CZAMANSKI, JULIUS		C	31st Infantry
COHEN, DAVID		B	39th Infantry
COHEN, ISIDOR		A	41st Infantry

Killed at Gettysburg.

NAME	RANK	COMPANY	REGIMENT
COHN, ISAAC		A	41st Infantry
COHN, ISIDOR		K	45th Infantry

Killed at Gettysburg.

NAME	RANK	COMPANY	REGIMENT
COHEN, JACOB		F	52nd Infantry
COHEN, JULIUS	Corporal	F	54th Infantry
COHEN, JOHN		C	62nd Infantry
COHEN, ABRAHAM		I	62nd Infantry
COHEN, JOSEPH		B	68th Infantry

NAME.	RANK.	COMPANY.	REGIMENT.
COHEN, LOUIS		B	68th Infantry
COHEN, ABRAHAM	Captain	E	68th Infantry

Entered as a Private; for his soldier-like qualities, strict discipline and gallantry on the battle-field was promoted in quick succession to Corporal, Sergeant, Sergeant-Major, 2d Lieutenant, 1st Lieutenant, and Captain of Company E, acting part of the time as Regimental Adjutant.

Besides participating in many skirmishes Captain Cohen took part in the battles at Cross Keys, Port Republic, Rappahannock Station, White Sulphur Springs, Slaughter Mountain, Manassas, Bull Run and Chantilly.

Being disqualified for further active duty he was honorably discharged, as shown by the annexed official order:

HEADQUARTERS OF THE ARMY,
ADJUTANT-GENERAL'S OFFICE,
WASHINGTON, December 23, 1862.

Special Order No. 408.

The following officer is honorably discharged from the military service of the United States on account of disability: Captain A. Cohen, Company E, 68th New York Volunteers.

By command Major-General Halleck,
(Signed)   E. D. TOWNSEND,
Assistant Adjutant-General.

HEADQUARTERS NEAR STAFFORD, C. H.

February 11, 1863.

I hereby certify that I have known Captain Cohen as acting Adjutant and subsequently as Captain in the 68th Regiment, New York Volunteers, and that I have known him to be an efficient officer, while the 68th Regiment was under my command; I recollect that his name was favorably mentioned in connection with the battle of Bull Run, August 30, 1862.

(Signed)   W. KRZYZANOWSKI,
Colonel Commanding 2nd Brigade, 3d Division, 11th Corps.

HEADQUARTERS 3d DIVISION, 11TH CORPS,

February 11, 1863.

From the reports that have reached me, I take pleasure in certifying to Captain Cohen's efficiency as an officer and his good conduct in action.

(Signed) C. SCHURZ,

Brigadier-General, Commanding 3d Division, 11th Corps.

HEADQUARTERS 1st DIVISION, 11TH CORPS,

STAFFORD, C. H., February 12, 1863.

I take pleasure in stating to all concerned that Captain Cohen is a very efficient officer and has conducted himself in action bravely.

(Signed) JULIUS STAHEL,

Brigadier-General, Commanding 1st Division, 11th Corps.

NAME.	RANK.	COMPANY.	REGIMENT.
COHEN, MOSES		B	73d Infantry
COHEN, LEOPOLD		A	102nd Infantry
COHEN, ——		E	113th Infantry
CORNELIUS, ABRAHAM		G	125th Infantry
CORNELIUS, JACOB		E	127th Infantry
COHEN, DAVID		B	131st Infantry
CORNELIUS, DAVID		F	134th Infantry
COHN, MAX		F	163d Infantry
COHN, WILLIAM		E	173d Infantry
COHEN, LEWIS		E	174th Infantry
COHEN, PHILIP, JR.			193d Infantry
COHN, ISAAC	Captain		8th S. V.
COHEN, COLEMAN		B	13th S. M.
COLEMAN, SAMUEL		B	7th Cavalry
COHN, HENRY		A	18th Cavalry
COHN, JOSEPH		G	5th Artillery
COHEN, SIMON		E	7th Artillery
COHEN, LOUIS		G	16th Artillery
COHNHEIM, MAX (the author)	Captain		41st Infantry
Promoted from Lieutenant.			
CASPAR, ——		B	1st Independent Battery
COHEN, MOSES S.			2nd Fire Zouaves

Name.	Rank.	Company.	Regiment.
Davis, Samuel		H	1st Infantry
Davis, David		H	1st Infantry
Davis, Charles		F	3d Infantry
Davis, Benjamin		D	4th Infantry
David, Simpson		D	5th Infantry
Davis, David P.		F	5th Infantry
Davis, Henry		D	6th Infantry
Davis, Gomperts		K	6th Infantry
Dampf, Meier			7th Infantry
Dantziger, ——		H	7th Infantry

Died from wounds received at Fredericksburg.

Name.	Rank.	Company.	Regiment.
Davis, G. D.	Lieutenant	I	7th Infantry
Dampf, Moritz			8th Infantry
David, Moritz	Corporal	E	8th Infantry
Davison, Gustav		K	8th Infantry
Dreyfus, Gustav		A	9th Infantry
Davis, David		H	9th Infantry
Davis, David M.		A	10th Infantry
Deutsch, J.		A	11th Infantry
Davidson, Jesse		K	13th Infantry
Davidson, Edmond		K	13th Infantry
David, B. Moritz			17th Infantry
Davis, Joseph		D	18th Infantry
Dryfus, Charles		A	20th Infantry
Davidson, Alfred		C	22nd Infantry
Davis, Benjamim		C	24th Infantry
Davis, Oscar C.		B	26th Infantry
Davidson, William		B	26th Infantry
Davis, Eugene M.	Sergeant	C	27th Infantry
Davis, Joseph L.		F	27th Infantry
Davis, Samuel		C	28th Infantry
Davis, Joseph		E	28th Infantry
Davis, Joshua C.		E	28th Infantry
Davis, Samuel H.		K	28th Infantry
Dondorf, Edward		A	29th Infantry
Davids, Samuel		A	34th Infantry
Davis, L. H.	Lieutenant		35th Infantry
Davis, Isaac H.		H	38th Infantry

NAME.	RANK.	COMPANY.	REGIMENT.
DAVIS, ISAAC		H	38th Infantry
DERNDINGER, LEO	Lieutenant		39th Infantry
DAVID, EMILE	Corporal	K	39th Infantry
DAVISON, GUSTAV		D	41st Infantry
DAVIS, HENRY		G	42nd Infantry
DAVIDSON, SAMUEL	Lieutenant	I	43d Infantry
DAVIS, ALEXANDER		C	44th Infantry
DAVIS, LEWIS W.		C	44th Infantry
DESSAUER, FR. A.	Captain		45th Infantry

Promoted from Lieutenant on General Howard's staff;
killed in action.

NAME.	RANK.	COMPANY.	REGIMENT.
DAVIDSON, DAVID C.		A	51st Infantry
DAVIDSON, CHARLES		D	53d Infantry
DREYFUS, HENRY		K	54th Infantry
DAVIS, DAVID C.		D	56th Infantry
DAVIS, MOSES		K	56th Infantry
DAVIDSON, SAMUEL		B	59th Infantry
DAVIDMEYER, LEWIN		A	68th Infantry
DAVIS, REUBEN		H	80th Infantry
DAVIS, DAVID A.		G	81st Infantry
DRYFUS, EMANUEL	Sergeant	C	83d Infantry
DAVIS, FRANK		E	87th Infantry
DAVIS, MOSES		H	89th Infantry
DE WOLF, D. C.		F	94th Infantry
DAVIS, DAVID		I	95th Infantry
DAVIS, DAVID		F	98th Infantry
DAVIS, JOSEPH		I	102nd Infantry
DAVIS, ABRAHAM		C	105th Infantry
DAVIS, JULIUS		G	110th Infantry
DAVIS, DAVID		G	111th Infantry
DAVIS, ABRAHAM L.		G	115th Infantry
DAVIS, ABRAHAM A.		B	118th Infantry
DAVID, REUBEN		C	118th Infantry
DAVIS, ISRAEL		F	119th Infantry
DAVIS, DANIEL		A	120th Infantry
DAVIS, DAVID		A	120th Infantry
DAVIS, ISAAC		A	120th Infantry
DAVIS, SIMEON		C	120th Infantry

NAME.	RANK.	COMPANY.	REGIMENT.
DAVIS, SIMEON J.		C	120th Infantry
DAVIDSON, D.	Corporal		121st Infantry
DRYFUS, JOACHIM	Sergeant	D	127th Infantry
DAVIS, BENJAMIN		A	129th Infantry
DAVIS, LEVI C.		I	130th Infantry
DAVIDSON, MORRIS	Adjutant	K	{ 130th Infantry
Lieutenant and Brevet Captain			{ 176th Infantry.
DAVIDSON, MORRIS M.,		K	{ 131st Infantry
	Quartermaster		{ 176th Infantry
DAVIS, EMANUEL		K	137th Infantry
DAVIS, EZEKIAH	Corporal	E	144th Infantry
DAVIS, JOSEPH A.	Lieutenant		149th Infantry
Killed at Chancellorsville.			
DANIELS, JOSHUA		F	150th Infantry
DANIELSON, WILLIAM E.		A	151st Infantry
DAVIS, ABRAHAM		D	153d Infantry
DAVIS, ISAAC L.		D	156th Infantry
DAVIDSON, JOSEPH B.		C	161st Infantry
DAVIS, AARON B.		C	169th Infantry
DAVIS, NATHAN M.		D	175th Infantry
DURST, JOSEPH		K	177th Infantry
DE WOLF, MOSES		H	184th Infantry
DAVIS, DAVID J.		C	185th Infantry
DAVIS, BENJAMIN		C	189th Infantry
DAVIDSON, DAVID B.		H	8th S. V.
DAVIS, ABRAHAM		L	3d Cavalry
DAVIDSON, SOLOMON		F	6th Cavalry
DAVISON, ALEXANDER		B	12th Cavalry
DAVID, SAMUEL		F	13th Cavalry
DAVID, SAMUEL	Lieutenant	F	25th Cavalry
DAVIS, EUGENE M.		A	1st Net. Cavalry
DAVIS, BENJAMIN		E	1st Net. Cavalry
DAVIS, SIMON		H	1st Mounted Rifles
DAVIS, ISAAC	Sergeant	C	2nd Artillery
DE SILVA, HENRY		B	4th Artillery
DE SILVA, HOMER		B	4th Artillery
DAVIS, ABRAHAM		K	7th Artillery

NAME.	RANK.	COMPANY.	REGIMENT.
DE SOUZA, W. H.		B	15th Artillery
DAUZER, CARL			30th Battery

Killed at Gaines' Mill.

NAME.	RANK.	COMPANY.	REGIMENT.
ECKSTEIN, SAMUEL		G	1st Infantry
ESAU, FERDINAND		E	5th Infantry
EICHBERG, JAMES T.		B	6th Infantry
ELSNA, CARL		C	7th Infantry
EPPENSTEIN, CARL		F	8th Infantry
ELSNER, CHARLES F.	1st Lieutenant		29th Infantry
EISNER, GUSTAV		I	29th Infantry
ENGEL, HERMAN		F	39th Infantry
EHRLICH, HERMAN		H	39th Infantry
ECKSTEIN, DAVID	Corporal	B	41st Infantry
ENGEL, MORITZ		I	41st Infantry
ENOCH, LEOPOLD		I	41st Infantry
EISEMAN, LOUIS	Corporal	C	46th Infantry
ENGEL, JOSEPH		C	46th Infantry
ELIAS, BENJAMIN		E	54th Infantry
ENGEL, GILBERT			61st Infantry
ELKAN, S.			62nd Infantry
EMANUEL, ULLMAN		E	66th Infantry
ELSAS, JACOB		H	68th Infantry
ETTINGER, JOSEPH		A	70th Infantry
ELLIS, DANIEL		C	94th Infantry
ELLIS, ISAAC		C	94th Infantry
EISMAN, FELIX		F	100th Infantry
EPSTEIN, DAVID		C	131st Infantry
ENGEL, ADOLPH		B	185th Infantry
ENGEL, HERMAN	Sergeant	C	7th S. V.
ELLINGER, ADOLPH		C	7th S. V.
EPHRAIM MORRIS	Sergeant	H	47th S. M.
ENGEL, ALBERT	Corporal	C	13th Cavalry
ELLINGER, CHARLES		D	18th Cavalry
ERLANGER, MARTIN			30th Independent Artillery
FULT, LOUIS		G	1st Infantry
FRIEDENBERG, JAMES A.		A	1st Infantry
FRIEDBERG, ALFRED	Ensign	I	1st Infantry

Name.	Rank.	Company.	Regiment.
FRANKFURTER, BENJAMIN E.		D	5th Infantry
FRANK, EMIL		E	5th Infantry
FRANK, AUGUST		C	6th Infantry
FREUND, AUGUST		C	6th Infantry
FRANK, LOUIS		B	7th Infantry
FRANK, JACOB		B	7th Infantry
FEDER, MAX		E	7th Infantry
FALKENBERG, HERMAN		E	7th Infantry
FISCHER, P. J.		E	7th Infantry
FRIEDMAN, ALBERT	Sergeant	D	8th Infantry
FRANKENSTEIN, L.			8th Infantry

Killed at Fredericksburg.

Name.	Rank.	Company.	Regiment.
FROHBACH, A.			8th Infantry
FROHBACH, GUSTAV		I	8th Infantry
FROHBACH, HERMAN		I	8th Infantry
FRIEDENTHAL, ABRAHAM	Sergeant	A	12th Infantry
FIX, MAX	Sergeant	B	12th Infantry
FELSENHEIMER, MARTIN		B	12th Infantry
FRANKENSTEIN, PHILIP			20th Infantry
FULD, MOSES		C	20th Infantry

Lost an arm in action.

Name.	Rank.	Company.	Regiment.
FLATTO, HARRIS		A	24th Infantry
FRIEDENBERG, WILLIAM		H	24th Infantry
FRANK, HENRY		B	26th Infantry
FRANK, JULIUS		D	29th Infantry
FRANKEL, LOUIS	Sergeant	F	29th Infantry
FREUND, LOUIS	Captain	G	29th Infantry

Promoted from Sergeant.

Name.	Rank.	Company.	Regiment.
FRANK, LOUIS	Lieutenant		29th Infantry
FLEISCHMAN, WILLIAM		G	29th Infantry
FRANKEL, HERMAN	Corporal	C	31st Infantry

Promoted from private.

Name.	Rank.	Company.	Regiment.
FRANKENBERG, JULIUS		C	31st Infantry
FREUDENTHAL, DAVID		C	31st Infantry
FREEMAN, JOSEPH	Sergeant	G	35th Infantry
FREDENBERG, DAVID			35th Infantry
FREDENBERG, J.			35th Infantry
FREUDENBERG, ALEXANDER		E	39th Infantry

NAME.	RANK.	COMPANY.	REGIMENT.
FREEMAN, SIMON		C	40th Infantry
FREEMAN, SIMON		E	40th Infantry
FLEISCHMAN, OSCAR	Captain	A	41st Infantry

Promoted from private.

FREUND, JOSEPH		B	41st Infantry
FRANK, JOACHIM J.		K	41st Infantry
FRANK, JACOB		C	46th Infantry
FLEISCHMAN, CARL		F	46th Infantry
FLEISCHMAN, JOSEPH		I	46th Infantry
FALK, JOSEPH		B	49th Infantry
FRIEDENFELD, CHARLES		C	49th Infantry
FRIEDENBERG, HENRY		C	49th Infantry
FRIEDENBERG, ABRAHAM		K	50th Infantry
FRANK, WILLIAM	Lieutenant	A	52nd Infantry
FRANK, EMIL	Lieutenant	A	52nd Infantry

Promoted from Sergeant.

FRIEDENBERG, DAVID		C	52nd Infantry
FRIEDENBERG, ADOLPH	Captain	E	54th Infantry
FLEISCHMAN, AUGUST		H	54th Infantry
FREUND, BERNARD		H	54th Infantry
FREUDENBERGER, L.			55th Infantry
FRANK, JACOB		K	57th Infantry
FRIEDLANDER, GOTTLIEB	Captain	C	58th Infantry

Promoted from private.

FLEISCHER, JULIUS	Lieutenant	D	58th Infantry
FREEMAN, HENRY			65th Infantry
FEDER, HENRY	(Three brothers)		66th Infantry
FEDER, ABRAHAM	Sergeant	C	66th Infantry
FEDER, ADOLPH	Corporal	C	66th Infantry
FISCHER, ——	Lieutenant	K	66th Infantry
FRIEDENBERG, NATHAN		E	66th Infantry
FALK, JACOB		C	68th Infantry
FRANKE, HERMAN		I	68th Infantry
FRANKE, JULIUS		F	68th Infantry
FELDSTEIN, THEODORE	Captain	I	68th Infantry
FRANK, GOTTLIEB		K	68th Infantry
FRANZ, ELI			68th Infantry
FRAENKEL, MOSES		A	72nd Infantry

NAME.	RANK.	COMPANY.	REGIMENT.
FRIEDMAN, WILLIAM		B	73d Infantry
FRANKENBERG, WILLIAM			83d Infantry
FRIEDENTHAL, R.			91st Infantry
FIRTH, ISAAC		E	91st Infantry
FRANKFURTER, ABRAHAM		E	91st Infantry
FRIEDMAN, JACOB		A	100th Infantry
FRANK, C. P.		E	100th Infantry
FRANK, JULIUS	Lieutenant	A	103d Infantry
Promoted from Corporal.			
FALK, JOSEPH		E	103d Infantry
FREUND, HEINRICH		D	119th Infantry
FRANKEL, JACOB		K	119th Infantry
FRIEDLANDER, MAX	Lieutenant		122nd Infantry
FIX, JULIUS		E	122nd Infantry
FRIEDENBERG, MORRIS		G	128th Infantry
FRIEDMAN, HENRY	Corporal	G	131st Infantry
FREEDMAN, DANIEL	Corporal	B	143d Infantry
FRANK, DAVID	Corporal	G	154th Infantry
FRANK, MOSES		F	160th Infantry
FLATTE, HARRIS			
FRANKLIN, MARCUS			178th Infantry
FRIEDENTHAL, FREDERICK		K	178th Infantry
FRANKEL, FRIEDRICH	Captain		187th Infantry
FERDINANDSON, JULIUS	Lieutenant		191st Infantry
FREUND, JOSEPH	2nd Lieutenant	C	1st Independent
Promoted from private.			
FRIEDMAN, PHILIP		K	5th S. V.
FRIEDMAN, JOSEPH		B	7th S. V.
FRIEDLANDER, DAVID	Major		25th S. M.
FRIEDENTHAL, JACOB	Captain	A	25th S. M.
FREEMAN, BENJAMIN		G	71st S. M.
FREEMAN, CHARLES		K	71st S. M.
FREEMAN, ABRAHAM		D	2nd Cavalry
FRANK, GUSTAV		M	4th Cavalry
FRANKENBERGER, H.			7th Cavalry
FREUND, JACOB		B	8th Cavalry
FRIEND, FRANK		E	13th Cavalry
FRIEND, ISAAC B.		B	13th Cavalry

NAME.	RANK.	COMPANY.	REGIMENT.
FRANK, LEOPOLD		G	18th Cavalry
FRANK, LEOPOLD		I	1st Mounted Rifles
FRANK, LEWIS		L	2nd Artillery
FRIEDMAN, HEINRICH			13th Artillery
FALK, JACOB		E	14th Artillery
FLEISCHMAN, GUSTAV		E	15th Artillery
FRANK, EMIL		F	15th Artillery
FRANK, JOSEPH		F	Marine Artillery
FELLEMAN, WILLIAM M.		G	1st Battery
FALK, JACOB		13th	Independent Artillery
FLECK, C. C.			30th Battery
FREUND, MAX.			30th Battery

NAME.	RANK.	COMPANY.	REGIMENT.
GANS, ALBERT		H	6th Infantry
GUMPRECHT, DAVID		K	6th Infantry
GOTTWALT, HERMAN		A	7th Infantry
GLAUBENKSLY, T. G.	Adjutant		7th Infantry

Promoted from Lieutenant.

NAME.	RANK.	COMPANY.	REGIMENT.
GUTMAN, HENRY		B	7th Infantry
GUMPRECHT, HENRY			8th Infantry

Wounded at Fredericksburg.

NAME.	RANK.	COMPANY.	REGIMENT.
GUMPRECHT, JULIUS			8th Infantry

Killed at Fredericksburg.

NAME.	RANK.	COMPANY.	REGIMENT.
GOTTLIEB, JULIUS		E	8th Infantry
GOLDSMITH, LEWIS		C	9th Infantry
GOLDSMITH, ISAAC		I	11th Infantry
GREENWALL, PHILIP			12th Infantry
GREENFIELD, ALBERT		K	19th Infantry
GREENFIELD, CHARLES		K	19th Infantry
GRUNEWALD, FRIEDRICH			20th Infantry
GRUNTHAL, EDWARD		I	29th Infantry
GRUNEWALD, GUSTAV		I	29th Infantry
GOLDFISCH, ADAM		C	31st Infantry
GREENFELD, MORRIS		H	31st Infantry
GOODMAN, LEVI		A	33d Infantry
GANS, AUGUST	Sergeant	C	38th Infantry
GOTTSCHALK, MICHAEL G.		D	39th Infantry
GOTTLIEB, HENRY E.	Captain		40th Infantry

NAME.	RANK.	COMPANY.	REGIMENT.
GANS, JACOB		G	39th Infantry
GOLDBERG, SAMUEL			40th Infantry
GOTTHOLD, ISAAC N.	Captain	F	42nd Infantry

Promoted from Lieutenant.

Mr. Gotthold was a gifted actor, whose impersonations of leading characters won for him high favor, and demonstrated his superior histrionic abilities.

GRUNBAUM, JOHN		K	45th Infantry
GOLDMAN, FRIEDERICH		H	46th Infantry
GOLDSMITH, ABRAHAM		I	47th Infantry
GOLDSCHMIDT, JULIUS		F	49th Infantry
GREENWALT, JOSEPH			50th Infantry
GOLDSMITH, CARL		I	52nd Infantry
GOLDSMITH, L.		G	54th Infantry
GOLDVOGEL, ALEXANDER		C	55th Infantry
GOODMAN, HENRY		K	56th Infantry
GOLDSMITH, CHARLES		K	56th Infantry
GOODMAN, BENJAMIN	Captain	B	77th Infantry

Promoted from private.

GOODMAN, ALBERT		B	57th Infantry
GOSLINE, HENRY S.		Colonel Pinckney's Regiment	
GOLDMAN, AUGUST		E	58th Infantry
GOLDMAN, WILLIAM		E	58th Infantry
GANS, EMIL		A	68th Infantry
GOTTHOLD, AUGUST		G	68th Infantry
GOLDSMITH, A.		F	70th Infantry
GOLDSMITH, LEOPOLD		C	71st Infantry
GOLDSMITH, H.			80th Infantry
GOODMAN, H. J.		C	82nd Infantry
GOODMAN, SAMUEL G.		H	93d Infantry
GOLDSMITH, WILLIAM		F	94th Infantry
GREENFELD, DAVID		F	97th Infantry
GREENHUT, S.			100th Infantry

Killed at Chancellorsville.

GUGGENHEIM, J.			100th Infantry

Killed in attack on Morris Island.

GOODMAN, HENRY S.		A	100th Infantry
GOLDSTEIN, PHILIP		F	103d Infantry

NAME.	RANK.	COMPANY.	REGIMENT.
GREEN, S.			107th Infantry
GOTTSCHALK, JACOB		K	115th Infantry
GANS, LOUIS		E	119th Infantry
GREEN, BENJAMIN H.		E	125th Infantry
GREEN, SOLOMON		D	126th Infantry
GOLDSMITH, JOSEPH W.		H	127th Infantry
GOODMAN, JOSEPH		H	131st Infantry
GOTTHELF, JACOB		F	146th Infantry
GREENWALT, HARRIS		K	152nd Infantry
GREENWAT, MARCUS		K	152nd Infantry
GREEN, OSCAR		G	153d Infantry
GOLDSMITH, HENRY		B	164th Infantry
GANS, ISAAC		A	175th Infantry
GANS, FREDERICK		B	185th Infantry
GOLDSMITH, ABRAHAM		A	1st Independent
GOLDSMITH, G. B.	Corporal	A	22nd S. M.
GOLDSMITH, J. W.	Sergeant	C	22nd S. M.
GOLDSMITH, M.		C	2nd Cavalry
GOLDSTEIN, A.		M	6th Cavalry
GREEN, DAVID		H	11th Cavalry
GOLDSMITH, S.		F	18th Cavalry
GOTTLIEB, LUDWIG	Corporal	K	1st Artillery
GOLDSMITH, WILLIAM		E	16th Artillery
GLASER, ADOLPH		K	15th Artillery
Killed in Virginia.			
GUMPEL, SAMUEL		C	15th Artillery
GREEN, MOSES S.	Captain		15th Engineers
HAAS, PHILIP			1st Infantry
HARRIS, JACOB		A	2nd Infantry
HIRSCH, ANDREW		K	2nd Infantry
HEYMAN PHILIP		D	4th Infantry
HESS, CHARLES		G	4th Infantry
HART, DAVID H.	Sergeant	F	5th Infantry
HEYMAN, NATHAN		F	6th Infantry
HIRSCHSON, EDMUND		B	7th Infantry
HESS, FRIEDRICH		B	7th Infantry
HEIMBERGER, CHARLES	Lieutenant		7th Infantry

NAME.	RANK	COMPANY.	REGIMENT.
HARTZHEIM, CHARLES		D	7th Infantry
HEIMBURG, JULIUS	Captain		7th Infantry (reorganized)
HELLER, FRIEDRICH		D	7th Infantry
HOCHHEIM, LOUIS	Captain	F	7th Infantry
HAAS, LEONARD J.			7th Infantry
HERZBERG, ALBERT	Lieutenant	C	8th Infantry
HERZFELD, JOSEPH		E	8th Infantry
HEINEMAN, THEODORE		E	8th Infantry
HOFFMAN, JACOB		H	8th Infantry
HIRSCH, JULIUS		I	8th Infantry
HART, JOSEPH A.	Drum Major		9th Infantry
HAYS, JACOB		C	9th Infantry
HARRIS, JOSEPH		B	10th Infantry
HARRIS, DANIEL		K	11th Infantry
HERSCH, J. S.	Corporal	G	13th Infantry
HARRIS, LOUIS		A	14th Infantry
HESSE, ADOLPH		C	14th Infantry
HAYS, MICHAEL		E	15th Infantry
HARRIS, DAVID		E	16th Infantry
HARRIS, JOSEPH		E	17th Infantry
HARRIS, DAVID		K	18th Infantry
HOYM, OTTO	Captain		20th Infantry
HOFFMAN, L.			20th Infantry
HERRMAN, AUGUST		C	20th Infantry
HERRMAN, WILLIAM		C	20th Infantry
HEINEMAN, CHARLES		D	20th Infantry
HEINEMAN, HENRY		F	20th Infantry
HESS, JACOB		K	20th Infantry

Lost an arm at Chancellorsville.

HARRIS, CHARLES		G	23d Infantry
HARRISON, SAMUEL		A	24th Infantry

Lost a leg at the Battle of New Hope Church.

HART, BENJAMIN B.		H	24th Infantry
HERRMAN, HENRY	Corporal	C	25th Infantry
HARRIS, ISRAEL	Corporal	E	25th Infantry
HAMBURGER, SIMON		I	25th Infantry
HARRIS, ISAAC		K	27th Infantry

NAME.	RANK.	COMPANY.	REGIMENT.
HERRMAN, JACOB		G	28th Infantry
HAHN, JACOB		B	29th Infantry
HUEBSCH, CHARLES		H	29th Infantry
HIRSCHBERG, CHARLES		A	31st Infantry
HIRSCH, MORRIS		C	31st Infantry
HOFFMAN, LOUIS		D	31st Infantry
HIRSCH, JACOB		E	31st Infantry
HAHN, JOSEPH	Sergeant	F	31st Infantry
HAHN, FERDINAND		G	31st Infantry
HAHN, GEORGE		G	31st Infantry
HEIMAN, HENRY		G	31st Infantry
HART, DAVID		B	33d Infantry
HOOFMAN, EUGENE		F	34th Infantry
HAYMAN, SAMUEL	Colonel	B	37th Infantry
HESS, ADOLPH		A	39th Infantry
HOCHHEIMER, CARL		B	39th Infantry
HEINE, LOUIS		H	39th Infantry
HAHN, CHARLES			39th Infantry
HERZOG, LOUIS		K	39th Infantry
HIRSCHFELD, HERMAN	Surgeon	B	41st Infantry
HIRSCHFELD, ERNST	Lieutenant	C	41st Infantry
HERZ, JACOB		C	41st Infantry
HIRSCH, GEORGE		C	41st Infantry
HIRSCH, JACOB		E	41st Infantry
HIRSCH, SELIGMAN		I	41st Infantry
HART, SAMUEL		F	43d Infantry
HAYS, JOEL		C	44th Infantry
HAYS, NATHANIEL		C	44th Infantry
HARRIS, DAVID S.		K	44th Infantry
HAHN, P.			45th Infantry
HEINEMAN, C.		B	45th Infantry
HESS, HENRY		F	45th Infantry
HEINEMAN, WILLIAM		G	45th Infantry
HAHN, CARL		B	46th Infantry
HAHN, CARL MORITZ		G	46th Infantry
HAHN, AUGUST		K	47th Infantry
HAYS, MICHAEL		B	48th Infantry

17

NAME.	RANK.	COMPANY.	REGIMENT.
HERRMAN, JACOB		E	49th Infantry
HAMMERSLAUGH, SAMUEL		A	54th Infantry
HAMMERSLAUGH, SIMON		A	54th Infantry

Died of wounds received at Chancellorsville.

HEINEMAN, GOTTLIEB		C	54th Infantry
HERSCHFELD, CHARLES		E	54th Infantry
HEINEMAN, HEINRICH		F	54th Infantry
HERTZ, ALEXANDER		F	54th Infantry
HIRSCHFELD, HERMAN		K	54th Infantry
HOTTHEIMER, HENRY			54th Infantry

Killed in action.

HARRIS, ISAAC C.		F	56th Infantry
HARRIS, JOSEPH		F	56th Infantry
HERRMAN, FERDINAND	Captain	D	58th Infantry
HERZBERG, ADOLF		C	59th Infantry
HERSCHFELD, ELIAS		I	59th Infantry
HERSCHFELD, JACOB		I	59th Infantry
HART, DAVID E.		A	60th Infantry
HARTFELD, ——			62nd Infantry
HIRSCHBERG, DAVID		F	62nd Infantry
HERZBERG, FRIEDRICH	Lieutenant	A	66th Infantry

Promoted from Sergeant.

HOCKSTER, MAYER			66th Infantry
HIRSCH, JULIUS		C	66th Infantry
HERRMAN, SIMON	Sergeant	K	66th Infantry
HESS, JACOB		K	66th Infantry
HARRIS, LEVI		H	67th Infantry
HERZBERG, RUDOLF		D	68th Infantry
HAYS, SAMUEL		E	70th Infantry
HESS, JACOB	Sergeant		71st Infantry

Color Sergeant and Commissary.

HESS, MORRIS		F	71st Infantry
HARRIS, FRANK	Corporal	G	77th Infantry
HERRMAN, ALEXANDER H.	Sergeant	C	80th Infantry
HOUSEMAN, N.			83d Infantry
HAYS, JACOB		C	83d Infantry
HART, LEWIS		A	86th Infantry

NAME.	RANK.	COMPANY.	REGIMENT.
HERRMAN, WILLIAM		C	86th Infantry
HAMBURGER, SIMPSON	Captain	D	91st Infantry
Promoted from Lieutenant.			
HART, ALEXANDER		D	91st Infantry
HARRIS, JOSEPH A.		H	95th Infantry
HAYS, OSCAR A.		G	97th Infantry
HERRMAN, LOUIS	Sergeant	H	97th Infantry
HECHT, BENJAMIN	Captain	B	98th Infantry
HEILBRUN, PHILIP			100th Infantry
HESS, JOSEPH		C	101st Infantry
HAYS, ABRAM		D	118th Infantry
HART, JOEL		G	113th Infantry
HERRMAN, JACOB		I	123d Infantry
HIRSCHLER, NATHANIEL			124th Infantry
HAYS, DANIEL		A	127th Infantry
HEINEMAN, OSCAR		A	132nd Infantry
HEINEMAN, CHARLES H.		A	134th Infantry
HERRMAN, DANIEL		E	136th Infantry
HART, B.			139th Infantry
HALLER, JACOB			140th Infantry
HAYS, JOSEPH	Lieutenant		142nd Infantry
HESS, JOSEPH		A	144th Infantry
HEINSFURTER, JOSEPH			149th Infantry
HYAMS, JACOB		A	149th Infantry
HARRIS, CHAPMAN A.		A	149th Infantry
HAYS, HENRY		E	149th Infantry
HAYS, DANIEL		E	149th Infantry
HAYS, SIDNEY		K	151st Infantry
HAYS, BENJAMIN E.		H	10th Zouaves
HEYMAN, R. B.	Corporal	A	153d Infantry
HARRISON, HENRY		K	158th Infantry
HERRMAN, ALEXANDER		C	162nd Infantry
HAHN, LOUIS		C	163d Infantry
HAHN, PHILIP		F	176th Infantry
HERZOG, CHARLES		B	178th Infantry
HIRSCH, HENRY		I	178th Infantry
HAYS, BENJAMIN T.		G	179th Infantry
HARRIS, LEVI E.		A	184th Infantry

Name.	Rank.	Company.	Regiment.
Hess, Jonah		K	192nd Infantry
Harris, Frank		H	194th Infantry
Holt, N.		B	1st Independent
Killed at Morris Island.			
Hirsch, John	Lieutenant	C	1st Independent
Holz, Louis		G	1st Independent
Hays, Benjamin J.		D	7th S. V.
Herzog, Joseph		G	7th S. V.
Herz, Carl			22nd S. M.
Harris, Samuel F.		H	37th S. M.
Hirsch, Herman	Corporal	E	1st Cavalry
Hirsch, Philip		E	1st Cavalry
Herzfeld, Moritz		I	1st Cavalry
Heidenheim, Henry		I	1st Cavalry
Hays, Michael	Lieutenant		4th Cavalry
Herman, Louis		K	4th Cavalry
Hahn, Henry		I	8th Cavalry
Hart, Isaac		E	12th Cavalry
Hart, Joseph		F	12th Cavalry
Haas, Louis	Lieutenant		12th Cavalry
Herrman, Charles T.	Corporal	K	12th Cavalry
Hess, Julian		L	14th Cavalry
Hahn, Adolph		F	16th Cavalry
Hays, Solomon E.		B	26th Cavalry
Hofheimer, Siegmund		F	1st Mounted Rifles
Hays, Isaac C.		C	2nd Mounted Rifles
Heineman, William		E	2nd Mounted Rifles
Herrman, Max		F	3d Artillery
Hart, Eli W.		G	6th Artillery
Hays, Abraham		D	7th Artillery
Hays, David H.		K	13th Artillery
Herzog, Charles	Adjutant		15th Artillery
Promoted from Lieutenant.			
Hess, David		A	15th Artillery
Hess, Herman		C	15th Artillery
Hess, Julius	Lieutenant		28th Battery
Promoted from private.			
Hess, Julius	2nd Lieutenant		1st Engineers

NAME.	RANK.	COMPANY.	REGIMENT.
HARTFIELD, ——		K	62nd Infantry
HYAMS, JACOB			——————
ISAACS, CHARLES L.		A	5th Infantry
ISAACS, JOSEPH	Corporal	A	9th Infantry
ISENSTEIN, GEORGE			24th Infantry
ISAACS, SOLOMON		A	40th Infantry
ISAACS, ISAAC		B	44th Infantry
ISRAELS, LEHMAN	Lieutenant	A	55th Infantry

Promoted from Sergeant.

NAME.	RANK.	COMPANY.	REGIMENT.
ISAYAH, E.			59th Infantry
ISIDOR, LEOPOLD		F	61st Infantry
ISAAC, JULIUS			De Kalle Regiment
ISAACS, J. J.		D	76th Infantry
ISAACS, LEVI		K	78th Infantry
ISAACS, MOSES M.		D	83d Infantry
ISAACS, ISAAC		I	83d Infantry
ISAACS, HENRY		G	90th Infantry
ISAACS, MICHAEL		G	90th Infantry
ISAACS, ALFRED S.	Color Sergeant	H	95th Infantry

Promoted from private; wounded at Gettysburg.

NAME.	RANK.	COMPANY.	REGIMENT.
ISAACS, SAMUEL		D	132nd Infantry
ISAAC, LEWIS	Captain		5th Cavalry

Promoted from private.

NAME.	RANK.	COMPANY.	REGIMENT.
ISAACS, DAVID		B	5th Cavalry
ISAACS, BENJAMIN		E	16th Artillery
ISAAC, V.		F	16th Artillery
JACOB, HENRY F.		B	1st Infantry
JACOBS, WILLIAM C.		I	3d Infantry
JACOBSON, PHILIP	Lieutenant		5th Infantry

Enlisted as private.

NAME.	RANK.	COMPANY.	REGIMENT.
JACOBS, JOHN		C	5th Infantry
JOACHIM, CHARLES		H	6th Infantry
JULIUS, OSCAR	1st Lieutenant		7th Infantry

Promoted from Sergeant.

NAME.	RANK.	COMPANY.	REGIMENT.
JOSEPH, GOTTFRIED		F	7th Infantry

NAME.	RANK.	COMPANY.	REGIMENT.
JACOBY, FRIEDRICH	1st Lieutenant	G	7th Infantry

Promoted from private; killed at Fredericksburg.

JUPITZ, F.		{	7th Infantry
		{ I	3d (New Jersey) Infantry
JACOBS, JOSEPH		A	8th Infantry
JACOBSON, IVOR	Captain	D	8th Infantry

Promoted from Lieutenant.

| JACOBY, JOSEPH | | E | 8th Infantry |
| JACOBS, EDWARD | | D | 9th Infantry |

Captured; died a prisoner of war.

| JACOBSON, LOUIS | Lieutenant | E | 9th Infantry |

Promoted from Sergeant.

JACOBS, GEORGE A.		H	17th Infantry
JACOBS, GEORGE M.		H	19th Infantry
JACOBS, CHARLES E.		H	19th Infantry
JACOBY, ADAM		F	20th Infantry
JACOB, W.		G	21st Infantry
JACOBS, HYMES		G	24th Infantry
JACOBS, MORRIS		E	25th Infantry
JOST, J.			29th Infantry
JACOBSON, HERMAN		C	29th Infantry
JONES, ABRAHAM		I	31st Infantry
JACOBUS, JESSE		I	34th Infantry
JACOBUS, HENRY		I	34th Infantry
JACKEL, JULIUS			39th Infantry
JACOBS, CARL		F	39th Infantry
JACOBSON, JULIUS		A	41st Infantry
JACOBS, B.		B	42nd Infantry
JACOBS, GOTTLIEB		K	45th Infantry
JACOBY, SAMUEL		K	50th Infantry
JONES, BENJAMIN		G	51st Infantry
JACOBS, SAMUEL		K	51st Infantry
JACOBY, LOUIS	Corporal	I	52nd Infantry
JACOBS, BENJAMIN		B	53d Infantry
JOSEPH, HENRY		F	54th Infantry
JOACHIMSEN PHILIP J.	Brevet Brigadier-General		59th Infantry

A New York paper makes the following remarks concerning this distinguished officer, under date of January 7, 1890:

"At the breaking out of the Civil War, the high virtues of this officer showed themselves in their brightest hue. He organized the 59th New York Volunteer Regiment and, appointed as its Colonel, was ordered to the front. The Regiment was stationed at Fortress Monroe. While there he was appointed as United States Paymaster. Subsequently he was ordered to New Orleans under the command of General B. F. Butler. While on duty he fell from his horse and was so severely hurt as to be sent to New York. Rendered disqualified for further military duty, he was honorably discharged. Governor Fenton, of the State of New York, in acknowledging his eminent services, appointed him Brevet Brigadier-General."

NAME.	RANK.	COMPANY.	REGIMENT.
JACOBS, GEORGE ALBERT		C	61st Infantry
JULIAN, THEODOR			62nd Infantry
JOSEPH, ——		E	66th Infantry
JACOB, JULIUS		K	66th Infantry
JOSEPH, JOSEPH M.	Corporal	K	66th Infantry
JACOBSIG, GUSTAV		A	67th Infantry
JOSEPH, J. ADOLPH	1st Lieutenant		68th Infantry
JACOBS, HENRY D.		K	70th Infantry
JOSEPH, LIONEL		C	72nd Infantry
JACOBSON, EUGENE P.	1st Lieutenant		74th Infantry
Promoted from Sergeant.			
JACOBS, BENJAMIN		I	82nd Infantry
JOEL, JULIUS		B	83d Infantry
JACOBS, JACOB	Captain	F	83d Infantry
Enlisted as private.			
JACOB, LOUIS		H	84th Infantry
JACOBS, ISRAEL P.	Corporal	E	89th Infantry
JACOBS, BENJAMIN		G	90th Infantry
JACOBS, CHARLES		G	90th Infantry
JACOBS, JOHN		G	90th Infantry
JACOBS, HENRY F.	Sergeant	G	91st Infantry
JACOBSON, ISAAC		H	91st Infantry
JACOBS, J. S.		H	92nd Infantry

NAME.	RANK.	COMPANY.	REGIMENT.
JONAS, DANIEL		E	100th Infantry
JACOBS, EDWARD		I	101st Infantry
JACOBY, MAX		A	103d Infantry
JACOBSON, HERMAN	Corporal	D	103d Infantry
JACOBS, ELI		B	109th Infantry
JACOBS, HENRY C.		H	110th Infantry
JACOBSON, HERMAN	Sergeant	K	119th Infantry
JONES, JOSEPH		F	124th Infantry
JACOBS, JOHN		F	127th Infantry
JACOBS, JOHN H.		K	127th Infantry
JACOBS, JOSEPH W.		K	127th Infantry
JACOBS, WILLIAM S.		K	127th Infantry
JACOBS, JOSEPH		A	129th Infantry
JACOBS, DANIEL T.	Captain	I	133d Infantry
JACOBS, HENRY P.		K	139th Infantry
JACOBS, REUBEN		G	141st Infantry
JONES, ISAAC		C	147th Infantry
JACOBS, GEORGE C.		A	149th Infantry
JACOBS, BERNHARD		D	156th Infantry
JACOBS, JOSEPH		D	156th Infantry
JACOBS, ALFRED		K	162nd Infantry
JACOBS, MORRIS		B	165th Infantry
JACOBS, CHARLES		C	173d Infantry
JACOBSON, A. D.		D	176th Infantry
JONES, LEVI		A	179th Infantry
JACOBS, JACOB		I	185th Infantry
JACOBSON, ABRAHAM		I	193d Infantry
JACOBSON, HERMAN		C	1st Independent
JOSEPH, A.		D	5th S. V.
JACOBSON, W. H.	Lieutenant		7th S. V.
JACOBS, MAURICE H.		F	17th S. V.
JACOBSON, A. C.		C	71st S. M.
JONES, ABRAHAM	Lieutenant	A	1st Cavalry
JACOBS, G.		B	1st Cavalry
JACOBSON, HENRY S.		H	10th Cavalry
JACOBS, CHARLES	Corporal	H	12th Cavalry
JACOBS, CARL		C	13th Cavalry
JACOBS, EUGENE		K	18th Cavalry

NAME.	RANK.	COMPANY.	REGIMENT.
JONES, HENRY		G	22nd Cavalry
JACOB, BENJAMIN		M	22nd Cavalry
JONES, JACOB T.		E	1st Veteran Cavalry
JACOBSON, HENRY		B	2nd Veteran Cavalry
JACOBS, ISAAC		G	4th Artillery
JACOBSON, W. C.	1st Lieutenant		5th Artillery

Promoted from 2nd Lieutenant.

JACOBS, JOSEPH		B	8th Artillery
JONES, ISAAC		F	13th Artillery
JOST, JACOB		I	15th Artillery
JACOBOWSKY, MARCUS		23d	Independent Artillery
JONES, MOSES		28th	Independent Artillery

KLUGEMAN, NATHAN		E	2nd Independent Artillery

Also Veteran Mexican War.

KUHN, JOSEPH		I	1st Infantry
KOHN, PHILIP	Captain		5th Infantry

Promoted from Lieutenant.

KAISER, WILLIAM			6th Infantry
KAUFMAN, WILLIAM B.	Sergeant	B	6th Infantry
KOERPEL, BENJAMIN			6th Infantry
KAUFMAN, WILLIAM B.	Captain	F	6th Infantry

Promoted from Lieutenant.

KUHN, FERDINAND		C	7th Infantry
KRUEGER, LOUIS		F	7th Infantry
KONIGSDORFER, L.			7th Infantry
KAUFMAN, JULES	1st Lieutenant		7th Infantry (reorganized)
KONIG, AUGUST	Lieutenant		7th Infantry (reorganized)
KESSLER, LEVI			7th Infantry (reorganized)

Wounded at Wilson Creek, N. C.; captured; confined in Libby Prison.

KOHN, HEYMAN		H	7th Infantry (reorganized)
KOLB, JACOB		I	7th Infantry (reorganized)

Name.	Rank.	Company.	Regiment.
Kohn, Joseph		F	7th Infantry (reorganized)
Kaufman, Norman			7th Infantry (reorganized)

Wounded at Fredericksburg on left leg, and shell wound on right hip.

Kaufman, Jacob		A	8th Infantry (reorganized)
Kohn, Hyman			8th Infantry (reorganized)

Killed at Fredericksburg.

Kaufman, P.			8th Infantry (reorganized)
Kahn, Henry		G	10th Infantry (reorganized)
Koch, Leopold		C	13th Infantry (reorganized)
Kaufman, William	Drum Major		20th Infantry (reorganized)
Kaiser, Jacob		A	20th Infantry (reorganized)
Kaufman, Adolph		B	20th Infantry (reorganized)
Krauskopf, George		B	21st Infantry (reorganized)
Kirsch, Jacob		E	21st Infantry (reorganized)
Katz, Michael		I	29th Infantry (reorganized)
Kohn, Barnet	Corporal	C	31st Infantry (reorganized)
Kassel, Joseph			31st Infantry (reorganized)
Kottner, L.			31st Infantry (reorganized)
Kaufman, Gustav		E	39th Infantry (reorganized)
Katz, Louis		B	41st Infantry (reorganized)

NAME.	RANK.	COMPANY.	REGIMENT.
KAUFMAN, GOTTLOB		D	41st Infantry (reorganized)
KIRITZ, MICHAEL			42nd Infantry (reorganized)
KAUFMAN, C.	Corporal		45th Infantry
KAUFMAN, LOUIS		D	45th Infantry
KAHN, CHARLES		G	45th Infantry
KAUFMAN, GOTTLOB	Sergeant	H	45th Infantry
KAUFMAN, FREDERICK		H	45th Infantry
KLINGENSTEIN, J.			45th Infantry
KOHN, JULIUS		D	46th Infantry
KING, FERDINAND		K	50th Infantry
KOHEN, NICOLAUS		D	51st Infantry
KARPELES, HENRY M.	Lieutenant-Colonel		52nd Infantry
Promoted from Major.			
KARPELES, R.	Lieutenant		52nd Infantry
Killed in action.			
KAHN, CARL		A	54th Infantry
KAHN, CHARLES		H	54th Infantry
KOCH, LEWIS		G	57th Infantry
KOHN, JACOB			57th Infantry
Wounded at Seven Pines.			
KAUFMAN, ALEXANDER		E	58th Infantry
KOHN, ISAAC	2nd Lieutenant	A	66th Infantry
KAHN, HERMAN		A	66th Infantry
KELLER, JULIUS		K	68th Infantry
KOHN, ADOLPHUS	Corporal	K	78th Infantry
KING, JOSEPH		A	81st Infantry
KING, JACOB		F	89th Infantry
KING, NOAH		H	100th Infantry
KING, JOSEPH		I	102nd Infantry
KRAUTH, HERMAN	Captain		103d Infantry
Promoted from Lieutenant.			
KOHN, CHARLES		A	103d Infantry
KAUFMAN, HEINRICH		A	103d Infantry
KAUFMAN, ADAM		F	104th Infantry
KOCH, JACOB		E	106th Infantry
KOHNSTADT, ISIDOR		G	132nd Infantry

Name.	Rank.	Company.	Regiment.
Kohn, Frederick		F	134th Infantry
Katzenstein, Joseph		F	140th Infantry
King, David		B	142nd Infantry
King, Levi	Corporal	I	150th Infantry
Kaufman, M.			159th Infantry
Kauffman, C.			163d Infantry
Katzenberg, Charles		F	163d Infantry
Kohn, Otto		C	173d Infantry
Kohn, Herman		C	178th Infantry
Katzenstein, Charles		D	178th Infantry
Kohn, Jacob		A	1st Independent
Kohn, Joseph		C	7th S. V.
Kohut, Jacob		H	7th S. M.
Kalish, Herman		D	1st Cavalry
Krauss, Henry		I	1st Cavalry
Krauss, Joseph		A	4th Cavalry
Kaufman, Jacob		K	1st Artillery
Kuhne, Levi			3d Artillery
Kaufman, Adolph		A	15th Artillery
Koch, Jacob			29th Independent Artillery

Leavy, Frederick	Sergeant		1st Infantry
Enlisted as private.			
Lilienthal, Johann		I	1st Infantry
Lipowitz, Herman	Lieutenant	K	1st Infantry
Promoted from Sergeant.			
Limberger, Augustus	Lieutenant		3d Infantry
Levy, Max		G	4th Infantry
Lisberger, D.		K	6th Infantry
Lowenthal, Siegmund	Lieutenant		6th Infantry
Levy, Joseph		F	6th Infantry
Leopold, Emil		B	7th Infantry
Lepman, Charles		D	7th Infantry
Lowenthal, Henry		D	7th Infantry
Wounded at White House Landing.			
Lowenstein, Julius		E	7th Infantry
Lichtenhahn, George		F	7th Infantry
Loeb, Max		K	7th Infantry

NAME.	RANK.	COMPANY.	REGIMENT.
LESTER, SIMON		H	8th Infantry
LIEBOLD, HERMAN	Captain		7th Infantry (reorganized)
LEVI, CARL		A	8th Infantry (reorganized)
LEVY, LOUIS		B	9th Infantry (reorganized)
LYON, MARK		B	11th Infantry (reorganized)
LYON, W.			11th Infantry (reorganized)
LAZARUS, JOHN		G	11th Infantry (reorganized)
LAZARUS, HARRY	Corporal	G	11th Infantry (reorganized)
LOWENTHAL, PHILIP		D	12th Infantry (reorganized)
LOEB, ABRAHAM			12th Infantry (reorganized)
LEDERMAN, WILLIAM		B	12th Infantry (reorganized)
LEVY, ABRAHAM			12th Infantry (reorganized)
LEWIS, DAVID J.		H	16th Infantry (reorganized)
LINDNER, B.		F	18th Infantry (reorganized)
LORCH, CHARLES	Adjutant		20th Infantry (reorganized)
Promoted for gallantry.			
LILIENTHAL, ADOLF	Sergeant	H	20th Infantry (reorganized)
LEHMAN, V.		I	20th Infantry (reorganized)
LYONS, JOSEPH		E	23d Infantry (reorganized)
LYONS, DAVID		K	23d Infantry (reorganized)

NAME.	RANK.	COMPANY.	REGIMENT.
LICHTENSTEIN, OSCAR		A	29th Infantry (reorganized)
LEWIS, EDWARD A.	Captain		26th Infantry

Promoted from Lieutenant.

LORCH, RUDOLPH	Sergeant	C	29th Infantry
LIEBMAN, FREDERICK		F	29th Infantry
LOWENSTEIN, MORITZ		H	29th Infantry
LICHENSTEIN, JACOB		I	29th Infantry
LEVY, HERMAN		C	31st Infantry
LEO, HENRY		G	31st Infantry
LEDERMAN, JOSEPH		H	31st Infantry
LEWIS, MARK A.		C	34th Infantry
LEWIS, ISAAC H		D	34th Infantry
LEWIS, SALOMON		E	34th Infantry
LOSHER, JOSEPH			38th Infantry
LOWENTHAL, BENJAMIN		D	39th Infantry

Wounded at Cross Keys; also at Bristow Station; captured at Spottsylvania and taken to Andersonville Prison.

LEIBNITZ, FERDINAND		B	39th Infantry
LEHMAN, HEINRICH		C	39th Infantry
LIESER, M.	Sergeant		39th Infantry
LEDERER, EMANUEL M.	Lieutenant	G	39th Infantry

Entered as private; twice wounded; promoted for gallantry.

LION, SIMON		I	39th Infantry
LEVY, ADOLPH		K	39th Infantry
LEWIS, D.			40th Infantry
LEWIS, J.			40th Infantry
LEVY, JOHN		A	40th Infantry
LOWENSTEIN, JOHN		B	41st Infantry
LEVY, REUBEN		C	41st Infantry
LEWIS, MOSES			42nd Infantry
LEVI, ABRAHAM		I	42nd Infantry
LIPPMAN, ——			Turner's Infantry
LEVY, BENJAMIN		B	40th Infantry

Wounded at the Wilderness. U. S. Congress awarded him a "medal of honor."

Benjamin B. Levy enlisted at the age of sixteen, in the First New York Volunteers, at the breaking out of the Rebellion, as a drummer boy, and while his regiment was stationed at Newport News, Virginia, he was detailed as Orderly for General Mansfield. While he was conveying dispatches on board the steamboat "Express" to General Wool at Fort Monroe, the steamboat was attacked opposite Norfolk, by the rebel gunboat "Seabird." The "Express," with all on board, was in imminent danger of capture, when young Levy saved the steamboat by cutting loose a water schooner they had in tow. The water schooner was captured, but the "Express" arrived safely at Fort Monroe. For this act Levy was highly complimented by Generals Mansfield and Wool.

On the retreat from Richmond, under General McClellan, his tent-mate was very ill, and to save him from being taken prisoner, Levy threw away his drum, and taking his comrade's gun and equipments, went into the fight with his regiment at Charles City Cross Roads and saved two of the colors of his regiment from capture. For this act he was promoted on the field by General Phil. Kearney to Color Sergeant of his regiment.

After the regiment's two years' service had expired, he re-enlisted in the Fortieth Few York (Mozart) regiment, and at the battle of the Wilderness he was distinguished for his gallantry. Here he was stricken down by a serious wound, receiving a compound fracture of the left thigh. Left on the field he was captured by Colonel White's Guerillas. He lay on the field with no shelter for two weeks, and was then recaptured by our troops that came from Fredericksburg. He was one of the first from this State to receive a medal of honor from Congress.

Mr. Levy is a member of Phil. Kearney Post, No. 8, New York.

NAME.	RANK.	COMPANY.	REGIMENT.
LEHMAN, ARTHUR	Sergeant	G	41st Infantry
LEHMAN, SAMUEL		H	41st Infantry
LOWENSTEIN, HERMAN		K	41st Infantry
LYONS, HENRY			43d Infantry

NAME.	RANK.	COMPANY.	REGIMENT.
LEWIS ISAAC		I	43d Infantry
LESTER, JOSEPH			44th Infantry
LEVY, SAMUEL	Corporal	A	45th Infantry
Enlisted as private.			
LIEBMAN, FREDERICK		A	45th Infantry
LEHMAN, GOTTLIEB		F	45th Infantry
LUDWIG, B.			45th Infantry
LOESCH, S.			46th Infantry
LEHMAN, WILLIAM		B	46th Infantry
LEWIS, LEWIS			47th Infantry
LEHMAN, LOUIS		B	49th Infantry
LYONS, EUGENE		K	50th Infantry
LUDWIG, JACOB		D	51st Infantry
LEWIS M.		B	51st Infantry
LICHTENSTEIN, PHILIP	Major		52nd Infantry
LORCH, HENRY	Sergeant	C	52nd Infantry
LEOPOLD, LOUIS	Lieutenant	F	52nd Infantry
Promoted from Sergeant.			
LEOPOLD, FRIEDRICH		I	54th Infantry
LEVY, LEON		A	55th Infantry
LEHMAN, CHARLES		F	55th Infantry
LEWIS, ABRAHAM		K	56th Infantry
LEWIS, BENJAMIN		K	56th Infantry
LICHTENSTEIN, THEO.	Major		58th Infantry
LEVYSON, ABRAHAM		F	58th Infantry
LEVY, ROBERT		G	58th Infantry
LOWENSTEIN, HENRY		H	58th Infantry
LEVY, HARRY		H	58th Infantry
LIPPMAN, FRIEDRICH		K	58th Infantry
LYON, DAVID H.		C	60th Infantry
LAWACH, ——	Lieutenant		62nd Infantry
LEO, FREDERICK P.		G	64th Infantry
LIEBERMAN, JOHN		F	65th Infantry
LIESER, JACOB		F	65th Infantry
LEVY, HERZ		E	66th Infantry
LEOROLDI, LEOPOLD	Captain	K	66th Infantry
LOEB, LOUIS		K	66th Infantry
LOWENSTEIN, JOSEPH		K	66th Infantry

NAME.	RANK.	COMPANY.	REGIMENT.
LOWENSTEIN, SOLOMON		K	66th Infantry
LOWENSTEIN, SELIGMAN	Corporal	B	68th Infantry
LASSNER, OTTO		C	68th Infantry
LEHMAN, ADOLPH		I	68th Infantry
LIEBMAN, GEORGE		K	68th Infantry
LOEWE, A.			68th Infantry
LEVI, WILLIAM	Sergeant	A	70th Infantry
LIPPERWITZ, HERMAN		F	71st Infantry
LICHENSTEIN, PHILIP G.	Lieutenant-Colonel		72nd Infantry
Promoted from Captain.			
LOEWE, MAX		A	72nd Infantry
LOEB, DANIEL	Adjutant	H	72nd Infantry
Promoted from Lieutenant.			
LOCHTE, DANIEL	Lieutenant		72nd Infantry
LEWIN, CHARLES		E	73d Infantry
LEHMAN, C.		F	74th Infantry
LEOPOLD, ISIDOR		A	78th Infantry
LEVIE, JOSEPH		H	82nd Infantry
LEVY, JAMES		E	87th Infantry
LYONS, MICHAEL		C	88th Infantry
LEVY, JOHN		I	88th Infantry
LOWE, WILLIAM		I	88th Infantry
LEWIS, I.			89th Infantry
LUDWIG, JACOB P.		H	89th Infantry
LEWIS, M.			96th Infantry
LEHMAN, PHILIP		I	97th Infantry
LEWIN, LEWIS		I	98th Infantry
LEWIS, EUGENE H.	Corporal	F	101st Infantry
LEWIS, ABRAHAM		B	102nd Infantry
LYON, DAVID E.		H	102nd Infantry
LEHMAN, ALBERT		C	103d Infantry
LEVY, ABRAHAM		H	103d Infantry
LEWIN, JOSEPH		I	103d Infantry
LEWIS, SAMUEL		C	107th Infantry
LEWIS, LEWIS		H	108th Infantry
LEWIS, SAMUEL		I	112th Infantry
LEWIN, N.	Lieutenant		114th Infantry

18

NAME.	RANK.	COMPANY.	REGIMENT.
LEDERER, CHARLES		D	116th Infantry
LEHMAN, WILLIAM	Corporal	E	116th Infantry
LEHMAN, P.			116th Infantry
LYON, DAVID	Sergeant	B	119th Infantry
LANDAUER, MOSES		C	119th Infantry
LAZARUS, JACOB		D	119th Infantry
LOWENSTEIN, EDWARD		I	119th Infantry
LIMBURGER, GUSTAV		E	121st Infantry
LAZARUS, LEVI		H	125th Infantry
LEWIS, L.			127th Infantry
LEIVY, ABRAHAM	Commissary Sergeant		132nd Infantry
LOWENSTEIN, LEVI		D	132nd Infantry
LEWIS, ISAAC		K	132nd Infantry
LYON, ABRAHAM		E	133d Infantry
LESTER, M.			134th Infantry
LEOPOLD, GEORGE		E	145th Infantry
LESTER, LEVY		E	147th Infantry
LEHMAN, JOSEPH		H	148th Infantry
LIGHT, SOLOMON	Captain		149th Infantry

Paralyzed in service.

LEVY, HYMAN		A	149th Infantry
LIGHT, LEWIS		A	149th Infantry

Wounded at Pine Mountain, Georgia; severely wounded at Lost Mountain.

LIEBMAN, HERMAN		A	149th Infantry
LAZARUS, NEWMAN		A	149th Infantry
LAUDERWITZBERG, LOUIS		A	149th Infantry
LEHMAN, MOSES		A	149th Infantry
LAZARUS, HARRY		A	149th Infantry
LOWITCH, MICHAEL		A	149th Infantry

Killed in action.

LEOPOLD, FRANK	Lieutenant	C	151st Infantry

Enlisted as private.

LEWIS, SIMON		A	156th Infantry
LEDERMAN, FRANK		C	161st Infantry
LEWIS, ISAAC J.		D	161st Infantry
LOESCHER, SAMUEL		C	162nd Infantry

NAME.	RANK.	COMPANY.	REGIMENT.
LICHTENFELZ, CHARLES		C	162nd Infantry
LIPOLD, ABRAHAM		A	168th Infantry
LESTER, FELIX		B	169th Infantry
LOEB, ABRAHAM		I	175th Infantry
LEHMAN, A.			176th Infantry
LOEWENTHAL, BARNEY		F	177th Infantry
LEHMAN, JOSEPH		B	178th Infantry
LEVY, ADOLPH		C	178th Infantry
LESTER, LOUIS		G	184th Infantry
LEVY, SIMON		Colonel	1st Independent
LEVY, FERDINAND	Father	Captain	1st Independent
Enlisted as Private.	and		
LEVY, ALFRED	three sons	Lieutenant	1st Indepen-
Enlisted as Private.			dent
LEVY, BENJAMIN C.			14th U. S. Infantry

The following are the records of these men:

Colonel Simon Levy was commandant of Camp "Sprague," Staten Island, and general recruiting officer during the year 1863. Afterwards he received his commission as Lieutenant-Colonel of the 1st Independent Battalion, New York Volunteers, and took command of that regiment at St. Helena Island, South Carolina, continuing in command of the same until its consolidation with the 47th and 48th New York Volunteers in February, 1864. The Battalion Regiment participated, while under the command of Colonel Simon Levy, in the capture of Folly and Morris Islands, South Carolina, and in several other engagements.

Captain Ferdinand Levy was in command of the skirmishing party of General Strong's Brigade at the capture of Morris Island, South Carolina, July 10th, 1863. This command was the first to land on the island, being the advance guard. Captain Levy was honorably mentioned for gallant services in brigade orders shortly afterwards. He is a well-known Israelite; and has served as Coroner, and is now Register of the city of New York; he is also active in Jewish institutions, secret societies, etc.

Lieutenant Alfred Levy enlisted as private in the 1st Independent Battalion; was promoted to Sergeant and subsequently to Lieutenant for meritorious conduct. After the consolidation of the regiment he joined the 5th United States Artillery and served until the close of the war.

Benjamin C. Levy enlisted in the 14th United States Infantry at the breaking out of the war and served until its close. He participated in fourteen general engagements and numerous skirmishes. His bravery on several occasions has been honorably mentioned.

NAME.	RANK.	COMPANY.	REGIMENT.
LYONS, C. H.	Adjutant		7th S. V.
LOWENTHAL, HENRY		B	7th S. V.
LEVY, JACOB		E	7th S. V.
LEVY, JACOB		F	7th S. V.
LIEBOLD, HERMAN	Captain	H	7th S. V.
LEVY, ADOLPH		C	8th S. V.
LEVY, ALEXANDER		F	8th S. V.
LEVY, JOSEPH C.		C	37th S. M.
LEOPOLD, DAVID		H	37th S. M.
LEWIS, FERDINAND		G	2nd Cavalry
LYON, ISAAC	Captain	B	5th Cavalry
LEVY, BERNHARD H.		B	5th Cavalry
LEON, ELIAS			5th Cavalry
LEWIS, DANIEL	Quartermaster-Sergeant		9th Cavalry
LEWIS, ISAAC B.		E	11th Cavalry
LEVI, CHARLES		E	11th Cavalry
LEHMEIER, G.			12th Cavalry
LUDWIG, EMIL		F	14th Cavalry
LOWENSTEIN, FREDERICK		K	14th Cavalry
LIEBMAN, FREDERICK		K	14th Cavalry
LOEB, EMIL		M	14th Cavalry
LEVI, FRANK		C	16th Cavalry
LAZARUS, H. LOUIS	1st Lieutenant	H	16th Cavalry
LEWIS, MORRIS	Captain		18th Cavalry

NAME.	RANK.	COMPANY.	REGIMENT.
LAZARUS, HENRY	Captain		25th Cavalry
LAUTERMAN, HENRY			3d Artillery
LESTER, JACOB		F	1st Veteran Cavalry
LEWIS, CHARLES E.		F	1st Veteran Cavalry
LOEB, SIEGMUND	1st Lieutenant		7th Artillery
Promoted from 2nd Lieutenant.			
LEVY, MEIER			7th Artillery
LEWIS, OSCAR		H	10th Artillery
LIEVY, JACOB		B	13th Artillery
LOWENSTEIN, MORITZ	2nd Lieutenant	F	15th Artillery
Promoted from Sergeant.			
LEVY, HENRY		E	16th Artillery
LOWENSTEIN, MORITZ		2nd Independent Artillery	
LEWIS, SAMUEL	Lieutenant	5th Independent Artillery	
LOWENTHAL, LEOPOLD			21st Artillery
LOWENTHAL, JACOB		31st Independent Artillery	
LIEBMAN, NEWMAN			———
LEHMAN, MOSES			———
LAZARUS, HARRIS			———
LEVY, HYMAN			———
LICHTENBURG, LOUIS			———
MORNINGSTEIN, HENRY		A	1st Infantry
MEYERS, JOSEPH		B	1st Infantry
MILETINSKI, MORITZ		I	1st Infantry
MANNHEIMER, MARTIN		K	1st Infantry
MORRIS, HENRY		K	1st Infantry
MYERS, SIMEON		A	2nd Infantry
MANN, A.	Ensign		3d Infantry
MEYERS, LEWIS F.			3d Infantry
MYERS, OSCAR		C	4th Infantry
MEYER, FREDERICK		B	5th Infantry
MARKS, WILLIAM		A	6th Infantry
MARKS, AUGUST		K	6th Infantry
MOSER, J.			6th Infantry
MEYER, HENRY		C	8th Infantry
MEYER, LOUIS		E	8th Infantry
MEYER, A.			8th Infantry

NAME.	RANK.	COMPANY.	REGIMENT.
MARX, GEORGE		G	8th Infantry
MEYER, LUDWIG		I	8th Infantry
MAY, MARCUS		A	9th Infantry
MEYERS, MARTIN		C	9th Infantry
MARTIN, J.			9th Infantry
MORRISON, WOLF			11th Infantry
MEYER, JACOB		C	13th Infantry
MEYERS, SIMEON		K	13th Infantry
MEYERS, JOSEPH		A	16th Infantry
MEYER, JOSEPH		E	16th Infantry
MORRIS, MOSES		K	16th Infantry
MENCKE, ISAAC	1st Lieutenant		17th Infantry

Promoted from 2nd Lieutenant.

NAME.	RANK.	COMPANY.	REGIMENT.
MAIER, J. JACOB		I	19th Infantry
MYERS, SAMUEL		I	19th Infantry
MAAS, JACOB		A	20th Infantry
MEYER, CARL	Corporal	B	20th Infantry
MARKOWSKY, AUGUST		B	20th Infantry
MANN, MAX	Corporal	C	20th Infantry
MASINS, LEOPOLD		C	20th Infantry

Lost an arm in action.

NAME.	RANK.	COMPANY.	REGIMENT.
MAYER, JOSEPH	Corporal	D	20th Infantry
MEYER, MARTIN		G	20th Infantry
MAYERS, HENRY		C	22nd Infantry
MOSES, MARCUS	Corporal	F	23d Infantry
MAY, D.			26th Infantry
MEYERS, JACOB		H	28th Infantry
MOSER, JOSEPH		A	29th Infantry
MEYER, LOUIS I.		D	29th Infantry
MORITZ, JOSEPH	Corporal	I	29th Infantry
MEYER, ADAM		K	29th Infantry
MEYERS, ISAAC		D	30th Infantry
MAYER, LEVI		F	31st Infantry
MANN, F.	Corporal		33d Infantry
MOSIER, L.			33d Infantry
MARKS, FRANK		E	35th Infantry
MENDEL, SIDNEY	Major		35th Infantry

Promoted from Captain.

NAME.	RANK.	COMPANY.	REGIMENT.
MARKS, JOSEPH		G	35th Infantry
MYERS, DAVID		E	36th Infantry
MYER, CHARLES		E	37th Infantry
MOSES, ISAAC	Adjutant-General		

Adjutant-General of the 3d Army Corps of the Army of the Potomac, commanded by General Heintzelman; participated in the battles of the Peninsular Campaign; subsequently served with General Banks.

NAME.	RANK.	COMPANY.	REGIMENT.
MAIER, A.			38th Infantry
MARSIN, F.			38th Infantry
MAIER, JOSEPH		C	38th Infantry
MAIER, DAVID		C	38th Infantry
MOSES, DAVID		F	38th Infantry
MAY, H.			39th Infantry
MEIER, HERMAN		B	39th Infantry
MAYER, CARL		G	39th Infantry
MEIER, FRIEDRICH		H	39th Infantry
MAYER, WILHELM		I	39th Infantry
MENTZ, S. D.		K	39th Infantry
MORRIS, DANIEL		E	40th Infantry
MORGENSTEIN, L.			41st Infantry
MEIERSON, MAX		B	41st Infantry
MEYERSTEIN, H.		C	41st Infantry
MEIER, JOSEPH		E	41st Infantry
MAY, HENRY	Hospital Steward		45th Infantry
MAYER, AUGUST		E	45th Infantry
MAYER, JACOB		K	45th Infantry
MORITZ, JOSEPH		K	45th Infantry
MAYER, CARL	Lieutenant		46th Infantry
MANTEL, LOUIS		A	46th Infantry
MEINHART, JACOB		B	46th Infantry
MILLER, EDWARD S.		H	46th Infantry
MARX, CARL		H	46th Infantry
MANDELL, J.		K	46th Infantry
MARKS, JOSEPH		D	49th Infantry
MOSES, AUGUST	Sergeant	G	49th Infantry
MORRIS, H.			50th Infantry
MEYER, ADOLPH	Quartermaster		52nd Infantry

Promoted from Lieutenant.

NAME.	RANK.	COMPANY.	REGIMENT.
MEYER, THEODORE		B	52nd Infantry
MOSES, GEORGE		H	52nd Infantry
MYERS, JOSEPH		A	53d Infantry
MAYER, FREDERICK		F	53d Infantry
MAYER, JACOB		G	54th Infantry
MOSES, HENRY		K	54th Infantry
MEYER, JACOB		H	55th Infantry
MEYER, GUSTAV		B	58th Infantry
MEIER, ISAAC		E	58th Infantry
MOSESSON, MAYER		E	58th Infantry
MARX, JOSEPH		G	58th Infantry
MARX, LOUIS		G	58th Infantry
MENDELSON, GUSTAV	Sergeant	D	59th Infantry
MARKS, SAMUEL		I	59th Infantry
MEYERS, LEVI		C	61st Infantry
MORRIS, BERNHARD	1st Lieutenant	D	62nd Infantry
Enlisted as private.			
MORRIS, A.	Lieutenant	K	62nd Infantry
MEYERSTEIN, H.		C	62nd Infantry
MEYERSTEIN, ——		F	62nd Infantry
MEYER, ISAAC		G	62nd Infantry
MEYERS, SIMEON		G	64th Infantry
MIELZINER, ISAAC			Zouaves
Killed at Bull Run.			
MEYER, ADOLPH	1st Lieutenant		66th Infantry
Promoted from 2nd Lieutenant.			
MANNHEIM, SIMON	Corporal	A	66th Infantry
MASIUS, LEOPOLD		A	66th Infantry
MANNHEIM, THEO.		C	66th Infantry
MOSES, J. HENRY	Captain	F	66th Infantry
MANDELBAUM, S.		K	66th Infautry
MARCUS, SAMUEL		K	66th Infantry
MELZHEIMER, SAMUEL		K	66th Infantry
MEYER, ALBERT		K	66th Infantry
MEIER, CARL		A	67th Infantry
MORRISON, WOLF			Ellsworth Zouaves
MEIER, GOTTLIEB		B	68th Infantry
MOSES, SELIG		B	68th Infantry

NAME.	RANK.	COMPANY.	REGIMENT.
MANTEL, LOUIS		E	68th Infantry
MEYER, FERDINAND		K	68th Infantry
MOSES, ISRAEL	Lieutenant-Colonel		72nd Infantry

Was appointed Assistant Surgeon of the U. S. Army in 1847, and served with the Army of Occupation at Vera Cruz and Toluca, Mexico, and at Fort Crawford, Fort Leavenworth, in Oregon, Washington Territory, and Texas until his resignation in 1855. In the Civil War he was appointed Lieutenant-Colonel of a regiment attached to Sickles' Brigade, but was soon compelled, by failing health, to resign. He was appointed Surgeon of the United States Volunteers and placed in charge of camp hospitals in the Army of the Potomac and subsequently served with General Gordon Granger, in the West. He was mustered out of service in 1865, after receiving the Brevet of Colonel for faithful and meritorious services.

NAME.	RANK.	COMPANY.	REGIMENT.
MASIUS, LEOPOLD		C	20th Infantry
MARCUS, LEOPOLD	Lieutenant	H	72nd Infantry
MEYERS, ABRAHAM		A	74th Infantry
MANN, GUSTAV		D	74th Infantry
MORRIS, P.		K	77th Infantry
MARKS, REUBEN		A	81st Infantry
MOSES, ABRAHAM		H	82nd Infantry
MEYERS, LEOPOLD		I	82nd Infantry
MOSES, J. C.	Corporal	C	83d Infantry
MEYER, ALBERT		K	83d Infantry
MOSS, B.			90th Infantry
MORRIS, J.			90th Infantry
MENDES, DAVID		G	90th Infantry
MENDES, JOHN		G	90th Infantry
MOSES, SAMUEL B.		I	90th Infantry
MEYER, MARTIN		C	97th Infantry
MENZ, JACOB		D	98th Infantry
MEYERS, MARKS H.		K	100th Infantry
MENDEL, FREDERICK	Quartermaster		103d Infantry

Promoted from Lieutenant.

NAME.	RANK.	COMPANY.	REGIMENT.
MORITZ, FRIEDRICH		A	103d Infantry

NAME.	RANK.	COMPANY.	REGIMENT.
MEYER, EMIL		A	103d Infantry
MAINSFIELD, MOSES	Corporal	D	103d Infantry
Enlisted as Private.			
MAYER, LIPPMAN		F	103d Infantry
MEYER, HERMAN		G	103d Infantry
MORITZ, WILLIAM		H	103d Infantry
MAYER, FERDINAND		I	108th Infantry
MACEY, JUDAH		B	110th Infantry
MESSENGER, MORRIS		H	112th Infantry
MORRIS, SAMUEL	Corporal	C	113th Infantry
MYERS, LEVI		C	115th Infrntry
MANN, DANIEL L.		E	115th Infantry
MEYER, ISIDORE	Sergeant	C	117th Infantry
MEYER, MOSES	Corporal	B	119th Infantry
MORRIS, J.			120th Infantry
MANNHEIMER, ISRAEL		E	122nd Infantry
MYER, AARON B.	Captain		125th Infantry
Died of wounds received in action.			
MORITZ, JOSEPH		I	125th Infantry
MEYER, JULIUS		G	132nd Infantry
MAYER, JACOB		K	138th Infantry
MEYER, AUGUST	Captain	B	140th Infantry
Promoted from Lieutenant.			
MARKS, DANIEL		H	147th Infantry
MAYER, ISAAC		I	154th Infantry
MARKS, SAMUEL N.			157th Infantry
MARKS, JOSEPH		F	160th Infantry
MEYER, JOSEPH	Sergeant	F	163d Infantry
MEYERS, BENJAMIN	Corporal	D	168th Infantry
MAYER, EDWARD		C	173d Infantry
MAYER, AUGUST		B	176th Infantry
MARKS, ABRAHAM		D	176th Infantry
MAYER, JACOB		K	177th Infantry
MEIER, JACOB		G	178th Infantry
MEIER, JOSEPH		I	178th Infantry
MEIER, LOUIS		E	179th Infantry
MEYER, ABRAHAM		I	179th Infantry
MARKS, DANIEL E.		H	184th Infantry

NAME.	RANK.	COMPANY.	REGIMENT.
MARBURGER, J.			188th Infantry
MYERS, ISAAC	2nd Lieutenant		193d Infantry
MEIERS, JACOB		H	193d Infantry
MORRIS, MARK		A	1st Independent
MAYER, JACQUES		F	1st Independent
MOSES, HERMAN		G	1st Independent

Wounded at Fort Wagner and at Petersburg.

MEYER, GUSTAV		B	5th S. V.
MAYER, FERDINAND	Captain	D	5th S. V.
MAYER, JACOB		A	7th S. V.
MORITZ, EDWARD		K	7th S. V.
MORITZ, DAVID	Sergeant	I	17th S. V.
MEYER, LOUIS		I	17th S. V.
MOSES, NATHAN F.	Major		7th S. M.
MAYER, BERNARD	Lieutenant	B	7th S. M.
MEIER, JACOB		E	7th S. M.
MEYERSON, FRANK G.		D	1st Cavalry
MAAS, AUGUST		I	1st Cavalry
MAYER, MAX			2nd Cavalry
MOSIER, LEVI	Corporal	E	3d Cavalry
MEYER, ADOLPH	Surgeon		4th Cavalry
MEYER, EMIL		M	4th Cavalry
MYERS, ——			5th Cavalry
MINZESHEIMER, MOSES	Adjutant	A	5th Cavalry

Promoted from Lieutenant.

MEIER, ELI		B	6th Cavalry
MEYERS, DAVID		C	8th Cavalry
MAIER, JACOB		H	8th Cavalry
MOAK, JULIUS			10th Cavalry
MOAK, HARRIS P.			10th Cavalry
MEYERS, MOSES		C	12th Cavalry
MENDELSON, BERNARD		E	13th Cavalry
MEYERS, ISAAC		L	15th Cavalry
MAAS, ADOLPH		I	16th Cavalry
MAAS, JACOB		L	16th Cavalry
MARKS, FRANK		B	20th Cavalry
MEIERS, ISAAC, JR.		A	21st Cavalry
MOSES, MARK E.	Sergeant	F	22nd Cavalry

NAME.	RANK.	COMPANY.	REGIMENT.
MEYER, RAPHAEL		E	25th Cavalry
MOSES, PHILIP		G	1st Veteran Cavalry
MANN, DANIEL P.	Captain		Independent Cavalry
MARKS, SAMUEL N.			Independent Cavalry
MAYER, ALEXANDER		E	15th Artillery
MAYER, LUDWIG		H	15th Artillery
MAYER, A			1st Mounted Rifles
MEIER, HERMAN		H	1st Mounted Rifles
MEYERS, JOSEPH		D	2nd Mounted Rifles
MYER, JOSEPH		K	2nd Mounted Rifles
MAX, SAMUEL	Corporal	E	2nd Artillery
MARKS, SAMUEL		F	2nd Artillery
MEYERS, JACOB B.		K	2nd Artillery
MENDELSON, MORITZ		E	4th Artillery
MEYERS, NATHAN		F	8th Artillery
MEYER, SAMUEL		B	9th Artillery
MAYER, JACOB		K	9th Artillery
MARKS, JOSEPH		I	10th Artillery
MEYERS, K.		A	13th Artillery
MARKS, LOUIS	Corporal	A	15th Artillery
MEIER, JOSEPH		H	15th Artillery
MEIER, JACOB		H	15th Artillery
MARK, ISAAC		E	16th Artillery
METZGER, SALOMON		E	Marine Artillery
MYERS, DAVID		H	Marine Artillery
MEIER, MOSES			2nd Independent Artillery
MEIER, LOUIS			9th Independent Artillery
MEIER, LOUIS			9th Independent Artillery
MOSES, JOSEPH		C	24th Independent Artillery
MAYER, WILLIAM	General		

During the Draft Riots at New York City he did heroic service for which he received an autograph letter from President Lincoln, thanking him for the eminent services rendered by him to our country during those days of darkness. Subsequently, he devoted himself to journalism, editing several leading German newspapers.

NAME.	RANK.	COMPANY.	REGIMENT.
NEWMAN, ABEL R.		I	3d Infantry
NEWMAN, HENRY		F	4th Infantry
NATHAN, MICHAEL		F	6th Infantry
NEWMAN, AUGUST		G	8th Infantry
NEUSTADTER, JOSEPH	Quartermaster		8th Infantry
NEWMAN, PHILIP		B	10th Infantry
NEWBURG, JOSEPH	Captain	G	10th Infantry

Wounded at Fredericksburg; joined service again after discharge from hospital.

NEUBURG, LIONEL C.	Sergeant	H	10th Infantry

Entered as private.

NUSSBAUMER, CHARLES		C	13th Infantry
NOAH, DAVID G.		G	20th Infantry
NOAH, MOSES D.		G	20th Infantry
NEWMAN, LAZARUS		A	24th Infantry

Lost a foot in action.

NEWMAN, LEOPOLD C. Lieutenant-Colonel

		B	31st Infantry

Was mustered in service as Captain; he rose to the rank of Lieutenant-Colonel. His term of service expiring a few days prior to the battle of Chancellorville, May 2, 1863, he expressed a desire to remain at the front and during that terrible struggle his foot was shattered by a cannon ball; was taken to Washington, where he died shortly after. President Lincoln visited him at his bedside, and brought his commission promoting him to the rank of Brigadier-General.

NEWMAN, WILLIAM		F	31st Infantry
NEWMAN, LEVI L.	Corporal	I	32nd Infantry
NIEMAN, CARL		H	39th Infantry
NEUBAUER, L.			46th Infantry
NEWMAN, LOUIS		G	53d Infantry
NEWMAN, CHARLES	Lieutenant		54th Infantry
NEUHAUSER, FERDINAND		C	54th Infantry
NEWMAN, ADOLPH		H	54th Infantry
NATHAN, WOLF		D	55th Infantry
NUSSBAUM, ABRAHAM	Quartermaster		58th Infantry

NAME.	RANK.	COMPANY.	REGIMENT.
NEUBERGER, AUGUST		C	58th Infantry
NEWMAN, ISAAC	Sergeant	I	61st Infantry
NEWMAN, CHARLES		A	66th Infantry
NEWMAN, SAMUEL		A	66th Infantry
NEWMAN, ABRAHAM		K	66th Infantry
NUSSBAUM HENRY		F	68th Infantry
NEWBERGER, LOUIS		G	70th Infantry
NEWBERGER, ANSEL		D	72nd Infantry
NATHAN, HENRY	Corporal	K	73d Infantry
NEELIS, ——	Captain		90th Infantry

Killed at Port Hudson.

NEWMAN, ABRAHAM D.		F	95th Infantry
NEWMAN, AUGUST	Lieutenant	D	103d Infantry

Died of wounds received in action.

NIEDERLANDER, F.			115th Infantry
NATHANSON, NATHAN		B	119th Infantry
NEWMAN, BENJAMIN F.	Sergeant	B	137th Infantry
NEWMAN, FERDINAND		G	140th Infantry
NEWMAN, MORRIS		D	146th Infantry
NEWMAN, JOSEPH	Corporal	F	162nd Infantry
NIEMAN, GOTTLIEB	Sergeant	K	174th Infantry
NOAH, D.			186th Infantry
NEWMAN, CARL		D	7th S. V.
NEWMAN, OSCAR		K	7th S. V.
NEWMAN, SIMON		F	47th S. M.
NIEBERGALL, JULIUS			3d Artillery
NEWMAN, ABRAHAM		F	4th Artillery
NUMBURGER, ALEXANDER			4th Cavalry

Regimental Quartermaster

NEUBERGER, MEIER		L	7th Cavalry

Captured; died in Andersonville Prison.

NEWMAN, SIMON		G	20th Cavalry
OPPENHEIM, JACOB		A	1st Infantry
OPPENHEIM, ARNOLD	Adjutant		7th Infantry

Promoted from Lieutenant.

OPPENHEIMER, LOUIS		H	8th Infantry
OCHS, JOHN		D	41st Infantry

NAME.	RANK.	COMPANY.	REGIMENT.
OPPENHEIMER, HENRY	Corporal	B	42nd Infantry
OCHS, JOSEPH		C	16th Cavalry
OPPENHEIM, DAVID	Sergeant	L	15th Artillery
OSTROSKY, LEOPOLD			1st Independent Infantry

Wounded at Alutra.

PINKSON, HENRY	Corporal	E	1st Infantry

Enlisted as Private.

PHILLIPS, LEWIS		G	2nd Infantry
PHILLIPS, JOSEPH		E	6th Infantry
PROSKAUER, HERMAN		H	7th Infantry
PHILLIPSON, FERDINAND		C	8th Infantry
PHILLIPS, MEYER D.		A	10th Infantry
PHILLIPS, ALFRED	Quartermaster		36th Infantry
POLLOCK, BERNHARD	1st Lieutenant		39th Infantry

Enlisted as Private; promoted for bravery at Cross Keys.

PECK, LOUIS		D	40th Infantry
PISKO, EDWARD		C	45th Infantry
PROSKAUER, ADOLPH	Sergeant	G	52nd Infantry
POTZNONSKY, MORITZ		E	54th Infantry
PINKSON, ISIDOR		K	59th Infantry
PHILLIPS, HENRY	Corporal	G	62nd Infantry
POLLOCK, JOSEPH B.		D	83d Infantry
POLLOCK, DAVID	Sergeant	E	96th Infantry

Enlisted as Private.

PHILLIPSON, ——			100th Infantry
PINKUS, L.	Sergeant	D	103d Infantry

Wounded at Stone Creek; promoted from Private; captured and sent to Libby Prison.

PHILLIPS, L.		E	115th Infantry
PEISNER, ELIAS	Colonel		119th Infantry

Killed at Chancellorsville.

PEISNER, FERDINAND	Captain		119th Infantry

Promoted from Lieutenant.

PEISNER, FRANCIS	1st Lieutenant		119th Infantry

Promoted from 2nd Lieutenant.

NAME.	RANK.	COMPANY.	REGIMENT.
PINKSON, ISIDOR			119th Infantry
PINKSON, HENRY		E	119th Infantry
POSNER, JACOB		E	131st Infantry
PHILLIPS, ABRAHAM		E	132nd Infantry
PHILLIPS, ISAAC		E	132nd Infantry
PLATTO, HARRIS		A	149th Infantry
POPPELSTEIN, SAMUEL		A	149th Infantry
POLLOCK, JACOB		I	149th Infantry
PEYSER, NATHAN	Sergeant	K	1st Independent
PEYSER, M.	Corporal	G	1st Independent
PEIXOTTO, MOSES L.	Captain	B	7th S. M.
Entered as Private.			
PHILLIPS, ——			5th Cavalry
ROSENTHAL, JOHN		G	1st Infantry
ROSENSTRAUS, SELIGMAN		D	4th Infantry
REIZENSTEIN, CHARLES		A	6th Infantry
ROSENTHAL, JACOB		B	6th Infantry
RHEIN, MORITZ	Captain		7th Infantry
RITTER, G.			7th Infantry
ROSENSTEIN, ADOLPH		D	7th Infantry
ROSENBERG, SAMUEL		G	7th Infantry
ROSENTHAL, AUGUST		I	7th Infantry
ROSENTHAL, M.		D	8th Infantry
RAUSCHER, J.			8th Infantry
ROSENBERG, HERMAN		F	8th Infantry
RAPHAEL, JACOB	Corporal	H	8th Infantry
REICH, SAMUEL		I	10th Infantry
ROSENTHAL, JOSEPH		K	10th Infantry
ROSENBERG, GEORGE		A	13th Infantry
ROSENBERG, LOUIS		D	17th Infantry
ROSENBERG, CHARLES		I	19th Infantry
ROSENFELD, JOSEPH		E	20th Infantry
ROSENBERG, I.		A	24th Infantry
ROSENTHAL, MILO		A	24th Infantry
ROTHSCHILD, MOSES		A	24th Infantry
Killed in action.			
ROSENBERGER, L.		C	25th Infantry

NAME.	RANK.	COMPANY.	REGIMENT.
RASZHE, JULIUS		C	31st Infantry
ROSENTHAL, MORRIS		C	31st Infantry
ROWE, MORRIS	Corporal	E	31st Infantry
REITLER, LOUIS	Sergeant		32nd Infantry

Killed at Crampton Pass, Maryland.

ROSENBAUM, JOSEPH D.		D	35th Infantry
ROWE, SAMUEL E.		H	37th Infantry
ROSENTHAL, LEWIS		C	38th Infantry
RICH, GEORGE L.		B	39th Infantry
ROSENTHAL, GUSTAV		F	39th Infantry
ROSENBERG, CARL		G	39th Infantry
RAPHAEL, ALFRED MAURICE	Lieutenant		40th Infantry

Recipient of testimonials for bravery at Gettysburg.

RACHEL, AUGUST	Quartermaster		41st Infantry

Promoted from Lieutenant.

ROSENBERG, SAMUEL		A	41st Infantry
ROSENTHAL, JACOB		I	41st Infantry
ROSENBERG, JOSEPH		C	47th Infantry
ROSENBERG, M.			50th Infantry
ROSENBERG, ANDREW J.		K	50th Infantry
ROSENBURG, MAX	Lieutenant		54th Infantry
ROSENTHAL, A.	Lieutenant		54th Infantry
ROSENBERG, GEORGE			54th Infantry
ROSENFELD, HENRY		C	54th Infantry
ROSENTHAL, DANIEL		K	54th Infantry
ROSENTHAL, BARNEY			55th Infantry
ROSENBERG, ISAAC		A	56th Infantry
ROSENTHAL, MOSES		B	58th Infantry
ROSENTHAL, LOUIS		K	58th Infantry
ROSENTHAL, K.		K	58th Infantry
REESE, J.			62nd Infantry

Seriously wounded at Gettysburg.

REES, ──		K	62nd Infantry
ROSENDALE, CHARLES H.			65th Infantry
ROSENBERG, EDWARD		A	66th Infantry
ROTHSCHILD, MORITZ	Lieutenant	K	66th Infantry

19

NAME.	RANK.	COMPANY.	REGIMENT.
ROSENDALE, SILAS	Captain		68th Infantry
Promoted from Lieutenant.			
ROSENTHAL, JOSEPH		G	79th Infantry
ROSENTHAL, JOSEPH		F	82nd Infantry
RAU, MAX		B	90th Infantry
ROWE, JOSEPH		C	91st Infantry
ROSENTHAL, GEORGE	Corporal	H	97th Infantry
ROSENBERGER, FREDERICK		K	105th Infantry
ROSENTHAL, EDWARD		G	113th Infantry
RICH, FRANK E.		I	115th Infantry
ROSENTHAL, LEVY		I	117th Infantry
ROSENSTEIN, DAVID		E	119th Infantry
REHMAN, MARCUS		E	119th Infantry
ROSENSTEIN, LOUIS		E	119th Infantry
REGENSBURGER, J.			119th Infantry
RICH, AARON P.		B	125th Infantry
ROSENDALE, DANIEL		F	131st Infantry
ROSENBURG, ADAM	Corporal	G	136th Infantry
ROWE, MOSES		K	137th Infantry
ROSE, ISAAC E.		D	141st Infantry
ROTHSCHILD, MOSES		A	149th Infantry

Killed at Lookout Mountain. Far in advance of his company he tore down the rebel flag, when he was killed by bullets.

ROSENBERG, ISAAC		A	149th Infantry
ROSE, DANIEL		I	149th Infantry
ROSENBURG, N. J.		I	151st Infantry
ROSENBURG, ISAAC		B	155th Infantry
ROSENDALE, SAMUEL	Corporal	D	177th Infantry
Enlisted as private.			
ROSENDALE, CHARLES H.		K	185th Infantry
ROSENBERG, D.		D	1st Independent
ROSENBERG, D.		D	1st Independent
ROTHSCHILD, SAMUEL		F	5th S. V.
ROSENBAUM, LOUIS		B	7th S. V.
ROSENBURG, ADOLPH		H	7th S. V.
REBHUN, JACOB			22nd S. M.
ROSENBLATT, M.		E	1st Cavalry

NAME.	RANK.	COMPANY.	REGIMENT.
REISS, NATHAN		M	2nd Cavalry
RICHTER, HERMAN	Lieutenant		4th Cavalry
ROSENTHAL, ISAAC		E	13th Cavalry
RICH, BENJAMIN		H	22nd Cavalry
ROSENBURG, JOSEPH		E	25th Cavalry
ROSENTHAL, EDWARD		G	7th Artillery
REISS, SOLOMON	Lieutenant		8th Battery
ROSENBURG, AUGUST		C	14th Battery
ROSENTHAL, MILO			————
ROSENBURG, ISRAEL			————
SILVA, FRANCIS	Captain		1st Infantry
SCOOLER, HENRY			1st Infantry
SEBESKY, WOLF			1st Infantry
STEINHARDT, ——			1st Infantry
STERNBERGER, J.		A	4th Infantry
SOLOMON, JAMES		B	4th Infantry
SCHWARZSCHILD, HERMAN		D	4th Infantry
SIMON, JACOB		B	6th Infantry
SCHEIER, IGNAZ,		K	6th Infantry
STERNBERG, SIEGMUND	Captain		7th Infantry
STERN, ALEXANDER	Lieutenant		7th Infantry (reorganized)
STERNE, LOUIS	Captain		7th Infantry
SIMONS, B.			7th Infantry
STRAUS, JACOB		F	7th Infantry
SACHS, LOUIS		H	7th Infantry (reorganized)
SCHIMMEL, AUGUST			8th Infantry

Captain and Assistant Quartermaster.

NAME.	RANK.	COMPANY.	REGIMENT.
SILVA, FRANK	Lieutenant		8th Infantry
STRAUSS, FRIEDRICH		A	8th Infantry
STERNFELD, PHILIP		D	8th Infantry
SOBESKY, WOLF		G	8th Infantry
SCHWARTZ, EDWARD		H	8th Infantry
STRAUSS, SOLOMON		H	8th Infantry
SPOREHASE, ALEXANDER			8th Infantry
SACHS, LOUIS			8th Infantry

NAME.	RANK.	COMPANY.	REGIMENT.
STEINER, JOSEPH N.	Captain		9th Infantry
SCHWEIZER, HERMAN P.		A	9th Infantry
SIMONS, HARRIS		H	9th Infantry
SOLOMON, BENJAMIN		K	10th Infantry
SIMPSON, FRANK H.		A	11th Infantry
	Commissary Sergeant		
SEIXAS, ISAAC G.	Lieutenant	C	11th Infantry
STEFFTER, WILLIAM			11th Infantry
STRAUSS, PETER	Captain	B	12th Infantry
Promoted from Lieutenant.			
SIMMONS, JACOB	Corporal	B	12th Infantry
SALMON, LEON N.		B	13th Infantry
SIMON, JACOB		I	15th Infantry
SCHOENBURGER, NAPOLEON	Quartermaster		20th Infantry
Promoted from Lieutenant.			
STERNBERG, MORITZ	1st Lieutenant		20th Infantry
SCHOENTHAL, JACOB		B	20th Infantry
SILBERSTEIN, MORITZ		C	20th Infantry
Wounded at Chancellorsville.			
SCHLESINGER, MORITZ		D	20th Infantry
SALOMON, LEOPOLD		H	20th Infantry
SIMON, JULIUS		H	20th Infantry
SCHWAB, GUSTAV		H	20th Infantry
SANDERS, HERMAN		G	21st Infantry
SALMON, DAVID		D	23d Infantry
STRAUSS, GEORGE		E	23d Infantry
STRAUSS, JOHN		E	23d Infantry
SHALENSKY, CHARLES			{ 24th Infantry { 149th Infantry
SALOMON, HENRY		K	25th Infantry
STRAUSBERG, AUGUST		K	28th Infantry
SPEAR, JACOB		D	29th Infantry
Seriously wounded.			
SONNENBERG, EDWARD	Sergeant	E	29th Infantry
SALOMON, LOUIS		F	29th Infantry
SIMON, CHARLES		G	29th Infantry
SIMONS, DAVID		A	31st Infantry
SALOMON, S.		C	31st Infantry

NAME.	RANK.	COMPANY.	REGIMENT.
SUMMER, SOLOMON		C	31st Infantry
STRAUSS, ABRAHAM		C	31st Infantry
SULMAN, S.		C	31st Infantry
SALEK, ADOLF		C	31st Infantry
STRAZNISKY, J.		C	31st Infantry
STERN, LOUIS		C	31st Infantry
SCHONFELD, E.			31st Infantry
STEINBACK, D.			31st Infantry
SIMPSON, J.	Lieutenant		35th Infantry
SIMONS, HENRY F.		B	35th Infantry
SALOMON, CORNELIUS			37th Infantry
SCHOENWALT, C.			38th Infantry
STERN, JACOB		C	38th Infantry
SPIEGEL, LUDWIG		C	38th Infantry
SIMONS, LEWIS		H	38th Infantry
SIMONS, NOAH		H	38th Infantry
SIEGMUND, OSCAR		F	39th Infantry
SACHS, LEOPOLD	Corporal	I	39th Infantry
SCHAINBERGER, ALEXANDER		A	41st Infantry
SCHWEITZER, JULIUS		B	41st Infantry
SCHWEITZER, HENRY		B	41st Infantry
SIMON, HENRY		B	41st Infantry
STRAUSS, FERDINAND		D	41st Infantry
SACHS, FRIEDRICH		H	41st Infantry
SCHOENFELDER, GUSTAV		K	41st Infantry
SIMON, FRIEDRICH		K	41st Infantry
STRASSBURGER, J.			41st Infantry
SCHLESSINGER, ANTON	Sergeant	B	42nd Infantry
SULCHMAN, ——	Lieutenant		44th Infantry
SIMPSON, L.			44th Infantry
STRAUSS, MAX		G	45th Infantry
SUSEDORF, CARL FREDERICK	Captain		46th Infantry
SCHLESINGER, AUGUST		B	46th Infantry
SELIG, JACOB	Captain	D	46th Infantry
Enlisted as Private.			
SELIG, ANDREAS			46th Infantry
SCHIFF, SIMON		C	47th Infantry

NAME.	RANK.	COMPANY.	REGIMENT.
SIMPSON, D.	Corporal		47th Infantry
STEIN, GOTTLOB		B	49th Infantry
SALMON, DAVID		E	49th Infantry
STEINBURG, SAMUEL		G	51st Infantry
SICKEL, M.	Quartermaster		52nd Infantry
STERNBERGER, JOSEPH		A	52nd Infantry
SAMUELS, ISAAC	Corporal	D	52nd Infantry
Enlisted as Private.			
SIMON, HENRY		E	53d Infantry
STERN, ADOLPH	Sergeant	I	53d Infantry
STERN, WILLIAM	Lieutenant	E	54th Infantry
STRAUSS, ABRAHAM	Sergeant	G	54th Infantry
SCHULER, J.	Sergeant		54th Infantry
SCHULER, F.			54th Infantry
STRAUSS, DANIEL		B	55th Infantry (S. M.)
SCHULER, CHARLES	Corporal		55th Infantry
SILBERMAN, HENRY		D	55th Infantry
SCHWAB, HERMAN		H	55th Infantry
SIMONS, LOUIS		H	56th Infantry
SILBERBERG, ANSELM			58th Infantry
SALOMON, JOSEPH		B	58th Infantry
STEINER, LEOPOLD		C	58th Infantry
STEINBERG, ALBERT		I	58th Infantry
SAMUELS, HENRY	Corporal	C	59th Infantry
STRAUSS, FRANZ		C	59th Infantry
STRAUSS, ABRAHAM		D	59th Infantry
SAMUELS, LOUIS	Sergeant	H	62nd Infantry
SALOMON, PHILIP		B	63d Infantry
SILBERMAN, JOSEPH		A	66th Infantry
STERN, FERDINAND		A	66th Infantry
STRAUSS, ADAM	Corporal	E	66th Infantry
STRAUSS, JACOB		E	66th Infantry
SIMON, LOUIS	Quartermaster		68th Infantry
SPITZER, LOUIS	1st Lieutenant		68th Infantry
Promoted from 2nd Lieutenant.			
SCHWERIN, HERMAN	Lieutenant	B	68th Infantry
SCHWEITZER, EMANUEL		C	68th Infantry

Name.	Rank.	Company.	Regiment.
Strauss, William		C	68th Infantry
Simon, Emil		D	68th Infantry
Simon, Louis	Captain	E	68th Infantry
Promoted from Lieutenant.			
Sinsheim, Gottlieb		E	68th Infantry
Sternberg, Franz		K	68th Infantry
Sulzberger, Jacob		K	68th Infantry
Solomon, Charles		B	70th Infantry
Solomon, Louis		B	70th Infantry
Schiff, David		B	70th Infantry
Steinberg, Henry		B	70th Infantry
Simon, Samuel		A	72nd Infantry
Solomon, Morris	Sergeant	K	72nd Infantry
Silva, Manuel	Captain		73d Infantry
Silberman, Louis		B	74th Infantry
Salmons, Charles Harmon		G	75th Infantry
Simon, Benjamin F.		B	77th Infantry
Solomon, A.		F	77th Infantry
Stein, Frank		B	83d Infantry
Strauss, Louis		G	84th Infantry
Spear, Leopold		E	87th Infantry
Simonson, Joseph	Corporal	H	87th Infantry
Sommer, Louis	Sergeant	D	89th Infantry
Sampson, Charles			91st Infantry
Strauss, George		G	95th Infantry
Steiner, Jacob		H	101st Infantry
Strauss, G.	Captain	A	103d Infantry
Promoted from Lieutenant.			
Steinbach, Friedrich		A	103d Infantry
Siebert, Julius		H	103d Infantry
Simon, Lewis		E	105th Infantry
Salmon, Joseph		H	105th Infantry
Samson, Levi C.		C	110th Infantry
Speyer, Morris	Corporal	A	119th Infantry
Schwerin, Henry R.	Captain		119th Infantry
Promoted from Lieutenant.			
Sussman, William	Sergeant	I	119th Infantry
Sternberger, T.	Quartermaster		121st Infantry

NAME.	RANK.	COMPANY.	REGIMENT.
SAX, JACOB		I	122nd Infantry
SIMMONS, LEWIS		C	128th Infantry
STRASS, MORITZ	Sergeant	G	128th Infantry
Enlisted as private.			
SACHS, LOUIS		B	140th Infantry
SCHONEMAN, HENRY		B	140th Infantry
STRAUSS, JOHN		B	149th Infantry
SCHOENTHAL, GOTTLIEB		K	152nd Infantry
STRAUSS, SIMON	Corporal	C	175th Infantry
STERNBERG, SIEGMUND	Lieutenant		175th Infantry
STERN, MOSES		C	177th Infantry
STEINER, D.			177th Infantry
SOLOMON, PHINEAS	Captain	D	178th Infantry
Promoted from Lieutenant.			
SOLOMON, LEVI		E	184th Infantry
STERNBERG, ABRAHAM	Major		186th Infantry
STERN, MOSES		A	191st Infantry
SOMMER, JACOB		C	1st Independent
SELIGMAN, LOUIS	Lieutenant	D	1st Independent
Enlisted as private.			
SCOOLER, HENRY			1st Independent
SIMON, JACOB		F	1st Independent
SEBESKY, WOLF		F	1st Independent
SIMON, L.		G	1st Independent
Enlisted as private.			
STEINHARDT, ——		G	1st Independent
SILVA, FRANK A.	Captain	E	7th S. M.
SCHLESSINGER, NATHANIEL F.		E	7th S. V.
STRAUSS, G. ADAM		F	7th S. V.
STRAUSS, SALOMON		F	7th S. V.
STERN, ALEXANDER		K	7th S. V.
STEIN, LEOPOLD		B	17th S. V.
SALOWSKY, HENRY	Adjutant		1st Cavalry
SCHWARZENBERG, J.			1st Cavalry
SACHS, HENRY		G	1st Cavalry
SWAAL, T. W.	Lieutenant		2nd Cavalry
SAMSON, JULIUS	Lieutenant		4th Cavalry
SACHS, H.		A	5th Cavalry

NAME.	RANK.	COMPANY.	REGIMENT.
SOLOMON, BENJAMIN		B	5th Cavalry
SAMUELSON, JOHN		F	9th Cavalry
SAMUELSON, SAMUEL A.		F	9th Cavalry
STERN, CHARLES H.		K	12th Cavalry
SCHWAB, SIMON		C	13th Cavalry
SHOLEM, LOUIS		K	13th Cavalry
SCHWAAB, FREDERICK W.	Lieutenant		16th Cavalry
STRASBURGER, JOSEPH		M	1st Mounted Rifles
SOLOMON, JOSEPH		D	2nd Mounted Rifles
STADEKER, JULIUS			1st Artillery

Wounded; captured; died in Libby Prison.

STEIN, HENRY		L	2nd Artillery
STEIN, ADOLPH		B	8th Artillery
SIMON, FRANK		K	14th Artillery
STEIN, GUSTAV		H	15th Artillery
STEIN, JULIUS		H	15th Artillery
SAMUELS, ALEXANDER R.			6th Independent Artillery
SIMON, HENRY			9th Independent Artillery
SOLOMON M.	Sergeant		27th Independent Artillery
SCHWEITZER, ABRAHAM			30th Battery
SHALMEK, CHARLES			———

TRAUB, ADOLPH			20th Infantry
TANNHAUSER, HERMAN			29th Infantry
TSCHOPICK, ADOLPH			45th Infantry
TRUFFINGER, PHILIP	Lieutenant		57th Infantry
THALHEIMER, JACOB		E	151st Infantry
THALHEIMER, ANTON		H	8th Cavalry

ULLMAN, BENJAMIN		A	55th Infantry

VIEXELBAUM, ———			1st Independent Infantry

Captured and sent to Andersonville Prison.

VAN ETTEN, DAVID		D	23d Infantry
VAN BAALEN, HENRY		E	49th Infantry

Killed at the Wilderness.

VEIT, MEYER			54th Infantry
VAN BOSH, MAX	Lieutenant		3d Artillery
VAN ETTEN, JACOB		I	5th Artillery

NAME.	RANK.	COMPANY.	REGIMENT.
WOLF, CHARLES		E	2nd Infantry
WOLF, JOSEPH		H	2nd Infantry
WOLF, WILLIAM		C	3d Infantry
WOLF, HENRY		C	4th Infantry
WOLF, MAX		D	4th Infantry
WOLF, CHARLES		G	4th Infantry
WEIL, OSCAR	Adjutant		5th Infantry (Veteran)
WEIL, CHARLES	Lieutenant		8th Infantry
WEISS, ADOLPH	Lieutenant		8th Infantry (Veteran)
WOLF, WILLIAM	Corporal	B	8th Infantry (Veteran)
WILDA, M.			8th Infantry
WOLF, WILLIAM		A	9th Infantry
WOLF, WILLIAM		A	9th Infantry (Veteran)
WOLF, EDWARD		B	12th Infantry (Veteran)
WOLF, W. W.		K	16th Infantry
WOLF, JOHN		I	17th Infantry
WOLF, MARK			18th Infantry
WISEMAN, SAMUEL		I	19th Infantry
WOLF, WILLIAM		A	20th Infantry
WEISS, ADOLPH		B	20th Infantry
WOLF, ADAM			20th Infantry
WENK, JOSEPH			20th Infantry

Lost an arm; Past Commander of Colt's Post No. 32.

WEISS, JULIUS A.		C	21st Infantry
WEYMAN, NATHAN			24th Infantry
WASSERMAN, IGNATIUS	1st Lieutenant		29th Infantry

Mustered out as Captain.

WEINBERG, THEO.	Sergeant	C	29th Infantry
WOLF, GUSTAV	Corporal	C	29th Infantry
WEINER, GUSTAV	Lieutenant	E	29th Infantry

Promoted from Corporal.

WOLF, EMIL		F	29th Infantry
WEISHEIMER, C.		C	31st Infantry

NAME.	RANK.	COMPANY.	REGIMENT.
WIENER, GUSTAV		E	39th Infantry
WEIL, JOSEPH		E	39th Infantry
WOLF, FRIEDRICH	Surgeon		39th Infantry
WOLF, JACOB		I	39th Infantry
WIENER, GUSTAV		B	41st Infantry
WOLF, JACOB		B	41st Infantry
WOLF, LEOPOLD		B	41st Infantry
WOLF, LOUIS	1st Lieutenant		52nd Infantry

Killed at siege of Petersburg.

WERTHEIMER, EDWIN   Captain   54th Infantry

Special mention is made of the heroic conduct of Captain Wertheimer at the battle on the plains of Manassas: With a small guide flag in his hands he advanced and cheered the men to follow him, while the enemy were pouring a perfect hail of lead into the Union lines. At the Battle of Chancellorsville, Captain Wertheimer particularly distinguished himself by gallantly rescuing the State flag during a murderous cross-fire of the enemy. While severely wounded, he proudly and nobly defended it until unable to bear up any longer, he placed the flag in charge of a brother officer.

NAME.	RANK.	COMPANY.	REGIMENT.
WOLF, A. B.			54th Infantry
WEINBURG, ISAAC			54th Infantry
WOLF, ARTHUR S.	Surgeon		55th Infantry
WORMS, A. C.	Quartermaster	K	58th Infantry

Promoted from the ranks.

NAME.	RANK.	COMPANY.	REGIMENT.
WORMS, CHARLES	2nd Lieutenant	K	58th Infantry
WERTHEIM, MORITZ	Corporal	K	66th Infantry
WENK, AARON		K	66th Infantry
WENK, AUGUST		K	66th Infantry
WENK, JOSEPH		K	66th Infantry
WERTHEIM, LOUIS		K	66th Infantry
WOLF, DAVID		K	66th Infantry
WOLF, CARL		A	68th Infantry
WOOG, EMANUEL		C	68th Infantry

Wounded at Bull Run.

NAME.	RANK.	COMPANY.	REGIMENT.
WOLF, SIMON		D	68th Infantry
WOLF, ADOLPH		I	68th Infantry
WOLF, LOUIS		C	71st Infantry

NAME.	RANK.	COMPANY.	REGIMENT.
WASSERMAN, MOSES		G	71st Infantry
WARNER, WILLIAM			72nd Infantry
WARNER, PHILIP		H	72nd Infantry
WOLFSOHN, CHARLES		B	74th Infantry
WOLFSKY, LOUIS		B	74th Infantry
WEIL, JOSEPH		B	78th Infantry
WERTHEIM, HENRY		F	84th Infantry
WATERMAN, CHARLES		E	86th Infantry
WOLFSOHN, LOUIS		C	87th Infantry
WOLF, PHILIP		K	87th Infantry
WATERMAN, SAMUEL H.		A	91st Infantry
WOLF, FREDERICK		K	97th Infantry
WEILER, JOSEPH		E	101st Infantry
WOLF, CHARLES H.		I	102nd Infantry
WOLF, CHARLES		F	117th Infantry
WEIL, JOSEPH		B	119th Infantry
WEIL, LYON		B	119th Infantry
WIENER, JOSEPH		I	119th Infantry
WEINSTEIN, JACOB		I	119th Infantry
WOLF, HERMAN		F	127th Infantry
WISE, SOLOMON S.		I	136th Infantry
WOLF, ABRAHAM B.		D	148th Infantry
WOLF, HENRY		B	154th Infantry
WOLF, JOSEPH		F	163d Infantry
WENZLICK, R.		G	173d Infantry
WOLF, WILLIAM	Lieutenant		178th Infantry
WOLF, ADAM		K	178th Infantry
WOLF, LEOPOLD		B	1st Independent
WOLF, HENRY		E	1st Independent
WOLF, GABRIEL		F	5th S. V.
WOLF, C.		H	5th S. V.
WOLF, JOSEPH		F	7th S. V.
WOLF, WILLIAM		B	7th S. M.
WIESBADEN, JULIUS		D	7th S. M.
WOLF, LOUIS		F	12th Cavalry
WEINBERG, MORRIS		D	14th Cavalry
WOLF, LEOPOLD		L	14th Cavalry
WOLF, JOSEPH		L	14th Artillery

NAME.	RANK.	COMPANY.	REGIMENT.
WOLF, CHARLES		F	15th Artillery
WERTHEIM, HENRY		32nd Independent Artillery	
WOLF, JOSEPH C.		I	2nd Cavalry
WISE, THEODORE			5th Cavalry
ZOLLER, OTTO			7th Infantry
ZIMMERMAN, B.		F	7th Infantry
ZABINSKI, GABRIEL	Corporal		4th Artillery

NORTH CAROLINA.

NAME.	RANK.	COMPANY.	REGIMENT.
AARON, MEYER			1st Infantry

Killed in battle; buried in Jewish cemetery, Richmond Virginia.

ABRAHAM, F.		B	6th Cavalry

Wounded at Gettysburg.

ALTMAN, NATHAN		G	40th Infantry

Captured; died and buried in Woodlawn Cemetery, Elmira, New York.

BEHRENDS, L.		C	1st Infantry
BRANDT, JACOB			5th Infantry
BASS, BENJAMIN		H	45th Infantry

Captured; died and buried at Woodlawn Cemetery, Elmira, New York.

COHEN, E. B.	Lieutenant	C	1st Infantry

DANIEL, HENRY		F	10th Infantry

Captured; died, and buried in Woodlawn Cemetery, Elmira, New York.

DANANE, JACOB		B	53d Infantry

NAME.	RANK.	COMPANY.	REGIMENT.
EIGENBRUN, I.		C	1st Infantry
ENGEL, JONAS		{ C	1st Infantry
		{	53d Infantry
ELIAS, LOUIS	Lieutenant		11th Infantry
EIGENBRUN, ISAAC			35th Infantry

FRIEDHEIM, ARNOLD   K   4th Infantry
Wounded at Seven Pines and at the Wilderness.

GOODMAN, HENRY   G   26th Infantry
Captured; died and buried in Woodlawn Cemetery, Elmira, New York.

HYMAN, S.   C   1st Infantry
HOFFLEIN, MARCUS   Captain   4th Infantry
Afterwards on the staff of General Grimes.

HEINEMAN, MORRIS   D   4th Infantry
HARRIS, EDWARD   G   36th Infantry
Captured; died and buried in Woodlawn Cemetery, Elmira, New York.

ISRAEL, J.   E   51st Infantry
Captured; died and buried in Woodlawn Cemetery, Elmira, New York.

JONAS, DANIEL   D   1st Infantry
Captured; died and buried at Woodlawn Cemetery, Elmira, New York.

JACOBY, NATHANIEL   25th Infantry

KATZ, I.   C   1st Infantry
KATZ, JACK   35th Infantry
KATZ, AARON   B   53d Infantry
Wounded at Gettysburg.

LEAVY, CHARLES M.   ———
Appointed Commissary by General Palmer in Special Order, Number 23.

NAME.	RANK.	COMPANY.	REGIMENT.

LURIA, ALBERT (MOSES)   Lieutenant   —— Infantry
Promoted from Sergeant. At the age of nineteen
years he was appointed Lieutenant in a North Carolina
Infantry Regiment. He was killed at Seven Pines, in
June, 1862, while rallying his Company, having
seized the colors falling from the hands of the dying
color-bearer.

An incident of this brave officer's career is worth
recording. At the engagement at Sewell's Point, in
May, 1861, an eight-inch shell, with fuse still burning, fell into the Company's gun-pit, and young
Albert without a moment's hesitation, seized it in his
arms and put it in a tub of water, quenched the fuse and
thereby saved his own and his comrades' lives. The
Company in recognition of his heroism had the shell
engraved with a history of the incident, and adding
the words, "The pride of his Regiment and the
bravest of the brave," sent it to his parents. It now
stands upon a pillar over his grave at the "Esquiline,"
near Columbus, Georgia, as a fitting monument.

LEVI, ISAAC C.		C	1st Infantry
LEON, L.		{ C	1st Infantry
		{	53d Infantry
LEVY, J. C.		C	1st Infantry
LEWIS, LOVET	Captain	D	4th Reserves
LEWIS, DAVID		C	22nd Infantry

Captured; died and buried in Woodlawn Cemetery,
Elmira, New York.

MEYER, AARON   1st Infantry
Killed; buried in Jewish cemetery, Richmond,
Virginia.

MYERS, MARCUS   2nd Infantry
MYERS, EZEKIEL   Reilly's Battery
MYERS, WILLIAM   Reilly's Battery

OPPENHEIMER, ——   { C   1st Infantry
                               {   44th Infantry

NAME.	RANK.	COMPANY.	REGIMENT.

OTTINGER, L.   2nd Infantry
Killed at Seven Pines.

OPPENHEIMER, S.   B   44th Infantry

PHELPS, H. M.   Sergeant   B   1st Infantry
PINNER, I. M.   E   3d Infantry
Captured; died and buried in Woodlawn Cemetery, Elmira, New York.

PINKUS, L.   D   103d Infantry

ROSE, JOSEPH   3d Infantry
RICE, IGNATIUS   B   8th Infantry
Commissary and Quartermaster-Sergeant
ROESSLER, J.   Captain   E   13th Infantry
Severely wounded at the Battle of the Wilderness; promoted.

ROESSLER, JACOB   Captain   F   13th Infantry

STERNGLANTZ, D.   D   4th Infantry
SOUTHAN, LEVI   A   28th Infantry
Captured; died and buried at Woodlawn Cemetery, Elmira, Mew York.

SELLERS, J.   Sergeant   G   36th Infantry
Captured; died and buried in Woodlawn Cemetery, Elmira, New York.

SIMON, JESSE   C   20th Infantry
Captured; died and buried in Woodlawn Cemetery, Elmira, New York.

SIMMONS, MOSES   G   20th Infantry
Captured; died, and buried at Woodlawn Cemetery, Elmira, New York.

TELLER, E.   18th Infantry

WOLF, G.   C   1st Infantry
Died from exposure; buried in Jewish Cemetery, Richmond, Virginia.

WEIL, HARMAN   D   4th Infantry

NAME.	RANK.	COMPANY.	REGIMENT.
WEISENFIELD, M.		A	4th Infantry
WERTHEIMER, HENRY			35th Infantry
WERTHEIMER, GEORGE		B	53d Infantry
WERTHEIMER, H.		B	53d Infantry

Died in the service.

OHIO.

NAME.	RANK.	COMPANY.	REGIMENT.
ABRAHAM, ALEXANDER		G	2nd Infantry
ASHER, ALBERT			3d Infantry

Wounded in action.

ADLER, MOSES			4th Infantry
ARNOLD, LEVI			4th Infantry

Served three years.

AMBURG, LOUIS C.	Sergeant		26th Infantry

Promoted from Corporal.

APPEL, JOSEPH			28th Infantry
AARON, THEODORE		F	34th Infantry
ADLER, JOSEPH		A	37th Infantry
AARON, HERMAN	Sergeant	F	37th Infantry
AARONSON, I.		I	37th Infantry
ABRAM, JOSEPH		C	39th Infantry

Died in the service.

APPEL, SAMUEL		F	39th Infantry
APPEL, DAVID H.			45th Infantry

Killed in action.

ABRAHAM, HENRY	Corporal	I	49th Infantry

Enlisted as Private; died in the service.

ADLER, JOSEPH			58th Infantry
ARNBACH, SIMON			74th Infantry
AUERBACH, HENRY H.		H	85th Infantry
AARON, LOUIS	Sergeant	A	108th Infantry

Enlisted as Private; served three years.

20

NAME.	RANK.	COMPANY.	REGIMENT.
BAER, ISAAC		B	1st Infantry
BAER, SAMUEL		I	1st Infantry
Served three years.			
BRANSTETTER, ABRAHAM		A	2nd Infantry
BERNHEIMER, SAMUEL.			4th Infantry
BACHMAN, ADAM		A	5th Infantry
Died of wounds received at Resaca.			
BAER, WILLIAM			5th Infantry
Wounded in action.			
BAUM, ISAAC		E	5th Infantry
BLUM, HENRY			8th Infantry
BLUHN, ERNST			9th Infantry
BAER, HENRY	Corporal		9th Infantry
BACHMAN, JACOB			12th Infantry
Died of wounds.			
BASH, SIMON		K	13th Infantry
BLUMBERG, JOSEPH		C	14th Infantry
BLUM, DAVID		K	18th Infantry
BUNZEL, W. J.			22nd Infantry
BERNSTEIN, LEWIS			24th Infantry
BAER, DAVID		G	25th Infantry
BAUM, JOSEPH		G	33d Infantry
BAUMGARDNER, SOLOMON		C	34th Infantry
BAER, HERMAN			37th Infantry
BLAU, EMIL			37th Infantry
BAUM, AUGUST			37th Infantry
Wounded in action.			
BLAU, A.			37th Infantry
Killed in Virginia.			
BENJAMIN, DAVID	Captain		39th Infantry
BAUM, J. C.		H	42nd Infantry
BENJAMIN, FRANK		D	48th Infantry
BING, JOSEPH			56th Infantry
BLOUT, HENRY			56th Infantry
BACHMAN, SOLOMON		F	58th Infantry
BACHMAN, JOSEPH		G	58th Infantry
Wounded in action.			

NAME.	RANK.	COMPANY.	REGIMENT.
BLUMENTHAL, FREDERICK			61st Infantry
BIEN, EMANUEL	Sergeant	I	61st Infantry

Enlisted as private.

NAME.	RANK.	COMPANY.	REGIMENT.
BLUM, MANUEL		E	67th Infantry
BAER, ABRAHAM		A	68th Infantry

Served three years.

NAME.	RANK.	COMPANY.	REGIMENT.
BAER, SAMUEL		G	68th Infantry
BENJAMIN, SAMUEL		F	69th Infantry
BLAUT, HENRY		E	75th Infantry
BENJAMIN, J. A.		C	76th Infantry
BAER, JONAS		C	80th Infantry
BAUM, HERMAN		C	80th Infantry
BAUM, KAUFMAN		C	80th Infantry
BERLIN, JACOB	Corporal	K	80th Infantry

Enlisted as Private; wounded at Mission Ridge.

NAME.	RANK.	COMPANY.	REGIMENT.
BERLIN, SOLOMON			80th Infantry

Served three years.

NAME.	RANK.	COMPANY.	REGIMENT.
BUSH, JACOB	Sergeant-Major		82nd Infantry

Promoted from Sergeant; served three years.

NAME.	RANK.	COMPANY.	REGIMENT.
BREYFOGEL, ISRAEL	Corporal	C	86th Infantry
BERNHEIMER, SAMUEL		H	91st Infantry
BERNHEIMER, WILLIAM		H	91st Infantry

Served three years.

NAME.	RANK.	COMPANY.	REGIMENT.
BENJAMIN, LEVI		D	97th Infantry
BAMBERGER, ADAM	Sergeant	E	104th Infantry

Promoted from Corporal; served three years.

NAME.	RANK.	COMPANY.	REGIMENT.
BAMBERGER, CYRUS			104th Infantry
BAER, JACOB	Corporal	F	106th Infantry

Served three years.

NAME.	RANK.	COMPANY.	REGIMENT.
BACHMAN, LEOPOLD	Sergeant	I	106th Infantry

Enlisted as Private.

NAME.	RANK.	COMPANY.	REGIMENT.
BERNHEIMER, AARON		D	107th Infantry

Wounded at Gettysburg.

NAME.	RANK.	COMPANY.	REGIMENT.
BIEN, MORDECAI P.	Lieutenant	G	113th Infantry
BAUMGARDNER, EMANUEL			114th Infantry

Served three years.

NAME.	RANK.	COMPANY.	REGIMENT.
BAER, JOEL			120th Infantry

Died in Louisiana.

BAER, JACOB P.	1st Sergeant	A	123d Infantry

Enlisted as Private; captured at Winchester.

BAMBERGER, JOHN		G	128th Infantry
BRAUNSCHWEIGER, JACOB		G	130th Infantry
BAER, JACOB		B	133d Infantry
BREYFOGEL, C. W.		F	9th Cavalry

COHN, HENRY S.		D	5th Infantry

Served three years.

COHEN, J.			12th Infantry
COHEN, JACOB			18th Infantry
COBLENZ, EPHRAIM			19th Infantry
COHEN, AARON		C	21st Infantry
COHN, BERNARD			22nd Infantry
COHEN, JACOB C.	Lieutenant		27th Infantry
COHEN, ISRAEL		A	30th Infantry

Died in the service.

COHN, JOSEPH		H	34th Infantry

Wounded at Winchester.

COHEN, ISAAC D.	Corporal	B	35th Infantry
COHN, HENRY		K	38th Infantry
COBLENZ, DANIEL			41st Infantry
COBLENZ, ADAM		C	50th Infantry

Served three years.

COHEN, WILLIAM F.		F	55th Infantry
COHEN, J. W.		C	69th Infantry

Killed at Jonesboro, Georgia.

COEN, REUBEN L.		D	77th Infantry

Killed in Tennessee.

COHEN, HENRY	Sergeant	G	106th Infantry

Wounded at Hartsville, Tennessee.

COHEN, WILLIAM	Corporal	H	114th Infantry

Died in the service.

NAME.	RANK.	COMPANY.	REGIMENT.
COBLENZ, NOAH		H	115th Infantry

Wounded in action.

COBLENZ, JOSEPH D.		C	128th Infantry

DURST, GABRIEL			1st Infantry

Served three years.

DAVIDSON, JOSHUA			5th Infantry
DARLEY, DAVID			7th Infantry
DAVID, LEWIS	Lieutenant		8th Infantry
DRYFUS, ARTHUR			9th Infantry
DANIELS, ABRAHAM		H	15th Infantry
DE SILVA, MANUEL	Lieutenant	E	16th Infantry
EZEKIEL, DAVID J.	Brevet Captain		{ 7th Infantry { U. S. Army

Wounded at Shiloh and promoted from Sergeant by order of General Banks for meritorious conduct.

EHRLICH, HENRY		H	22nd Infantry
EPPSTEIN, LEOPOLD			24th Infantry
EPHRAIM, W. H.		G	25th Infantry
ENGEL, SAMUEL	Corporal	K	85th Infantry

Enlisted as Private.

ELIAS, ISRAEL			108th Infantry
ELIAS, ELIJAH		A	115th Infantry
ERDMAN, CHARLES W.	Sergeant-Major		121st Infantry

Enlisted as Private.

ENGEL, DAVID A.	Corporal	C	131st Infantry
ENGEL, SAMUEL C.		K	131st Infantry
EISENSTAEDT, B.		E	146th Infantry

FRIEDMAN, DAVID	Captain		2nd Infantry

Enlisted as Private.

FOX, A.			2nd Infantry

Captured at Chickamauga; prisoner at Andersonville.

FRANK, JACOB		G	3d Infantry
FRANK, WILLIAM		D	5th Infantry
FRANK, SAMUEL			5th Infantry
FURST, JOSEPH		F	6th Infantry

NAME.	RANK	COMPANY.	REGIMENT.
FRANKS, HENRY			7th Infantry
Killed at Cedar Mountain.			
FRANK, A.			9th Infantry
FRANK, HERMAN			9th Infantry
FALK, NATHAN	Corporal	H	25th Infantry
Wounded in action.			
FALK, C.			28th Infantry
FOX, LEVI		E	31st Infantry
FALK, C.			35th Infantry
Died of wounds.			
FRIEDMAN, JACOB			37th Infantry
Served three years.			
FRANKFURTER, DAVID			37th Infantry
Served three years.			
FLEISCHMAN, MORITZ	Lieutenant	I	37th Infantry
FRIEDLEIN, JACOB		C	42nd Infantry
Died of wounds.			
FRANK, CHARLES	Corporal	E	49th Infantry
Died of wounds.			
FRANK, BENJAMIN			49th Infantry
FRANK, JACOB			57th Infantry
FLEISCHMAN, G.			60th Infantry
FISHEL, DANIEL	Corporal	A	61st Infantry
Enlisted as Private.			
FRANK, JOEL		E	61st Infantry
Killed in battle.			
FRANKHAUSER, D.			63d Infantry
FRANKHAUSER, S.			63d Infantry
FRANKHAUSER, L.			63d Infantry
FRANKHAUSER, SOLOMON		A	64th Infantry
Wounded in action.			
FRANKENFIELD, JOSEPH		K	66th Infantry
Died in service.			
FRANK, DANIEL		D	69th Infantry
Served four years.			
FRANK, DAVID		D	69th Infantry
Served three years.			

NAME.	RANK.	COMPANY.	REGIMENT.
FRANKFURT, H.			69th Infantry

Killed near Atlanta.

NAME.	RANK.	COMPANY.	REGIMENT.
FELDHEIM, EDWARD		K	70th Infantry
FREUND, JACOB		E	80th Infantry
FREIBERGER, DANIEL		H	83d Infantry
FLEISCHER, JACOB F.		B	86th Infantry
FRANKFURTER, JACOB		F	86th Infantry
FRANKFURTER, H.			86th Infantry
FRANKFURTER, ALEXANDER			90th Infantry

Served three years.

| FISHEL, SOLOMON | | H | 105th Infantry |

Served three years.

| FURST, JACOB | | B | 107th Infantry |

Served three years.

| FELS, JOSEPH | Corporal | F | 107th Infantry |

Promoted at Chancellorsville.

| FRANCK, C. | | | 107th Infantry |
| FLEISCHMAN, F. | 1st Lieutenant | | 108th Infantry |

Promoted from Corporal.

| FRANK, DAVID | | | 108th Infantry |
| FRIEDMAN, DAVID | Captain | E | 108th Infantry |

Promoted from Sergeant; served three years.

| FRANK, JACOB | | K | 110th Infantry |
| FELS, SAMUEL | | D | 114th Infantry |

Wounded at Thompson's Hill, Mississippi.

| FURST, JACOB H. | | E | 114th Infantry |
| FURST, JACOB H. | | D | 120th Infantry |

Wounded at Jackson, Mississippi.

FRANK, DANIEL		E	120th Infantry
FRIEND, LEVI		E	134th Infantry
FRANK, C.			137th Infantry
FRANK, JOSEPH		A	139th Infantry
FURST, SAMUEL		C	139th Infantry

| GUNTHER, A. | | | 7th Infantry |

Killed in action.

NAME.	RANK.	COMPANY.	REGIMENT.
GOLDSMITH, JOSEPH	Quartermaster		15th Infantry
GREENWALT, D			24th Infantry
GOLDSMITH, JAMES		K	29th Infantry
GUGGENHEIM, THEODORE		C	34th Infantry
GROSS, JACOB			34th Infantry
GROSS, D.			34th Infantry
GANS, DAVID M.	Captain	E	35th Infantry
GRATZ, MORRIS		F	35th Infantry

Wounded at Fort Donelson.

GRATZ, EMANUEL		I	35th Infantry

Died of wounds.

GOLDSMITH, GEORGE		E	42nd Infantry

Died in the service.

GORREL, LEVI		H	46th Infantry
GOLDSMITH, JACOB			47th Infantry
GOLDSMITH, HENRY M.	Lieutenant		56th Infantry

Enlisted as private.

GEIGER, JOSHUA		G	72nd Infantry

Died in the service.

GOLDSMITH, LEOPOLD		K	72nd Infantry

Died in the service.

GOLDSMITH, HENRY		K	76th Infantry

Served three years.

GOLDSMITH, JOHN		B	77th Infantry

Captured.

GOLDSMITH, B.		B	83d Infantry
GREENWALT, ABRAHAM		G	104th Infantry

Awarded by Secretary of War "Medal of Honor"
for capturing Rebel Corps flag in the battle of Franklin, Tennessee.

GOLDSMITH, WILLIAM		C	113th Infantry

Died at Nashville, Tennessee.

GOODMAN, ISAAC		A	125th Infantry

Died in the service at Franklin, Tennessee.

GREENWALT, MICHAEL		K	129th Infantry
GEIGER, JACOB		G	130th Infantry

Name.	Rank.	Company.	Regiment.
GREEN, SIMEON		Ġ	130th Infantry
GOLDSMITH, JOHN		C	133d Infantry
GOTTSCHALK, GUSTAV		D	138th Infantry
GREEN, SIMON	Corporal	F	177th Infantry
GANS, ISAAC	Corporal		2nd Cavalry

Received a Congressional "Medal of Honor" for bravery displayed on the battlefield.

GUGGENHEIM, S. S.			10th Cavalry

HART, BENJAMIN		H	2nd Infantry
HARRIS, SOLOMON S.		C	2nd Infantry
HARRIS, ISAAC		K	3d Infantry
HELLER, ELIAS		C	4th Infantry

Died in the service.

HIRSCH, J.		K	5th Infantry
HERMAN, HENRY		A	6th Infantry
HAHNEMAN, A.		H	6th Infantry
HOFMAN, HENRY			7th Infantry

Wounded at Chancellorsville.

HEILBRUN, ALEXANDER	1st Lieutenant		9th Infantry

Promoted from Corporal.

HERZOG, P.			9th Infantry

Killed at Chickamauga.

HEINEMAN, FREDERICK		B	9th Infantry
HESSBERG, ISAAC		C	9th Infantry
HERRMAN, JACOB		C	9th Infantry

Wounded at Chickamauga.

HIRSCHMAN, ——		F	9th Infantry

Killed at Chickamauga.

HIRSCHBAUM, A.			9th Infantry
HIRSH, J.			10th Infantry

Served three years.

HERZOG, JACOB		H	12th Infantry

Captured.

HIRSCH, WILLIAM			12th Infantry
HERRMAN, HENRY		A	17th Infantry
HESS, ISAAC		C	18th Infantry

NAME.	RANK.	COMPANY.	REGIMENT.
HIRSCHBERG, ISAAC			19th Infantry
Died in the service.			
HESS, JACOB			19th Infantry
HIRSCHBERG, DAVID		D	19th Infantry
HERRMAN, ADOLPH			22nd Infantry
HIRSCHMAN, JOSEPH		K	22nd Infantry
HERZOG, ADOLPH			24th Infantry
HEYMAN, JACOB		B	26th Infantry
HECHT, MOSES		H	27th Infantry
HIRSCH, JOHN W.			27th Infantry
HIRSCHMAN, JOHN		A	28th Infantry
HERRMAN, FERDINAND		C	28th Infantry
HERRMAN, BERNHARD			28th Infantry
HERRMAN, JOSEPH		K	29th Infantry
Died in the service.			
HIRSCH, JACOB		E	32nd Infantry
HOFMAN, LEVI			32nd Infantry
HOFFMAN, S.	Sergeant		33d Infantry
Enlisted as Private.			
HERZOG, BENJAMIN			33d Infantry
HESS, JACOB		A	33d Infantry
HIRSCHBERG, HENRY		B	33d Infantry
HIRSCH, HENRY		D	35th Infantry
HERRMAN, LEWIS	Sergeant	I	35th Infantry
Enlisted as Private.			
HELLER, EMIL	Quartermaster-Sergeant		37th Infantry
Enlisted as Private; served four years.			
HEINEMAN, HENRY			37th Infantry
HERRMAN, HENRY			37th Infantry
Wounded in action.			
HESS, FERDINAND		E	37th Infantry
HART, ABRAM		D	39th Infantry
HESS, JACOB			39th Infantry
HAHN, LEVI		A	40th Infantry
Served three years.			
HAHN, MORITZ		A	40th Infantry
Served three years.			

NAME.	RANK.	COMPANY.	REGIMENT.
HELLER, JOSEPH		C	41st Infantry
HOFMAN, REUBEN			41st Infantry

Died in the service.

| HELLER, HERMAN | | B | 46th Infantry |

Died of wounds.

| HOFMAN, LEVI | | | 46th Infantry |

Died in the service.

HERRMAN, JACOB		H	47th Infantry
HERRMAN, HENRY		K	47th Infantry
HOFMAN, JOSEPH	Sergeant	A	48th Infantry

Enlisted as Private.

| HEINEMAN, WILLIAM | | | 49th Infantry |

Killed at Stone River.

HELLER, SIMON P.			52nd Infantry
HEIMAN, JACOB		H	53d Infantry
HAHN, WILLIAM			56th Infantry
HERZOG, FELIX			57th Infantry
HESS, DAVID			57th Infantry

Died in the service.

| HERRMAN, ADOLPHUS | Corporal | B | 58th Infantry |

Wounded in action.

| HOFMAN, JACOB | | | 58th Infantry |

Killed in action.

HERRMAN, JACOB			58th Infantry
HEINE, JACOB		G	58th Infantry
HOFMAN, SAMUEL			59th Infantry
HAHN, REUBEN			60th Infantry
HELLER, ELIAS		F	63d Infantry
HAAS, MOSES	Corporal	G	63d Infantry
HIRSCHBERG, SAMUEL		K	64th Infantry
HESS, ABRAHAM		F	65th Infantry
HOFMAN, ABRAHAM		H	65th Infantry
HELLER, HENRY	Sergeant	A	66th Infantry

Enlisted as Private; received Congressional "Medal of Honor" for bravery and daring.

| HEINEMAN, AUGUST | | B | 68th Infantry |

Died of wounds received at Champion Hills.

NAME.	RANK.	COMPANY.	REGIMENT.
HERZFELD, JACOB		H	68th Infantry
Served four years.			
HAHN, W. C.		C	69th Infantry
Served four years.			
HESS, D.			69th Infantry
HAAS, JOSEPH			70th Infantry
Served three years.			
HAHN, HENRY			70th Infantry
HOFMAN, JACOB	Sergeant	C	72nd Infantry
Enlisted as Private; captured; served three years.			
HAHN, CHARLES		G	72nd Infantry
HOFMAN, JACOB			73d Infantry
HIRSCHMAN, ISAAC	Corporal	F	74th Infantry
Enlisted as Private.			
HELLER, WILLIAM	Commissary Sergeant		78th Infantry
Enlisted as Private.			
HART, ISRAEL		G	78th Infantry
HERZOG, D.			80th Infantry
Served four years.			
HERZOG, JACOB		D	80th Infantry
Served three years.			
HESS, MOSES		D	80th Infantry
Died in the service.			
HART, SAMUEL		K	82nd Infantry
HAYS, AARON		C	84th Infantry
HEYMAN, FRANK	Adjutant		84th Infantry
HELLER, GEORGE		K	84th Infantry
HIRSCHBERG, HENRY		B	86th Infantry
HELLER, CHARLES		I	90th Infantry
Died at Murfreesboro.			
HEINEMAN, ADAM		K	92nd Infantry
HOFMAN, LEVI			96th Infantry
Died at Young's Point, Louisiana.			
HAHN, JACOB		D	106th Infantry
HAHN, HENRY		D	107th Infantry
Captured at Chancellorsville.			

NAME.	RANK.	COMPANY.	REGIMENT.
HAAS, JACOB		A	108th Infantry
HERRMAN, CHARLES	Sergeant	D	108th Infantry

Enlisted as Private; died from wounds at Resaca.

HOFMAN, JACOB		H	108th Infantry
HART, LEVI		H	110th Infantry

Wounded at Winchester and at Monocacy, Maryland.

HELLER, NATHAN		D	111th Infantry

Served three years.

HAHN, HENRY		I	111th Infantry

Served three years.

HARRIS, ISRAEL		K	111th Infantry
HUHN, JOSEPH S.	Sergeant	F	114th Infantry

Promoted Corporal; wounded at Vicksburg.

HEIDELBACH, JACOB		F	114th Infantry
HEIDELBACH, HENRY		F	114th Infantry
HEIDELBACH, DAVID		G	114th Infantry

Died in the service.

HEIDELBACH, H.			114th Infantry
HOFMAN, L.			115th Infantry
HAYS, ABRAHAM		F	118th Infantry

Served three years.

HEIDELBACH, C.			122nd Infantry

Captured; served three years.

HEIDELBACH, A-			122nd Infantry
HEYMAN, SAMUEL	Sergeant	F	123d Infantry

Enlisted as Private; captured at Winchester.

HEYMAN, JACOB		F	123d Infantry
HAAS, JACOB		K	123d Infantry

Died at Clarksburg, West Virginia.

HELLER, MOSES	Corporal		———

Captured at Winchester; served three years.

HERRMAN, SIMON		K	123d Infantry

Captured at Winchester.

HESS, DAVID K.		F	125th Infantry
HELLER, CHARLES		G	125th Infantry
HART, MARKS		K	128th Infantry

NAME.	RANK.	COMPANY.	REGIMENT.
HAMBURGER, FRANCIS		D	131st Infantry
HOFMAN, EPHRAIM		K	131st Infantry
HERRMAN, JOSEPH		I	137th Infantry

Was honorably mentioned by President Lincoln.

HESS, NATHAN		C	167th Infantry
ISRAEL, P.			3d Infantry

Wounded at Chaplin Hills.

ISRAEL, ALFRED			19th Infantry
ISRAEL, ELISHA		F	77th Infantry

Captured.

ISRAEL, DAVID			97th Infantry

Died at Murfreesboro.

ISRAEL, WILLIAM			97th Infantry
ISRAEL, ELIAS		K	108th Infantry
JOSEPH, JOSEPH		F	15th Infantry

Enlisted as Private.

JACOBY, BENJAMIN			35th Infantry
JACOBSON, OTTO			39th Infantry
JOSEPH, NATHAN B.			47th Infantry
JACOB, JULIUS		F	47th Infantry
JUDELL, D.		G	47th Infantry
JACOBSON, DANIEL	Corporal	F	49th Infantry

Enlisted as Private.

JACOBY, DAVID		K	49th Infantry
JACOBY, DAVID H.		K	49th Infantry
JACOBY, HENRY		K	49th Infantry

Died in the service.

JACOBS, FERDINAND	Corporal		57th Infantry

Served three years.

JACOBS, JACOB		C	57th Infantry
JOSEPH, NATHAN		C	59th Infantry
JACOBS, JOSEPH	Lieutenant	B	67th Infantry

Promoted from Sergeant.

JACOBS, HENRY	Sergeant	B	67th Infantry

Enlisted as private.

NAME.	RANK.	COMPANY.	REGIMENT.
JACOBY, FRANK		F	69th Infantry
JACOBS, BENJAMIN		F	70th Infantry
JACOBS, DANIEL		G	71st Infantry
JACOBS, LEWIS W.	Sergeant	I	71st Infantry

Enlisted as private; served four years.

JACOBS, M.	Sergeant		71st Infantry
JACOBS, ALEXANDER		E	75th Infantry

Wounded at Bull Run.

JACOBS, HENRY	Sergeant	F	75th Infantry

Enlisted as private; died from wounds received at McDowell.

JACOBS, DAVID		H	75th Infantry
JACOBS, FRANK	Corporal	I	76th Infantry

Enlisted as private; served four years.

JOSEPH, JACOB		A	80th Infantry

Wounded and captured.

JACOBY, HENRY	Lieutenant	D	82nd Infantry

Promoted from Sergeant; killed at Gettysburg.

JACOB, MARTIN			82nd Infantry

Killed at Gettysburg.

JACOBS, BERNHARD		C	83d Infantry

Served three years.

JACOBS, HENRY		I	86th Infantry
JULIAN, S.			88th Infantry
JACOBS, HENRY		A	91st Infantry

Served three years.

JACOB, JOSHUA		B	94th Infantry
JUDAH, EMANUEL		F	94th Infantry
JUDAH, JOHN H.		F	94th Infantry

Served three years.

JONES, S.			95th Infantry
JACOBS, HENRY		A	99th Infantry
JACOBS, JACOB		H	107th Infantry
JACOB, LOUIS	Corporal	C	108th Infantry
JACOB, HENRY J.	Sergeant	K	110th Infantry

Promoted from Corporal; served three years.

NAME.	RANK.	COMPANY.	REGIMENT.
JACOBS, CHARLES		B	111th Infantry
Served three years.			
JACOBS, MICHAEL		H	111th Infantry
Served three years.			
JACOBS, A.			125th Infantry
JACOBY, N.			115th Infantry
JACOBS, S.			125th Infantry
JACOBS, ABRAHAM		I	128th Infantry
JACOBY, EDWIN	Sergeant	B	130th Infantry
JACOBS, GUSTAV		F	130th Infantry
JACOBS, S.			135th Infantry
JACOBS, BENJAMIN T.		A	135th Infantry
JACOBS, LOUIS C.		A	138th Infantry
KLINE, M.	Lieutenant	K	1st Infantry
KLINE, MOSES		A	2nd Infantry
Captured at Chickamauga.			
KIEFER, WILLIAM		A	2nd Infantry
KAUFMAN, DAVID		B	2nd Infantry
KAUFMAN, SAMUEL		F	4th Infantry
Wounded at Chancellorsville.			
KOHN, SIEGMUND		G	5th Infantry
Killed at Port Republic.			
KAUFMAN, JOSEPH			5th Infantry
Served three years.			
KING, SAMUEL			7th Infantry
KOCH, MICHAEL			9th Infantry
KUHN, ISIDORE		H	9th Infantry
Served three years.			
KUHN, JACOB		F	10th Infantry
Served three years.			
KAUFMAN, G.			12th Infantry
Wounded in action.			
KAUFMAN, JACOB		K	16th Infantry
Served three years.			
KAUFMAN, DAVID		G	18th Infantry

NAME.	RANK.	COMPANY.	REGIMENT.
KAUFMAN, JONATHAN			21st Infantry
Died in the service.			
KLEIN, MOSES	Captain	H	22nd Infantry
Served three years.			
KLEIN, FRANK		H	22nd Infantry
KLEIN, DAVID	Corporal		24th Infantry
KAHN, SIMON		G	25th Infantry
Wounded at Cross Keys.			
KOENIGSBERGER, HERMAN	Lieutenant		28th Infantry
KOCH, LEWIS			28th Infantry
KAUFMAN, FRANK		A	28th Infantry
KAHN, LEWIS		F	28th Infantry
KAUFMAN, FRANK		K	28th Infantry
KOCH, JACOB		H	30th Infantry
KAUFMAN, SOLOMON	Quartermaster		32nd Infantry
Enlisted as private.			
KOCH, SAMUEL		H	33d Infantry
Died in the service.			
KAUFMAN, JOSEPH C.			36th Infantry
KLEIN, MORITZ		E	37th Infantry
KAUFMAN, SAMUEL		C	38th Infantry
KAUFMAN, FRANK	Sergeant	K	42nd Infantry
Promoted from private.			
KING, EMANUEL		E	44th Infantry
KAUFMAN, BENJAMIN			44th Infantry
KLEIN, DAVID	Sergeant		47th Infantry
Enlisted as private; captured.			
KLEIN, ABRAHAM		B	48th Infantry
KLEIN, JACOB W.	Lieutenant		49th Infantry
Enlisted as private; captured at Stone River.			
KLEIN, DAVID			49th Infantry
KOCH, JOSEPH	Sergeant	G	50th Infantry
KING, JACOB		H	50th Infantry
KLEIN, DAVID			51st Infantry
KAUFMAN, W. H.	1st Lieutenant	A	52nd Infantry
Promoted from 2nd Lieutenant.			

21

NAME.	RANK.	COMPANY.	REGIMENT.
KOCH, HENRY		K	52nd Infantry
KLEIN, JACOB			58th Infantry
KING, DAVID			62nd Infantry
Killed in action.			
KAUFMAN, LEVI	Lieutenant	B	68th Infantry
Promoted from Corporal.			
KAUFMAN, DAVID		H	71st Infantry
KAUFMAN, ISAAC			72nd Infantry
Wounded at Shiloh.			
KLEIN, JOSEPH		H	73d Infantry
KLEIN, DAVID B.		B	74th Infantry
KLEIN, D. J.			75th Infantry
Wounded and captured at Gainesville.			
KLEIN, ISAAC		A	76th Infantry
KLEIN, LOUIS		E	76th Infantry
KLEIN, ISAIAH	Sergeant	G	77th Infantry
Enlisted as Private; died in the service.			
KLEIN, FRANX			82nd Infantry
KLEIN, FRANK			83d Infantry
KAUFMAN, HENRY		I	83d Infantry
Served three years.			
KOCH, JACOB		E	84th Infantry
KAUFMAN, DAVID		C	86th Infantry
KAUFMAN, HERMAN S.	Corporal	I	86th Infantry
KAUFMAN, FRANK		I	87th Infantry
KLEIN, D.			91st Infantry
KLEIN, S.			92nd Infantry
Served three years.			
KAUFMAN, ABRAHAM		A	94th Infantry
KAUFMAN, FRANK			94th Infantry
KLEIN, JACOB	Sergeant	A	96th Infantry
KLEIN, JACOB	Sergeant	A	96th Infantry
Enlisted at Private; served three years.			
KLEIN, JONAS		C	96th Infantry
Captured.			
KLEIN, JACOB	Sergeant	F	96th Infantry
Enlisted as Private.			

NAME.	RANK.	COMPANY.	REGIMENT.
KAUFMAN, JACOB J.	Corporal	F	96th Infantry

Enlisted as Private.

KAUFMAN, EMANUEL	Captain		100th Infantry

Died at Knoxville, Tennessee.

KAUFMAN, DANIEL		D	102nd Infantry

Captured at Athens; died in rebel prison.

KLEIN, JOSEPH			102nd Infantry

Served three years.

KAUFMAN, HENRY		A	106th Infantry
KAUFMAN, LOUIS	Captain	C	106th Infantry
KOCH, HENRY		C	108th Infantry

Killed at Hartsville, Tennessee.

KING, DAVID	Sergeant	I	108th Infantry

Enlisted as Private; wounded near Petersburg; served three years.

KAUFMAN, PHILIP		E	110th Infantry

Wounded near Petersburg.

KAUFMAN, HENRY		I	110th Infantry

Captured at Winchester, and wounded at Cedar Creek.

KLEIN, JONAS L.	Corporal		111th Infantry

Enlisted as Private.

KLEIN, ISAAC N.		A	116th Infantry
KAHN, JACOB		I	124th Infantry
KOHLER, DANIEL		K	125th Infantry
KING, SOLOMON	Corporal	I	126th Infantry

Enlisted as Private; served four years.

KOCH, MAX		F	103th Infantry
KLEIN, EMANUEL		D	131st Infantry
KLEIN, LEVI J.		D	131st Infantry
KAUFMAN, HENRY		K	131st Infantry
KAUFMAN, FRANK	1st Lieutenant	B	132nd Infantry
KRAUSKOPF, SOLOMON	Corporal	B	132nd Infantry
KLEIN, SOLOMON		D	132nd Infantry
KING, LEVI		B	133d Infantry
KRAUSKOPF, JUSTIS		I	138th Infantry
KLEIN, JACOB		F	139th Infantry

NAME.	RANK.	COMPANY.	REGIMENT.
KLIPPSTEIN, MEYER			7th Cavalry
KOCH, MOSES			150th Infantry
KOCH, HERMAN	(three brothers)		4th Artillery
KOCH, JOSEPH			177th Infantry
KOCH, JACOB			164th Infantry
LEVI, CHARLES		G	2nd Infantry
LEHMAN, LEWIS			4th Infantry
LOSER, JOSEPH		B	4th Infantry
LAZARUS, ED.	Sergeant	G	7th Infantry

Promoted from Corporal; wounded at Winchester;
also at Cedar Mountain.

| LAZARUS, MARTIN | | | 7th Infantry |

Killed at Antietam.

| LOWENTHAL, JACOB | | G | 8th Infantry |

Died from sickness contracted in camp.

| LANDAUER, SAMUEL | Sergeant | | 9th Infantry |

Promoted from Corporal.

| LOVENSTEIN, NATHAN | | C | 9th Infantry |

Served three years.

| LOWENSTEIN, J. | | C | 9th Infantry |
| LEHMAN, JOSEPH | Corporal | F | 9th Infantry |

Enlisted as Private; wounded at Chattanooga.

LEVY, NATHAN		K	9th Infantry
LIEBERMAN, WILLIAM			14th Infantry
LEHMAN, BENJAMIN	Corporal	C	15th Infantry

Killed at Pickett's Mills.

LOWENSTEIN, GEORGE		D	23d Infantry
LEOPOLD, WILLIAM		H	23d Infantry
LICHENFELD, ADOLPH	Corporal	A	24th Infantry
LOESER, LEWIS		A	26th Infantry
LEHMAN, THEODORE		G	26th Infantry
LEHMAN, JACOB	Sergeant		28th Infantry
LEHMAN, HERRMAN		B	28th Infantry
LEHMAN, FERDINAND		D	28th Infantry
LEOPOLD, FRANK		G	28th Infantry
LEHMAN, JACOB		E	32nd Infantry

NAME.	RANK.	COMPANY.	REGIMENT.
LEHMAN, HENRY	Sergeant	H	32nd Infantry
Served three years.			
LYONS, JOSEPH			33d Infantry
LYONS, DAVID		A	34th Infantry
LEVY, WILLIAM		F	38th Infantry
LEHMAN, DANIEL		F	39th Infantry
LYONS, JACOB			40th Infantry
Killed in battle.			
LEHMAN, ALEXANDER		F	41st Infantry
Died of wounds.			
LEHMAN, ABRAHAM		G	41st Infantry
LEHMAN, SAMUEL		F	42nd Infantry
LEVY, J. J.			43d Infantry
Served three years.			
LIEBMAN, FREDERICK		I	43d Infantry
LEHMAN, JOSEPH		A	46th Infantry
Served three years.			
LEVY, B.			46th Infantry
Wounded; served four years.			
LEHMAN, NOAH		D	48th Infantry
LEHMAN, ALEXANDER		K	54th Infantry
LUDWIG, BENJAMIN			58th Infantry
LEVY, JOHN A.		A	77th Infantry
LEHMAN, ISAAC		D	81st Infantry
Served three years.			
LOWENTHAL, THEODORE		I	81st Infantry
LOWENTHAL, J.			81st Infantry
LEHMAN, NATHAN		C	83d Infantry
Served three years.			
LEHMAN, LEWIS	Sergeant	D	86th Infantry
LEHMAN, SAMUEL S.		D	86th Infantry
LICHTENSTEIN, JOSEPH		F	87th Infantry
LEHMAN, DANIEL		A	93d Infantry
LEHMAN, JULIUS		H	93d Infantry
Served three years.			
LEHMAN, HENRY M.	Corporal	H	99th Infantry
Enlisted as private.			

NAME.	RANK.	COMPANY.	REGIMENT.
LOWENTHAL, THEODORE		E	101st Infantry
LEHMAN, HENRY		F	102nd Infantry
Served three years.			
LEHMAN, DANIEL		F	102nd Infantry
Served three years.			
LEHMAN, HENRY		A	107th Infantry
LEOPOLD, GUSTAV	Corporal	C	107th Infantry
Killed at Chancellorsville.			
LEHMAN, NOAH		I	107th Infantry
Served three years.			
LEHMAN, HERMAN		C	108th Infantry
Served three years.			
LOWENSTEIN, DANIEL		G	108th Infantry
LUDWIG, FRANK	Corporal	E	111th Infantry
Enlisted as private ; captured at Stone Mountain, Georgia.			
LEHMAN, JACOB	Sergeant	D	114th Infantry
LEHMAN, SAMUEL			114th Infantry
Died at Vicksburg.			
LEHMAN, JUDAH		H	115th Infantry
Served three years.			
LEHMAN, JACOB	Sergeant	A	120th Infantry
Promoted from Corporal; captured.			
LEHMAN, SALOMON		H	131st Infantry
LEHMAN, DAVID E.	Corporal	H	134th Infantry
LEVY, W. H.		D	137th Infantry
LEVY, SAMUEL		C	139th Infantry
LINDERMAN, J.		C	1st Artillery
LEVI, HENRY I.			2nd Cavalry
MACHNER, EMANUEL		E	1st Infantry
MOSES, WILLIAM		E	1st Infantry
MEYERS, SAMUEL		B	2nd Infantry
MORRIS, AARON			2nd Infantry
Served three years.			
MICHELS, ABRAHAM		F	2nd Infantry
MESSNER, LEVI			3d Infantry

NAME.	RANK.	COMPANY.	REGIMENT.
MILLER, JONAS AARON		E	5th Infantry
MEYER, BERNARD		C	6th Infantry
MOSLER, HERMAN		C	6th Infantry
MARKS, JACOB	Corporal	B	7th Infantry

Wounded at Cedar Mountain and at Dallas, Georgia.

MARKS, WILLIAM			8th Infantry

Killed at Antietam.

MARIENTHAL, SIMON			8th Infantry
MAIER, LOUIS		C	9th Infantry
MANGOLD, AD.	Lieutenant	K	9th Infantry

Promoted from Sergeant.

MANDEL, CHARLES			9th Infantry

Wounded in action.

MAYER, HENRY			9th Infantry
MAYER, JOSEPH			10th Infantry

Served three years.

MEYER, JACOB			11th Infantry
MARKS, SAMUEL		F	11th Infantry
MAURICE, ISAAC		I	11th Infantry
MANN, FREDERICK			14th Infantry
MOSES, SAMUEL		F	16th Infantry

Served three years.

MANN, JOSEPH			18th Infantry
MAAS, DAVID			18th Infantry
MEIER, LEOPOLD		A	22nd Infantry

Died in the service.

MILLER, ALEXANDER		H	22nd Infantry
MILLER, WILLIAM		H	22nd Infantry
MYERS, ABRAHAM			24th Infantry
MEYER, HENRY			24th Infantry
MEIER, FRANK			24th Infantry
MORRIS, NATHAN		C	25th Infantry
MEYER, ADOLPH			25th Infantry

Wounded at Cross Keys.

MARX, EMIL			25th Infantry
MEIER, HENRY			25th Infantry
MENKEN, JACOB	Captain	B	27th Infantry

NAME.	RANK.	COMPANY.	REGIMENT.
MAYER, LOUIS H.	Commissary Sergeant		27th Infantry

Afterwards Corporal of Company B, 27th Infantry; subsequently detached for staff duty.

MAYER, ADOLPH	Sergeant	B	27th Infantry
MOAK, J. H.	Lieutenant	A	28th Infantry

Enlisted as Private.

MARX, J. H.		A	28th Infantry
MEYER, FRANK		B	28th Infantry
MEYER, FRANK		G	28th Infantry
MEYER, HERMAN			28th Infantry

Wounded in action.

MEIER, LEOPOLD			28th Infantry
MEYER, HERMAN			28th Infantry
MAYER, JOSEPH			28th Infantry
MAY, DAVID	Corporal		32nd Infantry
MARKS, ABRAHAM		E	32nd Infantry

Killed in action.

MANN, SAMUEL			33d Infantry
MORRIS, ISRAEL			34th Infantry
MEYERS, JACOB			34th Infantry
MEYERS, NOAH		D	34th Infantry
MEYERS, SAMUEL			34th Infantry
MEYER, EDWARD			34th Infantry
MEYER, JOSEPH	Sergeant		35th Infantry

Enlisted as Private; served three years.

MEYERS, JACOB T.		B	35th Infantry
MAIER, ISIDORE			35th Infantry

Died in the service.

MANDELBAUM, SOLOMON			35th Infantry
MAINZ, ABRAHAM			36th Infantry
MYERS, DAVID			36th Infantry
MORITZ, CARL	Captain		37th Infantry
MAY, JACOB			37th Infantry

Died in the service.

MARCUS, FREDERICK			37th Infantry

Wounded in action.

MORITZ, JOSEPH			37th Infantry
MEIER, BERNHART		L	37th Infantry

NAME.	RANK.	COMPANY.	REGIMENT.
MAYER, FREDERICK			37th Infantry
MANN, DAVID		D	39th Infantry

Wounded in action.

MORITZ, JACOB	Sergeant	H	46th Infantry

Entered as Private; served four years.

MANN, AARON B.		I	46th Infantry
MYERS, SOLOMON			47th Infantry
MEYER, JACOB	Sergeant		49th Infantry

Enlisted as Private.

MARKS, SAMUEL	Sergeant	K	51st Infantry
MEYERS, JACOB		B	52nd Infantry
MEYER, SAMUEL			54th Infantry
MEYERS, JOSEPH			54th Infantry
MANN, SAMUEL		I	54th Infantry
MEYERS, ALEXANDER		I	54th Infantry

Captured; died in rebel prison.

MEYER, JACOB	Corporal		———

Enlisted as Private; wounded in action.

MENDEL, WILLIAM			56th Infantry
MEYER, HENRY			56th Infantry

Wounded.

MEYERS, JACOB			57th Infantry

Died in the service.

MARKS, HENRY			57th Infantry
MEYER, JACOB		E	60th Infantry
MARKS, SAMUEL A.		E	60th Infantry

Killed at Petersburg.

MARKS, ISAAC N.		H	60th Infantry
MARKS, SAMUEL		H	60th Infantry
MEYER, HERMAN			61st Infantry
MEIER, MARCUS	Lieutenant	I	64th Infantry
MEYERS, JOSEPH		B	65th Infantry
MARKS, JONAS S.		H	66th Infantry
MARKS, ISAAC		H	66th Infantry
MAIER, ISAAC		I	66th Infantry
MANN, ABRAHAM		A	68th Infantry
MANN, AARON		D	70th Infantry

NAME.	RANK.	COMPANY.	REGIMENT.
MANN, ISAAC	Lieutenant	C	71st Infantry

Promoted from Sergeant.

| MANN, JACOB | Sergeant | C | 71st Infantry |

Promoted from Corporal; served three years.

| MAAS, HENRY | | | 72nd Infantry |

Died in the service.

| MAY, SAMUEL | | B | 73d Infantry |

Died in the service.

| MAY, JOSEPH | | C | 73d Infantry |
| MAYER, SIMON | | D | 73d Infantry |

Killed at Gettysburg.

| MANN, ISAAC | | | 75th Infantry |

Served three years.

| MYERS, ISRAEL | | A | 76th Infantry |

Died in the service.

| MEYERS, JACOB | | E | 76th Infantry |

Died in the service.

MYERS, FRANK			76th Infantry
MARX, EMIL		I	78th Infantry
MENDEL, WILLIAM		I	78th Infantry

Served three years.

MANN, JACOB		K	83d Infantry
MAIERS, SOLOMON		A	98th Infantry
MEYERS, DAVID			99th Infantry

Died in the service.

MANN, SAMUEL		H	102nd Infantry
MEYERS, DAVID			102nd Infantry
MEYERS, LEWIS H.			102nd Infantry
MANN, SAMUEL		K	104th Infantry

Served three years.

| MAIER, WILLIAM | | B | 105th Infantry |

Served three years.

| MEYER, SERAPHIM | Colonel | | 107th Infantry |

Captured at Chancellorsville.

| MEIER, JOSEPH | | H | 107th Infantry |

Served three years.

NAME.	RANK.	COMPANY.	REGIMENT.
MANN, JACOB	Corporal	K	107th Infantry

Died in the service.

MAIER, JOSEPH			107th Infantry
MEYERS, HENRY	Commissary Sergeant		108th Infantry

Promoted from Sergeant; served three years.

MEYERS, JACOB, JR.	1st Sergeant	B	108th Infantry

Enlisted as Private; served three years.

MEYER, JOSEPH		B	108th Infantry
MEIER, DANIEL		D	108th Infantry
MOSLER, MAX	Lieutenant.	E	108th Infantry
MEYER, HENRY		F	108th Infantry
MENKE, HENRY		G	108th Infantry
MEYER, JOSEPH		H	108th Infantry
MANTEL, LEWIS		I	113th Infantry
MANN DAVID		C	116th Infantry

Captured at Winchester; died in the service.

MAY, SIMON	Corporal	E	118th Infantry

Enlisted as Private; served three years.

MANN, JACOB		E	118th Infantry

Served three years.

MANN, SAMUEL		E	118th Infantry

Killed at Kennesaw Mountain, Georgia.

MYERS, DAVID		I	120th Infantry

Died in the service.

MAY, SAMUEL		B	121st Infantry
MANN, JOSEPH		H	121st Infantry

Served three years.

MEYERS, HENRY		I	122nd Infantry
MEYERS, JOSEPH		D	123d Infantry

Wounded at Opequan, Virginia; served three years.

MEYERS, JOSEPH P.	Corporal	I	123d Infantry

Served three years.

MEYER, ANSELM	Corporal	H	125th Infantry
MOSES, HENRY S.	Sergeant-Major		126th Infantry

Enlisted as Private; served three years.

MOSES, DAVID		G	126th Infantry

Died of wounds received at Spottsylvania, Virginia.

NAME.	RANK.	COMPANY.	REGIMENT.
MYERS, DAVID H.		H	126th Infantry

Captured at Monocacy, Maryland.

NAME.	RANK.	COMPANY.	REGIMENT.
MARKS, ALBERT		B	128th Infantry
MEYERS, JACOB		B	128th Infantry
MYERS, JACOB C.		B	128th Infantry
MARX, LOEB		C	128th Infantry
MAYER, ALBERT		K	128th Infantry
MOSES, FRANK A.		E	130th Infantry
MEYER, JOSEPH			130th Infantry
MANN, CHARLES		E	131st Infantry
MEYERS, DAVID		A	132nd Infantry

Died in the service.

NAME.	RANK.	COMPANY.	REGIMENT.
MEYERS, JACOB		K	132nd Infantry
MEYERS, SAMUEL		K	132nd Infantry
MORGENTHAL, HENRY		B.	136th Infantry
MEYERS, MICHAEL		D	136th Infantry
MOSES, GEORGE		B	137th Infantry
MEYER, JACOB		A	138th Infantry
MANN, JOSEPH B.	Sergeant	C	138th Infantry
MEYER, HENRY		C	138th Infantry
MEYERS, ISAAC			169th Infantry
MEYERS, SAMUEL			169th Infantry
NEUBERGER, FREDERICK			28th Infantry
NEUBERGER, SAMUEL			44th Infantry
NEUSTAT, DAVID			58th Infantry
NEUMAN, CHARLES			61st Infantry
NIEMAN, DANIEL		C	83d Infantry

Served three years.

NAME.	RANK.	COMPANY.	REGIMENT.
NUSSBAUM, FRANK		A	88th Infantry
NEWHOUSE, DAVID K.		K	101st Infantry

Killed at Stone River.

NAME.	RANK.	COMPANY.	REGIMENT.
NUSSBAUM, FREDERICK	Sergeant	C	107th Infantry

Promoted from Corporal; served three years.

NAME.	RANK.	COMPANY.	REGIMENT.
NATHANS, HENRY		K	107th Infantry
NEUMAN, HENRY		F	108th Infantry
NUSSBAUM, HENRY		A	113th Infantry

NAME.	RANK.	COMPANY.	REGIMENT.
NEWBAUER, JACOB B.		E	115th Infantry

Served three years.

| NAUMAN, JACOB | Corporal | G | 120th Infantry |

Enlisted as Private; served three years.

NEUMAN, JACOB		H	123d Infantry
NEUBERGER, WILLIAM M.		F	134th Infantry
NEWMAN, JOSEPH	Lieutenant		4th Cavalry

| OCHS, FERDINAND | Sergeant-Major | | 1st Infantry |

Promoted from Private; served three years.

OCHS, GEORGE		K	13th Infantry
OPPENHEIMER, BENJAMIN			19th Infantry
OPPENHEIMER, J.		C	28th Infantry
OCHS, JOHN			37th Infantry
OCHS, JULIUS			52nd Infantry
ORBANSKI, DAVID		B	58th Infantry

Was awarded a Congressional " Medal of Honor " for distinguished bravery at Shiloh, Tennessee, and at Vicksburg, Mississippi.

| OCHS, HENRY | | B | 82nd Infantry |

Served three years.

| OPPENHEIMER, ALEXANDER | | K | 108th Infantry |
| OCHS, THEODORE | | G | 123d Infantry |

Killed at Petersburg.

| OCHS, JULIUS | Captain | | Independent Company |

| POLLOCK, HENRY | Corporal | A | 4th Infantry |

Enlisted as Private; served three years.

| POLLOCK, JOSEPH | | | 7th Infantry |
| PERLEY, VICTOR | | | 7th Infantry |

Killed at Chancellorsville.

| PASSAUER, JOSEPH | | | 9th Infantry |

Wounded at Chickamauga.

| PARADISE, SOLOMON | | G | 13th Infantry |

Killed in battle.

| PHILLIPS, ISRAEL | | I | 13th Infantry |

Served three years.

NAME.	RANK.	COMPANY.	REGIMENT.
POLLOCK, WILLIAM			15th Infantry

Died in the service.

POLLOCK, DAVID	Corporal	E	48th Infantry
PEIXOTTO, MOSES L.	Captain	G	103d Infantry

Brother of Honorable Benjamin Franklin Peixotto.

PIKE, HENRY C.	Lieutenant	G	2nd Cavalry

RHEINHEIMER, JACOB		E	1st Infantry

Wounded at Resaca.

RICE, ASHER			4th Infantry
RICE, SIMPSON			6th Infantry
ROSENFELD, WILLIAM		C	9th Infantry
ROSENBERG, ABRAHAM			10th Infantry

Died of wounds.

ROTHSCHILD, DAVID		A	11th Infantry
ROSENAU, G.			13th Infantry

Wounded at Chattanooga; captured; died of wounds.

ROSE, HENRY		B	13th Infantry

Served three years.

ROSENBERG, DAVID		A	21st Infantry

Killed at Chickamauga.

RICHMIRE, SOLOMON		G	23d Infantry
ROSENTHAL, SAMUEL	Lieutenant		28th Infantry

Promoted from Corporal.

ROSENBERG, GUSTAV		I	28th Infantry
ROSENBERG, JACOB		G	29th Infantry

Killed at Port Republic.

ROSENBERG, W.		C	34th Infantry
ROSENBAUM, HERMAN	Captain		37th Infantry

Promoted from Sergeant.

ROSENFELD, GUSTAV			38th Infantry

Served four years.

RAPP, JACOB			49th Infantry
ROSENBERG, GUSTAV			57th Infantry
ROSENFELD, ALEXANDER		D	58th Infantry

Died in the service.

NAME.	RANK.	COMPANY.	REGIMENT.
ROSENBAUM, WILLIAM		D	58th Infantry
ROSENBERG, GUSTAV			61st Infantry
RUBEL, WILLIAM			63d Infantry
RICE, SIMON P.		K	66th Infantry

Died in the service.

| RICE, ISAAC L. | | C | 67th Infantry |

Killed at Winchester.

| ROSENBERG, HENRY | | I | 69th Infantry |
| RAU, LOUIS | | | 72nd Infantry |

Served three years.

| ROSENBERG, DAVID | | G | 76th Infantry |
| ROSE, GERSHOM | Corporal | B | 78th Infantry |

Enlisted as private; served three years.

ROSE, REUBEN			
ROSENBAUM, SAMUEL		K	82nd Infantry
ROSENBAUM, ISAAC		D	89th Infantry

Served three years.

| ROSENBAUM, JACOB | | D | 89th Infantry |
| REICHMAN, BENJAMIN | | | 8th Infantry9 |

Served three years.

| ROSE, JACOB | | G | 102nd Infantry |

Captured; died in the service.

| ROSE, DANIEL | | | 104th Infantry |

Served three years.

| ROSENBAUM, G. W. | | | 104th Infantry |

Served three years.

| RUBEL, ISAAC | | F | 106th Infantry |

Served three years.

| ROSENBERG, JOSEPH | | H | 106th Infantry |

Served three years.

| ROSENFELD, SIEGMUND | Corporal | E | 107th Infantry |

Captured at Gettysburg.

| ROSE, D. | | | 113th Infantry |

Killed at Chickamauga.

| RICE, ESAU | | F | 113th Infantry |

Served three years.

NAME.	RANK.	COMPANY.	REGIMENT.
ROSENDALE, CHARLES		G	113th Infantry

Died in the service.

ROSE, EZEKIEL		F	114th Infantry
ROSE, DANIEL		B	116th Infantry

Captured at Winchester; served three years.

RICH, SOLOMON		H	116th Infantry

Died of wounds at Piedmont, Virginia.

RICE, LEVI	Sergeant	B	118th Infantry

Enlisted as private; killed at Nashville, Tennessee.

ROSE, LEVI B.		H	118th Infantry

Served three years.

ROSE, JESSE		H	118th Infantry

Served three years.

RUHRMAN, ABRAHAM		K	120th Infantry
ROSENBAUM, OSWALD H.	Sergeant	G	123d Infantry

Promoted from Corporal; captured at Winchester.

SCHERCK, SOLOMON		D	1st Infantry
SCHANE, ABRAHAM M.		G	1st Infantry
SUMMAS, JACOB		G	2nd Infantry
SCHWAB, CHARLES			3d Infantry
SOLOMON, J. S.			5th Infantry
SOMMER, LEVI		F	6th Infantry
STERN, CHARLES H.		A	7th Infantry

Killed at Winchester.

STEIN, DAVID G.			7th Infantry
STRAUSS, J.			7th Infantry

Killed at Cedar Mountain.

SIMON, LEWIS		F	8th Infantry
STERN, WILLIAM		F	9th Infantry
STRAUSS, ERNST		F	9th Infantry

Served three years.

SOMMER, JACOB			9th Infantry

Served three years.

SOMMER, JULIUS			10th Infantry

Served three years.

SUSMAN, MAURICE	Lieutenant		13th Infantry

Enlisted as private; three years service.

NAME.	RANK.	COMPANY.	REGIMENT.
SCHELT, MOSES	Sergeant	B	13th Infantry
STRAUS, LEHMAN	Corporal	C	14th Infantry

Served three years.

NAME.	RANK.	COMPANY.	REGIMENT.
SAMPSON, SAMUEL	Corporal		15th Infantry
SIEGMUND, EPHRAIM		D	17th Infantry
SCHLOSS, JACOB		G	17th Infantry
SACHS, JACOB		C	28th Infantry
SILBERMAN, CHARLES		G	28th Infantry
SCHWARTZ, LOUIS HENRY			28th Infantry
SAMPSON, JOSEPH	Corporal		31st Infantry
SCHWAB, JACOB			33d Infantry
SOLOMON, R.		K	33d Infantry

Died in the service.

NAME.	RANK.	COMPANY.	REGIMENT.
SACHS, JOHN			34th Infantry
SCHWARZ, ISAAC			34th Infantry
SAMUELS, NATHAN		C	35th Infantry

Wounded at Chickamauga.

NAME.	RANK.	COMPANY.	REGIMENT.
SIEDENBERG, HENRY		B	37th Infantry

Killed in action.

NAME.	RANK.	COMPANY.	REGIMENT.
SCHWARZ, ADODPH		D	37th Infantry

Wounded; served four years.

NAME.	RANK.	COMPANY.	REGIMENT.
SCHWAB, ADOLPH			37th Infantry

Served four years.

NAME.	RANK.	COMPANY.	REGIMENT.
SIMON, AUGUST	Sergeant	F	39th Infantry
SANGER, GEORGE	Corporal		41st Infantry

Enlisted as Private; served three years.

NAME.	RANK.	COMPANY.	REGIMENT.
SAMPSON, SAMUEL			41st Infantry

Served four years.

NAME.	RANK.	COMPANY.	REGIMENT.
SCHWARZ, DAVID		H	46th Infantry
STERN, SOLOMON	Sergeant	K	46th Infantry

Enlisted as Private.

NAME.	RANK.	COMPANY.	REGIMENT.
STERNBERG, HENRY			47th Infantry
SOLOMON, J. E.			48th Infantry
STRAUSS, EDWARD		G	51st Infantry
SALTSMAN, BENJAMIN			52nd Infantry

Served three years.

22

NAME.	RANK.	COMPANY.	REGIMENT.
SALTSMAN, JOSHUA			52nd Infantry

Served three years.

SAMPSON, DAVID W.			53d Infantry
STRAUSS, WILLIAM		B	57th Infantry
SALOMON, JOSEPH		H	57th Infantry
SEELIG, SAMUEL	Sergeant		58th Infantry

Enlisted as Private; wounded.

| STRAUS, FREDERIC | | | 58th Infantry |

Killed in action.

| STEIN, JACOB | | | 58th Infantry |
| SAMLUNG, EDWARD | | B | 58th Infantry |

Died of wounds received at Shiloh.

| SCHLESINGER, DAVID B. | | | 58th Infantry |

Served four years.

STRAUS, DAVID		B	63d Infantry
STRAUS, AARON		K	63d Infantry
SOLOMON, ABRAHAM		H	64th Infantry

Killed in action.

| STRAUS, FREDERICK | | | 66th Infantry |

Captured.

STERN, ISAAC		K	72nd Infantry
SIMON, JOSEPH			81st Infantry
STERN, JACOB G.		G	82nd Infantry

Wounded at Bull Run.

| SCHWARZ, ABRAHAM | | | 82nd Infantry |

Wounded at Chancellorsville.

| SCHWARZ, JOSEPH | | | 82nd Infantry |

Wounded at Dallas, Georgia.

STEIN, LEWIS			84th Infantry
STEIN, L.			85th Infantry
STRAUSS, ABRAHAM		D	86th Infantry
STERN, JOHN		K	86th Infantry
STEIN, LOUIS		A	88th Infantry
STERNBERG, JACOB		H	88th Infantry
SAMPSON, SAMUEL			92nd Infantry

Served three years.

NAME.	RANK.	COMPANY.	REGIMENT.
STRAUSS, GEORGE		I	93d Infantry

Killed at Chickamauga.

SCHWAB, SOLOMON		A	94th Infantry
SCHARFF, NATHAN		B	94th Infantry

Captured near Lexington, Kentucky.

SOLOMON, JOSEPH		K	95th Infantry

Died in the service.

STINER, ABRAHAM			96th Infantry

Wounded in Louisiana.

STEIN, REUBEN D.		K	100th Infantry

Captured at Limestone Station, Tennessee.

SOLOMON, ISAIAH	Corporal		101st Infantry

Enlisted as Private; served three years.

SAMPSON, FRANKLIN		D	103d Infantry
SCHREIER, FRANK		G	103d Infantry
STEIN, JACOB		A	105th Infantry
STEIN, HENRY	Lieutenant	B	105th Infantry

Promoted from Private.

SACHS, WILLIAM		K	106th Infantry
STRAUSS, JACOB		A	107th Infantry
SCHWAB, SAMUEL		I	107th Infantry

Wounded at Gettysburg.

SCHIFF, SIMON			108th Infantry
STEINBERG, A.	Corporal		108th Infantry

Enlisted as Private; died at Chattanooga.

SIMON, ALBERT			108th Infantry

Died at Rossville, Georgia.

SIMPSON, SAMUEL		G	110th Infantry
SCHWARZ, Joseph	Corporal		111th Infantry

Wounded at Resaca; served three years.

STRAUSS, PHILIP		E	111th Infantry
SCHWARZ, ABRAHAM		B	113th Infantry
STRAUSS, NATHAN	Captain	I	113th Infantry
STRAUSS, ABRAHAM	Sergeant	I	113th Infantry

Served three years.

SCHWARZ, LEVI		D	115th Infantry

Served three years.

NAME.	RANK.	COMPANY.	REGIMENT.
SACHS, JACOB C.		I	115th Infantry
SULZBERGER, LEWIS	Corporal	C	116th Infantry

Enlisted as Private; served three years.

STEIN, JOSEPH		C	118th Infantry

Served three years.

SPIEGEL, MARCUS M.   Colonel   120th Infantry
Enlisted in the 67th Ohio Infantry; was soon promoted to 2nd Lieutenant, Captain, Lieutenant-Colonel,
and for bravery manifested on the battle-field, was
appointed Colonel of the 120th Ohio Infantry. This
brave officer was wounded at Vicksburg, Mississippi,
and notwithstanding entreaties, rejoined his regiment,
but to fall at Snaggy Point, on the Red River, Louisiana. But for his untimely death, Colonel Spiegel
would have been promoted to Brigadier-General, for
which position he had been recommended by his
superior officers. Colonel Spiegel was the son of a
well-known Rabbi, of Oppenheim-on-the-Rhine, and
a relation of the Greenbaum family, of Chicago.

STEINER, JOSEPH		A	121st Infantry

Served three years.

STRAUSS, JOHN		G	121st Infantry
STEINBERG, MORRIS		D	124th Infantry

Served three years.

STRAUSS, JOSEPH J.	Corporal	E	126th Infantry

Enlisted as private; served three years.

SOLOMON, CHARLES		D	128th Infantry

Served three years.

SCHWAB, JACOB		B	129th Infantry
STERNBERGER, MARK		F	129th Infantry
STRAUSS, DAVID		F	130th Infantry
STRAUSS, JOHN		F	130th Infantry
SOMMER, CHARLES		F	130th Infantry
SOLOMON, EDWARD B.		A	131st Infantry
STEINER, HARRY		G	131st Infantry
STEINER, HENRY		G	131st Infantry
STRASBURG, J.			133d Infantry

NAME.	RANK.	COMPANY.	REGIMENT.
STERNBERG, NATHAN		D	138th Infantry
SIMON, ISAAC		E	138th Infantry
STRAUSS, DAVID W.		E	140th Infantry
TANNHAUSER, A.		B	6th Infantry
Served three years.			
TANNHAUSER, MOSES		B	6th Infantry
TACHAN, HENRY G.	Lieutenant	K	6th Infantry
TYROLER, SIGO			7th Infantry
TROWNSTEIN, PHILIP	Captain	B	5th Cavalry
ULLMAN, JOSEPH		G	16th Infantry
ULLMAN, ISAAC		A	23d Infantry
ULLMAN, FRANK		K	28th Infantry
ULLMAN, AUGUST			43d Infantry
ULMAN, ISAAC	Captain	A	80th Infantry
Promoted from Lieutenant.			
ULMAN, FREDERICK			80th Infantry
Died of wounds received at Vicksburg.			
VOGEL, ISRAEL		D	32nd Infantry
VOGEL, FRANK			39th Infantry
VOGEL, ELISHA		C	41st Infantry
VOGEL, NOAH			57th Infantry
WITKOWSKY, H.			1st Infantry
Served three years.			
WISE, JACOB			3d Infantry
WISE, SAMUEL		G	4th Infantry
WOLF, ALBERT			5th Infantry
WENDELSTEIN, MORITZ			5th Infantry
Died in the service.			
WOLF, JULIUS			7th Infantry
WIESNER, LOUIS		G	10th Infantry
WOLF, SAMUEL			17th Infantry
WOLF, DAVID			18th Infantry
WEIS, JACOB			19th Infantry
WOLF, DAVID		F	21st Infantry

NAME.	RANK.	COMPANY.	REGIMENT.
WOLF, SAMUEL		G	21st Infantry
WOLF, MAX			24th Infantry
Died in service.			
WISE, SAMUEL		G	25th Infantry
WOLF, ADOLPH		G	28th Infantry
Wounded in action.			
WOLF, ADOLPH A.			30th Infantry
Killed at Antietam.			
WISE, JOSEPH			31st Infantry
WATKOWSKY, KAN.		K	35th Infantry
WISE, SAMUEL			36th Infantry
WEILER, JACOB		C	37th Infantry
WEINBERG, LEWIS		D	37th Infantry
Wounded in action.			
WOLF, ADOLPH	Sergeant	K	37th Infantry
Enlisted as private.			
WISE, LEVI		K	39th Infantry
WOLF, AARON			39th Infantry
WISE, BENJAMIN L.		I	40th Infantry
Served three years.			
WATERMAN, HENRY			46th Infantry
WEIL, JACOB			47th Infantry
WOLF, JACOB	Lieutenant	F	49th Infantry
Promoted from Sergeant; Killed at Chattanooga.			
WOLF, ISAAC		A	50th Infantry
WOLF, DAVID			51st Infantry
Died in the service.			
WISE, JOSEPH M.		B	53d Infantry
Captured; died in hospital.			
WOLF, ISAAC		H	54th Infantry
WISE, JACOB			55th Infantry
Died in the service.			
WOLF, ISRAEL			57th Infantry
Died in the service.			
WEISS, LEWIS		E	57th Infantry
WOLF, LEVI		H	57th Infantry
Died in the service.			

NAME.	RANK.	COMPANY.	REGIMENT.
WATERMAN, HENRY		H	60th Infantry
WOLF, JACOB		I	67th Infantry

Died in the service.

WOLF, LEVI M.		C	68th Infantry
WISE, ABRAHAM		A	71st Infantry
WIEN, ALEXANDER			71st Infantry

Died in the service.

WOLF, MARCUS			72d Infantry

Captured.

WEIS, LOUIS		B	73d Infantry

Served four years.

WOLF, JACOB		I	80th Infantry
WISE, DANIEL W.			82nd Infantry
WISE, HENRY		K	82nd Infantry
WERTHEIMER, ANDREW		B	83d Infantry

Served three years.

WISE, SAMUEL		K	87th Infantry
WEINSTEIN, CHARLES W.		E	88th Infantry
WOLF, JACOB		I	94th Infantry

Died of wounds at the siege of Atlanta.

WISE, LEVI		I	101st Infantry

Served three years.

WOLF, EMANUEL			101st Infantry
WISE, EMANUEL	Corporal	A	104th Infantry

Enlisted as Private; served three years.

WOLF, M.		I	104th Infantry
WISE, JACOB		D	107th Infantry

Captured at Chancellorsville.

WEINMAN, LEOPOLD	Sergeant	F	107th Infantry

Enlisted as Private; wounded at Gettysburg.

WEIS, JOSEPH		H	107th Infantry

Wounded at Gettysburg.

WOLF, JACOB	Sergeant	K	107th Infantry

Promoted from Corporal; captured at Chancellorsville.

WISE, LEVI	Corporal	E	115th Infantry

Enlisted as Private; served three years.

NAME.	RANK.	COMPANY.	REGIMENT.
WOLF, JACOB		G	121st Infantry
WENTZ, JACOB	Sergeant	G	123d Infantry

Enlisted as Private; captured at Winchester; died in Rebel prison.

WOLF, JACOB	Sergeant	K	123d Infantry

Enlisted as Private; captured at Winchester.

WORMSER, NATHAN		A	128th Infantry

Served three years.

WOLF, LEVI		H	128th Infantry
WISE, JOSEPH A.	Lieutenant	E	131st Infantry
WEISS, SAMUEL		K	135th Infantry
DE WOLF, ISRAEL		A	135th Infantry
DE WOLF, SIMON	Lieutenant	B	136th Infantry
WIENER, MICHAEL			150th Infantry
WOLF, SOLOMON B.	Surgeon		165th Infantry

Served through the war.

WOLF, LEOPOLD		C	1st Cavalry

PENNSYLVANIA.

NAME.	RANK.	COMPANY.	REGIMENT.
ARNOLD, AMOS	Sergeant	A	14th Infantry
ARNOLD, BENJAMIN		B	17th Infantry
APPLE, JACOB	Corporal	G	22nd Infantry
ASH, SOLOMON		C	25th Infantry
ARNOLD, MAX		A	27th Infantry
ADELSHEIMER, JACQUES	Captain	B	27th Infantry

Enlisted as Private; promoted step by step to Captaincy; wounded at Chancellorsville; mentioned in special orders for gallantry.

ADLER, NOAH		B	27th Infantry

Captured at Gettysburg; sent to Belle Island.

ADLER, JACOB N.		B	27th Infantry

NAME.	RANK.	COMPANY.	REGIMENT.
ALEXANDER, JASTROW	Lieutenant	H	27th Infantry

Enlisted as Private; promoted to Regimental Adjutant subsequently Adjutant on staff of General von Steinwehr; mentioned in special orders for gallant conduct at Chancellorsville.

APPEL, FRANCIS		H	27th Infantry
APPEL, HENRY		H	27th Infantry
ADELSHEIMER, S.			27th Infantry
ALEXANDER, J.			27th Infantry
ARNOLD, AARON			40th Infantry
ABRAHAMS, ABRAHAM		G	48th Infantry
APPLE, SAMUEL A.	Sergeant	B	51st Infantry

Served four years.

ALLABACH, C. H.		E	54th Infantry

Subsequently in the United States Army as Assistant Surgeon.

ARNOLD, GEORGE			63d Infantry
AARONS, SOLOMON		B	69th Infantry

Served through the war.

ASHER, ASHER		I	69th Infantry

Killed on picket duty near Richmond.

ASHER, MORRIS		B	71st Infantry

Wounded at Gettysburg; Served three years.

APPLE, DAVID A.	Captain	B	83d Infantry

Promoted from Sergeant, Lieutenant and Captain in Veteran Reserve Corps. Died of wounds.

ABRAHAM, ISAAC M.	Major		85th Infantry

Promoted from Captain; wounded near Deep Bottom, Virginia.

APPEL, CHARLES A.	{ Lieutenant	A	
	{ Captain	F	92nd Infantry
AARONS, JOSEPH		B	109th Infantry

Enlisted as a drummer boy while quite young; captured while delivering a dispatch in second Battle of Bull Run; after release appointed "orderly" on staff of General Geary, 2nd Division, 12th Army Corps; served until close of war.

ARNOLD, JACOB E.	Corporal	E	114th Infantry

Served three years.

NAME.	RANK.	COMPANY.	REGIMENT.
ABEL, JACOB W.			115th Infantry

Also in Veteran Reserve Corps; served as army-hospital steward.

ARNOLD, HENRY		F	133d Infantry

Wounded at Fredericksburg.

ARNOLD, ELI		I	137th Infantry
ARNOLD, SIMON		G	140th Infantry

Killed at Gettysburg.

ARNOLD, LEVI	Sergeant	F	143d Infantry

Also Veteran Reserve Corps; served three years.

ARNOLD, SIMON J.	Sergeant-Major		151st Infantry

Promoted from Sergeant of Company K; Wounded at Gettysburg.

ARNOLD, SIMON		I	151st Infantry

Wounded at Gettysburg.

ARNOLD, MOSES P.	Sergeant	A	172nd Infantry
ANSTEIN, JACOB		D	194th Infantry
APPLE, BENJAMIN	Corporal	I	209th Infantry
ALEXANDER, SAMUEL	Assistant-Surgeon		1st Cavalry

Killed at Dranesville, Virginia.

ALLEN, MICHAEL MITCHELL	Chaplain		5th Cavalry
AUB, JACOB	Quartermaster		5th Cavalry
ARMHOLD, MAX		A	5th Cavalry

Captured.

APPEL, HENRY		B	5th Cavalry
ALTMAN, SOLOMON		K	14th Cavalry
ARNOLD, HENRY	Corporal	Battery I	5th Artillery
ASCH, CHARLES J.			Independent Battery

BARNET, MOSES		A	1st Infantry
BIRNBAUM, CHARLES		I	22nd Infantry
BLUMENTHAL, SIMON		A	27th Infantry
BACH, LOUIS		D	27th Infantry
BIGGARD, ISAAC		K	27th Infantry
BELSINGER, LAZARUS		D	28th Infantry

Served three years.

BEAR, ABRAHAM E.		B	30th Infantry

NAME.	RANK.	COMPANY.	REGIMENT.
BERNARD, AARON A.		H	30th Infantry
BRANDON, ISAAC M.	Corporal	K	30th Infantry
BENJAMIN, OSCAR H.	Sergeant	B	41st Infantry
BLOOM, NATHANIEL F.	Corporal	F	45th Infantry

Wounded at Petersburg.

| BACHENHEIMER, JACOB | Sergeant | | 51st Infantry |

Wounded at Cold Harbor.

BARNETT, PHILIP A.	Corporal	B	51st Infantry
BAHNEY, MOSES	Corporal	B	54th Infantry
BERKOWITZ, LEON	Corporal	H	59th Infantry
BARNETT, NATHANIEL P.	Assistant Surgeon		72nd Infantry
BAIR, JOSEPH		A	79th Infantry

Wounded at Chickamauga; Served four years.

| BAMBERGER, HENRY | Corporal | E | 79th Infantry |

Died of disease contracted in the service.

| BARNETT, DAVID A. | Corporal | B | 99th Infantry |

Died of wounds received at Kelly's Ford, Virginia.

BLOOM, SAMUEL S.	Lieutenant	H	111th Infantry
BEAR, ELIAS		C	122nd Infantry
BAER, BENJAMIN F.	Captain	F	122nd Infantry

Served three years.

BENEDICT, JACOB	Corporal	H	122nd Infantry
BAER, MICHAEL	Major	{ F	123d Infantry
			204th Infantry

Promoted from Lieutenant.

| BENEDICT, JOSEPH | Sergeant | K | 126th Infantry |

Severely wounded.

BEAR, HENRY		H	133d Infantry
BLUM, AARON		B	153d Infantry
BUSH, ASHER		B	153d Infantry
BEAR, JOSEPH	Sergeant	I	153d Infantry

Wounded at Gettysburg.

BLOOM, DAVID S.		I	137th Infantry
BAIR, ISRAEL	Sergeant	F	195th Infantry
BACHMAN, JOSEPH	Sergeant	H	195th Infantry
BAUM, SAMUEL	Corporal	G	200th Infantry

Wounded at Fort Steadman, Virginia.

NAME.	RANK.	COMPANY.	REGIMENT.
BACHMAN, H.		C	2nd Cavalry
BLOOM, DAVID H.		A	5th Cavalry
BIRNBAUM, HENRY F.	Hospital Sergeant	H	5th Cavalry

Promoted from Private; served about four years.

BERG, HENRY   Corporal   D   11th Cavalry
Enlisted as Private; wounded near Richmond; served three years.

BLUM, JULIUS   Corporal   A Independent Battery
Enlisted as Private; served three years.

COHEN, JACOB DA SILVA SOLIS   26th Infantry
Assistant Surgeon
Subsequently in United States Navy, in Commodore Du Pont's expedition to Port Royal.

CAHN, LOUIS   27th Infantry
CROMELIEN, WASHINGTON   Sergeant-Major   27th Infantry
Discharged to accept Commission as Lieutenant 65th Infantry

COHN, IGNATZ   { Lieutenant   C   27th Infantry
           { Captain   B

CALKER, ISAAC   B   33d Infantry
Died from effects of wounds.

CASNER, ABRAHAM		I	38th Infantry
COHEN, J.	Sergeant		62nd Infantry
COHEN, LEWIS		F	122nd Infantry
CANTNER, JACOB		C	126th Infantry
CONSTINE, LEWIS		C	143d Infantry

Killed at White Oak Church.

COHEN, A. J.   Captain   A   5th Cavalry
Seriously wounded.

CROMELIEN, ALFRED   1st Lieutenant   C   5th Cavalry
Promoted from 2nd Lieutenant; elected to Loyal Legion U. S. Commandery of Pennsylvania; acting Recorder of Commandery; titled Major.

CROMELIEN, JAMES   Lieutenant   G   5th Cavalry
Also Quartermaster.

NAME.	RANK.	COMPANY.	REGIMENT.
COHEN, LEON SOLIS	Corporal		Keystone Battery

Wounded in action.

COONS, JACOB — Captain — Wyoming Jägers.

DINBACHER, S.		B	6th Infantry
DURLACHER, S.		H	6th Infantry
DE YOUNG, WASHINGTON R.	Lieutenant	I	17th Infantry

Brevetted Captain for bravery.

DAVID, LOUIS N.		E	18th Infantry
DOON, THEODORE	Sergeant		23d Infantry
DUSCH, ABRAHAM		C	27th Infantry

Also Veteran Reserve Corps.

DAVIDSON, JOSEPH — Sergeant — 28th Infantry

Enlisted as Private; killed at Chancellorsville.

DAVIDSON, ISAAC — H — 122nd Infantry

Died at Falmouth, Virginia, in 1862.

DAVIS, EVAN — D — 125th Infantry

Promoted from Sergeant; died of wounds received at Chancellorsville.

DAVIDSON, JOSEPH A. — I — 134th Infantry

Killed at Fredericksburg.

DAVIDSON, ELIAS B.		G	136th Infantry
DASHER, SAMUEL		D	192nd Infantry
DINKELBERGER, J. R.		E	1st Cavalry
DE HAAN, AARON		A	2nd Artillery
DE HAAN, HENRY	Sergeant	M	3d Artillery

Transferred to United States Veterans, 2nd Regiment.

ELLENGER, JACOB — I — 26th Infantry

Served three years.

| ELLENGER, WILLIAM | | I | 26th Infantry |
| EINSTEIN, MAX | Colonel | | 27th Infantry |

Born at Buchau, Wurtemberg, Germany, October 10, 1822; 1st Lieutenant of Washington Guards, 1852; Captain of Philadelphia (Flying) Artillery Company, 1853; Aide-de-Camp (with rank of Lieutenant-Colonel) to Governor James Pollock, of Pennsylvania, and Paymaster-General of Pennsylvania (with rank of Brigadier-General) 1856; Brigadier-General 2nd Brigade, Pennsylvania Militia, 1860; Colonel of 27th Regiment of Volunteers (Pennsylvania) 1861. This Regiment, under Colonel Einstein's command, succeed in covering the retreat of the Union Army in the first battle of Bull Run, and won credit by its conduct. Colonel Einstein was subsequently appointed by President Lincoln, United States Consul at Nüremburg, Germany, and since then served as United States Internal Revenue Agent in Philadelphia, where he still resides.

NAME	RANK.	COMPANY.	REGIMENT.
ELLINGER, EMANUEL		C	27th Infantry
EPPSTEIN, DANIEL	1st Lieutenant	D	27th Infantry

Promoted from 2nd Lieutenant.

EISENMAN, JACOB		H	27th Infantry
EMANUEL, LYON LEVY	Major		82nd Infantry

Promoted from Lieutenant and Captain; distinguished for bravery; served three years.

EMANUEL, LOUIS MANLY	Brigade Surgeon		82nd Infantry

Promoted from Surgeon; rendered valuable services; served three years.

ETTING, CHARLES EDWARD	Captain	D	121st Infantry

Promoted from 2nd Lieutenant; Regimental Adjutant on Brigade Staff; assigned to 1st Brigade, 3d Division, 1st Army Corps; served three years.

ECKERMANN, JACOB B		E	139th Infantry

Wounded at Salem Heights and at the Wilderness.

EISENBERG, DANIEL		⎧ I	5th Cavalry
Transferred to		⎩ B	

FRAUENTHAL, ABRAHAM	Corporal	⎧ C	8th Infantry
		⎩ D	9th Cavalry

At expiration of service, Lieutenant, Company I, 83d Infantry. Served nearly four years.

FLOERSHEIM, HENRY	Lieutenant	A	27th Infantry
FRANKEL, MAYER		A	27th Infantry

Honorably mentioned by Secretary of War.

NAME.	RANK.	COMPANY.	REGIMENT.
FUCHS, JACOB		B	27th Infantry

Transferred to 109th Regiment.

FRANK, CHARLES		I	27th Infantry
FRIEDHEIM, ADOLPH		E	98th Infantry
FELLENBAUM, DAVID		K	122nd Infantry
FRANKENFIELD, E.		B	153d Infantry
FRANKENFIELD, GEORGE		B	153d Infantry
FROMM, NATHAN	Corporal	A	167th Infantry
FRANK, JACOB	Corporal	C	197th Infantry
FRIEDMAN, MAX	Colonel		5th Cavalry

Born in Mühlhausen, Bavaria, Germany, March 21, 1825. He was Major of a regiment in Pennsylvania Militia before the Civil War; Colonel of 65th Regiment (5th Pennsylvania Cavalry) 1861 ; severely wounded in battle of Vienna, Virginia, in February, 1862. After his resignation, Colonel Friedman was commissioned to organize other Cavalry Regiments in Pennsylvania. He was Special Inspector of the Revenue Department (1867-1868); he started the Union Square National Bank, of New York City, in 1869, and became its cashier. He is President of the Veteran Corps of "Cameron Dragoons" (by which title the 65th Regiment has been known). Colonel Friedman resides in New York City.

FRANK, JACOB		I	5th Cavalry
FISHBLATT, LEWIS	Lieutenant	E	8th Cavalry
FRANKEL, REV. JACOB	Chaplain	United States Hospital	

GROSS, J. L.		E	1st Infantry
GOODMAN, AARON		A	14th Infantry
GOLDSMITH, JAMES		F	26th Infantry

Served three years; captured at Gettysburg.

GOLDBERG, SAMPSON,	Sergeant	A	27th Infantry
GROSS, LEOPOLD		A	27th Infantry

Died of wounds received at Cross Keys, Virginia.

GOODMAN, BENJAMIN B.	Lieutenant	B	27th Infantry

Promoted from Sergeant.

NAME.	RANK.	COMPANY.	REGIMENT.
GENTER, NATHAN		B	27th Infantry

Wounded in action.

| GASSENHEIMER, GUS | | | 27th Infantry |
| GLASER, ADOLPH | | | 27th Infantry |

Transferred to 15th Heavy Artillery, New York.

| GOODMAN, DAVID J. | | A | 33d Infantry |

Served three years.

| GROSSMAN, LEWIS | | C | 40th Infantry |

Served three years; lost an arm and leg at Spottsylvania; died from wounds; buried in National
Cemetery, Arlington.

| GROSS, ABRAM | | F | 41st Infantry |

Transferred to 190th Infantry; served over three
years.

GROSS, ISAAC		H	50th Infantry
GOLDSTEIN, LOUIS		B	61st Infantry
GREMITZ, ——	Captain		62nd Infantry
GOLDSMITH, JOSEPH	Captain	A	74th Infantry

Promoted from the ranks.

| GOODMAN, DAVID | Sergeant | B | 78th Infantry |

Served four years.

| GOODMAN, ISAAC | Sergeant | | 91st Infantry |

Promoted from Private; wounded at Petersburg;
served four years.

GOLDBERG, ——	Corporal	A	91st Infantry
GASSENMAIER, JOSEPH		D	98th Infantry
GOLDENBERG, C. D.		F	110th Infantry
GOLDENBERG, HENRY		F	110th Infantry
GALLINGER, JOSEPH		B	123d Infantry

Enlisted at eighteen years of age.

GISNER, GEORGE	Corporal		142nd Infantry
GOLDBACHER, ISAAC	Sergeant		150th Infantry
GROSS, AARON		C	153d Infantry

Captured at Gettysburg.

| GOLDSTROM, LEOPOLD | | E | 5th Cavalry |

Quartermaster-Sergeant
Entered as Private; served four years.

NAME.	RANK.	COMPANY.	REGIMENT.
GERSCHEL, ADOLPH		I	6th Cavalry

Served three years, until expiration of term.

| GOLDSCHMIDT, ANTON | Lieutenant | A | 12th Cavalry |

Promoted from Sergeant; served three years and until the close of the war.

| GOLDSMITH, JAMES | Sergeant | H | 18th Cavalry |

Promoted from Corporal; served three years.

HAYS, DAVID		C	2nd Infantry
HIRSH, JACOB	Lieutenant	G	18th Infantry
HIRSH, MORRIS	Corporal	G	18th Infantry
HIRSCH, ISIDOR	Lieutenant	A	22nd Infantry
HELLER, HENRY	Surgeon		27th Infantry
HELLER, MAXIMILIAN	Surgeon		27th Infantry
HEYMAN, HERMAN		A	27th Infantry
HARRIS, B.		B	27th Infantry
HEIMBURG, JULIUS	Quartermaster	B	27th Infantry

Promoted from Lieutenant.

| HERRMAN, FRANK | Lieutenant | C | 27th Infantry |

Promoted from Corporal.

HELLER, DAVID		C	27th Infantry
HOUSEMAN, JACOB		E	27th Infantry
HERMAN, PHILIP		H	27th Infantry
HOCHSTETTER, A.			27th Infantry
HIRSCH, A.			27th Infantry
HERTZOG, JOEL J.		{ M	28th Infantry
	Corporal	{ D	147th Infantry

Served three years.

HERTZOG, JOSEPH		E	29th Infantry
HENRY, B.		D	32nd Infantry
HESS, JACOB		H	36th Infantry

Captured.

| HESS, MICHAEL | | H | 36th Infantry |

Died of wounds received at Fredericksburg.

HASSLER, AUGUSTUS	Sergeant	{ F	41st Infantry
		{	190th Infantry
HERMAN, JACOB		G	57th Infantry

23

NAME.	RANK.	COMPANY.	REGIMENT.
HIGHTULL, ISRAEL	Sergeant		61st Infantry
HOFFMAN, S.			67th Infantry
HARRIS, BENJAMIN	Sergeant	G	72nd Infantry

Enlisted as private.

HAMBERG, ANSEL	Lieutenant	A	91st Infantry
	Major		44th Infantry
	Colonel		12th Infantry

He has been Junior and Senior Vice-Commander of
George G. Meade Post, No. 1, Grand Army of the
Republic.

HART, ABRAHAM		I	73d Infantry

Captain and Brigade Adjutant-General.

Captain Abraham Hart, at present commander of Kit
Carson Post, Grand Army of the Republic, one of the
large Posts of the District of Columbia, was born in
Hesse-Darmstadt, Germany, in 1832. At the age of
eighteen years he came to the United States and was
employed in a large house in Philadelphia, where he
was residing at the outbreak of the Rebellion in 1861.

He volunteered as a soldier in the 73d Regiment of
Pennsylvania Infantry, commanded by Colonel John
A. Koltes; he aided Colonel Koltes in enlisting other
volunteers, and as early as August, 1861, was on his
way with the regiment to help in the defences of
Washington on the Virginia side. While there, Lieutenant Hart—for he had been promoted to a lieu-
tenancy — was frequently sent out on reconnoitring
expeditions, and in one of these he had a sharp brush
with a body of Confederate cavalry which was also
out reconnoitring. Subsequently, Lieutenant Hart
was promoted to a captaincy, and when Colonel Koltes
was elevated to the command of a brigade in General
Blenker's Division of the Army of the Potomac,
Captain Hart was detailed as Adjutant-General of the
Brigade. In this capacity he participated in the
battle of Cross Keys, in numerous skirmishes, and in
the second battle of Bull Run.

At the battle of Cross Keys, the commanding

General desired information as to the position and movements of the opposing force under "Stonewall" Jackson, and Captain Hart undertook to obtain it for him. In pursuance of this undertaking, and in company with a squad of picked men, he successfully made the circuit of the rebel camp, obtained the desired information, and reported it to the General.

At Sulphur Springs he was entrusted by General Sigel with the command of a force to destroy a bridge over the Rappahannock which was defended by rebel artillery, and he succeeded in destroying it. At another time he had the good fortune to rescue several hundred Union soldiers who had been captured by the Confederates.

But perhaps Captain Hart's most important service was done at the second battle of Bull Run. General von Steinwehr's (Blenker's) Division was in advance, and engaged in the first day's battle, as well as in the second and third. In the afternoon of the third day (August 30) of the fight, Koltes' Brigade was ordered to silence a rebel battery which was doing us great damage. The Brigade was several times driven back, but each time rallied, and finally captured and spiked the guns. It was here that the Brigade Commander, Colonel Koltes, was killed, and here that the Brigade suffered the heaviest loss.

NAME.	RANK.	COMPANY.	REGIMENT.
HERRMAN, JACOB	Sergeant	C	98th Infantry

Enlisted as private; wounded at Cedar Creek; served four years.

HIRSCH, M. L.			101st Infantry
HIRSCH, AUGUST	Corporal	A	102nd Infantry

Wounded at the Wilderness; three years service.

HERMAN, EMANUEL	Captain	D	103d Infantry
HOFFMAN, LEOPOLD		C	113th Infantry

Regimental Quartermaster Sergeant; promoted from private.

NAME.	RANK.	COMPANY.	REGIMENT.
HYNEMAN, JACOB EZEKIEL		G	119th Infantry

Wounded at Fredericksburg; also at Brandy Station and Mine Run; transferred to United States Signal Corps; served three years (1862-1865); has served since during riots in Pennsylvania; has held several military ranks.

HOFFMAN, ABRAHAM	Corporal	E	186th Infantry
HYNEMAN, ELIAS LEON	Sergeant	C	5th Cavalry

A reference to this brave soldier and the sacrifice which cost him his life is contained in our "Introduction," page 5, so that little is left to record. Hyneman voluntarily enlisted in the 5th Cavalry, after the first Battle of Bull Run. He was promoted from Corporal to Sergeant, and was always eager for active service, distinguishing himself in several battles, and being one of twelve skirmishers who advanced on the enemy in the Battle of Gettysburg. He fought dismounted in the Battle of the Wilderness. His term expired in 1864, but so anxious was he to serve his country that he re-enlisted, only to meet so untimely a fate as recorded. He died on January 7, 1865, at Andersonville, of starvation and sickness, and his body was brought for interment to Philadelphia five months later.

As to Hyneman's course as a soldier, no stronger testimony than that contained in the following official paper is required:

"I hereby certify on honor that I was well and personally acquainted with Elias Leon Hyneman, who was a Sergeant of Company C, 5th Regiment, Pennsylvania Cavalry, Volunteers, that the said Elias L. Hyneman was a thorough and efficient soldier, and a person of excellent habits, and known and respected as such by all in the regiment. That he was ever foremost in the line of duty and at the post of danger, and vigilant and patient in the prosecution of his patriotic services. That by his zeal and enthusiasm to be foremost among the defenders of his flag he was unhappily captured by a merciless foe, and consigned to an ignominious and beastly prison house, there to suffer for many months and at last to yield up his noble spirit in death. Even his last life scenes were worthy of a soldier and full of true manfulness. That I, being a prisoner of war at the same time with said Elias L. Hyneman, heard of his many sufferings with deepest regret. I sympathize sincerely with his afflicted relatives and all who mourn his loss. He fought and fell in the glorious cause of freedom and justice omnipotent

"Given at Camp, Fifth Pennsylvania Cavalry, near Richmond, Va., this 1st day of May, 1865.

J. FRANK CAMERON,

"*Capt. Com'd'g Company C, Fifth Penn. Cavalry.*"
"Approval:

"Colonel Commanding Regiment."

NAME.	RANK.	COMPANY.	REGIMENT.
HARRIS, ABRAHAM B.	Lieutenant	F	5th Cavalry
HOFFMAN, DAVID B.		G	5th Cavalry
HASSLER, JACOB	Sergeant	D	9th Cavalry

Served about four years.

HERZOG, JACOB	Captain	E	12th Cavalry
HAMBURGER, HERMAN	Lieutenant	L	18th Cavalry

Assistant Adjutant-General, 1st Brigade, 3d Cavalry Corps, Army of the Potomac; has been Judge in Carbon County, Pennsylvania, etc., etc.

ISRAEL, DANIEL		F	10th Infantry
ISAACS, HENRY		I	18th Infantry
ISRAEL, JACOB		B	27th Infantry
ISAACS, HENRY		{ M { C	72nd Infantry

JOSEPHS, GUSTAV		C	3d Infantry

And one year in Hancock's Veteran Corps; served three years.

JACOBS, HENRY		B	4th Infantry

NAME.	RANK.	COMPANY.	REGIMENT.
JACOBS, JACOB	Corporal	K	11th Infantry
JACOBY, HENRY	Corporal	I	18th Infantry
JOSEPHS, AARON		F	19th Infantry
JACQUES, HENRY	Lieutenant	G	26th Infantry

Wounded in second Battle of Bull Run, and other battles.

JACOBSON, AUGUSTUS		A	27th Infantry

Transferred to United States Navy.

JACOBY, HERMAN		A	27th Infantry

Wounded at Missionary Ridge; served throughout the war.

JACOB, JOHN		B	27th Infantry
JOSEPHS, ABRAHAM		F	27th Infantry

And one year in Hancock's Veteran Corps; served three years.

JACOBY, HUGO	Sergeant	{ A	27th Infantry
Promoted from Corporal; transferred to		{	109th Infantry

JACOBY, H.		H	27th Infantry
JACOBS, HENRY		F	28th Infantry

Served three years.

JACOBS, SAMUEL		H	29th Infantry

Served four years.

JACOBS, ISRAEL		D	30th Infantry

Served three years.

JACOBS, ABRAHAM B.		{ A	34th Infantry
Subsequently		{	6th U. S. Cavalry
JACOBY, MOSES	Corporal.	E	47th Infantry

Enlisted as Private.

JACOBS, HENRY	Lieutenant	F	51st Infantry

Promoted from Sergeant; served four years.

JACOBS, SIMON		D	99th Infantry

Served three years.

JACOBS, HENRY H.	Sergeant	F	165th Infantry
JACOBS, ALEXANDER	Corporal	F	165th Infantry
JACOBY, JOSEPH	Sergeant	I	167th Infantry
JACOBS, THEODORE	Assistant Surgeon		187th Infantry
JACOBY, SIMON P.		E	3d Artillery
JACOBS, S. H.		1st Troop, Philadelphia City Cavalry	

NAME.	RANK.	COMPANY.	REGIMENT.
KOENIGSBERG, MAX	Lieutenant	A	12th Infantry

Wounded at Gaines' Mills; captured and sent to Libby Prison.

KAUFFMAN, ISAAC B.	Lieutenant	C	16th Infantry
KIRSCHHEIMER, JOSEPH	Sergeant		27th Infantry
KUHN, MAGNUS		A	27th Infantry
KUHN, MARCUS		A	27th Infantry
KOHN, IGNAZ	Captain	B	27th Infantry

Enlisted as Private.

KUHN, ABRAHAM		B	27th Infantry
KAHN, LOUIS		C	27th Infantry
KATZ, JACOB F.		C	35th Infantry

Served three years.

KAUFFMAN, SAMUEL		A	46th Infantry
KAUFFMAN, LEVI H.	Corporal	H	52nd Infantry
KLINE, JOSEPH		I	61st Infantry

Killed at Fair Oaks, Virginia.

KARPEL, JACOB		C	63d Infantry

Died of wounds received at Bull Run.

KOHEN, FRANK P.	Lieutenant	I	67th Infantry
KAUFFMAN, BENJAMIN L.	Corporal	{ D	90th Infantry
		{ H	11th Infantry
KOSHLAND, NICHOLAS N.		A	91st Infantry
KAYSER, MORRIS	Captain	B	91st Infantry

Promoted from Lieutenant; served about three years.

KATZ, EMANUEL			98th Infantry
KAUFFMAN, JACOB	Corporal	A	101st Infantry
KLINE, NATHAN		K	119th Infantry

Served three years.

KAUFFMAN, SOLOMON B.	Corporal	F	126th Infantry
KRAMER, SOLOMON H.	Sergeant	G	128th Infantry
KAUFFMAN, JONAS H.	Assistant Surgeon		151st Infantry
KAUFFMAN, JOSEPH A.	Lieutenant	B	154th Infantry
KAUFFMAN, JACOB	Corporal	F	171st Infantry
KAUFFMAN, DAVID S.	Sergeant	F	179th Infantry
KAUFFMAN, SOLOMON B.	Sergeant	B	202nd Infantry

NAME.	RANK.	COMPANY.	REGIMENT.
KAUFFMAN, ISAAC B.	2nd Lieutenant	H	9th Cavalry

Died of wounds received at Moore's Hill, Kentucky.

KARPELES, LEO			2nd Artillery

LIVERMAULI, MOSES		B	2nd Infantry
LEVY, DAVID		I	5th Infantry
LEVY, ABRAHAM		E	6th Infantry
LEVI, CHARLES	Corporal	F	7th Infantry
LOWENTHAL, SAMUEL		G	9th Infantry

Served four years.

LAZARUS, DAVID		F	23d Infantry
LEWENBERG, JOSEPH		I	23d Infantry
LEVY, AARON		A	26th Infantry

Transferred to Signal Corps.

LUESCHER, JACOB	Sergeant	A	27th Infantry

Served three years.

LEO, CHARLES	Lieutenant	H	27th Infantry

Regimental Adjutant.

LOWENSTEIN, M.			27th Infantry
LAZARUS, AARON	Brevet Captain	D	28th Infantry

Enlisted as Private, and promoted to Corporal, Ser-
geant, 1st Sergeant, 2nd Lieutenant, 1st Lieutenant,
Regimental Adjutant, and Brevet Captain, United
States Volunteers; served three years; has since been
Captain and Major; member of Loyal Legion of the
United States (Commandery of Pennsylvania).

LACHENHEIMER, F.		K	29th Infantry
LYON, ABRAHAM	Corporal	H	35th Infantry
LANG, PHILIP		I	37th Infantry
LOWENTHAL, SAMUEL		G	38th Infantry

Served three years.

LEBENGOOD, JACOB		E	40th Infantry

So seriously wounded as to be disabled for further
service.

LEVI, WILLIAM P.	Sergeant	C	54th Infantry
LICHTENBERGER, DANIEL	Sergeant	I	76th Infantry

Enlisted as Private.

NAME.	RANK.	COMPANY.	REGIMENT.
LEO, HENRY F.	Captain	B	115th Infantry

Promoted from Sergeant; served three years.

LAZARUS, HENRY		C	119th Infantry

Also Veteran Invalid Reserve Corps; served through the war.

LEVY, HERMAN			119th Infantry
LEHMAN, EMANUEL		D	127th Infantry
LEHMAN, JACOB		D	127th Infantry
LILLIENSTINE, CHARLES		I	127th Infantry
LEVI, JOSEPH	Corporal	G	129th Infantry
LAZARUS, WILLIAM		E	132nd Infantry

Killed at Antietam.

LOEB, JACOB		H	151st Infantry
LOEB, SAMUEL B.		H	151st Infantry
LOEB, WILLIAM C.		H	151st Infantry

Died at Fairfax Seminary, Virginia, June 27, 1863.

LONG, ISAAC		H	151st Infantry
LEVY, PHILIP	Sergeant	G	193d Infantry

Promoted from Corporal.

LIPOWITZ, HERMAN	Sergeant	H	215th Infantry
LANGSDORF, SIMON	Corporal	B	5th Cavalry

Discharged for injuries received at Williamsburg.

LEVY, MEYER S.		C	5th Cavalry
LEVY, SAMUEL		C	5th Cavalry
LEVY, THEODORE		C	5th Cavalry
LANG, ERNST		E	5th Cavalry
LEVI, SIMON		I	5th Cavalry
LINDHEIMER, BARNEY			6th Cavalry
LANG, MORRIS			12th Cavalry

Captured at second Battle of Bull Run.

LEVY, BENJAMIN J.	Brevet-Major		21st Cavalry

Promoted from Commissary of Subsistence.

LIEBSCHUTZ, ADOLPH	Lieutenant		2nd Artillery

Promoted from the ranks for gallantry; served three years.

Name.	Rank.	Company.	Regiment.
Miller, Jonas		E	5th Infantry

Served three years.

May, Samuel F.		K	8th Infantry
Mayer, Louis H.	Sergeant	C	13th Infantry

Also in Ohio Infantry, and staff officer in Regular Army.

Myers, Solomon	Lieutenant	A	16th Infantry
Miller, Moses		K	19th Infantry
Miller, Samuel		K	19th Infantry
May, Solomon W.			19th Infantry
Meyer, C.		B	21st Infantry
Miller, Alexander		H	22nd Infantry
Mayer, Jacob	Corporal	B	23d Infantry
Mitchell, M.		F	23d Infantry
Moritz, Joseph		C	26th Infantry
Moss, John		{ E	26th Infantry

Served three years. Transferred to { 99th Infantry

Meyer, Joseph		I	26th Infantry

Wounded at Gettysburg; transferred to 99th Infantry; served four years.

May, Louis		A	27th Infantry
Moser, Leo	Sergeant	C	27th Infantry
May, Meyer		D	27th Infantry
Mayer, Herman		D	27th Infantry
Meyer, Moses		E	27th Infantry
Meyer, Emil	Lieutenant	G	27th Infantry
Marx, David		G	27th Infantry
Maier, Jacob		H	27th Infantry
Moser, David		H	27th Infantry

Died at Winchester, Virginia.

Max, Jacob			27th Infantry
Meyer, Max			27th Infantry
Myers, Simon P.		G	28th Infantry
Marks, Emanuel		K	28th Infantry

Died at Rectortown, Virginia.

Miller, Aaron		I	36th Infantry

Served three years.

Myers, Levi		I	36th Infantry

Served three years.

NAME.	RANK.	COMPANY.	REGIMENT.
MOSES, JOSHUA		I	42nd Infantry
MILLER, JACOB		A	45th Infantry

Killed at South Mountain.

MOSES, DANIEL	Corporal	K	48th Infantry
MOSES, DAVID	Lieutenant	K	52nd Infantry

Promoted from Sergeant; served until the close of the war.

MILLER, SOLOMON C.	Sergeant	A	57th Infantry

Served three years.

MILLER, JACOB		C	61st Infantry
MILLER, JACOB	Corporal	H	61st Infantry

Disabled at Malvern Hill.

MYERS, EMANUEL	Sergeant		62nd Infantry
MAZUR, F.			63d Infantry
MYERS, ISRAEL	Corporal	E	67th Infantry

Enlisted as Private; served three years.

MOSS, WILLIAM	Surgeon		70th Infantry

Surgeon United States Volunteers.

MYERS, ISAAC	Corporal	G	74th Infantry
MYERS, SIGMUND	Corporal	I	76th Infantry

Served three years.

MAYER, JACOB	Sergeant	F	82nd Infantry

Promoted from Corporal.

MYERS, SOLOMON	Captain	E	87th Infantry

Served over three years.

MOSER, HENRY	Corporal	F	107th Infantry

Transferred to Veteran Reserve Corps.

MOSS, JACOB			119th Infantry
MYERS, HENRY		H	122nd Infantry
MYERS, DANIEL S.		I	127th Infantry
MYERS, ALBERT	Sergeant	H	128th Infantry
MILLER, AARON		F	129th Infantry
MYERS, BENJAMIN F.		C	130th Infantry
MYERS, JACOB		A	150th Infantry

Also Veteran Reserve Corps.

MARKS, ISRAEL		E	151st Infantry

NAME.	RANK.	COMPANY.	REGIMENT.
MYERS, AARON J.	Sergeant	I	153d Infantry

Died of wounds received at Gettysburg.

MYERS, HERMAN	Corporal	A	155th Infantry

Served three years.

MOYER, EMANUEL	Sergeant	H	162nd Infantry

Killed at White House, Virginia.

MYERS, EMANUEL	Sergeant-Major		165th Infantry
MARX, AARON J.		F	169th Infantry
MYERS, LEVI	Lieutenant	E	178th Infantry
MYERS, DAVID	Corporal	H	183d Infantry

Enlisted as private; seriously wounded at Cold Harbor.

MILLER, AARON	Corporal	K	190th Infantry

Enlisted as Private.

MICHAELS, DAVID	Lieutenant	I	210th Infantry

Promoted from Corporal and Sergeant.

MENKEN, NATHAN D.	Captain		—— Cavalry

At the outbreak of the Civil War he organized a body of cavalry and was chosen Captain. At the Second Battle of Bull Run his horse was shot under him. As commander of General Pope's body-guard, he won the esteem and admiration of his brother officers for his bravery, courtesy and firmness. In 1878, during the yellow fever scourge in Memphis, Tennessee, Captain Menken refused to quit that city, but remained at his post, attending to the suffering until the terrible plague made this hero also a victim.

MILLER, JACOB			3d Cavalry

Died of wounds received at Mine Run, Virginia.

MOSS, JOSEPH L.	Major		5th Cavalry

Lieutenant-Colonel 12th Cavalry; served three years.

MOSS, JACOB		{ C { H	5th Cavalry
MYERS, EMANUEL		K	5th Cavalry
MAX, CHARLES		E	6th Cavalry
MOELER, MAX	Lieutenant	E	11th Cavalry
MEYER, LEOPOLD	Captain	C	12th Cavalry

Served over three years.

NAME.	RANK.	COMPANY.	REGIMENT.
MILLER, MOSES	Corporal	H	14th Cavalry
MOSER, HENRY	Quartermaster-Sergeant		19th Cavalry

Served three years.

MARKS, SIMON		Custer's	Division of Cavalry
MENDEL, HERMAN	Sergeant	L	{ 3d Artillery

Subsequently in United States Army.   { 4th Cavalry

MESSING, BERNHARD	Sergeant	M	3d Artillery

Transferred 62nd Regiment, U. S. V.

NATHANS, OSCAR S.		H	18th Infantry
NATHANS, THEODORE		H	18th Infantry
NATHAN, LEWIS		A	51st Infantry
NEYMAN, JACOB			Signal Corps

OTTENHEIMER, SOLOMON		A	19th Infantry
OSTHEIMER, NATHAN		K	62nd Infantry

Killed at Harrison's Landing.

OCHS, JOSEPH		E	5th Cavalry
OPPENHEIMER, LOUIS		E	5th Cavalry

PINHEIRO, SOLOMON		G	26th Infantry

Enlisted quite young as a drummer boy; subsequently entered United States Navy; served there three years and took part in a number of engagements.

PICKARD, M.			27th Infantry
POLLOCK, A.			27th Infantry
PROSKAUER, A.			27th Infantry
PHILLIPS, ISAAC W.		K	29th Infantry

Captured.

PHILLIPS, ISAAC H.		F	36th Infantry
PHILLIPS, DAVID J.	Adjutant { Captain { I		81st Infantry
PODOLSKY, THEODORE			101st Infantry

Promoted from 2nd Lieutenant, etc.

ROSENSTEEL, JACOB		I	11th Infantry

Wounded at Rappahannock Station; served four years.

NAME.	RANK.	COMPANY.	REGIMENT.
ROSENFELT, NATHAN	Sergeant	D	26th Infantry

Died of wounds received at Gettysburg.

ROSENTHAL, MAX		⎰ D	26th Infantry
Transferred to		⎱	99th Infantry
ROSENSTEIN, WILLIAM		F	26th Infantry
ROSENTHAL, ARNDT	Major		27th Infantry
ROEDELSHEIMER, SOLOMON	Captain	A	27th Infantry
ROSENGARTEN, HENRY	⎰ Corporal	A	27th Infantry
	⎱ Sergeant	K	
RINGETSTEIN, JACOB		A	27th Infantry
ROSENHEIM, BERNARD		A	27th Infantry
ROTH, LEWIS		A	27th Infantry
REINHARD, FRANCIS		B	27th Infantry
ROSENBERG, MAURICE	Sergeant	C	27th Infantry

Wounded at Lookout Mountain.

ROSENTHAL, ABRAHAM		E	27th Infantry
REINHART, NATHAN F.	Corporal	F	27th Infantry
ROSENSTEIN, DAVID		I	27th Infantry
ROSENSTOCK, JACOB		A	28th Infantry

Wounded at Chancellorsville; served three years.

ROSENBAUM, MICHAEL		F	29th Infantry
RASHKE, MORITZ	Sergeant		63d Infantry

Killed at Chancellorsville.

ROSENFELT, NATHAN		A	72nd Infantry

Wounded and captured at Antietam; when released,
transferred to Veteran Reserve Corps.

ROTHSCHILD, SAMUEL	Sergeant	I	74th Infantry

Enlisted as Private.

ROSENBERG, LOUIS	Corporal	K	82nd Infantry
ROTHSCHILD, LEWIS		K	99th Infantry
ROSENBERGER, L. A.	Lieutenant	D	104th Infantry

Enlisted as Private; captured at Gloucester Point,
Virginia; served three years.

ROSENGARTEN, JOSEPH GEORGE		D	121st Infantry
	Lieutenant		

Major on staff of General John F. Reynolds, Army
of the Potomac; Brevet Captain in United States
Volunteers; served three years.

NAME.	RANK.	COMPANY.	REGIMENT.
ROWE, SAMUEL W.	Captain	B	122nd Infantry

Promoted from Lieutenant.

ROSENBERGER, SAMUEL		G	126th Infantry
RICH, ISAAC B.	Sergeant	B	129th Infantry

Promoted from Corporal.

ROSENSTEEL, JACOB	Sergeant	F	139th Infantry

Enlisted as Private; wounded at the Wilderness; served three years.

RINEHARD, ALFRED A.	Captain	D	148th Infantry

Promoted from Sergeant; wounded at Po River, Virginia; served three years.

ROSENSTEIN, MICHAEL	Lieutenant	K	173d Infantry
ROSENSTEEL, TOBIAS	Lieutenant		4th Cavalry

Served three years.

ROWLAND, ADOLPHUS	Major		5th Cavrlry

Promoted from Lieutenant for distinguished bravery.

ROSENTHAL, LEOPOLD	Captain	A	5th Cavalry

Wounded at Fort Magruder.

RHINE, MICHAEL		G	5th Cavalry
ROSENTHAL, EPHRAIM	Sergeant	A	12th Cavalry

Enlisted as Private; served three years, and until close of war.

REUBENTHAL, ELIAS	Sergeant	I	12th Cavalry

Served over three years.

ROSENGARTEN, ADOLPH G.	Major		15th Cavalry
			(Anderson Troop)

Promoted from Sergeant; killed at Stone River, Tennessee.

ROSENBERGER, S.	Assistant Surgeon		2nd Artillery

SONTHEIMER, BERNARD			6th Infantry
SCHWARZ, S. F.		I ˙	16th Infantry
SCHONEMAN, ABRAM P.	Lieutenant	⎧ E	19th Infantry
		⎨	65th Infantry
		⎩	Keystone Battery
STERN, ABRAM E.	Corporal	G	19th Infantry

NAME.	RANK.	COMPANY.	REGIMENT.
STERN, CHARLES			19th Infantry
STERNBERGER, CHARLES			19th Infantry
STEIN, JACOB	Corporal	B	21st Infantry
SELIGMAN, MARCUS		F	26th Infantry
Transferred to			99th Infantry
SALINGER, B.	Lieutenant		27th Infantry

Enlisted as private.

SCHLOSS, ABRAHAM		A	27th Infantry
SCHONEMAN, EMANUEL		B	27th Infantry
SPAETH, HENRY	Sergeant	B	27th Infantry
SHEIER, MOSES		B	27th Infantry
SIEDLER, JOSEPH		B	27th Infantry
SILBERBERG, MAX		B	27th Infantry

Enlisted at eighteen years of age; took part in battles
in Pennsylvania, incuding Gettysburg; served twice as
Commander of August Willich Post, G. A. R.; also
as President of Employment Bureau of Grand Army
of the Republic Association of Hamilton County,
Ohio.

STRAUS, JONAS		B	27th Infantry
STEIN, LOUIS		D	27th Infantry
SCHOEN, DAVID		G	27th Infantry
STERN, JULIUS	Sergeant	H	27th Infantry
SCHLOSS, MOSES		K	27th Infantry

Served three years.

SCHLOSS, DAVID			27th Infantry
SELKER, ADOLPH			27th Infantry
STROUSE, CYRUS	Major		28th Infantry

Killed at Chancellorsville.

SNOWBERGER, ELIAS		K	29th Infantry
STERN, DAVID			32nd Infantry
SNELLENBURG, ISAAC		B	33d Infantry

Killed at Charles City Cross Roads, Virginia, buried
on the battle-field.

STROUS, JACOB		G	34th Infantry

Served three years.

NAME.	RANK.	COMPANY.	REGIMENT.
STEIN, JACOB		A	37th Infantry
SIGMUND, ALBERT M.	Assistant Surgeon		38th Infantry
STEIN, LEWIS		E	41st Infantry

Served three years.

SILBERMAN, MARX	Corporal	A	51st Infantry

Raised a company of men in three days and became Corporal of the company; started the company by signing first.

STINE, JACOB		C	54th Infantry
STEINER, JACOB		G	55th Infantry

Also Veteran Reserve Corps.

STROUSS ELLIS C.	Captain	K	57th Infantry

Entered as private; wounded at Charles City Cross Roads and at Wilderness; served four years.

STROUSE, HENRY	Corporal	D	76th Infantry
STERN, HENRY	Captain	G	77th Infantry

Enlisted as private.

STERN, HERMAN		B	83d Infantry
SOLOMON, AUGUSTUS	Sergeant	B	93d Infantry

Promoted from private; also in Veteran Reserve Corps.

STEINBRUN, J.		D	98th Infantry
SNOWBERGER, ALBERT LEOPOLD			99th Infantry

Born in Philadelphia, April 4, 1845. He was sent to the Military Academy, at Portsmouth, Virginia, when but fifteen years of age. When the war broke out he enlisted in the Union Army, despite his youthful age. He took part in a number of engagements with the enemy, but at the Battle of Fredericksburg, Virginia, December 13, 1862, he was mortally wounded, yet even in his agonies this young hero "waved his cap and urged his comrades on to victory." He died January 6, 1863. Of this gallant boy the lad's commander wrote to his mother that "his bravery and heroism were remarkable for one so young."

SALISBURG, DAVID S.	Corporal	B	102nd Infantry
STRAUSS, HENRY	Surgeon		115th Infantry

24

NAME.	RANK.	COMPANY.	REGIMENT.
STINE, DANIEL		I	126th Infantry
STROUSE, LEHMAN K.	Corporal	F	128th Infantry
STERN, JACOB		E	133d Infantry
SALISBURG, SAMUEL B.	Sergeant	G	138th Infantry

Wounded at Monocacy, Maryland; served three years.

NAME.	RANK.	COMPANY.	REGIMENT.
STROUSE, FERDINAND K.		E	151st Infantry
STRAUSE, JOEL S.		H	151st Infantry
STRAUSE, SALOMON		H	151st Infantry

Wounded at Gettysburg.

STRAUSE, WILLIAM S.		H	151st Infantry

Wounded at Gettysburg.

STRAUSE, WILLIAM T.		H	151st Infantry

Wounded at Gettysburg.

NAME.	RANK.	COMPANY.	REGIMENT.
SIMON, MICHAEL		I	151st Infantry
STERNBERGER, LEVIN		I	151st Infantry
SULZBACH, MILTON	Quartermaster		166th Infantry
STRAUS, DANIEL	Corporal	F	167th Infantry
SILVA, DAVID	Corporal	G	181st Infantry
SIMON, JACOB	Corporal	E	183d Infantry

Promoted from private.

STEINER, LEVI A.		H	194th Infantry
SCHLESINGER, MORRIS	Adjutant		210th Infantry

Promoted from Sergeant; died from wounds received
at Gravelly Run, Virginia.

SCHLOSS, HENRY	Corporal	E	5th Cavalry

Wounded near Richmond; served four years.

SCHLOSS, ABRAHAM		E	5th Cavalry

Wounded before Richmond.

SONTHEIMER, MORRIS		K	11th Cavalry

Served four years.

SCHOENFELD, J.			15th Cavalry
STEIN, JACOB	Corporal	K	3d Artillery
SALZMAN, ADAM	Corporal	G	5th Artillery
STRASSMAN, A.			2nd Battery

Wounded twice.

SCHONEMAN, R. A.			Keystone Battery

NAME.	RANK.	COMPANY.	REGIMENT.
THALHEIMER, ALBERT		B	23d Infantry

Captured at Cold Harbor; served about four years.

TSCHOPEK, JOSEPH		D	27th Infantry
TAFEL, ADOLPH	Lieutenant	H	27th Infantry
TELLER, MICHAEL,		K	119th Infantry

Served three years.

TRAUTMAN, JACOB	Sergeant	E	5th Cavalry

Served four years.

ULMAN, JOHN	Sergeant	D	27th Infantry

Served three years.

ULLMAN, JACOB		E	75th Infantry

Served four years.

ULLMAN, ——	Captain	E	5th Cavalry

Was noted for his bravery; served throughout the
Civil War; he was also engaged in the war with the
Sioux Indians in 1876, and was one of those in the
command of General Custer on thot fatal day in June;
in which the entire command was surrounded by the
Indians, every man being slaughtered.

VOGEL, L.	Captain	E	27th Infantry

WIMPFHEIMER, MAX		F	19th Infantry
WOLF, JACOB	Corporal	H	19th Infantry
WOHL, SAMUEL	Lieutenant	B	27th Infantry
WEINBERGER, PAUL		B	27th Infantry

Transferred to 29th Infantry, New York Volunteers.

WARBURG, SIGMUND		D	27th Infantry
WEINSTOCK, BERNARD		D	27th Infantry
WEIL, JACOB		H	27th Infantry
WARBURG, MOSES			27th Infantry
WETZLAR, MORRIS	Lieutenant	K	37th Infantry

Promoted; wounded at Pea Ridge; disabled.

WATERMAN, ISRAEL		I	40th Infantry

Transferred to United States Regulars.

NAME.	RANK.	COMPANY.	REGIMENT.
WOLF, DAVID	Sergeant	H	89th Infantry

Served nearly four years.

WOLF, MORRIS		A	3d Cavalry

Served three years.

WEINBACH, ABRAHAM			
	Quartermaster-Sergeant	A	12th Cavalry

RHODE ISLAND.

NAME.	RANK.	COMPANY.	REGIMENT.
FROINSOHN, SAMUEL			2nd Infantry
HARRIS, BENJAMIN			10th Infantry
PHILLIPS, JOSEPH S.			2nd Infantry

On staff of Commander General Sexton, of the Grand
Army of the Republic.

SIEGEL, M.		I	3d Infantry

SOUTH CAROLINA.

NAME.	RANK.	COMPANY.	REGIMENT.
ALEXANDER, ISAAC		A	10th Infantry
ALEXANDER, ISIDORE		A	10th Infantry
ALEXANDER, S.		A	10th Infantry
ALTMAN, JAMES P.		A	21st Infantry

Captured; died and buried at Woodlawn Cemetery,
Elmira, New York.

ASHER, HENRY			Hampton Legion
ASCHER, ABRAHAM			1st Cavalry
ASHER, HARRIS			Washington Artillery

NAME.	RANK.	COMPANY.	REGIMENT.
ABRAHAMS, E. H.			Reserves
ABRAHAMS, THEODORE H.			Sumter Guards.

BOWMAN, LOUIS		E	1st Infantry
BALL, BARNEY			2nd Infantry

Lost his life at Port Royal.

BAUM MANUS		A	7th Infantry
BARUCH, H.		K	7th Infantry

Enlisted a mere lad.

BROWN, MENDEL	Sergeant	F	10th Infantry

Wounded at Murfreesboro, Tennnessee, and mortally
wounded at Griffin, Georgia; died in Griffin Hospital.

BENJAMIN, SOLOMON		L	10th Infantry
BROWN, JOSEPH			10th Infantry
BROWN, SIMON			10th Infantry
BAUM, MARX			15th Infantry

Killed at the Battle of the Wilderness.

BARUCH, B. S.		G	16th Infantry
BARUCH, HERMAN		A	7th Cavalry

Courier to General Robert E. Lee.

BLANKENSEE, D.			Hampton Legion

Killed at Manassas.

BELITZER, JACOB			Washington Artillery

Mortally wounded.

BELITZER, THEODORE			German Hussars

Killed in action.

CASHBY, A.			3d Infantry
COHEN, MORRIS			7th Infantry

Enlisted when not quite sixteen years old.

CLARK, H.			10th Infantry
COHEN, GRATZ			10th Infantry

Killed at Malvern Hill.

COHEN, LAWRENCE L.			2nd Cavalry

Enlisted 1861.

COHEN, ASHER D.			Hampton's Cavalry

Enlisted 1861.

NAME.	RANK.	COMPANY.	REGIMENT.

COHEN, ISAAC   Hampton's Cavalry
Killed in action; buried in Jewish cemetery, Richmond, Virginia.

COHEN, McDUFF   Hampton's Cavalry
COHEN, ANSLEY D.   Walter's Battery
COHEN, PHILIP I.   Washington Artillery
Enlisted 1861.

COHEN, GUSTAVUS   Washington Artillery
COHEN, HENRY   Washington Artillery
Killed at Savage Station, Virginia, June 29, 1864; buried in Jewish cemetery, Richmond, Virginia.

COHEN, AARON   ⎧ Six brothers; ⎫ ⎧ Washington Artillery
COHEN, JACOB H.   ⎪ three serving in ⎪ Washington Artillery
COHEN, JULIUS   ⎪ South Carolina, ⎬ Washington Artillery
COHEN, C. S.   ⎬ one in NorthCar- ⎪ Washington Artillery
COHEN, FISHEL   ⎪ olina, and two ⎪   10th Infantry
COHEN, DAVID D.   ⎩ in Virginia.   ⎭ ⎩ Hampton's Cavalry
                                         Jefferson Rangers

Enlisted 1861.

COHEN, DR. MARX E., JR.   Washington Artillery
One of the heroes of the Civil War was Dr. Marx E. Cohen, Jr., of Charleston. He enlisted at the age of twenty-one. At the battle of Bentonville, North Carolina, towards the close of the the war, some shells containing explosive material were thrown into the Confederate lines from the guns of the Union forces. The captain of Hart's Battery called for volunteers to hurl them aside before they should burst and cause destruction to the command. Three men volunteered to undertake the task; Dr. Cohen being one of them. He and his companions were successful, but while returning to their own lines all three were shot dead by Federal bullets.

DANIELS, L.   B   15th Cavalry
Captured; died and buried in Woodlawn Cemetery, Elmira, New York.

DREYFUS, HERMAN   Cameron's Battery

NAME.	RANK.	COMPANY.	REGIMENT.
EMANUEL, EDWIN	Sergeant	A	10th Infantry

Died from exposure contracted in service.

EMANUEL, J.		A	10th Infantry
EMANUEL, SOLOMON		A	10th Infantry
EMANUEL, WASHINGTON		A	10th Infantry

Enlisted when a mere boy; died from wounds received
at Atlanta, Georgia.

EMANUEL, H.		10th Infantry
ELLBAUM, G.		14th Infantry
ESDWA, ARTHUR A.		Culpepper Battery

FOX, WILLIAM		K	1st Infantry

Wounded at Gettysburg and captured.

FOX, M. SR.	A	3d Infantry
FRIEDMAN, BENJAMIN	A	3d Infantry

GUNDHAUS, S.	I	4th Infantry
GUNDHAUS, J. L.	I	6th Infantry
GOLDSMITH, ISAAC	G	16th Infantry

Killed in action.

GOLDSMITH, MICHAEL	G	16th Infantry
GOLDSMITH, ISAAC P.		24th Infantry

Died in the service.

GOLDSMITH, A. A.	Kershaw's 2nd

Wounded at Antietam. Regiment

GOLDSMITH, M. M.	Reserves

HEYMAN, I.	F	6th Infantry

Wounded at Owensboro, North Carolina.

HORNET, J. D.	2nd Battalion
HAMMERSLOUGH, A.	3d Battalion
HAMMERSLOUGH, H.	3d Battalion
HARTZ, H.	10th Battalion
HIRSCH, MELVIN J.	Beauregard Infantry

Commissary Sergeant

Promoted from Private; served throughout the war.

HOLZHAUER, C.	Washington Artillery

NAME.	RANK.	COMPANY.	REGIMENT.
HOFFMAN, JULIUS		A	Kershaw's 1st Regiment
HIRSCH, I. W. Wounded.		B	Kershaw's 2nd Regiment

JOEL, JULIUS   C   1st Infantry
Lost an arm in the battle of the Wilderness.

JACOBS, ISAIAH   Lieutenant   D   2nd Infantry
Promoted from the ranks; killed at Knoxville, Tennessee.

JOSEPHUS, JOSEPH   1st Cavalry
JAMES, ——   Surgeon   7th Battalion
Promoted to Brigade Surgeon.

JACOBS, EMANUEL   Washington Artillery
JACOBUS, J. J.   Washington Artillery
JACOBS, FREDERICK   Palmetto Artillery
JACOBS, REID   Palmetto Guards
Wounded in action.

JACOBS, A. L.   C   Hampton Legion
Called "Little Jake;" wounded at Sharpsburg; killed in Tennessee.

JACOBS, ABRAHAM   Hampton Legion
Killed in action.

JACOBS, LOUIS   Hampton Legion
JACOBS, MITCHELL   Hampton Legion
JACOBS, H.   ——
Killed in battle; buried in Jewish cemetery, Richmond, Virginia.

KAPHAN, THEODORE   Hagood 1st Infantry
KAHN, DAVID   8th Infantry
KAMINSKI, H.   Sergeant   B   10th Infantry
KAHN, ISAAC   12th Infantry
KOHN, THEODORE   F   25th Infantry
From a newspaper clipping: "Theodore Kohn of Orangeburg, a veteran of the Edisto Rifles, 25th

Regiment, South Carolina, will carry to his grave the wounds he received at Drewy's Bluff while gallantly fighting for his adopted country.''

NAME.	RANK.	COMPANY.	REGIMENT.
KOHN, AUGUST			25th Infantry

Served throughout the war.

LEVI, LEOPOLD			5th Infantry
LEVIN, G. W.		A	15th Infantry
LEVIN, SAMUEL		A	15th Infantry

Killed at Sharpsburg, Maryland.

LOWENBERG, DAVID	Sergeant	A	16th Infantry

Served three years.

LEVY, MOSES   23d Infantry

He is spoken of by his former Colonel Benhon as one of the bravest, truest and most devoted men in his command; he was captured at the last battle at Petersburg, Virginia.

LEVIN, L. C.	2nd Cavalry
LEVIN, L. J.	Wheeler's Cavalry
LEVY, LIONEL C. JR.	Fenner's Battery
LAZARUS, M. H.	Walter's Battery
LAZARUS, B. D.	Washington Artillery
LAZARUS, BENJAMIN	Washington Artillery
LAZARUS, MARX	Washington Artillery
LAZARUS, SOLOMON	Washington Artillery

Enlisted 1861; served until the close of the war.

LEVY, LIONEL L.   Washington Artillery

Promoted to Judge Advocate.

LOPEZ, JOHN   Palmetto Guards

From 1861 until the close of the war.

LOPEZ, MOSES   Palmetto Guards

From 1861 until the close of the war.

LEVIN, S. M.   Sumter Guards

Wounded at Secessionville.

LYONS, J. C.	Company Cadets
LEHMAN, A.	————

Killed; buried at Jewish Cemetery, Richmond, Virginia.

NAME.	RANK.	COMPANY.	REGIMENT.
MOSES, H. C.	1st Lieutenant		2nd Infantry

Promoted from Private, Lucas Battalion; wounded at Manassas.

MOSES, PERRY		D	2nd Infantry

Killed at Malvern Hill, aged 17 years.

MOSES, CLAREMONT		E	2nd Infantry

Wounded in action.

MOSES, P.		E	2nd Infantry

Seriously wounded.

MOSES, MEYER			2nd Infantry
MOSES, EDWIN L.			27th Infantry

Captured; died prison, Camp Chase.

MORDECAI, J. RANDOLPH   Washington Artillery
        Lieutenant and Assistant Quartermaster.
        Promoted from the ranks.

MOISE, CAMILLUS   Washington Artillery
        Served four years.

MORDECAI, G. L.   Washington Artillery
        The father of this soldier, the late Benjamin Mordecai,
        was the first contributor to the Southern cause, donating $10,000 to South Carolina.

MOSES, JOSHUA L.   1st Lieutenant ⎫   ⎧ Culpepper Battery
        Wounded at Manassas; killed │   │
        at Mobile, commanding Bat- │   │
        talion.   │   │

MOSES, JACKSON   │ Five brothers. │ Culpepper Battery
MOSES, HORACE   │   │ Culpepper Battery
        Entered service at 17 years ; ⎬   ⎨
        captured at Mobile.   │   │

MOSES, PERRY, JR.   │   │ Culpepper Battery
        Wounded at Mobile.   │   │

MOSES, I. HARBY   │   │ 6th Cavalry
        Graduate of Citadel Academy; │   │
        served throughout the war. ⎭   ⎩

MOSES, DANIEL   Culpepper Battery
MOSES, DAVID L.   Culpepper Battery

NAME.	RANK.	COMPANY.	REGIMENT.

MOSES, I. L.   Culpepper Battery
  Wounded at Manassas; killed at Fort Blakely

MOSES, M. P.   Culpepper Battery
MOSES, T. J. JR.   Culpepper Battery
MOSES, Z. P.   Culpepper Battery
MOSES, MEYER B.   Culpepper Battery
MORDECAI, THOMAS W.   Hampton's Cavalry
  Killed at Brandy Station, Virginia.

MANNING, JACOB   Hampton Legion
  Killed at Brandy Station, Virginia.

MOSES, A. D. L.   Hampton Legion
  Wounded at Seven Pines.

MOSES, A. J. SR.   Mellet's Regiment
MOISE, EDWARD   Palmetto Guards
  Enlisted 1861; served until the close of the war.

MOISE, ISAAC   Palmetto Guards
  Enlisted 1861; served until the close of the war.

OPPENHEIMER, EDWIN   Sergeant   G   16th Infantry
OPPENHEIMER, JULIUS H.   Sergeant   G   16th Infantry
OPPENHEIMER, SAMUEL   Sergeant   G   16th Infantry
OPPENHEIMER, H. D. H.   G   16th Infantry

POLLOCK, B. C.   A   1st Infantry
POLLOCK, CLARENCE   A   1st Infantry
  Killed at Spottsylvania, Virginia.

POLLOCK, J. L.   A   1st Infantry
POLLOCK, T. M.   A   1st Infantry
PEIXOTTO, S. C.   1st Infantry
PHILLIPS, ISIDORE   Hampton Legion
PHILLIPS, MICHAEL A.   Hampton Legion
POSNANSKI, GUSTAVUS   Sumter Guards

ROBERTSON, ABRAHAM   A   3d Infantry
ROBINSON, CHARLES C.   7th Infantry
  Served throughout the war.

NAME.	RANK.	COMPANY.	REGIMENT.
RICHARDS, MEYER			21st Infantry
ROSENDORF, JACOB			1st Cavalry
ROTHSCHILD, BENJAMIN			Hampton Cavalry

Killed at Gaines' Mills, Virginia.

SOLOMON, J. L.			2nd Infantry
SUMMERS, AD.			2nd Infantry

Drowned near Port Royal.

SULZBACHER, WILLIAM		E	3d Infantry
SPIEGELBERG, MORRIS			16th Infantry
SEIXAS, B. M.			20th Infantry
SOLOMON, J. F.			20th Infantry
SCHILLER, LOUIS			1st Cavalry
SOMMERS, ISAAC			Heavy Artillery

Killed at Siege of Fort Moultrie.

SHAPIRA, L. D.			Hampton Legion
SAMPSON, HENRY			Stuart's Command
SAMPSON, E. J.			————

Killed on June 27, 1864; buried in Jewish Cemetery, Richmond, Virginia.

TRIEST, MAIER			24th Infantry

VALENTINE, JACOB	Captain		Infantry

Served while a mere youth in the Palmetto Regiment during the Mexican War and was wounded in the storming of Cherubusco. He was believed to be the youngest pensioner of the United States Government. He lived in Philadelphia at the passage of "Secession," and immediately went to Charleston, offering his services to his native State. He was appointed Lieutenant in the first South Carolina regular infantry and took part in the bombardment of Fort Sumter, in April, 1861. He served in this regiment from that time continuously until December, 1863, when he was severely wounded while in command of Fort Moultrie. This wound was of so serious a character as to prevent him from performing any further active service. He was detailed to the recruiting department in which he served until the close of the war. During the Mexican War he received two medals; one for bravery on the battle-field, and another for being the youngest soldier in the regiment.

NAME.	RANK.	COMPANY.	REGIMENT.
VALENTINE, ISAAC R.			Sumter Guards

Killed at Secessionville.

VALENTINE, H. M.			Sumter Guards

Wounded at Secessionville.

VALENTINE, HERZ			Palmetto Guards

Wounded in action.

VALENTINE, I.			Palmetto Guards

Seriously wounded.

WITKOWSKI, ADOLPH			2nd Infantry

Severely wounded at the Wilderness.

WACHTEL, M.			4th Infantry
WERTHEIM, HERMAN	Lieutenant		7th Infantry

Killed at Spottsylvania.

WERTHEIM, BERTHOLD		G	16th Infantry
WETHERHORN, SOLOMON		E	25th Infantry
WOLF, D.		G	25th Infantry

Captured; died and buried at Woodlawn Cemetery, Elmira, New York.

WERTHEIM, LEVI			German Artillery
WERTHEIM, JULIUS			Hampton Legion
WILSON, J. C.			Hampton Legion
WOLF, W. M.	Lieutenant		Hagood's Brigade

Killed; buried in Jewish Cemetery, Richmond, Virginia.

WARNER, HENRY			Colleton Rifles
WERTHEIM, HEYMAN			Kershaw's Command

Killed at Gettysburg.

ZACHARIAS, DAVID		C	5th Cavalry

Killed at Mechanicsville.

TENNESSEE.

NAME.	RANK.	COMPANY.	REGIMENT.
BIEBER, ——		I	15th Infantry
BURG, FELIX		I	15th Infantry
COOK, JOEL		K	63d Infantry

Captured; died and buried at Woodlawn Cemetery, Elmira, New York.

NAME.	RANK.	COMPANY.	REGIMENT.
DAHLSHEIMER, M.	Corporal	I	15th Infantry
DANHEISER, CHARLES		I	15th Infantry
FREED, JULIUS		I	15th Infantry

Wounded at Perryville, Chickamauga, and Dallas.

FOLTZ, BENJAMIN			15th Infantry

Killed at Shiloh.

FOLTZ, LEON			15th Infantry

Lost a leg in battle

FOLTZ, MOSES			15th Infantry

Lost a leg in battle.

FREEMAN, MAX			15th Infantry

Killed at Murfreesboro.

GUTMANN, EMANUEL		A	3d Infantry
HIRSCHBERG, SIMON			1st Infantry
HOBER, G.	Major		8th Infantry

Taken prisoner at Port Hudson.

HANSMAN, SAMUEL		I	15th Infantry
HECHT, SAMUEL		I	15th Infantry
JACOBY, EMIL G.			3d Infantry

Killed at Shiloh.

NAME	RANK.	COMPANY.	REGIMENT.
KUHN, MAX			15th Infantry
Killed at Shiloh.			
LIEBSCHUTZ, JACOB			8th Infantry
Killed at Resaca.			
LIEBSCHUTZ, JOSEPH			8th Infantry
Killed at Franklin, Tennessee.			
LANG, ——		I	15th Infantry
LENBRIL, L.		I	15th Infantry
LOEB, JACOB		I	15th Infantry
MINKUS, J.			1st Infantry
MARTIN, MORDECAI		I	15th Infantry
NASSAUER, LOUIS			1st Infantry
NATHAN, JULIUS	Sergeant	I	15th Infantry
Promoted.			
PARAIRE, ISAAC			1st Infantry
SCHIFFMAN, SIMON			3d Infantry
SANDERS, MARK			4th Infantry
SEELIG, SIMON			4th Infantry
STRAUS, S.	Lieutenant	I	15th Infantry
SEESEL, HENRY, JR.		I	15th Infantry
SIMONSON, ——		I	15th Infantry
Killed at Shiloh.			
WRONKER, MORRIS			4th Infantry
WOLF, FREDERICK	Corporal	I	15th Infantry
WASSEMAN, CHARLES		I	15th Infantry
WACHENHEIM, S.			40th Infantry
ZUCKER, SIMON		K	10th Cavalry

TEXAS.

NAME.	RANK.	COMPANY.	REGIMENT.
ALEXANDER, A. S.	Captain		1st Infantry

Commander Oswald's Battalion; served until close of war.

| ANGEL, A. | | A | 5th Infantry |

Killed at Manassas.

| AUERBACH, Doctor J. | | A | 5th Infantry |
| AUERBACH, E. | | B | 5th Infantry |

Killed at Wilderness.

| ASH, HENRY | | C | 5th Infantry |

| BENEDICT, JACOB | | F | 1st Infantry |

Killed at Malvern Hill.

BACHARACH, WOLF		A	5th Infantry
BILLIG, ISAAC		A	5th Infantry
BUCK, ROBERT			1st Artillery

| COHEN, HENRY | | L | 1st Infantry |
| CRAMER, JOSEPH | | | 1st Infantry |

Wounded at Gettysburg; served until close of war.

| COBMAN, LOUIS | | A | 5th Infantry |

Wounded at Gettysburg.

| COHEN, S. | | A | 5th Infantry |

Killed at Gettysburg.

| COLEMAN, LOUIS | | A | 5th Infantry |

Wounded at Gettysburg.

CRAMER, A.	Lieutenant	B	8th Infantry
			(Flourney's Regiment)
COLEMAN, MEYER		A	26th Infantry

| DREYFUS, SAMUEL | | B | 1st Infantry |
| DEUTSCH, SOLOMON | | | 1st Infantry |

Wounded; served until close of war.

NAME.	RANK.	COMPANY.	REGIMENT.
DAVIDBURG, DAVID D.		B	6th Infantry
DAVIDSON, DAVID H.		B	6th Infantry
DEUTSCH, S.		C	6th Infantry
DANIELS, J.		C	8th Infantry
DAVIDSON, HENRY		A	26th Infantry
DREYFUS, CHARLES		A	26th Infantry
DANNENBAUM, JOSEPH		C	Cook Regiment
ELSASSER, I.		A	5th Infantry

FRANK, J. W.   L   1st Infantry
    Enlisted 1861; killed at Sharpsburg.

FRANK, L.   B   Elmore's Infantry

FRIEDBURGER, G.   9th Cavalry
    Killed at Corinth.

FRIEDLANDER, N.   A   26th Cavalry
FRIEDBERGER, GABRIEL   Terry's Cavalry
FRIEDBERGER, SAMUEL   Terry's Cavalry
FISCHEL, LEON   Wirt Adams Cavalry
FOX, ALLEN   C   Heavy Artillery
FOX, A.   B   Waul's Legion

GLASER, WOLF   1st Infantry
GOLDSTICKER, J.   A   4th Infantry
    Killed at Sharpsburg.

GOETZ, JULIUS   A   14th Infantry
    Wounded and taken prisoner.

GANS, SAMUEL   26th Cavalry
    Wounded at Cane River.

GANS, LEON   A   Parson's Cavalry

HINES, A.   B   4th Infantry
    Lost an arm at Gaines' Mills; wounded at New Hope
    Church.

HIEF, CHARLES   B   6th Infantry
    Enlisted 1861; captured.

25

NAME.	RANK.	COMPANY.	REGIMENT.
HELLER, LOUIS			6th Infantry
HOLDSTEIN, ISIDORE		A	8th Infantry
HIRSCHBERG, J.		A	26th Cavalry
HYAMS, S.		A	26th Cavalry
HARBY, HENRY J.		C.	26th Cavalry

Enlisted at the age of sixteen years; served until close of war.

| HIRSCHFIELD, H. | | | Parson's Brigade |

| JACOBY, MAX | | A | 1st Infantry |

Lost right leg at Gains' farm.

KAUFMAN, EDWARD			1st Infantry
KEMPER, H.			1st Infantry
KELLER, THEODORE	Colonel		2nd Infantry

Promoted; wounded at Corinth.

| KLOPMAN, L. | | A | 8th Infantry |

Killed at Jenkins' Ferry, Arkansas.

| KOHLMAN, M. | | A | 26th Cavalry |

| LEAVE, R. B. | | B | 1st Infantry |

Wounded at Malvern Hill.

| LAZARUS, S. S. | | L | 1st Infantry |

Wounded at Chickamauga.

LAZARUS, B.		E	4th Infantry
LEVY, ROBERT		A	5th Infantry
LEWIS, ISAAC		C	5th Infantry
LACHMAN, E.		D	5th Infantry

Wounded at Manassas.

LASKER, M.			2nd Cavalry
LEOPOLD, W.			1st Heavy Artillery
LEVY, ISAAC		B	Light Artillery
LEVISON, A		B	Waul's Legion
LEVISON, PAUL		B	Waul's Legion

| MORRIS, LEHMAN | Sergeant | D | 1st Infantry |

Killed at Gettysburg.

NAME.	RANK.	COMPANY.	REGIMENT
MAAS, LOUIS		D	5th Infantry

Killed at Manassas.

MICHEL, HENRY			15th Infantry
MELASKI, J.		A	26th Cavalry
MEYER, JOSEPH		C	Heavy Artillery

OPPENHEIMER, J.		B	2nd Infantry
OPPENHEIMER, A.			22nd Infantry
OPPENHEIMER, BENJAMIN			22nd Infantry
OPPENHEIMER, S.			22nd Infantry
OPPENHEIMER, D.	Captain		3d Cavalry

PICKARD H.		H	5th Infantry
PEPPER, L. S.		A	8th Infantry
PEPPER, SAMUEL		A	8th Infantry
POHALSKI, G. D.		G	11th Infantry

Served throughout the war.

POHALSKI, P.		G	11th Infantry

Served until the close of the war.

ROSENFIELD, ALEXANDER		A	26th Cavalry
ROSENFIELD, HENRY		A	26th Cavalry
ROSENFIELD, MICHAEL		A	26th Cavalry
RICH, LOUIS M.		C	Cook's Cavalry

SHOWLSKI, CHARLES		E	5th Infantry

Wounded at Gettysburg.

SAMUSH, J.		A	8th Infantry

Wounded at Sabine River.

SIEGEL, JOSEPH			8th Infantry
SILBERBERG, GEORGE		B	9th Infantry

Served four years.

SAMPSON, EDWARD J.			10th Infantry

Killed at Hanover Court House; buried in Jewish
cemetery, Richmond, Virginia.

SOLOMON, JOSEPH A.		G	11th Infantry

NAME.	RANK.	COMPANY.	REGIMENT.
STEIN, ISAAC	Colonel		Marshall's Regiment

Lost his right arm at second battle of Manassas.

STEINER, VICTOR			Texas Rangers
SEELIGSON, HENRY	Lieutenant		Cavalry

[*See record in Mexican War Lists.*]

TEAH, ABRAHAM			8th Infantry

Promoted to Corporal, Sergeant-Major, and Aid-de-camp to Colonel Overton Young, commanding 1st Brigade, Walker's Division.

TEAH, ABRAHAM			22nd Infantry

NAME.		COMPANY.	REGIMENT.
WALKER, A.		K	1st Infantry
WOLF, SIMON		F	4th Infantry

Killed at Manassas.

WOLF, A.		A	5th Infantry

Wounded at Seven Pines.

WOLF, A. F.		A	5th Infantry

Killed at Sharpsburg.

WOLF, BENJAMIN		A	5th Infantry
WETMORE, JAMES		C	8th Infantry
WEIS, ALBERT			2nd Cavalry
WEIS, LEOPOLD			2nd Cavalry
WIENER, SOLOMON			Terry's Scouts

VERMONT.

NAME.	RANK.	COMPANY.	REGIMENT.
SELIGSON, H. A.	Colonel		————

VIRGINIA.

NAME.	RANK.	COMPANY.	REGIMENT.
ADLER, HENRY		{ E	1st Infantry 14th Infantry

Enlisted 1861; killed at Roanoke Island; buried in Jewish Cemetery, Richmond, Virginia.

ABRAMS, ISAAC		G	1st Infantry
ARCHER, LEWIS		H	1st Infantry

Enlisted 1861; honorably discharged on account of wound.

ANGLE, MEYER		D	12th Infantry

Enlisted 1861; captured at Sailors' Creek.

ANGLE, M.		E	46th Infantry
ANGLE, BUCK			46th Infantry
ANGLE, JOSEPH			59th Infantry
ADLER, A.		A	1st Artillery

BEAR, ALEXANDER	Lieutenant	D	4th Infantry

Subsequently Surgeon.

BACHARACH, M. —————

Killed before Richmond; buried at Jewish Cemetery, Richmond, Virginia.

BACARACH, S. —————

Killed before Richmond; buried at Jewish Cemetery, Richmond, Virginia.

BAACH, SIEGMUND Longstreet's Corps.

Captured by Union troops.

BAACH, SELIGMAN Longstreet's Corps

Captured.

BAACH, SOLOMON H. Longstreet's Corps

Killed in battle at Salem Church, near Fredericksburg, Virginia.

NAME.	RANK.	COMPANY.	REGIMENT.
BERNHEIM, SAMUEL	Sergeant-Major		City Battalion
BARNETT, B. J.			Engineer Corps

COHEN, JACOB		B	12th Infantry
COHEN, DAVID			Richmond Hussars
COHEN, MORRIS			Richmond Hussars

DAVIS, BENJAMIN   B   6th Infantry
Killed before Richmond; Buried at Jewish Cemetery,
Richmond, Virginia.

DANIEL, JOSEPH   B   12th Infantry
Wounded at Gettysburg; served until surrender.

DEGEN, SAMUEL   A   19th Infantry
DREYFUS, LEON   A   10th Cavalry
DAVIS, ANSLEY S.   Reserves
DEICHS, WILLIAM   Norfolk Blues
Detailed on special service.

EZEKIEL, E. M.   { A   1st Infantry
                         { A   46th Infantry
Served until the close of the war.

EZEKIEL, JOSEPH K.   B   46th Infantry
Killed at Petersburg.

EISEMAN, LOUIS   Wise's Brigade
EZEKIEL, JACOB   1st Militia
EZEKIEL, MOSES J.   Lieutenant   Cadets Virginia Institute
Promoted from Private.

FRANKENTHAL, SIMON   B   46th Infantry
Enlisted 1861; honorably discharged for disability on
account of wounds.

FRIEDENWALD, ISAAC   A   53d Infantry
FRIEDLAND, A.   Richmond Light Blues

GOLDSTEIN, BERNARD   E   46th Infantry
Enlisted 1861; disabled by wounds; honorably discharged.

GUGGENHEIM, SIMON   E   46th Infantry

NAME.	RANK.	COMPANY.	REGIMENT.
GUNST, MICHAEL		E	46th Infantry
GOLDSTEIN, J.			46th Infantry
GUNST, HENRY			—— Cavalry
GERSBERG, HENRY			——

Killed June 2nd, 1864; buried at Jewish Cemetery, Richmond, Virginia.

HIRSCHBERG, JOSEPH		A	1st Infantry
HUTZLER, SIEGMUND L.		A	1st Infantry
HEXTER, SIMON		{ E	1st Infantry
		{ A	46th Infantry
HESSBURG, JULIUS			3d Infantry

Killed at Gaines' Mills; buried at Jewish Cemetery, Richmond, Virginia.

HEILBRONER, HENRY		H	27th Infantry

Wounded at Port Republic.

HESSER, S.		E	46th Infantry
HIRSCH, HERMAN		A	1st Cavalry

Enlisted 1861; assigned to 12th Infantry.

HESSBURG, M.			—— Cavalry
HARRIS, MOSES			Richmond Hussars

ISAACS, ABRAHAM		E	46th Infantry

Enlisted 1861; wounded at Petersburg; served through-the war.

KUH, E. S.		H	8th Infantry
KULL, M. E.		A	12th Infantry
KAYTON, N. N.		E	46th Infantry
KEYTON, LOUIS		E	46th Infantry
KADDEN, A.		A	10th Cavalry
KALTEN, AARON			Wise's Brigade

LICHTENSTEIN, ISIDORE		H	1st Infantry
LOWENSTEIN, WILLIAM			{ 1st Infantry
			{ 46th Infantry

Enlisted 1861; detailed to Medical Department; a member of the State Legislature, November, 1892.

NAME.	RANK.	COMPANY.	REGIMENT.
LEVY, LEWIS		A	12th Infantry
LOWENSTEIN, ISIDORE		A	12th Infantry
Wounded at Malvern Hill.			
LORSCH, HENRY		A	19th Infantry
Seriously wounded at Seven Pines.			
LEVY, EZEKIEL J.	Captain	E	46th Infantry
Promoted for gallantry; served four years.			
LEVY, ISAAC J.		E	46th Infantry
Killed at Petersburg.			
LEVY, ALEXANDER H.		E	46th Infantry
Served four years.			
LEVY, JOSEPH		E	46th Infantry
Enlisted 1861; wounded at Petersburg, and disabled.			
LEVY, EMANUEL G.		E	46th Infantry
LYON, THOMAS			46th Infantry
LEVY, LEOPOLD		G	1st Cavalry
LEVY, SAMPSON		G	1st Cavalry
LEVY, SOLOMON	(Three brothers)		23d Infantry
Died of wounds.			
LICHTENSTEIN, K.			19th Reserves
LEVY, E.	Captain		Richmond Blues
LOWENSTEIN, I.			Richmond Grays
LITERMAN, SIMEON			Young's Battery
MYERS, WILLIAM		A	1st Infantry
MYERS, MARKS			12th Infantry
Killed at Manassas.			
MYER, MAX		B	12th Infantry
Disabled in action.			
MIDDLEDORFER, CHARLES		E	12th Infantry
MYERS, A.			17th Infantry
MYERS, SOLOMON			18th Infantry
MOSES, J. C.		E	46th Infantry
Seriously wounded.			
MYERS, C.		E	46th Infantry
Disabled in service.			

NAME.	RANK.	COMPANY.	REGIMENT.
MYERS, LEWIS			46th Infantry
MYERS, HERMAN			1st Cavalry
MYERS, BENJAMIN		C	Wise's Brigade
MIDDLEDORFER, MAX			Fayette Artillery

NEWMAN, JOSEPH		K	20th Infantry

Captured; died of wounds; buried in Woodlawn
Cemetery, Elmira, New York.

NEWMAN, ISAAC			46th Infantry
NEWMAN, JACOB			59th Infantry

OBERMAYER, H.			2nd Infantry
OETHENGER, DAVID		B	18th Infantry
OBERNDORFER, B.			Young's Battery

PYLE, HARDY		G	1st Infantry
PLAUT, HUGO			46th Infantry

ROSENBERG, M.		G	6th Infantry

Specially detailed at Richmond.

ROSENFELD, SIMON		A	12th Infantry
REINACH, A. S.		B	12th Infantry
REINACH, ISADORE		B	12th Infantry
ROSENHEIM, HENRY		E	46th Infantry
ROSENBERG, MICHAEL			Norfolk Blues Infantry
REINACH, MORRIS			Petersburg Grays

SELDNER, ISAAC	Lieutenant		6th Infantry

Promoted from Private for bravery; killed at Chancellorsville, May 3, 1863; buried in Jewish Cemetery,
Richmond, Virginia.

SCHWARTZ, ——			17th Infantry
SEMON, JACOB S.		E	46th Infantry
SCHOENTHAL, JOSEPH		E	46th Infantry
SON, JACOB		E	46th Infantry
STRAUSS, DAVID			7th Cavalry
SIMON, ISAAC			Richmond Hussars

NAME.	RANK.	COMPANY.	REGIMENT.
SIMON, NATHAN			Richmond Hussars
SMITH, HENRY			Otoy's Battery

Killed in first battle.

SELIGMAN, H.			Petersburg Grays

TRIESDORFER, G.		B	14th Infantry
TUCKER, ——			10th Cavalry

UNSTADTER, M.		A	6th Infantry

Wounded at Gaines' Mills; discharged for being disabled for service.

WHITLOCK, P.		A	12th Infantry

Discharged for being disabled for service.

WILZINSKY, LEWIS		H	12th Infantry
WOLFF, W. M.	Lieutenant		25th Infantry
			(Hagood's Brigade)

Killed before Richmond; buried in Jewish Cemetery, Richmond, Virginia.

WASSEMAN, LEVY		E	46th Infantry

Wounded and captured at Roanoke; when discharged served on hospital duty.

WAMBACH, LEOPOLD			Norfolk Blues Infantry

Killed at Vicksburg.

WHITEHEAD, HENRY			Wise's Brigade

WASHINGTON TERRITORY.

NAME.	RANK.	COMPANY.	REGIMENT.
STEINBERGER, JUSTUS	Major		——

Captain and Assistant Adjutant-General, Major and Paymaster.

WEST VIRGINIA.

NAME.	RANK.	COMPANY.	REGIMENT.
EDDELMAN, G. H.		K	6th Infantry
HEIDELSHEIMER, W. H.	Lieutenant	G	7th Infantry
KRAUS, SAMUEL	Captain	B	7th Infantry

Promoted from the ranks.

MAYER, DANIEL   Captain   5th Infantry

The following letter is of interest:

STATE OF WEST VIRGINIA,
WHEELING, May 30th, 1866.

ADJUTANT-GENERAL'S OFFICE.

DOCTOR DANIEL MAYER, Charleston, W. Va.

SIR:

I am directed by his Excellency, the Governor, to present to you the enclosed medal in accordance with a joint resolution of the Legislature of the State of West Virginia, adopted February 1st, 1866, as a slight testimonial of the high appreciation by the State of your devotion, patriotism and services in suppression of the late rebellion.

Very respectfully,
Your obedient servant,
J. H. DUVAL,
Adjutant-General.

RAUSCH, C. M.   11th Infantry
ROSE, ABRAHAM   A   1st Light Artillery

STEINACHER, WILSON   { 2nd Infantry
                                      { 5th Cavalry

Wounded.

WISCONSIN.

NAME.	RANK.	COMPANY.	REGIMENT.
ABRAHAMSON, MARTIN		B	1st Infantry
ASH, REUBEN,	1st Lieutenant	E	2nd Infantry

Enlisted as Corporal; wounded at Bull Run; captured at Gettysburg.

AUERBACH, GUSTAV		F	3d Infantry
ABRAHAMSON, MARTIN		{ H	3d Infantry
			21st Infantry

Served four years.

ABRAHAM, AUGUST		A	6th Infantry
ARNSTEIN, EMIL		F	6th Infantry
AARON, JACOB		C	8th Infantry
ABRAHAMSON, JACOB		I	13th Infantry
ABRAHAMSON, JACOB		A	15th Infantry
ALEXANDER, JACOB		F	16th Infantry
AARON, MICHAEL		K	20th Infantry

Wounded at Prairie Grove, Arkansas.

ABRAHAMSON, JOHN		E	21st Infantry

Served three years.

ALEXANDER, LEVI	Corporal	G	43d Infantry
ADLER, FREDERICK		G	45th Infantry
ABEL, HERMAN		A	48th Infantry
ADLER, MAX			2nd Battery

BLUM, FERDINAND		E	1st Infantry
BEAR, ISAAC		C	3d Infantry
BIRNBAUM, CHARLES		I	6th Infantry

Killed at Gainesville, Virginia.

BERNHARD, JULIUS		B	7th Infantry
BAUM, CHARLES F.		E	8th Infantry

Wounded in action.

BAHR, JULIUS		H	8th Infantry

NAME.	RANK.	COMPANY.	REGIMENT.
BLUM, JACOB		G	9th Infantry
BENJAMIN, CYRUS		H	11th Infantry
BENJAMIN, SAMUEL		I	11th Infantry

Wounded; served four years.

BAER, AARON		A	14th Infantry
BENJAMIN, EPHRAIM		D	16th Infantry
			(reorganized)
BEHREND, JOSEPH		C	17th Infantry
BAER, HERMAN		D	17th Infantry
BLUM, FERDINAND		B	21st Infantry

Wounded in action.

BAUM, DANIEL		I	22nd Infantry
BEHRENS, S. BEHREND		H	26th Infantry
BLUM, JACOB		I	26th Infantry

Enlisted as Private; wounded in action.

BAUMGARTEN, HENRY		K	26th Infantry

Captured.

BLUM, SAMUEL		D	27th Infantry
BLUM, CHARLES		G	28th Infantry

Served three years.

BENJAMIN, EPHRAIM		G	32nd Infantry
BLUMENSTEIN, CHARLES F.	Lieutenant	E	34th Infantry

Enlisted as Private.

BERNHARD, MAX		G	35th Infantry
BERNHARD, CARL		G	35th Infantry
BACHMAN, JACOB		I	42nd Infantry
BAUM, JULIUS		G	44th Infantry
BAUM, JACOB		D	45th Infantry
BAHRENT, JOSEPH			45th Infantry
BAUM, OSCAR		D	48th Infantry
BENJAMIN, ISAAC		C	51st Infantry
BAUM, JULIUS		M	1st Cavalry

Captured.

BAMBERG, CARL			Milwaukee Cavalry
BEHREND, GUSTAV		C	1st Heavy Artillery
BENJAMIN, DANA	Corporal		9th Battery

Enlisted as Private; served three years.

NAME.	RANK.	COMPANY.	REGIMENT.
COHEN, WILLIAM		D	49th Infantry

DAVISON, NATHAN S. 1st Lieutenant B 37th Infantry
Promoted from Sergeant, 20th; wounded at Petersburg and at Weldon Railroad.

DAVIS, ISAAC		H	38th Infantry
DAVIS, LEVI		F	40th Infantry
DAVIS, ISAAC		H	43d Infantry

Died in the service.

DAVISON, JOSEPH		E	44th Infantry
DANIELSON, JACOB		A	48th Infantry
DAVIS, DAVID A.		K	49th Infantry
DAVIS, DAVID		G	50th Infantry
DAVIS, DAVID		F	51st Infantry
DAVIS, LEVY P.		E	52nd Infantry
DAVID, ALEXANDER	Captain	B	3d Cavalry

ERDMAN, HERMAN Commissary-Sergeant 9th Infantry
Enlisted as Private. (reorganized

ERDMAN, GOTTLIEB C 14th Infantry
Wounded at Spanish Fort.

ERDMAN, THEODORE		C	14th Infantry
EISEMAN, JACOB		E	25th Infantry

Wounded at Decatur, Georgia.

ERDMAN, HENRY Sergeant C 26th Infantry
Enlisted as Private; wounded at Bentonville, N. C.;
served three years.

ESSLINGER, EMANUEL Corporal K 33d Infantry
Served three years.

ESSLINGER, SAMUEL K 33d Infantry
Served three years.

ERDMAN, GOTTLIEB Sergeant E 34th Infantry

FALKENSTEIN, CHARLES		H	1st Infantry
FREUND, JOSEPH		F	6th Infantry
FRANK, SALOMON S.		C	11th Infantry

NAME.	RANK.	COMPANY.	REGIMENT.
FRANK, SIMON		C	16th Infantry
FALK, JACOB			17th Infantry

Died in the service.

FRANK, JOSEPH S.		F	18th Infantry

Captured.

FLESH, MOSES		I	23d Infantry

Wounded at Vicksburg and at Carrion Crow Bayou.

FROHLICH, JULIUS	Corporal	B	26th Infantry

Enlisted as Private.

FELDMAN, PHILIP		I	26th Infantry

Died of wounds received at Gettysburg.

FRANKE, HERMAN		E	34th Infantry
FRIEDLAND, FREDERICK		D	2nd Cavalry
FRIEBERG, HEINRICH		H	2nd Cavalry
FURST, LUDWIG		H	2nd Cavalry
FALKENBURG, ELIAS	Sergeant	M	2nd Cavalry
FRANK, OSCAR		E	4th Cavalry
FRANK, GUSTAV			8th Battery

Veteran; served four years.

GANS, ADAM		H	6th Infantry
GANS, ISAAC		K	22d Infantry

Captured.

GRUNEWALD, HEINRICH		F	34th Infantry
GOODMAN, JOSEPH		I	45th Infantry
GANS, ARNOLD		K	58th Infantry

Died in the service.

HORWITZ, PHILIP	Lieutenant	H	1st Infantry
HART, BENJAMIN		D	2nd Infantry
HESS, DAVID		B	3d Infantry
HERRMAN, GOTTLIEB		A	5th Infantry

Wounded at Gettysburg and at Fredericksburg.

HAAS, JACOB		A	9th Infantry

Served three years.

HEINEMAN, FREDERICK		B	9th Infantry

Served three years.

NAME.	RANK.	COMPANY.	REGIMENT.
HERRMAN, ALBERT		C	9th Infantry
HESS, ADOLPH		I	9th Infantry
Wounded in action.			
HIRSCH, JOHN			9th Infantry
HARRIS, ISAAC		B	10th Infantry
HERRMANSON, HERMAN		K	10th Infantry
HARRIS, SIMON		D	11th Infantry
HARRIS, JOEL		H	11th Infantry
HERRMANN, JACOB			14th Infantry
HIRSCHMAN, FERDINAND		C	16th Infantry
HIRSCH, WILLIAM		F	19th Infantry
HERRMAN, HENRY		H	19th Infantry
HERZBERG, AUGUST		H	20th Infantry
Died in the service.			
HERRMANSON, HERMAN		D	21st Infantry
HEINBERG, LOUIS		I	23d Infantry
Served three years.			
HAHN, HERMAN		I	24th Infantry
HORWITZ, PHILIP	Major		26th Infantry
HUBSCHMAN, FRANCIS	Surgeon		26th Infantry
HERRMAN, HERMAN			26th Infantry
Died of wounds at Chancellorsville.			
HIRSCH, FREDERICK		I	26th Infantry
Captured.			
HEINEMAN, JOSEPH		E	27th Infantry
Died in the service.			
HART, LEVI		F	27th Infantry
Died in the service.			
HART, BENJAMIN		K	29th Infantry
Died in the service.			
HART, DANIEL	Sergeant	A	32nd Infantry
Enlisted as private.			
HART, BENJAMIN		A	32nd Infantry
HERRMAN, JACOB		D	32nd Infantry
HEINEMAN, JOSEPH		C	33d Infantry
Died in the service.			
HEINEMAN, AUGUST		I	37th Infantry

NAME.	RANK.	COMPANY.	REGIMENT.
HARRIS, ERWIN W.		F	39th Infantry
HIRSCHMAN, DAVID	Captain	G	44th Infantry
HUEBSCH, JOSEPH		C	45th Infantry
HAAS, JACOB		I	46th Infantry
HERRMAN, LEOPOLD		D	48th Infantry
HART, FRANK J.		A	1st Cavalry

Died in the service.

HARRIS, SIMON		F	2nd Cavalry
HERZFELD, JOHN		G	2nd Cavalry

Served three years.

HEINEMAN, JOSEPH		H	2nd Cavalry
HEYMAN, WILLIAM		D	2nd Cavalry

Served three years.

HERZBERG, ERNEST F.	Captain		2nd Battery
HESS, HENRY E.			3d Battery

Captured; died in the service.

HOFMAN, JOSEPH			5th Battery

Served four years.

ISRAEL, ABRAHAMS	Sergeant	A	14th Infantry

Enlisted as private; Veteran; served four years.

ISAACSON, ISAAC		D	15th Infantry
ISRAELSON, J. G.		K	50th Infantry
ISAACSON, LEWIS C.			4th Battery

Killed at Darby Road, Virginia.

JACOBY, ADOLPH		H	9th Infantry
JACOBSON, JACOB		B	15th Infantry

Wounded at Chickamauga.

JACOBSON, SALOMON		C	15th Infantry

Served four years.

JACOBSON, JACOB L.		D	15th Infantry

Wounded at Hope Church.

JACOBS, JUSTIN		C	16th Infantry

In Veteran Reserve Corps; served four years.

JACOBSON, MARTIN		F	18th Infantry

26

NAME.	RANK.	COMPANY.	REGIMENT.
JONAS, ELIAS		C	19th Infantry
JACOBSON, JOHN		B	22nd Infantry

Killed at Peach Tree Creek.

JOACHIMSTHAL, JOSEPH		F	26th Infantry

Wounded at Chancellorsville; served three years.

JACOBSON, JACOB		I	27th Infantry

Served three years.

JACOBSON, JULIUS		C	28th Infantry

Served three years.

JACOBS, LYMAN C.	2nd Lieutenant	B	36th Infantry

Promoted from Corporal.

JACOBY, FREDERICK		B	45th Infantry
JACOBSON, ADOLPH			2nd Cavalry
JACOBSON, DAVID		B	4th Cavalry
JACOBSON, JACOB		G	4th Cavalry
KLAUBER, CHARLES		K	1st Infantry
KOHN, JACOB			5th Infantry
			(reorganized)
KOHN, JULIUS		D	9th Infantry
KAUFFMAN, BENJAMIN		E	12th Infantry
KAUFMAN, JOSEPH		B	18th Infantry
KAUFMAN, ELI M.		I	20th Infantry
KAUFMAN, BENJAMIN		F	25th Infantry
KOHN, MARTIN	Corporal	H	26th Infantry

Wounded at Resaca, Georgia.

KAUFMAN, JOSEPH L.		H	33d Infantry
KAUFMAN, MICHAEL		I	43d Infantry
KAISER, FELIX		D	44th Infantry
KOHN, RUDOLPH		A	45th Infantry
KAUFMAN, FREDERICK		G	45th Infantry
KAUFMAN, ELI		H	50th Infantry
KAHNS, FREDERICK		C	1st Cavalry
KOHN, FREDERICK		C	1st Cavalry
KAUFMAN, JULIUS		H	2nd Cavalry

Died in the service.

NAME.	RANK.	COMPANY.	REGIMENT.
KLEIN, ADOLPH		L	3d Cavalry
KOHN, FRANZ			2nd Battery
KAUFMAN, JACOB A.			Permanent Guard
LOWENSTEIN, CHARLES		D	1st Infantry
LIEBENSTEIN, WILLIAM		B	3d Infantry
LISNER, HENRY		F	5th Infantry

Killed at Petersburg.

LOEBE, MICHAEL		C	6th Infantry
LIEBMAN, LOUIS		I	7th Infantry

Wounded at Hatchers' Run.

LEVY, THEODORE			10th Infantry
LEVI, ISIDORE		I	14th Infantry
LEVISON, ISAAC		E	18th Infantry

Died in the service.

LEWISON, LEWIS		L	22nd Infantry
LYON, BENJAMIN			23d Infantry

Died in the service.

LYONS, MOSES J.		G	24th Infantry
LIEBENSTEIN, PHILIP		B	26th Infantry
LIEBENSTEIN, W.		B	26th Infantry
LIPPMAN, HENRY			
	Commissary Sergeant	F	26th Infantry

Died of wounds.

LOEB, HENRY		C	35th Infantry
LOEB, LEWIS		E	36th Infantry
LANGSTAAT, GOTFRIED	1st Lieutenant	H	2nd Cavalry

Re-enlisted as Veteran; promoted from Sergeant;
served four years.

LIVERMORE, JOSEPH L.		L	2nd Cavalry

Wounded and captured.

LICHTENBERG, FREDERICK	Corporal	M	3d Cavalry

Served three years.

LOEB, ISAAC		C	4th Cavalry

Died in the service.

NAME.	RANK.	COMPANY.	REGIMENT.
MARX, FREDERICK		C	1st Infantry
MARKS, JACOB		H	1st Infantry
METZLER, JACOB		K	2nd Infantry

Wounded and captured at Gainesville.

| MOSES, EDGAR | | F | 7th Infantry |

Served four years.

| MARX, JACOB | | H | 9th Infantry |
| MARKS, JOSEPH B. | | G | 10th Infantry |

Died in the service.

MOSES, ALBERT		H	10th Infantry
MAAS, MARTON		B	11th Infantry
MEYER, SIMON		I	11th Infantry
MEYER, BERNARD	2nd Lieutenant	B	17th Infantry

Enlisted as Private.

MEYER, EMANUEL		B	17th Infantry
MAAS, FREDERICK		C	17th Infantry
MAAS, WILLIAM		D	17th Infantry

Wounded in action.

| MARX, PHILIP | | E | 18th Infantry |

Captured.

MOSES, RICHARD		C	21st Infantry
MOSES, JOHN		C	21st Infantry
MARX, JACOB		D	21st Infantry
MAYER, JOSEPH		C	24th Infantry
MAYER, LOUIS	Corporal	C	24th Infantry

Enlisted as Private; killed at Resaca, Georgia.

MAYER, JACOB		K	24th Infantry
MOSES, MARTIN		E	25th Infantry
MANN, NATHAN		G	25th Infantry

Died in the service.

| METZEL, ALEXANDER | Sergeant-Major | B | 26th Infantry |

Enlisted as Private.

| MEYER, LEOPOLD | | C | 26th Infantry |

Served three years.

| MANGOLD, NATHAN | | K | 26th Infantry |

Killed at Chancellorsville.

NAME.	RANK.	COMPANY.	REGIMENT.
MANDEL, THEOEORE		D	27th Infantry
Served three years.			
MANDEL, HEINRICH		D	27th Infantry
Wounded; captured; died as prisoner.			
MANDEL, FREDERICK		D	27th Infantry
Served three years.			
MARX, HENRY P.		C	33d Infantry
Served three years.			
MAIER, JACOB		K	48th Infantry
MAIER, HERMAN		A	50th Infantry
MAAS, FRITZ		K	51st Infantry
MOSES, ALFRED		D	52nd Infantry
MARCUS, BERNARD		A	1st Cavalry
MAYER, JOHN T.		B	1st Cavalry
MARX, FREDERICK		B	2nd Cavalry
Served three years.			
MORITZ, OSCAR		H	2nd Cavalry
MARKS, THEODORE		A	3d Cavalry
MOSES, REUEL E.		C	4th Cavalry
MARKS, HENRY	2nd Lieutenant		12th Battery
Enlisted as private; served three years.			
MAYERS, JACOB			13th Battery
MAIER, DAVID		C	1st Heavy Artillery
MANN, JACOB		C	1st Heavy Artillery
NAUMAN, MORITZ	Corporal	E	9th Infantry
Captured; served three years.			
NAUMAN, FREDERICK		E	9th Infantry
Served three years.			
NEWMAN, CARL		B	17th Infantry
NATHAN, DANIEL		I	24th Infantry
NEWSTADFOR, NATHAN		H	24th Infantry
Killed at Chickamauga, Georgia.			
NUSSBAUM, GEORGE		C	33d Infantry
Served three years.			
NATHAN, ADOLPH		A	41st Infantry

NAME.	RANK.	COMPANY.	REGIMENT.
NEWBAUM, MICHAEL		G	44th Infantry
NUSSBAUM, DANIEL		D	51st Infantry
NEUBERG, JACOB		H	2nd Cavalry
Died in the service.			
PERLEWITZ, HERMAN		H	1st Infantry
PERLEWITZ, H.	Sergeant	A	26th Infantry
POLASHAK, ADOLPH		H	26th Infantry
POLLACK, FREDERICK J.		B	3d Cavalry
Died in the service.			
RICE, MORRIS S.		C	1st Infantry
RICHTENSTEIN, JULIUS	Corporal	C	1st Infantry
Entered as Private.			
ROSE, ALEXANDER			5th Infantry
ROTHSCHILD, MAX			5th Infantry
ROSENBERG, HENRY		D	6th Infantry
RICE, JACOB		C	7th Infantry
Captured; died at Andersonville.			
ROSENBACH, CHARLES		F	8th Infantry
Veteran; served four years.			
ROSENTHAL, RUDOLPH		B	9th Infantry (reorganized)
ROTHSCHILD, WILLIAM		F	10th Infantry
ROSENAU, CHARLES B.		F	21st Infantry
ROSENBAUM, ARNOLD		C	24th Infantry
Died of wounds received at Kenesaw Mountain.			
ROSENTHAL, HENRY		D	26th Infantry
Wounded at Gettysburg.			
ROSENTHAL, WILLIAM		E	26th Infantry
Wounded in action.			
ROSENTHAL, EUGENE		K	31st Infantry
ROSENAU, CHARLES		A	35th Infantry
Died in the service.			
ROSENBERG, JAMES		C	36th Infantry
ROSENBERG, FREDERICK	Corporal	C	45th Infantry
ROSENFELD, LEOPOLD	Corporal	D	48th Infantry

NAME.	RANK.	COMPANY.	REGIMENT.
ROSENTHAL, AUGUST		E	48th Infantry
ROSENTHAL, WILLIAM		F	50th Infantry
ROSENHEIM, MAX		H	2nd Cavalry

Wounded at Grand Gulf, Missouri.

RICE, SIMON			1st Battery
RICE, NATHAN P.			5th Battery

Veteran; served four years.

ROSE, MOSES			6th Battery
RICE, NATHAN B.			12th Battery

STEINER, HENRY		D	1st Infantry
STEINER, FREDERICK		D	1st Infantry
STEINBERGER, JACOB		E	1st Infantry
SAMPSON, SAMUEL		I	2nd Infantry

Captured.

SCHWAB, SIMON		I	3d Infantry
SAMUELS, ALEXANDER		D	3d Infantry
	Commissary-Sergeant		

Enlisted as Private.

SAMUELS, ALEXANDER	Quartermaster		5th Infantry (reorganized)
SCHOENFELD, JOSEPH		A	5th Infantry
SAMUELS, DAVID		D	5th Infantry
SCHONEMAN, AUGUST	Corporal	D	9th Infantry

Enlisted as Private; served three years.

SOLOMON, JAMES F.		E	12th Infantry
SELIGMAN, LOUIS		{ K	13th Infantry
		{	24th Infantry
SAMPSON, SAMUEL		A	15th Infantry

Died in the service.

SOLOMON, EDWIN A.		D	16th Infantry
STEINMAN, JACOB		E	16th Infantry

Captured.

SIMON, JACOB		C	17th Infantry
SOLOMON, JAMES		C	17th Infantry
STEIN, SAMUEL		K	17th Infantry

Died in the service.

NAME.	RANK.	COMPANY.	REGIMENT.
SOLOMON, G. W.		E	19th Infantry
SAMSON, JOEL J.		E	21st Infantry
SEMISCH, JULIUS		A	26th Infantry
STEIN, JULIUS		C	26th Infantry

Killed at Chancellorsville.

SOLOMON, LEVI H.		A	29th Infantry
SAMPSON, REUBEN			33d Infantry
STERN, WILLIAM		F	33d Infantry

Served three years.

STERN, CHARLES		F	33d Infantry

Wounded; captured; died of wounds.

SELIG, LUDWIG			45th Infantry
SCHOENEMAN, DAVID		F	49th Infantry
SACHS, LEWIS			49th Infantry
SALMON, JOSEPH		H	1st Cavalry

Captured.

SEIDENBURG, HENRY		D	1st Cavalry
SACHS, LOUIS		H	2nd Cavalry

Served three years.

SCHLESINGER, WILLIAM		M	3d Cavalry
SACHS, WILLIAM G.		A	4th Cavalry
STEINMAN, WILLIAM		A	1st Heavy Artillery
SIMON, CHARLES		K	1st Heavy Artillery
SACHS, SAMUEL			9th Battery

Served four years.

VOGEL, CARL		I	34th Infantry
VOGEL, JULIUS	Sergeant	K	45th Infantry

WISE, SOLOMON		K	1st Infantry
WOLF, VICTOR	Captain	C	8th Infantry

Promoted from Lieutenant.

WEISS, JACOB		G	10th Infantry

Served three years.

WOLF, JACOB		B	11th Infantry
WOLF, ABRAHAM		G	11th Infantry

NAME.	RANK.	COMPANY.	REGIMENT.
WOLF, FRANK	Sergeant	D	12th Infantry

Enlisted as Private.

WETZEL, ALEXANDER	Major	B	26th Infantry

Enlisted as a Private in the 20th Wisconsin Volunteers; promoted to Corporal, Sergeant and Major for bravery at Chancellorsville; he was mortally wounded at Gettysburg.

WOLF, ALBERT		G	26th Infantry

Died of wounds.

WOLF, ABRAHAM		I	38th Infantry

Leg amputated.

WENK, THEODORE		H	45th Infantry
WOLF, SAMUEL		A	51st Infantry
WOLF, ADAM		A	51st Infantry
WOLF, JACOB		C	51st Infantry

WYOMING TERRITORY.

NAME.	RANK.	COMPANY.	REGIMENT.
JUDELL, H.		D	1st Infantry

SOLDIERS OF THE CIVIL WAR UNCLASSIFIED AS TO COMMANDS.

Absent from their respective places in the foregoing rolls are the names of a large number of men whose participation in the Civil Conflict is found of record, but of whom the connection with their respective commands remains unnoted. These names are printed in the following list—a supplement to the ample quota of Jewish soldiers who did duty during the Civil War.

ALABAMA.

BRISK, ISAAC

ARKANSAS.

ADLER, BENJAMIN   FEIST, MARCUS
FEIST, SAMUEL

GEORGIA.

ALEXANDER, JOSEPH   HILZHEIM, ALEXANDER
BREN, ROBERT   Killed at Missionary Ridge.
BRAND, HERMAN   KRAUS, WILLIAM
BUSH, GEORGE   LEVY, ALBERT
  Killed in action.   LEVY, ABRAHAM
BLANKENSEE, J.   LEVY, W. E.
  Killed in action.   Killed in action.
COHEN, ISAAC G.   MOISE, E. W.
COHEN, ISAAC S.   MARCUS, M.
COHEN, M.   MINIS, P. H.
COHEN, M. S.   MAGNUS, ——
FRANK, ISAAC   ROSE, GEORGE
GOODMAN, A.   RUSSEL, W.
HEYMAN, A.   SOLOMON, W. C.

SOLOMONS, L.
WEIL, E. A.
WEIL, HENRY
WEISS, S.
  Buried at Richmond.

WEISS, H.
WEISS, L.
  Died of wounds; buried at Richmond.
WEISS, HENRY W.

ILLINOIS.

CAHN, AL.
CASS, ——
FRÜHLING, ——
HIRSCH, WOLF
HECHT, ——
HELDMAN, MORITZ
HEFLER, ——
KLEIN, ——
KAHN, S.
JONES, BENJAMIN
JONES, DAVID
JONES, ABRAHAM
JONES, ADOLPH
JONES, ISAAC
JONES, JOSEPH
JACOBS, BERNARD
JONES, MOSES
JONES, SOLOMON

JONES, LEVI
JONES, HENRY
KING, ASA
KARLENBACH, MORRIS
KAHN, S.
LEDERMAN, MOSES
LEDERMAN, DAVID
LIPPOLD, JULIUS
LESTER, JOSEPH
LEDERMAN, DANIEL
LEDERMAN, SOLOMON
LESTER, MARCUS
LIPPOLD, GOTTLIEB
LESTER, SIMON
LILIENFIELD, ——
LEDERMAN, JOSEPH
LESTER, ISAAC
MENKE, HERMAN

MENKE, HENRY

INDIANA.

ABRAHAMS, J.
ANCHUTZ, G.
ANSPACH, NOAH
ACKERMAN, FRANK
BALL, LEVI
DAVIDSON, ELIAS
DAVIS, NATHAN
DAVIS, ISAAC
DAVIS, LEVI
DAVIS, AARON

DAVIS, MOSES
DAVIS, ABRAHAM
FRANK, GOTTLIEB
FRIEDMAN, FRANK
FREEMAN, NATHAN
FRANK, DAVID
FRANK, ISAAC
GREEN, AARON
GREEN, JACOB
GOODMAN, ISAAC

GREEN, HEYMAN
HALLER, NATHAN
HALLER, JOSEPH
HART, ISAAC
HAMMERSLEY, MOSES
HAMMERSLEY, JACOB
HALLER, DAVID
HARRIS, LEVI
HEINEMAN, CHARLES
ISRAEL, JOSEPH
ISAACS, PHILIP
ISAACS, SIMPSON
ISAACS, REUBEN

ISRAEL, ELIJAH
ISAACS, M.
JUDAH, ANDREW
JACOBS, ISAAC
JONES, ISRAEL
LEHMAN, B.
LEHMAN, JACOB
POLLOCK, J.
ROSENBERG, D.
SANDERS, ISAAC
SANDERS, SAMUEL
SANDERS, AARON
WALLACH, B.

WISE, LOUIS

KANSAS.

DAVIS, ABRAHAM

COHN, DAVID

FRANK, HARRY I.

KENTUCKY.

DAVIS, ISAAC
DAVID, ABRAHAM
EHRLICH, MAYER
EHRLICH, WILLIAM

MOSES, ABRAHAM
MAYER, JACOB
MAYER, ISAAC
WOLF, ABRAHAM

LOUISIANA

AARON, ISAAC
ARONSTEIN, MOSES
BLUM, MOSES
BAER, HERMAN
COHEN, JOSEPH
KAUFMAN, MORRIS

LEON, ALEXANDER
LEVENSON, ——
ROSENAU, HERMAN
RIED, ——
ROSENAU, SIEGMUND
WOLF, ABRAHAM

MARYLAND.

KAUFMAN, ISAAC
MOSES, JOSEPH

NEWGARTEN, HARRY
WOLF, JACOB

MASSACHUSETTS.

ARNOLD, O.
ACKERMAN, JOSEPH
ARNOLD, ISAAC
ACKERMAN, DANIEL
BENJAMIN, MARK
BENDER, JACOB
BENJAMIN, SAMUEL
BENJAMIN, JOSEPH
COLEMAN, JOSEPH
COLEMAN, MOSES
DANIELS, MARCUS
DAVIS, MOSES
DAVIS, LEVI
FRIEDMAN, GOTTLIEB
FRANK, GUSTAV
FREEMAN, ABRAHAM
FREEMAN, NATHAN
GREEN, DAVID
GOLDSMITH, JOSEPH
GREEN, LEVI
GREEN, AARON
HARRIS, ISAAC
HARTMAN, MORITZ
HALLER, DAVID
JACOBS, JACOB
JACOBS, DAVID

JACOBS, DANIEL
LEHMAN, FREDERICK
LEHMAN, DANIEL
MEIER, JOSEPH
MAIER, HERMAN
MOSES, SAMUEL
MANN, BENJAMIN
MANN, ISAAC
MANUEL, FRANK
MEYERS, ISAAC
MEYER, LUDWIG
MAYER, FREDERICK
NEWMAN, FRANK
PHINNEY, ISAAC
PHILLIPS, SAMUEL
RICE, MOSES
RICH, SAMUEL
RICE, OSCAR
RICE, JACOB
SAMUEL, SOLOMON
SANDERS, LEWIS
SIMONS, BENJAMIN
SANGER, DANIEL
SANGER, THEODORE
SANDERS, NATHAN
WIESENBACH, GUSTAV
WISE, JOSEPH

MICHIGAN.

ACKERMAN, SAMUEL
ARNOLD, LEWIS
ARNOLD, MARCUS
ACKERMAN, ABRAHAM
ACKERMAN, JACOB
BALL, DAVID
BENJAMIN, M.

BENJAMIN, E.
COLEMAN, LEVI
COLEMAN, ISAAC
COLEMAN, DAVID
DAVIS, OSCAR
DAVIS, DAVID
DAVIS, ISAAC

Davis, Aaron
Davidson, Isaac
Freeman, Phineas
Fuchs, David
Freeman, Levi
Green, Isaac
Green, Benjamin
Green, Nathan
Hart, Isaac
Hart, Samuel
Harris, Israel
Harris, Abraham
Jones, Jacob
Jones, Abraham
Jones, David
Jones, Isaac

Jones, Henry
Jacobs, Lewis
Kaiser, Jacob
King, Aaron
King, Jacob
Karlenbach, Joseph
King, Marcus
Lehman, Gottlieb
Meyers, Joseph
Myers, David
Newman, Moses
Newman, Joseph
Phillips, J.
Rose, David
Rich, Levi
Sanders, J.

MISSISSIPPI.

Levy, Meyer
  Killed in action.
Lichtenstein, S.

Morse, Charles
Rosenau, Marx
Weil, J.
  Died of wounds.

MISSOURI.

Adler, George
Adolph, Philip
Arnold, Nathan
Baer, Isaac
Baer, William
Block, David
Ball, Leon
Baum, Louis
Cline, Charles
Cline, Henry
Clifman, Asa
David, Daniel
Davidson, Isaac
David, Ephraim

Davis, Emanuel
Gottschalk, Louis
Gottschalk, Frederic
Green, David
Green, Adolph
Hammer, Isaac
Hartman, Jacob
Holzinger, Charles
Jacobson, A.
Joel, E.
Joel, Benjamin
Jones, Isaac
Jones, Henry
Lehman, M.

LEIBOLD, GUSTAV
LEUPP, JACOB
MEYERS, JOSEPH
NEWMAN, G.
NOGEL, E.

REXINGER, MOSES
RIA, MORRIS
SEGAL, BENJAMIN
TRIBURG, EUGENE
WOLF, CHARLES
WOLF, JOSEPH

NEW JERSEY.

ACKERMAN, JOSEPH
ALEXANDER, ADOLPH
ABRAHAM, JACOB
ACKERMAN, DAVID
ACKERMAN, AARON
ALEXANDER, CHARLES
ADLER, WILLIAM
ADLER, HENRY
ARNOLD, JACOB
ACKERMAN, JOSEPH
ACKERMAN, MORRIS
ABRAMS, ELIAS
ACKERMAN, AARON
ACKERMAN, ABRAHAM
ABRAMS, JACOB
ARNOLD, MICHAEL
ABRAMS, CHARLES
BUXBAUM, WILLIAM
BAER, JOSEPH
BEHRENS, CHARLES
BAUER, JOSEPH A.
BALL, ABRAHAM
BACHMAN, JACOB
BAUER, JACOB S.
BRILL, JACOB
BAUER, MORRIS
BACHMAN, WILLIAM H.
COLEMAN, MOSES
COLEMAN, REUBEN
DAVIS, ISAAC
DAVIS, NATHAN

DIAZ, HENRY
DAVIS, ISAAC C.
DAVISON, LEWIS
FREEMAN, MORRIS
FREEMAN, ALEXANDER
FREEMAN, AARON
FREEMAN, SAMUEL
FUCHS, JACOB
FUCHS, MICHAEL
FRANKS, HENRY P.
GREEN, AARON
GREEN, MOSES
GEIGER, GEORGE
GEISINGER, JACOB
GEISINGER, ISAAC
GEISINGER, FREDERICK
GOTTSCHALK, SAMUEL
GREEN, AARON S.
GEIGER, JACOB
GREEN, JOSEPH
GOODMAN, MARCUS
HARRIS, DAVID
HARDENDORF, JACOB
HARRIS, ISAAC
HOLZMAN, GEORGE
HARRIS, DAVID
HARRIS, BENJAMIN
HERRMAN, HENRY
HAHN, MARTIN
HESS, CHARLES
HESS, SAMUEL

HAHN, CHARLES	KLEIN, SAMUEL
HARRIS, ABRAHAM	KING, JACOB
HOFMAN, LEWIS	KOHLER, ELIAS
HAHN, MORRIS	LOEB, BENJAMIN
HOFMAN, DAVID	LOZIER, ALEXANDER
HARRIS, SAMUEL	LYON, EBENEZER
HOFMAN, BENJAMIN	LYON, LEWIS
HOFMAN, ISAAC	LEHMAN, JOSEPH
HART, DAVID	MYERS, JULIUS
HOFMAN, JACOB	MEYER, ALEXANDER
HARRIS, JOSEPH	MEYER, HENRY
HARTMAN, GUSTAV	MEYER, FRANK
HARRIS, JACOB B.	MEYER, JOSEPH
HART, ISAAC	MEIER, CHARLES
HART, JACOB C.	MEYER, JOSEPH
ISAAC, HENRY	MEIER, CHARLES
JACOBS, HENRY	MEYERS, SAMUEL
JACOBS, WILLIAM	MEYER, JACOB
JOSEPHS, FREDERICK	MORITZ, GEORGE
JACOBS, JOSEPH	MEYERS, ADOLPH
JACOBS, CHARLES	MEYER, ISAAC
KING, MOSES	MEYERS, JOSEPH
KOENIG, MAXIMILIAN	MEYERS, LOUIS
KUHN, THEO.	MARX, CHARLES
KOHLER, HENRY	MEYER, JOSEPH P.
KUHN, FERDINAND	MOSES, WILLIAM
KLEIN, LUDWIG	MOSES, A.
KING, ISAAC	MARKS, JOSEPH
KING, ISAAC M.	MEIER, HERMAN
KING, JOSEPH	MEIER, LEWIS
KONIG, GUSTAV	NEWMAN, JOSEPH
KLEIN, JOSEPH	NEWMAN, JACOB
KOCH, FREDERIC	NEWMAN, JULIUS
KING, ALEXANDER	NAUMAN, JULIUS
KUHN, JACOB	NEWMAN, DAVID
KING, ABRAHAM	NEWMAN, LEVI
KING, LEWIS	NEWMAN, JOEL
KOHLER, JACOB	NEWMAN, DAVID

SOMINSON, FREDERICK
SANGER, CARL
SIMONS, JOSEPH
SIGAL, BENJAMIN
SIMON, SAMUEL
SIMONS, LEVI
SIMONS, JOSEPH
STEIN, LOUIS
SIMONSON, JESSE
STEINBACH, JOSEPH
SIMONS, ISAAC

SIMON, HENRY
STAHL, LEOPOLD
VOGEL, FERDINAND
VOGEL, LOUIS
VOGEL, JOSEPH
VOGEL, LEWIS
WOLF, AUGUST
WEISS, ADOLPH
WOLF, CHARLES
WOLF, FREDERICK
WOLF, JOSEPH
WOLF, WILLIAM

NEW YORK.

ASHER, MOSES
ASHER, ISAAC
ASSENHEIMER, ISAAC
ADLER, MOSES
ASHER, DAVID
ADLER, MARCUS
ASH, ISAAC
ARNHEIM, OSCAR
ADLER, DAVID
AARON, DAVID
ASH, MOSES
ARNHEIM, GUSTAV
ASH, LEWIS
AARON, LOUIS
AARON, MOSES
ARNOLD, FRANK
ALTMAN, ISAAC
AUERBACH, GOTTLIEB
ACKERMAN, ADOLPH
ALTMAN, CHARLES
ACKERMAN, GUSTAV
AUERBACH, MOSES
BUNSTEIN, MOSES
BACHARACH, MARCUS
BLUMENSTEIN, MAYER

BACHARACH, MORITZ
BERNSTEIN, DAVID
BLUM, ADOLPH
BRILL, HENRY
BLUM, ISAAC
BARUCH, M.
BAER, ABRAHAM
BALL, SIMON
BACHMAN, ABRAHAM
BAER, MOSES
BIEN, MORITZ
BERLINER, A.
BRESLAUER, ALEXANDER
BAUER, JULIUS
BAUM, C.
BLUMENTHAL, CHARLES
BAUM, WILLIAM
BACHARACH, SIMON
BAMBERGER, LOUIS
COHEN, MOSES
DAVIDSON, JACOB
DAVIDSON, ISAAC
DAVIDSON, OSCAR
DAVID, MOSES
DAVID, ISAAC

27

Eppenstein, Morris

Ehrlich, J.

Eiseman, Max

Friedberg, H.

Friedman, Isaac

Fleischman, M.

Friedman, Adolph

Fleischman, George

Goodman, Mayer

Gottlieb, Moses

Goodman, M.

Gottlieb, A.

Goodman, Lewis

Goldsmith, I.

Harris, M.

Harris, George

Harris, Adolph

Heineman, Adolph

Hochheim, M.

Jacobson, M.

Jacobson, A.

Jones, David

Jones, Meier

Jones, Oscar

Jones, Adolph

Jones, Martin

Kohn, Mayer

Kohn, Alexander

Kaufman, Isaac

Kahn, Oscar

Koch, J.

Katz, Jacob

Kong, Isaac

Loeb, Jacob

Loeb, Moses

Lichtenstein, Jacob

Limburger, Isaac

Levy, Bernhard

Lippman, Moses

Lazarus, Edward

Lowenthal, Simon

Lederman, Moritz

Lowenstein, Isaac

Landauer, Joseph

Mannheimer, Moses

Mann, Joseph

May, Adolph

Maas, Frederick

Mantel, Lewis

Mendelson, Joseph

Marcus, Oscar

Mandelbaum, Isaac

Nathan, Simon

Nathanson, Jacob

Nussbaum, Moses

Oppenheimer, Maier

Ochs, Moses

Pinkson, Gustav

Proskauer, Jacob

Pollock, Isaac

Pollock, Moses

Posner, Joseph

Rosenbaum, Joseph

Rothschild, Meyer

Rothschild, Jacob

Rosenfeld, Abraham

Raphael, Joseph

Rosenblatt, Julius

Strauss, Moses

Strauss, Oscar

Sinzheimer, Gustav

Schoenthal, George

Selignan, Joseph

Schoenberg, Mayer

Schoeneman, Harry

Silberman, Moses

Spiegel, Louis

Schiff, Daniel

SCHONEWALT, MORITZ
SCHWAB, ADOLPH
SCHWAB, HENRY
STERN, FREDERICK
SACHS, LEWIS
SCHLESSINGER, ELI
SCHWARZSCHILD, HENRY

WEINBERG, JULIUS
WIENER, MORITZ
WEIL, JULIUS
WASSEMAN, MORRIS
WASSEMAN, SIMON
WEINSTEIN, JOSEPH
WISE, SIMON

NORTH CAROLINA.

ABRAHAM, S.
COHEN, MOSES
MAYER, NATHAN

MEYER, SAMUEL
OPPENHEIM, DAVID
WOLF, JOSEPH
    Killed in action.

OHIO.

AARONSTEIN, I.
ALTMAN, FRANK
ABRAHAM, ALEXANDER
ACKERMAN, HENRY
ALEXANDER, JACOB
ALEXANDER, ISAAC
ACKERMAN, JOSEPH
ALEXANDER, DAVID
ALTMAN, SAMUEL
ALTMAN, SOLOMON
BAUER, GUSTAV
BALL, LEWIS
BAUER, JACOB
BALL, ABRAHAM
BASH, MOSES
BRILL, DAVID
BALL, SOLOMON
BASH, BERNARD
BAER, ISAAC
BAUM, CHARLES
BLAU, EMIL
BLAU, A.
CLINE, JACOB

COLEMAN, ABRAHAM
COLEMAN, JACOB
COLEMAN, DAVID
DAVIS, JOSEPH
DAVIS, ASA
DAVIS, SAMUEL
DAVIS, FRANK
DAVIS, DAVID
DAVIS, HENRY
DAVIS, LEVI
DAVIS, ABRAHAM
DAVIS, OSCAR
DAVIS, ELI
DAVIS, ISAAC
DAVIS, LEWIS
DAVIS, BENJAMIN
DAVIS, JACOB
DAVIS, ISRAEL
DAVIS, NATHAN
EHRLICH, ADOLPH
EHRLICH, CHARLES
EHRLICH, LEWIS
FIX, BERNARD

Franks, Gustav	Hahneman, J.
Frank, Heyman	Isaacson, Henry
Friedburg, Philip	Isaacs, Moses
Fix, Lewis	Israel, Elias
Fuchs, David	Jones, Isaac
Freund, Daniel	Jones, Henry
Freeman, Abraham	Jones, Jacob
Freund, Jacob	Jones, David
Freeman, Samuel	Jones, Aaron
Fuchs, Salomon	Jones, Benjamin
Friedman, Jacob	Jones, Julius
Fuchs, Jacob	Jones, Levi
Frank, David	Klein, Jesse
Green, Isaac	Klein, Lewis
Green, Jacob	Koch, Charles
Goodman, Joseph	King, Benjamin
Goodman, David	Klein, Charles
Green, Levi	King, Joseph
Green, David	Klein, Henry
Green, Abraham	Konigsburger, Henry
Harris, Solomon	Lippold, Jacob
Harris, Levi	Ludwig, Lewis
Hart, Isaac	Lederman, Joseph
Hofman, Henry	Ludwig, Jacob
Harris, Ephraim	Lester, Benjamin
Hays, Alexander	Ludwig, Isaac
Heller, Charles	Lederman, Samuel
Harris, Abraham	Ludwig, Daniel
Haller, Benjamin	Lester, David
Harris, Simon	Ludwig, Samuel
Hochstedter, Hugo	Lippold, Frederick
Heine, Henry	Ludwig, Noah
Hart, Frank	Lowenstein, J.
Harris, Benjamin	Lowenthal, I.
Harris, Samuel	Levi, Nathan
Hart, Benjamin	Levi, Henry I.
Harris, Lewis	Moses, Henry
Heller, Jacob	Marks, Lester
Hays, David	Mangold, Henry

Moses, Perry
Mann, Lewis
Marienthal, Simon
Michels, Abraham
Moses, Asa
Mangold, Jacob
Marks, Jacob
Munz, Gottlieb
Moses, Charles
Manuel, James
Metzger, Jacob
Mangold, George
Moses, James
Marx, J. H.
Moses, Enoch
Mangold, Joseph
Mann, Alexander
Moses, William
Moak, J.
Moses, Enoch
Nieman, Theodore
Nieman, Charles
Ochs, Julius
Orbanski, Abraham
Phillips, Emanuel
Philip, Noah
Phillips, Lewis
Phillips, Daniel
Pike, H.

Perley, V.
Rapp, David
Rich, Charles
Rapp, Adolph
Rose, Aaron
Rapp, Jacob
Rose, Nathan
Rose, David
Rubd, William
Schweitzer, Jacob
Switzer, Henry
Sampson, Frank
Schenk, Salomon
Schwarz, Gottlieb
Schlosser, S.
Schiff, Simon
Tachan, Henry G.
Tannhauser, A.
Utz, Jacob
Utz, Joseph
Utz, Samuel
Yost, Ephraim
Yost, David
Yost, Charles
Yost, Daniel
Yost, Henry
Wisner, Henry
Wittkowsky, H.
Wittkowsky, K.

PENNSYLVANIA.

De Young, Charles
Fleisher, Moyer
   32nd Regiment of Pennsylvania State Militia.
Highhill, Israel
Highhill, Solomon
Lehman, Solomon

Levy, Elias
Lewi, David
Samuel Abraham
Stern, Israel W.
   Served four years and three months.
Stern, Simon

SOUTH CAROLINA.

BARUCH, D.

COHEN, O.
  Killed in action.

COHEN, HENRY
  Buried at Richmond.

GOLDSMITH, ABRAHAM

HIRSCH, ISAAC

JACOBS, HENRY
  Killed in action.

LEHMAN, ABRAHAM
  Killed in action.

LEOPOLD, JACK
  Wounded in action.

LYONS, ISAAC L.
  Seriously wounded.

MOSES, A. I.

MOSES, ISAAC C.

MENKEN, NATHAN

MILLER, EZRA B.
  Killed in action.

MOSES, DR. FRANK J.

NATHAN, JULIUS

SIMON, A.

SOLOMON, H.

WEISS, SAMUEL
  Killed in action.

TENNESSEE.

FELSENTHAL, —
FELSENTHAL, — } (Brothers)

FRAUENTHAL, M.

SOLOMON, ERNST

TEXAS.

FLEISCHEL, CAPTAIN

KAUFMAN, C.

KAUFMAN, K.

MAYER, LEO E.
  Captured.

VIRGINIA.

BACHARACH, M.
  Buried at Richmond.

BACHARACH, S.
  Buried at Richmond.

EICHEL, JACOB

EICHEL, A.

FALK, EMANUEL

FLEISCHMAN, SOLOMON

GOLDBERG, ——

GANS, LEON

HOLZINGER, E.

HESSBERG, I.
  Killed in action.

KAYTON, HERRMAN

KROMER, C. H.

LEVIN, SOLOMON M.

MOISE, WILBORN

MARCUS, MADISON

MILLER, CHARLES

WEIL, CHARLES

WEST VIRGINIA.

BLONDHEIM, H.

ADDENDA TO LISTS OF SOLDIERS.

[Additional names received after printing of lists, and before close of present form.]

CHARLES BAUM served in the 80th Ohio Infantry, during the Civil War. Mr. Baum is now a resident and a leading merchant of Washington, D. C.

SOLOMON POLOCK and LOUIS POLOCK, two brothers, served in the Army during the Mexican War.

LIEUTENANT LAUCHHEIMER, serves as Judge Advocate-General in the Regular Army of the United States.

JACOB LYON enlisted in June, 1854, in Battery E, 2nd Regiment, United States Artillery. He re-enlisted in June, 1859, and was honorably discharged in June, 1864. Participated in eighteen engagements.

CHARLES STEIN enlisted in the United States Marine Corps, June 22nd, 1864, at Philadelphia, Pa., became sergeant and was honorably discharged, June 22nd, 1868. He died on March 6th, 1881, from disease contracted while in the service.

MORITZ AUGENSTEIN served in Company E, 52nd Regiment, New York Infantry, during the Civil War.

SIMON FLEISHER served in Company A, 18th North Carolina Infantry, during the Civil War.

MORRIS M. KATZ served in Company A, 18th North Carolina Infantry, during the Civil War.

ABRAHAM MAYER served in Company A, 18th North Carolina Infantry, during the Civil War.

AARON STERN served in the Regular Army before and during the Civil War. Now attached to the Record and Pension Division of the War Department, at Washington, D. C.

CHARLES KATZENSTEIN, Regular Army, now connected with the Record and Pension Division of the War Department.

BENJAMIN JACOBS, Regular Army, now in Adjutant General's office, at Washington, D. C.

STATISTICAL.

NUMBER OF JEWISH SOLDIERS WHO SERVED IN DIFFERENT WARS OF THE UNITED STATES.

In the Continental Armies (including patriots)   46
In the War of 1812   44
In the Mexican War   58
In the United States Regular Army   96
In the United States Navy   78

IN THE CIVIL WAR.

Staff Officers in the Union Army   16
Staff Officers in the Confederate Army   24
Officers in the Confederate Navy   11
Soldiers classified in Regiments from different States who served
    in the Union and Confederate Armies during the Civil
    War 7038
Soldiers unclassified as to States who served during the Civil
    War 834
Other Soldiers (indicated in Addenda)   12

Total in all wars 8527

IN THE CIVIL WAR.

NUMBER OF SOLDIERS CLASSIFIED ACCORDING TO STATES.

Alabama	135	Nevada	3
Arkansas	53	New Hampshire	2
California	28	New Jersey	277
Connecticut	17	New Mexico	2
District of Columbia	3	New York	1996
Florida	2	North Corolina	58
Georgia	144	Ohio	1004
Illinois	702	Pennsylvania	527
Indiana	475	Rhode Island	4
Iowa	12	South Carolina	182
Kansas	9	Tennessee	38
Kentucky	22	Texas	103
Louisiana	224	Vermont	1
Maine	1	Virginia	119
Maryland	7	Washington Territory	1
Massachusetts	174	West Virginia	7
Michigan	130	Wisconsin	331
Mississippi	158	Wyoming Territory	1
Missouri	86		

Total 7038

JEWISH PATRIOTISM IN CIVIL LIFE.

The foregoing lists of Jewish soldiers in the armies of the Civil War may well be supplemented by a review of Jewish activity in civil walks in connection with that momentous struggle. In the political movements for the abolition of slavery there were not lacking many Jews who took an active and at times a leading part in the moulding of public opinion, and the fact that the influence of these men did not become more widespread may be regarded as almost wholly due to their having been but recent immigrants from foreign lands and therefore comparative strangers in the communities in which they settled. Such men were Michael Heilprin, the scholar and philanthropist whose devotion to liberty had previously been attested by his activity as a member of Kossuth's civil staff during the Hungarian Revolution; Dr. Edward Morwitz, then a writer and afterwards publisher of the "Demokrat," a German newspaper of Philadelphia, and Rev. Dr. Sabato Morais, then and still at present the Rabbi of a Philadelphia congregation. Dr. David Einhorn's ardent advocacy of the abolition of slavery led to his removal from Baltimore; and in New York, Rev. Samuel M. Isaacs, then Rabbi of a congregation of that city and editor of the "Jewish Messenger," took an earnest part in the movement.

In the West, among the pioneers of the Jewish community, are to be named in this connection Dr. James Horwitz, of Cleveland; Rabbi Liebman Adler, then of Detroit; Henry Greenebaum, then a member of the City Council of Chicago Edward Salomon, afterwards County Clerk of Cook county and subsequently Brigadier-General in the army, and Leopold Mayer and Michael Greenebaum, likewise of Chicago. In an article on the German pioneers of Chicago, published in a late issue in the "Times-Herald" of that city (June 9th, 1895), are printed some interesting reminiscences of ante-bellum times, wherein Mr. Mayer is quoted as follows :

"The fugitive slave law set us at loggerheads with the powers that were. It was sometime in 1853 when a United States Marshal, on the corner of Van Buren and Sherman streets, arrested a poor devil of a negro as a fugitive. A crowd of citizens, led by Michael Greenebaum, liberated the prisoner and on the same evening a big meeting was held to ratify this act. The enthusiasm in this meeting reached its highest pitch when Long John Wentworth entered the hall and publicly declared from the platform that he would be with us in resisting the enforcement of the barbaric law. From that time we slowly but steadily marched up hill. The first official call for a German mass meeting to join the Republican party appeared in the 'Staats Zeitung' signed by George Schneider, Adolph Loeb, Julius Rosenthal, a cigar dealer by the name of Hanson and my humble self."

Here we find four Jews among five leaders of the German population of Chicago in a great political movement.

In another portion of the same article another of the old pioneers, William Vocke, Esq., referring to the record of the 24th Illinois regiment, is quoted as follows:

"Our regiment served three years and three months. With recruits taken in from time to time, fully 1200 men had joined it. Only 240 of us returned. One company of this regiment consisted exclusively of Hebrews. It was led by Captain Lasalle, who stuck it out with us to the last."

Another striking incident of the forcefulness of Jewish sentiment in the great agitation that preceded the outbreak of the war is recorded by Rear Admiral George Henry Preble, U. S. N., in his "History of the Flag of the United States of America," (Houghton, Mifflin & Co., Boston, fourth edition, 1894.) We quote as follows: (Page 406).

"On the 11th of February, 1861, Mr. Lincoln, the President-elect of the United States, left his home in Springfield, Illinois, for the seat of government, accompanied by a few friends. His fellow-citizens and neighbors gathered at the railway station to wish him God-speed. He was visibly affected by this kind attention, and addressed the assembly of his friends in a few words, requesting they would all pray that he might receive the Divine assistance in the responsibilities he was about to encounter, without which he could not succeed, but with which success was certain. Before leaving Springfield, he received from Abraham Kohn, city clerk of Chicago, a fine picture of the flag of the Union, bearing an inscription in Hebrew on its folds. The verses being the 4th to 9th verses of the first chapter of Joshua, in which Joshua was commanded to reign over a whole land, the last verse being: 'Have I not commanded thee? Be strong and of a good courage; be not afraid, neither be thou dismayed; for the Lord, thy God, is with thee whithersoever thou goest.' "

In a recent speech at Ottawa, Kansas, on June 20, 1895, (quoted in the *Reform Advocate*, of Chicago, July 13, 1895,) Governor William McKinley, of Ohio, referred to this incident as follows:

"What more beautiful conception than that which prompted Abraham Kohn, of Chicago, in February, 1861, to send to Mr. Lincoln, on the eve of his starting to Washington, to assume the office of president, a flag of our country, bearing upon its silken folds these words from the first chapter of Joshua: 'Have I not commanded thee? Be strong and of good courage. Be not afraid, neither be thou dismayed, for the Lord, thy God is with thee, whithersoever thou goest. There shall not any man be able to stand before thee all the days of thy life. As I was with Moses so shall I be with thee. I will not fail thee nor forsake thee.'

"Could anything have given Mr. Lincoln more cheer, or been better calculated to sustain his courage or to strengthen his faith in the mighty work before him? Thus commanded, thus assured, Mr. Lincoln journeyed to the capital, where he took the oath of office and registered in heaven an oath to save the Union. And the Lord, our God, was with him, until every obligation of oath and duty was sacredly kept and honored. Not any man was able to stand before him. Liberty was the more firmly enthroned, the Union was saved, and the flag which he carried floated in triumph and glory from every flagstaff of the republic."

In reply to a letter addressed to him by the daughter of Abraham Kohn, Mrs. Dankmar Adler (whose husband, the architect of the Auditorium building and one of the architects of the Columbian Exposition, had fought through the war and been wounded at Chickamauga), Major McKinley wrote: ''The incident deeply impressed me when I first learned of it, and I have taken occasion to use it, as in my speech at Ottowa, to which you refer.

'' I am very glad to have been able to give publicity to this striking incident, and I am sure that the family of Mr. Kohn should feel very proud of his patriotic act.''

The patriotism of the Jewish people in the support of the soldiers in the field was no less positive than their participation in the fray itself. The various bodies organized at the North for the support of the government, such as the Sanitary Commissions, counted a full quota of Jewish citizens among their membership everywhere.

Prominent in the West among these earnest co-workers in the cause of the Union was the lamented Benjamin F. Peixotto, of Cleveland, who severed the affiliations of an active political career and took an earnest part in arousing the patriotic sentiment of the people. He contributed largely of his means to the furtherance of the civil movements in support of the men at the front and attained a recognized position as a leader. When in 1872, the Jews of Roumania were subjected to persecutions by the Government of that principality, Mr. Pexiotto was selected as Consul of the United States at Bucharest,* in

---

* The appointment of Mr. Peixotto to the Roumanian Consulate was initiated and brought about by Hon. Simon Wolf, who afterwards made a tour among the lodges of the Order of B'nai B'rith for the purpose of raising funds to strengthen the Consul's position at Bucharest and to enable him to more effectively exert his influence in behalf of the persecuted Roumanian Jews.

In this connection mention may well and properly be made of Mr. Wolf's untiring efforts, both in his early home in Ohio and later in Washington, in behalf of the Union cause. The movements organized by Mr. Wolf in Washington for the systematic aid of the sick and wounded in the numerous hospitals then established in and

which capacity his services were of marked importance to the cause of humanity and won for him the gratitude of the Jewish people at large, as well as the confidence and support of our government. Other Jewish patriotic leaders in the West during the war were Isidor Busch, of St. Louis; Henry Mack, of Cincinnatti; Nathan Bloom, of Louisville, and others that ought, perhaps, to find mention here.

Notable in this connection at the East was Hon. A. S. Solomons, now the General Agent of the Baron de Hirsch Trust in the United States. Before the war and during its early years he was a leading Jewish citizen of Washington and enjoyed the confidence and esteem of President Lincoln, of Secretaries Stanton and Chase, and of many other leading spirits of the time. His home was a centre of patriotic activity and he made heavy sacrifices of his personal interest in behalf of the Union cause.

In the South, during the dark and trying days of the Confederacy, the Jewish citizens of that section displayed to the full their devotion to the cause which they held at heart. The Jewish Southerners were as zealous in their efforts as were their neighbors all about them, and however mistaken was their contention, they adhered to it tenaciously. A Jew, it is said, fired the first gun against Fort Sumtner, and another Jew gave the last shelter to the fleeing President and Cabinet of the fallen Confederacy.

Throughout the country, North and South, the earnestness of the Jewish character found expression through an active participation by Jewish citizens in the great movements of the time. A closer examination of this feature of our subject would involve a detailed reference to the leading members of the various Jewish communities throughout the land, and carry

about Washington gained for him the recognition of the Government and the friendship of General Grant. In this work Mr. Wolf enlisted the support of the mass of the Jewish citizens of the District and especially the active co-operation of the women of the Jewish community. General Grant, when he became President, appointed Mr. Wolf Recorder of the City of Washington and he was subsequently appointed by President Garfield to the mission at Cairo as Diplomatic Agent and Consul General in Egypt.—EDITOR.

us into fields beyond our present scope, which have already received the careful attention of other writers.*

One specially significant example of American Jewish citizenship and manly worth yet claims our attention. In New York, foremost in every patriotic movement, were the brothers Joseph and Jesse Seligman. The place that they filled in the affairs of that time and since has become a part of our country's history. Their influence in maintaining the financial credit of the Government during the war was of far reaching import for the cause of the Union, and the recognition of their services led President Grant to offer to Joseph Seligman, who died in 1880, a place in his Cabinet as Secretary of the Treasury. The universal esteem in which Joseph and Jesse Seligman were held, not alone as men of affairs, but as patriots, citizens and philanthropists, was well betokened by the expressions given to the public feeling when Jesse Seligman died. Some of these expressions may well be cited here, for Jesse Seligman was, *par excellence*, as perfect a type of the American Jew as he was typically an American citizen. He died in April, 1894, and from among the innumerable tributes to his worth, we cite a few of the expressions of some of the leading men of the metropolis, whose stations are a guarantee of their judgment and sincerity, and most of whom had known him through a generation of years.

Lengthy, comparatively speaking, in view of the necessary limitations of this volume, as are these several presentations, they yet command our full consideration by reason of their great significance.

Hon. Carl Schurz, on the occasion of the Memorial Services at the New York Hebrew Orphan Asylum, Decoration Day, May 30, 1894, painted for his audience in the following deeply

---

*See Marken's "The Hebrews in America," New York, 1888; Judge Charles P. Daly's "Settlement of the Jews in North America," edited by Max J. Kohler, New York, 1893; "History of the Jews of Boston and New England," by A. G. Daniels, Boston, 1892; "Eminent Isralites of the 19th Century," by Henry S. Morais, Philadelphia, 1880; "The Jews of Philadelphia," by the same author, Philadelphia, 1894, and the publications of the American Jewish Historical Society.

thoughtful utterances a vivid picture of a model Jew and a model man :

"It is most fit that the memory of Jesse Seligman should be celebrated here, on this very spot. I see him now, as he stood here years ago, when the corner-stone of this magnificent building was laid, and when, owing to his friendly invitation, I enjoyed the privilege of taking part in the dedication ceremonies, I see him, his face beaming with joy over the good that had been accomplished, and with glad anticipation of the greater good still to be done, for his whole heart was in this noble work. And here, where his monument stands—not a mere monument of stone or brass, but a living monument in grateful human hearts—here, where he still lives and will not die, the lessons of his life may be most worthily learned, not to be forgotten.

" Indeed, the legacy not only of benefactions, but of lessons which that life has left behind it, may be, especially to the young among us, if they understand well and treasure them up to inspire and guide their hearts and minds, of far greater value than any amount of his money that Jesse Seligman might have bequeathed to them. Some of us may, perhaps, have envied him while he lived, as an eminently successful man. But do we consider him worthy of envy now, since he is dead? Why do we honor his memory, and wish that, when we shall be gone, we should, in many respects, be remembered as he is? Because he was a rich man? Certainly not ; for that is in itself nothing to be proud of. The ambition to be merely rich is only a small and vulgar ambition. It may be gratified by the accident of birth or of good fortune; it may be gratified by the diligent and constant exertion of faculties, which do not by any means belong to the higher attainment of human nature. Of those who, in the history of mankind, left most fragrant memories behind them, only very few were distinguished by great wealth, and the mere possession of that wealth never constituted their title to affection and reverence.

" Are we honoring Jesse Seligman because he was a successful, self-made man? This is especially in our country of great opportunities, not in itself a distinction deserving uncommon esteem. I know, and no doubt you know, self-made men so inordinately puffed up with their own success, so forgetful of the merits of others in comparison with their own, so oppressive with the ostentations and unceasing display of their riches as their self-appreciation, that they rank among the most disagreeable members of human society, making us wish that they had made anything else but themselves.

" Or do we admire Jesse Seligman above others because he

was a patriotic man? No, for under ordinary circumstances it is only a natural thing to be patriotic. Especially a citizen of this Republic is more apt to attract attention and to be blamed when he is not patriotic, than to be praised when he is.

"All these things, therefore, are in themselves not sufficient to make a life valuable as a memory, and as an inspiration. Jesse Seligman's life, as we look back upon it, is such a valuable memory and inspiring lesson because he was above the ordinary level of the merely rich, self-made, liberal and patriotic men.

"The ideal rich man is he, who not only has come by his wealth honestly, but who uses his riches in such a fashion as to silence the voice of envy, and to make those who knew him glad and grateful that he was rich. To reach this ideal completely is given to but few. But it may truly be said that Jesse Seligman approached it. No doubt, he wished to be rich and worked for it. He valued the acquisition of wealth, but he valued it most as the acquisition of opportunities for something larger and nobler. He saw his business success but not his higher ambition and his happiness in his balance sheets. He felt himself greater and happier in this orphan-home than in his bank. He made his wealth a blessing to others; he enjoyed it the more, the greater the blessing to others it became, and there were many who wished him to be much richer, knowing that his greater wealth would only have become to many others greater relief and comfort. He was such a self-made man as it is a joy to meet. In a high degree he had the self-made man's virtues and was remarkably free from his faults. He never forgot his lowly beginnings, but never boasted of them, to contrast his success with other people's failures. His recollections only stimulated his sympathy with those less fortunate than himself. He did not in his affluence affect the rough simplicity and contempt of refinement in which upstarts sometimes demonstratively please themselves and which is only a coarse form of vanity; and still less was he an ostentatious swaggerer bent upon letting the world perceive that he possessed his millions. He lived with his family in a style becoming his means, but with the modesty becoming a gentleman. There was no gaudy display of riches, no obstrusive flashing of diamonds on hotel piazzas, and no flaring exhibition in opera boxes. But there was nothing mean about him or his. The hospitality of his house was hearty and most generous, but it abstained from anything that might have made one of his guests feel poor or small. Nor was there anything in him of that superciliousness not unfrequently met with in rich men which claims for them much wisdom, because they have much money.

"In all my experience I have never met a rich man, more

modest, more generous more tolerant of adverse opinion, or a self-made man less overbearing, less vain-glorious, and less conceited, more sympathetic and more helpful. As a matter of fact, he was thought much richer than he really was—richer not because of his display, but because of his benefactions. To judge from the good he did, his wealth should have been much greater. He was a liberal giver, but he gave much more than money. That rich man only manifests the true spirit of benevolence who not only gives to the needy, but who also thinks for them and works for them. It was by this that Jesse Seligman proved the genuine gold of his humanity, and nowhere did this gold shine more brightly than on this very spot. There was indeed no charitable enterprise within his reach that did not feel the generosity of his open hand, and, when needed, the kindly thoughtfulness of his counsel, from the hospital and the home for the aged up to that remarkable triumph of wisely directed energy, the Hebrew Technical Institute, which not only successfully demonstrates that the Jew, when well guided, will take to skilled handicraft with enthusiasm and with the whole force and ingenuity of his nature, but which also in its plan, organization and conduct may serve as a noble model of its kind to the educators of any country and of any creed.

" All such endeavors could count upon Jesse Seligman's bountiful aid; and when his last will was opened and the community saw the list of the benevolent institutions to which he had left bequests, without regard to religion or nationality, with unsurpassed catholicity of spirit, people asked with wonder, not what opportunities for doing good he had thought of, but whether there was any he had failed to remember. It was, however, here in the Orphans' Home that his heart found its favorite field for beneficent work. Here he lived on the best of his nature. It was truly touching to see this man, loaded down with the enormous responsibilities and cares of a vast financial business, at least once a week, every Sunday morning, wend his way to this house, forget all about bonds and stocks and syndicates and chances of gain and financial crises in which fortunes might be lost, and to give all his thoughts to the little ones who are cast upon the mercy of the world, and study and scheme and work—as indeed he did often also when he was not here to turn sunshine upon their bereaved existence—to arm them for the struggles of life, and to enable them to become useful, self-reliant, self-respecting and happy citizens of a free country. This was the work he loved most, which satisfied his fondest ambition and in which he found the most genuine happiness. In the best sense of the word he was the father of the fatherless and it was his active,

28

untiring and unceasing care for the welfare of these children, more than any other of his benefactions, that stamped him as a truly benevolent man, a genuine friend of humanity and therefore this is the noblest and most enduring of his monuments.

"He was a patriotic man—not in the sense merely that he cheerfully performed all his duties as a citizen, or that he gave the government valuable advice and aid as a financier whenever called upon—but that he ardently loved his adopted country, was proud of it and was not only willing but eager to serve it. Some gentlemen of high standing among us here have in their published tributes to Jesse Seligman's memory, regretfully mentioned the fact that he and his son, too, have been struck at by anti-Semitic hostility, by that narrow-minded, contemptible spirit which revived the prejudices of dark ages and which seeks in barbarous persecution the remedy for evils, for which popular ignorance, sloth and improvidence are in the largest manner responsible; a spirit so utterly abhorrent to justice and enlightened reason, that it is difficult to understand how a person of self-respect can share it or behold it in others without shame and indignation.

"I have heard it said that a Jew cannot be a patriot because he has no fatherland. Those who say so do not want the Jew to have a fatherland and would, if they had their way, make it impossible for him to be a patriot. A country can hardly expect those of its inhabitants to be ardent patriots whom it treats as aliens or outcasts. In the same measure as an anti-Semitic spirit prevails, a Jew is a patriot under difficulties. If he is a patriot under anti-Semitic persecution, that patriotism is in him a virtue of especial merit. And this virtue Jesse Seligman possessed in the highest degree. I saw him and spoke with him when the smart he had suffered was fresh. I know how keenly he felt it, but I know also that had at that moment the country, or what he understood to be the public interest, demanded of him any service or any sacrifice he would have offered it with the same enthusiastic devotion that ever had animated him. He would have remained a patriot in spite of any difficulty—a shining example for his own race to follow, putting to shame its revilers; indeed, an example to every citizen of whatever creed or origin.

"And now he lies in an honored grave, and by it stand with sadness, but also with pride, his dear ones whom he loved so much, and who so warmly returned his love. And you all have come, rich and poor, native and foreign born, Christian and Jew and Gentile, with hearts full of respect and affection for the man who understood the great truth, and whose life has taught the greatest lesson, that our truest and most enduring happiness springs from the contributions we make to the happiness of others— a lesson that every one may follow according to his means and opportunities, each in his sphere and in his way, to win the same happiness and to deserve the same honor. It may well be said that he had not lived in vain whose life has left its mark in the advanced well being of his kind; and there are multitudes of human beings whose tears he has dried, whose distress he has relieved, whom he has helped to make strong for the struggle of life who now and ever will gratefully affirm and proclaim that Jesse Seligman has surely not lived in vain, and who will never cease to bless his memory.''

Ex-Postmaster General Thomas L. James, President of the Lincoln National Bank of New York City, wrote the following graphic and affecting tribute :—

" I have received the news of the death of Jesse Seligman with the shock which comes only with the announcement of the sudden loss of an old and valued friend. My acquaintance with him commenced away back in the sixties; and I dearly learned to value his sturdy honesty, his integrity, untiring industry, and his genial, warm-hearted friendship. Moreover, I was impressed, in those dark days when I first knew him, with his sterling patriotism, he being one of those men of foreign birth who seemed to go beyond those of us of native birth, in the all-consuming zeal and devotion for our common flag. I think that is what particularly attracted me towards Mr. Seligman; and I soon found that he really did understand more fully and completely, perhaps, than many of us did, what the war meant and what the result would be. He was one of those men, too, who, when some were anxious, speaking hesitatingly about the outcome, gave by his courageous faith and heroic example, a grand impulse of which we afterwards saw the results in that impressive tender by the financiers of New York of their credit and their gold to the government in its extremity.

" He had undying faith in General Grant, too, in those dark hours. He was one of the few men in New York who knew him personally, and he never wavered in his confidence in the great commander's ability to carry the war through to a successful issue. Later on we learned the grounds of his faith; for he was probably the oldest acquaintance of General Grant in New York, having become acquainted with him in Watertown, N. Y., where Grant was then stationed as a Second Lieutenant; and he had afterwards renewed the friendship, when General Grant was sent as First Lieutenant to the Pacific Coast, where he found his old friend Seligman one of the argonauts of California.

"It was given to me, in an especially affecting and touching manner, to see some of those traits in Mr. Seligman's inner life and his family surroundings, which made his home one of the most delightful in New York, and gave to him unusual charms in social and friendly intercourse. I saw those qualities displayed in that sad, sad summer of 1881, when General Garfield, stricken with an assassin's bullet, lay on his deathbed in a cottage at Elberon. Mr. Seligman's summer home was at Long Branch; and, with that thoughtful consideration and tenderness which distinguished the man he showed the official family of the dying President courtesies and kindnesses that were very grateful and which can never be forgotten. A more pleasant family circle than Mr. Seligman's I never met; and I will never cease to remember the charm of that fireside. There, perhaps, Mr. Seligman was seen in the highest display of the beautiful qualities of head and heart that made him not only foremost as a great financier, but as a faithful friend.　.　.　.　.

＊　　＊　　＊　　＊　　＊　　＊　　＊

.　.　.　"Of course, I do not need to speak of his genius as a financier. His name and fame in that particular are secure; and his achievements will become traditions in the history of those influences which have made this country the great financial power among the nations of the earth."

Ex-Judge Noah Davis wrote as follows :

"By the death of Jesse Seligman our country loses a loving and faithful citizen and friend. He loved America, though not his native land, with all the ardor of a native, enhanced by a keen and tender sense of gratitude for what it had done for his race and for him and his brothers ever since they became its adopted sons.

"I have never met any foreign-born American citizen more prompt to express warmly and gratefully this sentiment; and yet it will be rare to find one who has so amply and generously repaid it. His gratitude was not confined to words. His deeds preceded his words; and if it had ever been necessary, he would have staked his whole fortune and his life as well, for our country and its institutions.

"I recall an occasion, when he and I left the Union League Club together, at a late hour one evening, and walked arm in arm up the avenue to our homes. I listened as he gave me some happy reminiscences of his busy life. When we reached the street, I stopped to part with him. "No," said he, "I will walk further with you," and he kept on till he reached my home on 50th street. "Now," I said, "it is my turn to walk with you, sir," and we walked slowly back to his own street, where we compromised by his walking half way back with me. In that delightful walk he developed to me his loving nature toward our country, its government and its people. I was chiefly a listener, but a deeply interested and pleased one, for I could see and feel that a pure-hearted and patriotic man was talking from the inmost bosom of a noble and tender nature.

"A few days before General Grant sailed on his tour around the world, the brothers Seligman gave him a farewell dinner at Delmonico's. There were forty or fifty people present. General Grant was then fully relieved from all public cares, and felt that the honors shown him on that occasion were the tribute of pure and disinterested esteem and affection. He talked with me as I sat near him of the services his hosts had rendered the government during the war and to himself during his administration, with a warm sense of what was due to their genuine patriotism. It happened afterwards, and after his return from his Eastern tour, that I met with General Grant in Paris. He spoke on that occasion of that dinner and his great enjoyment of the evening, and gave a warm expression of his esteem for the Seligmans and for their services to the country and himself.

"It was a merited tribute of a noble man to worthy citizens and friends, and I am glad to lay it now where General Grant would have placed it—on the bier of Jesse Seligman, his devoted friend. . . .

. . . "With all his skill, ability and success in business, with all his love for his country, his devotion to order and good government, his deep and tender attachment to his family and friends, I think his chief virtue was ' Charity,' and that most comprehensive and beautiful word should be inscribed on his tomb.

From General Horace Porter:

"The news of the death of Jesse Seligman has fallen upon many of the most prominent business men in New York with something akin to the quiet of a personal bereavement. Few of our citizens have been more generally known or more highly esteemed. His sudden removal from the company of his friends and from the active walks of business life brings a deep regret to many hearts and recalls the admirable traits which adorned his character. My personal acquaintance with him began a few years after the war. I had before that time heard officers of the army and others speak in admiring terms of him during his sojourn on the Pacific Coast, where he had displayed so much public spirit and such indomitable courage at the time the law-abiding citizens were trying to redeem that community from the domination of the criminal class. I found him displaying the same qualities in the metropolis which had commended him to his fellow-citizens in the West. He had been loyally devoted to the cause of the Union in the great struggle for the preservation of its integrity, and was always an ardent laborer in all great works. He was never known to be anything but fearless in the advocacy of the principles he believed to be right, and always manifested his faith by his works.

* * * * * * * * *

" His death removes a foremost figure in our national and business life; and we shall long look for one to take the place of this man, who by his genius as a financier, his broad liberal charity, and his loving kindness towards suffering humanity, will long be remembered; for Mr. Seligman's life and work have made him one of the benefactors of mankind."

From E. B. Harper, President Mutual Reserve Fund Life Association:

" Few names in the financial and business world of New York are better known than that of Jesse Seligman, financier, banker, philanthropist, and citizen. It may truly be said of Mr. Seligman that he attained one of the highest positions of good citizenship in the metropolis of the nation. While, strictly speaking, a financier, he was ever ready to bring capital, business experience and financial ability into the broader industrial enterprises of the nation which, in their building up, employ labor, pay out vast sums in wages, add comfort to the masses, and bring prosperity to the country. He was not a mere banker, but closely identified with sound enterprises, which have built up the Empire State and developed the resources of the republic. He was a man to be respected, to be looked up to, and his career, as it seems to me, is one that may well be studied to advantage by the youth of his race and his country. The Hebrew race has undoubtedly given to the world more of the most extraordinary instances of great wealth, but at the same time it has produced many of the greatest philanthropists the world has ever known.

* * * * * * * * *

" It is difficult to sum up in a few words such men as Mr. Seligman. He was a man who, by his example, as well as his action benefitted the community of which he was an honored member, and his death will be greatly regretted, not only by those who knew him intimately, but the whole community, because his demise will be a real loss to them. Our wealth of humanity is not so great, even in this great city, that we can afford to lose many such citizens."

From Henry G. Marquand, Esq., President, Metropolitan Museum of Art:

"I was not brought in contact with the late Jesse Seligman as often as some others, but during twenty years or more I saw enough of him to form a very high opinion of his work as a citizen of this republic. His views were always of the broad and generous stamp. They were not confined to the various schemes of philanthropy, but extended to the enterprises relating to high culture at home and abroad, and by contact with him it was easy to see how quickly his sympathies were aroused in favor of everything good. . . . . ''

Ex-Mayor Abram S. Hewitt, expresses himself as follows:

" The story of Jesse Seligman's life should be produced as the best commentary on his career, and as an encouragement to all young men who are starting out on the journey of life. * * * Perhaps the most admirable point of his character was his catholic charity for the opinion of others and his willingness to co-operate in every great movement without regard to creed or race."

From Cornelius N. Bliss :

. . . . "No truer friend, once in Jesse Seligman's confidence did man ever have. With his partners, his brothers, he has been of inestimable service to the United States Government from the time of the Civil War.

"A believer in Republican principles, he was a quiet but all-important influence in the councils of his party. Sagacious in counsel, always for peace and unity, liberal in view, rendering to all their just dues, he will be sorely missed in all circles—social, charitable, business and political.

The foregoing may be fitly supplemented by the following extract from a sermon delivered by the late Henry Ward Beecher, June 14, 1877. Mr. Beecher's pointed references to the absurd prejudices which so frequently manifest themselves at summer resorts have not yet lost their force or application:

"I have the pleasure of the acquaintance of the gentleman whose name has been the occasion of so much excitement—Mr. Seligman. I have summered with his family for several years. I am acquainted with him, with his honored wife, and with his sons and daughters; and I have learned to respect and love them. During weeks and months I was with them at the Twin Mountain House; and not only did they behave in a manner becoming Christian ladies and gentlemen, but they behaved in a manner that ought to put to shame many Christian ladies and gentlemen. They were my helpers and they were not only present at the Sunday services at the Twin Mountain House, but they were present at the daily prayer meetings on week days, volunteering services of kindness. I learned to feel that they were my deacons and that in the ministration of Christian service they were beyond the power of prejudice and did not confine themselves to the limitations which might be prescribed by their race."

Hon. Carl Schurz makes reference, as the reader will have noted, to the "unsurpassed catholicity of spirit," manifested by Jesse Seligman's "bequests without regard to religion or nationality." Among the beneficiaries of his concluding bounty were numbered no less than thirty-six different non-Jewish institutions, the aggregate of these legacies amounting to a very large sum. Unsurpassed as was this breadth of liberality, it was by no means the first time when a Jew gave signal evidence of the supreme catholicity of Judaism and the Jewish spirit. Adverting but passingly to the story of Hyam Salomon's liberality, we may stop to remember that Judah Touro,

whose patriotism had been attested with his blood in the
defense of New Orleans, in 1815, left in his last will and testament in 1854, an example of catholic munificence unequalled
before his time and unsurpassed since. Over and above the
various bequests made by him to Jewish institutions in
different cities of the Union, he left amounts averaging $5000
to fourteen charitable institutions under the control of various
Christian denominations, besides $80,000 to the municipality
of New Orleans for the poor of that city, and $10,000 to the
city of Newport, R. I., for a public improvement. This latter
formed the nucleus of the public park of that city, which has
commemorated in its "Touro Avenue" the public spirit of this
Jewish citizen, who has yet another memorial on Bunker Hill
monument, to the erection of which he so largely contributed.*

Michael Reese, of San Francisco, who died in 1878, bequeathed amounts aggregating $70,000 to a number of non-
Jewish charities, besides $50,000 to the University of Califor-
nia, and left provisions which eventuated in the establishment
of the non-sectarian Michael Reese Hospital of Chicago. Ro-
senna Osterman, of Galveston, and Isidor Dyer, of the same
city, divided their estates among charitable institutions without
distinction of creed.

Miss Ellen Phillips, of Philadelphia, whose long and useful
life, constantly devoted to the cause of charity, closed on February 2, 1891, after aiding the cause to which she was devoted
by her unceasing munificence during her lifetime, bequeathed
the bulk of her property to various charitable institutions.
She left the large collection of paintings and statuary which
she inherited from her brother, the late Henry M. Phillips, to
the Commissioners of Fairmount Park, as an addition to the
collections in Memorial Hall, and divided a very large sum of
money among numerous charities, naming ten different non-
Jewish institutions among her beneficiaries.

The will of Dr. J. D. Berndt, of Pittsburg, Pa., divides a
considerable estate almost equally between Jewish and non-
Jewish institutions, over twenty of the latter class being named,
and the residuary estate of nearly $35,000 is equally divided

* See pages 63–4.

between the American Hebrew College of Cincinnati and Carnegie Library of Pittsburg.

Simon Muhr, of Philadelphia, whose untimely death in February, 1895, was mourned by Jew and Gentile alike, after making certain personal bequests and devoting a fund of $10,000 for the support of scholarships in the University of Pennsylvania, left the residue of his large estate to be divided into three parts, one part to be allotted among Jewish charities, one part among non-Jewish charities, and the third part for the improvement of the public school system of Philadelphia.

The Philadelphia *Times* concluded an editorial reference to the death of Simon Muhr as follows:

" It was his broad and simple tolerance, his unfailing charity of heart as well as hand, his willingness and even eagerness to take personal trouble, not only to relieve distress, but to right wrong, and to defend the victim of oppression, however humble or disreputable, that gave Simon Muhr a peculiar position in the community and a peculiar usefulness. He was an example in this way to many a professing Christian, whose reading of the parable leads him only to condemn the priest and the Levite, and not to imitate the Good Samaritan."

The instances of Jewish citizenship and catholicity here cited are but the more prominent examples of that spirit. Only less conspicuous, but with equal breadth and depth of feeling are many more that would likewise point a moral for us all.

JEWS IN LATIN AMERICAN SETTLEMENTS.

The preceding pages have dealt with various aspects of Jewish influence in Anglo-Saxon America, and we have yet to consider the extent of that influence in the Latin American settlements. Here in this Western Hemisphere, where the Jew has sought an asylum from the historic oppressions and repressions of Old World prejudices, and where, in the very year that saw him expelled from Spain a new future was opened for him and all humanity, here the Jew has been at the fore from the very landing of Columbus to the present day.*

In the following pages is presented a review of Jewish activity and influence in the South American Colonies and the West Indies, which has been collated for this volume by Mr. George Alexander Kohut. His careful studies and scientific investigations in this hitherto almost untrodden field of historical research have resulted in the development of many highly interesting facts, and his work affords a most welcome contribution to our general subject. It will be found to command very justly the space accorded to it.

---

* See Dr. M. Kayserling's "Christopher Columbus and the Participation of the Jews in the Spanish and Portuguese Discoveries." Translated from the German by Charles Gross, Ph. D., Assistant Professor of History in Harvard College. New York, 1894.

SKETCHES OF JEWISH LOYALTY, BRAVERY AND PATRIOTISM IN THE SOUTH AMERICAN COLONIES AND THE WEST INDIES.

By George Alexander Kohut, New York City.

I

Services Rendered to the Dutch by the Jews of Brazil
(1623–44).

In 1624, when the Dutch conquered Brazil, several Jews, desirous of joining their co-believers in the newly acquired Dutch dominions, where our brethren flourished for many decades previously in the guise of New Christians or Marranos, enlisted in the Hollandish fleet as volunteers. Encouraged by this show of patriotism on the part of their newly arrived co-religionists, who, under the reign of the United Provinces, enjoyed all the blessings of peace and equality, many *Nuevos Christianos* openly renounced their sham faith and re-avowed Judaism, happy once more to breathe the air of freedom without suffering persecution. It is said that the Jewish soldiers in the navy displayed so much zeal and courage in the taking possession of Brazil that the government protected them ever after.[1] Even

---

[1] See H. J. Koenen's prize essay, *Geschiedenis der Joden in Nederland* (Utrecht, 1843), pp. 277–78: "Machtig breide zich deze bevolking uit als de Nederlanders omstreeks het jaar 1624 Brazilie veroverden. Op de Hollandsche vloot hadden verscheiden Joden vrijwillig dienst genomen, om zich in het te vermeesteren gewest met hunne geloofsgenooten te vereenigen. Deze ontmoeting, en de voor hen aanlichtende vrijheid onder Hollandsche Bestuur, maakten, dat vele Braziliaansche Nieuwe Christenen wederom opentlyk het Jodendom beleden; en dat zij eerlang eene tweede volkplanting hunner geloofsgenooten te Cayenne stichteden, waar David Nassi, een geboren Braziliaan, zich met goedkeuring der West-Indische Compagnie nederzette. Inmiddels hadden de Joden die met 's lands vloot in 1624 naar Brazilie overgestoken waren en de Nederlanders dat land hadden helpen vermeesteren, aan hunne te Amsterdam woonachtige broederen geschreven, en hen uitgenoodigd om zich in het nieuw veroverde gewest op den pas ontgonnen koophandel te komen toeleggen ; waartoe eene ruime

before putting to sea, remarks a French historian of Brazil,[2] the Dutch admirals obtained much useful information concerning the political situation of Brazil, from the Israelites there settled, and who were all eager to remain, or rather, to pass over to the Dutch, whose liberal spirit and religious tolerance seemed much more inviting to them than the cruel sceptre of Spain or Portugal. This is furthermore corroborated by another (English) writer, Mr. Robert G. Watson, in his excellent work: *Spanish and Portuguese South America during the Colonial Period* (London, 1884), Vol. II, p. 1, where we read: "The religious intolerance from which the Dutch had themselves so terribly suffered at the hands of their Spanish rulers had taught them to be tolerant in such matters towards others, *and to this circumstance they were now (1623–24) indebted for much valuable information respecting Brazil, which they received from the Jews who had taken refuge amongst them.*"

It is apparent from these and other items to be mentioned later that the Jews rendered not only military and naval service to the Dutch in their struggle against Portugal in Brazil, but

gelegendheid was, sedert de Hollanders, na het sluiten van eenen wapenstilstand met de Portugezen, eene publicatie hadden afgekondigd, dat het den Joden voortan volkomen zoude vrijstaan, zich in Brazilie te vestigen, etc."

We have copied this in full, as Koenen, whom recent historians all follow, is the only authentic source, although in this case no authorities are given. This point, and others in connection with the early Jewish settlements in Brazil were discussed by the present writer in two papers: *Early Jewish Literature in America*, in *Publications of the American Jewish Historical Society* (=*P. A. J. H. S.*), No. 3 (1895), pp. 103–47 (cf. esp. pp. 104, 105, 134–40) and *Jewish Martyrs of the Inquisition in South America*, to appear simultaneously with this volume, in the same place, No. 4.

[2] See Pieter Marinus Netscher's *Les Hollandais au Brésil, Notice Historique sur les Pays-Bas et le Brésil au XVIIe siècle* (La Haye, 1853), p. 14: "Avant de mettre en mer (1623?), les amiraux Hollandais obtinrent sur la situation politique du Brésil les informations les plus utiles *par l'intermédiaire des Juifs* qui s'y étaient établis, et qui presque tous, désiraient avec ardeur passer sous le gouvernement des Provinces-Unies, à cause de sa tolérance en matière de religion." Cf. also De Beauchamp's *Histoire du Brésil*, vol. II, p. 159; Southey's *History of Brazil* (2nd ed.) I, pp. 477, 479, 495, supplem. note 135; vol. II, p. 241; Judge Daly's *Settlement of the Jews in North America* (2nd ed. New York, 1893) p. XVII.

diplomatic counsel of no little weight, by means of which Holland could conquer the American possessions and establish herself most firmly there. The inhabitants of Brazil at about that time (1623-38) were not very yielding. In fact R. Southey, the reliable and painstaking historian, says[3] that "The Portuguese were held in subjection only by fear, but many Portuguese Jews from Holland had taken their abode in a country where they could speak their own language as well as enjoy their own religion. *These were excellent subjects;* they exercised the charitable industry of their original nation secure of enjoying its fruits under a free government." The Dutch, upon taking possession of Brazil, issued a proclamation, no doubt with a view of attracting the Jews, whose accession would prove beneficial to the interests of the government, whereby they offered full possession of their property, and freedom of worship to all such as would submit. Amongst those who were thus brought under Dutch rule were *two hundred Jews.* (cf. Watson, *l. c.*, II, p. 2.) This liberal charter of religious freedom lasted as long as the Dutch supremacy until the Portuguese re-conquest of Brazil in 1654, with more or less privileges, according to the whim of the public whose dictates even the government had to obey, as we may see from what took place in 1638, as recorded by Southey (*l. c.*, Vol. I, p. 566): " Some of the Portuguese-Brazilians also, gladly throwing off the mask which they had so long been compelled to wear, joined their brethren in the synagogue. The open joy with which they now celebrated their ceremonies attracted too much notice; it excited horror in Catholics, and *even the Dutch themselves,* less liberal than their laws, pretended that the toleration of Holland did not extend to Brazil; the senate conceded to, and perhaps partook of the popular feeling, and hence arose the edict, by which the Jews were ordered to perform their rites more in private.''[4]

Under Count Maurice's gentle reign our coreligionists lived in peace and they appear to have benefited by this temporary respite and acquired much wealth, for we find on record a

[3] *History of Brazil* (London, 1810), Vol. I, p. 566; cf. also the quotation in R. G. Watson's *Spanish and Portuguese South America*, etc., *op. cit.*, Vol. II, p. 29.

[4] See also Netscher's *Les Hollandais au Brésil*, etc., (La Haye, 1853), p. 94: " Les synagogues furent fermées, et les Juifs durent se

petition from the Jews of Mauritsstad, dated May 1, 1642, offering an annual present of 3000 florins to Count Maurice if he would be induced to remain as their Governor in Brazil.[5] In 1642, at the urgent invitation of their coreligionists (cf. Koenen, *l. c.*, p. 278), 600 Jews, headed by Moses Raphael de Aguilar and Ishac Aboab de Fonseca, came from Amsterdam[6] and formed a prosperous colony in Recife, which gave promise of glorious development, had not the wars between Holland and Portugal, in which our brethren took noble part, destroyed their hopes. In 1642, it must be noted, they again were permitted to worship publicly, a privilege which did not remain unrewarded, for we soon hear of certain state services rendered by the Jews in 1644 and later, when many mean conspiracies against the government were afoot, concocted, no doubt by the Portuguese under Dutch rule. Watson (*Spanish and Portuguese South America*, etc., London, 1884, Vol, II, p. 47) says: "At length, however, the time came when his (the chief conspirator's, Fernandes) practices could no longer be ignored by the government, *who were set on their guard chiefly by the Jews.* These are certainly not to be blamed for wishing a continuance of the *status quo*; since, in the event of an outbreak, they were certain to be plundered by both parties with complete impartiality; whilst, in the event of a victory on the part of the Portuguese, they had before them the image of the fiendish agents of the Inquisition,'' which, as we have elsewhere shown,[7]

borner à célébrer leur culte dans l' intérieur des maisons. Le mal fut d' autant plus sensible qu' un grand nombre de commerçants respectables et d'autres habitants du Brésil-Hollandais étaient des Juifs, qui depuis nombre d'années s'étaient réfugiés au Recife ou qui récemment y avaient été attirés par la tolérance du comte Maurice.'' Cf. also *ibid.*, pp. 128, 202, note 82 ; and Judge Daly's work, op. cit., p. 6. On the subject of religious freedom enjoyed by Jews in Brazil, more at another time.

⁵ Cf. Netscher's work, *op. cit.*, p. 127. The document is preserved in *Le rapport détaillé de Tolner, contresigné par le Comte, avec tous les appendices, se trouve aux Arch. du Roy., Liasse Ind. Occ.*, 1641–1644. The contents of this letter will be communicated elsewhere.

⁶ See Dr. M. Kayserling's article in *P. A. J. H. S.*, No. 3, (1895), p. 14 sq. Geo. A. Kohut, *ibid* , pp. 103, 105, 137 sq.

⁷ Proofs for these statements may be found in my study on *The Jewish Martyrs of the Inquisition in South America, P. A. J. H. S.*, No. 4, (1895.)

they had good reason to fear. We read later (*l. c.*, p. 48) that Fernandes could not be captured and summoned troops. Many obeyed the call and fell upon such Dutchmen and Jews as happened to be within their reach.

The loyalty of the Jews in the matter of revealing the various state conspiracies is thus alluded to by Pieter Marinus Netscher in his admirable work *Les Hollandais au Brésil*, (La Haye 1853), p. 145: "Fortunately, national and religious fanaticism did not smother the sentiments of humanity and justice in the hearts of all the conspirators. Two Portuguese [Jews?] Sebastian Carvalho and Fernando Vale, with *five Jews*, fearing that their lives and fortunes were at stake, resolved to disclose the secret of the plot to the Grand Council.[8] Another conspiracy was brought to light and denounced to the government by a Jew named *Moise Accoignes*, who, against his will, was forced to become an accessory to the plot.[9] He is no doubt alluded to by Prof. H. Graetz, who, in his *History of the Jews* (English version, Philadelphia, 1895, Vol. IV, p. 693. Jewish Publication Society of America) writes: "Of course, the Brazilian Jews enjoyed perfect equality of rights with other citizens, *for they rendered the Dutch essential services as advisers and warriors.* When the native Portuguese, who bore the yoke of the Dutch impatiently, formed a conspiracy to get rid of the Dutch authorities at a banquet in the capital, and attack the colony bereft of government [?], *a Jew gave warning, and*

---

[8] We give the text in full: "Heureusement le fanatisme national et religieux n'avait pas étouffé les sentiments d'humanité et de loyauté dans les coeurs de tous les conjurés. Deux Portugais, Sébastian Carvalho et Fernando Vale, *avec cinq Juifs*, craignant d'ailleurs aussi pour leurs jours et leur fortune, se décidèrent en commun à révéler le secrèt de la conspiration au grand conseil."

[9] Cf. Montanus Arnoldus, *De nieuwe en onbekende wereld of beschrijving van Amerika en't Zuidland*, Amsterdam, 1671, fol. 81; Netscher, *l. c.*, p. 144, says: "*Un Juif, Moise Accoignes*, qu'on avait forcé à prendre part à cette conspiration le dénonça au grand conseil." N. G. van Kampen, in his *Geschichte der Niederlande*, vol. II, p. 118 and Frankel in *Monatsschrift*, vol. XII (1863) p. 323-324, record, that the ringleader in this conspiracy was Joan Fernandes Vinira (?), who intended to poison the government officials at a dinner given at his own home, and the plot would have succeeded had not a Jew raised the alarm.

saved the colony from certain destruction.'' Southey, whom at the present writing we are unable to consult, (cf. his *History of Brazil*, Vol. II, pp. 60–70), and Koenen, also chronicle the the timely intervention of a faithful Israelite,[10] who, at the risk of his life, for the conspirators would not have scrupled to put him out of the way, informed the authorities of the impending calamity to the state.

We also know that a Jew in Lisbon proved instrumental in intercepting some official papers in reference to the revolt in Brazil.[11]

The execution of one, Jacob Rabbi, an agent of Holland, who must have been a Jew, is mentioned by Netscher in the following terms: `` . . . . . The cause of this desertion [from the Portuguese troops?] was that the Lieutenant-Colonel, Garstman, had been sufficiently impolitic to put to death (in 1645 or 1646?) for a real or supposed crime, a certain Jacob Rabbi, German by birth, of a ferocious character. He had lived for many years among the savages as agent of the Hollandish government.'"[12]

It is evident that the Dutch Government and especially the Governor, Count Maurice de Nassau, was not backward in appreciating the services of the Jews. An ordinance from the States-General reads:

`` . . . The persons, goods and rights of the Jews in Brazil are taken under the special protection of the Govern-

---

[10] Cf. *Geschiedenis der Joden*, p 279: De terugroeping van Johan Maurits, wiens edele afkomst en schitterende eigenschappe zelfs den Portugezen eerbied inboezemden, en wiens ongelookige opvolgers, meestal kooplieden (merchants), leden de Westindische Maatschappij, door hunne bekrompenheid, hebzucht en onmenschelijkheid algemeenen afkeer verwekten, deed onder de Portugesche ingezetenen een sluw beraamde zamenzwering tegen de Hollanders onstaan, die op het punt was van te gelukken, *toen een Joodsche geneesheer* haar door het schrijven van een naamloozen brief aan den dag bracht," etc.

[11] Netscher, *l. c.* p. 153. : `` . . . . . Mais on parvint enfin en Hollande, à se procurer, par un Juif qui demeurait à Lisbonne, le moyen d'intercepter quelques lettres du roi, qui prouvèrent au soulèvement dans le Brésil." (Ces lettres se trouvent aux Arch du Roy., Liasse Ind. Occ. 1647 et 1648.)

[12] Cf. *ibid, l. c.*, p. 154 ; See also *Lettre de Justif. de Garstman aux Etats-généraux en date du 27 Septembre, 1646.* Arch. du Roy., Liasse Ind. Occ. 1645 et 1646.

ment, because of the fidelity and courage which that nation had on every occasion displayed toward the said Government.'"[13]

II.

Brave Defense of the Jews in Brazil in 1645–1646.

The best evidence of Jewish loyalty to their lenient Dutch rulers was given at a time when the Hollandish Government was contending with the Portuguese for the possession of Brazil. The numerous conspiracies years previous were only a foretaste of what followed and when at last, in the year 1645, war actually broke out, our co-religionists lost no time in siding with their generous patrons, regardless of consequences. Among those that distinguished themselves for their noble patriotism and whose co-operation in behalf of the needy and distressed won all hearts, was a wealthy Israelite, Abraham Coen by name, whose fame is recognized in the following verses written in his honor by one of the greatest Portuguese Jewish poets of Holland, Don Miguel Levi de Barrios, who visited Cayenne[14] in 1660 and remained there until 1662 :

> *Abraham Coen en el Brasil remoto*
> *del principe Mauricio halló el agrado*
> *prospero y noble, y oy del Rey Empireo*
> *goço la luz en ideal palacio.*
> *Cerco al Brasil el luso balicoso*
> *en nueve años continuos, que empeçaron*
> *en el de mil seiscientos y quarenta*
> *y cinco, contra el valeroso Holandio.*
>
> Y en todos con magnanima grandeza
> el grande Abraham Coen sustento à quantos
> Judios y Cristianos de su auxilio
> en la miseria atroz necesitaron.
> *Entonces los Señoras del Supremo*
> *Consejo sobre el Pueblo Brasiliano*
> *vieron del fiel Coen la piedad grande.*[15]

[13] Cf. Dr. A. Hahn, in *American Jews' Annual* for 1886–1887, p. 35; see also Isaac de Costa, *Israel und die Voelker* (Frankfort o. M., 1855), p. 319 ; and Dr. Z. Frankel, in his *Monatsschrift*, vol. XII, (1863), p. 323.

[14] Cf. Kayserling's *Sephardim, Romanische Poesien der Juden in Spanien* (Leipzig 1859) p. 266; *P. A. J. H. S.*, No. 3, p. 18.

[15] *P. A. J. H. S.*, *l. c.*, p. 15, note. Jacob Coen, Abraham's eldest son, was afterwards appointed "Contador Mayor," Receiver—General of Duke Moritz of Nassau. Cf. *ib. l. c.*

29

Dr. Hahn informs us that "in the perilous times of 1645 and 1648 great services were rendered to the government by the Portuguese family of Cohen in furnishing ammunition and provisions.'"[16]

The Portuguese besieged Recife, near Pernambuco, which boasted of a large Jewish population (among them several fine scholars: David Senior Coronel, Dr. Abraham de Mercado, Jahacob Mucate, Ishac Castanho and others)[17] and the inhabitants thus deprived of every possible communication, endured much suffering. The Jews, encouraged by their learned and eloquent Rabbi Isaac Aboab, the friend of Menasse ben Israel, bore their tribulations bravely, and though almost famished for want of nourishment, defended the fort with such remarkable skill and heroism, as to evoke the praise and gratitude of the Government. Had it not been for the dauntless resistance offered by them, the garrison would have been compelled to surrender.

Aboab commemorated his thrilling experiences of war in the introductory chapter of his Hebrew version of Abraham Cohen Herrera's *Porta Coeli* (Sha'ar Ha'shamayîm) which he began to translate in June, 1655 (22nd of Siwan 5415). Besides this, he wrote nine years before (anno 1646) a poetical account of the siege in a work entitled *Secher Rab;*[18] *Prayers and Confessions and Supplications, which were composed for appealing to God in his trouble and in the distress of the Congregation, when the troops of Portugal overwhelmed them during their sojourn in Brazil in the year 5406* [*1646*]. *And I have caused the wonderful works of God to be remembered in songs and praises, when he released them from the hands of their enemies.* It is written in Hebrew. The Ms. is still extant in Amsterdam, in possession of the "Arbol de las Vidas" Theo-

---

[16] Cf. *American Jews' Annual* for 1886–1887, p. 35; Isaac de Costa, *l. c.*, p. 318; see also Hon. Oscar S. Straus's address in *P. A. J. H. S.*, No.3, p 3.

[17] See Kayserling in *P. A. J. H. S., l. c.*, p. 14 ; Graetz, *History of the Jews* (Engl. transl.) vol. IV, p. 693.

[18] See full particulars concerning this work in our study on *Early Jewish Literature in America*, *P. A. J. H. S.*, No. 3, pp. 105, 106 139, No. 9, and Dr. Kayserling's paper, *ibid. l. c.*, p. 16.

logical Society.[19] The part played by the Jews in the defense of the colony is described by eminent Jewish and Christian historians.[20] Dr. Kayserling's and Prof. Graetz's accounts are worth citing *in extenso.* The former, who is engaged in copying this earliest specimens of American Jewish literature, the work of Isaac Aboab, for the American Jewish Historical Society, writes as follows: "Aboab became *Chacham* (Chief) of the congregation in Recife, which would have become one of the largest and richest, had it not been hindered in its development by the disturbances of war; it was dissolved after a short existence. The new settlers enjoyed tranquility only for a few years, for already in 1645 the sanguinary struggles, for the possession of the colony, between the Portuguese and the Hollanders began. The Jews stood faithfully on the side of the Hollanders, who had granted them perfect equality, and distinguished themselves by courage and heroism, as well as by succor to the distressed. During the war Abraham Coen, a rich and high-minded man of Amsterdam, who was in great favor with Duke Moritz of Nassau, supported Jews and Christians in such a magnanimous way that the Supreme Council of the Brazilian people looked with admiration at the great work of mercy. Isaac Aboab faithfully discharged the duties of his office; he ordered days of fasting and prayer, and his fiery speeches encouraged his co-religionists to perseverance and devotion. It was a fierce struggle of nine years which brought much suffering on the Jews. Recife was besieged and the garrison decimated by hunger. ' Many of the Jewish immigrants were killed by the enemy, many died of hunger. The remainder were exposed to death from similar causes. Those who had been accustomed to delicacies were glad to be able to satisfy their hunger with dry bread; soon they could not obtain even this; they were in want of everything, and were preserved alive as by a miracle.' "

[19] Cf. *l. c.,* p. 16, No. 3.

[20] Cf. Van Kampen, *Geschichte der Niederlande,* vol. II, p. 120 ; *apud* Frankel, *Monatsschrift,* vol. XII (1863), p. 324 ; Koenen's *Geschiedenis der Joden in Nederland* (Utrecht, 1843) p. 280 sq.; Isaac da Costa, *Israel und die Voelker* (Germ. ed. by K. Mann, Frankfort, A. M., 1855) p. 318 ff.; Graetz's *History, l. c.,* p. 693–4; Kayserling, *ib., l. c.,* pp. 17–18.

Prof. Graetz, still more explicit, writes to the following effect: "In 1646, when open war broke out between the Portuguese and the Dutch, and the garrison of Recife, exhausted by famine, was on the point of surrendering unconditionally, the Jews encouraged the governor to brave resistance. A fanatical war of race and religion between the Portuguese and the Dutch devastated fair Brazil, and a famine ensued. The Jews vied with the Dutch in suffering and bravery. Isaac Aboab, the Chacham of the Brazil community, paints the suffering of the war, which he himself endured, in lurid colors: 'Volumes would not suffice to relate our miseries. The enemy spread over field and wood, seeking here for booty and there for life. Many of us died, sword in hand, others from want; they now rest in cold earth. We survivors were exposed to death in every form; those accustomed to luxuries were glad to seize mouldy bread to stay their hunger.'

"At last, the States-General were compelled by European wars to surrender the colony to the Portuguese. The devoted zeal of the Jews for the political welfare of the Dutch was a firm band, never afterwards dissolved, between them and the Republic. The toleration and equal position of Jews in the Netherlands were ensured forever."

Southey relates (*History of Brazil*, Vol. II, p. 241; *apud* Koenen's *Geschiedenis*, p. 281), that when the Dutch in Recife were besieged the second time,[21] the Jews manifested much courage and bravery in its defense. One of the Pintos (Jewish stock also in Surinam, where Isaac Pinto, a member of this family, likewise displayed zeal and heroism in resisting the enemy), is said to have manned the fort *Dos Affrogados* single handed, until, overwhelmed by superior force, he was compelled to surrender.

"In the wars of the Dutch against the Spaniards," says Dr. A. Hahn, "one of the Pintos was killed at his post while bravely defending one of the fortresses." His death is nowhere else recorded, however.[22]

[21] Cf. Southey's *History of Brazil*, Vol. II, pp. 202–230; Van Kampen, *Geschichte der Niederlande*, Vol. II, pp. 120–122; also the same writer's *Geschiedenis der Nederlanders buiten Europa;* Isaac de Costa, *op. cit.*, p. 319.

[22] See the *American Jews' Annual* for 1886–1887, p. 35.

The supremacy of the United Provinces now came to an end in America. On the 23d of January, 1654, Recife, together with the neighboring cities of Mauritsstad, Parayba, Itamarica, Seara, and other Hollandish possessions, was ceded to the Portuguese conquerors, with the condition that a general amnesty be granted. (Koenen, *l. c.*, p. 282). Although, as Netscher[23] remarks, this stipulation was agreed upon, and the Jews, who were loyal supporters of Holland, were promised every consideration, the Portuguese governor, heeding the treacherous advice of jealous persons, ordered the Jews to quit Brazil at once. It must be admitted, in justice to Portugal, that he treated them kindly, inasmuch as he placed at their disposal sixteen vessels to carry them and their property anywhere they chose, and furnished them with passports and safeguards. Thus after a residence of several decades, Aboab, Aguilar, the Nassys, Pereiras, the Mezas, Abraham de Castro, Josua Sarfati, both surnamed *el Brasil*,[24] returned to Amsterdam, and many others went to New York, where they formed the nucleus of a prosperous colony. They arrived in safety, although one of their vessels, attacked by pirates, was rescued by the French and escorted to New Holland.[25]

[23] *Les Hollandais au Brésil*, p. 163, *ad ann.* 1653–1654: "Une amnistie pleine et entière était accordée aux Portugais et aux Juifs, qui avaient pris cause pour le gouvernement Hollandais, et les Juifs et autres personnes non-catholiques qui resteraient au Brésil y seraient traités de la meme manière, qu'au Portugal (ce qui cachait une arriere-pensée digne de l'intolérance relígieuse de ces jours-là." Here he adds a note which is hardly correct: "Aujourdhui il ne se trouvent presque pas des Juifs au Brésil."

[24] Cf. Koenen, *l. c.*, p. 282; Kayserling, *P. A. J. H. S.*, No. 3, p. 17.

[25] See the *Measseph* for 1784; *ap.* Jost, *Geschichte der Israeliten*, Vol. VIII, pp. 241–242; Da Costa, *Israel und Die Voelker, l. c.*, pp. 321–322; Dr. Hahn in *The American Jews' Annual* (1886–1887) p. 36; Rev. E. M. Myers' *The Centurial* (New York, 1890), p. 105; *P. A. J. H. S.*, No. 2, p. 99. More fully in our paper on *Early Jewish Literature in America, l. c.*, p. 138–139.

III.

SAMUEL NASSY OF SURINAM.

Not all the Jews, who were by royal order expelled from Brazil in 1654, when the Dutch possessions in South America were ceded to Portugal, left their adopted country, where they, for a brief span of years enjoyed all the privileges of their fellowmen. Many were so much attached to American soil that they dared remain, despite the edict of banishment, in Brazil and elsewhere.

In Dutch Guiana, a thrifty colony was formed as early as 1644,[26] two years after the influx and settlement of Amsterdam Jews in Brazil under Aboab and Aguilar. These were undoubtedly the original colonists of Brazil. This colony soon increased by a second settlement of Jews hailing, likewise, from Brazil, who were undoubtedly persuaded to migrate thither by their Dutch coreligionists in Cayenne. The President of the West Indian Company, recognizing their influence as a commercial and political body, granted a most liberal charter of rights[27] in 1659 (September 12th), wherein freedom of thought, and liberty of conscience and worship were duly accorded to them through their able representative, David Nassy, a native Brazilian, who, by force of his personality, culture and intelligence, was destined to play a most important part in the political and social development of this and other colonies subsequently formed in the Guianas. So enticing was this generous programme, that already in the following year, 1660, 152 Jews

----

[26] Cf. Koenen's *Geschiedenis der Joden in Nederland*, p. 283; Dr. M. Kayserling, *Sephardim, Romanische Poesien der Juden in Spanien*, (Leipzig, 1859), p. 265.

[27] The Dutch text of this valuable document is published in the *Essai Historique sur la Colonie Surinam*, Paramaribo 1788 [Amsterdam 1791], Vol. II, pp. 113–122 and in Koenen's work on the *History of the Jews in Holland, l. c.*, pp. 460–466. The present writer intends to reprint the original text with an English translation in the *P. A. J. H. S.*; cf. his paper on *Early Jewish Literature in America* in the *Publications* No. 3 (1895), p. 104, 136, 137.

of both sexes,[28] embarked at Livorno, Italy,[29] bound for the land of freedom, where they arrived in the ship *Monte del Cisne*, having set sail on the memorable 9th day of Ab (August) 1660, in order to build up their temple under more favorable auspices in another hemisphere.[30]

Among their number was the famous Spanish poet and historian De Barrios (see above), to whom we owe many important items of early American Jewish history. His visit to America was not a happy one, for shortly after his arrival his wife, Deborah, died in Tabago (West Indies).[31]

The continuous wars between Holland and Portugal caused the colonists no little grief and annoyance. The frequent devastations of the French, too, who were equally zealous and greedy for conquest, gave them so much anxiety that they decided to transplant the colony to Surinam—a plan which was carried out on May 15th, 1664.[32]

As the writer is engaged in compiling an extensive work on

[28] Cf. Kayserling *Sephardim*, etc., *l. c.*, p. 266; his paper on the *Earliest Rabbis and Jewish Writers in America*, in *P. A. J. H. S.*, No. 3, p. 18; Koenen, *l. c.*, pp. 283–284.

[29] From this it would appear that the Jews in South America were corresponding and perhaps commercially connected with their brethren in Italy. We have elsewhere proven that the Marranos in Hispañiola were carrying on an extensive trade between various large sea-ports of Italy (see our forthcoming paper on *The Jewish Martyrs of the Inquisition in South America*, to appear in *P. A. J. H. S.*, No. 4, 1895), and that the Jews of Brazil as early as 1636 wrote to Rabbi Chayim Sabbathai, of Salonica, in reference to disputes arising in their midst concerning Jewish customs and ritual Cf. the notes in our study quoted above, *P. A. J. H. S.*, No. 3, pp. 104–105, 137.

[30] Cf. Barrios' reference at the end of his Opuscula: "En Tisa beab (sic) sali de Liorne año de 1660 con 152 Almas de Israel en la nave llamada Monte del Cisne para ir apoblar a Cayana conquista de Holandeses en America." Koenen, *l. c.*, p. 283, numbers only 112 passengers, which is evidently erroneous. Cf. also Kayserling, *Sephardim*, etc., p. 266, note 1; 355, n. 402; *P. A. J. H. S.*, No. 3, p. 18.

[31] Cf. Kayserling *Sephardim*, *l. c.*, and *P. A. J. H. S.*, 3, p. 18; see more fully in my paper on a *Contribution to the History of the Jews in the Islands of St. Thomas, Jamaica and Barbadoes*, to appear in *P. A. J. H. S.*, No. 4.

[32] See Koenen's *Geschiedenis*, p. 284. The date 1654, there given is probably a misprint for 1664.

the Jews of Surinam he refrains now from entering into details concerning their early career. Suffice it to say that the spirit of their Dutch masters followed them thenceforth for more than a century and a half. The English government then ruling the colony, true to their traditional standard of tolerance ever since the days of Cromwell and Menasseh ben Israel, endowed them with equal civil rights and granted them not only full exercise of their religion, but excused them from public and military service on the Sabbath day. The document is a precious chapter in the history of religious liberty in America. It was published recently by the present writer.[33] Without further prolegomena, we desire to introduce one of the members of the famous family of Nassy, all of whom fully deserved the distinction of nobility implied in their name,[34] for their bravery and statesmanship.

History records the estimable services of Samuel Nassy, who but for some unlucky circumstance would have occupied the highest official position in Surinam. De Barrios, who probably knew him personally, remembers him in the following words: " *Del pueblo de Sariñam Samuel Nasi (sic) Señorea El coraçon con los dones y et estudio con la ciencia.*"[35] Dr. Kayserling, in a recent article says: " Of great influence upon the free development of the colony, as on the condition of the Jewish inhabitants, was the activity of Samuel Nasi, a talented and scientifically trained man, who is designated as ' Citizens' Captain,' and was a candidate for the position of governor."[36] It is said that

---

[33] Cf. Appendix II to my paper on *Early Jewish Literature in America, P. A. J. H. S.*, No. 3, pp. 145–147, cf. also pp. 125–132 where some points in their history are given.

[34] Dr. E. Carmoly, in his essay on *Don Joseph Nasi, Duc de Naxos* (Brussels, 1855), traces the relationship of this eminent personage even to American shores, where the Nasis flourished. The word Nasi in Hebrew indicates chief, or prince. See also Fuerst's *Orient*, XII (1851–2), p. 335; Steinschneider's *Hammaskir*, II (1859), p. 33.

[35] See Don Miguel Levi de Barrios, *Arbol de las Vidas*, p. 90; apud Kayserling, in *P. A. J. H. S.*, No. 3, p. 18, note 2.

[36] Cf. Kayserling, *ib.*, *l. c.*; and his article: *Die Juden in Surinam*, published in Frankel's *Monatsschrift für die Geschichte und Wissenschaft des Judenthums*, Vol. VIII, (1859), p. 207; also Van Sijpenstein, *Beschrijving van Suriname, historisch-geographischen statistisch overzigt. Uit officiele Bronnen bijeengebragt* (Gravenhage, 1854,) p. 22.

Governor Aerssens, with whom the Jews of Surinam had some little difficulty,[37] sealed a treaty of peace with the Indians, who molested the early settlers quite often, and in order to make it of a more durable character, he formed an alliance with the chieftain's daughter.[38] While he lived there was no disturbance at all, but almost immediately after his death, the savage tribes returned to their former aggressive attitude and made a furious onslaught on the colony. With the help of the Jewish inhabitants, who were headed by Captain Samuel Nassy, the Indians were promptly repulsed.[39]

Nassy soon acquired influence and prominence among his co-religionists in particular. He strove to introduce a few necessary reforms in ritual and ceremony—the first traces of the reform movement in America—especially in the abrogation of certain festivals which were perhaps too burdensome to the community. It seems, however, that in this he met with considerable opposition, although he had the sanction and support of the Rabbis in Amsterdam, with whom he corresponded.[40] The authority with which he was vested by reason of his executive ability and earnest zeal soon diminished with the arrival of the newly appointed governor, Heer Van Scherpenhuizen, the successor of Aerssens,[41] a fact which tended much to embitter his days and aroused sharp controversy between him and his rival. He had the satisfaction of being instrumental in his recall soon after his accession.[42]

[37] See Koenen's *Geschiedenis der Joden*, etc., pp. 291–92.

[38] Cf. *ibid, l. c.*, p. 293; *Essai Historique sur la Colonie Surinam*, etc., Vol. I, p. 42.

[39] Koenen, *l. c.*: "Zij werden vooral door de Joden, aan wier hoofd zich als Kapitein Samuel Nassy bevond, teruggedreven."

[40] Koenen, *l. c.*, says: "Deze Nassy verkreeg van tijd tot tijd veel invloed onder zijne geloofsgenooten, en trachtte eenige hervormingen bij hen tot stand te brengen, in zonderheid met opzicht tot hunne zoo menigvaldige feestdagen; doch hij vond daarin niet weinig tegenwerking, ofschoon hij door brieven der Amsterdamsche Rabbijnen werd ondersteund."

[41] Koenen, *l. c.*: "Zijn gezag verminderde zeer, toen de Kolonie op nieuw een Bewindhebber verkreeg in den Heer Van Scherpenhuizen, die Aerssens in het bestuur opvolgde."

[42] See Kayserling, in *Monatsschrift, l. c.*, Vol., VIII, p. 207: "*Samuel (Cohen) Nasi* wird als Bürger-Capitaen bezeichnet und trieb

Nassy flattered himself that his personal influence was necessary to the welfare and prosperity of the colony.   And he was
right.   The Jews relied so implicitly upon his counsels and
were so certain that he would be proclaimed governor, for he
enjoyed the esteem of Jew and Gentile alike, that it was an
unpleasant shock to them all when quite another person, comparatively unknown, was chosen in his stead.   It is, therefore,
not surprising that Samuel Nassy, seeing the loss of his public
prestige, thought fit to betake himself to Amsterdam, unwilling
to remain in a country which owed all its present affluence to
his sterling honesty and wise management, and was yet so slow
in showing its gratitude to the able statesman.   His disappointment and dissatisfaction in not succeeding Heer Van Sommelsdyk as governor infected the whole Jewish community.   The
rupture which eventually followed between the Jews and
Governor Scherpenhuizen resulted in the latter's removal.[43]
This was chiefly occasioned by the unfriendly treatment of the
Jews at the governor's hands, who, seeing in them only the
partisans of his former rival, took care to harrass them with
unjust taxation.   This exasperated them so much that they
lodged a complaint against him with Baron de Belmonte and
their '' Citizens' Captain '' Samuel Nassy, both in Amsterdam,
and demanded the immediate recall of their prejudiced governor
from the State-Council.   Strangely enough, Nassy's influence

nicht allein die stets wieder neu einbrechenden Indianer mit starkem
Arm zurück, sondern bewirkte auch, dass der neu ernannte
Gouverneur Jan (Johann) van Scharphuisen von seinem Posten
abberufen wurde.'' Cf. also Isaac de Costa's work, *op. cit.*, p. 321.

[43] See Koenen's *Geschiedenis*, etc., p. 294: '' Ongelukkig ontstond
er een scherpe naijver tusschen den nieuwen Gouverneur en Samuel
Nassy, die vóór zijne komst bijkans alle gezag in zich vereenigd had,
en wellicht had gehoopt den Heer Van Sommelsdyk in het bestuur
te zullen opvolgen; ten gevolge waarvan hij goedvond de nieuw
wereld te verlaten, en zich onder zijne broederen te Amsterdam te
gaan nederzetten.   Ook na zijn vertrek bleef de spanning tusschen de
hoofden der Israelitische bevolking en den Heer Van Scherpenhuizen
voortduren, zoodat de eersten zich bij den Baron de Belmonte en
Samuel Nassy te Amsterdam over hem beklaagden, hun bijstand
verzochten, en de terugroeping van den Bewindhebber op die wijs
wisten te bewerken.   Hij werd in 1696 vervangen door Paulus Van
Der Veen, en deze op zijne beurt in 1706 door Willem de Gooyer.''

was still powerful, for he was replaced, in 1696, by another governor, Paulus van der Veen by name, shortly after the petition was filed. Scherpenhuizen embarked for Holland. Having been taken prisoner by the French on his way thither, he arrived there only after several months. Hardly had he landed at Amsterdam, before he was arraigned by Samuel Nassy before the civil court and he was compelled to vindicate his conduct.[44] The record of that trial and defense, in which Nassy took a leading part, is still extant, published in 1697.[45]

IV.

DEFENSE OF THE JEWS IN SURINAM AGAINST THE FRENCH IN 1689 AND 1712.

The loyalty of the Jews to their new settlement is unparalleled in American history. Every emergency found them ready to show their allegiance to Holland. Thus, when in 1689, a French fleet, under Admiral Cassard, made a sudden attack on the colony, they were met with brave resistence by

[44] Cp. Dr. M. Kayserling's sketch on "The Jews of Surinam," in *Monatsschrift, l. c.,* p. 207: " Ehe noch Scharphuizen auf Surinam landete, hatte Samuel Nasi die Kolonie verlassen. Nasi konnte es nicht ertragen, einen andern Mann in der Stellung zu sehen, welche er selbst zu erlangen hoffte und welche er, vermoege seiner dem Lande erwiesenen Dienste und Fähigkeiten mit Recht beanspruchen konnte. Er verliess Surinam und schiffte sich nach Amsterdam ein. In Folge der Mitbewerbung des Juden um die Gouverneurstelle hatte Scharphuizen die jüdischen Kolonisten mit weniger Freundlichkeit behandelt und sie hoeher besteuert als die uebrigen Bewohner der Kolonie, so dass jene bei dem Grafen de Belmonte und ihrem Bürger-Capitän Samuel Nasi Klage führten und die Rückberufung des Gouverneurs aufs dringenste von der Regierung verlangten. Wirklich wurde ein anderer Gouverneur in der Person des Paulus van der Veen bestellt. Scharphuizen schiffte sich nach Holland ein; unterwegs von den Franzosen zum Gefangenen gemacht, gelangte er erst nach mehreren Monaten in die Heimat. Kaum aber in Amsterdam angekommen, wurde er von Nasi vor Gericht gefordert und gezwungen sich oeffentlich zu vertheidigen."

[45] *Punten en articulen, und Bericht en antwoord van den Gouverneur Jan van Scherpenhuizen.* (Amsterdam, 1697.) It would be very interesting to have a copy of this important trial, in which Samuel Nassy figured so prominently.

the Jews.   Van Chattillon, son of the previous governor, displayed great heroism on this occasion.[46]   Two Dutch historians make mention of the valor of the Jews.   Verburg and Fr. Holf.   Merkurius relate in their *Histories of the East and West Indies*, that "after the death of Governor Aersen (*sic*) and the arrival of the new representative Scherpenhuizen, word was received that a French fleet was nearing Surinam.   All soldiers and sailors were ordered out and summoned to appear at the fort.   The call was obeyed by the Jews, of whom there were many in Surinam, and despite the fact that it was a Sabbathday, they fought valiantly for their colony.   Two letters eulogizing their action in the matter were sent to the Society *Felix Libertate*, by a worthy citizen, H. L. Bromet, who lived for many years in Surinam." [47]

[46] Cf. Koenen, *l. c.*, p. 293–294 : " De Joden van Surinam bewezen de Kolonie wederom groote diensten, toen zij in den jare 1689 eenen aanval te verduren had van het Fransche Eskader, onder bevel van den vlootvoogd Cassard; in welke verdediging de Heer Van Chatillon, zoon van den vorigen Bewindhebber, zich bijzonder onderscheidde." See also Isaac de Costa's *Israel und die Voelker* (1855), p. 321; Frankel in his *Monatsschrift*, vol. XII (1863), p. 362. *Révue des Études Juives*, Vol. IV (1882), p. 131.

[47] Dr. E. Carmoly, in a brief note entitled: "Patriotismus der Juden in Surinam," published in Dr. Leopold Loew's journal, *Ben Chananju* (Szegedin, 1861), Vol. IV, No. 20, p. 178, n. 37, writes: "Niemand wird ihnen den Ruhm streitig machen, nicht nur ihre Soldatendienste zu thun, sondern auch bei Zuegen gegen ihre in die Wälder geflohene Sklaven ihre Religionsgesetze den Interesse ihrer Buergerpflichten nachzusetzen; sogar aberglaubische Juden werden es ihnen nicht als Suende anzeichnen.   Man sehe davon einen Beweis in Verburg's O [*st*] *en* W [*est*] *Ind. Geschied* [*enis*], 11 D. 8, *Cyd bestek*, 35 hoofild. § 45, v. d. J. 1689, und Fr. Holf. Merkurius 40 D. wo erzählt wird, dass, da nach dem Tode des Gouverneur Aersen (*sic*) der Bevollmächtigte Scherphuizen bei seiner Ankunft in Surinam die Nachricht von der Annäherung der franzoesischen Flotte erhalten habe, sogleich alle Soldaten, nebst den Matrosen und den Bürgern auf das Kastell erboten und diesem Befehl Gehorsam geleistet worden sei, selbst von den Juden, deren viele in Surinam wohnen, ungeachtet es Sabbat war.   Auch hat man darueber zwei sehr schoene Briefe an die Gesellschaft: *Felix Libertate* von dem kuendigen Bürger H. L. Bromet der 20 Jahre lang in Surinam wohnte." These letters may yet be extant in the State library at Amsterdam, where many documents on Surinam are preserved.

The colony, unmolested by strife and war, soon began to thrive and prosper. Their respite was of short duration, however, for already in in 1712, Admiral Cassard, at the head of another powerful squadron advanced upon the settlement. A fierce attack made in June, 1712, was manfully repulsed. In October of the same year, Cassard's fleet again appeared on the coast, and endeavored to sail up the Commawine River. The inhabitants, and particularly the Jews, under Captain Isaac Pinto [48] offered a stubborn resistance, and although they fought valiantly, they could not prevent the enemy from landing, bombarding the city of Paramaribo, and devastating the country. The treaty of Utrecht sealed soon after between the French and Dutch put an end to these vagaries. [49]

A recent writer on American Jewish history says: "In the war against the French in 1689, members of the families Pinto da Fonsera (read *Fonseca*), Arias, Naar, De Brito and D'Avilar fought valiantly.'' [50]

[48] See my paper in the *P. A. J. H. S.*, No. 3, p. 121, note 1; also *Révue des Études Juives*. Vol. IV (1882), p. 131.

[49] See Van Kampen, *Geschiedenis der Nederlanders buiten Europa*, Dl. II, bl. 416–420; *apud* Koenen's *Geschiedenis*, etc., p. 294–495: " De Kolonie was van jaar tot jaar in bloei en welstand toegenomen, sedert de heilzame hervormingen van Aerssens hare talrijke vruchten begonnen af te werpen. Geen wonder, dat ire opkomende welvaart de Franschen, die op dat pas met de Republiek in oorlog waren, geweldig in de oogen stak. In Junij des Jaars 1712 waagden zij een vrij hevigen aanval, die echter manmoedig werd afgeslagen. In October verscheen de Fransche vlootvoogd Cassard op nieuw voor de kust, en trachte de rivier Commawine binnen te zeilen. De ingezetenen, in zonderheid de joden onder hun Kapitein Isaac Pinto, boden een hardnekkigen wederstand, doch konden niet beletten, dat de vijand het land afliep, de stad Paramaribo bombardeerde, en de volkplanting op een gruwzame wijs brandschattede. Kort daarop werd de vrede van Utrecht gesloten, waardoor de Kolonie van dezen vijand gelukkig voor het vervolg verlost werd." See also Dr. Kayserling, in the *Monatsschrift, l. c.*, p. 208. His remarks being substantially the same, we forbear citing in full.

[50] Cp. Dr. A. Hahn's article on *Primitive Jewish Settlements in America*, in the *American Jews' Annual* for 1886–1887, p. 36; also Isaac de Costa, *op. cit.*, p. 321; *Révue des Études Juives*, Vol. IV (1882), p. 131. We are inclined to think that the families mentioned, distinguished themselves in subsequent engagements in Surinam, during the negro revolts of which we shall speak in the next rubric.

V.

Hardly were the colonists freed from the depredations of the French before danger menaced them from another direction. An anonymous writer, cited by Hannah Adams,[51] says: "'The great check to the prosperity of Surinam has arisen from the inhabitants being exposed to the invasion and lawlessness of the Maroons, or runaway negroes, who have formed several communities in the inaccessible parts of the woods, and were the most implacable and cruel enemies of the colonists. *The Jewish militia have often signalized themselves against them, and have been of great use to the colony;* one-third of whom were of this (Jewish) nation.''

Already in the year 1690 the negro slaves on the plantation of a wealthy Jewish landowner, *Machado*, rebelled against their master and murdered him. Governor Scharphuizen, who entertained bitter feelings against the Jews, refused to lend them the slightest assistance, so that they were thrown entirely upon their own resources.[52] More than once the Jews, exasperated

---

[51] Cp. a review of the *Essai Historique sur la Colonie Surinam*, etc., quoted often in this ˙essay, in the *Monthly Review* for 1792; Frankel in his *Monatsschrift*, vol. XII (1863), p. 362; and Hannah Adams' *History of the Jews* (Boston, 1810) p. 457. On pp. 455–458, a fair résumé of the History of the Jews in Surinam is given.

[52] Koenen, *l. c.*, p. 295: "Reeds in het jaar 1690 waren de slaven op de plantagie van eenen rijken Israeliet, Machado genaämd, opgestaan, en hadden hun meester vermoord. Van toen af waren de Negers, die kans zagen om zich van hunne heeren te ontslaan, begonnen naar de binnenlanden te vluchten, alwaar zij zich in de bosschen nestelden. De Gouverneur Van Scherpenhuizen vond niet goed, den Joden bij dergelijke gelegenheden eenigen bijstand te verleenen, maar beval hun, om up hunne eigene verdediging bedacht te zijn. Dit was een groote misslag ; want, eensdeels leerde hij daardoor de Israelitische bevolking zich onderling tot hare eigene handhaving te verbinden, hetgeen lichtelijk voor de Christenen bij eenige botsing gevaarlijk had kunnen worden; anderdeels liet hij daardoor langzamerhand eene macht opkomen, die gelijk de ervaring geleerd heeft, niet slechts voor de rust en veiligheid, maar voor het bestaan der volkplanting zelve hoogstgevaarlijk moest worden." Cp. also Kayserling, *l. c.*, p. 208.

by the governor's neglect, took matters into their own hands, and defended themselves with great success. The negroes, nothing daunted by this spirited show of resistance assumed a still more threatening attitude, their numbers, and hence their audacity, increasing more and more each day. The natives knowing full well that their advantage lay in their endurance of climate and similar local circumstances, understood how to utilize the fact to their benefit, and during the following years harassed the colony very much. This state of affairs, however, could not last long. In 1730 a desperate effort was made by the Jewish militia, which was determined to punish the slaves, under the lead of an under-officer followed by fourteen volunteers and thirty-six negroes. They exhibited no little courage and bravery in the taking possession and guard of an important post situated in the vicinity of the devastated negro villages.[53] This determined stand of the Jews did not, by any means, intimidate the lawless hordes who were intent upon rebellion and plunder. On the contrary it only roused their anger all the more. In 1731 it was again deemed imperative to check their depredations. The Citizens' Captain *Boeyê* and the spirited David Nassy, (who more than any one else before and after him worked for the prosperity of Surinam) were chosen leaders of this campaign. David Nassy is described by historians as a man of power and integrity. He is said to have drilled the negro slaves on his plantation so thoroughly for such enterprises, that his co-operation was of the utmost necessity. He was the nephew of David Nassy who first settled in Surinam and received (in 1659), the famous charter of privileges to settle in Cayenne.[54] (See above.) It seems that he entertained friendly relations with his negro slaves who, in 1717 were offered perfect freedom by the Political Council

[53] Koenen, *l. c.*, pp. 295–296: " De Joden verdedigden zich meer dan eenmaal net goed gevolg. . . . . Evenwel deed men in 1730 eene krachtvolle poging, bij welke zich eene Joodsche compagnie, onder aanvoering van een Onderofficier met veertien blanken en zes-en-dertig Negers, onderscheidde door het bezetten en bewaken van een belankrijken post, na het verwoesten van de gehuchten der Bosch-negers." Cp. also Kayserling, *l. c.*, p. 208.

[54] Cp. Kayserling in *Monatsschrift, l. c.*, p. 208.

(*Raad van Politie*) if they volunteered to fight against the Maroons, who made frequent assaults on the colonists. Already in the year 1718, Nassy enlisted in the Jewish Corps, commanded by Captain *Jacob D'Avilar*, and distinguished himself in a combat of a similar nature. So impetuous and brave was he in battle that he was speedily promoted from a regular to the office of Lieutenant, and later to that of Captain of the Jewish Citizens' Company (*Kapitein der Joodsche burger compagnie*). He was, therefore, well qualified by dint of personal bravery and diplomatic skill to take so important a part in the expedition against the Maroons.

In the present campaign he was not less fortunate and heroic. Undaunted by the treacherous trick of Boeyé, who abandoned him in the middle of the fray, he attacked the foe in their own retreats, killed several and took as many more prisoners. Boeyé, who was his envious rival, fearful perhaps of the consequences of his own cowardice, accused Nassy of indiscretion and disobedience, but so universal was the esteem and sympathy felt for the latter, who had before earned laurels on the field and was thought incapable of such folly, that he had but little difficulty in proving his innocence. The result was that Nassy was honorably acquitted, whilst his jealous rival, the real culprit, was duly punished. He added to his fame most decisively by this new stroke of bravery and military prowess and had the honor of being praised and glorified by the Spanish-Jewish poetess *Benvenida Belmonte*,[55] who composed a fitting eulogy in verse on his deeds of valor.[56] Nassy was the

---

[55] Koenen, *l. c.*, p. 297, has erroneously *Ben Venida del Monte*—a name unknown in Spanish-Jewish literature. Dr. Kayserling, *l. c.*, p. 208, note 6, corrects the mistake, and identifies him with the same authoress, who wrote in praise of the Spanish translation of the Psalter by *Daniel Israel Lopez Laguna*, of Jamaica. Cp. the present writer's papers on *Early Jewish Literature in America*, in *P. A. J. H. S.*, No. 3, p. 110–112; 140–141; and *Jewish Martyrs of the Inquisition in South America*, in *P. A. J. H. S.*, No. 4, (1895) where full references are given on this famous American-Shephardic poet.

[56] See Koenen's *Geschiedenis l. c.*, p. 296–297: " . . . . .
Reeds in 1718 had hij, (David Nassy) onder bevel van den Joodschen Kapitein Jacob d'Avilar, aan een welgelukten aanslag van dien aard deel genomen: ten gevolge van welken hij van Onderofficier tot eersten Luitenant, straks tot Kapitein der Joodsche burger-compag-

second South American Jew, whose nobility of character and state services were commemorated in Spanish-Jewish literature. (Cp. *supra*, rubric II, on Abraham Coen of Brazil.) His generalship and scientific tactics were called into requisition about two decades afer his above detailed victory, in another expedition against the marauding band of negroes, who troubled the peace of the colony for nearly a century at various intervals. As previously noted, in the case of Machado, anno 1690, the slaves of another wealthy Jewish planter, *Manuel Pereira*, rebelled against their master, in 1738, and, thinking to shake off the yoke of slavery, cruelly murdered him. Hereupon, *Isaac Arias*, a former officer of the Jewish militia, who lived in the victim's neighborhood, sent out a detachment of Jewish volunteers, headed by *David Nassy* and *Abraham De Brito*, to wreak vengeance upon the rebels. The troops remained away for six weeks in the enemy's camp,[57] and it began to be feared that they were utterly routed and destroyed, when the company returned, bringing with them the trophies of a most successful onslaught made against the Maroons, namely six hands severed from fallen negroes, and forty-seven prisoners of war.

As a reward for their bravery every officer received from the Council (*Raad*) 75 f. (florins?); every citizen (Jewish regular) 36 f.; each armed negro 20 f.; and each colored man who was in needy circumstances, 5 f.[58]

nie, benoemd was. Thans was hij niet minder voorspoedig; en ofschoon door Boeyé verlaten, trof hij den vijand in zijne woningen aan; versloeg er velen, en nam een aantal anderen gevangen. Boeyé, die den Israelitischen Hoofdman wegens gebrek aan ondergeschiktheid, had aangeklaagd, werd zelf gestraft, en Nassy oogstte van dezen tocht zoo groot eenen naam in, dat hij door den Spaansch-Joodschen dichter (*sic*) Ben Venida del Monte (sic) in fierlijke lofdichten werd bezongen en gevierd." See also Kayserling, *l. c.*, p. 208. His notes based on Koenen's are not as full.

[57] Van Kampen, in his *Geschiedenis der Nederlanders buiten Europa*, Dl. III, bl. 116, says, curiously enough, that they were away about six *months* instead of six *weeks*.

[58] Cp. Koenen, *l. c.*, p. 297: " In 1738 standen de Negers der plantagie van den Joodschen eigenaar Manuel Pereira op, vermoorden hunnen meester. Hierop zond Isaac Arias, voormalig Officier der Joodsche compagnie die zijne bezittingen in de nabuurschap had,

30

Five years later, in 1743, brave old Captain David Nassy, who had conducted thirty like expeditions against the Maroons, sallied forth for the last time to fight for his people and, according to some, to die on the battlefield the death of a hero.[59] This time he was arrayed against the Creoles, who by reason of their more acute intelligence and culture (having been long associated with Europeans) were yet the most dangerous of all their foes. Endowed with a noble Macabbean spirit, he fell like his ancestor Matathias, in the moment of victory. It was on the *Day of Atonement* that the venerable sage and warrior sallied forth to war. It must have been urgent indeed, for David Nassy regardless of the solemnity of the festival put himself at the head of his trusty men, crossed over the Surinam River; penetrated further inland; pursued the enemy, set their huts ablaze; tore their fruits out of the ground; killed many on the spot and dragged about forty slaves along with them as captives. Nassy, who had already passed his three score years and ten, fell a victim to the treachery of his foes. It was told him that the negroes had poisoned all the wells in the village, so that he was compelled to turn homeward, in order to quench the burning thirst which afflicted him and his troops, without awaiting the orders of the Council. This most

eenige, vrijwilligers van zijne natie, onder aanvoering van David Nassy en Abraham De Brito, tegen de Boschnegers uit. Zes weken lang bleef deze bende op vijandelijken grond, zoodat niemand wist wat van haar geworden was; doch bij hunne terugkomst bleek het, dat zij een allervoorspoedigsten aanval hadden gedaan terwijl zij de afgehouwene, handen van zes gesneuvelde Negers, en zeven-een-veertig krijgsgevangenen medevoerden. Jeder Officier ontving daarop van den Raad voor dezen tocht f. 75 ; jeder burger f. 36; elk gewapende Neger f. 20, en jeder zwarte die met levensmiddelen belast geweest was, f. 5 ter belooning." See also Dr. Kayserling, *l. c.*, pp. 208–209. He does not state what the rewards were.

[59] Cf. Dr. Hahn's article on *Primitive Jewish Settlements in America*, in *The American Jews' Annual* for 1886–87, p. 36, who says that "among those who fell on the battlefield was David Nassi, in 1743, at the age of seventy. That was his thirty-first campaign against the French." We are inclined to believe that this is wrong, for earlier historians (see the following note) state that he died of a broken heart—a victim of slander. Furthermore, he did not fight against the French, but the Maroons. See also Isaac de Costa, *op. cit.*, p. 321.

natural step gave his opponents a good excuse for lodging a complaint against him with the authorities, who are usually ready to listen to malice and dispute. His defense was scarcely heard and he was pronounced guilty. Such wanton ingratitude the good old soldier hardly expected as a reward for his services for the welfare of his fellow-men. Bitter disappointment and grief undermined his health. He was seized with fever, and soon after at the age of seventy, or thereabouts, death released him from his sufferings. With him died the flower of the Jewish colony, an Israelite indeed, in whom there was no guile. His co-religionist, *Isaac Carvalho*, was chosen Captain of the Jewish Citizens' Company, in his place.[60]

A few years later, a treaty of peace was made with the Western Maroons, who were getting more and more perilous to the safety of the colonists. But a new danger threatened them from another side. In 1749 the Maroons in the east, known as *Tempati (?) Negroes* (*Tempati-negers*), broke forth in mutiny, plundered a plantation completely and carried off all the negro slaves who lived there. This plantation (as in fact

[60] Cf. Kuenen, *l. c.*, p. 297–98: Vijf jaren later deed dezelfde onvermoeide Israelit (David Nassy), die wel dertig tochten tegen de Boschnegers heeft ondernomen, ofschoon reeds bejaard, nog eenen aanval op het dorp der kreoolsche Negers, die door hunne meer dere beschaving en hun omgang met de Europeers de gevaarlijkste van alle waren. Deze strooptocht had plaats op den grooten Verzoendag der Joden. Zonder dat zij zich door de heiligheid van het feest lieten terug houden, trokken deze, de rivier Suriname langs, het binnenland in vervolgden den vijand, staken zijne hutten in vlam, roeiden de veldvruchten uit den grond, brachten een aantal Negers om, en voerden viertien krijgssgevangenen met zich. Doch Nassy werd het slachtoffer van een list des vijands. Men maakte hem diets, dat de waterbronnen door de Negers vergiftigd waren; een hij, door gebrek aan de noodige verversching gedwongen, neemt op zich om terug de keeren, zonder den last of de orders ven deen Raad af te wachten. Zijne benijders en tegenstanders wisten hem deswege bij den Raad in een kwaad gerucht te brengen; zijne verdediging werd naauwelijks aangehoord; zijn proces opgemaakt. Dit krenkte den wakkeren man zoo geweldig, dat hij door eene koorts werd aangetast, die hem in den ouderdom van zeventig jaren ten grave sleepte. Na zijnen dood werd zijn geloofsgenoot, Isaac Carvalho, in zijne plaats tot Kapitein der Joodsche burger—compagnie benoemd." Cp. also, Kayserling, *l. c.*, p. 209.

all others in Surinam) belonged to a Jewish land-owner, and was called *Auka*. Henceforth the insurrection which originated there was named after the *Auka-negroes*. Against these marauders, an expedition, partly under the Christian chief, Rijsdorp, and parly in command of the Jewish captain, *Moses Naar*, was organized and dispatched in 1757. It deserves to be mentioned, by the way, that this was Naar's *seventeenth campaign* against the Creoles. The result of this undertaking was likewise favorable. Naar burned down a whole negro-village, made a number of captives, among them being a certain Corydon, the leader of the insurrection. For his bravery and skilful capture he was presented with a worthy gift by the Council.[61]

We are informed by David J. C. Nasi (or Nassy), the third descendant of the original settler of Surinam, who compiled with other intelligent men of his age, an exhaustive and comprehensive chronicle of the Jews in Surinam in French,[62] that

[61] See Koenen, *l. c.*, p. 298–299: "Eenige jaren daarna werd een verdrag van vrede met de meer en meer gevaarlijk wordende westelijke Marrons gesloten. Doch nu vertoonde zich en nieuw gevaar van den kant der oostelijke of Tempati-negers, die in het jaar 1749 eene plantagie plonderden, en de Negerslaven die zich aldaar bevonden, met zich voerden. Deze plantagie behoorde eenen Joodschen eigenaar, en heette *Auka*; van daar bleef aan deze opstandelingen de naam van *Auka-negers*. Tegen dien vijand was het, dat in 1757 een tocht werd ondernomen, gedeeltelijk onder den Christenoverste Rijsdorp, gedeeltelijk onder den Joodschen Kapitein *Naar*, die reeds vroeger zestien malen tegen denzelfden vijand opgetrokken was. De uitslag ook van deze onderneming was allergunstigst. *Naar* verbrandde een groot Negerdorp, maakte een aantal gevangenen, waaronder zich zekere Corydon, de belhamel der opstandelingen, bevond, en werd voor zijn manmoedig bedrijf door den Raad met een aanzienlijk geschenk begiftigd." See also Dr. Kayserling, *l. c.*, p. 209: "Im Verein mit dem obersten Rijsdorp bekriegte Naar die noch immer Verheerung anrichtenden Neger. Er verbrannte eine ihrer groessten Doerfer, nahm ihren Häuptling gefangen und wurde wegen seiner an den Tag gelegten Tapferkeit ansehnlich belohnt."

[62] See the *Essai Historique sur la Colonie de Surinam*, etc., (Paramaribo, 1788; Dutch version, Amsterdam, 1791), Vol. I, p. 123. Of this rare and valuable work, which was called forth by the writings of Dohm on the *Emancipation of the Jews*, only one copy (in the British Museum) is known to be in existence. The writer of these lines is having the volumes copied in view of his *History of the Jews in*

already in 1750, *Moses Naar* and *Gabriel de La Fatte*, in recognition of their active zeal in suppressing a revolt of the negroes in their colony, were presented with silver cups and a vote of thanks from the government.[63]

The fame achieved by his co-religionist, *Naar*, so enthused and electrified the young and ambitious *Isaac Nassy* that he was eagerly anticipating another outbreak on the part of the Maroons, in order to show his courage and reckless heroism. The impetuous youth met with a noble, but pathetic end:

Thinking that against a well-regulated army, however small, no valor or charge of the negroes could possibly prevail, he hastily collected twelve of his followers upon the rumor of their approach; armed his and their most trusty slaves; provided himself with the barest necessities of war, sufficient for about ten or twelve days, and pursued the retreating foe with an ardor which, if imprudent, is at least a virtue in one so young and war-thirsty. He was, however, suddenly confronted by a much more considerable number of negroes than he reckoned upon. His little band stood ground but for a short while. Nassy himsely displayed great bravery, and although severely wounded by a rifle shot in his right limb, he began to fight with a still more marvelous energy in order to rally his terrified men and to re-arouse their fleeting courage. But in vain. He was captured alive by the sanguinary horde and brutally murdered. Two of their chief officers and twenty soldiers fell with him on the battlefield.[64]

Surinam. See for further references his paper in the *P. A. J. H. S.*, No. 3, pp. 126–30. It is worthy of mention that this is the *first* work published in Paramaribo.

[63] Cf. Rev. E. M. Myers' *Centurial* (New York, 1890), p. 117, *ad ann.* 1750.

[64] Cp. *Essai Historique sur la Colonie de Surinam*, etc. (Paramaribo, 1788), Vol. I, pp. 98, 99; Kuenen, *l. c.*, pp. 299, 300 gives a graphic account: "Zoodanige belooning, de eerzucht ook van den nog jeugdigen *Isaac Nassy* prikkelende, berokkende dezen moedigen jongeling zijn ondergang. Naijverig op de onderscheiding, door zijnen geloofsgenoot verworven, en wanende, dat de Boschnegers tegen een' geregelden aanval geen moed noch kracht wisten over te stellen, verzamelt hij in haast een twaalftal zijner vrienden, wapent hunne beste slaven en de zijnen, voorziet zich met een onbeduidenden voorraad van krijgsbehoeften en levensmiddelen voor tien of twaalf

At last, the authorities saw that it was advisable and imperative again to make a treaty of peace with the relentless Maroons, or fugitive negroes, (*gevluchte Negers*) whose ravages
for over half a century spread ruin and terror throughout the
land. Accordingly, on the 23d of May, 1761, peace was established, to last for a good many years, apparently.[65] It was
not long, however, before hostilities were resumed. In 1772
the State Council found it imperative to call in the aid of the
mother country against the Maroons, who grew more audacious
in proportion as they advanced in culture and education.[66]
The State General, roused to action by the serious state of
affairs in the colony, sent a company of 500 men, under command of Captain Forgeoud, who had previously shown much
courage and ingenuity in suppressing a revolt of negroes in the
Barbary States. Two years later, a series of military posts
was established, beginning from the *Savannah of the Jews* to
the banks of the Commawine River and from there to the sea.
Forts, strengthened by means of palisades were constructed
from plantation to plantation, and when finally peace was
enforced, the colony was spared from any further molesta-
tion at the hands of the unruly negroes.[67] Koenen, though very

dagen en vervolgt alzoo den op de vlucht gedreven' vijand. Doch hij
stutte op een veel grooter aantal dan hij berekend had. Eenen tijd
lang hielden de blanken zich nog stande. *Nassy* leide groote dapper-
heid aan een dag, en ofschoon hij een geweerschot in het rechter-
been bekomen had, deed hij nog groote moeite om zijne lieden te
hereenigen en hun zinkenden moed weder aan te wakkeren. Doch
te vergeefs. Hij werd levend door de Negers gevat, en wreedaardig
vermoord. Wellicht zouden zij hem nog het leven gespaard hebben,
ten einde de voldoening te smaken van zich door een' blanke te laten
dienen; maar 'de wraakzucht, die al te hevig in hun woesten boezem
blaakte, liet hun zelfs deze wreede barmhartigheid niet toe. Zij
verloren echter bij deze gelegenheid een tweetal hunner opperhoof-
den, en nog wel twintig gemeenen." See also Kayserling, in *Monatsschrift, l. c.,* pp. 209, 210.

[65] Cf. Koenen, *l. c.,* p. 300–301: "Den 23 sten Mei, 1761, werd er
een vrede met hen gesloten, die thans een einde maakte aan de
gewapende tochten," etc., etc.

[66] See *Essai Historique sur la Colonie de Surinam*, etc., Vol. I,
p. 130.

[67] Cf. *Essai Historique*, etc., Vol. I, p. 135; Koenen, *l. c.,* p. 301–
302.

fair and just to the Jews in his *History*, sees fit to reproach them for their unkind treatment. of slaves,[68] which, he opines, was the chief cause of the rebellion, lasting over seventy years. We are inclined to think that this rebuke is unwarranted, inasmuch as the rigid Mosaic and Rabbinic laws regarding them, were always strictly followed by the Jews and those in Surinam, who had men like the family of Nassy at their head, could not have trespassed these ordinances. He admitted, however, in his summary, that the colony in her defense was always deeply indebted to the Jewish militia, and in social and commercial matters especially beholden to them, for the Jews were the cultivators of the marshy and often dangerous soil and the masters of commerce, the chief factors of the welfare and prosperity of the settlement,[69] since its foundation. Not desiring to anticipate our conclusions in a larger work, we content ourselves with saying that nowhere else in the history of America is such devotion, disinterestedness and loyalty on the part of Jewish citizens so marked, and let us add, so gratefully recognized as in the little Dutch Province of Surinam. And nowhere else in the New World did the Israelites thrive more in culture, learning and religion than in the *Jewish Savannah* of Guiana, as their community was called. Small wonder, then, in view of their attachment to their Hollandish masters, when we hear that in 1785, on the occasion of the reconsecration of their synagogue, then 100 years old, the Governor Wichers, with all the provincial magistrates and other eminent citizens, attended in a body the impressive ceremonies, which

[68] See Koenen, *l. c.*, p. 300: " . . . De afkeer des verdrukten Negers was veel grooter voor den Israelitischen meester dan voor den Christenplanter; en de Jood was harder tegen den armen slaaf, dan zijn landgenoot van verschillend geloof." etc.

[69] Cf. Koenen, *ibid.*, *l. c.*, p. 300–301: " . . . . Haasten wij ons intusschen, tegenover deze treurige bedenkingen de aangenamer opmerking te maken, dat de volkplanting wegens hare verdediging niet minder verplichtingen aan hare Joodsche bevolking in die dagen gehad heeft, dan vroeger wegens de oorbaarmaking harer woeste gronden, of als het moederland door de herlevendiging van deszelfs handel; en dat dus de Jood in de kolonien door het beoefenen van den landbouw en het waarnemen der landsbeveiliging, die verdiensten verworven heeft, die hem in het Gemeenebest zelve nog schenen te ontbreken."

are graphically narrated in a little volume published by an eye witness.[70] And that two Christian philo-Semites wrote beautiful verses in Dutch in honor of these festivities, republished by the writer, elsewhere.[71] Nor does it now seem strange that the Jews loved to glorify their governors, J. G. Wichers,[72] Sir Chas. Green,[73] and Abraham De Veer,[74] in pretty songs and hymns, written in Hollandish and Hebrew. These were but poetic tokens of their patriotism. As late as 1853, the records inform us of their prosperity and constantly growing activity and interest in the colony. In that year we find them in the courts (Ellis, Juda, Fernandes, and others); among thirteen advocates, notaries, and procurators, there were seven Jews (Heilbronn, Colaço, Belmonte, de Granada, Abendañon, etc.); many served in the army as captains, lieutenants, colonels, majors, and chaplains.

[70] *Beschrijving van de plechtigheden, nevens de lofdichten en gebeden uitgesproken op het eerste Jubelfeest van de Synagogue der Portugeesche Joodsche gemeente, op de Savane in de Colonie Suriname, genaamd Zegen En Vrede.* [*Berakha Ve-Shalom*] *op den 12 den van Wijnmaand 1785.* (Amsterdam, Hendrik Willem en Cornelis Dronsberg, 1786). The volume is described at length in my paper on *Early Jewish Literature in America, P. A. J. H. S.*, No. 3, pp. 126–129, where the Hebrew title is also given.

[71] See the writer's *Literary Gleanings on American Jewish History*, No. II, in the *Menorah Monthly* for September, 1895 (Vol. XIX), pp. 149–152.

[72] See S. J. Rudelsom's *Lofzang op den bleyde dag der inhuldiging van. . . . . J. G. Wichers, gouverneur-generaal over de colonie v. Suriname, 2 Juni, 1785.* The Ms. of this interesting pamphlet will soon be printed, with other works of Surinam Jews, in the French Jewish periodical, *Révue des Etudes Juives*, published in Paris. See also *P. A. J. H. S.*, No. 3, p. 127.

[73] *Plechtigheden, vreugde gezangen en gebeeden in de Hoogd. Joodsche Synagogue Neve Salom, te Suriname, op d. dag d. dinhuldig. van Sir Charles Green, Gouverneur-Generaal over Suriname, opgesteld en gezongen d. J. M. De Vries, Voorzanger.* (Paramaribo, 1804.) See also *P. A. J. H. S.*, No. 3, p. 130.

[74] See *Plechtige Vreugde Gezangen, en Gebeden, Verricht in de Hoogduitsche Israelitische Sinagogue Neve Salom. . . . . te Suriname, ter gelegenheid, en op den blydendag der Inhuldiging van Zynen Hoog Edelen Gestrengen, Heer Abraham De Veer, Gouverneur-Generaal der gemelde kolonie,—Gezongen door den Erwaarden Heer Tobias Tall.* The Hebrew title and other particulars are given in the writer's paper, *P. A. J. H. S.*, No. 3, pp. 130–131.

In fact they minister to the public weal in every conceivable capacity.[75] In their hands the colony still prospers. Recent reports, made by a correspondent of the *Jewish Chronicle* in London, are aglow with enthusiasm for the prosperity of their now thrifty and intelligent colony, and reassure us of the vigor and tenacity of our faith in that distant land.

VI.

EXTRACTS FROM A LETTER OF DAVID EBRON (DATED 1597) TO KING PHILIP II, GIVING AN ACCOUNT OF HIS DISCOVERIES AND SERVICES TO THE STATE, IN SOUTH AMERICA.

Among the numerous letters, documents and registers of the Albaic archives,[76] which bear special reference to the discovery and colonization of America, is particularly noticeable the culture-historic, perhaps valuable memorial address of DAVID EBRON from Constantine, Algeria (dated December 9th, 1597), to the Emperor, Philip II. The writer introduces himself in the preliminary note as an Israelite, who, at a tender age, fled to Africa, and rendered important services to the King of India and other personages of rank in various sections of Africa.

He enumerates many items of surprising significance, apparently anxious to array them as an overwhelming evidence of his abilities and reliability, and eager to impress upon the august reader the great amount of gratitude due him for his achievements. He prepared accurate sketches of distant

---

[75] Cf. Dr. Kayserling, *Monatsschrift, l. c.*, p. 213.

[76] For completeness' sake we reproduce this chapter from a recent sketch in the *Menorah Monthly* (Vol. XIX), for September, 1895, pp. 145–148, entitled: *A 16th Century document written by David Ebron, a Jewish financier in America.* This newly discovered letter is perhaps the most important evidence yet furnished of the services rendered by the Jews in the discovery and financial improvement of America, and deserves to be incorporated in this work. The book containing a copy of this document was lately published in Madrid (1891), under the title: *Documentos Escogidos del Archivo de la Casa di Alba.* See for other particulars the above quoted article in *Menorah*, note. We intend publishing Ebron's letter soon in the orginal.

regions and established settlements, dependent upon his
generous bounty; he discovered countries and conquered them,
and whatsoever had been attempted in Santa Marta, South
America, within the last five years, may be safely attributed
to his energetic activity and perseverance. Thence he repaired
by land to Peru, and enlisted in the service of the monarch in
Huancabelica. The last remarkable harvest in quicksilver,
which was so advantageous to the king, was chiefly due to his
judicious management. By careful husbanding of material
and laudable zeal he was instrumental in not only saving sixty
and some odd thousand pesos (!) involved in the annual transportation of small fleets from Lima and Panama but equally as
much by causing galleys to be constructed there.

Through the personal malice and mean manœuvers of two
officials, the well-merited reward for the last mentioned benefits
was withheld from him. '' But,'' affirms the abused victim of
ingratitude with a dignified emphasis, which seemed to restore
his confidence, '' my accomplishments in this regard may easily
be ascertained by application to Gutierrez Florez, the Indian
minister of commerce in Seville.''

'' I do not bring these facts to your notice,'' continues the
self-vindicator in haughty terms, '' in order to obtain reward
from your Majesty, but that your serene highness might perceive how zealously and indefatigably, I, a *secret Hebrew*,[77]
travelled everywhere, despite harassing circumstances, obstacles
end even imminent perils, and have forsaken your realm out of
pure fear to die outside of my faith, which, according to my
conception is the only true creed appointed by the Almighty,
the Creator of heaven, sun, moon, sea and all things therein,
you, gracious Sire included. I do not revive these recollections in order to deplore my ill-fortune or petition for the proper
remuneration and recognition denied me for the various favors
rendered, for such great and weighty benefits I am yet in a
position to offer from here, without necessitating my residence
there; only out of simple attachment to your royal highness,

---

[77] On the Marranos in Hispañiola and South America, Dr. Kayserling has published some interesting data in the *P. A. J. H. S.*, No.
2; see also his *Christopher Columbus and the Participation of the
Jews in the Discovery of America* (New York, 1894).

whom I desire to serve and in order that the memory of this Israelite and his faithful acts be not wholly eradicated from yóur heart, I am quite satisfied to continue the diligent execution of projects confided to my trust. O, would it please the Heavenly Father, that the Jews in your dominion could enjoy the same liberties and privileges accorded to them by the exemplary toleration of the Pope in Rome, Venice Milan, Naples, in the whole of Apulia, Ragusa, Florence, Pisa, Ferrara, Mantova and Italy and *here in Constantine* and the Barbary States.

Would that they were permitted to migrate from one portion of your realm to the other and live under the same circumstances as elsewhere. Then I would not resign from the office I so loyally occupied, and your countries would considerably increase in commercial opulence—it is inconceivable why your Grace should not participate in the profits reaped by others— then your armies, military exploits and campaigns against Lutherans, heretics and other enemies would be much more successful than they have been heretofore.

" And as regards the Spanish Inquisition against the Jews," [78] further declares this remarkable champion of the Mosaic faith, " I have absolutely no objection to urge, if it is directed against such as voluntarily embrace Christianity and secretly profess the ancient religion." He calls the King's attention to the fact that within two months he could at command transport 200,000 pesos cash money into the state treasury without injuring anyone; in a similar manner he is able in one single day, whenever the King willed it, to obtain more than one million pieces of gold from Santa Fe in the new kingdom of Granada. Other treasures are spoken of as accessible to the all-conquering genius of *David Ebron*, and obtainable by him for the King, whom he is intent on reconciling to his Jewish subjects.

[78] The writer of these pages, in another paper, treats of the sufferings of the *Marranos* or New Christians in Mexico, Peru and Brazil from 1570 to 1750. See his article on "The Jewish Martyrs of the Inquisition in South America," in *P. A. J. H. S.*, No. 4, (1895). Dr. Cyrus Adler furnishes in the same *Publications*, No. 4, a valuable sketch on the "Trial of Jorge de Almeida by the Inquisition in Mexico," 1590–1609, which sets forth the social condition of the secret Jews in that country at the end of the sixteenth century.

His eloquence reaches the fever heat of indignation, however, when he alludes to the thievish officials in the King's employ. " What a pity, your Majesty, that so much money is stolen in India and Spain. I could aggravate myself to death when I contemplate upon the mass of wealth wrongfully acquired by your representatives and ministers. Were I to enumerate all the outrageous robberies committed against you, O mighty Sovereign, in Seville, and apprise you of the doings of that infamous horde there stationed, and admitted into your court! . . . O lips, if only you would divulge the secrets which oppress the heart! O tongue! why not reveal what you know and feel?" In concluding his remarks, he places himself at the disposal of the government as confidential agent in the affairs of Portugal, the marriage of the Oranian, and similar matters, and enjoins upon the King to communicate with him under the seal of strictest privacy, should he require his co-operation or assistance at any future time. "The God of Abraham, Isaac and Jacob," says he, "who created the universe, protect and exalt your Majesty and inspire you to deal leniently and indulgently with your Hebrews, whom God never totally ignores or forgets, but inflicts with penalties and disasters only to try their fortitude and allegiance!"

This quite forgotten explorer and financier, whose eloquent plea in behalf of his race can not fail to appeal to every one, and whose only demand for the enormous service rendered to his king is more tolerance toward his people, deserves an honorable place in the annals of American Jewish History as a loyal, patriotic subject.

VII.

Enterprise and Influence of the Gradis Family in the West Indies, and During the Canadian Wars.

This is not to be a series of biographical sketches on the Rothschilds of the Eighteenth Century, for neither the space nor the scope of this work would permit of such an elaborate history. This chapter aims merely to set forth the political prominence attained by the family of Gradis,[79] to whose hands the fortunes of two continents were entrusted, and whose labors of love and patriotic services during the war-times of France in America, deserve to be chronicled in our annals. Reserving the elaboration of the family's antecedents, and other interesting particulars for another large paper on the *History of the Jews in Martinique*—the seat of their chief activity—we shall here detail those fa ts which concern our topic the most.

We may begin with *David Gradis*, who, in 1731, was naturalized in Bordeaux,[80] and who died in 1751. Already in 1696 he founded the great mercantile house which had commercial connections with England, Holland, Paris, southern France and the West Indies. The exports were linen, wine and alcohol. In the year 1715, David Gradis tided over the financial crisis under Louis XIV., after paying a draft of 150,000 francs, which his house endorsed. In fact the hard times did not affect him much, for we know that only two years after he conducted all the transatlantic commerce. He fitted out three ships, one bound for Cayenne and two for the Island of Martinique (or *Martinico*). His cargo consisted of wine, alcohol, meal and pickled meat, which he exchanged for sugar and indigo in the West Indian ports. Another money-crisis in 1719, passed without materially injuring his prospects, although he lost heavily. In spite of it, however, he again undertook foreign expeditions and was, as before, successful. In 1724, his business expanded to such an extent that he opened a branch on the island of St. Domingo. His name and fame grew in pop-

---

[79] The sources whence the materials contained in this chapter are taken, being for the most part accessible, and, as in a forthcoming essay on the *Jews of Martinique*, all the references will be incorporated in full, the writer merely quotes the following authorities: *Notice sur la famille Gradis et sur la maison Gradis ét fils de Bordeaux, par Henri Gradis* (1875), *apud* Graetz, " Die Familie Gradis," in his *Monatsschrift*, etc., Vol. XXIV (1875), pp. 447–459; XXV (1876), pp. 78–85; his *Geschichte der Juden*, Vol. XI (Leipzig, 1870), pp. 190, 200, 202, 223; see also Ad. Thierry: *Dissertation sur cette quest. est-il des moyens de rendre les juifs plus heureux et plus utile en France—(ouvrage couronné)* Paris, 1788; and several books on the history of the Jews in Bordeaux. In our narrative of the career of the Gradis family we follow Prof. Graetz, in his *Monatsschrift, l. c.*

[80] Cf. also Dr. Graetz, in *Monatsschrift*, Vol. XXIV, p. 557.

ularity and opulence, and French America was glad to acknowledge the enterprise of this energetic man who passed under the name of *the Portuguese Merchant*. And, although Jews were not tolerated in the French colonies, by the stern and scheming Jesuits, as we shall have ample occasion to show elsewhere, the government was constrained to overlook his origin and belief, in view of his vast influence and commercial importance. So universal was the esteem felt for the house of David Gradis that when his son Samuel, who conducted the interests of the business in St. Pierre, Martinique, died there in 1732, his remains were interred in the garden of the *frères de la Charité*, and masses were held in the cloisters for the repose of his soul. True, the monks dared not erect a monument to mark the spot. The lieutenant of the colony urged in argument of their expulsion the fact that were any of the members of the house of Gradis, there established, to die, their property would have to be confiscated, for Jews were not permitted to have possessions. Nevertheless he shut his eyes on their prolonged residence on the island. Abraham, eldest son of David Gradis, succeeded his father as senior member of the firm, of which he was previously a partner. He achieved even more fame than his predecessor. Endowed with wonderful ability and speculative genius, he also controlled the trade of France with the West Indies. He received important official contracts from the government; became intimate with personages of the highest political rank; obtained the protection and friendship of M. Maurepas, the confidant of Louis XVI., and added much to the glory and renown of the house of "*David Gradis, et fils.*" His extensive correspondence with the greatest men of the reign of Louis XV. and XVI., is still extant.

Through the friends who were influential in his behalf at court, his ships were fitted out at the cost of the government, and this gave him further opportunity to enlarge his business connections. Nor was he ungrateful for these privileges and for the consideration shown him by his royal patron. Thus we hear of remarkable exploits undertaken in behalf of his country. In the wars between England and France for the possession of Canada, he displayed extraordinary activity. In order to expedite matters, he fitted out ships to Canada, although the insurance on the cargo, because of the war then pending, was most exorbitant. If his freight vessels were captured by the armed cruisers of the enemy, he built and replenished new ones, without caring for losses thus incurred for France. In 1748, he organized the society of Canada, under the auspices of the government, in order to test the possibilities of the land, and thereby again widened the sphere of his mercantile activity. Important missions were entrusted to him. His ships carried valuable cargo (presumably military ammunition, etc.), always at the expense of the firm. He even erected magazines in Quebec. Later on the goverment defrayed these costs, but *David Gradis et fils* had no little share in the success of these projects.

After his father's death in 1751, Abraham Gradis' financial interests were still more extended. To give an idea of the scope of his commercial activity we will cast a momentary glance into the private accounts of the firm. In 1758, the commerce of the house with the French colonies alone, amounted to 2,369,326 francs. In the following year, the firm received the commission to forward 4500 tons of goods and ammunition for the French troops in Canada. Twelve ships, among them *eight of his own* were called into service for the purpose. From 1759 to 1763, when Canada ceased to be a French possession, the export trade of the firm of Gradis was worth *nine million francs*. These merchant vessels, on account of the war, had to be manned by a goodly company of soldiers, who had frequent occasion to defend themselves from attacks on the sea, and saved quite often the honor of their flag by their fearlessness and bravery.

During the struggle between England and France for the occupation of Canada, the house of Gradis dispatched thither many heavily laden ships at the order and expense of the French Government, which was their debtor to the amount of several millions on more than one occasion. Of course these obligations could not be liquidated for some time. Gradis & Co.'s drafts were not promptly paid, for France was impoverished by the American wars and had no means at her disposal. Although these noble financiers suffered heavy losses from the capture and detention of richly cargoed vessels sent out in the

name of France, they did not lose faith and preserved their
balance with a skill and energy which is remarkable. Far from
fearing to sacrifice too much for the fatherland, they strove
more and more to merit the good will and esteem of the king
and the aristocracy. It was indeed a work of charity and
patriotism on their part to ransom French captives.[81] Abraham
Gradis, we are told, authorized an influential business friend in
London, to supply the captains and commanders held as
prisoners in England with everything necessary to ease and
comfort their condition.[82]

He more than once was compelled to appeal to the government for the necessary funds due him, in order to carry on his
trade 'with the colonies, which was increasing in dimensions
every year. The road to the audience-chamber of the King
was not always clear to even so influential a personage as Abraham Gradis. On one occasion, being hard pressed for money
to fill a large order received from the West Indies, he presented
his claim to Minister Berryer—well known for his harsh and
imperious demeanor. The latter, hesitating to comply, Gradis
assured him that unless his demands were soon satisfied he would
be prevented from accomplishing his duties. Whereupon the
stern minister cuttingly replied: *" That will not be such a great
misfortune ; you merchants are accustomed to such things ; in fact
you become rich through them !"* Abraham Gradis straightened
himself up at this insult, and looking steadily at the great man,
said: "The name of Gradis, better known in four quarters of
the globe than that of the Minister of France, is free from dis-
honor. No taint of any kind covers its escutcheon!" With

---

[81] This important fact is thus recorded by Prof. Graetz: (*Geschichte der Juden*, vol. XI, p. 190) " Gradis aus einer reichen und
angesehenen Familie in Bordeaux, die grosse Bank- und ueber-
seeische Geschaefte fuer die franzoesischen Colonien betrieb, eigene
Schiffe ausruestete und dem franzoesischen Staate in den entfernten
Besitzungen *durch Ausloesung franzoesischer Gefangener aus den
Haenden der Englaender Dienste geleistet hatte.*" See also the following note, which is still more explicit.

[82] Cf. Graetz, in *Monatsschrift*, vol. XXIV., p. 452: " . . *Abraham Gradis gab einem Geschaeftsfreunde in London den Auftrag,
den gefangenen franzoesischen Capitaenen und Commandanten auf
seine Rechnung Alles zu verabreichen, was sie noethig haben sollten,
um ihre Lage zu erleichtern.*"

this he urged the minister with even greater persistence to render him satisfaction by appealing to the King in his behalf. Berryer, unused to such show of courage and firmness, could not but comply with his request, and Gradis' claims were duly honored.

It was no conceit that prompted his reply to the haughty representative of King Louis XV. His sovereign gave frequent sign of his favor and gratitude for the diplomatic skill and rare tact as well as noble devotion with which Gradis managed the business affairs of the empire in these revolutionary days. The minister once wrote in the following strain to Gradis & Co.: "I considered it my duty to remind his Majesty that your conduct was both unselfish and zealous for the welfare and services of the state on all occasions and under all circumstances. His Majesty commissions me to express to you his utmost satisfaction and recognition."

As a reward for his untiring interest in behalf of the French nation, exceptional privileges were granted to him (Abraham Gradis), and his family in the colonies. The right of owning real estate and civil equality in common with the other citizens of France on the Island of Martinique, were accorded to him in 1779. It is interesting to note that he was associated with the Superior of the Jesuit Missionaries in Martinique—the famous *pater Lavalette*, who had charge of the largest and most influential congregation there, and who conducted an immense business with foreign countries. Gradis once advanced him 400,000 francs. He often received him in his own home socially, and was charmed by the personal merits of the enterprising Jesuit. This did not prevent Gradis—a shrewd and careful merchant who knew just how much to risk—from severing all connections with him, for he rather early suspected the utter collapse of Lavalette's colossal undertakings, and thus avoided the bankruptcy which would inevitably have resulted, had he, like other careless firms, allowed himself to be drawn into the vortex of speculation. Similar causes of self-preservation prompted him to withdraw from further commercial relations with the State, as another financial crisis warned him of the outbreak of the Revolution.

Much more of interest might be told of Abraham Gradis and
31

other members of the same stock. Thus for instance of his acts of kindness during the famine in the French Colonies, at which time he sent seventeen ships laden with nourishment and merchandise for the relief of the suffering—a fact used by the Abbe Gregoire as a plea and an argument in favor of the emancipation of the Jews.

A rebellion in St. Domingo and in Martinique where the Gradis family (among them David II, Benjamin, Moses Gradis, etc.), owned extensive territory, together with the losses in the mother country during the French Revolution, caused the downfall of this princely house. Their possessions in St. Domingo, valued at three million francs, were utterly ruined. The slaves in their employ were (unknown to them) misused by their representative, hence the "habitation," as his property was called, began to yield but sad results. The younger brother, Moses, saved at least a meagre portion of the vast wealth once commanded by the house of Gradis, by visiting the island and caring for the negroes, who, in gratitude for his kind treatment of them—eulogized by the abolitionist Schoelcher—strove to make good their former losses. The family of Gradis is immortalized in the history of the commerce of two continents. "Their works are their monuments."

VIII.

THE CIVIL AND MILITARY STATUS OF THE JEWS IN JAMAICA.

In the West Indies, the Jews, though debarred from public office until late, contributed much to the public good. Their constancy and restless activity in behalf of the Government under which they served are chronicled by many historians. It were useless to give an elaborate account of their influence for good in the islands. It would lead us much too far to recount them, and in fact many things have been recorded of this nature by the present writer elsewhere.[83] If we mention the case of *Daniel Cordoso*, who was killed while defending Cura-

---

[83] Cf. G. A. Kohut's article on *Jews in St. Thomas, Jamaica and Barbados*, in the *P. A. J. H. S.*, No. 4.

çao, from an attack of the English in 1805,[84] it is because his is the only one referred to by name in the history of that island. No doubt other researches will be made by the active members of the *American Jewish Historical Society*, in this direction, which will silence all calumny against our patriotism. As a fitting epilogue to these pages, we subjoin a "List of Jews appointed to civil and military offices in Jamaica, since the act of 1831," extracted from the official gazettes of the island, and presented by Sir F. H. Goldsmid, in his *Arguments advanced against the enfranchisement of the Jews, considered in a series of letters*, Second Edition, London 1833, pp. 39–40 (First Ed., London, 1831), arranged in the following chronological order:

1831.

October 15th	MYER BENJAMIN, Gent., to be a Quartermaster.
October 24th	MOSES GOMES SILVA, ESQ., to be a Provost Marshal-General.[85]
October 27th	ALEXANDER BRAVO, Esq., to be a Magistrate and Assistant Judge of the Court of Common Pleas for the Parish of Clarendon.
November 2nd	PHILIP LUCAS, Esq., to be a Magistrate and Assistant Judge of the Court of Common Pleas for the Parish of Kingston.
December 13th	AARON GOMES DACOSTA, Gent., to be an Ensign.
December 31st	DANIEL JACOBS, Gent., to be an Ensign.

1832.

January 19th	ALEXANDER JOSEPH LINDO, Gent., to be a Quartermaster.
March 8th	JACOB DE PASS, Esq., to be a Magistrate and Assistant Judge of the Court of Common Pleas for the Parish Port Royal.

[84] See Koenen's *Geschiedenis*, etc., p. 307–8: ". . . . . Toen in 1805 de Engelschen een vruchteloozen aanval op dit eiland deden, de Joden, aldaar woonachtig, hun plicht ter verdediging van hetzelve moedig betracht hebben, zoodat een van hen, zijnde *Daniel Cardoso*, geboortig van Amsterdam, bij die gelegenheid gesneuveld is." Cf. also Van Hamelsveld, *Geschiedenis der Joden*, p. 363.

[85]This is analogous to the English office of Sheriff.

1832.

March 9th	SAMUEL DELISSER, Gent., to be an Ensign.
April 27th	ISAAC GOMES DACOSTA, Gent., to be a Quartermaster.
May 1st	GEORGE ISAACS, Gent., to be a Quartermaster.
May 5th	BARNET ISAACS, Gent., to be an Ensign.
July 6th	DAVID LOPEZ, Gent., to be a Lieutenant of Artillery.
July 26th	ABRAHAM ISAACS, Esq., to be a Magistrate and Assistant Judge of the Court of Common Pleas for the Parish of St. Ann.
August 4th	MOSES Q. HENRIQUES, Gent., to be an Ensign.[86]

It is evident from this brief and insufficient summary of our subject, that the Jews on American soil, north and south, east and west, were loyal, law-abiding citizens, noble philanthropists and exemplary patriots.

[86] This list was already published by the writer in an article on *The Civil and Military Status of American Jews*, in *Menorah Monthly*, Vol. XVIII, No. 4, pp. 256–7.

JEWS IN THE ARMIES OF EUROPE.

The purpose of the present volume, as its title indicates, is a review of the record and the status as patriot, soldier and citizen of the *American* Jew. But the Jew is co-extensive with civilization, not only historically but geographically as well, and wherever civilization makes its way, there the Jew will be found exerting a positive influence in furthering its progress. He will be found at the nucleus and core of conservatism and order wherever order is akin to right, but he has never been wanting at the front of Revolution when wrong could no longer otherwise be righted.

Avoiding more than a passing advertence to Jewish military achievements in the beginning of Israel's history, in the later struggles against the Greeks and subsequently against the Romans; stopping but a moment to remember Joshua, and Gideon, and Deborah, the successive Maccabæan heroes, and the last desperate struggle for freedom that was led by Bar Cochba against Hadrian; passing down through all the martyrdoms of the Dark Ages to the present "nineteenth century," we come face to face with the fact that Jews have been present in European armies since the time of the Napoleonic wars. They were to be found in the ranks of all the combatants during that bloody prelude to the great political regeneration that is yet going on before us, and they have risen as far above the ranks as the prejudices of the Christianity-professing majority would admit.

In the successive Polish uprisings, in all the great political upheavals of 1848, and especially in the Hungarian revolution of that time, the Jews of their respective nationalities took a vigorous and aggressive part.* Their position in this regard

* . . . "It is a gratifying proof of progress that the President of the Magyars (Kossuth) has promised freedom to those who equally with himself are struggling for the independence of their country,

was so positive and unmistakable that when those great socio-
political disturbances had been quieted through the partial
concession of popular rights by the monarchies of Europe, the
Jews of Germany and Austria had reached a position where
they could logically demand their political enfranchisement
and the abolition of the mediæval restrictions which remained
imposed on them. That they did not obtain a full measure of
citizenship until after the establishment of the German Empire
in 1871, is indeed true, and even yet the spirit of the Dark
Ages is so far prevalent in Germany and in Austria (leaving
Slavic Europe out of consideration as not yet modernized) as to

since it is said that there are no less than 35,000 Israelites in the Hungarian army." *Extract from a French newspaper reprinted in " The
Occident," August, 1849. Phila.; Edited by Isaac Leeser.*

. . . . . "It cannot be denied that already at that time the
majority of the Magyar Jews were patriotically inclined towards
the country which they called their home. As by magic, they
felt themselves drawn towards the man who preached liberty
and eqality, and at whose hands they were expecting redemption
from the Ghetto and from civil and political degradation. As a matter of fact, thousands of Jews, among them a general, fought in the
Magyar army. . . . . The contribution which the notorious
Haynau levied upon the Jewish congregations was but a consequence
of the loyalty to the man of the New Era, attributed to the Jews."
*Dr. Adolph Kohut on " The Relations of Kossuth to the Jews," in
the American Hebrew, N. Y., March, 1894.*

To the above may be added the following testimony of General
Julius Stahel, one of the active participants in the Hungarian Revolution, and who subsequently made a distinguished military record
in our civil war.

NEW YORK, MAY 22d, 1895,
 Hon. Simon Wolf, Washington, D. C.,
DEAR SIR:

I know from personal knowledge that many Jews fought in the
battles for the independence of Hungary in 1848, with as much
bravery and gallantry as the American Jew fought here during the
late strife between the North and the South, and I also know that
the late humane and illustrious apostle of liberty, Louis Kossuth,
always fully appreciated the patriotism, loyalty and devotion of the
Jews to the cause of Hungary during that great struggle for freedom.

Patriotism and bravery are not the birthright of one nation or race,
but of all mankind.

Very sincerely yours,
J. STAHEL.

preclude the advancement of Jews to the higher posts of the army. In France, however, since the French Revolution, and in Italy since the consolidation of the Kingdom, Jews have been advanced to the highest military commands. In both countries and especially in France, several Jewish soldiers at present hold the rank of General of Division, and quite a number, proportionately, that of Brigade and Regimental Commander.*

The part played by the Jews of Europe in all the various avenues of progress need not detain us here. The recurrent ebullitions of unreasoning prejudice against them which become manifest from time to time, are ultimately traceable as but distorted expressions of the unrest which the European social organism is suffering under its abnormal political and economic conditions. What there is left of this spirit on American soil is but a reflex of that of Europe, but there, as here, the record made by the Jewish people in politics and in war, in commerce and in industry, in science, art and literature, has placed beyond question their position as patriots, soldiers and citizens.

---

* Referring to a newspaper item regarding the rumors of a duel between Capt. Cremieux Foa, a French cavalry officer, and a certain anti-Semite editor of a Paris newspaper, General Franz Sigel wrote as follows:

NEW YORK, MAY 31st, 1892.

Hon. Simon Wolf, Washington, D. C.,
DEAR SIR:

Not knowing whether you have seen or will see the inclosed item, I send it to you. It shows at least that there are no less than 300 Jewish officers serving in the French army, probably the highest number in any of the great European armies, which speaks well for France and her republican government.

Hoping that you are well, I am,

Truly yours,
FRANZ SIGEL.

THE JEWISH PEOPLE BEFORE THE WORLD.

As already noted by the author in the introduction to this work, it was in December, 1891, that another of the numberless public villifications of the Jewish people which have appeared from time to time had demanded a no less public refutation of its falsities. It has furthermore been noted that this refutation was dictated not by anything specially remarkable in the nature of the slander itself, nor of its source, inasmuch as the former was commonplace and the latter obscure, but that the reply had been called forth wholly by reason of the extraordinary condition of the public mind with regard to the subject at that particular juncture. It was the time and the occasion that gave the slander prominence, rather than any peculiarity of its own.

It has been so for a long time past. From the time, nearly 1900 years ago, when Philo of Alexandria appeared before Caligula in defence of his people, down along the centuries to the date of Menasseh ben Israel's appeal to Cromwell in 1656, there were repeated occasions for such defenses and appeals, and there have been many since. These contingencies have repeatedly arisen in the course of the slow process of popular enlightenment which makes up the history of Man, and as that process is yet far from accomplishment it is not at all unlikely that they may be repeated in the future.

It is, however, more than passingly remarkable that in the closing decade of the 19th Century, when

" the thoughts of men have widened with the process of the suns,"

an occasion of this nature should have arisen. That such exigencies occur but rarely in the midst of our Western civilization, and that rare as they are, their occurrence is always traceable to foreign impulses, only renders more apparent the liberalizing influences of our free American institutions, while on the other hand further emphasizing the lessons taught us by the spectacle of Monarchic Europe. There the remnants of the mediæval system, political, ecclesiastic and social, that remained as historic *debris* after the cataclysm of the French Revolution, still clog the advance of true enlightenment. In Germany and in Austria a considerable portion of the populace is still affected by a taint of monkish fanaticism, and in Russia only a comparatively few individuals appear to be free from it. Schools are numerous in Austria and universities flourish in Germany, but the prejudices which form the obverse side of folly find still some teachers in the schools and preachers in the pulpit.

" Knowledge comes, but wisdom lingers,"

and the dictates of reason, the teachings of political and economic science, the lessons of history, will have to be yet more than once repeated before that umbra of the Dark Ages, the so-called " anti-Semitism " of Slavic and Teutonic Europe, and its penumbra in America, will have been lost in historic space.

These lessons have been learned and these teachings taught by the foremost minds of every epoch and latterly of every generation. From the time of Reuchlin's defense of the Talmud and Jewish literature generally against the fanatics of his day, a defense which caused a religious and political agitation that became the prelude to the Reformation, down to our present time, there have not been wanting Christian men of learning and of understanding who strove successfully in the defense of Jewish polity against the prejudices of ignorance. The great Renaissance of German letters in the latter half of the 18th century afforded numerous instances of men of this character, among whom need but be cited Lessing, Herder, Schiller, and Goethe. These writers and thinkers carried on their polemics in the domain of idealism, in poetry and philosophy, and their thoughts were soon re-echoed in the outgivings of the succeeding generation of scientists, students and statesmen. We will not attempt here to adduce all the great array of leading minds who have been impelled to express themselves on this theme, but will limit our citations to a few of the most authoritative thinkers and a quotation of the most positive utterances on the subject.

In marked contrast with the accusation of the passing school of anti-Semitic writers against Judaism as materialistic in its tendencies, there may be cited an expression by the great German and cosmopolitan philosopher, ALEXANDER von HUMBOLDT. In a letter to a Jewish friend regarding the natural idealism expressed in Hebrew literature, he refers him to the following passage in his *Cosmos* (*Vol. III, p. 44*), and closes his letter as below.

" It is a characteristic sign of the natural poetry of the Hebrews, that, as a reflex of Monotheism, it always comprises the whole of the universe in its unity, both life on earth and the bright realms on high. It seldom dwells upon single phenomena, but rejoices in the contemplation of great masses. Nature is not described as self-existent, or glorified by a beauty of her own; to the Hebrew singer she always appears in connection with an over-ruling spiritual power. Nature to him is ever a thing created and ordained, the living utterance of God's Omnipresence in the works of the world of matter. Therefore, the lyrical poetry of the Hebrews, by reason of its subject, is grand and grave in its solemnity."

" Stand fast by your brethren who have accomplished so remarkable a course of martyrdom through centuries and now stand on the threshold of their liberation; devote all the energies of yonr intellect to the spiritual labor wherewith your millennial history is instinct; success cannot, will not fail you and the rich results that you, my young friend, will obtain from the mines of science, will calm and comfort you in many a sad experience in the dull and cloudy present, that is but the precursor of the bright dawn of the day of liberty."

Another world-famous scientist, ALPHONSE L. P. PYRAME De CANDOLLE, in his *Histoire des sciences et des savants depuis deux siècles*, Geneva, 1873, makes the following very remarkable observations:

" If Europe had been peopled by Jews only we might have witnessed a curious spectacle. There would no longer be any wars; hence the moral sensibility would be violated much less and millions of people would not be torn away from useful occupations. Public debts and taxes would decrease. The cultivation of science, of literature, of fine arts, especially music, for which the Jews have a great predilection, would be furthered to the highest extent. Industry and commerce would flourish. Few crimes of personal violence would be committed, and those against property would but seldom be accompanied by violence. The wealth of the community as a whole and of individuals would largely increase by the effect of intelligent and regular labor, combined with economy. This wealth would have a beneficent effect. The clergy would not come in collision with the State. Perhaps there would be less corruption among the officials and greater firmness.''

The above passage is approvingly quoted by another great leader in the world of science, Professor Carl Vogt, in an article published in *Westerman's Monatshefte,* wherein the writer, treating of the habits and qualities acquired by European peoples through hereditary transmission, speaks of the Jewish people as having attained the highest civilization notwithstanding their having lived for ages under oppression.

On the occasion of the centennial anniversary, in 1891, of the political enfanchisement of the French Jews, the celebrated leader of the French Liberal Catholics, PERE HYACINTHE, addressed to the Grand Rabbi of Paris the following express- ive communication:

"MONSIEUR LE GRAND RABBIN: — You will have seen from the papers that our Gallican Catholic church intends to commemorate the centenary of the emancipation of the Jews by the Constituent Assembly. The 27th of September, 1791, is a date of even greater glory to France than it is to the Jews. It was a day that witnessed the reparation of a long and cruel injustice; it inaugurated for the whole world an era of liberty and brotherhood from which no evil disposed person has since been able to make us swerve. We are too enlightened and too liberal-minded to become anti-Semites. Besides, we are Christians, and as such we must not forget that it is from Irael's bosom that we have sprung. Israel, the grand old olive tree from which we have been grafted. For the French Jews the inter- regnum which commenced with Sedecias ended with Napoleon. Napoleon it was, who boasted of being the King of the Jews, and the Jews accordingly treated him as their political Messiah. Than him they could not have had a greater.

"But Napoleon's empire, like the kingdom of David, is no more, and the French Republic now has the keeping of these two illustrious necropoles, that at Jerusalem wherein reposes the race of David, that at Paris wherein rests the hero who was in himself his own sole dynasty.

"But none the less, France has remained, as Bonaparte remarked, the new tribe of Judah, where Frenchmen and Jews constitute one people.

"Republicans by virtue of the Mosaic legislation, I would almost say socialistic, in the best sense of the term, before they became monarchists by Samuel's dispensation, the traditions of the Jews comprise all the essentials for the service of France.

"'Hear, Lord, the voice of Judah and bring him unto his people; let his hands be sufficient for him, and be Thou a help to him from his enemies.'

"These are my wishes, Monsieur le Grand Rabbin and may the God of the Jews, who is also the God of the Christians, cause them to be fulfilled speedily.

"Accept, monsieur, the assurance of my fraternal friendship.

HYACINTHE LOYSON,
Priest."

As focussing effectively the most salient aspects of this general subject, we will here cite a thoughtful statement from a strictly orthodox Roman Catholic source, the French clerical journal, *Le Monde:*

"The immortality of the soul has been repudiated by the Academie des Inscriptions and Belles-Lettres. The Jews had to serve as the occasion. The Old Testament, however, was vindicated. But in how many feeble minds was not an uncertainty left? How many will take the trouble to read over the Sacred Books, when the reading of the daily papers absorbs all their time? Voltaire knew well enough that to sustain his iconoclastic views he had to discredit the Jewish people, to falsify their history, and to take up again the pagan theory of presenting them as the most degraded of people.

"Such, indeed, was the opinion of the Greeks and Romans in regard to the Jews. The Greeks, given over to all conceivable turpitude and tyranny, to an anarchy without bounds and without end, incapable of even simulating a defence against Rome, despised the Jewish people, and the Romans entertained the same feelings. They despised them for the same reason that the economists, the capitalists, the modern free-thinkers, despise the Catholics. The Jews did not worship idols; they alone did not prostrate themselves before nature; they condemned, despised that pantheism, that idol-worship, which sanctified the vices and the passions and which the Greeks and Romans embraced with such ardor. The dignity and regularity of their habits formed a striking contrast to pagan dissipation. They opposed in their individuality, the beauty of their rigorous law to the impure teachings of paganism. They never presented a disgraceful spectacle in the time of their prosperity ; they never participated in the bloody games of the ring; they held human sacrifices in horror.

"The Jews did not profess the principle of equity, of which the Greeks and Romans boasted so much—themselves absolute partisans of Slavery. They simply upheld the institution of family hiearchy, the paternal authority. Their habits and institutions, inspired by the parental sentiment — were they not full of kindliness and foresight? Could they overlook the feeble and the poor? Amongst them brothers could not know contention and strife, because they were equals in reality. Without the parent, fraternity would disappear.

"In order to subsist it is necessary that children should always have before them the image, the memory, the principle of the paternity from which they emanated, which formed the bonds of their friendship. Their unity proceeds from thence, a unity, sweet, lively, inculcated in infancy, formed by the heart before the mind could grasp it. The law-giver had no occasion, therefore, to enjoin fraternity, but needed only to submit it to that law of nature which organizes the paternal authority. The Jews were ignorant of those social ideas that desolated the ancient cities and that spring up again in modern times. The poor had no demands to make upon the rich. The Jews never forget, and had they done so, the law reminded them that the earth belongs to the Lord and that in God they are all brothers. The constitutional wars between the poor and the rich in Rome and Athens were caused by extortion. This question of extortion fills Roman history with its pale shadow; it is at the bottom of all the troubles, dissensions, periodical massacres and revolts. It has again taken possession of society with the reform of the Nineteenth Century. Only in 1789 France passed from under the yoke of extortion. The Jewish fraternity condemned extortion as a principle of tyranny.

"This fraternity, so powerful a principle, led the Jews to love their fellow-beings, to see in them colleagues and brothers ; they received the stranger willingly, extended to him their hospitality, even a share in the benefits of their law—something that was foreign to all other nations. With these other nations the stranger was regarded simply as an enemy ; "enemy" and "stranger" were expressed by one and the same word. Pantheism, denying the principle of unity, as indicated in the Divine origin, left men in a continual state of war. And war never ceased; the cities fought with each other, until the strongest had subdued the others, and in their turn were conquered and absorbed by a greater. This is the invariable history of Greece and Rome. The dogma of Divine creation exhibited to the Jews all men as brethren. They did not treat the stranger therefore as a barbarian. They, the Israelites, alone of all the nations of antiquity, did not carry on aggressive wars; once established upon their soil, they had no other desire than to live in peace by living out their laws. This is the object of all their institutions. They do not make war upon the stranger, because they had no hate against him.

"Their God, greater than the gods of the Olympus, neither flattered nor served their passions. He was a jealous God, who exacted the submission of the heart. He chastised his rebellious children. And this people purified by persecution and misfortune, returned to the laws of their fathers, to the observance of their precepts. No city in ancient, no people in modern times could have passed through like vicissitudes and recovered again. It is not through progress that they endured and were capable of resistance, but by holding fast to the past; by rallying around the law, which they had never abandoned and which they never modified, hard as it was. It often became irksome, it never bargained with its conscience. What else existed, before the laws of Moses, than that paganism which legalized all vices? The Jews defended their law with their lives; they fought for it against the Greek kings of Syria; they preferred to be buried under the ruins of Jerusalem to making a compact with Roman pagan ism The Greeks and Romans never had the idea that one can die for one's religion.

" By their habits in the government of the State the Jews were separated completely from Greece and Rome. They never brooked the insults of the ancient or modern mobocracy, because they respected the principle of the family, the foundation of their political, judicial, administrative and military organization. They alone in antiquity repudiated slavery. They practiced a national brotherhood which the Christian people are hardly capable of comprehending; it is so sublime, and almost beyond human nature. The institution of the jubilee, of the seventh year, the seventh day, was the perfection of social order; but even with Christianity these institutions could not maintain themselves. Dispersed, reduced to direst need and to the humiliation of exile, the Jews have never abandoned these first principles. Tacitus remarked the close ties of brotherhood that united them in his time. *Inter ipsos obstinata fides.* Since then and up to this time is it not the same sentiment? Are there many dissensions amongst them? This moral greatness of the Jewish people made them the target of pagan enmity. The policy of Rome was to be enforced upon all nations. The Jews share with the Christians the honor of having been singled out as the victims of utter extermination.

"The Jewish nation has survived all its victors; it alone, says Jean-Jaques Rousseau, withstood the power of time, fortune and defeat. Greece and Rome were enveloped in a system of superstition which weighed heavily upon the actions of public and private life. The Jews lived beyond the pale of that ignominy. The causes of this intellectual and moral superiority became the subject of jealous depreciation generally."

The essential spirit of the Jewish polity has seldom, if ever, been more effectively portrayed than by REV. DR. HENRY M. FIELD, in his scholarly work, *On the Desert*, published by Charles Scribner's Sons, New York, 1883. It deals with the system of law instituted by Moses, which became ingrained in the Jewish people through long centuries of victorious contention against barbarism in all its historic forms, and which remains to-day the guiding principle of Jewish life in all the relations of man to man.

We quote from Dr. Field's work as follows:

THEOCRACY AND DEMOCRACY.

" Perhaps it does not often occur to readers of the Old Testament that there is much likeness between the Hebrew Commonwealth and the American Republic. There are more differences than resemblances, at least the differences are more marked. Governments change with time and place, with the age and the country, with manners and customs; yet at the bottom there is one radical principle that divides a republic from a monarchy or an aristocracy; it is the natural equality of men—that " all men are born free and equal " —which is as fully recognized in the laws of Moses as in the Declaration of Independence Indeed the principle is carried further in the Hebrew Commonwealth than in ours; for not only was there equality before the laws, but the laws aimed to produce equality of condition in one point, and that a vital one—the tenure of land—of which even the poorest could not be deprived, so that in this respect the Hebrew Commonwealth approached more nearly to a pure democracy.

" Of course the political rights of the people did not extend to the choice of a ruler, nor did it to the making of the laws. As there was no king but God, it was the theory of the State that the laws emanated directly from the Almighty and his commands could not be submitted to a vote. No clamorous populace debated with the Deity. The Israelites had only to hear and to obey. In this sense the government was not a popular, but an absolute one.

" But how could absolutism be consistent with equality ? There is no contradiction between the two, and indeed, in some respects, no form of government is so favorable to equality as a theocracy. Encroachments upon popular liberty and the oppression of the people do not come trom the head of the State so often as from an aristocratic class which is arrogant and tyrannical. But in a theocracy the very exaltation of the Sovereign places all subjects on the same level. God alone is great and in His presence there is no place for human pride. Divine Majesty overawes human littleness, and instead of a favored few being lifted up above their fellows, there is a general feeling of lowliness and humility, in the sight of God, in which lies the very spirit and essence of equality.

" As the Hebrew law recognized no natural distinctions among the people, neither did it create any artificial distinctions. There was no hereditary class which had special rights; there was no nobility exempted from burdens laid on the poor, and from punishments inflicted on the peasantry. Whatever political power was permitted to the Hebrews belonged to the people as a whole. No man was raised above another; and if in the making of the laws the people had no voice, yet in the administration of them they had full power, for they elected their own rulers.

" Moses found soon after he left Egypt that he could not administer justice in person to a whole nation, so he directed the tribes to choose out of their number their wisest men, whom he would make judges to decide every common cause, reserving to himself only the more important questions. Here was a system of popular elections, which is one of the first elements of a republican or democratic state.

"In the administration of jusiice a Theocracy is an ideal government, for it is Divinity enthroned on earth as in Heaven, and no other form of government enforces justice in a manner so absolute and peremptory. In the eyes of the Hebrew lawgiver the civil tribunal was as sacred as the Holy of Holies. The office of the judge was as truly authorized, and his duty as solemnly enjoined, as that of the priest. The judgment is God's, said Moses, and he who gave a false judgment disregarded the authority of Him whose nature is justice and truth. The judgment seat was a holy place, which no private malice might profane. Evidence was received with religious care. Oaths were administered to give solemnity to the testimony. Then the Judge, standing in the place of God, was to pronounce equitably, whatever might be the rank of the contending parties. 'Ye shall not respect persons in judgment, but ye shall hear the small as well as the great; ye shall not be afraid of the face of man, for the judgment is God's.' He recognized no distinctions, all were alike to him. The judge was to know no difference. He was not to be biased even by sympathy for the poor. ' Neither shall thou countenance a poor man in his cause. Thou shalt not respect the person of the poor, nor honor the person of the mighty; but in righteousness shalt thou judge thy neighbor.' Magistrates were not allowed to accept a gift; 'for the gift blindeth the wise, and perverteth the words of the righteous.'

"The humanity of the Hebrew code is further seen in its mitigation of slavery. This was a legal institution of Egypt, out of which they had just come. They themselves had been slaves. Their ancestors, the patriarchs, had held slaves. Abraham had over three hundred servants born in his house. The relation of master and slave they still recognized, but by how many limitations was this state of bondage alleviated! No man could be subjected to slavery by violence. Man-stealing was punished with death. The more common causes of servitude was theft or debt. A robber might be sold to expiate his crime, or a man overwhelmed with debt might sell himself to pay it; that is, he might bind himself to service for a term of years: still he could hold property, and the moment he acquired the means might purchase back his freedom, or he might be redeemed by his nearest kinsman. If his master treat him with cruelty; if he beat him so as to cause injury the servant recovered his freedom as indemnity. At the longest his servitude came to an end in six years. He then recovered his freedom as a natural gift; ' If thou buy a Hebrew servant, six years he shall serve, and in the seventh he shall go out free for nothing.' A Hebrew slave was therefore merely a laborer hired for six years. Nor did the law permit the servant to go forth in naked poverty, and with the abject feeling of a slave still clinging to him. He was to be loaded with presents by his late master — sheep, oil, fruits, and wine — to enable him to begin housekeeping. Thus for a Hebrew there was no such thing as hopeless bondage. The people were not to feel the degradation of being slaves. God claimed them as his own, and as such they were not to be made bondmen. Every fiftieth year was a jubilee, a year of universal emancipation. Then ' liberty was proclaimed throughout all the land to all the inhabitants thereof.' This was the time of the restitution of all things. Though a man had sold himself as a slave, his right in the land was not alienated. It now returned to him free of encumbrance. At the year of jubilee all debts were extinguished. His native plot of ground, on which he played in childhood, was restored to him in his old age. Again he cultivated the paternal acres. He was not only a free man but a holder of property. Says Michaelis: ' The condition of slaves among the Hebrews was not merely tolerable, but often extremely comfortable.'

" That the sympathies of the law were with the oppressed appears from the singular injunction that a foreign slave who fled to a Hebrew for protection should not be given up: ' Thou shalt not deliver unto his master the servant which is escaped from his master unto thee.' No Fugitive Slave Law remanded the terror-stricken fugitive to an angry and infuriated master and to a condition more hopeless than before.

Such was the democracy of Theocracy — a union in which one sprang out of the other. Men were equal because God was their Ruler—a Ruler so high that before him there was neither great nor small, but all stood on the same level. But the Hebrew Law did not stop with equality; it inculcated fraternity. A man was not only a man, he was a brother. That law contains some of the most beautiful provisions ever recorded in any legislation, not only for the cold administration of justice, but for the exercise of humanity. The spirit of the Hebrew law was broader than race, or country, or kindred. What liberality, for example, in its treatment of foreigners. Against race hatred Moses set up this command, ' Thou shalt not oppress a stranger,' which he enforced upon the Israelites by the touching remembrance of their own bitter experience, ' for ye know the heart of a stranger seeing ye were strangers in the land of Egypt.' But not only were foreigners to be tolerated ; they were to receive the fullest

32

protection. ' Ye shall have one manner of law as well for the stranger as for one of your own country.'

" In several requirements we discern a pity for the brute creation. Long before modern refinement of feeling organized societies for the prevention of cruelty to animals, Moses recognized dumb beasts as having a claim to be defended from injury. Birds' nests were protected from wanton destruction.

" But perhaps the most beautiful provision of the law was for the poor.

" ' When ye reap the harvest of your land, thou shalt not wholly reap the corners of thy field, neither shalt thou gather the gleanings of thy harvests. And thou shalt not glean thy vineyard, neither shalt thou gather every grape of thy vineyard; thou shalt have them for the poor and the stranger.' If the reaper dropped a sheaf in the field, he might not return to take it. Whatever olives hung on the bough, or clusters on the vine, after the first gathering, were the property of the stranger, the fatherless and the widow. Under the shelter of this law came many a Ruth, gleaning the handfuls of golden corn to carry home to her mother, who was thus saved from utter destitution. By these means the law kept the poor from sinking to the extreme point of misery. At the same time, by throwing in their path these wayside gifts, it saved them from theft or vagabondage. As a proof of its successful operation, it is a curious fact that, in the five books of Moses, such a class as beggars is not once mentioned. The tradition of caring for those of their own kindred, remains to this day and it is an honorable boast that among the swarms of beggars that throng the streets of the Old World or the New, one almost never finds a Jew.

" The law took also under its care all whom death had deprived of their natural protectors; ' Ye shall not afflict any widow or fatherless child.' They were sacred by misfortune. God would punish cruelty to them. ' If thou afflct them in any wise, and they cry unto me, I will surely hear their cry; ' and your wives shall be widows and your children fatherless.'

" Thus the Hebrew law took the poor and the weak under its special protection; death, sorrow, widowhood, orphanage, all threw a shield of protection over the desolate and the unhappy. By this spirit of humanity infused into the relations of life, all the members of a community — the rich and poor, the strong and the weak—were united in fellowship and fraternity. One sacred tie bound them still closer; not only were they of the same race and nation, but they had the same religious inheritance; all were fellow-citizens with the saints and of the household of God."

As a supplement to Dr. Field's effective presentation of his subject we add here an extract from the *Christian Union*, on '' Moses and his Laws,'' by HARRIET BEECHER STOWE:

" The strongest impulse in the character of Moses appears to have been that of protective justice, more particularly with regard to the helpless and down-trodden classes. The laws of Moses, if carefully examined, are a perfect phenomenon ; an exception to the laws of either ancient or modern nations in the care they exercised over women, widows, orphans, paupers, foreigners, servants and dumb animals. No so-called Christian nation but could advantageously take a lesson in legislation from the laws of Moses. There is a plaintive, pathetic spirit of compassion in the very language in which the laws in favor of the helpless and suffering are expressed, that it seems must have been learned only of superhuman tenderness. Not the gentlest words of Jesus are more compassionate in their spirit than many of these laws of Moses. Delivered in the name of Jehovah, they certainly are so unlike the wisdom of that barbarous age as to justify of them to Him who is Love."

Another woman of commanding authority, GEORGE ELLIOT, speaks on this topic as follows:

" Unquestionably the Jews, having been more than any other race exposed to the adverse moral influences of alienism, must, both in individuals and in groups, have suffered some corresponding moral degradation ; but in fact they have escaped with less abjectness, and less of hard hostility toward the nations whose hands have been against them, than could have happened in the case of a people who had neither their adhesion to a separate religion founded on historic memories, nor their characteristic family affectionateness. Tortured, flogged, spit upon, the *corpus vile* on which rage or wantonness vented themselves with impunity, their name flung at them as an opprobrium by superstition, hatred, and contempt, they have remained proud of their origin. Does any one call this an evil pride ? The pride which identifies us with a great historic body is a humanizing, elevating habit of mind, inspiring sacrifices of individual comfort, gain, or other selfish ambition, for the sake of that ideal whole ; and no man swayed by such a sentiment can become completely abject. That a Jew of Smyrna, where a whip is carried by passengers ready to flog off the too officious specimens of his race, can still be proud to say, ' I am a Jew,' is surely a fact to awaken admiration in a mind capable of understanding what we may call the ideal forces in human history.

"And again, a varied, impartial observation of the Jews in different countries tends to the impression that they have a predominant kindness, which must have been deeply ingrained in the constitution of their race to have overlasted the ages of persecution and oppression.

The concentration of their joys in domestic life has kept up in them the capacity of tenderness ; the pity for the fatherless and the widow, the care for the women and the little ones, blent intimately with their religion, is a well of mercy, that cannot long or widely be pent up by exclusiveness, and the kindness of the Jew overflows the line of division between him and the Gentile.

"On the whole, one of the most remarkable phenomena in the history of this scattered people, made for ages 'a scorn and a hissing,' is that, after being subjected to this process, which might have been expected to be in every sense deteriorating and vitiating, they have come out of it (in any estimate which allows for numerical proportion) rivaling the nations of all European countries, in healthiness and beauty of physique, in practical ability, in scientific and artistic aptitude, and in some forms of ethical value. A significant indication of their natural rank is seen in the fact, that at this moment the leader of the Liberal party in Germany is a Jew, the leader of the Republican party in France is a Jew, and the head of the conservative ministry in England is a Jew.

THOMAS BABINGTON MACAULEY (afterwards Lord Macauley) delivered a celebrated oration in the British House of Commons on April 17, 1833, in support of the bill for the removal of the disabilities of the Jews. After a destructive criticism of the arguments and reasons which were then being advanced by the opponents of liberalism, arguments which have since then been so completely outlived as to be no longer, in any Anglo-Saxon community, deemed worthy of consideration, the great statesman concluded his masterly presentation in a lucid statement and eloquent peroration, as follows:

"Whatever the sect be which it is proposed to tolerate, the peculiarities of that sect will, for the time, be pronounced by intolerant men to be the most odious and dangerous that can be conceived. As to the Jews, that they are unsocial as respects religion is true; and so much the better; for surely, as Christians, we cannot wish that they should bestir themselves to pervert us from our own faith.

"But that the Jews would be unsocial members of the civil community, if the civil community did its duty by them, has never been proved. My right honorable friend who made the motion which we are discussing has produced a great body of evidence to show that they have been grossly misrepresented; and that evidence has not been refuted by my honorable friend, the member for the University of Oxford.

"But what if it were true that the Jews are unsocial? What if it were true that they do not regard England as their country? Would not the treatment which they have undergone explain and excuse their antipathy to the society in which they live? Has not similar antipathy often been felt by persecuted Christians to the society which persecuted them?

" While the bloody code of Elizabeth was enforced against the English Roman Catholics, what was the patriotism of Roman Catholics? Oliver Cromwell said that in his time they were Espaniolized. At a later period it might have been said that they were Gallicised. It was the same with the Calvinists. What more deadly enemies had France in the day of Louis XIV, than the persecuted Huguenots?

" But would any rational man infer from these facts that either the Roman Catholic as such, or the Calvinist as such, is incapable of loving the land of his birth? If England were now invaded by Roman Catholics, how many English Roman Catholics would go over to the invader? If France were now attacked by a Protestant enemy, how many French Protestants would lend him help? Why not try what effect would be produced on the Jews by that tolerant policy which has made the English Roman Catholic a good Englishman and the French Calvinist a good Frenchman?

" Another charge has been brought against the Jews, not by my honorable friend, the member for the University of Oxford — he has too much learning and too much good feeling to make such a charge —but by the honorable member for Oldham, who has, I am sorry to see, quitted his place.

"The honorable member for Oldham tells us that the Jews are naturally a mean race, a money-getting race; that they are averse to all honorable callings; that they neither sow nor reap; that they have neither flocks nor herds; that usury is the only pursuit for which they are fit; that they are destitute of all elevated and amiable sentiments.

"Such, sir, has in every age been the reasoning of bigots. They never fail to plead in justification of persecution the vices which persecution has engendered. England has been, legally, a home to the Jews less than half a century, and we revile them because they do not feel for England more than a half patriotism.

" We treat them as slaves, and wonder that they do not regard us as brethren. We drive them to mean occupations, and then reproach them for not embracing honorable professions. We long forbade them to possess land, and we complain that they chiefly occupy themselves in trade. We shut them out from all the paths of ambition, and then we despise them for taking refuge in avarice.

" During many ages we have, in all our dealings with them, abused our immense superiority of force, and then we are disgusted because they have recourse to that cunning which is the natural and universal defense of the weak against the violence of the strong. But were they always a mere money-changing, money-getting, money-hoarding race? Nobody knows better than my honorable friend, the member for the University of Oxford, that there is nothing in their national character which unfits them for the highest duties of citizens.

"He knows that, in the infancy of civilization, when our island was as savage as New Guinea, when letters and arts were still unknown to Athens, when scarcely a thatched hut stood on what was afterward the site of Rome, this contemned people had their fenced cities and cedar palaces, their splendid temple, their fleets of merchant ships, their schools of sacred learning, their great statesmen and soldiers, their natural philosophers, their historians and their poets.

"What nation ever contended more manfully against overwhelming odds for its independence and religion? What nation ever, in its last agonies, gave such signal proofs of what may be accomplished by a brave despair? And if, in the course of many centuries, the depressed descendants of warriors and sages have degenerated from the qualities of their fathers, if, while excluded from the blessings of law and bowed down under the yoke of slavery, they have contracted some of the vices of outlaws and slaves, shall we consider this as a matter of reproach to them?

"Shall we not rather consider it as a matter of shame and remorse to ourselves? Let us do justice to them. Let us open to them the door of the House of Commons. Let us open to them every career in which ability and energy can be displayed. Till we have done this, let us not presume to say that there is no genius among the countrymen of Isaiah, no heroism among the descendants of the Maccabees.

"Sir, in supporting the motion of my honorable friend, I am, I firmly believe, supporting the honor and the interest of the Christian religion. I should think that I insulted that religion if I said that it cannot stand unaided by intolerant laws. Without such laws it was established, and without such laws it may be maintained.

"It triumphed over the superstitions of the most refined and of the most savage nations, over the graceful mythology of Greece and the bloody idolatry of the northern forests. It prevailed over the power and policy of the Roman Empire. It tamed the barbarians by whom that empire was overthrown. But all these victories were gained, not by the help of intolerance, but in spite of the opposition of intolerance.

"The whole history of Christianity proves that she has little indeed to fear from persecution as a foe, but much to fear from persecution as an ally. May she long continue to bless our country with her benignant influence, strong in her sublime philosophy, strong in her spotless morality, strong in those internal and external evidences to which the most powerful and comprehensive of human intellects have yielded assent, the last solace of those who have outlived every earthly hope, the last restraint of those who are raised above every earthly fear!

"But let us not, mistaking her character and her interests, fight the battle of truth with the weapons of error, and endeavor to support by oppression that religion which first taught the human race the great lesson of universal charity."

Here is an utterance on this subject by OTTO von BISMARCK. This man, whose iron hand puddled the smelt of the furnace wherein, with fire and blood, the German people were fused into political unity, was—or rather, is, for he is yet living, and will long remain a power—this man is no friend of the Jews. His spirit crystallized, and his nature drew its inspiration out of the time when " *Polen, Juden und Franzosen* " were a trinity of bugbears for the worshippers of royal divinity in Europe. Bismarck never fully recovered from that nightmare of his youth and early manhood, but he towered above his fellows, and he had the faculty of perceiving the truth and a habit of telling it which, notwithstanding his diplomatic training, he was wont to indulge. In a notable debate in the Prussian Landtag during the session of 1871, he expressed himself as follows:

"In my position as President of the Ministry I must repudiate any obligation to fill the places in the civil service with Roman Catholics according to their proportionate number in the population of the country. . . . The existence of a distinctively religious body in a political assembly is in itself a monstrous phenomenon. . . This tends to make religion the subject of parliamentary debates. . . I adhere to the principle that every religion should be allowed perfect freedom, without considering it, for that reason, necessary that it should be represented in the executive departments in the same ratio as in the population. Every religious body would have as much right as the Catholics to claim this; the Lutherans as well as the Jews, and *I have found that it is the latter particularly who are most distinguished by their special intelligence and capacity for administrative functions.*"

As an estimate of Jewish citizenship by a man whose life experience has afforded him a rare insight into social and political conditions on both sides of the Atlantic, we quote the following expression by CARL SCHURZ, on the occasion of the dedication of the Montefiore Home for Chronic Invalids, in New York City:

" Honor to the men and women who have accomplished this and who are bound to accomplish still more. They do honor to the community which calls them its own; for any community, whatever its pretensions, will be honored by citizens who take so high a view of their duties to humanity.

" And who are these citizens? They are Jews. This is not the only monument the Jews of New York have planted to their benevolence and public spirit. There are others—some even far exceeding this in costliness and grandeur. But none — none of their own and none instituted by any other class of citizens excells it, nay, perhaps none equals it in beauty of sentiment and devotion. And for whom is this done? Hear the noble words of the President of the Society as found in last year's report: ' As Israelites we are compelled, both by circumstances and inclination, to provide for the needy of our own faith; but this must not induce us to exclude any human being because of his religious belief from the benefit of an institution charged with the improvement of bodily ailment.' Thus it is done for the brotherhood of men. This is the true spirit, worthy of him whose name this edifice bears. It is the spirit, too, which more than any other, has created the brightest, the most stainless glories of our great American Republic — the spirit which, without any governmental action, out of the spontaneous initiative of the patriotic citizen, through private munificence, through individual solicitude for the welfare of all, has covered this land all over with educational institutions and enterprises of benevolence. In our school days we read of the Roman matron Cornelia, who, when other noble ladies exhibited to her their stores of pearls and precious stones, called in her children, and pointing to them, said: ' These are my jewels.' So when the Old World shows to us the magnificence of its baronial halls and royal castles, the American Republic may point to her colleges and hospitals and asylums founded by the patriotic generosity of simple citizens, and say, ' These are my palaces.'

" And to entitle the American people to this proud distinction, the Jews have done as much as any other class of citizens—nay, I may repeat in their presence what I have frequently said in the presence of others — the Jews have, in proportion to their numbers, done far more. I repeat this with all the greater willingness, as I have recently had occasion to observe the motive springs, the character and the aims of the so-called " anti-Semitic " movement, a movement whose dark spirit of fanaticism and persecution insults the humane enlightenment of the 19th century; whose appeals are addressed to the stupidest prejudice and the blindest passion, whose injustice affronts every sense of fairness and decency and whose cowardice—for cowardice is an essential element in the attempt to suppress the competing energies of a mere handful of people—whose cowardice I say, should provoke the contempt of every self-respecting man.

"In the face of this movement, which for years has stirred some European countries, and thrown its shadows even across the ocean, upon our shores, it is most grateful to the human heart to hear the President of the Montefiore Home say, that while this roof is to shelter the neediest of Israel, no human being because of his religious belief shall be excluded from its protection. He might take the clamorous anti-Semic by the hand, show him the hospitals, orphans homes, charity schools, founded and sustained by Jewish money, Jewish labor, Jewish public spirit, benevolence and devotion and say to him: 'If you have any sick, any aged, any children who cannot find help elsewhere, here we shall have room for them, and they are welcome.' What has the anti-Semite to answer? No, no, that movement cannot survive. It must perish in shame. It will be consigned to an ignominious grave by the generous impulses of human nature and the civilization of this age. And what will remain will be the beneficent influence and the sweet memory of such good actions as yours, and the brotherhood of mankind."

On the same occasion as that noted above, the opening of the Montefiore Home for Chronic Invalids, HON. ABRAM S. HEWITT, Mayor of New York City, spoke as follows:

"No other people, so far as I have observed, no sect or denomination or party have done so much as the Jews, to relieve distress, give education and elevate the standard of morality in our midst, and I make that statement after a good deal of observation and attention, particularly that part of it concerning the subject of education.

"I have never found the Jews lacking in public spirit. It is said of them that they have the art of getting wealth. If but a part of what is said of them be true, they understand well the use of wealth when once acquired. They are found among the first admirers of art, they love music and have since the daughters of Judah hung their harps on the willows by the waters of Babylon.

"This charity is unique, and it is a link in the chain of Jewish institutions. So long as there are calls by suffering humanity, the Jews will year by year add new links to their beautiful chain until it embraces every need of society regardless of race and religion.

"I have read at the door as I entered, that the Israelites erected this building to the chronic sick in honor of Moses Montefiore, a Jew, who for nearly a hundred years set an example to other people and creeds of a broad charity that affects all people and all lands.

"This institution was one long wanted in New York for a class for whom there is no hope save such offered by the poor-house or Blackwell's Island. They were here given instead a home in which love reigned and religion presided, religion which opened the portals of the other world where all must go, rich and poor, Jew and Christian, where reigns the Heavenly Father whose chosen people have proven steadfast amid all oppression and persecution, and who has so long preserved them, but who nevertheless knows no difference between His children.

From a deeply thoughtful address before the Young Men's Hebrew Association of Philadelphia, by JUDGE F. CARROLL BREWSTER, on the Valley of Baca as referred to in Psalm lxxxiv, we quote the following as the expression of a Nestor among jurists:

" Perhaps, then, the very dreariness of this barren place was intended as a prophecy of the woes which God's chosen people should encounter on their march through the history of many ages. And the water to be found in the midst of this desolation might prefigure the refreshing deliverance which the centuries were to bring. Of bitterness and of persecution, of suffering beyond man's power to describe, of its depth, of all that is sad and sorrowful, the history of the Jewish nation bears tearful testimony. The student has two marvels, as he turns these weary pages of the very monotony of cruelty. He wonders how the ferocity of man could ever enact this horrible tragedy, and then he wonders how the race survived.

" It would be a vain and painful task to recite here the thousandth part of what history tells us, and it is certain that history does not, in this case as in many others, falsify the facts. These narratives were all written by the actors who took a horrid pride in recounting their own infamy. The man who has but a moderate installment of feeling in his breast must cry out with indignation as he reads of these outrages. To the jurist they are especially repugnant, for they tell not only of the slaughter of human beings, but of the murder of justice."

The following is from the pen of GEORGE WILLIAM CURTIS, the life-long editor of "Harper's Weekly" and "Harper's Magazine." As a prominent actor in the stirring events of his generation he has left a marked impress on our national life, but great as was his influence in the councils of the nation he was yet best known to the large mass of the American people as the genial, persuasive writer of the "Easy Chair" in the magazine which he so ably edited. The extract which we print is from that department of Harper's Magazine, where it appeared in July, 1877, vol. 55, p. 300.

WHAT WE OWE TO THE JEWS.

"One beautiful June evening in Paris the 'Easy Chair' strolled with a friend into a café on the Boulevard. They had been to hear 'Robert le Diable' at the French Opera, and gaily humming and gossiping they sat upon the broad walk that was still thronged on the still summer night. Presently a dark-haired man came quietly along and seated himself at a table near by. He was alone, and seemed not to care for recognition. He was simply dressed and was entirely unnoticeable except for the strong Jewish lines of his intellectual face. The 'Easy Chair's' companion whispered, 'That is the man to whom we owe the delight of this evening; that is Meyerbeer.' After a little while he added with feeling, 'How much we owe to the Jews and how mean Christendom is !'

"It was remarkable how much of the conspicuous work and influence on that evening was due to the genius of a people whose name is so constantly used as a word of reproach. A few months before, Mendelssohn had been buried in Leipsic, and in Berlin the 'Easy Chair' had heard the memorial concert of his music at the Sing-Akademie. Rossini was still living, and Verdi was writing operas, but Mendelssohn and Meyerbeer were the recognized masters of music. The evening before, the 'Easy Chair' had seen the Jewess Rachel in 'Phedre'—the one woman who contests the laurel with Mrs. Siddons, and who was then the great living actress. Beyond the channel, Disraeli, the child of Spanish Jews, was just about to kiss hands as Chancellor of the Exchequer, and to become the political leader of the British Tories. In the vast city in which they were sitting, the 'Easy Chair' knew that the Jewish Heine was living, breathing his weird and melancholy song, while in Paris and London and Frankfort and Vienna the great masters of the mainspring of industrial activity, the capitalists, who held peace and war in their hands, and by whose favor kings ruled, were Jews. The philosophy, the arts, the industry, the politics of Christendom were full of the Jewish genius, the gayety of nations, the delight of scholars, the scepters of princes, the movements of civilization, hung in great degree upon it. It is as true to-day as in that long summer night, and the words of the 'Easy Chair's' friend are still as shamefully true. 'How mean Christendom is !'

"Recently in New York an estimable and accomplished gentleman was rejected as a member of the Bar Association 'for no other reason that can be conceived,' indignantly said one of the leading members, 'except that he was a Jew.' Doubtless a few votes would procure the rejection. But the Association is not a social club, and presumptively a man who is an honorable member of the Bar is a fit member of the Association. The few hostile votes, however, represent the prejudice. It is very old and very universal. To the audience of to-day there is nothing in Shakespeare more vital and intelligible than the fervent

appeal of 'Shylock' to the common humanity of the world around
him. The Jew is still separate, and the prejudice which has pursued
him for generations is but slightly relaxed. The lines of demarcation
are fine. They are often almost invisible. But they are deep, and
apparently absolute. It is one of the most common and most tenacious
of the objections to " Daniel Deronda " that it deals with Jews and
Jewish life and character. The fact is sometimes almost resented as
an offence to the mass of readers. Even in ' Ivanhoe,' although tor-
rents of Christian tears have flowed over the closing pages, where the
noble and beautiful ' Rebecca ' asks to see the face of the fair
'Rowena,' yet such is the fell and weird outlaw of the Jew from
general sympathy, that the catastrophe seems to be an inevitable
fate. There is no doubt that this prejudice is as cruel in its effects as
it is unreasonable in its origin. . . . . .
    " The legend of the ' Wandering Jew ' has a pathos beyond the
usual interpretation. The story is told that the Jew, who refused to
comfort Christ as he toiled under the weight of the cross, was condemned to tarry until he came, and so wanders around the world
until the second coming. But it is the symbol also of the restlessness
of the race, roaming through Christendom, homeless and rejected. It
is the curse, says many a Christian heart, of the people that crucified
the Redeemer. This is the common theory of the origin of the
traditional antipathy to the Jews, and, undoubtedly, this is with
many persons a vague justification of the feeling with which a Jew is
regarded. But should it be nothing to such persons that when, as
they believe, the Creator would incarnate himself, He became a Jew?
Or, again, do they reflect that if it was in the eternal decrees that the
sins of men were to be atoned and condoned by the innocent
sacrifice, those who accomplished the sacrifice were but the agents of
the Divine will? Are all such ingenious speculations other than
devices to explain and justify a mere prejudice of race, such as some
African tribes cherish against people of white skins ? Those who find
in such prejudice a profound significance will continue to plead the
feeling as its own sufficient reason. But honorable men will be careful how they carelessly use the name of a race to which the religion,
the literature, the art, the civilized progress of humanity, are so
greatly indebted, as a term of utter derision and scorn."

Mr. Curtis in his reference to Shakespeare's "Shylock" truly
says that "there is nothing in Shakespeare more vital and intelligible than the fervent appeal of Shylock to the common
humanity around him." Much has been said and written concerning this remarkable creation of the dramatist's genius, and
often and again it has been remarked that Shakespeare's Jew
was not the real Jew, not even the Jew of his own imagination,
but the Jew as mirrored in the distorted consciousness of

mediæval Europe. The great pathologist of human feeling only then failed in his diagnosis when he sought to realize the Jew, the real Jew and his attributes were beyond his ken.

One of the grandest and most cherished of our poets, WILLIAM CULLEN BRYANT, long the editor of the New York *Evening Post*, in a trenchant criticism of the character of Shylock on the occasion of a presentation of the drama by Edwin Booth, wrote as follows: *

"In terming Shylock 'the Jew whom Shakespeare drew,' there is a perfect logic, for Shylock is, of all Shakespeare's characters, the only one untrue to nature. He is not a Jew, but a fiend presented in the form of one; and whereas he is made a ruling type, he is but an exception, if even that, and the exception is not to be met with either in the Ghettos of Venice or of Rome. Shakespeare holds up the love of money that marks the race, although he does not show that this passion was but the effect of that persecution which, by crowding the Jew out of every honorable pursuit, and thus cutting off his nature from every sympathy with the world around, sharpened and edged the keen corners of his brain for the only pursuit left to him.

"It is true that money-changers once spat on in the Ghetto are now hugged in the palace. But we fear that it is not so much that the prejudice against the Jews has ceased, but that the love of money among the Christians has increased. Shakespeare was not true in the picture he has drawn of the Jew's cravings for revenge, and in the contempt with which he is treated by his daughter. Revenge is not a characteristic of the Jew. He is subject to sudden fits of passion, but that intellect which always stands sentinel over the Hebrew soon subdues the gust. However strong in Shylock's time might have been the hatred of the Jew towards the Christian, the lust of lucre was more strong, and Shakespeare might have ransacked every Ghetto in Christendom without finding a Jew, or a Christian either, who would have preferred a pound of flesh to a pound sterling; and Jews also shrink from physical contests. Their disposition is to triumph by intellect rather than violence. It was this trait more than any other that rendered them, in the Middle Ages, so repulsive to the masses, who were all of the Morrissey and muscular Christianity school. The contempt of a daughter for her parent is equally uncharacteristic of the Jew. The Jews are universally admired for the affections which adorn their domestic life. The more they have been pushed from the society of the family of man the greater has been the intensity with which they have clung to the love of their own family.

"No one can ever have visited the houses of the Jews without having been struck by the glowing affection with which the daughter greets the father as he returns from the day's campaign and the

* See note, next page.

slights and sneers his gaberdine and yellow cap provoke, and without observing how those small, restless eyes that sparkle and gleam,
shine out in a softened, loving lustre as they fall upon the face of
Rebecca, or Jessica, or Sarah, and how he stands no longer with
crooked back, but erect and commanding, as he blesses his household
gods with an exultation as vehement as the prejudices which during
the day have galled and fretted his nature. To do justice to the
grandeurs of the Jewish race, and to brand with infamy its infirmities,
it is not enough to produce a repulsive delineation of the latter. It
would only be just to give expression to the former, and to exhibit
that superiority of intellect which has survived all persecution, and
which, soaring above the prejudices of the hour, has filled us with
reluctant admiration on finding how many of the great events which
mark the progress of the age or minister to its improvements, or
elevate its tastes, may be traced to the wonderful workings of the soul
of the Hebrew, and the supremacy of that spiritual nature which
gave to mankind its noblest religion, its noblest laws, and some of its
noblest poesy and music."

Treating the same subject the great German critic, ROBERT
BENEDIX, writes as follows: *

" Let us look at this Shylock closer. Antonio calls him an usurer;
the proof he fails in. Shylock takes high interest; so did all the
merchants of Venice. Shylock deals in money; to-day we call him a
banker. Why does he deal in money? Because it is the only trade
permitted. He does not carry on an industry, has no agricultural
pursuits, no official station—only trade. If the Jews, under centuries
of restriction, ostracised from social life, did cling to money and its
uses, whose fault was it? No one can say anything dishonorable of
Shylock. He is penurious; in no law-book of the world is that
denominated as a crime. What is against this man? Simply nothing
more than that he is a Jew. But for the poet, who, enthroned on
Olympian heights, there should exist only *the man, not the Jew.*
Shylock is revengeful. Well, who has instigated it? Only they who
have despised him. After persecuting and deriding him, they crown
their infamy by asking him to turn Christian. That is the very depth
of baseness. What is left to the poor Jew, whom you have trodden
under foot, when you rob him of his faith? It is the bond that binds
him to his fathers, to his home. It has been his solace in persecutions a thousand times repeated. To this faith Israel clings with
devoted love, and from this faith shall Shylock turn to become a
Christian? No wonder he turns with abhorrence from those who

* These citations are gleaned from the notable lecture by Hon.
Simon Wolf, on "The Influence of the Jews on the Progress of the
World," delivered before the Schiller Bund in Washington, April 1st,
1888.

torture him so cruelly. Christians they may be. Men they are not. And is there no feeling for a father? To exalt a daughter who absconds and robs him whom she should honor? Is that Jewish or Christian? The grand speech, 'Has not a Jew eyes,' etc., is the exclamation of a martyr people who for centuries had been the victims of debauched, bigoted priests.

"It is impossible to acquit Shakespeare of the prejudice of his age. He has morally sinned; artistically erred. Contrast Lessing; and he wrote in an age of equal intolerance. His 'Nathan the Wise' is an embodiment of morality and and sublime virtues; his figures are apostles of true humanity. Nathan is an evangelist of true worth; and Lessing, taking for his hero a Jew, made thereby the amende honorable in the name of humanity."

As a veritable anti-climax to these utterances of poet and critic, we may here consider the views of the representative proletary of America, who deals with the Shylock theme from an entirely different standpoint. This dissertation is by Mr. TERRENCE V. POWDERLY, long the leader of the organization of wage-earners known as the Knights of Labor, and as such will command the attention of the reader. Under the caption of "*The Real Shylock*," he writes in the *Journal of the Knights of Labor* as follows :

"Flings at the Jews are flying about promiscuously on every hand, and it seems to me that this practice is neither just nor manly. Turn the pages of history backward to the dawn of Christianity and notice how the Jew has been persecuted by those who professed to be actuated by Christian charity. Notice how he has been driven from country and home, how he has been driven ahead of the advanced guard of Christianity, and then pause for a moment to ask if the Christian is not in some small measure to blame for the money-lending characteristics of the Jew of this day and generation. Driven from all other branches of trade, with a price on his head, and his home at the mercy of others, how could the Jew protect himself? It is well enough to single out Rothschild and to point to him as a fit representative of an usury-taking class, but when he is pointed to as 'Rothschild the Jew,' the bounds of propriety are overstepped and common justice is violated.

"What right has a Christian to drive a man from every walk in life but that of money-lending and then insult his race and religion because of that fact, in sneeringly calling him a Jew. It is proper to call a money-lender a 'Shylock,' for that is a term that is applicable to men of all races and religions if they practice usury, but to single the Jew out as the only one who should wear that appellation is an outrage. I know Christians, and the reader knows them, who on every

Sunday morning will walk slowly down the middle aisle in the
Christian church, and with sanctimonious mien bend the knee before
the altar of God with no more of Christianity in their hearts than
may be found in the stone steps leading up to the church door. If a
living representative of 'Shylock' is to be singled out, one whose
talon-like fingers itch for usury and stretch out toward your pocket
for the principal as well, let us be honest enough to admit that we
can throw a stone into any of our temples of Christianity and hit
such a sinner. Do not lay it all to the Jew. I admit that he knows
how to deal in money, but who gave him points in the game of
usury? Look over the United States to-day. Contrast the acts of
pretended Christians with the principles of Christ, and then dare to
lay the blame of all the wrong that usury has wrought, to the door
of the Jew. Look at our American Congress and tell us if those who
obey the voice of greed in that body are all Jews. . . . . . . Are
all who have cornered lands, railroads and homes Jews? Let the
reader whose home is mortgaged inquire who it is holds the mortgage,
and if he happens to be a Christian, as in nine cases out of ten he will
be, ask him to be lenient with you, and you will learn that he wants
his 'pound of flesh,' and will be anxious to go old Shylock one
better, by sucking the blood along with it."

The Jewish Question and the Mission of the Jews, published
by Harper and Brothers, New York, 1894, contributes a valuable addition to historical literature. The work ably elucidates
its comprehensive subject matter and deserves the careful
perusal of every student of whatever creed. A few characteristic extracts are collated in the following :—

"If we turn to Europe, in which we are chiefly interested, we find
that the Jews were settled there as early as Roman times, and lived
on terms of perfect equality with all their neighbors, until religious
intolerance set itself to repress them or directed and intensified the
jealousy which their success elicited. When the west of Europe was
raised out of its barbarism by Charlemagne, this great leader of
modern civilization also took account of the valuable civilizing influence of the Jews, especially as regarded commerce and learning. He
granted them privileges, and even made use of them for diplomatic
services ; and as he transplanted learned men from Italy into France
and Germany in order that their wisdom might be diffused among
those people, so he also desired to engraft the learning of the Jews in
these districts. He encouraged them to found Talmudic Schools and
transplanted from Lucca the learned family Kalonymos to Narbornne
about the year 787, gave them a large tract of land, where the chief of
the family and his successors were called princes, while the part of
the town where they lived was called 'The Court of the King of the

Jew.' The position which the Jew, Isaac, held in the embassy of Charlemange to Haroun al Rashid is a matter of history."

* * * * * * * * *

" As to the pluck and courage of the Jews it certainly did not die out with the Maccabees and the Zealots. I will not mention the spiritual courage it required for the whole race to survive at all during the persecutions which might have been avoided by the simple act of conversion, or of the thousands that burned at the stake singing. I should say, even numerically, more than the whole Christian martyrology has to show. The numbers who heroically during the Spanish Inquisition, and at other times and places, preferred burning at the stake to baptism, the perfidy which often met their heroic resistance, would fill volumes. In the history of the Spanish Jews more than in that of any other of their numerous communities do we meet with heroism, courage and chivalry. They fought in the Spanish battles as the bravest knights. Alfonso X of Castile, rewarded them *en masse* for their war-like assistance against Seville and gave them, when the enemies' land was divided, a village which was called "Aldea de los Judeos." They fought desperately for Dom Pedro, even after the Black Prince had forsaken him, defended Burgos to the last man, so that even their opponent, Dom Enrico, recognized publicly their valor."

* * * * * * * * *

" Even in Germany during the Black Death and the butchery of Jews, and in Poland, the spirit of the Maccabees and the Zealots had not forsaken them. It very often met with the basest treachery on the part of their enemies and allies. One instance is a striking, if not a typical one. During the onslaught of the Cossacks into Poland in the Thirty Years' War the Jews were brave defenders of the Polish territory. When a horde of Hadamaks attacked the town of Tulczyn, six thousand Christians and about two thousand Jews retreated to the fortress. Nobles and Jews pledged themselves by oath to defend the fortress to the last man. The Cossacks resorted to a stratagem, and assured the Nobles that they were only fighting against their real enemies, the Jews. If they were handed over to them they would withdraw. The nobles asked the Jews to give up their arms ; and when they complied, they opened the gates to the Cossacks. When the Cossacks had plundered the Jews, they proposed to them the alternative of death or baptism. Not one of them accepted the latter, and they were put to the sword. But the nobles suffered the same fate, as the Cossacks held that there was no cause to hold faith by the faithless."

* * * * * * * * *

" The late James Russell Lowell was wont to say that a large proportion of the great families of the English aristocracy had some

33

admixture of Jewish blood, while some of the great names were in a direct line to be traced back to Jewish ancestors. So, for instance, he believed, and he must have had good grounds for his belief, that the families of the Cecils and the Russells were originally Jewish. Of course such conversational statements must not be taken literally. Many years ago I met a Russian scholar, deeply read in literature and science—the pure Russian, without any associations with Jews— who told me he was engaged upon a work which set itself the task of tracing the origin of most of the great men in letters and science that were then living in Germany, and that he was coming to the conclusion that, not only were a great many of them actually Jews, but that a large proportion of the best known among the Christian dignitaries had also some admixture of Jewish blood."

Our symposium could not be more effectively and fitly rounded out than by a quotation of the Preface to M. Anatole Leroy Beaulieu's celebrated work, " *Israel chez les nations*," and of the Preface written by the author for the English translation by Mrs. Theodore Hellman, which has just been announced as soon to be published by Messrs. G. P. Putnam's Son's, New York. M. Leroy Beaulieu, whose mastery of the philosophy of history has commanded universal recognition, makes clear his standpoint in the preface to the original work, and in the preface to the English translation he evinces his thorough insight, not only into his general subject, but furthermore into its American phases especially.

We copy these extracts from the columns of the *American Hebrew*, New York, September 13, 1895, and from its editorial reference to the subject we gladly quote the concluding paragraph, as follows:

"The publication of M. Leroy Beaulieu's work in its English dress will be timely for two reasons: Its Jewish readers will find it an eloquent appeal for renewed devotion to the noble cause of Israel's mission; its Christian readers, recognizing the important part Judaism has played in the production of our present-day civilization, will recognize how baseless is the prejudice that reigns against the Jew. May the book find many readers."

ISRAEL AMONG THE NATIONS.

THE PREFACES TO M. LEROY-BEAULIEU'S " *Israel chez les nations.*"

[*Copyrighted, 1895, by* G. P. PUTNAM'S SONS.]

I. PREFACE TO THE ORIGINAL WORK.

The author of this book is a Christian and a Frenchman. As a Christian, he is one of those who believe that a spirit of intolerance is repugnant to Christianity, and nothing appears to him less consistent with the Gospel than race-hatred. Be it a war of races or a war of classes, popular jealousy can never screen itself behind the robe of Christ. Be it Aryan or Semitic, a nation should never purchase its salvation at the cost of another's rights.

As a Frenchman, the author is one of those who are convinced that France ought to remain true to her traditions of justice and liberty. They are the only glory and the only wealth which the fortunes of war cannot wrest from her. The more severe the trials that she has undergone, the more menacing the dangers that await her, the more essential is it to her honor that she should remain herself and not belie, in the eyes of the nations, those great ideas which she was the first to proclaim. To abjure them would be not only an act of apostasy, but a forfeiture of her place in history. A France that should stoop, more than a century after 1789, to abridge religious and civil liberty and to establish among her inhabitants distinctions based upon name or birth, would no longer be the France that the world has thus far known.

The inheritance of the Revolution, which we have come to regard with so much reverence, may possibly include rash postulates and exaggerated inferences that tend to intoxicate, almost to madness, a people infatuated with its title of sovereign; but surely neither religious liberty nor civil equality is likely to produce such effects; neither the one nor the other can have any tendency to turn the people's heads; and, after having been the first to preach these principles to Europe, France will not disavow them now, when, thanks to our propaganda or our example, they have conquered almost all the countries of both hemispheres. On others be the shame of such a recantation !

Anti-Semitism is consistent with neither the principles nor the genius of our nation. It came to us from the outside, from countries which have neither our spirit nor our traditions. It came to us from across the Rhine, from old Germany, always ready for religious quarrels, and always imbued with the spirit of caste; from new Germany, all inflated with race-pride and scornful of whatever is not Teutonic.

Anti-Semitism may be traced also to Russia, to that huge and shapeless Russia, which, with its steppes and forests, has remained isolated from the great currents of modern life; to holy, Orthodox

Russia, half Oriental, half Asiatic, which endeavors to find its national unity in its religious unity, and which regards the Catholic and the Lutheran with little more favor than the Israelite; to that autocratic Russia, which differs from us in all its institutions, as well as in all its conditions, be they economic, political, religious or social. Whatever sympathy we may feel with the Slavonic mind or the Russian spirit, the Russians, who so often emulated us, would be greatly surprised to see us copying them; as well might one propose to the Czar to model the government of his moujiks and cossacks on that of the French Republic.

Men of my age, who have grown up under the Second Empire and in the worship of liberty — it was fashionable then among the young — have witnessed many distressing sights. How often was the lie given to our youthful faith in right and justice! How many truths which we thought established forever were again called into question by the selfish passions or the ignorant claims of new generations! How many of the conquests won by reason and liberty were we unable to maintain against the encroachments of power or the delusions of political sophistry! Popular rights trodden under foot in the name of the principle of nationality, everywhere heralded as a principle of emancipation; European states transformed, for half a century, into entrenched camps and separated once more from each other by custom-house barriers and ramparts of prejudice almost as high as the Wall of China; freedom of thought and religious toleration cynically overridden or hypercritically evaded by those very political parties that professed to be their champions; laws passed to the detriment of special persons; decrees of exile or confiscation promulgated in the name of liberty, within so-called free countries and by self-styled liberals; appeals to secular power, demands for legal restriction, for paternalism, addressed to the government by all manner of clashing interests and passions. And all this, not only in Eastern Russia, buried neck-deep in the Middle Ages or rather in the *ancien régime*, but in the West, in France, in Germany, among nations said to be the most advanced of ancient Europe. Oh, how old she is, this ancient Europe, and how difficult it is for her to slough her skin and regain her youth! What an effort it is for her to strip off her old prejudices and practices and clothe herself in the spirit of a new age!

And this new age, the age that we have so ardently invoked, what will it bring us and how will it fulfil its boasted promises? To judge by the methods and the teachings extolled by those who proclaim themselves its representatives, this new age is in great danger of reviving the worst practices of the past. Men who boast of being the pioneers of the future openly praise deeds of absolutism, and smile sanctimoniously at legal brutalities borrowed from the *ancien régime* by the jurists of the Revolution. Visions of the future and mediæval prejudices; Utopias conceived by dreamers deluded with misty ideals and belated memories of a superannuated past; unceasing race-competition and ever-recurring class jealousies, all these have become confused and entangled in the minds of the learned as well as in those of the masses. And something of all this is contained in anti-Semitism; something of the old and of the new, of the far-off Middle Ages and of visionary socialism, of reactionary instincts and of revolutionary passions; and it is because of this that anti-Semitism finds an echo in such different quarters, from the drawing-rooms of society to the grog-shop of the working-man.

Let us confess it once again: we have presumed too much on reason, and relied too confidently on civilization. This brilliant civilization, which inspires our idlers with such ludicrous pride, is often shallow and unsound, even in the most advanced countries of the continent. In our proudest capitals it is barely thicker than a light veneer, underneath whose surface, if we scratch it ever so little, we shall find all the ignorance and savagery of the ages that we deem barbarous. Thus, in Paris, Vienna and Berlin, the close of our century suffers the disgrace of seeing measures of proscription and confiscation advocated by people who are really good-natured and ordinarily harmless.

It must not be inferred from what has been said that the complaints of the anti-Semites are wholly imaginary. By no means. Whether they attack our private or our public morals and customs, many of their complaints are but too well founded. Abroad, as well as at home, and most especially, perhaps, in our republic France, they are right, these noisy anti-Semites, in loudly denouncing certain governmental methods, certain practices which seem about to take root in the life of modern nations. Anti-Semitism may have been, in its time, a protest, on the part of public conscience, against culpable concessions of men in office, against the venality of politicians, and the domination, at once mysterious and contemptuous, of stock-jobbing interlopers. Despite its excesses and outrages, anti-Semitism is within its rightful province when it assails the worship of money, the scandalous barter of political influences, and the shameless exploitation of the people by the men whom they have elected; or, again, when it unmasks the hypocritical intolerance of inconsistent free-thinkers, who have erected irreligion and corruption into a method of government.

Modern society is ailing indeed, more ailing that the most honest anti-Semite imagines. The error of anti-Semitism lies in its misapprehension of the origin and the seat of the evil. It sees, or is willing to see, but one of the symptoms, and it calls this symptom the cause of the disease. Anti-Semitism is essentially "simple-minded," in the literal sense of the word. It fails to grasp the complexity of social phenomena. But this failure, which should prove its ruin, is largely the cause of its success with the masses, who in their simplicity are always carried away by that which they deem simple.

Even if the Jews had all the vices and all the power which the hatred of their enemies sees fit to ascribe to them, it were none the less childish to discover in a handful of Semites the source of the evils that afflict modern society.

It is not true that, in order to restore it to health, we need but to eliminate the Semite, as the surgeon's knife eradicates a cyst or a malignant excrescence. The extent and gravity of the evil are of a different nature. The evil is in ourselves, in our blood, in the very marrow of our bones. To cure us, it will not be enough to remove a foreign body from our flesh. Though every Jew be banished from French soil, though Israel be swept from the face of Europe, France would be not one whit more healthy, nor Europe in any better state. The first condition of a cure is a knowledge of the nature of one's malady. Now, anti-Semitism deceives us; it blinds us to our condition by trying to make us believe that the cause of the evil is external, instead of internal. There is no more dangerous error. We are afflicted with an internal trouble, due to our constitution and our entire mode of living; and the anti-Semites insist upon telling us, over and over again, that it is but a superficial ailment, brought on by chance, and foreign to our race and blood. Even when they boast of exposing our secret wounds, they misconstrue their nature; consequently, instead of furnishing a cure for them, they are in great danger of inflaming them still more.

Such will be, I doubt not, the feeling of every reader who is sufficiently thoughtful and independent to base his opinions upon reflection, and not upon the antipathies of the mob. Anti-Semitism, even when most justified in its complaints, is mistaken as to the source of our evils. It would be easy for me to prove this conclusively, could I, in this volume, have treated of finance, capital, and the ascendancy of the stock-exchange. Unfortunately, I have been obliged, for the present, to omit a part of my subject — that which in these days of subserviency to material interests so completely engrosses the public mind—the money question. I had intended at first to devote one or two chapters to it. But this money-question has assumed so prominent a place in our democratic society; it so easily takes the lead everywhere, it is so complex, and so liable to give rise to confusion, that it seemed to me worthy of separate treatment. Therefore this volume will be followed by another, in which I shall attempt to define the role played by money among the nations of to-day. On that occasion I shall take up again some of the views set forth in my book on *Papacy, Socialism, and Democracy*. There may, perhaps, seem to be no connection between these two subjects. That is a mistake, for anti-Semitism, too, is a social question. And as for myself, in studying the influence of the Jew and of modern Israel, as well as in examining the teachings of the Pope on socialism and democracy, I have always the same object in view: religious liberty and social peace. *Caritas et Pax*, such is ever my motto; and, if I mistake not, it is a Christian motto, not unbecoming a Frenchman.

II. PREFACE TO THE ENGLISH VERSION.

Our age will constitute a critical, a supreme epoch in the long history of Israel. To-day the prophecies of the seers are at last approaching fulfilment, and Israel is really being scattered to the ends of the earth. We are witnessing a new *diaspora*, the great and final dispersal.

The tree of Israel, the ancient vine of Judah, transplanted to the Sarmatian plains, has again been rudely shaken by the blast of persecution; its branches have fallen and its seeds have blown afar, over the hills and across the deserts and oceans.

As in earlier times, the wrath of their persecutors is forcing Jews and Judaism into countries where the Sabbath-lamp has never yet been lighted. The spectacle witnessed during the Renaissance and at the end of the fifteenth century, in consequence of the edicts of Isabella of Castile—the exodus of a people driven forth, without means of existence, from the land of its ancestors because it clung to the faith of its fathers — this spectacle disgraces the closing years of our nineteenth century, in consequence of the ukases of a Russian czar.

What will be the verdict of history as to the effects upon Judaism of the harsh policy of Alexander III? Possibly in years to come, when the tears of her exiles and their present sufferings shall be forgotten, the historians of Israel may affirm that the Russian autocrat contributed, more than any other man, to the expansion and renovation of Judaism.

The Jews who are driven from Slavic soil by the law or by their own poverty, are forced to begin a new life under kindlier skies and in freer lands. They are torn from the old Jewries where, closely herded together, they had barely air enough to breathe; and this painful expatriation may well prove of equal benefit to their souls and their bodies.

The majority of these exiles have gone to America, and especially to the United States. To their brethren already established between the Atlantic and the Pacific this sudden influx of a whole people, in the main poor and ignorant, who demand from them shelter and support, must indeed prove a very heavy burden. The Jews of the United States have been confronted here with an enormous task, to which, however, they have shown themselves equal. Fortunately, the most trying years seem to be over. The accession of the young emperor, Nicholas II, to the throne of Russia gives rise to the hope of some mitigation of those antiquated laws which, under Alexander III, had furnished official intolerance with the means of hypocritical persecution. The stream of emigration, whose volume is already lessening, will probably slacken. It will not wholly cease, for free America will long continue to attract the victims of persecution.

I, for one, do not believe that the United States ought to view this Jewish immigration with any disquietude; I cannot see what there is to fear from it. Among all the races and nations that have furnished the United States with colonists and have thus helped to advance its marvelous growth, I can find none more intelligent or more industrious; nor can I find any that is more capable of assimilating American civilization and of introducing into it a useful competition.

I am told that one of the charges brought against the Jews of America is that they frequently manifest leanings toward socialism; or rather toward anarchism. This may be the case with many Russian and Roumanian Jews—we have some in Paris who show such tendencies—but the fact is due less to the racial character of the Jews than to the conditions under which they have long been forced to live in Europe, and to which they are still subjected in Russia and Roumania. If Lassalle and Karl Marx were the prophets of German socialism, one of the causes of their revolt against the old social order lay in the sort of life which that order imposed upon the sons of Israel, even in Germany. This is still more evident in the case of the Jews who have been infected in Russia by the germs of nihilism and anarchy. The Jew of the old secluded Jewry is—as I have shown in this book—essentially conservative. If, in the past twenty or twenty-five years, a certain number of young Jews and Jewesses have joined the ranks of the nihilists, if some of them have been concerned in the conspiracies against the person or the authority of Alexander II and of Alexander III, this is due to the social conditions imposed on the Jews by the Russian laws. This I think I have conclusively proved, both in my present volume and in my larger work: "The Empire of the Tsars."

Only the most systematic vexations and humiliations could have aroused the children of Abraham to this spirit of revolt, to these political conspiracies, so opposed to Jewish ideas and traditions. A further proof of this, which ought to appeal to the most furious anti-Semites, is that in Russia conspiracy can lead to nothing, as yet, but transportation or the gallows.

Moreover, I have often noticed that all the Israelites implicated in political trials were what I call "de-Judaized" Jews—that is to say, Jews who have renounced the beliefs and practices of Judaism. It was Christian contagion that gave the Jews their revolutionary ideas. Some of the Jewish emigrants from Russia and other parts of Europe have been obviously degraded and corrupted by centuries of oppression. Many years — perhaps one or two generations — will be needed to raise their moral plane, to imbue them with a sense of honor and dignity. It is a great mistake to believe that this moral uplifting can be facilitated by detaching them from their religion. On the contrary, the least praise-worthy Jews that I have met have generally been "de-Judaized" Jews, those who had ceased to observe the Mosaic law. The Jew—such. at least, is my opinion — stands in even greater need of religious support than the Christian; and, as a rule, he can find that support only in the faith of his fathers. There are indeed, Israelites who become converts to Christianity. But, in order to be morally efficacious, such conversion should be genuine and disinterested. Its object should be to find favor, not in the eyes of society or of man, but of God. Now, it is well known that such true conversions are rare, and this accounts for the fact that the baptized Jews are often the least commendable.

I must confess that, in many cases, thé Christian missionaries are to blame. They are too often satisfied with purely external, nominal conversions, and, for the winning of souls, they too often employ means that are neither holy nor honest. I have been told that there are missionaries — mainly of the Protestant faith — in London, New York, and the East, who angle for Jewish souls with the coarse bait of worldly benefits, taking unfair advantage of the poverty, abandonment, and loneliness of immigrants driven out of their country by want or persecution, to lead them to the Christian font. These conversions by seduction, if I may venture so to call them, are not a whit less odious than conversions by force. Such proselytizing is unworthy of the Christian ministry and is a disgrace to the churches that encourage it. It can result only in making bad Christians and in educating bad citizens.

I need say little, in addressing my English-speaking readers, of the fear entertained by some persons, that the Jewish newcomers are likely to monopolize the national wealth. Although these apprehensions are quite common among the simple souls of the old world, I do not imagine that they have crossed the Channel or the Atlantic. Englishmen and Americans have too much faith in themselves to share such visionary fears. However great may be the commercial talents of the Jews, the Anglo-Saxons feel themselves by no means inferior to them; and when it comes to "making money," the Yankee does not fear the competition of the Semite.

Nor do I believe that, in extending hospitality to the sons of Israel, the United States, or Australia, or even old England herself, has reason to apprehend what German anti-Semites call the "judaizing" of modern society.

This expression is often used in Europe to indicate the growing ascendancy of material interests and the encroachment of the mercantile spirit. I do not think that the Jew can be held responsible for this tendency, and I shall attempt to show this in my forthcoming work: "Le Règne de l'Argent." What the anti-Semites call the "judaizing" of society might, as I have taken the liberty of asserting, be more correctly called the "Americanizing" of morals. I trust that this remark will not bring down the resentment of my American readers. That would be unfair, for I am, in many respects, a sincere admirer of their great Republic. If I have ventured to speak of the

"Americanizing" of modern society, it is simply because the typical characteristics of democratic industrial society were first revealed in the United States, and have there been developed on a larger scale than in any other country. This form of social organization, new to history, is gradually becoming dominant in all parts of the old world, as well as the new. If it has its advantages, it has also its faults, which we are all in duty bound to correct. The ascendancy of material interests, the greed for money, the frantic race for wealth, are the most deplorable characteristics of our modern industrial and democratic society. These are not social characteristics; they are peculiar neither to the Yankee nor to the Jew, although they some-times seem to be most pronounced in the Jew and the Yankee. They are the result of our social conditions, and it is not by proscribing any particular race or any faith, but only by appealing to moral forces and by bringing all such forces to their highest development that our modern democracies can escape from the practical materialism that threatens to engulf them.

Paris, April, 1893.

RUSSIA'S CRIME AGAINST THE JEWS AND CIVILIZATION.

The closing citation in the symposium of general opinion which we have presented under our preceding rubric, the preface to the English translation of Leroy Beaulieu's work on "Israel among the Nations," may serve almost without further comment as an effective introduction to our present subject. It deals directly with the great wrong committed by the government of Russia against Israel and Humanity, and it deals with it from the vantage ground of an impartial authority.

The proscriptive policy adopted by Russia against the Jewish people, a policy whose animus appears to be a mixture of political and religious fanaticism, has erected the provinces along the Western frontier of the Empire, on the German and Austrian borders, into a " Pale of Jewish Settlement" and thus created a Ghetto-country, into which the Jews of the interior provinces have been driven, to live as best they may. Even in these confines they are forbidden to apply themselves to agriculture and forced into various towns and cities, there to huddle and if need be to starve.

It has been held that this seemingly inexplicable policy has been deliberately directed to the end and with the purpose of crowding a mass of helpless and impoverished population on the Western borders of the Empire, to be utilized as an abattis against a foreign foe or as a cushion against foreign invasion, but it seems incredible that Russian fanaticism, shortsighted and ruthless as it is, should reach such a degree of turpitude and folly. It would seem, on the contrary, to be persisted in notwithstanding the manifest political and military dangers which the unreasonable procedure harbors and which, since its inception in 1879–80 has not ceased to bring about widespread economic and social disorganization, not to speak of the political disturbance of the Empire. The "russification" of the Empire, the retaining of "Russia for the Russians" (as though the Jews who are conscripted in disproportionate numbers into the army, who fought valiantly for their native land in the Crimea and on the Balkans, were not to be regarded as Russians), is the ostensible purpose of the proscription. With this purpose the ruling power of Russia continues to drive out its Jewish subjects; the historic tragedy wrought out by Spanish bigotry and fatuousness 400 years ago is being re-enacted by Russia at the present day, and the political and economic lessons taught by that example, not to mention the admonitions of humanity and the protests of an outraged civilization remain unheeded. The end of this wicked folly is apparently still afar, and seems likely to be brought nearer in point of time only by a political explosion. It were difficult to arrive at a conclusion as to which prospect is the worst.

The facts concerning the persecution of the Russian Jews have constantly been belied by the Russian authorities, in conformity with the historic methods of Russian diplomacy, but have for some years past been placed beyond question through the efforts of our own government. In view of the positive contradictions between the Russian official statements and the constantly reported and seemingly well-established facts, it was deemed expedient by the administration of President Harrison, in 1891, to send an official American Commission to investigate the condition of affairs in Russia, and the report of this Commission, referred to below by Ambassador White, gave official confirmation to the previously published details of the relentless and heartrending cruelties practiced by the Russian officials in the name of the Czar. Into these details we will not here enter. The Commissioners' Report has been widely published and has become historic.*

---

* This Commission was appointed, under direction of the President, by Secretary of the Treasury Charles Foster, by virtue of authority of the act of Congress (Sundry Civil Appropriation Bill) of March 3, 1891, and its Report was transmitted by the Secretary to Congress, February 25, 1892. The Commission consisted of Hon. John B. Weber, Commissioner of Immigration at the port of New York, Chairman, and the following named special immigrant inspectors: Judson N.

A statement of the general subject has, however, been formulated in another official report, made subsequently to that noted above, by our Ambassador at St. Petersburg, Hon. Andrew D. White, in a despatch to the Secretary of State, the late Walter Q. Gresham. In this document Mr. White summarizes the conditions relating to the persecution of the Russian Jews in a manner so concise and lucid, and in a spirit so entirely dispassionate, that it may properly be cited here as a statement whose authority is entirely beyond question.*

Cross, of Minnesota; Walter Kempster, M. D., of Wisconsin; Joseph Powderly, of Pennsylvania, and Herman J. Schultheis, of Washington, D. C. The investigations with which the Commission was charged were made in the various countries of Europe by the Commissioners in severalty, those relating to Russia and the persecution of its Jewish subjects being made by the Chairman, Col. Weber, with the assistance of Dr. Kempster.

Col. Weber's report on the condition of affairs in Russia affords the most detailed and exhaustive statement of the subject that has been given to the world. It followed closely upon the publication in the New York *Times*, (Sept.–Dec., 1891,) of the masterly review of Russian affairs generally, by Harold Frederic, in a series of articles entitled " An Indictment of Russia," and these two publications finally disposed of the glossing with which Russian diplomacy had attempted to hide the facts.

---

*This subject had on frequent occasions previously received the attention of our State Department. In a despatch under date of July 29, 1881, Secretary of State Jas. G. Blaine directs our minister at St. Petersburg. Mr. John W. Foster, to demand of the Russian Government the due rights of American Jewish citizens travelling or temporarily sojourning in Russia, in compliance with treaty obligations. From this document we quote the following salient paragraphs:

" From a careful examination of the causes of grievances heretofore reported by your legation, it appears that the action of the Russian authorities toward American citizens, alleged to be Israelites, and visiting Russia, has been of two kinds:

" First. Absolute prohibition of residence in St. Petersburg and in other cities of the Empire, on the ground that the Russian law permits no native Jews to reside there, and that the treaty between Russia and the United States gives to our citizens in Russian jurisdiction no other rights or privileges than those accorded to native Russians. The case of Henry Pinkos may be taken as a type of this class.

" Second. Permission of residence and commerce, conditionally on belonging to the first guild of Russian merchants and taking out a license. The case of Rosenstrauss is in point.

"The apparent contradiction between these two classes of actions becomes more and more evident as the question is traced backward. The Department has rarely had presented to it any subject of inquiry in which a connected understanding of the facts has proved more difficult. For every allegation, on the one hand, that native laws, in force at the time the treaty of 1832 was signed, prohibited or limited the sojourn of foreign Jews in the cities of Russia, I find, on the other hand, specific invitation to alien Hebrews of good repute to domicile themselves in Russia, to pursue their business calling under appropriate license, to establish factories there, and to purchase or lease real estate. Moreover, going back beyond 1832, the date of our treaty, I observe that the imperial ukases concerning the admission of foreigners into Russia are silent on all questions of faith; proper passports, duly viséd being the essential requisite. And, further back still, in the time of Empress Catharine, I discover explicit tolerance of all foreign religions laid down as a fundamental policy of the empire.

" It would be, in the judgment of this government, absolutely inadmissible that a domestic law restraining native Hebrews from residence in certain parts of the empire might operate to hinder an American citizen, whether alleged or known to profess the Hebrew faith, from disposing of his property or taking possession thereof for himself (subject only to the laws of alien inheritance) or being heard in person by the courts which, under Russian law, may be called upon to decide matters to which he is necessarily a party. The case would clearly be one in which the obligation of a treaty is supreme, and where the local law must yield. These questions of the conflict of local law and international treaty stipulations are among the most common which have engaged the attention of publicists, and it is their concurrent judgment that where a treaty creates a privilege for aliens in express terms, it cannot be limited by the operation of domestic law without a serious breach of the good faith which governs the intercourse of nations. So long as such a conventional engagement in favor of the citizens of another state exists, the law governing natives in like cases is manifestly inapplicable.

" I need hardly enlarge upon the point that the Government of the United States concludes its treaties with foreign states for the equal protection of all classes of American citizens. It can make absolutely no discrimination between them, whatever be their origin or creed. So that they abide by the laws, at home or abroad, it must give them due protection and expect like protection for them. Any unfriendly or discriminatory act against them on the part of a foreign power with which we are at peace would call for our earnest remonstrance whether a treaty existed or not. The friendliness of our relations with foreign nations is emphasized by the treaties we have concluded with them. We have been moved to enter into such international compacts by considerations of mutual benefit and reciprocity, by the same considerations, in short, which have animated the Russian Government from the time of the noble and tolerant declarations of the Empress Catharine in 1784 to those of the ukase of 1860. We have looked to the spirit rather than to the letter of these engagements, and believed that they should be interpreted in the broadest way; it is, therefore, a source of unfeigned regret to us when a government, to which we are allied by so many historical ties as to that of Russia, shows a disposition in its dealing with us to take advantage of technicalities, to appeal to the rigid letter and not the reciprocal motive of its international engagements, in justification of the expulsion from its territories of peaceable American citizens resorting thither under the good faith of treaties and accused of no wrong-doing or of no violation of the commercial code of the land, but of simple adherence to the faith of their fathers."

OFFICIAL DISPATCH OF AMBASSADOR WHITE TO SECRETARY OF STATE GRESHAM.

LEGATION OF THE UNITED STATES,
ST. PETERSBURGH, JULY 6, 1893.
(Received July 27.)

SIR:—Your telegram, presumably of May 17, was received on the morning of May 18, and answered at once.

Since telegraphing you I have made additional inquiries with reference to your question, and am persuaded that there has been no new edict banishing Israelites from Poland, as was stated in some of the papers of Western Europe; but for some time past the old edicts and regulations against them have been enforced in various parts of the Empire with more and more severity.

Soon after my arrival at this post it was rumored that there was to be some mitigation in the treatment of them, but the hopes based on this rumor have grown less and less, and it is now clear that the tendency is all in the direction not only of excluding Israelites more rigorously than ever from parts of the Empire where they were formerly allowed on sufferance, but to make life more and more difficult for them in those parts of the Empire where they have been allowed to live for many generations.

As you are doubtless aware, there are about 5,000,000 Israelites in Russia, forming, it is claimed, more than half of the entire Jewish race, and these are packed together in the cities and villages of what was formerly Poland and adjacent governments, in a belt extending along the western borders from northwest to southeast, but which for some years past has been drawn back from the frontier about forty miles, under the necessity, as it is claimed, imposed by the tendency of the Israelites in that region to conduct smuggling operations. In other parts of the Empire they have only been allowed to reside as a matter of exceptional favor. This alleged favor, under the more kindly reign of Alexander II, was largely developed and matured into a sort of *quasi* right in the case of certain classes, such as Israelites who have been admitted to the learned professions, or have taken a university degree, or have received the rights of merchants of the first or second guild, paying the heavy fees required in such cases. Certain skilled artisans have also been allowed to reside in certain towns outside the Jewish pale, but their privileges are very uncertain, liable to revocation at any time, and have in recent years been greatly diminished. Besides this, certain Israelites are allowed by special permits to reside as clerks in sundry establishments, but under the most uncertain tenure. This tenure can be understood by a case which occurred here about a month since.

At that time died an eminent Israelite of St. Petersburg, a Mr. —— ——, who had distinguished himself by rescuing certain great companies from ruin by his integrity and skill in various large operations, and by the fact that, while he made large and constant gains for those interested in these companies and operations, he laid up for himself only a moderate competence. He had in his employ a large number of Jewish clerks, and it is now regarded here as a matter of fact that at the expiration of their passes, say in a few months, all of them must leave St. Petersburg.

The treatment of the Israelites, whether good or evil is not based entirely upon any one ukase or statute; there are said to be in the vast jungle of the laws of this Empire more than one thousand decrees and statutes relating to them, beside innumerable circulars, open or secret, regulations, restrictions, extensions, and temporary arrangements, general, special, and local, forming such a tangled growth that probably no human being can say what the law as a whole is — least of all can a Jew in any province have any certain knowledge of his rights.

From time to time, and especially during the reign of Alexander II, who showed himself more kind to them than any other sovereign had ever been, many of them were allowed to leave this overcrowded territory, and, at least, were not hindered from coming into territory and towns which, strictly speaking, they were not considered as entitled to enter; but for some time past this residence on sufferance has been rendered more and more difficult. Details of the treatment to which

they have been subjected may be found in the report made by
Mr. J. B. Weber and his associate commissioners entitled,
"Report of the Commissioners of Immigration upon the Causes
which incite Immigration to the United States," Government
Printing Office. I must confess that when I first read this
report its statements seemed to me exaggerated, or at least,
over-colored, but it is with very great regret that I say that
this is no longer my opinion. Not only is great severity exercised as regards the main body of Israelites here, but it is from
time to time brought to bear with especial force on those
returning to Russia from abroad. The case was recently
brought to my notice of a Jewish woman who, having gone
abroad, was stopped on her return at a frontier station, and, at
last accounts, had been there three days, hoping that some
members of her family in Russia might be able to do something
to enable her to rejoin them.

Israelites of the humbler classes find it more and more
difficult to re-enter Russia, and this fact will explain the case
of Mrs. Minnie Levin, referred to in Mr. Wharton's dispatch
No. 60 as being refused a visa at the Russian Consulate-
General in New York, and it will also throw light on various
cases we have had in which the legation has been able to
secure mitigation of the application of the rules.

On this latter point we have been successful in obtaining
such mitigation in cases of many Israelites who have been subjected to annoyance by over-zealous local authorities.

It may appear strange that any nation should wish to expel
a people who, in other parts of the world, have amassed so
much wealth. The fact is that but a very small fraction of
them in Russia are wealthy; but few even in comfortable
circumstances. The vast majority of them are in poverty, and
a very considerable part in misery — just on the border of
starvation.

Nearly forty years ago, when, as an attaché of this legation,
I was for seven days and nights on the outside of a post coach
between St. Petersburgh and Warsaw — there being then no
railway to the frontier—I had an ample opportunity to see
something of these Israelites and of the region in which they
live. They exist for the most part in squalor, obliged to resort
to almost anything that offers, in order to keep body and soul
together. Even the best of them were then treated with contempt by the lowest of the pure Russians. I myself saw two
Israelites, evidently of the wealthier class and richly clad, who
had ventured into the enclosure in front of the posthouse to
look at the coach in which I was, lashed with a coach whip and

34

driven out of the enclosure with blows by one of the postilions —evidently a serf.

A very few millionaire Israelites are to be found among the merchants of the first guild in some of the larger cities, but there is no such proportion of wealthy men among them as in the United States, Great Britain, France, and Germany. In the smaller towns, in some of which they form the majority of the residents, their poverty is so abject that they drag each other down, making frequently a ruinous competition with each other in such branches of business as they are allowed to pursue. This is now even more the case than ever before, since recent regulations have swept the Israelites living in many rural districts into the towns.

A case was a few days since mentioned to me in which a small town of 8000 or 10,000 inhabitants had recently received into its population nearly 6000 Israelites from the surrounding country.

The restrictions are by no means confined to residence; they extend into every field of activity. Even in the parts of the Empire where the Israelites are most free they are not allowed to hold property in land, or to take a mortgage on land, or to farm land, and of late they have even been, to a large extent, prevented from living on farms, and have been thrown back into the cities and villages.

As to other occupations, Jewish manufacturers have at times, even under the present reign, been crippled by laws or regulations forbidding them to employ Christian workmen, but these are understood to be not now in force. They are relics of the old legislation which, in the interest of the servant's soul, forbade a Jew to employ a Christian servant under pain of death, and which, in a mitigated form, remained on the statute book until 1865, when it was abolished by Alexander II.

There are also many restrictions upon the professions considered more honorable. A few Israelites are allowed to become engineers, and they are allowed to hold 5 per cent of the positions of army surgeons, but no more; and this in spite of the fact that from the Middle Ages until now their race has been recognized as having a peculiar aptitude for medicine and surgery. As a rule, also, they are debarred from discharging any public functions of importance, and even as to lesser functions, a Jew can not be elected mayor of a village or even member of its council.

Not more than one man in ten of those summoned to do jury duty can be a Jew, and even in the cities within the pale, where the Jews form the great majority of the population, they can not hold more than one-third of the places on a municipal council.

Perhaps the most painful of the restrictions upon them is in regard to the education of their children. The world over, as is well known, Israelites will make sacrifices to educate their sons and daughters, such as are not made, save in exceptional cases, by any other people. They are, as is universally recognized, a very gifted race, but no matter how gifted a young Israelite may be, his chances of receiving an education are small.

In regions where they are most numerous, only 10 per cent of the scholars in high schools and universities are allowed to be Jews, but in many cases the number allowed them is but 5 per cent, and in St. Petersburgh and Moscow only 3 per cent. Out of the seventy-five young Israelites who applied for admission to the University of Dorpat in 1887 only seven were allowed to enter. A few days since the case was brought to my notice of a well-to-do Israelite who wished to educate his son, whom he considered especially gifted, but who could not obtain permission to educate him in St. Petersburg, and was obliged to be satisfied with the permission to enter him at one of the small provincial universities remote from the capital.

To account for this particular restriction it is urged that if freely allowed to receive an advanced education they would swarm in the high schools, universities, and learned professions; and, as a proof of this, the fact is mentioned that some time since, in the absence of restrictions, at Odessa from 50 to 70 per cent of the scholars in sundry Russian colleges were Jews.

As to religious restrictions, the general policy pursued seems to an unprejudiced observer from any other country so illogical as to be incomprehensible. On the one hand great powers are given to the Jewish rabbis and religious authorities. They are allowed in the districts where the Israelites mainly live to form a sort of state within the state, with power to impose taxes upon their co-religionists and to give their regulations virtually the force of law. On the other hand, efforts of zealous orthodox Christians to proselyte Israelites, which must provoke much bitterness, are allowed and even favored. The proselytes, once brought within the orthodox Russian fold, no matter by what means, any resumption of the old religion by them is treated as a crime.

Recent cases have occurred where Jews who have been thus converted and who have afterwards attended the synagogue have been brought before the courts.

So, too, in regard to religious instruction it would seem to an unprejudiced observer, wishing well both to Russia and to the Israelites, that the first thing to do would be to substitute instruction in science, general literature, and in technical branches for that which is so strongly complained of by Russians generally — the instructon in the Talmud and Jewish theology. But this is just what is not done, and indeed, as above stated not allowed.

The whole system at present in vogue is calculated to make Talmudic and theological schools — which are so constantly complained of as the nurseries and hotbeds of anti-Russian and anti-Christian fanaticism — the only schools accessible to the great majority of gifted young Israelites.

As to the recent interferences of which accounts have been published in the English newspapers and especially as to a statement that a very large number of Jewish children were, early during the present year, taken from their parents in one of the southern governments of Russia and put into monastic schools under the charge of orthodox priests, this statement having been brought to my notice especially by letters addressed to me as the representative of the United States, I communicated with our consuls in the regions referred to and also obtained information from other trustworthy sources, and the conclusion at which I arrived was that the statement was untrue; it probably had its origin in the fact that much anxiety has recently been shown by certain high officials, and especially ecclesiastics, to promote education in which orthodox religious instruction holds a very important part.

In justification of all these restrictions various claims are made. First of all it is claimed that the Jews lend money to peasants and others at enormous rates of interest. But it is pointed out, in answer to this, that sundry bankers and individuals in parts of Russia where no Jews are permitted have made loans at a much higher rate than Jews have ever ventured to do; while it is allowed that 100 per cent a year has not unfrequently been taken by the Israelites, there seems to be no doubt of the fact that from 300 to 800 per cent, and even more sometimes, has been taken by Christians.

This statement seems incredible, but it is unimpeachable. In a general way it is supported by the recent report of a Russian official to Mr. Sagonof; and a leading journal of St. Petersburg, published under strict censorship, has recently given cases with names and dates where a rate higher than the highest above named was paid by Russian peasants to Christian money lenders.

Those inclined to lenity towards the Jews point to the fact that none of them would dare take any such rates of interest as Christians may freely demand; that to do so would raise against the Israelites in their neighborhood storms which they could not resist, and it is argued that, as their desire for gain is restricted in this way, their presence in any part of Russia tends to diminish the rate of interest rather than to increase it. On the other hand it is claimed that they will not work at agriculture and, indeed, that they will do no sort of manual labor which they can avoid.

As to the first of these charges, the fact is dwelt upon, which has so impressed Mr. Mackenzie Wallace and other travelers, that the Jewish agricultural colonies founded by Alexander I, in 1810, and by Nicholas I, in 1840, have not done well.

But in answer it may be stated as a simple matter of history that, having been originally an agricultural people they have been made what they are by ages of persecutions which have driven them into the occupations to which they are now so generally devoted; that in Russia they have for generations been incapacitated for agricultural work by such restrictions as those above referred to; that even if they are allowed here and there to till the land, they are not allowed, in the part of the Empire which they most inhabit, to buy it or even to farm it, and that thus the greatest incentive to labor is taken away.

As to other branches of manual labor, simply as a matter of fact, there are very large bodies of Jewish artisans in Poland, numbering in the aggregate about one-half the entire adult male Israelite population. Almost every branch of manual labor is represented among them, and well represented. As stone masons they have an especially high reputation, and it is generally conceded that in sobriety, capacity, and attention to work they fully equal their Christian rivals.

Complaint is also made that they, as far as possible, avoid military service. This is doubtless true, but the reasons for it are evident. For the Jewish soldier there is no chance of promotion, and when he retires after service, he is, as a rule, subject to the same restrictions as others of his race. In spite of this fact the number of them in the conscription of 1886 was over 40,000.

I find everywhere in discussing this subject, a complaint that the Israelites, wherever they are allowed to exist, get the better of the Russian peasant. The difficulty is that the life of the Israelite is marked by sobriety, self-denial and foresight; and, whatever may be the kindly qualities ascribed to the Russian peasant, these qualities are rarely, if ever, mentioned among them.

It is also urged against the Israelites in Russia that they are not patriotic, but in view of the policy pursued regarding them the wonder is that any human being should expect them to be patriotic.

There is also frequent complaint against Jewish fanaticism, and recently collections of extracts from the Talmud have been published here as in western Europe, and even in the United

States, to show that Israelites are educated in bitter and undying hate of Christians, and taught not only to despise but to despoil them; and it is insisted that the vast majority of the Israelites in Russia have, by ages of this kind of instruction and by the simple laws of heredity, been made beasts of prey with claws and teeth especially sharp, and that the peasant must be protected from them.

Lately this charge has been strongly reiterated, a book having appeared here in which the original Hebrew of the worst Talmudic passages, with translations of them, are placed in parallel columns. It seems to be forgotten that the Israelites would be more than human if such passages did not occur in their sacred writings. While some of these passages antedate the establishment of Christianity, most of them have been the result of fervor under oppression and of the appeal to the vengeance of Jehovah in times of persecution; and it would be but just to set against them the more kindly passages, especially the broadly and beautifully humane teachings which are so frequent in the same writings.

An eminently practical course would be to consider the development of Judaism in the United States, Great Britain, and other countries where undeniably those darker features of of the Talmud have been more and more blotted out from Jewish teaching, and the unfortunate side of Talmudic influence more and more weakened.

But this charge of Talmudic fanaticism is constantly made, and Russians, to show that there is no hatred of Israelites, as such, point to the fact that the Karaites, who are non-Talmudic, have always been treated with especial kindness.

To this the answer would seem to be that the Karaites are free from fanaticism because they have been so long kindly treated, and that this same freedom and kindness which has made them unobjectionable to Russian patriotism would, in time, probably render the great mass of Israelites equally so.

There is no need of argument, either in the light of history or of common sense, to prove that these millions of Israelites in Russia are not to be rendered less fanatical by the treatment to which they are subjected.

To prove that the more bitter utterances in the Talmud complained of do not necessarily lead Israelites to hate Christians, and indeed to show that the teachings which the Israelites receive in countries where they have more freedom lead to a broad philanthropy of the highest type, I have been accustomed, in discussing the subject with Russians, to point to such examples of the truest love for human kind as those shown by Judah Touro in the United States, Sir Moses Montefiore in England, Nathan de Rothschild in Austria, James de Rothschild and Baron Hirsch in France, and multitudes of other cases, citing especially the fact of the extensive charities carried on by Israelites in all countries, and the significant circumstance that the first considerable contribution from the United States to the Russian famine fund came from a Jewish synagogue in California, with the request that in the use of it no discrimination should be made between Jews and Christians. Cases like these would seem to do away effectually with the idea that Jewish teachings necessarily inculcate hostility to people of other religious beliefs.

There is also a charge closely connected wtth the foregoing which undoubtedly has much to do with the present severe reaction. It is constantly repeated that, in spite of the fact that the late Emperor Alexander II had shown himself more kindly toward the Israelites than had any of his predecessors— relaxing the old rules as to residence, occupation, education, and the like, and was sure, had he lived, to go much farther in the same direction, probably as far as breaking down a mass of the existing barriers, and throwing open vast regions never before accessible to them—the proportion of Israelites implicated in the various movements against him, especially in the Nihilistic movement, and in the final plot which led to his assassination, was far beyond the numerical proportion of their race in Russia to the entire population. This feeling was certainly at the bottom of the cruel persecutions of the Israelites by the peasants just after the death of the late Emperor, and has no less certainly much to do with the prejudices of various personages of high influence as well as of the vast mass of the people which still exist.

The remarkable reaction now dominant in Russia is undoubtedly in great measure, if not entirely, the result of the assassination of Alexander II; it is a mere truism to say that this event was the most unfortunate in its effects on well-ordered progress that has occurred in this Empire; but, so far as the Israelites are concerned, the facts at the bottom of this charge against them can be accounted for, without imputing anything to the race at large, by the mass of bitterness stored up during ages of oppression, not only in Russia, but elsewhere. The matter complained of must certainly be considered as exceptional, for it cannot hide the greater fact that the Jews have always shown themselves especially grateful to such rulers as have mitigated their condition or even shown a kindly regard for them.

I was myself, as minister at Berlin, cognizant of innumerable evidences of gratitude and love shown by the entire Jewish population toward the Crown Prince, afterwards the Emperor Frederick III, who, when Jew-baiting was in fashion, and patronized by many persons in high positions, set himself quietly but firmly against it.   And this reminiscence leads me to another in regard to the oft-repeated charge that the Israelite is incapable of patriotism, is a mere beast of prey, and makes common cause with those of his race engaged in sucking out the substance of the nation where he happens to be.   It was my good fortune to know personally several Israelites at Berlin, who as members of the Imperial Parliament showed their patriotism by casting away all hopes of political advancement and resisting certain financial claims in which some of their coreligionists, as well as some leading and very influential Christians, were deeply engaged.   There is nothing nobler in recent parliamentary history than the career of such Israelites as Lasker and Bamberger during that period, and at this moment no sane man in Germany hesitates to ascribe to the Israelite Simson all the higher qualities required in his great office, that of chief justice in the highest court of the German Empire.

The same broad and humane characteristics have been shown among the vast majority of Israelites eminent in science, philosophy, literature and the arts.   Long before the Israelite Spinoza wrought his own ideal life into the history of philosophy, this was noted, and it has continued to be noted in Russia. During my former residence here there were two eminent representatives of the proscribed race in the highest scientific circles, and they were especially patriotic and broad in their sympathies; and to-day the greatest of Russian sculptors, Antokolski, an Israelite, has thrown into his work not only more genius, but also more of profound patriotic Russian feeling, than has any other sculptor of this period.   He has revived more evidently than has any other sculptor the devotion of Russians to their greatest men in times past, and whenever the project of erecting at St. Petersburg a worthy monument to the late Emperor shall be carried out, there is no competent judge who will not acknowledge that he is the man in all Russia to embody in marble or bronze the gratitude of the nation.   This is no mere personal opinion of my own, for when recently a critic based an article against Antokolski's works, evidently upon grounds of race antipathy, a brilliant young author, of one of the oldest and most thoroughly Russian families in the Empire, Prince Sergius Wolkonsky, wrote a most cogent refutation of the attack.   It is also charged that in Russia, and, indeed, throughout Europe, an undue proportion of Jews have been prominent in movements generally known as "socialistic," and such men as Ferdinand Lasalle and Karl Marx are referred to.

When this statement has been made in my hearing I have

met it by the counter statement of a fact that seems to me to result from the freedom allowed in the United States, namely, the fact that at a meeting of the American Social Science Association in 1891, in which a discussion took place involving the very basis of the existing social system, and in which the leading representatives of both sides in the United States were most fully represented, the argument which was generally agreed to be the most effective against the revolutionary and anti-social forces was made by a young Israelite, Prof. Seligman, of Columbia University, in the city of New York. Here, again, results are mistaken for causes; the attitude complained of in the Israelites is clearly the result of the oppression of their race.

But there is one charge which it is perhaps my duty to say that I have never heard made against Israelites even by Russians most opposed to them—the charge that they are to be found in undue or even in any considerable proportion among inebriates or criminals. The simplest reason for this exception in their favor is found in the official statistics which show that in the Governments where they are most numerous diseases and crimes resulting from the consumption of alcoholic drinks are least numerous, and that where the number of Israelites is greatest the consumption of spirits is least. It is also well known, as a matter of general observation, that the Russian Israelites are, as a rule, sober, and that crimes among them are comparatively infrequent.

Yet, if in any country we might expect alcoholism to be greatly developed among them it would be in this Empire, where their misery is so great and the temptation to drown it in intoxicating beverages so constant; and if we might expect crime to be developed largely among them it would be in this Empire, where, crowded together as they are, the struggle for existence is so bitter. Their survival under it can only be accounted for by their superior thrift and sobriety.

It would be a mistake to suppose that religious hatred or even deeply religious feeling is a main factor in this question. The average Russian believes that all outside the orthodox Greek Church are lost; but he does not hate them on that account, and though there has been of late years, during the present reaction, an increase of pressure upon various Christian organizations outside the established church, this has been undeniably from political rather than religious reasons; it has been part of the "Russifying process," which is at present the temporary fashion. The rule in Russia has always been toleration, though limited by an arrangement which seems to a stranger very peculiar. In St. Petersburg, for example, there are churches for nearly all the recognized forms of Christian belief, as well as synagogues for Hebrews, and at least one Mohammedan

mosque; but the only proselytism allowed is that between themselves and from them to the established church; in other words,
the Greek church may proselyte from any of them, and, within
certain limits, each one may proselyte from its orthodox neighbors, but none of them can make converts from the Greek
Church.

This regulation seems rather the result, on the whole, of
organized indifference than of zeal, its main purpose being undoubtedly to keep down any troublesome religious fervor.   The
great body of the Russian peasantry, when left to themselves,
seem to be remarkably free from any spirit of fanatical hostility
toward religious systems differing from their own, and even
from the desire to make proselytes.   Mr. Mackenzie Wallace,
in his admirable book, after showing that the orthodox Russian
and the Mahommedan Tartar live in various communities in
perfect peace with each other, details a conversation with a
Russian peasant, in which the latter told him that just as God
gave the Tartar a darker skin, so he gave him a different religion ; and this feeling of indifference, when the peasants are
not excited by zealots on one side or the other, seems to prevail
toward the Roman Catholics in Poland and the Protestants in
the Baltic provinces and Finland.   While some priests have
undoubtedly done much to create a more zealous feeling, it
was especially noted during the fierce persecution of the Jews
early in the present reign that in several cases the orthodox
village priests not only gave shelter to Israelites seeking to
escape harm, but exerted themselves to put an end to the
persecutions.   So, too, during the past few days the papers
have contained a statement that a priest very widely known
and highly esteemed, to whom miraculous powers are quite
generally attributed, Father John, of Cronstadt, has sent some
of the charity money, of which he is almoner, to certain Jewish
orphanages under the control of Israelites.

The whole present condition of things is rather the outcome
of a great complicated mass of causes, involving racial antipathies, remembrances of financial servitude, vague inherited
prejudices, with myths and legends like those of the Middle
Ages.

But, whatever may be the origin of the feeling toward the
Israelites the practical fact remains that the present policy
regarding them is driving them out of the country in great
masses.   The German papers speak of large numbers as seeking the United States and the Argentine Republic—but especially the former—through the northern ports of that Empire,
and, as I write, the Russian papers state that eight steamers
loaded with them are just about leaving Libau for America.

It is, of course, said in regard to these emigrants that they have not been ordered out of the country, that they can stay in Russia if they like, and that Russia has simply exercised her right to manage her own internal affairs in her own way; but it is none the less true that the increasing severity in the enforcement of the regulations regarding the Israelites is the main, if not the only, cause of this exodus. In order that this question may be understood in its relations to the present condition of political opinion in the Empire, there is need to make some additional statement.

There has never been a time, probably, when such a feeling of isolation from the rest of the world, and aversion to foreign influence of every sort, have prevailed in Russia as at present; it is shared by the great majority from the highest to the lowest, and it is echoed in the press. Russia has been, during the last ten years, in a great reactionary period, which now seems to be culminating in the attempted ''Russification'' of the Empire, involving such measures as increasing pressure upon Poland, increasing interference with the Baltic provinces and the German colonies, in the talk of constitutional changes in Finland, in the substitution of Russian for German names of various western towns, in the steadily increasing provisions for strengthening the orthodox Russian Church against all other religious organizations, in the outcry made by various papers in favor of such proposals as that for transferring the university at Dorpat into the Muscovite regions of the interior, for changing the name of St. Petersburg, and for every sort of Russifying process which the most imaginative can devise.

In this present reaction, connected as it is with bitter disappointment over the defeat of Russian aspirations in the Berlin treaty and since, reforms which were formerly universally considered honorable and desirable for Russia are now regarded with aversion ; the controlling feeling is for ''Russification.''

Peter the Great is now very largely regarded by Russians as having taken a wrong road, and, while monuments are erected to Alexander II, his services as emancipator of the serfs are rarely alluded to, and the day formerly observed in remembrance of the emancipation has ceased to be publicly noticed. This reaction shows itself in general literature, in paintings, in sculpture, in architecture, in everything. Any discussion regarding a change in the present condition of things is met by the reply that strangers do not understand Russian questions, and that these questions are complicated historically, politically, economically and socially to such a degree that none but those having personal experience can understand them. If the matter is still further pressed and the good effects of a different policy in the United States, Great Britian, and elsewhere are referred to, it is answered that in those countries a totally different state of things exists, and that no arguments can be made from them to Russia. Any continuance of the discussion is generally met by the statement that Russian questions are largely misrepresented by the press of western Europe; that there is a systematic propaganda against Russia in England, Germany, Austria, and Italy; that England does or allows worse things in her Irish evictions and in her opium traffic, and the United States in lynch law proceedings and treatment of the Chinese, than any done or allowed in Russia; that, in short, Russia is competent to take charge of her own internal policy, and that other powers will do well to mind their own business. This feeling is closely akin to that which was shown sometimes in the United States before the civil war toward foreign comments upon our own "peculiar institution," when representations by such philanthropists as the Duchess of Sutherland, George Thompson, M. P., and others were indignantly repelled.

This condition of opinion and the actions resulting from it are so extreme that it naturally occurs to one who has observed Russian history that a reaction cannot be long deferred.

The progress of Russia thus far has been mainly by a series of reactions. These have sometimes come with surprising suddenness. In view of that which took place when the transition was made from the policy of restriction followed by the Emperor Nicholas to the broadly liberal policy adopted by Alexander II, of which, being connected with this legation at that time, I was a witness, a reaction at present seems by no means impossible or even improbable. It is by no means necessary that a change of reign should take place. A transition might be occasioned as others have been, by the rise of some strong personality bringing to bear upon the dominant opinion the undoubted fact that the present system of repression toward the Israelite is from every point of view a failure, and that it is doing incalculable harm to Russia.

This dispatch ought not, perhaps, to close without an apology for its length; the subject is one of great importance, and it has seemed to me a duty to furnish the Department, in answer to the Secretary's question, with a full report regarding the present stage in the evolution of the matter concerned as my opportunities have enabled me to make.

I am, etc.,
ANDREW D. WHITE.

NOTE:—The attitude of our Government with regard to the general question here involved has respeatedly been manifested through our State Department. On the occasion of the Mohammedan outrages against the Jews in 1840, and under date of August 19th of that year, Secretary of State John Forsyth addressed to our Minister to Turkey, David Porter, a dispatch as follows:

Sir: In common with the people of the United States, the President has learned with profound feelings of surprise and pain, the atrocious cruelties which have been practised upon the Jews of Damascus and Rhodes in consequence of charges, extravagant and strikingly similar to those, which in less enlightened ages, were made pretexts for the persecution and spoliation of these unfortunate people. As the scenes of these barbarities are in the Mohammedan dominions, and as such inhuman practises are not of infrequent occurrence in the East, the President has directed me to instruct you to do everything in your power with the Government of his Imperial Highness, the Sultan, to whom you are accredited, consistent with discretion and your diplomatic character, to prevent or mitigate these horrors, the bare recital of which has caused a shudder throughout the civilized world, and in an especial manner to direct your philanthropic efforts against the employment of torture in order to compel the confession of imputed guilt. The President is of opinion that from no one can such generous endeavors proceed with so much propriety and effect as from the Representative of a friendly power whose institutions, political and civil, place upon the same footing the worshipers of God, of every faith and form, acknowledging no distinction between the Mohammedan, the Jew and the Christian. Should you in carrying out these instructions find it necessary or proper to address yourself to any of the Turkish authorities, you will refer to this distinctive characteristic of our government, as investing with a peculiar propriety and right the interposition of your good offices in behalf of an oppressed and persecuted race among whose kindred are found some of the most worthy and patriotic of our citizens. In communicating to you the wishes of the President I do not think it advisable to give you more explicit and minute instructions, but earnestly commend to your zeal and discretion a subject which appeals so strongly to the universal sentiments of justice and humanity.

I am, Sir,
Your obedient servant,
J. FORSYTH.

In 1870, when the persecution of the Roumanian Jews, which had been started in 1868, was growing from bad to worse, our government, at the instance of the Order of B'nai B'rith, (as noted on page 428), established a diplomatic agency at

Bucharest. On this occasion President Grant furnished Consul-General Peixotto with a special authorization, as follows:

EXECUTIVE MANSION, WASHINGTON, D. C.,
December 8th, 1870.

The bearer of this letter, Mr. Benjamin F. Peixotto, who has accepted the important, though unremunerative, position of United States Consul to Roumania, is commended to the good offices of all representatives of this Government abroad.

Mr. Peixotto has undertaken the duties of his present office more as a missionary work for the benefit of the people he represents than for any benefit to accrue to himself — a work in which all citizens will wish him the greatest success. The United States, knowing no distinction of her own citizens on account of religion or nativity, naturally believes in a civilization, the world over, which will secure the same universal views.

U. S. GRANT.

President Grant's interest in the subject was furthermore evinced when, in 1871, at the earnest request of Hon. Simon Wolf, he called a special Cabinet meeting to consider the reported expulsion of the Jews of Russian Bessarabia. This meeting resulted in the sending of a cable dispatch to Minister Andrew G. Curtin at St. Petersburg, protesting against the ukase of banishment. The protest was heeded by the Czar and the ukase was rescinded.

As a further indication of the position taken by our Government in regard to the matter, we quote the following dispatch from Secretary of State Hamilton Fish to Consul General Peixotto:

DEPARTMENT OF STATE,
WASHINGTON, D. C., April 10, 1872.

SIR:—Among the large number of Israelites in this country there are probably few whose sympathies have not been intensely excited by the recent intelligence of the grievous persecutions of their co-religionists in Roumania. This feeling has naturally been augmented by the contrast presented by the position of members of that persuasion here, who are equals with all others before the law, which sternly forbids any oppresion on account of religion. Indeed, it may be said that the people of this country universally abhor persecution anywhere for that cause, and deprecate the trials of which, according to your dispatches, the Israelites of Roumania have been victims.

This Government heartily sympathizes with the popular instinct upon the subject, and while it has no disposition or intention to give offence by interfering in the internal affairs of Roumania, it is deemed to be due to humanity to remonstrate against any license or impunity which may have attended the outrages in that country.

You are consequently authorized to address a note to the Minister of Foreign Affairs of the Principality in which you will embody the views herein expressed, and you will also do anything which you can do discreetly, with a reasonable prospect of success, toward preventing a recurrence or continuance of the persecutions adverted to.

I am, Sir, etc., etc.,

HAMILTON FISH.

As a plain and unmistakable summary of the attitude of the American people with regard to the brutalities deliberately perpetrated by Russia, we close these citations with that of the Resolution of Congress, introduced by Representative Amos J. Cummings of New York, December 19th, 1890, and adopted unanimously by the House.

Resolved, etc.: "That the members of the House of Representatives of the United States have heard with profound sorrow and feelings akin to horror the reports of the persecutions of the Jews in Russia, reflecting the barbarism of past ages, disgracing humanity and impeding the progress of civilization ; that our sorrow is intensified by the fact that such occurrences should happen in a country which has been, and is now, the firm friend of the United States, and in a nation that clothed itself with glory, not long since, by the emancipation of its serfs and by its defence of helpless Christians from the oppression of the Turks; that a copy of this resolution be forwarded to the Secretary of State with a request that he send it to the American Minister at St. Petersburg and that said Minister be directed to present the same to His Imperial Majesty Alexander III, Czar of all the Russias."

THE RUSSIAN JEWISH REFUGEES IN AMERICA.

CONSIDERED IN CONNECTION WITH THE GENERAL SUBJECT OF IMMIGRATION IN ITS HISTORICAL AND ECONOMIC ASPECTS.

(Note.—In the preparation of the following article the editor has utilized the contents of a paper read by him before the Board of Presidents of the National Societies of Philadelphia, as a member of that body, December 12th, 1891).

A review of the subject of American Jewish citizenship necessarily involves a consideration of the recent accretions to the Jewish population in this country through the immigration of those of the expatriated Russian Jews who have found and are yet finding their way to our shores. The influx and settlement here of this practically new element of the population has attracted a large measure of public attention, notwithstanding the fact that it comprises an average of not over 8 per cent. of the total immigration. This has been due not only to the extraordinary causes of the influx, but also to the fact that the settlement of a large number of the newcomers in the seabord cities has caused some disturbances in the labor market at those points.

The influence of this movement on the future development of American Judaism is beyond our immediate purview, and its present bearing on the Jewish community need be considered but incidentally. In view, however, of the repeated changes in our immigration laws since 1882, when the immigration of the Russian Jews began to reach its present marked proportions by reason of their expulsion from their homes, and of the agitation for such further legislation as will result in a practically complete disbarment of these and other unfortunate victims of European oppression, we may here properly proceed to a brief consideration of the social, political and economic aspects of the question, both as regards the Russian Jewish immigrants and immigration in general.

The earliest immigration movement of which a record has come down to our day is that which carried the Hebrew Abram from "Ur of the Chaldees" westward to the plains of Canaan. It carried with it the latent energy whose force has been the most potent in the world's affairs; which has become the moving spirit of the Caucasian race, and which afforded the vehicle of development for Judaism, Christianity and Islam. The far-reaching consequences of that first of recorded immigrations need not be dwelt upon; it forms the prologue to the history of civilization, a history whose epilogue is yet to be enacted, and whose processes are not only still a living reality in the present, but are proceeding towards an infinitely greater compass in the future.

The migration of Abraham is to be regarded, not only from the historic standpoint, but in the most abstract scientific sense, as a force, resulting as all forces must, from some cause of equal or greater potentiality, and moving, as all forces do, along the lines of least resistance. The movement proceeded, as we know, from the East, away from, if not out of, the cradle of the Caucasian race; from where expansion was hemmed and development was hampered, towards the West and South where the possibilities of both were greater and the requisite conditions more favorable. This was forty centuries ago; from that time to the present the movement has still been westward and southward, and by virtue of the same natural law that operated in the early dawn of history, its course is manifestly destined to trend in the same direction for some time longer.

In the meantime, throughout all the course of the historic past, migration after migration has successively marked the greatest epochs in the annals of mankind. The migration of Abraham was followed by many others, none indeed of more far-reaching significance, but all or nearly all of greater magnitude, and not a few of them of vast importance as factors in the history of man. Some centuries after Abraham's time the

35

migration of the Canaanite Cadmus westward to the Isles of Greece, or perhaps the migration of the Pelasgic tribes westward from Asia Minor, opened the first chapter in the history of Europe. Still later, through the great migrations at the close of the Roman period, and in the early Middle Ages, the barbarians of Europe became imbued with the leaven of Jewish ideals in the form of Christianity, and further still in the course of time the migrations of the hunted Jews from Germany to Poland, and from Spain to Holland and to England, influenced permanently the current of the world's affairs. Subsequently, the migration of the Pilgrim Fathers to North America left an indelible impress in our modern civilization, and finally the migrations of yesterday and to-day, trending still westward to the Pacific, and the offshoots of the current to Australia, to New Zealand and to South America, have opened in the history of mankind a chapter which the Twentieth Century will not complete.

It is remarkable that of all these notable migrations, that of Abraham may be considered as not only first in point of time, but also as altogether normal in its character. In all the later historic movements of this kind, the element of force is more or less definitely manifest, but Abraham's migration was a peaceful one, and when he took up the sword at all, it was only to benefit the people among whom he dwelt. We find him earnestly pleading the cause of his adopted countrymen, notwithstanding their great wickedness; he bought and paid for even his last resting place rather than accept it as a gift, and in general he figures on the historic horizon as in all respects not only a typical but a model immigrant.

Had the great migrations of later times been as peaceful as that of Abraham, the annals of humanity would have been less troubled than we find them. But the subsequent movements of population were migrations of masses of people, forced from their native soil by extraneous pressure or lured away by the incitements of conquest, or by both agencies combined, and such movements must in their very nature, be violent and sanguinary.

The earliest peoples required for their sustenance far more space than do equal numbers in a more civilized state. They had no developed means of subsistence; the most primitive inhabitants relied solely on the products of unaided nature, and these they found mainly in the chase. As this became more difficult, or its produce scarcer, they betook themselves to herding, a culture in itself, the first step in civilization, and the first expedient to support an increasing population. In this respect the inhabitants of the Eastern plains were far in advance of their Western contemporaries; the Asiatic herdsman was more favorably situated than the huntsman in the forests of primeval Europe, and hence we find both culture and population first evolved in the East and flowing thence by natural sequence towards the West. Culture, the outgrowth of population, was first planted in the East; there it rooted and there it blossomed, and there humanity gathered its first fruits, but its ripened products have fructified upon its Western grafts. Westward indeed the star of Empire has made its way, and here on our Western Continent, under the ægis of our great Republic, under the influence of American liberty and freedom, it seems destined to reach its ascendant.

In the upbuilding of this Republic the decendants of the first great emigrant have taken, as we have recorded in the preceeding pages, an ample share, and among these descendants the compatriots of the present victims of Russian barbarity were by no means wanting. The emigration of the Slavic Jews to America had been going on in a normal manner, and therefore to a limited extent, for a long time before the present exodus, and in fact, so to speak, from the beginning. After each of the successive uprisings of Poland against the barbarous tyranny of its Russian oppressors, from the time of Pulaski, who after leading his countrymen vainly against the Russian hordes in 1768, came to America to die in the struggle for liberty here; from the time of Kosciuszko, who came here to fight successfully for the independence of our country and then returned to fight vainly for the independence of his own, there have been Polish emigrants to America and among them were many Jews. Haym Solomon, who afforded one of the noblest examples of devotion to American liberty that is recorded in our annals, was as we have seen* a Polish Jew and an intimate of the two patriots named above, and on Pulaski's staff was a

*Page 15.

Jewish officer* and others of his Jewish countrymen were doubtless serving in his command.

Down to the bloody outbreak of Russian fanaticism in 1879–
1880, followed by the officially decreed expulsions of the succeeding years, the influx of the Slavic Jews, was, as we have
noted, a normal tide, like that which brought to these shores
millions of immigrants from every European country. Nor-
mally, without being forced, and of their own volition they
had come, as had the Sephardic Jews from England and
Holland during our Colonial period and in the early decades of
our independence, and as the German Jews came with the
stream of German immigration after the beginning of steam
navigation and the Revolution of 1848. The English Sephardim
ceased to emigrate after their enfranchisement in 1850; the
German Jews have ceased to emigrate since their enfranchisement in 1871, and the Polish and Russian Jews would come in
fewer numbers if they were not driven from their homes, and
would scarcely come at all if but the boon of unhampered domicile, not to mention political liberty, were accorded to them
there.

The calamitous condition of general suffering into which the
Russian Jews were plunged by the proscriptive policy of their
government, appears to have passed its acute stage. While the
expulsion of the Jews from the interior of the Empire and their
settlement, permanent or temporary, in the "Pale" of the
Western Russian provinces, including Poland, was in the
height of its progress a few years ago, the number of those
who were eventually forced to emigrate was very large,
aggregating, it is estimated, nearly two hundred thousand in a
single year. The newcomers in the Pale, nearly all of them
utterly impoverished through pillage by the low element of the
populace and by the extortion of the officials, disorganized the
economic condition of the older settlers in the district and
caused a most excessive competition for the means of livelihood. The emigration of some of the surplus population and
the gradual reorganization of the remainder, has tended to
render the general condition less acute, and while a considerable

* See page 51.

emigration from the Pale must, in the nature of things, be looked for until the existent conditions are fully ameliorated, the great exodus that marked the years 1891–2 is not likely to be repeated unless further measures of oppression and repression are adopted by the Russian government.

Meanwhile the world looks on while the Jews of Western Europe and America are laboring to help those of their Russian brethren who, unable to gain a foothold in the Pale, are forced out from their wretched surroundings. The world looks on while the philanthropist, Maurice de Hirsch, emulating the spirit of Montefiore, is devoting his wealth to the succor of his co-religionists and striving to found an asylum for them on the plains of Argentina. It looks on while the Alliance Israélite Universelle, from its headquarters in Paris, is establishing and maintaining primary schools for the Jews throughout the Orient, and agricultural schools for the Russian refugees in Palestine, while this educational work is being seconded by both the American and European branches of the Order of B'nai B'rith, and while Edmond de Rothschild is fostering agricultural colonies near Jaffa and Jerusalem and aiding Russian Jews to gain a foothold in the land of their forefathers.

In our own country agricultural colonies of Russian Jews have been founded, educational institutions built up, distribution of the refugees effected, through the efforts of Jewish communal organizations or by means of the funds devoted for the purpose by Baron de Hirsch, or by both in unison. The de Hirsch Trust dispenses in this manner the income of $2,500,000 donated for this purpose by the great-hearted and open-handed philanthropist, supplementing to this large extent the charitable efforts of the American Jews in their work of succor. That work is carried on by independent local organizations both in Europe and America, ramifying from the Vistula westward to the Golden Gate; centering in Königsberg, Memel, Lemberg and Brody, in Berlin and Vienna, Hamburg and Bremen, in Paris, London and Liverpool, in New York, Philadelphia, Boston and Baltimore, in Chicago, San Francisco and Portland, and at other intervening points. These organizations are apart from the great movement organized by Baron de Hirsch and chartered in England under the title of "The

Jewish Colonization Association." That institution, which
the Baron has endowed with the sum of $10,000,000, has its
headquarters in St. Petersburg and affiliated centers throughout the Jewish Pale, and is devoted exclusively to furthering
the Jewish emigration to the Argentine Republic. The Russian Jewish emigrants to other lands proceed wholly by dint
of their own means or those of their relatives already in the
haven of rest, and these wayfarers are frequently impoverished
and always in need of protection and counsel. Onerous as has
been the burden which the wickedness of Russian folly has
imposed on the Jewish people at large, they have thus far coped
with a reasonable degree of success against the almost overwhelming difficulties of the situation.*

During the progress of this movement a hue and cry has repeatedly been raised all along the roads which the Russian
refugees have taken in escaping from their oppressors and in
seeking an asylum and resting place. Here in our country,
where many of our State governments have made organized
efforts to induce immigration into their borders, where numerous towns and hamlets in the interior are organizing "booms"
to increase their population, here, where the single State of
Texas, with less than two and a half millions of population,
extends over an area greater than Germany and England together; where a state like Montana, larger than England, Scotland, Wales, and Ireland combined, has a population of but
132,000, only half as many as the single English town of Leeds,
here there have not been wanting those who have constantly
urged in Congress and in the press, that European immigration
should be not only regulated, but largely restricted and even
entirely debarred. All this because in the metropolitan centres
and at times at other points, a surplus of wage workers in one
or two industries was causing friction and disturbance.

This agitation, by reason of its obvious causes, may well
claim our attention in connection with our present subject.

The effort towards better material conditions which has
formed the main impulse of all emigration movements, has, as
we learn from history, been always fraught with suffering and

* See note, p. 559.

misery for the populations first effected, and frequently for several of the succeeding generations, but, in the end, improvement has resulted to the greater number at least. Even when the natural surroundings of a migrated population are not more favorable than those of their previous experience, the mere change of environment has generally furthered an improvement of their social arrangements. The change of their location may disappoint an immigrant people in their hopes of material betterment, but they never fail to take advantage of their new beginnings to eliminate from their new organization such conditions as their previous experience had proved objectionable. Migrations, whether peaceful or otherwise, and for that matter sudden changes of material conditions generally, inevitably consume a large part of the existing powers of those effected, but where those powers are not totally exhausted and destroyed, where enough energy remains to form a nucleus of recuperative force, and especially where the new material surroundings are more favorable than those which were left behind, there a marked improvement of all the conditions of life, physical and intellectual, material and social, becomes developed. It would be superflous to cite the proofs of this proposition ; the history of civilization is a record of its examples, and its latest annals are but statements of this fact.

Palpable as is this fact, and nowhere is it more so than on this Western Continent, and especially in our own country, there are yet many who regard an immigrant with the narrow prejudice of mediæval ignorance, and to whom a stranger is still, as to the barbarians of old, an enemy. Over and over again in the course of the great new departure which the establishment and growth of these United States has made in the world's history, over and over again in the course of our development, has the debarment of immigrants been proposed and advocated. At times the opposition to the new comers has been born of Old World animosities, at other times of religious prejudice, and latterly we hear most frequently of restrictions proposed on political and economic grounds.

That political reasons may justify a restriction, or even dictate the entire debarment of certain defined classes of immigrants, is to be admitted. Thus the exclusion of Chinese immigrants may be defended on the grounds of a broad public policy, with reasons which cannot logically be adduced with regard to any branch of the Caucasian race. The most cogent of these reasons, and the one that has afforded the only rational basis for the policy adopted, is not the economic element of the subject, not that the Chinese live cheaply and work cheaply, but that their assimilation with the rest of the population is practically impossible. To what extent the theoretical possibility of their being merged in the general population could be realized, to what extent its realization would be desirable or the contrary; to what extent a mixture of the Caucasian and Mongolian races would enhance or deteriorate their respective qualities, physical and psychical, we need not here stop to inquire. Suffice it to re-state the fact that political, or perhaps ultimately ethnological reasons may here be considered as prompting a course which could not reasonably be adopted on any other ground. But in the case of immigrants of the Caucasian race, such opposition as has been made from time to time, though frequently insisted upon as a political necessity, can only, in the absence of any broad ethnological basis, be argued on economic grounds.

The discussions engendered by propositions to restrict immigration have recurred at various periods of our history and have been factors in our politics from the beginning of our institutions. There was indeed already in the old Colonial times an anti-immigration or Nativist Party, almost before there were any natives to make it up. In fact, the subject has cropped out whenever some slight occasion offered, and particularly whenever politicians on the in or the outside needed a new string to harp upon. Some of us are old enough to remember something of the native American agitation which began as far back as 1835, and which took shape in the so-called "American" party, afterwards generally known as the "Know-Nothings," about 1844. In that year the Know-Nothing Party carried the city of New York on a mayoralty election by a large majority, and for a time the movement spread widely throughout the country. It developed strong religious prejudices, and was marked by the memorable anti-Catholic riots in Philadelphia.

The odium which those disgraceful outrages brought on the " American " party was attempted to be overcome by making it a secret organization, and in the political confusion resulting from the breaking up of the old Whig party, the former grew to such proportions, that in 1855 it carried no less than nine state elections. That the movement then had no vital force, but was only a political stalking-horse for partisan purposes, became manifest in the Presidential election of 1856, when the Know Nothing candidates carried only the State of Maryland, and that only by aid of the remnant of the Whig party and the bludgeons of the "Plug-Uglies." The outcome of the whole movement, politically considered, was the complete extinction of the party organization which had fostered, and the permanent discredit of the party leaders who had promoted it.

But the lessons of the past, the arguments and considerations which have repeatedly led to the rejection of a proscriptive policy, have now to be gone over again in this later generation, and the reason for this is plain enough. The economic aspect of the question is more permanent than the political, and the economic argument more plausible than the other. The objectionable features inseparable from a considerable influx of newcomers into a community, large or small, are palpable and on the surface, while the inestimable value of these newcomers, by virtue of the added material and social forces with which they endow the community, becomes perceptible only upon a closer investigation of the subject. It thus happens that when an unusually large number of new arrivals disturbs for a time some existing economic condition, the community is startled by those immediately affected with an outcry against the intruding force, and it is then only on investigation that it becomes apparent that while indeed a comparatively few individuals suffer, and even they but temporarily, the new element is of far-reaching benefit to the community at large.

A quite parallel instance, as far as it goes, is the effect of the introduction of machinery in substitution of hand labor. The history of inventions is burdened with the details of opposition which gathered at every step of the process through which Man has brought to his service the forces of Nature. So too, the practical aid of immigration in subduing the domain of Nature on this Western Continent has often been decried as inimical to the interests of those native to the soil, notwithstanding that even a cursory analysis of the question proves clearly the fact that the immigrant not only does not travail against the native's interest, but on the contrary, aids and enhances that interest beyond all computation. Just as the throng of new inventions temporarily disarranges existent conditions of commerce and of industry, with the immediate result of causing economic distress to some groups of individuals, so the tide of immigration temporarily affects existent conditions in the centers of population, but the eventual benefit of the new force is as certain to be felt in the latter case as in the former.

Let us for a momemt consider the character and extent of the impulses which the influx of the newcomers imparts to the social organism. The nature of these impulses is two-fold ; the increase of numbers adds power to the community, and the diversity of interests which is an inevitable concomitant of increased population, brings wealth, culture, and all the higher gains of human effort.

To elucidate these propositions we cannot do better than here quote the carefully considered statements of the foremost of American publicists, Henry C. Carey, himself an American of Americans, and the great expounder of the protective system of political economy. As Chairman of the Committee on Industrial Interests and Labor, in its report to the Constitutional Convention of Pennsylvania in 1873, referring to the Immigration question, he writes as follows:

" Closing their eyes to the important facts which have been thus presented, very many of our working men look with jealous eyes at every measure tending toward bringing those of other countries to take a place side by side with them, believing, as they do, that the more the supply of labor the lower must certainly become the price. Nevertheless, could they but be pursuaded to study carefully the facts of even the last twenty years they could not fail to become impressed with the fact, that growth of wages has always kept even pace with growth of immigration ; the reward of labor on the contrary declining as immigration has been arrested or destroyed. At no previous period had the demand for labor, or its reward, grown so rapidly as in the early years of the great California one, say from 1850 to 1854, when immigration grew to 400,000. At none, has labor been more in excess of the demand than in the years that followed the great crisis of 1857, when immigration declined to figures scarcely greater than had been attained 20 years before; and when, as in 1860–61, not one out of five of the skilled workmen of the country was steadly employed. Here, in Philadelphia, when it was desired to build a street railroad they advertised for two hundred and fifty hands at but sixty cents a day, and had more than five thousand offered, a majority of whom were skilled artisans who were wholly out of work. In the neighborhood of one great establishment, a rolling mill, the number of unemployed men was so great that the county authorities, to save its skilled workmen from open pauperism, determined to build a turnpike, employing experienced hands at breaking stone, for fifty cents a day, rather than supporting them as paupers. At no period of our history has the reward of labor grown so rapidly as in the last ten years, when the exodus of European working men has so rapidly increased that the states of Central and Western Europe now find themselves forced to consideration of the measures required for retaining their countrymen at home; and when the highest German authorities admit that the pecuniary loss resulting from training and educating men for export to this country has now already more than counterbalanced the French indemnity of $1,200,000,000. To all appearance the immigration of the present year will closely approach to half a million; and yet it is at this moment, in face of so wonderful an addition to our stock of working men and women, that we have a determined agitation for bringing about a reduction of time and increase of wages. In the years prior to the rebellion, when immigration so largely declined, the agitation was for employment at almost any price. Why is this? Why is it that, contrary to the rule elsewhere observed, demand for labor goes ahead of supply when this latter is great, and falls behind it when the supply is small? To this the answer is, that the power to compel nature to labor in man's service increases almost geometrically as numbers increase arithmetically; as employment becomes diversified; and as men are more enabled to combine their efforts for attainment of that object."

*   *   *   *   *   *   *   *   *   *   *

" As a consequence of the great increase in the power of combination that has thus been brought about, we find the manufacturing product of the country to have grown in the period 1860 to 1872, from 1800 to 5000 millions, the mere increase having been almost twice the total amount to which the country had attained in the centuries that had preceded the war of the rebellion. Adding to the figures the foreign manufactures consumed, we obtain for the first—a period when immigration was rapidly declining—a total consumption of about $65 per head; whereas in the period which since has passed, and in which immigration has so greatly grown, it has risen to more than $130 per head. So far, therefore, is the working man from having occasion to dread the competition of the immigrant, that he needs, night and morning, to pray for maintenance of that policy which is now making demand on Europe for so much of its half fed and half clothed population, thereby compelling both landed and manufacturing capitalists to the adoption of measures tending so to improve the condition of them who are left behind as to induce them to forego the idea of abandoning their native land. Never in the world's history has there been furnished such conclusive evidence of the fact, that measures tending to benefit the working man anywhere tend toward raising his condition everywhere ; and that, therefore, there is a perfect harmony in the real and permanent interests of mankind at large.''

As still more directly bearing on this subject, I quote from the same report as follows:

'' Less than a dozen years since, our working men looked jealously upon the negro, believing that any measure tending toward his emancipation would certainly be followed by such an influx of cheap labor as must seriously affect themselves. Directly the reverse, the negro migrates to Texas and there becomes a customer for manufactured products of a class greatly higher than that of those which his master had been accustomed to purchase for his slave.''

Carey here reaches the very pith of the question. Every newcomer becomes a customer for those already on the ground, for all that he needs for his maintenance, just as the new born babe furnishes a new customer for the dry goods store, the milk man, not to mention the doctor and sometimes the lawyer. The baby, it is true, does not, as the phrase goes, '' enter into competition'' for a living, while the immigrant does, but in this respect the latter is the more valuable acquisition, for unless the immigrant is supported by charity, he has to produce at least as much as he consumes, and thus the community is an inevitable gainer by his presence. Inasmuch as a very large proportion of the immigrants produce more than they consume, in other words, save something of their earnings, it is manifest that the community gains doubly by their presence. It gains through the increase by the immigrant of the general social force, in his contribution to the total of the community's traffic and exchange, and also gains through the newcomer's addition to the general capital stock.

But, it is urged on the other hand, this may all be true of some kinds of immigrants, and not be true of others who are low in the scale of moral worth and of physical and intellectual capacity, and it is these whose coming should be restricted. Be it so; we may safely admit this proposition, and proceed thence to the sole remaining problem of drawing the line.

Where shall this line be drawn ? The native American agitation proceeded on the very ground we have postulated, and grew to the proportions of carrying a majority in no less than nine states. It grew to these proportions as the result of an agitation that arose from the influx of impoverished Irishmen after the famine of 1847, and of their followers from Scotland and England in the succeeding decade. Has the agitation been justified by time? Have the prophecies of the Know Nothings that our people could not possibly assimilate the great mass of foreigners who were then thronging hither, whose proportion to the native population was even greater than it is now, who were alien to our institutions and our laws, in habits and in religion at variance with the great majority of the citizens, been fullfilled? Of course not; the facts have but developed what the common sense of the people soon perceived to be true. These immigrants have all been assimilated. Those of them that survive, and their children assuredly, have become thoroughly Americanized and effectually welded into the commonalty of our republic.

How was it with the Germans who came hither in such swarms under the allurements of the great gold finds in the West, and the growth of steam navigation on the ocean after 1850? They too have been assimilated, notwithstanding that through their variance in language they were even more differentiated from the native inhabitants than the immigrants from the British Isles. How about the Scandinavians and the Holland Dutch, the French and Italians? Has the grafting of these scions on the rooted stem degenerated the stock? We have ample evidence to the contrary, sufficiently palpable to need no citation in detail.

Where then shall we draw the line? We have seen that the immigrant, though he arrives penniless as tens of thousands of them have done and do, does certainly not impoverish the community. We have seen, on the contrary, that though he arrives penniless, he enhances the wealth of the community by bringing with him the germ of all commodities, Labor. Where then shàll we draw the line? Shall we exclude the poor Roman Catholic Pole, who is driven from his home by the vindictive policy of his barbarous conquerer? Does he not bring energy and labor? Shall we exclude the Russian Jew, who is driven from his native soil by the stupid villany of the same Tartar barbarism? Is his thrift and industry likely to impoverish our community? The pious fools who, four hundred years ago, drove three hundred thousand of such people from the Iberian Peninsula had a bigger majority than the Know Nothings of later date who wanted to do as much for the Roman Catholics fifty years ago, and they had their way. They diminished the population according to their wish, but they wrought the ruin of the then richest nation of Europe, a ruin from which it has even to this day not yet arisen.

No; let the immigrants come, as they have come. Let us but guard ourselves against the preventable evils which are likely to attend their coming, by the careful enforcement of the laws that are enacted to that end. Let us draw the line so as to exclude the habitual paupers, the habitual criminals, the incurably insane; the rest will take care of themselves and add to our well being and our wealth by filling up the waste stretches of the great expanse behind us; they will but follow in the way trodden by the immigrants who landed two hundred and seventy years ago at Plymouth Rock, and will work out their salvation as did their predecessors by making the desert to blossom as the rose.

NOTE:—Various movements for the relief of the Russian refugees have been organized independently from 1882 on by the Jewish communities throughout the country and especially in the seabord cities. The renewed severity of the Russian persecutions in 1890 called forth a general movement for the relief of the sufferers which was focused at a convention held in Philadelphia, February 16, 1891, and which resulted in the formation of the "Jewish Alliance of America."[1] This organization was composed in the main of Russian Jews already settled in this country, but the increasing demand on the Jewish people by the extraordinarily large influx of the refugees during 1891 necessitated a more general organization of the measures for their relief. To that end the Trustees of the Baron de Hirsch Fund issued a call[2] for a general convention of representatives of the Jewish organizations throughout the country, which accordingly met in New York City on September 23, 1891. This convention[3] resolved itself into "The American Committee for Ameliorating the Condition of Russian Refugees," and

[1] The officers of this organization were as follows:
President: Simon Muhr, Philadelphia.
Vice Presidents: Hon. Ferdinand Levy, New York; Rev. Dr. H. W. Schneeberger, Baltimore; Dr. Chas. D. Spivak, Philadelphia.
Secretary: Bernard Harris, Philadelphia.
Treasurer: Hon. Simon Wolf, Washington, D. C.
Board of Directors—Philadelphia: Louis E. Levy, Chas. Hoffman, Dr. Solomon Solis-Cohen ; *Baltimore:* Jacob J. H. Mitnick, Joseph Eisner, S. L. Auerbach ; *New York:* Daniel P. Hays, Dr. Henry M. Leipziger ; *Chicago:* Dr. A. P. Kadison, A. Bernstein ; *Boston:* David Blaustein ; *Pittsburg, Pa.:* Wm. Hoffman ; *Albany, N. Y.:* Louis Aronowitch ; *Troy, N. Y.:* H. Kuschevsky ; *Omaha, Neb.:* B. Kohn.

[2] The call was signed by the officers of the Baron de Hirsch Fund as follows:
President: Myer S. Isaacs.
Vice President: Jacob H. Schiff.
Treasurer: Jesse Seligman.
Honorary Secretary: Julius Goldman.
Trustees: Oscar S. Straus, Henry Rice, and James H. Hoffman, of New York; Mayer Sulzberger, and Wm. B. Hackenburg, of Philadelphia.
General Agent: Adolphus S. Solomons, Washington, D. C.

[3] The convention was organized with the following named officers:
President: Lewis Seasongood, Cincinnati; *Vice Presidents:* Lazarus Silverman, Chicago, Joseph Fox, New York; *Secretaries:* Adolphus S. Solomon, Washington, and Bernard Harris, Philadelphia.

elected an Executive Committee[1] to carry out its plans.   With this organization the Jewish Alliance of America was merged in February, 1892, but with the diminution of the influx in the course of that year the united organization devolved its functions on a '' Central Committee '' composed of members of the American Committee, the Baron de Hirsch Trust and the United Hebrew Charities of New York.

The several organized movements above noted elicited earnest expressions of sympathy from many leading men in our community.   A number of these are so pointed and revelant to our present subject matter as to dictate their citation in this connection.

On the occasion of the movement for the formation of the Jewish Alliance, CARDINAL GIBBONS wrote as follows, under date of Baltimore, Dec. 15th, 1890.

"Every friend of humanity must deplore the systematic persecution of the Jews in Russia.

"For my part, I cannot well conceive how Christians can entertain other than kind sentiments towards the Hebrew race, when I consider how much we are indebted to them.   We have from them the in-spired volume of the Old Testament, which has been a consolation in all ages to devout souls.   Christ, our Lord, the Founder of our religion, His blessed mother, as well as the Apostles, were all Jews

---

[1] The Executive Committee thus elected, in addition to the general officers, was composed of representatives of various organizations in different sections of the country, as follows:

New York : Henry Rice, Julius Bien, Jacob H. Schiff, Morris Tuska, Ferdinand Levy, Isaac Hamburger, M. Warley Platzek; *Philadelphia :* Simon Muhr, Louis E. Levy ; *Baltimore :* Aaron Friedenwald; *Boston :* Jacob Ḥecht; *Cincinnati :* Julius Freiburg; *Chicago :* Adolph Loeb, Julius Rosenthal; *Peoria, Ill.:* Samuel Woolner; *Washington, D. C.:* Simon Wolf; *Milwaukee :* Bernard Gross; *St. Louis, Mo.:* Marcus Bernheimer; *Portland, Or.:* David Solis-Cohen; *Detroit, Mich.:* Martin Butzel; *Minneapolis, Minn.:* Emanuel Cohen; *Atlanta, Ga.:* Aaron Haas; *Galveston, Tex.:* Leo. N. Levi; *Memphis, Tenn.:* Elias Loewenstein; *Ex-Officio*, Myer S. Isaacs, *New York.*

The Committee organized by electing as Chairman, M. Warley Platzek, of New York, and as Vice Chairman, Julius Freiburg, of Cincinnati, the Secretaries of the General Committee acting in the same capacity on the Executive Committee.

according to the flesh.   These facts attach me strongly to the Jewish race ''

The call for the convention which resulted in the organization of the American Committee for Ameliorating the Condition of Russian Refugees, elicited the following letter from Judge DILLON to Mr. Seligman :

Dear Sir: Coming to this place (Saratoga) on the train from New York, I saw in the *Evening Post* a statement that prominent Hebrews in all parts of the United States have been invited by the Trustees of the Baron de Hirsh fund to meet in this city on Wednesday, September 23rd in the building of the Hebrew Educational Alliance at East Broadway and Jefferson streets, for the purpose of co-operating in the formation of an American Relief Committee to make the best possible disposition of the exiled Russian Jews coming to this country.

The persecution of your people with mediæval cruelty, whereby they are exiled without cause, suddenly and *en masse*, with all the multiplied and nameless hardships and sufferings which must necessarily attend such an exodus, from a country in which they had lived for generations and had the right to peacefully remain, has awakened among all right-thinking persons sympathy for the victims and indignation against their oppressors.   This is not a matter that appeals alone to the people of your race.   It appeals to every man with a heart of flesh in his bosom.   There remains no longer any place for prejudice or selfishness.   Reports are made that some Jewish refugees have already been sent back from this country for fear that they may become a public charge.   This must not be.   Without shame we cannot remain idle and cold spectators and see this done under our very eyes.   Ever since the establishment of our nation, it has been its just boast that it was the asylum of the toiling and oppressed people of all other countries, who in good faith sought our shores with a view of permanent residence and citizenship.   I am not criticising necessary or provident defensive modification of this policy, but the former considerations have a rightful application to your fugitive people, who in their necessity come from preference to this land of freedom to find and make themselves homes.

I would as soon shut my door against a benighted wanderer seeking refuge from the merciless blizzard as to shut our national ports against those of your people, who, stricken like wild beasts, are driven here in the stress of the raging storm which threatens their destruction. Let us receive them with welcome and hospitality.   Let us show to the nations of the world that there is one spot on God's earth where these unfortunate exiles may rest their tired feet, set up again their household goods, reconstruct their ruined homes and worship in peace the God of their fathers.

I notice in the article referred to that it is proposed ''to appeal to

36

the Jews of the United States to unite in a co-operative plan to find homes and employment for Russian immigrants." I beg to suggest that this concerns not your people alone. It quite as deeply concerns the good name of the American people to see that no refugee shall be returned for poverty, or for any cause, save for crime, or shall be allowed to suffer until he can find work.

I do not rest these sentiments upon the unfeigned respect I feel for the immemorial traditions and glorious history of your people, who in theology, ethics, philosophy, arts, literature, jurisprudence and legislation have either led the thought of the world or kept abreast with it. I prefer to rest them upon the broader, higher and truer ground, that these exiles are men, with all the inprescriptable rights that belong to men because they are men, irrespective of religion, race or nationality, rights which governments do not create or confer, so they cannot rightfully deny or destroy. I enclose my check for the cause (would it were more), and in doing so, I could not refrain, before resting my head upon my pillow, to thus state the reasons why I did it.

With great respect, I am as ever,
Very truly yours,
JOHN F. DILLON.

To JESSE SELIGMAN, ESQ.

On the same occasion as that noted above, HON. CHAUNCEY M. DEPEW expressed himself as follows:

"We behold to-day in Russia with horror the amazing spectacle in the nineteenth century of the whole power of the government brought to bear upon three millions of Hebrews to treat them as aliens and enemies. They have been for three hundred years the subjects and the citizens of the Russian Empire, and yet the whole power of the state, of its army, of its civil force, is brought to bear to deprive them of the opportunities of employment and to refuse them, except within certain limits, the right to live in the country where their ancestors have lived for ten to twenty generations. It is because monarchical institutions, autocratic institutions, class institutions do not possess the power of assimilation and of homogeneity.

" In the past fifty years, fifteen millions of people have come to this country from abroad. They belonged to every race, they spoke every language but our own. They worshipped in every form, under every symbol and in every creed. But American liberty solved the problem. These people did not know about our institutions, or understand them. They had been taught to believe that liberty was license, and yet the solvent power of American liberty made them citizens and gave to the immigrants of a few years ago, the same rights before the law and in making the law that is possessed by the descendants of the Pilgrim Fathers. These fifteen millions of people, under the operation of this glorious principle, have become bone of our bone, flesh of our flesh. They have aided in the development of the country; they have assisted in increasing its wealth, its power and its glory, and have marched with equal step and equal love under the old flag for the preservation of the glorious Republic which had made them free."

Following is an extract from a letter written to Hon. Simon Wolf by Father Sylvester Malone, of St. Peter and Paul Church, Brooklyn:

I have listened to St. Patrick's Day discussions in time past in which your co-religionists were likened to the Irish. Both suffered because of their holding with such tenacity to what was their belief. This was true in the case of the Hebrew in his own native land and in every other land whither tyranny forced him to emigrate. The Irish have been the victims of cruel persecution in their own native land. Here, however, they are free, and are always successful when they do not by some fault of their own mar their best hopes of success. The Jewish people too have had great success in America, but the later emigration, directly from Russia, has not been acceptable to many of our citizens. They have run the gauntlet, as my countrymen had to do some fifty years ago. They must learn wisdom and patience."

As an instructive conclusion to our present subject we add the following extract from the New York *Sun* of September 1st, 1894. It needs no further comment:

" In the Jews, Judaism is deeply ingrained. As many as 10,000 or 12,000 of the Jewish tailors of this city were on a strike for higher wages all last week ; and day after day they loitered in the streets, or congregated in their hall, or sat down any where to talk in their jargon. But upon the forenoon of Saturday last the strikers, who had been highly excited the day before, were not to be found at their usual places of rendezvous. Nearly all of them had gone to their synagogues. They were engaged in Divine worship. They were at prayer. They were listening to the voice of the rabbi. They were following a custom established by Moses, and kept up through all the ages ever since his time. In the hundreds of garrets, rear halls, and rickety old edifices which are used as synagogues in what is called the "ghetto," on the east side of New York, the Jews on strike celebrated the everlasting name of "JAHVEH" last Saturday forenoon, the holy Sabbath.

"This is Judaism in New York and the world over.

" Lots of workingmen, who are called Christians, go on a strike from time to time, but who is there that ever heard of any body of strikers other than Jews, giving heed to the ceremonies of their religion during the heat of a strike? We are told that nearly all of these Jewish strikers are orthodox, and all wore their hats in the synagogues. Many of them, we are assured, are familiar with the Torah and the Talmud, and can quote Ben Ezra and Maimonides. . . . . . .

"Judaism is in the bones of the Jews, and of all Jews, from the equator to the poles.

"Was there ever any crowd of Presbyterian strikers, or of Baptist, Methodist, or Unitarian strikers, or of Roman Catholic strikers, who made it their business to go to church in a body, for the purpose of engaging in worship and prayer, during a strike? Let us ask Rev. Dr. John Hall, or Bishop Simpson, or that learned and mirthful priest, Father Flattery, not to speak of the eminent Dominican, Father O'Neil, or our three Universalist preachers.

"The Jews of New York, like the Jews of all the rest of the world, believe in Judaism, and are rooted and grounded in it.

"Oh, that we could say that the people who call themselves Christians believe in Christianity and practise it, either at work or when on strike!"

CONCLUSION.

The project of the present volume had contemplated a lesser number of pages than it now includes, but it has been restricted to its present bounds only by eliminating much that was germane to its subject. The grand fabric of Jewish charity, whose broad expanse extends throughout the land, compassing every element of society, responsive to every call of humanity, expressive of every trait of civilization and conducive to every avenue of culture, has been adverted to but incidentally. In the field of philanthropic effort the Jewish citizens of the American Union may unhesitatingly claim to have built for themselves monuments more numerous and larger by far than their proportionate share; in this field the historic spirit of Judaism continues even increasingly to manifest itself. In this field and in this alone the Jewish spirit has been materialistic. Its forces have been directed not to saving souls by a change of creed, but by bettering the conditions of human existence. The great ideals of Judaism, the universal fatherhood of God, the universal brotherhood of men, and the direct responsibility of every human being to the Maker of all, have steadfastly been upheld, but its forces have not been exerted in striving to make good the seeming shortcomings of the Divine nature, but in striving to make good the essential shortcomings of our human nature, by alleviating the distresses arising from the constitution of society and by lessening the sufferings that are inevitably incident to the conditions of life. To this end the American Jewish citizens have organized a widely diversified system of relief for the sick and the needy, and while so doing have not restricted their efforts within denominational bounds, but have opened their doors and stretched out their hands to all humanity. Not alone, however, in dealing with conditions that are inseparable from the social system, but furthermore in dealing with such as are removable, in educating and lifting up those of the community who are in need of fostering care, in furthering the spread of intelligence and in raising the standard of citizenship, the Jewish people have been unceasingly active, and especially so in free America, where, as the foregoing pages have recorded, they have stood from the very beginning '' shoulder to shoulder '' with their fellow citizens of every creed, in every movement that has made for freedom and for liberty, for culture and for charity. And well they might. To no others of the Old World denizens was the New World more completely new; for no other people has the promise of the Columbian epoch been more completely fulfilled than for the Jews.

And, therefore, more especially while the closing years of the nineteenth century have seen its brilliant promise darkened by a broad shadow of the Middle Ages; while the ghastly tragedy that marked in Spain the opening year of American discovery is being rehearsed in Russia with all the effects of modern aggrandizement, we may not better close this book than with the grand apostrophe of the Columbian year that has been left us by the Jewish poetess, Emma Lazarus:

> Thou, two-faced year, mother of Change and Fate,
> Didst weep when Spain cast forth with flaming sword
> The children of the prophets of the Lord.
> Prince, priest and people spurned by zealot hate,
> Hounded from sea to sea, from state to state,
> The West refused them and the East abhorred,
> No anchorage the known world could afford,
> Close locked was every port, barred every gate.
> Then smiling, thou unveil'dst, O two-faced year,
> A virgin world where doors of sunset part,
> Saying, ' Ho, all who weary, enter here !
> Here falls each ancient barrier that the art
> Of race or creed or rank devised, to rear
> Grim-bulwarked hatred between heart and heart.'

INDEX.

The Pennsylvania Academy of The Fine Arts

Album of Reproductions of Selected Works From the Permanent Collections

A highly artistic Livre-de-Luxe, 66 pages, large quarto, enamelled paper, bound in card-board covers, cloth back. Price, $1.00

This standard publication of the Pennsylvania Academy of the Fine Arts contains 28 faithfully copied reproductions of selected and typical works in the Permanent Collections of the Academy, together with a view of the exterior of the building and one of the interior of the gallery. The pictures selected for compilation in this album, comprise characteristic works of every epoch, from the Renaissance (Bennozzo Gozzoli's "Virgin and Child," ca. 1450) down to the present time.

The successive subjects are elucidated by brief but comprehensive references to the various painters and their notable works, collated under the direction of the Academy, and are prefaced by a compendious history of the institution.

Engraved and Printed for the Academy by the Levytype Company, Philadelphia

Forty Works of Art

FROM THE

Sixty-Third Annual Exhibition

OF THE

Pennsylvania Academy of the Fine Arts

OCTAVO, 44 LEAVES; 88 PAGES; ARTISTICALLY PRINTED
AND BOUND IN HEAVY PAPER COVERS.
PRICE, 25 CENTS.

These reproductions of art works from the Sixty-third Annual Exhibition of the Fine Arts were collated with the view to affording a souvenir of the most notable exhibition of distinctively American art productions held within recent years. From the large collection of famous subjects, many of them fresh from the walls of the Art Palace of the World's Fair, a series of works were selected for illustration as embodying in a due measure the representative character of this special exhibition.

Published under the Auspices of the Pennsylvania Academy of the Fine Arts, Philadelphia

For Sale by all Booksellers

PUBLICATIONS OF THE LEVYTYPE COMPANY, PHILADELPHIA
628–630–632 Chestnut Street, Cor. Seventh Street

Catalogue OF THE

W. P. Wilstach Collection

Memorial Hall, Fairmount Park, Philadelphia

Edited by CAROL H. BECK

104 PAGES, 12 MO., BOUND IN HEAVY PAPER COVER, CLOTH BACK

Full Descriptive Catalogue of the Wilstach Art Gallery, illustrated, with 28 autoglyphic engravings on India tint, sumptuously executed throughout.

Engraved and Printed for the Commissioners of Fairmount Park, Philadelphia, by the Levytype Company, Philadelphia

Price, - - - - - - **25 Cents**

Washington The... Federal City

AN ILLUSTRATED GUIDE BOOK FOR THE CITY OF WASHINGTON, DESCRIPTIVE OF ITS HISTORY, OFFICIAL LIFE, POINTS OF INTEREST, AND ENVIRONS

By EUGENE MURRAY AARON

Illustrated by 100 Photo-engravings of principal objects of interest in the Capital City and two maps, 88 pages, 12mo, paper covers, cloth back, Levytype Edition.   Price 25c.

This is the most compendious and accurate guide book to Washington, Mount Vernon, and the District of Columbia thus far published.   A complete historical and topographic encyclopædia of its subject.

FOR SALE BY ALL BOOKSELLERS.
THE UNION NEWS COMPANY
NEW YORK CITY, GENERAL AGENTS

PUBLICATIONS OF THE LEVYTYPE COMPANY, PHILADELPHIA
628-630-632 Chestnut Street, Cor. Seventh Street

The Golden Day

And Miscellaneous Poems

By WILLIAM T. DUMAS

Broad Octavo.   144 pp.   Cloth.   Price, $1.00

"THE GOLDEN DAY," the first portion of the work, is a series of poems beginning with "Cock-Crowing" and leading the reader through various scenes to the evening. The design of this portion is to portray the day in the Sunny South, as is evinced by such titles as "The Fox Hunt," "The Dinner Horn," "Corn Husking." etc. Interwoven with these are sonnets and longer pieces on a variety of themes, sentimental, humorous, lyrical.

Of the miscellaneous poems, undoubtedly the finest, in phrasing, meter and conception is "The Cyclone." It is in a strong dactylic verse and is a gem. "Joy; an ode" is of a different type, but full of fine expression. In this portion of the work is also contained an "Ode on the death of Jefferson Davis" and a tribute to Gen. Joseph E. Johnston entitled "From the Valley of the Shadow." A number of the author's earlier poems are also included in the volume.

This production, taken as a whole, stamps the author as possessing in a high degree the true poetic spirit, and his renditions cannot fail to find an appreciative audience, not only throughout the South, but wherever the memories of its former times are harmonized with the realizations of to-day. The book is a well bound and superbly printed octavo of 144 pages. Price $1.00. For sale by all booksellers.

The Dinner Horn

By WILLIAM T. DUMAS

Illustrated by PAUL T. HILL

An Album of 24 leaves, embracing a pictorial title page and the 16 stanzas of "The Dinner Horn," admirably illustrated, each stanza and illustration on a seperate leaf.

AN ARTISTIC LIVRE-DE-LUXE

sumptuously printed and bound, gilt edges. Long octavo, album style.

Price, ~ ~ ~ One Dollar

PUBLICATIONS OF THE LEVYTYPE COMPANY, PHILADELPHIA
628–630–632 Chestnut Street, Cor. Seventh Street

FROM...
INDEPENDENCE HALL

Around the World

BY

F. CARROLL BREWSTER, LLD.

216 Pages, 12mo., Copiously Illustrated, Enamelled Paper, Fine Cloth Binding. Price, $1.50.

THIS itinerary of Judge Brewster's recent tour around the world contains the notes of his journey from San Francisco to Brindisi, and records his impressions of the countries and people of Hawaii, Japan, China, Mallacca, Ceylon and India. The report of such a journey by so trained and unprepossessed an observer as Judge Brewster will be welcomed by all who have become acquainted with the accurracy of his observations through his other published works, and will be read with interest by the public generally.

The book is fully illustrated with over 70 photo-types of salient and interesting subjects, which have been selected especially with the view to supple-menting the traveler's narrative to the fullest possible extent.

FOR SALE BY ALL BOOKSELLERS

PUBLICATIONS OF THE LEVYTYPE COMPANY, PHILADELPHIA
628–630–632 Chestnut Street, Cor. Seventh Street

IN PREPARATION.—To be Published December, 1895

Cuba and the Cubans

BY

RAIMUNDO CABRERA

MEMBER OF THE CENTRAL EXECUTIVE COMMITTEE OF THE
AUTONOMIST PARTY OF CUBA, ETC., ETC.

Author of " MIS BUENOS TIEMPOS," " LOS ESTADOS UNIDOS," " IMPRESIONES DE VIAJE "
ETC., ETC.

TRANSLATED FROM THE EIGHTH SPANISH EDITION OF
"CUBA Y SUS JUECES"

By LAURA GUITÉRAS

REVISED AND EDITED BY

LOUIS EDWARD LEVY

ILLUSTRATED WITH 91 LINE ENGRAVINGS OF PORTRAITS AND LOCALITIES,
AND 16 LARGER PORTRAITS IN PHOTOTYPE.

396 Pages, 12 Mo., Bound in Cloth . . . . PRICE $1.50

This translation of Señor Cabrera's masterly work on Cuba renders accessible to English readers the most authentic, comprehensive and thorough statement of the Cuban question that has emanated from the press. It has the advantage of presenting the subject in a spirit free from the rancors of the present armed conflict between the Cuban colonists and the mother country, the original work having been published in Cuba and throughout Spain some years before the present struggle began. It commanded the universal attention of the Spanish-speaking world from its first publication in 1887, since which time it has gone through eight editions in the Spanish, successively amplified by the author with notes, appendices and illustrations.

Señor Cabrera deals with his subject-matter from the vantage ground of an acknowledged leadership of the Autonomist party of Cuba, and his work, although voicing the demands of the Cuban people for reforms which Spain has constantly postponed or absolutely refused, has commanded the recognition and the respect of Spanish statesmen of the first rank.

With scholarly insight and a thorough analysis, Señor Cabrera traces the existing social, political and economic condition of Cuba and its people with an impartial pen, in brief but effective outlines and in a lucid and trenchant style. No other contribution to the literature of this important subject compares with this work as an authoritative presentation, and as such it appeals to the attention of the American public.

For Sale by all Booksellers.   Price $1 50

PUBLICATIONS OF THE LEVYTYPE COMPANY, PHILADELPHIA
628–630–632 Chestnut Street, Cor. Seventh Street

THE JEWISH YEAR

Illustrated by Pictures of Old-Time Jewish Family Life, Customs and Observances. From the Paintings by

PROFESSOR MORITZ OPPENHEIM

With Historical and Explanatory Text by

LOUIS EDWARD LEVY

An Imperial Folio Volume (17 x 21)

Containing 20 Levytype Autoglyphic Reproductions of the original Paintings, mounted on boards, and some 50 folio pages of superbly printed text, securely bound in heavy half Russia covers.

In addition to the 20 Autoglyphs of Oppenheim's celebrated paintings, this sumptuous volume contains a line reproduction of a notable work by Leopold Horovitz, and the text itself is furthermore embellished and illustrated by numerous effective relief etchings representing various incidents and accessories of Jewish religious observance.

The twenty-one impressive compositions are collated in illustration of the Jewish year; they represent the successive festivals, fasts and holidays of the religious year, the various aspects of the Sabbath, and the distinctive customs and observances of Jewish family life.

The following is a list of the subjects :—

1. Passover, the Feast of Unleavened Bread.
2. Shabuoth, The Feast of Weeks.
3. Tisha B'Ab, The Feast of the Ninth Day of Ab.
4. Kal Nidre, Eve of The Day of Atonement.
5. Succoth, The Feast of Tabernacles.
6. Hanukah, The Feast of the Dedication.
7. Purim, The Feast of Esther.
8. Beginning of Sabbath.
9. Sabbath Eve.
10. Sabbath Afternoon.
11. Sabbath Rest.
12. Close of Sabbath.
13. The Rite of the Covenant (B'rith Milah).
14. The First Birthday.
15. The Rabbi's Blessing.
16. The Examination.
17. The Confirmation (Bar Mitzva.)
18. The Wedding.
19. The Village Vender.
20. The Anniversary of Mourning (Minyan.)
21. The Return of the Volunteer.

The complete cycle of Oppenheim's masterly Pictures of Jewish Life is included in this work, the original paintings being reproduced with all the fidelity and effectiveness of the most advanced reproductive art.

The text has been written with a special regard to its educational import. Each subject is elucidated by a brief citation of the historic data bearing on it, and by a consideration of those of its features which are directly or indirectly traceable in their origin and development. The various articles thus make up a succession of historic monographs, each one presenting, so to speak, a different cross-section of the outline perspective of Jewish history which the text in its entirety affords.

In the preparation and arrangement of this work the Publishers have endeavored to maintain for its various elements, artistic, literary and mechanical, a standard commensurate with the dignity of the subject. They believe that they have measurably succeeded in their purpose, and they bring the work before the Jewish public with a confident reliance on its support.

The Oppenheim Album of the Jewish Year is furnished at $20,

a price which, while necessarily greater than that of ordinary books, is far below the usual cost of art books of equal magnitude. This has been rendered possible through the economies resulting from the concentration of all the requisite facilities for its production and the compassing of all the latest advances in the heliographic and typographic arts. The work forms a magnificent *livre de luxe.* The pictures are mounted on artistically matted boards, hinged on guards, and bound in heavy covers with fine cloth and half Russia leather binding. It may be ordered through any bookseller, and if ordered direct it will be sent by express prepaid to any address in the United States or Canada on receipt of the subscription price.

LEVYTYPE COMPANY, PUBLISHERS,

7th and Chestnut Streets,

PHILADELPHIA, PA.

The Jews of Philadelphia

THEIR HISTORY FROM THE EARLIEST SETTLEMENTS TO THE PRESENT TIME

By HENRY SAMUEL MORAIS

Author of "EMINENT ISRAELITES OF THE NINETEENTH CENTURY," ETC., ETC.

This work describes the history of the Jews in America from their earliest arrival with Columbus, and their subsequent settlement in Pennsylvania and Philadelphia; their growth in the chief city of the Keystone State in every sphere of Congregational, Institutional and Communal activity. Every religious corporation and society existing among the Jews of Philadelphia is traced from its beginning up to the date of publication of this work. Many rare historic subjects are introduced. Biography is a special feature of the work.

Part I, treats of history and biography. Part II deals with biographical and miscellaneous data, subdivided into sections as follows: In Communal Affairs; In Literature, Science and Journalism; In Art; In Music and Drama; In Politics; In Law; In Medicine, Dentistry, etc.; In the University of Pennsylvania and In Old Philadelphia. Part III treats of Pennsylvania Jews in the United States Regular Army; In the United States Navy; In Pennsylvania Volunteers during the Civil War, embracing Field and Staff Officers, Company Officers and Privates; In Other Regiments and in European Armies, etc., etc.

A copious index is supplied. The volume is handsomely printed and substantially bound. It comprises 592 pages, large octavo. The price has been set at $2.50 per volume; the edition is limited and only a fraction of the edition remains for disposal. Those desiring copies should send in their orders without delay.

FOR SALE THROUGH ALL BOOKSELLERS

PUBLICATIONS OF THE LEVYTYPE COMPANY, PHILADELPHIA
628-630-632 Chestnut Street, Cor. Seventh Street

The American Jew

AS

Patriot, Soldier and Citizen

By HON. SIMON WOLF

Edited by LOUIS EDWARD LEVY

THIS timely work on a timely topic, called forth by recent magazine discussions regarding the position of Jewish citizens as patriots and as soldiers, contains an alphabetical register and numerous detailed notices of American citizens of the Jewish faith who have been enrolled in the armies of the country from the earliest period of American history to the present time, including those in the Confederate armies during the War for the Union.

In elucidation of this subject there are included in this volume, besides a prefatory introduction by the author, a number of historical papers on the part taken by American Jews in the upbuilding of this Republic, and a special contribution on the same subject in relation to the South American Countries, the West Indies and Canada. The book furthermore contains a carefully collated series of articles, discussions and letters bearing upon the question at issue, from eminent Christian writers and publicists of Europe and America, and a brief but comprehensive review of the subject of the Russian Jewish immigrants.

The various matters are successively prefaced with introductory references by the editor, and the book affords a thorough and complete refutation of the falsities and misstatements regarding Jewish citizenship which have been put forth from time to time through ignorance, bigotry or selfish interest.

This work has been undertaken by the author in response to suggestions arising out of recently published contentions on this subject, and THE NET PROFITS OF ITS SALE ARE DEVOTED WHOLLY AND EXCLUSIVELY TO THE ENLARGEMENT OF THE HEBREW ORPHAN'S HOME, ESTABLISHED IN ATLANTA, GA., under the auspices of the Order of B'nai B'rith, of which Mr. Wolf is President.

The work contains 592 pages large octavo, bound in cloth, blue back and gray sides, and is offered at the low price of $2.00 per copy.
For sale by all booksellers.